Alfred A. Knopf presents

DAVID C

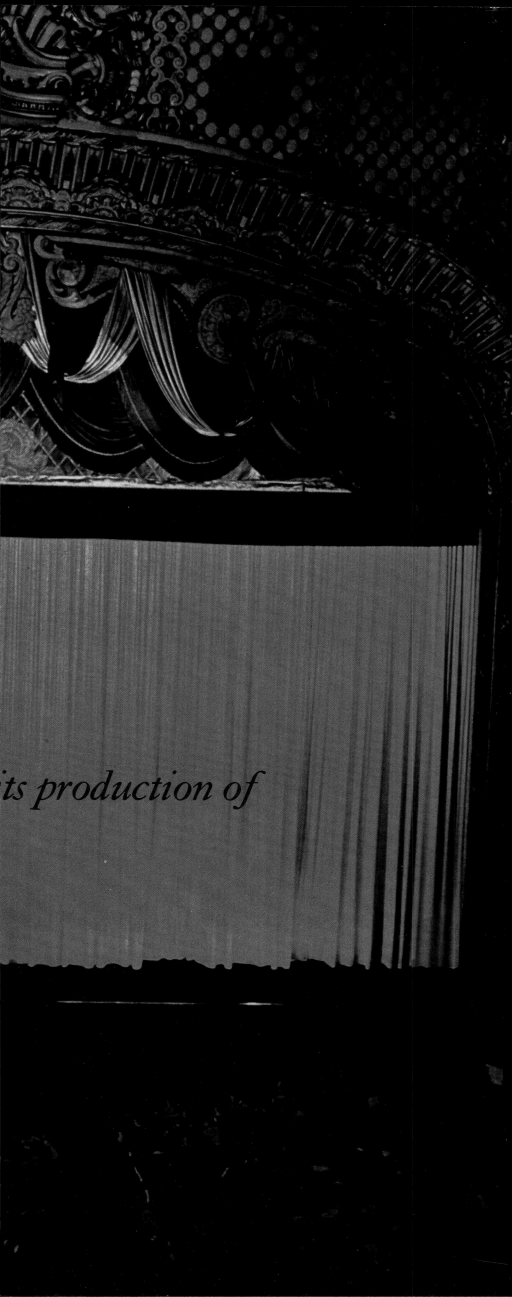

its production of

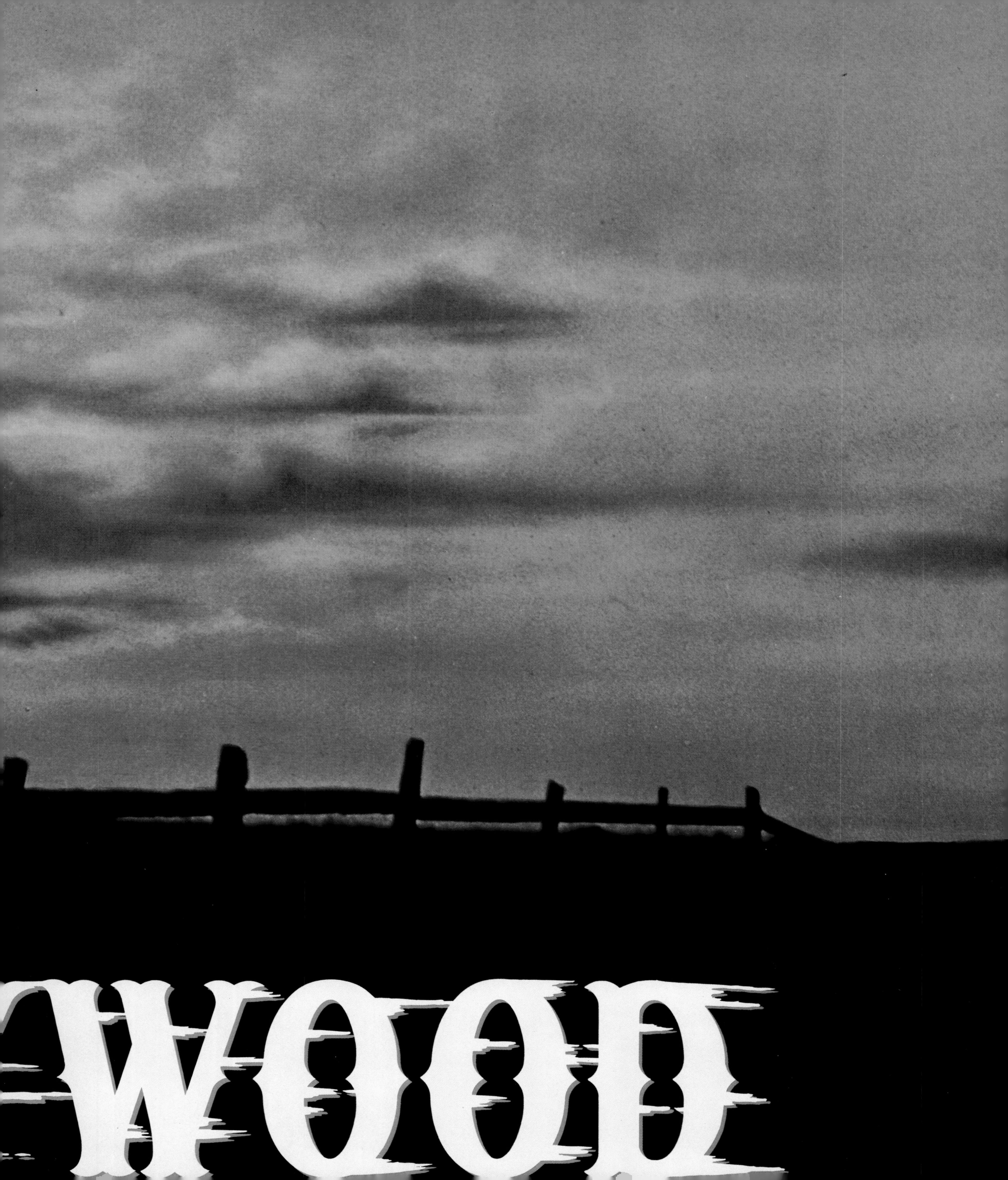
WOOD

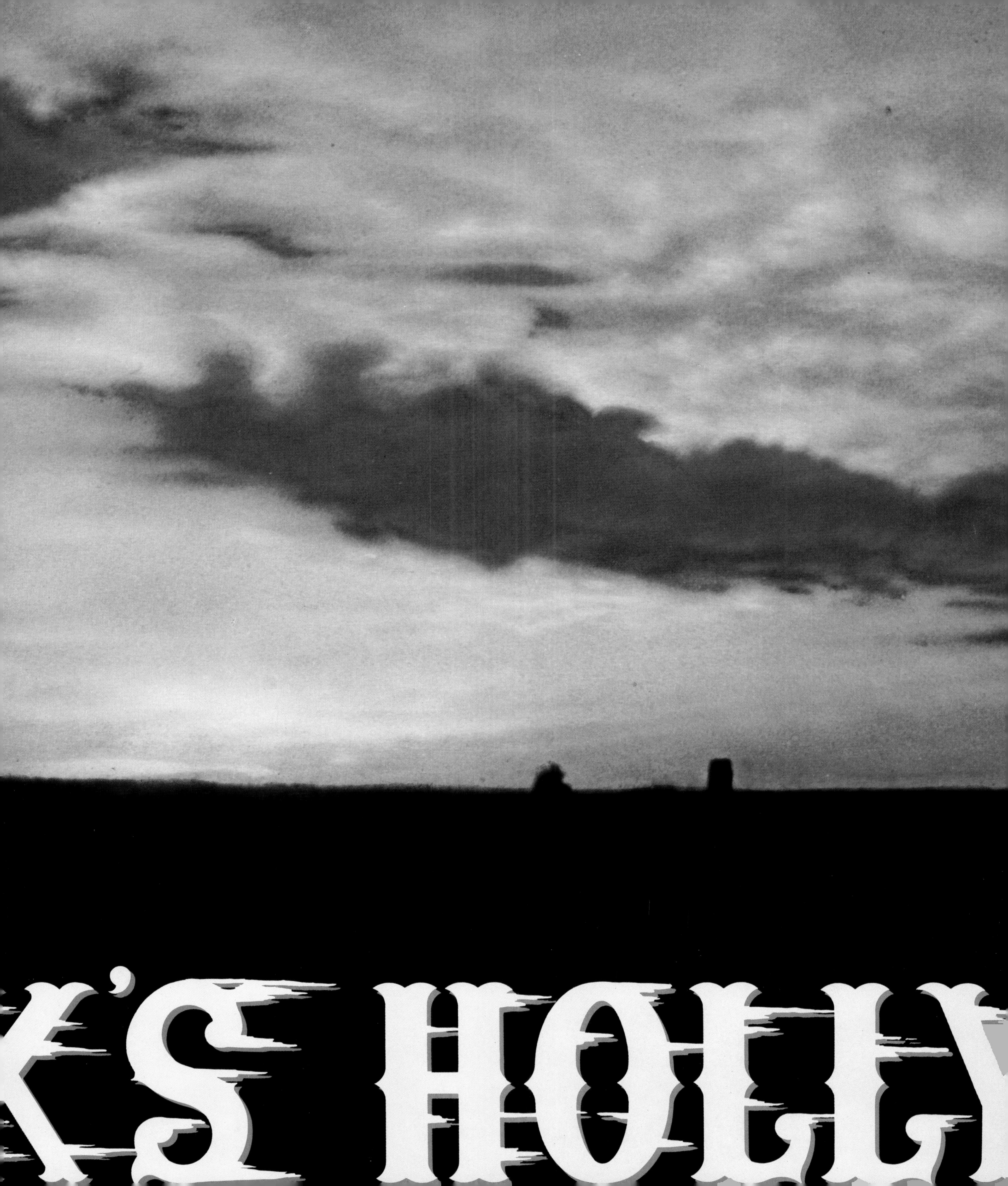
K'S HOLL

David O. Selznick's
HOLLYWOOD

Written & Produced by
RONALD HAVER

Designed by
THOMAS INGALLS

Alfred A. Knopf
New York
1 9 8 0

Portions of the material in the chapters on Paramount
and RKO appeared originally in somewhat different
form in *American Film* magazine, published by the
American Film Institute.

All of the quoted remarks by, and correspondence to
and from, David O. Selznick in this book are copyrighted by Selznick Properties, Limited, and are used
by permission.

Library of Congress Cataloging in Publication Data
Haver, Ronald
    David O. Selznick's Hollywood.
    Bibliography: p.
    Includes index.
    1. Selznick, David O., 1902–1965.   I. Title.
PN1998.A3S397   1980   791.43′0232′0924   79-2224
ISBN: 0-394-42595-2

Manufactured in the United States of America
First Edition

Cover photograph adapted from the 1940 black-and-
white MGM campaign book cover for *Gone With The
Wind.* Color adaptation and airbrushing by Ray Price for
ReproColor; cover typography by Michael Schwab, airbrushed by Carson Smith, adapted from Jack Cosgrove's
titling for *A Star Is Born* (1937).

Borzoi color art by Lucinda Cowell.

Gatefold title page artwork by William Cameron Men-
zies and Jack Cosgrove, adapted and rephotographed by
ReproColor; lettering by Lance Anderson, airbrushed by
Ray Price.

King Kong copper page reproductions executed by Paul
Miller.

Technicolor display page by Paul Miller, airbrushed by
Carson Smith.

For my mother, Ann Spikula Calistro, who introduced me to *Gone With The Wind,* novel and film, and who has remained steadfast in her belief both in me and in this project.

For Gary Essert, who has shared my adolescent obsessions with encouragement, enthusiasm, and friendship for these many years.

AND

In Memoriam

My father, George Calistro, whose taciturn exterior masked a poet's sensitivity.

Shirley Harden Diaz, who encouraged my Selznick obsession.

Peter Kemeny, a gentle and trusting man, who introduced me to Robert Gottlieb.

Contents

Preface

This is not a biography of David O. Selznick, nor is it a critical appraisal of his films. It is rather a history of his career in the film business, a career that began in 1913 and ended in 1965—fifty years that coincide with the rise to prominence of the American motion picture, both as an industry and as an art form. Selznick's most active years of production, 1932 to 1958, correspond to what most historians generally acknowledge as Hollywood's second Golden Age, the most creative and productive period in its seventy-year history as a film production center. This was the era in which the American film industry reached its peak—artistically, financially, and, most importantly, in the emotional and intellectual grip it had on millions of people.

Selznick's significance during these years has been attributed to the fact that he produced *Gone With The Wind,* and while this monolithic creation should not be underestimated, it unfortunately has tended to obscure his other accomplishments, both as a picturemaker and as a creative and innovative businessman. Selznick's success and influence in these areas make him the most important figure in American films after D.W. Griffith, who was the first strong voice in the infant film industry. This nineteenth-century rural Victorian Southerner gave the motion picture its syntax and its respectability, elevating it to an art form and then using it to show his contemporaries how to mold audience reactions—and, in the process, make unparalleled amounts of money.

These two strains, the artistic and the financial, came together in David Selznick. He was the first real twentieth-century movieman. His sensibilities were shaped by the forces of the new century: writers such as Michael Arlen, F. Scott Fitzgerald, Ben Hecht, Ernest Hemingway, George S. Kaufman, and Edna Ferber—strongly idiomatic voices that spoke eloquently, humorously, sarcastically, and romantically about new ideas and new attitudes—and the purveyors of this modern popular culture: tabloid journalism, mass-circulation magazines, four-color printing, and, of course, the movies. All of these had a strong influence on the adolescent Selznick, but their impact was tempered by his childhood fascination for literary classics, something instilled in him by his father, the movie pioneer Lewis J. Selznick. This sort of cultural crossbreeding is what gives the best of David Selznick's films their sense of impudence and reverence, a concern for the values and traditions of the past, for human strengths and weaknesses. And it is these intangibles that inspired Selznick's constant efforts not only to raise his own standards of excellence, but to upgrade the taste of his audiences; and that is how he succeeded so consistently at what eluded so many of his contemporaries, and indeed most of his successors: creating motion pictures with class and imagination that appealed to a large and devoted paying audience. He was deeply, almost obsessively, involved in every aspect of his films, from the planning to the making to the selling, and it was his taste and his particular psyche that gives these films their handcrafted look and feel.

Selznick's romantic, glossy style of moviemaking dominated Hollywood for more than a quarter of a century. Arguments have been raised on behalf of others from this period—Samuel Goldwyn, Irving Thalberg, Darryl Zanuck, Hal Wallis, even Cecil B. DeMille—and they all are valid up to a point; some of these men did oversee almost all aspects of their productions. But none of them carried the function of motion picture producer to the logical extreme where David Selznick carried it, nor did any of them create quite the personal body of work Selznick did. In a medium that is uniquely collaborative and primarily dominated by the writer or the director, Selznick's films more often than not reflected his own sensibilities far more than they did those of any of his collaborators.

Which brings us to one of the two reasons this book is called *David O. Selznick's Hollywood.* There have been two previous books on Selznick. The first, *Selznick,* by the veteran Holywood newsman Bob Thomas, gave a good general outline of the man's career; but with its anecdotal approach and erratic sense of history, it was superficial in its presentation of the reasons for Selznick's success, defining his importance in the history of film primarily as the producer of *Gone With The Wind.* The second book, *Memo from David O. Selznick,* exhaustively researched and intelligently edited by the film historian Rudy Behlmer, was much more detailed, accurate, and exciting in its approach. Behlmer culled from thousands of Selznick's letters and memos a near-comprehensive compendium of the function of the producer, as Selznick dictated his way through the making of his films. I say "near-comprehensive" because the book exists in a vacuum. Admirable as it is as a work of research (probably the best of its kind), it is basically a monologue. One hungers for the other side, the replying voice, the thoughts of the people to whom those memos and letters were directed—what they were doing to implement Selznick's desires, or what their arguments were against doing things his way. For Selznick, dogmatic as he was in his pursuit of what he wanted, evidently had a completely open mind insofar as his collaborators and employees were concerned. Over and over again the people who worked with him mention his accessibility and his receptiveness to ideas. He hired what he considered to be the best, and he wanted their best thoughts and their best efforts. His files are stuffed with thousands of responses to his memos, each one carefully check-marked and with the salient points underlined for discussion. It was this back-and-forth dialogue that was responsible in large part for the textual and sensual richness that characterizes so much of Selznick's work, charging his films with a dramatic force and energy that jumps off the screen and envelopes the viewer.

Selznick's films have an opulent, stylish look to them that makes them larger than life—images projected in rich blacks and lustrous whites and grays on huge pearly, translucent screens, or in colors as bright and as emotionally charged as the stories they illusrate. Motion picture technology was one of the tools of Selznick's trade. He was an enthusiastic pioneer in the dramatic uses of sound and one of the earliest advocates of color: his Technicolor productions make extravagant use of the advantages of the legendary—now vanished—process. To see these films is to be forcefully reminded of the contributions of Selznick's co-workers, and to be curious as to just how they achieved their results, how they were able to function not only within the confines of the much-maligned studio system, but also under the benevolent dictatorship of the autocratic Selznick. Neither of the two previous books on Selznick satisfied these curiosities, nor did they manage to present visually the excitement, glamour, and mystery inherent in the craftsmanship of moviemaking during this era. For more than just being about Selznick, this book is about Hollywood in its prime and about all the elements that once made movies alluring: the advertising that often promised more than was ultimately delivered; the sound, look, and feel of the actual film; the technological advances that spawned new crafts to back up new styles of filmmaking. It's about all these things and about the people who took the tools of a craft and created an art form within an art form.

This book is also called *David O. Selznick's Hollywood* because Selznick was my childhood idol. In the early fifties, when I was not quite a teenager, my fascination with movie history and production was fueled when I read a magazine article about Rudolph Valentino and was intrigued enough to ask the local librarian if she had anything else about him. She came up with a book called *A Pictorial History of the Movies,* by Deems Taylor, Marcelene Peterson, and Bryant Hale. It didn't tell me much more about Valentino, but it did open my eyes to the movies' past. From its account of Griffith and *Intolerance* to its picture of a giant ape atop the Empire State Building, the book stimulated my imagination and made my mouth water to see these films. But at that time, this was almost an impossibility. Television had barely gotten off the ground. Occasionally *Stagecoach* or *To Be or Not to Be* or *A Star Is Born* would show up on TV, whetting my appetite even more, and my local movie theatre in East Oakland—the Granada—would sometimes give us a kiddie matinee of *The Long Voyage Home* under the mistaken impression that it was a John Wayne western. But mostly I had to make do with books: *Talking Pictures: How They Are Made,* by Barrett Kiesling; *We Make the Movies,* by Nancy Naumberg; *Merely Colossal,* by Arthur Mayer; *A Tree Is a Tree,* by King Vidor; *The Lion's Share,* by Bosley Crowther; and, most satisfying of all, *The Movies,* by Richard Griffith and Arthur Mayer. From these books I learned not only the history of an art but, even more excitingly, the history of the business of the movies and how this affected the making of films. I learned also how a film was put together: the functions of the writer, the director, and most intriguing it seemed to me, the producer. And then, during a long illness, I read *Gone With The Wind.* It was the most engrossing piece of fiction I had ever read, light years ahead of the Hardy Boys and *Treasure Island. A Pictorial History of the Movies* told me that a movie had been made from it and that it was supposedly the best picture ever made. Suddenly, it was announced that the picture would return to San Francisco, and the original anticipation felt by audiences in 1940 could not have been half so rabid as mine in 1954. I cut school to journey across the Bay and sat all day in Loew's Warfield on Market Street, seeing the picture twice. It had a profound effect on me. It dealt with history and adult passions in a more attractive and intelligent manner than I had ever encountered in American films. Clark Gable's "damn" was as audacious then as it had been fifteen years earlier, and the film's use of color and design, with massive cloudscapes and epic struggles against fate, underscored by the overwhelmingly romantic music—well, to a moviestruck kid it was like dying and going to a Technicolor heaven. Even after more than twenty-five viewings, *Gone With The Wind* still had enough narrative power to keep me engrossed in its story. Along about number thirty, I began to be very aware of the picture as a work of the art of production, and its fascination on that level has carried me through another 118 screenings. I've seen the film under every conceivable condition: from Market Street fleapits with an audience of winos to reserved seats at first-run theatres to middle-class suburban theatres to the drive-ins of southern California to the ghetto theatres of Harlem (with audiences alternately outraged and delighted at the film's treatment of blacks) to the hysterical "recite-alongs" of *GWTW* camp followers in Greenwich Village. The night of its first commercial television broadcast, I drove around the nightspots of Los Angeles to the bars, the bowling alleys—any place that had a television set and a cross-section of people. I watched bits and pieces of the film here and there, fascinated at the silences and surges of enthusiasm coming from the knots of people, hearing them comment on things they remembered, liked, or didn't like, and their disappointment with what it looked like on TV.

Forty years after its first showing, *Gone With The Wind* is still the standard by which Hollywood and the American film industry measure their efforts. Its particular combination of excellences is still able to attract and satisfy audiences on a scale that cannot be matched by many contemporary films, let alone any other that is almost half a century old. The durability of *Gone With The Wind* gives it a meaning and resonance far beyond the sum of its parts. Aside from the Disney classics, it is one of the few films that have been handed down from generation to generation; people to whom it was an important movie event in the late thirites and early forties are now grandparents, even great-grandparents. People like myself, who were kids when we saw it for the first time in the fifties, took it for our own—one of the few things we had in common with our parents.

It was after my first few viewings of the film that I began the research that ultimately resulted in this book. I was curious to know why there were differences between the book and the film, and as I delved through old magazines and newspapers, I began to fall under the spell of David O. Selznick and his accomplishments. Over the years I amassed a huge store of clippings, photos, and other trivia related to his career. I bombarded him with letters, telegrams, and personal appearances, begging for a job. In one memorable encounter, after trying for several months to get an appointment with him, I presented myself at his home late one night insisting that he hire me to work on his new film, *A Farewell to Arms.* I was given a polite brush-off, and the closest I ever came to my goal was sitting behind him at the two sneak previews of the picture, where I strained to hear every word he mumbled to his two secretaries as the film unreeled. It was only after his death, when I went to work at the new American Film Institute Center for Advanced Film Studies in Beverly Hills, that this book began to take shape.

The AFI in its initial years was the most exciting place in the film world. It was there I was finally able to meet and interview all the people whose names and accomplishments were already so familiar to me: directors George Cukor, King Vidor, and John Cromwell; Lyle Wheeler, Lee Garmes, and Ray Rennahan, all of whom made *Gone With The Wind* look the way it did; Lee Zavits, who burned Atlanta; James Wong Howe, who photographed *The Adventures of Tom Sawyer* and *The Prisoner of Zenda;* and, most importantly, Danny Selznick, who listened patiently as I tried to explain what his dad represented to me. Fortunately, David Selznick had been a pack rat; he saved just about everything that pertained to the way his films were produced, even from as far back as 1920. Not just memos, but script drafts, set and costume sketches, production schedules, photos, ads, and letters. His sons had preserved all this material, and Danny, after the publication of *Memo from David O. Selznick,* gave me carte blanche to examine this collection in depth and to use whatever was relevant to this project. This material was supplemented by interviews with many of Selznick's collaborators. Every quote in this book is taken from letters, memos, or interviews, published and unpublished. All of the factual material has been checked and cross-checked, and I believe it is as historically accurate as time, money, and resources have allowed. The Louis B. Mayer Oral History Program of the American Film Institute and the oral history archives of the University of California at Los Angeles and the University of Southern California were extremely valuable in providing additional material, as were the production files of RKO Radio Pictures and Metro-Goldwyn-Mayer, and the archives of the Academy of Motion Picture Arts and Sciences.

There are any number of people who gave unselfishly of their time, energy, and talents in the long and arduous task of researching and assembling everything in this book. First is Danny Selznick, whose enthusiasm and patient encouragement have contributed enormously to the completion of this book in the Selznick manner. Irene Mayer Selznick graciously took time out from writing her autobiography to read portions of the manuscript, pointing out errors of fact and judgment; I'm extremely grateful to her not only for this but for her many other kindnesses in the preparation of this book. The work Rudy Behlmer had done for *Memo from David O. Selznick,* as well as the book itself, simplified the searching through the hundreds of boxes of Selznick papers, and his careful and detailed perusal of the manuscript was responsible for the elimination of many errors. Kevin Brownlow, whose book *The Parade's Gone By* inspired me to undertake this project, was extremely kind to a tyro historian; his championing of the cause of film research at the AFI (which, unfortunately, the powers that be have decided to abandon) was enormously helpful, and his introducing me to

Merian C. Cooper was the impetus that started me on this book. The importance of Cooper, not only to this project but to the motion picture industry in general, cannot be overestimated, and, after Selznick, he is the most fascinating and important figure in this book. I'm also grateful to David Shepard for his confidence in my abilities, which led to my present position as head of the Film Department at the Los Angeles County Museum of Art, and I must express my appreciation to the Board of Trustees of the Museum and to Morton Golden, the Deputy Director, for granting me a leave of absence from my duties there to complete this project. Frank Davis and Herbert Nussbaum and their respective staffs at MGM were also enormously helpful, not only in research but, especially in the case of Frank Davis, in allowing use of frame enlargements from a Technicolor print of *Gone With The Wind*. Al Korn, vice-president of RKO General, was exceedingly generous in allowing use of material from the RKO archives, and Marshall Flaum, who wrote, produced, and directed the excellent TV documentary "Hollywood' The Selznick Years," kindly gave permission for use of transcripts of interviews done for that production. Arthur Shimmel of ABC Entertainment, the owners of most of the Selznick International films, was also generous with permissions for use of stills and frame enlargements. James Bigwood's unpublished honors' thesis of the film work of Salvador Dali added greatly to the section on the making of *Spellbound*.

A research project of this magnitude could not have been accomplished without the dedication of several people, chief among them Joan Cohen, who spent several years of her life, both here and in England, digging up facts, checking for accuracy, and making suggestions that invariably improved the quality of the work we were all doing. She was aided in this by Sharon McCormick, who organized much of the research material and generally kept everything operating smoothly during the several years of research and writing. Her sister Kathy patiently typed, and re-typed, and re-typed again the various drafts of the manuscript, making legible my somewhat inchoate pages; what she wasn't able to handle was done by Marilynne Garrison and Janet Brunie; the two of them, along with Barbara Lauter, were also invaluable to the research efforts. Anne Schlosser generously allowed me access to much of the material in the AFI's Charles K. Feldman Library, as did Mildred Simpson, Bonnie Rothbart, Sam Gill, and Robert Cushman at the Academy of Motion Picture Arts and Sciences, probably the finest motion picture research library in the United States, if not the world. Photographic and other material also came from the Lincoln Center Library for the Performing Arts in New York, the archives of Technicolor Incorporated, Mark Wanamaker's Bison Archives, Paula Klaw's *Movie Star News*, Collector's Book Store, Eddie Brandt's Saturday Matinee, and Larry Edmunds' Book Shop. Permission to reproduce pages from *The Hollywood Reporter* was graciously supplied by Tichi Wilkerson Miles; the New York *Times*, the Atlanta *Journal-Constitution*, the Los Angeles *Times*, the Los Angeles *Herald-Examiner, Time, House & Garden*, and photographer Anton Bruehl all generously supplied material and the necessary permissions for its inclusion in these pages. Mary Corliss and Carlos Clarens at the Museum of Modern Art Stills Archive added greatly to the pictorial effectiveness of this book, as well as boosting my flagging spirits with their enthusiastic response to the work at hand. To Rod Dwyer and Irene Maltman Fis I owe particular thanks because for years both of them put up with what must have been an exasperating set of personality quirks. The same must be said of Claudie Kunze and Jonathan Benair, Neal Aberman, Gary Abrahams, and Ruth Gribin, who have listened patiently all these years to my doubts, complaints, and insecurities and kept assuring me that everything would be fine. My sister, Pat Calistro McCauley, read portions of the manuscript, and her intelligent comments and suggestions helped keep me on an even keel.

But all of these contributions and all of the work done by dozens of individuals would be for naught were it not for two people at Alfred A. Knopf who gave me the financial and moral support that was so necessary to complete this project. It's impossible to adequately express my gratitude to Robert Gottlieb, who convinced me that I could do this book and who backed me all the way down the line as expenses mounted, deadlines were missed, and chapters were re-written because of his conviction that this was a book worth doing and that it should be done in a manner and style befitting the Selznick tradition. One of his most valuable contributions, aside from his ability to make people transcend themselves, was his introduction of Martha Kaplan to this enterprise. Week by week, page by page, telephone call after telephone call, she cajoled, encouraged, wheedled, threatened, and quietly and calmly managed to turn me into a writer fit to be published, and she deserves more credit than these few lines could possibly give her. Also at Knopf, my gratitude to the delightful Eva Resnikova, whose ability to "think pink" brought a discerning intelligence to the function of production editor, correcting grammatical, factual, and stylistic errors with the same ease with which she sharpened her pencils and charmed a weary author. And finally at Knopf, a deep bow of affectionate appreciation to Ellen McNeilly, for without her dedication to this project, it would have been impossible to adequately demonstrate the beauty of David O. Selznick's Hollywood. Her encyclopedic knowledge of printing and book production combined with a connoisseur's appreciation of craftsmanship and her unerring eye for beauty in all its forms has given this book an opulent glow that reflects not only the films but also Ellen's own commitment to standards of excellence that are as high as David Selznick's. Her contribution is ultimately the most significant, for it was she who maintained and even improved the quality of the images. How she managed to do all this and still be a terrific cook, an even better photographer, and a dedicated squash player is one of the mysteries of Manhattan life. And finally, as you will see as you go through this book, the work of Tom Ingalls is of incalculable importance. For five years his talent, taste, patience, and lust for exciting visuals has been one of the delights of assembling this volume. Together we examined close to ten thousand photographs, posters, advertisements, and other visual materials; we spent endless hours huddled over a Movieola, isolating black-and-white and Technicolor frames from these films, having them blown up, and then repeating the process until we got as near to the Selznick standard as possible. Without Tom, this book would not be the visual feast that I believe it is, and my admiration for his abilities is matched only by my gratitude and affection.

This book tells of a group of fascinating individuals who went through war, death, earthquake, and social and technical revolution, led by David Selznick in pursuit of what one Los Angeles phrasemaker has referred to as *The Art Form of the Century*." Its aim is to entertain, instruct, and inspire, with a little sex thrown in too, just like the films it celebrates.

Ronald Haver
Hollywood, California

Acknowledgments

It would have been impossible to put together a book of this scope and complexity without the kindness and cooperation of the following people, who were all a part of David O. Selznick's Hollywood. They gave generously of their time and their memories, aiding this project with their enthusiasm, their belief, and, most importantly, their trust:

Pandro Berman

Dewitt Bodeen

Ridgeway Callow

Merle Chamberlain*

J. J. Cohn

Dorothy Jordan Cooper

Merian C. Cooper*

Stanley Cortez

John Cromwell*

George Cukor

Frank Davis

Olivia de Havilland

Howard Dietz

Linwood Dunn

Lee Garmes*

Elsa Neuberger Grossman

Alan Handley

James Wong Howe*

Hal C. Kern

Barrett C. Kiesling

Raymond Klune

John Lee Mahin

Darlene O'Brien

Daniel T. O'Shea*

Fred Parrish

Walter Plunkett

Merrill Pye*

David Raksin

Ray Rennahan*

Alan Rivkin

Lydia Schiller

Helen Gregg Seitz

Murray Spivack

Max Steiner*

Howard Strickling

Dimitri Tiomkin*

King Vidor

William Wellman*

Lyle Wheeler

Fay Wray

Lee Zavits*

To all of them, I offer my gratitude and my appreciation, not only for their efforts on my behalf but for the quality of their accomplishments in the films and during the era covered here. Without their achievements, this book would have no reason for existence.

*Deceased

David O. Selznick's Hollywood

There are only two kinds of class:
first class and no class.

DAVID O. SELZNICK

Smithfield Street, Pittsburgh, Pa., as it
looked in 1905 when Harris and Davis
opened the world's first nickelodeon, located two blocks to the right of
this photo—and a block farther on was
the Keystone Jewelry Store of Lewis J.
Selznick.

Introduction

ON MAY 10, 1902, in Pittsburgh, when the family of jeweler Lewis J. Selznick announced the birth of their third son, David, there was no such thing as a movie industry or a movie theatre. If you said the word "movie" to people, they wouldn't know what you were talking about. They knew "peep shows" in the penny arcades and dime museums; they knew "motion pictures," or "films," which were used as gimmick attractions in the vaudeville theatres; but nobody had yet affectionately called these things "movies." And the only business aspects of these peep show novelties were represented by the handful of small companies that manufactured the films and the equipment to make and show them.

In May 1902 in Pittsburgh, in addition to the Lewis J. Selznick family, there were two enterprising gentlemen named John Harris and Harry Davis, owners of various amusement enterprises, one of which, a penny arcade, was located on Smithfield Street several doors away from Mr. Selznick's Keystone Jewelry Store. The Harris and Davis operation was patronized mainly by newly arrived European immigrants, those whom a well-meaning Emma Lazarus had labeled "wretched refuse." They were anything but that; mostly they were energetic, ambitious, and on the lookout for the opportunity America was the land of. While they watched for it, they worked. And in Pittsburgh, the work was in the foundries—work that lasted fourteen hours a day, six days a week, for an average weekly wage of $14. For an immigrant family of four, after life's other necessities were deducted, this left about $1.50 for recreation.

In Pittsburgh a great deal of this money found its way into the arcades and museums of Harris and Davis. Most of their customers seemed to be especially attracted to the six-year-old peep show cabinets. For a penny, and for less than a minute, they could watch a picture that moved. In the landlocked city, with the furnaces blasting twenty-four hours a day, the sight of waves breaking on an anonymous shore was a wonder beyond comprehension. Even more so was *The Execution of Mary, Queen of Scots,* which gave hundreds of credulous Pittsburghers their first, and probably only, look at a beheading. The lines at these cabinets were always the longest, a fact not lost on Messrs. Harris and Davis. They reasoned that if the pictures were longer and bigger and more people could see them, they could charge more than a penny. The duo invested $150 in the necessary equipment, partitioned off a section of one of their arcades, installed ninety-six folding chairs, and on the day before Thanksgiving 1905 offered the Pittsburgh working classes a two-year-old vaudeville attraction, *The Great Train Robbery,* for 5 cents, thereby giving the world its first nickelodeon.

Harris and Davis didn't know it, but they had made history. *The Great Train Robbery* also turned out to be the first motion picture blockbuster; within two weeks the doors of the new theatre on Smithfield Street had to open at eight in the morning and stay open until midnight to accommodate the crowds. For ten minutes they sat enthralled, staring at an optical illusion: a series of still photographs that flashed in front of their eyes so quickly the pictures seemed to move and tell a story. The images on the screen were larger than life, the action was vivid in its depiction of danger, treachery, and heroism, with justice reassuringly triumphant.

1898—This very first advertisement for an Edison motion picture machine set the pattern for the fine art of movie advertising, and its basic precepts are still in use. Superlatives ("the latest marvel"); production expense ("large outlays of money," etc.); years in preparation; exhibition formulas ("four or five minutes is better"); promise of large profits; and even the world's first actual "tie-in," with the Edison phonograph, which was, in these early years, connected to the Vitascope by a belt.

THE LATEST MARVEL

"Vitascope"

A NEW MACHINE is now ready to be exhibited to the public, which is probably the most remarkable and startling in its results of any that the world has ever seen. Several marvels of inventive genius have, in past years, gone forth from the Edison Works, located at Orange, New Jersey. "The Wizard of Menlo Park" has conceived and in due course perfected the Phonograph, the Kinetoscope and the Kinetophone, each of which in turn, has excited the wonder and amazement of the public and, from a practical standpoint, opened up opportunities for exhibition enterprises, many of which are paying handsomely to this day.

THE NEW MACHINE

which is now to be launched upon the wave of public curiosity, promises to be a greater marvel and to bring larger material results to exhibitors than any of its predecessors which have been constructed at the Edison Works . . . .

This latest scientific wonder has been named the "VITASCOPE," as it projects apparently living figures and scenes upon a screen or canvas before an audience. In bringing this machine to its present state of perfection, many months of experiment and expert labor, as well as large outlays of money have been devoted to the work . . . .

The new machine will be made by the Edison Manufacturing Company, where the Phonograph and Kinetoscope are made. *Several years ago Mr. Edison conceived the idea* of projecting moving figures and scenes upon a canvas or screen, before an audience . . . . . .

A *Subject* can be shown for ten or fifteen minutes if desired, although four or five minutes is better

THEREFORE

It is apparent that the field covered by the "Vitascope" is vastly greater than that of the Kinetoscope, in which the length of exhibition of a subject is practically limited to about one minute. Almost any happening or occurrence; any subject having motion of living beings or other objects, singly or in groups, in city or country, in-doors or out, and in any part of the world, will, in our judgment, be within the scope of the new machine, and can be reproduced, true to life in size, movement and every detail, before an audience, however large. We need not dilate upon the tremendous possibilities which these facts involve, although they may be even more far-reaching, scientific and advantageous to mankind than any of us now imagine, to say nothing of their practical benefit. and their . .

 promise of large profit to those who control the exhibition of the "Vitascope"

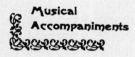

Musical Accompaniments

MUSIC CAN BE VERY APPROPRIATELY AND EFFECTIVELY RENDERED SIMULTANEOUSLY WITH THE EXHIBITION OF MANY VITASCOPE SUBJECTS.

ALL SUBJECTS MADE UP OF DANCING, MARCHING, OR OTHER ACTS AND SCENES WHERE MUSICAL SELECTIONS IN TIME WITH THE MOVEMENT ARE IN PLACE, CAN BE MADE MORE INTERESTING AND REMARKABLE BY THE ADDITION OF MUSIC.

THE EDISON . . . . PHONOGRAPH

CAN THUS BE UTILIZED TO RENDER BAND AND ORCHESTRA SELECTIONS. A PIANO; A GROUPE OF MANDOLINS OR GUITARS; A COMBINATION OF VIOLINS AND WIND INSTRUMENTS, OR EVEN AN ORCHESTRA OR BAND (WHERE THE EXHIBITION IS GIVEN IN A THEATRE OR LARGE HALL) WILL, IN EITHER CASE, ADD MATERIALLY TO THE NOVELTY AND ATTRACTIVENESS OF THE VITASCOPE.

And when, as an added final thrill, one of the desperadoes fired a gun point-blank at them, the audience was hooked forever and completely by the excitement of what would come to be known as the "movies." Within two years there were five thousand of these nickelodeons all over the country.

A few doors up Smithfield Street, unaware of the larger ramifications of this working-class epiphany, the Selznicks lived the life of a successful middle-class family. Their prosperity flowed from the father and his uncanny ability for making people want "the finer things in life." Lewis J. Selznick was a jeweler by trade, but at heart and soul he was a gambler. He'd gambled at age twelve when he left Russia on the chance that life for a peasant Jewish boy would be better in the United States. His gamble had paid off. The streets weren't exactly paved with gold, but they were lined with opportunities for anyone shrewd and quick enough to recognize them. Lewis Selznick apprenticed himself to a jeweler, and within several years, by dint of hard work and an aggressive and winning personality, he had his own jewelry store in downtown Pittsburgh. In line with his philosophy of wanting only the best, he met, charmed, and married Florence Sachs, daughter of a prominent Jewish family and a young lady of unimpeachable quality. They had three sons: Myron, born in 1898, pugnacious, bullheaded; David, born in May 1902, who took after his mother in his quiet sensitivity, imagination, and love of reading; and the eldest, Howard, who, having no ambition and no "chutzpah," consequently has no place in this story.

Chutzpah means nerve, and it's one of the several virtues that Lewis J. schooled his sons in. Among the others were a fierce family pride, an aggressive self-confidence, a love of the classics that he read to them at home in the evenings, and of course, an appreciation for "the finer things in life." The Selznicks were, by all accounts, a tightly knit, loving family, held together by the daring and optimistic talking of Lewis and the quiet, affectionate intelligence of the mother. Florence Selznick always encouraged her husband and her children in their ambitions, never in a nagging, domineering fashion but in the quiet, more effective way of support, advice, and the ability to deal, in a practical manner, with misfortune and adversity. The boys were brought up with the belief that it was the woman who kept marriage and home together, even at the cost of pain, self-sacrifice, and pride. In line with this, the Selznick children were also taught not to take nonsense or abuse from anyone, not an easy lesson in an era when anti-Semitism was as much a way of life as the corner saloon. But Lewis J. constantly reminded his sons that America was the land of opportunity, that the possibilities for making something of yourself were inexhaustible as long as you weren't afraid of taking chances, had a healthy confidence in yourself, and above all, kept your sense of humor.

Practicing what he preached, Lewis J. in 1910 packed up his family and his stock of gems and left Pittsburgh for the opportunities offered by New York City. This manifested itself in "The World's Largest Jewelry Store," which Lewis J. confidently offered to a completely indifferent city. Within a year the store was gone, but the Selznicks lingered on. New York was bursting at the seams with vitality, optimism, and money. The city was a golden goose of opportunities; if you dropped one egg,

Lewis J. and Florence Sachs Selznick, 1913.

another would be along shortly. And in 1912, the best place in the world to grow up was New York City, with its theatres, libraries, museums, and concert halls; it offered anything and everything to the inquisitive, the adventurous, and the ambitious.

The Selznicks arrived in New York just as the motion picture business was getting its first hints of respectability. Adolph Zukor, an ex-furrier, nickelodeon owner, and, like Lewis J., a man with a taste for the finer things in life, was challenging the monopoly of the Edison-dominated Motion Picture Patents Company, which refused to consider the idea of letting films run longer than one reel, or twelve minutes. Zukor imported a French film, *Queen Elizabeth,* starring the legendary and very prestigious Sarah Bernhardt. He made arrangements with Daniel Frohman, the leading theatrical impresario of the time, to exhibit the film in one of Frohman's heretofore sacrosanct Broadway theatres at advanced admission prices, treating it in the style of a dignified cultural event. The film drew the upper classes, the carriage trade of the time, and their acceptance and the film's success took away some of the lower-class stigma previously attached to movies. It was partly this new snob appeal, and of course the money to be made, that attracted Lewis Selznick to the otherwise contemptible movies.

New York, in 1912, was the financial and production center of the ten-year-old film business. It was a brawling, boisterous free-for-all, which Lewis Selznick was quick to catch on to. One of the legends of these early years tells how Selznick, with what was left of his stock of gems, called on a vice-president of the Universal Film Manufacturing Company, hoping to interest him in a sale. The company was divided into two warring factions. Selznick didn't make a sale, but he took advantage of the fact that neither side seemed to know what the other was doing, and appointed himself general manager and set out to learn what he could about the business of making and selling films. He said he learned in the six months before he was found out and bounced that "it takes less brains to be successful in the film business than in any other."

When David Selznick was ten, his life began to revolve around the movies. At night he would listen to his father alternately plan, denounce, and cajole his way into the film business. He tells of how Lewis J. "used to take Myron or myself or both of us to the most important kind of business meetings . . . at the age of ten or eleven I was dragged down to a big Long Island estate where I sat on the porch while my father organized the World Film Company, with my father occasionally directing questions at me."

As an industry, the film business was still strictly an unstructured cottage affair in 1912. Films were made in lofts and converted brownstones in and around Manhattan. Across the Hudson, Fort Lee, New Jersey, with its scattering of laboratories and open-air "stages," was the closest thing there was to a production "center." A few enterprising showmen had begun to look for new, fresher locations for background and had gone as far west as California, where some filming was being done around the cities of Niles in the north and Los Angeles in the south. The pictures that were being ground out by all these small concerns were still fairly primitive. Scenes were enacted as if on a theatre stage, with exits, entrances, and all the other conventions of live performances. Reputable stage actors were paid to "pose" for the camera in "picturizations" of their stage successes; film actors were largely anonymous, their employers not allowing their identities to be publicized for fear of their demands for more money. But audiences began to discern faces, personalities, believability; they wanted to know who these people were. When they found out, they began to look for those particular performers and the star system was born.

From the working classes, the movie infection spread upward into the native-born American middle class. As the quality of the customers improved, so did the halls used for exhibition: the day of the nickelodeon was over when Mitchell Mark opened the Strand, the world's first deluxe film theatre, on Broadway in 1914. Seating almost three thousand, the house was patterned after the "legitimate" theatres in its opulence, and marked the acceptance of moviegoing as a middle- and upper-class diversion. But even in this dazzling setting, even with their new-found respectability, films remained crude. The staging was largely unimaginative. Settings were generally painted backdrops, another borrowed stage technique, although the exteriors were usually real, giving the films an immediacy the stage could not offer.

At the American Biograph, one of the more famous small companies, David Griffith, its chief director, was changing the position of the camera arbitrarily in the middle of scenes, then cutting the film up into little bits and pieces and rearranging them into a more dramatic order, a technique he credited Charles Dickens with inspiring. Dickens was also influencing the young David Selznick, who later related that at this period in his life, "my father used to lecture us on the wonders of Dickens, Tolstoi; when most people were reading Frank Merriwell . . . my father encouraged my reading of *Anna Karenina* and *David Copperfield."* This pre-teen fascination with the classics was shared by the moviemakers of the time, and young Selznick was more than likely going to adaptations of such classics as *A Tale of Two Cities, Enoch Arden, Jane Eyre, The Count of Monte Cristo,* and *The Prisoner of Zenda,* the filmic alterations of which must have startled and disappointed someone to whom the scenes in the originals "had engraved themselves indelibly on my mind." His early readings, coupled with his romantic nature, developed in the youngster a fondness for what the French Surrealists called *l'amour fou:* mad, or doomed, love. It was a taste that was to build over the years as he grew older and more experienced, dominating and giving a distinct elegiac quality to much of his adult work.

Selznick's other grand passion was writing. He had begun by writing down what he thought of the various books his father had him read: "My father was very proud of my 'compositions,' even when I was extremely young." These "compositions" were largely analyses of books he had read, pointing out the ways an author achieved effects, the approach to characterization, and the strengths and weaknesses of the work. Selznick always felt that "from this came . . . an understanding and appreciation of style. I can still tell the exact details of scenes from books that I read when I must have been between 10 and 12 years old."

Anyone who loves the movies has had one primal moviegoing experience in which he gave himself over completely to his lifelong passion; the kind of experience described once by Samuel Goldwyn as "making the hair stand up on the edge of my seat." For twelve-year-old David Selznick, this was probably a viewing of D. W. Griffith's *The Birth of a Nation.* Selznick never commented on the film publicly, but circumstances all point to its being a work that influenced him greatly, as it did a whole generation of his contemporaries. The film was the sensation of New York during most of 1915, and Selznick was at the perfect age and impressionable, romantic state of mind to be overawed by the sweep and power of the film's style and its thunderous musical score. *The Birth of a Nation* was also the first film to have any kind of widespread social impact, causing racial disturbances in many areas and being banned

Myron, Howard, and David Selznick on the sidewalks of New York, 1913.

A series of ads from the *Motion Picture News* published in New York the week of March 30, 1915. The Paramount distribution combine set up by W. W. Hodkinson was selling production. Chaplin had just left Mack Sennett to go out on his own with Essanay, and at the Liberty Theatre, a legitimate playhouse on 42nd Street, *The Birth of a Nation* ("conceived, inspired, and created in America") was giving an entire generation its first taste of the awesome power of the movies.

October 24,1916.

RAOUL A. WALSH,
Director.

In a short time,Walsh has risen to become one of the screen's foremost
and best directors. A few years ago he played the role of John Wilkes
Booth in Griffith's "The Birth of a Nation." He later joined Fox and
directed Theda Bara in "Carmen",and other pictures for that concern. A
list of these follows.

"Carmen," with Theda Bara. A very good picture.

"The Serpent," with Theda Bara.

"The Regeneration," with Rockcliffe Fellowes and Anna Q. Nilsson.
A very fine feature.

"Blue Blood and Red," with George Walsh (brother).

"The Honor System," a ten reel production,about prison life,which
has not yet been released.

Walsh's work,as a whole,is masterful.

Very truly yours,

Mr. Lewis J. Selznick,
729 Seventh Avenue,New York City.

October 26,1916.

MAURICE TOURNEUR,
Director.

Tourneur is one of America's greatest film directors. He came here
from France,where he had produced several pictures for Eclair,a few
years ago and joined the Peerless-World forces. He later joined the
Paragon company in the capacity of vice-president and general manager,
but continued to produce features,released through World. He is now
directing,at the Paragon's studios,the second Artcraft feature with
Mary Pickford. The following are a few of the films he has directed.

"Trilby," (Peerless-Equitable,) with Clara Kimball Young and Wilton
Lackaye. There is no need of my telling of the remarkable success
of this film.

"The Pit," with Wilton Lackaye,(Peerless,) another successful feature.

"The Ivory Snuff Box," (Peerless-World,) was very good(-with H.Blinn)

"The Pawn of Fate," with George Beban. A fair picture,but Tourneur's
worst since coming to America. (Peerless-World.)

"A Butterfly on the Wheel," with Holbrook Blinn and Vivian Martin.
Very good,with one of the most realistic courtroom scenes,and one
of the best fire scenes ever shown in a feature. (Peerless-World.)

"The Wishing Ring," with Vivian Martin. One of the best of World pictures.

"Alias Jimmy Valentine" and "The Man of the Hour," with Robert Warwick,
and "The Hand of Peril," and "The Closed Road," Paragons with House
Peters,were also very fine. "The Rail Rider," with Peters,was good.

"The Cub," with Martha Hedman,(Peerless,) was considered rather poor.

Very truly yours,

Mr.Lewis J. Selznick,729 7th Ave.,N.Y.C.

outright in others. The young Selznick may not have been affected by the
film's racial bias; certainly he was impressed enough by its spectacle and
its imagery to refer years later to a scene in his own *Duel in the Sun* as
"the gathering of the Clans" and to pattern it after the climactic rescue
sequence in *Birth of a Nation*.

While David was going to the movies and learning film's grammar
and style, the rest of his education was being taken care of by the New
York City public school system, which was then the best in the country.
His report cards show average marks, with a strong interest in history
and English. In the seventh grade he started a school paper, serving as
editor, printer, and distributor. All this was watched with a careful eye by
his father, with the result that by 1916 David was leaving school at 2:30
in the afternoon and going directly to work in the publicity offices of
Selznick Pictures, which his father had formed after being forced out of
the World Film Company. David later described Lewis J. as "the industry's biggest advertiser ... he had, at one time, eight huge electric
signs on Broadway. I did a great deal of the designing of the advertising
and posters." The fourteen-year-old's shrewdness and developing sense
of publicity are evident in a letter sent to his father's publicity chief,
Vivian Moses, in which he chides the man for the fact

that Clara Kimball Young is being favored in the publicity sent out by
you ... your reason for this preference is beyond me ... certainly Miss
Young is not in more need of publicity than the other stars. Also, I
have noticed several times in the stories concerning Constance Talmadge you mention "Morosco Studios." In the same stories you omit
the name Selznick ... this to my mind is absurd, when you undoubtedly know that Miss Talmadge's contract specifically states that all
publicity ... on her ... shall bear the wording "Lewis J. Selznick
presents." These stories of yours confuse not only the lay mind, but the
well-informed magazine editor.... Witness stories in *Variety* and
Motion Picture stating that Miss Talmadge has deserted Selznick for
the Famous-Players Morosco forces.

While the teenaged Selznick was learning the ins and outs of the
movie world, the business itself was going through its own adolescent
phase, and Lewis J. was adding to its folklore. The historian Terry
Ramsaye characterized him at this time as "the chief disturbance of the
business," and the description seems apt; he took very few things about
the motion picture business seriously. A game player, he played it well
enough, better than most for a while; but it was never his life's work,
never the kind of all-consuming passion that it was for men like Adolph
Zukor, William Fox, or Marcus Loew, his contemporaries and chief
rivals. These were the men who built the industry; they had their eye
upon the whole and not just the doughnut. Their aims were the time-
honored ones of wealth and power, but they soon began to sense themselves as the statesmen and leaders of a new industry, becoming conscious
of the potential of a developing art form, a little taken aback at the
discovery but secretly pleased to have found respectability. Zukor in
particular was laying the foundations upon which would be built the
interlocking structure of production, distribution, and exhibition that
would prove the industry's greatest strength for the next fifty years.

David was fourteen when he began writing these reports for his father. Whether or not
he saw the films or just researched reviews is hard to say—probably the latter—but
young Selznick was still seeing several pictures a week.

David is engrossed in the newspaper, Howard is nonchalant, Myron is pensive, and Mother Selznick looks rather dubious. The family, informal, about 1915–16.

A composite advertising still showing Zena Keefe, a Selznick star, surrounded by any number of Selznick billboards, on Broadway, circa 1920.

Lewis J., on the other hand, didn't give much credence to the idea of movies as art; that role was reserved for opera, theatre, painting, and the other diversions of the wealthy. His one act of statesmanlike conduct came in 1922, near the end of his career, when he was instrumental in setting up the Motion Picture Producers and Distributors Association, personally persuading politician Will Hays to head the new "regulatory organization." But mainly Lewis J. delighted in twitting his rivals. He was mischievous, grandiose, and had a genius of a kind for organization and self-promotion, usually one in service of the other. He loved battles, spending huge amounts of money on ad campaigns in the early trade publications sometimes just to call his competitors names and insult their product. He ruthlessly raided other companies for their stars, and was especially contemptuous of Adolph Zukor's efforts to make his Famous Players-Paramount the dominant force in the business. The two men tried to outmaneuver each other in a game of oneupmanship that was played throughout the years of World War I when the decimation of the European film industry saw the rise to world domination of movies made in America.

It was in the years immediately after the war that David began to be infected by the film business itself: the fun, the vitality, and the hurly-burly of the industry in the early twenties had a kind of intoxicating excitement to them that Selznick would not be able to shake off until near the end of his life. Out of school now, and preparing for college, he was spending his days in the Selznick Pictures studio with his father, learning distribution, exhibition, and publicity. It was here that he first met many of the people he was to work with later on in his own career.

During those early years of the twenties, David flourished. He was young, wealthy, working in a business he liked, getting a sense of himself and in the process becoming, in his words, "the young man of Manhattan," getting around the upper-class high life of New York. The war was over, Prohibition was in full flower, the speakeasies were jammed, the theatre, literature, and the older arts were loosening up and coming fully into the twentieth century. The movies capitalized on this revolution in manners and morals, reflecting it in a series of lurid sex comedies and melodramas which, while paying lip service to the new freedoms, still held fast to the Victorian code of conduct and beliefs. Sin was punished and a good woman always saw the error of her new ways, ending up once more subservient to her husband and family. In *The Sheik,* a sensational success first as a novel and then as a film, the very independent young heroine was first captured, then tamed after one night of rape by the hard-breathing, handsome hero. Playing the title role in the movie version of this effusion was a good-looking, sensuous young Italian named Rudolph Valentino, who became the embodiment of the erotic daydreams of most American women anywhere between puberty and senility.

"Selznick Pictures Make Happy Hours" was the slogan that Lewis J. used to seduce his audiences into seeing such pictures as *The Foolish Virgin, The Savage Woman, Woman and Wife, His Bridal Night, The Better Wife, The Flapper,* and, in a more spiritual vein, *The Woman God Sent.* Eighteen-year-old David was now running the entire Selznick Pictures publicity department. He also began publishing a weekly news magazine for Selznick employees. Dubbed *The Brain Exchange,* its number-one contributor was David Selznick, and he had some comments on the titles of Selznick Pictures:

Lewis Selznick pioneered the concept of financing independent productions under his corporate umbrella. These ads of the time give an idea of the scope and appeal of the Selznick product, made with some of the era's biggest stars and directors.

11

You can take my word that we don't pick titles for the fun of it. *The Nobleman* was clearly a poor title for a Eugene O'Brien picture; the home office and the studio all agreed ... after much discussion we decided on *The Thug* ... a few weeks passed and the sales manager returned from a tour of the branches ... and excitedly informed us that exhibitors thought *The Thug* was a terrible title ... it wasn't too late, so we changed it to *The Wonderful Chance* ... in another episode *Regret* was a working title only. Two or three others were considered ... *His Wife,* for example, was turned down because we had already made *His Wife's Money.* ... so we finally decided on *Worlds Apart.*

Another correspondent for *The Brain Exchange* wrote of a talk David gave to a group of six hundred women in Indiana on "The Motion Picture—Its Present and Future." Making allowances for company hyperbole, the account still manages to give a vivid impression of the lucid and engaging eighteen-year-old:

He let them have it straight from the shoulder, and did not resort to the usual honey-toned flattery they have been accustomed to hear. It was a clean-cut, comprehensive discussion of how the industry can be helped by the women of the country. He brought out frankly and fully the fact that producers were more anxious to please women than men, as they believed their influence accounted for ninety percent of the attendance at theatres. He urged that they be constructive in their criticism ... pointing out that it had been the practice of all sorts of bodies to harass, malign and hinder the greatest gift of the ages to the common people—the motion picture.

In 1923 Selznick Pictures went broke, bankrupted by Lewis J.'s lavish spending methods and the inability to get adequate distribution for his films on the larger exhibition circuits, now primarily controlled by Adolph Zukor and William Fox. These two men, with whom he had less than cordial relations, were delighted to see the disappearance of the Selznick name from Broadway's electric signs. They were not alone. Lewis J. had alienated many important and powerful men, and his

Constance ("Dutch") Talmadge and her sister Norma, two of the reigning screen queens of the teens and twenties.

A 1922 list of twenty-year-old David's screen favorites.

collapse was as complete as it was sudden; it seemed to both Myron and David that everybody in the business had ganged up on their father, maneuvered him into bankruptcy, then turned their backs on him, refusing to help him get back on his feet and in some cases even actively working against him. Loving their father as they did, they couldn't bear to see him thus humbled. For David, it was a psychic shock; he had always lived like a prince, had plenty of spending money and everything else he needed or wanted. Suddenly, there was no money to pay bills, and the bills kept coming in. David began to get dunning letters from his creditors, then letters threatening legal action. The family moved from their palatial Park Avenue apartment to what David later described as "a three room flat, where my mother did all the housework and cooking. Even though everything we owned personally had been taken away from us, my mother wasn't disturbed in the least by my father's defeat. She said not a word when we had to give up the seventeen room apartment, the enormous staff of servants, a flock of Rolls-Royces; she even gave up her jewelry; and two weeks later the five of us were in the three room flat."

For Myron, the collapse and, to his mind, disgrace, left wounds and grievances that never healed. Largely through Myron's lust for revenge, the family events of 1924 were to have unforeseen and unsettling effects on the film business over the next twenty years.

Both boys began looking for work. David now started seriously considering writing as a career. Out of Chicago had come the tough, rampant prose of Ben Hecht, which made a considerable impression on

Olive Thomas, one of Lewis J.'s most popular stars. In 1920 she married Jack Pickford, Mary's brother, and they went off to Paris on their honeymoon, where she died under mysterious—some say scandalous—circumstances. The eighteen-year-old David was infatuated with the actress and her death was a severe shock to him.

13

Lewis J. Selznick was instrumental in setting up the Motion Picture Producers and Distributors Association of America (MPPDA) and in persuading Postmaster General Will Hays to head it. Here is the first formal gathering of the organization's members. Lewis J. is seated at far left; Myron is standing fourth from left. Samuel Goldwyn is standing third from right. Will Hays is seated center; to the right of him are Adolph Zukor, William Fox, and Universal's Carl Laemmle, Sr.

Selznick. The two met, forming a close friendship that lasted until Hecht's death in 1964. The relationship seriously affected David's writing, but the discipline involved plus the lack of immediate financial reward were evidently more than he cared to inflict on himself, for, after several rejections, he decided to go into publishing. With Arthur Brentano, he organized a small outfit with the idea of "doing some publishing and revolutionizing distribution of books around the country. We finally dropped it, because we had very little capital." His father, meanwhile, tried rather listlessly to get into the nine-day wonder that was the Florida land boom, arriving on the ninth day, and also discovered America's new toy, the radio. Convinced that fortunes were to be made, he talked himself into the franchise for the distribution of Radak Receivers. His enthusiasm was infectious, and both Myron and David dipped a toe into the General American Radio Company, as the new outfit was called. But the manufacturing end was not well organized, and within a year the Selznicks were all seeking new associations.

Myron went out to California, while David rounded up some investors and for the next two years bummed around the movie jungles of New York. On one occasion he paid prizefighter Luis Firpo $1,000 a day to make a short two-reel film, firing him at the end of the first day. Entitled *Will He Conquer Dempsey?*, the film showed the Wild Bull of the Pampas boxing on roofs and other places because, as Selznick explained, "That way I didn't have to pay any rentals or pay for any lights." Selznick's shrewdness was even more evident in his next short effort, which took advantage of the fact that "Rudolph Valentino had been off the screen for some time as a result of a fight with Paramount, and the public was clamoring to see him. He was going to be judging a beauty contest in Madison Square Garden for the Mineralava Beauty line. What I did was to sell the Mineralava people on the value of having a motion picture on the finals of the contest; by convincing them of the advertising value of this, I didn't have to give them anything. Accordingly, I had a two-reel Valentino picture for the cost of the film, plus lights. I made $15,000 on it." What made the money even sweeter was the knowledge that he had made it with Adolph Zukor's biggest star, when Zukor himself couldn't get Valentino in front of a camera. This delighted his father, who, far

The Official Journal of the Organization — **The Brain Exchange** — OF BY And FOR Selznick Employees.

Published Weekly — New York, Wednesday, May 19, 1920 — Vol. II. No. 23

I-M-P-R-E-S-S-I-O-N-S

By RANDOLPH BARTLETT

DAVID SELZNICK

A young eagle.

A mountain stream.

Playing truant from school to go home and saw wood.

Nothing but the truth.

A steel mushroom.

Sir Galahad.

A machine gun.

A chip of the old block.

Perpetual motion.

Now.

SELZNICK
REG. U.S. PAT. OFF.
PICTURES

LEWIS J. SELZNICK Presents

ELAINE HAMMERSTEIN
AND CONWAY TEARLE IN
"ONE WEEK of LOVE"

BY EDWARD J. MONTAGNE AND GEORGE ARCHAINBAUD
Directed by GEORGE ARCHAINBAUD
Produced by MYRON SELZNICK

from being humbled by defeat, was still up to his old mischievous ways.

In the winter of 1925–26, Lewis J. made a move that was to have a direct bearing on his son's formal entry into the film business. As David told it:

> My father had heard about the deal [MGM] had on *Ben-Hur,* which called for them to pay fifty per-cent of the gross of the film to Klaw and Erlanger, who owned the theatrical rights. MGM had inherited this deal when they took over the old Goldwyn Company.... My father conceived the idea of buying up the Klaw and Erlanger half and got a man by the name of Pat Powers to back him, with the profits to be divided fifty-fifty.... When MGM heard about it they were frantic. Nick Schenck [president of MGM] asked my father to come to see him, and my father took me along, saying: "I think we'll have some fun." The atmosphere got rather thick, with Nick insisting that my father had no place in the deal and no right to inject himself into it. My father said, "You did everything possible to break me, and refused to help me since. I see no reason why I should do you a favor." Nick was insistent, and my father finally said, "I'll put it up to David. Anything he says, I'll do." Needless to say I was frightened and flabbergasted. Nick turned to me and said, "Well, Davie, my boy, what's it to be?" I said, "I think you ought to drop out of it, Pop." My father said, "That's it, Nick," and as we rose to leave, Nick said if there was ever anything he could do for me, to call on him. My father never said another word to me about it.

Instead, Lewis J. got himself involved with Associated Exhibitors, a new distribution outfit badly in need of products. Myron was already in Los Angeles working with him, and at his urging, David, still vacillating between the movies and a writing career, went out to California in the summer of 1926 to help Myron line up some films for release. He had been to Los Angeles before on Selznick Pictures business, but this time he stayed long enough to let himself fall under the charm of a quiet, sunny lifestyle, different from the fast-paced, untidy New York. He

---

FIFTEEN REASONS FOR HATING A JEW

by David O. Selznick

1: Because he is a Jew.

2: Because he is a Jew.

3: Because he isn't eligible at the country club.

4: Because he is a Jew.

5: Because he is a Jew.

6: Because he disagrees with you as to whether a certain Jew had a father or a Father.

7: Because he is a Jew.

8: Because he is a Jew.

9: Because a couple of thousands of years ago some Jews had something to do with the death of a Jew.

10: Because he is a Jew.

11: Because he is a Jew.

12: Because, Jew though he is, he thinks he's as good as you are.

13: Because he is a Jew.

14: Because he is a Jew.

15: Because your friends have fifteen reasons for hating a Jew.

Myron Selznick (front, far right) in 1923 on the set of *The Passionate Adventure,* an early Gainsborough production filmed at the Islington studios in England. Two of the film's stars were Clive Brook (front, far left, looking dazed) and Marjorie Daw (rear, looking demure with the teapot), whom Myron later married. The gentleman with the snappy socks is director Graham Cutts. Missing are one of the story's writers, the assistant director, and the art director, all of whom were Alfred Hitchcock.

Rudolph Valentino and five of the eighty-eight American Beauties served up by the Mineralava company in Madison Square Garden, 1923.

knew some of the people in the film world there from the Selznick Pictures days in Fort Lee; one old friend, Harry Rapf, was with the new MGM outfit.

In July 1926 Associated Exhibitors folded, before they could release anything, leaving David Selznick broke and without a job, not quite stranded in Los Angeles but not knowing what to do next. In New York City, a month later, Rudolph Valentino died suddenly in a Manhattan hospital. His was the first great death of the movie industry, and the crowds of thousands of weeping, screaming fans nearly destroyed Campbell's Funeral Parlor, where the body lay in state before being sent to California for interment. After the race riots over *The Birth of a Nation,* the epic hysteria that surrounded Valentino's death was the second tangible demonstration of the movies' power to arouse unchecked emotional responses, this time in minds that had been conditioned by twenty years of romantic force-feeding from the Hollywood studios and roused to heights of emotional excess by the tabloids of the time.

Selznick, along with everyone else in town, was shocked by Valentino's unexpected death. The two had met only briefly during the filming of the Mineralava short, and Selznick remembered him as "a good-looking quiet boy of enormous charm." The actor's body finally reached Los Angeles on September 8, and Selznick was amazed and repelled by the clamor and bad taste of the circus atmosphere surrounding the burial. The animal frenzy of the thousands of fans confronted him for the first time with the hold that movies had on the libidinous fantasies of the female American moviegoer; the spectacle was something he couldn't comprehend but never forgot.

In the weeks immediately after the Valentino funeral, Selznick made a concerted effort to get work in the Hollywood film business. In his favor were ten years of experience in all phases of the business, and his youth. It was to Louis B. Mayer's studio, the year-old Metro-Goldwyn combine in Culver City, that Selznick turned to try to get a job. At his brother Myron's insistence, David went out to the studio to see Harry Rapf, who had been Myron's assistant at Fort Lee and also during the short-lived Associated Exhibitors days. Rapf didn't exactly know what David could do; if ever a person was overqualified to start at the bottom, it was David. But he was persuasive, convincing Rapf to let him have a two-week trial.

But the Selznick name was not always an asset when dealing with some of his father's enemies, of whom Louis B. Mayer was one of the

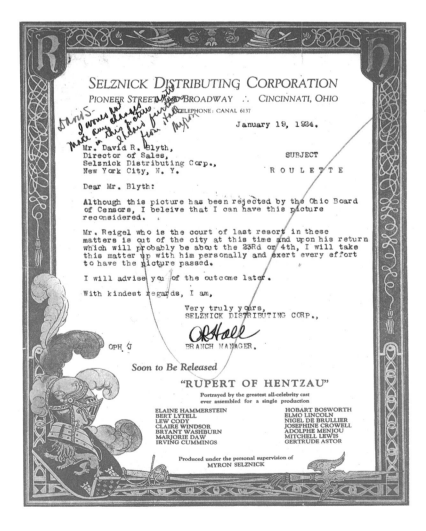

There were several hundred local censorship boards throughout the country, each of which could, and did, demand its own set of changes before a picture could be released in the area. It was partially to combat this situation that the MPPDA had been organized in 1922; but independent producers like Selznick were left to their own devices in contending with the boards. This letter concerns the Ohio censorship problems of *Roulette,* young Selznick's first produced feature, but it's also an elaborate coming attraction for *Rupert of Hentzau* (a sequel to *The Prisoner of Zenda*), the last picture to be completed by the Selznicks before bankruptcy ruined them.

earliest. When Mayer heard that David had been hired, he is reported to have said he would not have any Selznicks in his studio. This was a momentary setback, but David's chutzpah and resourcefulness came to the rescue. He had read in the paper that Nicholas Schenck, MGM's president and Mayer's boss, was in town staying at the Ambassador Hotel. As Selznick tells it:

I waited for him outside the barbershop. After I introduced myself, he remembered me, and I reminded him of the *Ben-Hur* incident and his promise. For once, a Schenck remembered and he asked what he could do. I told him about the situation at the studio and asked him to invest $150 on the basis of a two week job at $75 per, and assured him that he wouldn't ever hear of me after that if the studio didn't keep me, despite Mayer's antagonism. I told him I only wanted two weeks to make good, and he said to call him the next day at the studio, which I did, and he said that I had my two weeks.

So, on October 4, 1926, David Selznick took the forty-minute bus ride from Hollywood southwest to the Metro-Goldwyn-Mayer studios in Culver City, where he was going to start at the very bottom of the Hollywood ladder as a reader in the story department.

Twenty-four-year-old David O. Selznick just after the collapse of Associated Exhibitors, going places in Hollywood.

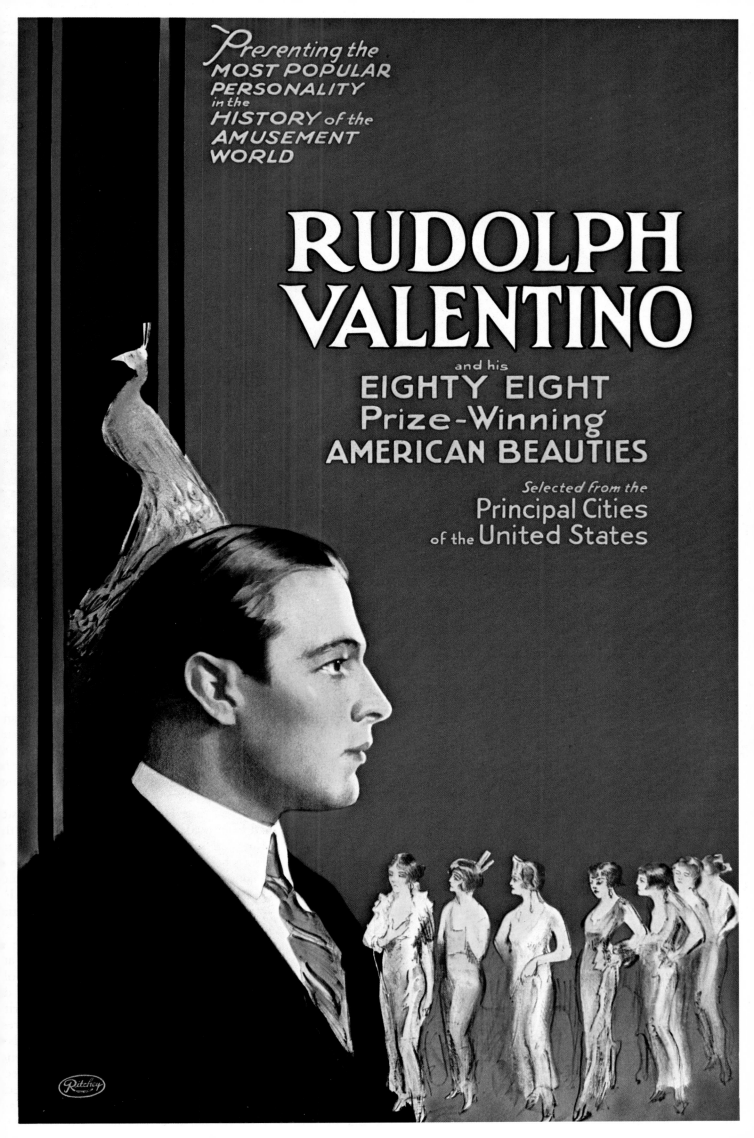

Hollywood—1926

IN OCTOBER 1926, when David Selznick went to work at MGM, cars, trains, buses, and an airplane a week were delivering to southern California a relentless stream of people from everywhere: tourists hoping to see a movie star and seldom being disappointed. Many, lured by the weather and the promise of cheap land, stayed on, settling in small surrounding communities that would eventually spread out and form the world's first twentieth-century city—Los Angeles.

By 1926, Los Angeles had grown significantly since the days when the Nestor Film Company, in 1911, had first brought the movie business to the "drowsy little resort village" of five thousand residents called "Holly-Wood." The name had come from Mrs. H. H. Wilcox, a prominent local resident who had appropriated it from an Eastern country estate because she liked the sound. In the intervening fifteen years Hollywood had grown into the most famous place on earth, vying with Rome and the Holy Land as a Mecca for pilgrims. Forty thousand people now lived and worked in the booming little town of streets fringed by pepper trees and tall palms that swayed in the warm winds blowing in from the desert, blanketing the area with the fragrance of the surrounding orange and citrus groves. The streets were lined with stucco bungalows, shops, restaurants, and theatres, while the surrounding low hills were dotted with the larger, more expensive homes of the well-to-do.

In the flood tide of twenties prosperity, Hollywood was riding the crest of the wave. Downtown at the new Biltmore Hotel, at a convention of the American Bankers Association, six thousand delegates cheered as financier Otto Kahn lauded President Coolidge for allowing "prosperity to run rampant throughout the land" and extolled Los Angeles as "the city of the future." Across the continent in Rochester, New York, film industry watchdog Will Hays told another convention, this time of film

engineers, that "in ten years Hollywood may well be the art center of the world." Hollywood business leaders took heed of this and that same October embarked on a $25 million expansion program: streets were being widened, new buildings were going up. Sid Grauman, one of the town's leading showmen, was spending $1 million to construct his massive new Chinese Theatre, which, with its handprints and footprints of the famous, would eventually become a concrete symbol of Hollywood's history.

At that time Hollywood's history consisted solely of the movies that had been made there, and the films, once they had played, were locked away and seldom seen again. Since the motion picture industry has always been prone to that unique American custom of destroying its past to construct its future, old films were melted down to retrieve the silver chemicals, which would then be recycled. Films and what was on them were considered as transient and insubstantial as the delicate celluloid on which they were printed.

So, in Hollywood, there was no sense of things accomplished, no continuity with the past, unless you stood at the corner of Sunset, Prospect, and Talmadge near the eastern end of Hollywood Boulevard and looked across the flat bungalows to the decaying remains of ancient Babylon, the towering set from D. W. Griffith's 1916 epic, *Intolerance*, already ancient history. Griffith, who was responsible for the maturation of the movies and also for the rise of Hollywood as a center of production, had given up after a decade of independence, and in 1926 had gone to work for Paramount as a contract director, ostensibly a prestigious replacement for the recently departed Cecil B. DeMille. There was a popular theory that Griffith had suffered a decline as an artist, but the truth was that audiences' tastes had changed, and Griffith was a victim of his own innovations. Audiences had rushed past him in their ability to absorb new styles and techniques, something he was unable or unwilling to furnish them with.

Hollywood was just then coming out of its fascination with the foolish, romantic, exotic melodramas that had been a staple of audience appeal for the past twenty years—and none too soon. Box-office receipts, for the first time in years, showed an alarming drop, and more and more theatres were adding live entertainment to their programs to bolster attendance.

Everybody blamed the novelty—radio—for this, and indeed it was partly to blame, being new, exciting, and easily accessible, just as the movies had been. But it wasn't just the radio. After twenty-six years, the movies held few surprises any more, except for the big specials like *Ben-Hur* and *The Big Parade*. The silent film had reached a cul-de-sac, although no one yet knew it: neither the audiences, who never gave it any thought, nor the critics, who did, nor the studios, whose livelihood and expansion rested on the smug assumption that nothing could possibly change the status quo.

For a time they were right. Old habits die hard, and enough people still poured into the theatres every week to allow the film industry to publicize itself as the nation's fourth largest industry. And the leaders of this industry, who were seriously beginning to consider themselves artists, had just decided to form the Academy of Motion Picture Arts and Sciences to reward "excellence in all branches of production."

David Selznick and the others who were coming to town in the hopes of getting into the movies were the vanguard of a new generation who had grown up on the movies and been nurtured on their excitement and razzle-dazzle. It was to be a generation whose attitudes and endeavors would have a profound effect on the structure and methods of moviemaking in Hollywood for the next thirty years.

In the late fall of 1926 more than 75,000 people were engaged in some aspect of film production in Hollywood. The year before, the ten studios around town had spent $175 million to make 775 features that were shown to 100 million movie fans a week, close to the total population of the United States. These fans paid $750 million at an average admission price of 25 cents to get into the 20,000 theatres across the country.

(Opposite) Hollywood Boulevard, looking east in late 1926. The excavation site for Sid Grauman's new Chinese Theatre is at the bottom center.

(Below) The same general area as it looked in 1903, when Hollywood Boulevard was called Prospect. The Pacific Electric streetcar is stopped at the intersection of Prospect and Highland.

Art director Harold Grieve drew this topically humorous map of Hollywood and its environs in 1925—capturing perfectly the charm, geography, and attitudes of the ten-year-old boom town.

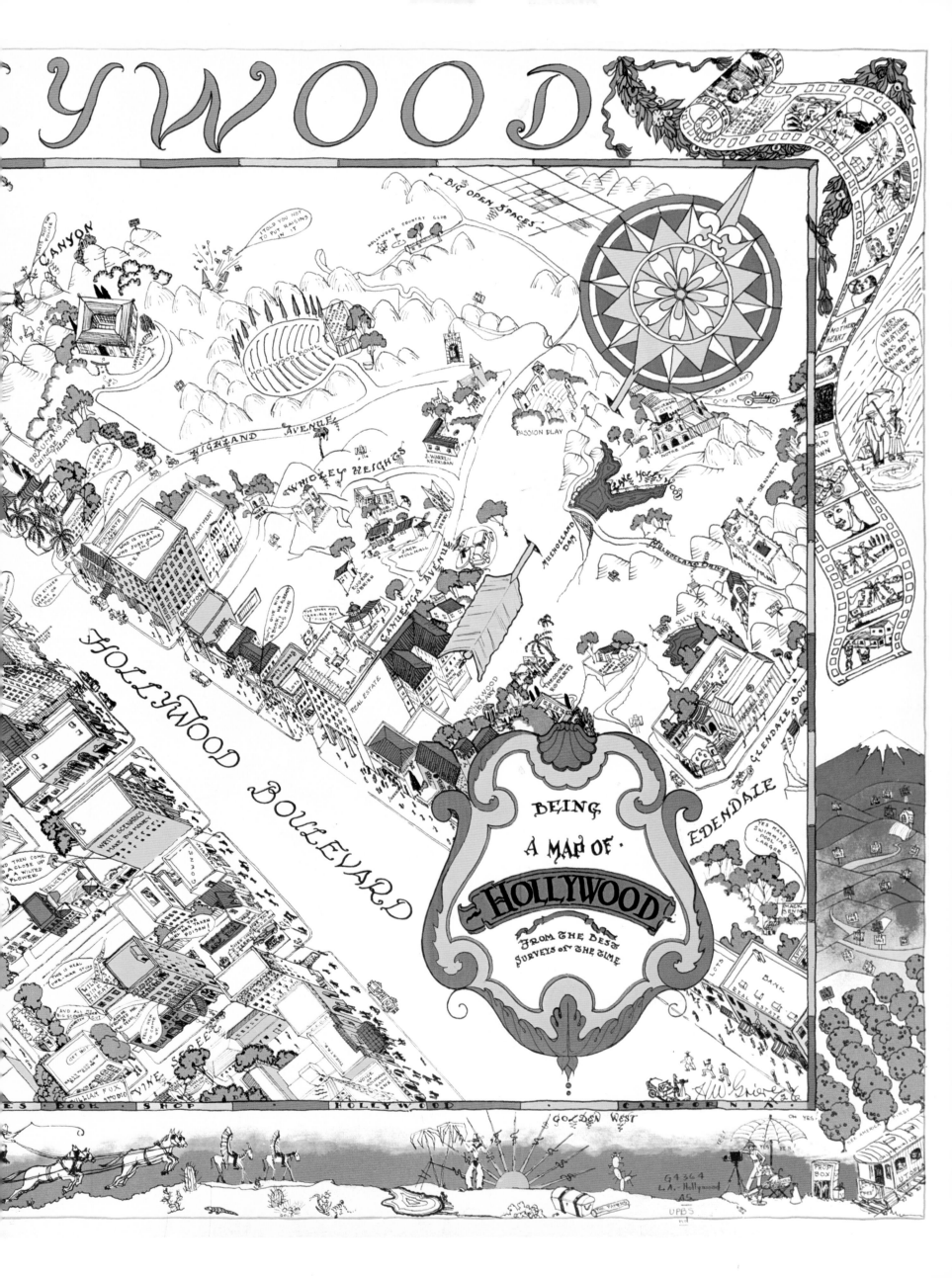

BEING
A MAP OF
HOLLYWOOD
FROM THE BEST
SURVEYS OF THE TIME

Sid Grauman and Jack Warner with the truck delivering the Vitaphone equipment to Grauman's Egyptian for the second "premiere" of *Don Juan.*

Sid Grauman (with hands in pockets) and the cast of real Indians he used in his stage prologue for Paramount's epic *The Covered Wagon* in 1924. Jesse Lasky is standing between Grauman and Colonel Tim McCoy, who, on the strength of his appearance in this prologue, was signed to a contract by the new firm of Metro-Goldwyn-Mayer.

On Hollywood Boulevard there were seven theatres. One, the new El Capitan, was devoted to the "legitimate drama." The other six were film theatres, ranging from the tiny Apollo near Western Avenue to the exotic Grauman's Egyptian near Highland, where first-run films sometimes played for as long as a year and where, in October 1926, Sid Grauman and Warner Bros. were about to launch for the second time John Barrymore in *Don Juan*—this time with the Warner Bros. novelty sound device, the Vitaphone, which had recently caused a mild sensation in New York. When the film had originally opened at the Egyptian in August 1926, Grauman had not wanted to use the recorded Vitaphone orchestral accompaniment, believing that his audience would feel cheated without the live orchestra that usually accompanied films. So *Don Juan* premiered sans Vitaphone and played that way for two months, until business dropped off. The canny Grauman then gave the film a second "premiere," this time with the Vitaphone's own prologue,

offering a potpourri of operatic excerpts, popular songs, and a concert by the New York Philharmonic, all introduced from the screen by the indefatigable Will Hays, who declared the invention a milestone.

It was, but not in the way that either he or the audience envisioned. Evidently very few people that night made the connection between the new device, "legitimate" or spoken drama, and the future of the movies, for the heavily advertised debut of Vitaphone sound didn't immediately affect picturemaking in Hollywood at all. Production continued in much the same way as before. Most films announced for 1927 were program pictures built around star appeal. There were, however, a larger number of specials announced: Paramount was letting William Wellman spend $2 million on an aviation drama, *Wings;* Warner Bros. was spending a like amount on a biblical spectacle, *Noah's Ark;* and out in Culver City at the Pathé studio Cecil B. DeMille was topping even this by taking on nothing less than the life of Christ in *King of Kings.* The towering sets he erected for this film were visible to David Selznick as he passed the studio on his way to MGM, a quarter mile away from the Pathé lot.

Selznick was one of eleven hundred people at MGM who labored around the clock six days a week to turn out fifty-two pictures a year. They worked in a ten-year-old, 40-acre complex of buildings built originally by pioneer Thomas Ince. Ince had sold it to one of the early anemic giants, Triangle; after its demise, the studio was taken over by the Samuel Goldwyn interests, which had the name but not the man. Then in April 1924 the studio facility and the Goldwyn corporate name were merged with Marcus Loew's Metro Pictures, and the new company was put under the management of Louis B. Mayer, ex–theatre owner turned independent producer. For a time the company was called Metro Goldwyn, and the credits on the films read "A Metro Goldwyn Picture, Produced by Louis B. Mayer." This lasted several months. Then in the interests of brevity, along with pride and ego, the name became officially Metro-Goldwyn-Mayer. Mayer was fiercely insistent about the use of the full name. Joe Cohn, his production manager at the studio, remembers Mayer berating a telephone operator who was still answering calls with "Hello, Metro Goldwyn." Mayer told her: "It's Metro-Goldwyn-Mayer, and the next time you forget it, you won't have a job."

Mayer's main strength as an executive was his ability to pick talent. He had a sixth sense about creative people; he appreciated them and paid them well, whether they were in front of the camera or behind it. That included Cohn, who, as production manager, organized the various departments to turn out a picture a week at a set cost with a minimum of wasted time and effort. Mayer was in charge of overall business arrangements for the studio. He hired and fired, decided how much money should be spent, and generally formulated studio policy. Irving Thalberg was his creative right hand. Even in 1926, at a time of anonymous studio executives, the frail twenty-six-year-old Thalberg had a well-deserved reputation as a maker of outstanding films. He had, from all contemporary accounts, an instinctive and unerring knack for story construction and casting, seemingly knowing at any given moment what would please an audience. Before joining Mayer in 1923, his grasp of film technique had been nurtured by seven years of working for Carl ("Papa") Laemmle at Universal. After the 1923 move his perceptive talent appreciably improved the quality of Mayer's films.

Mayer placed Thalberg in charge of all creative aspects of production; he decided which stories to make, how to cast them on both sides of the camera, and when to send a project back for more work. He did all this with just two assistants: Harry Rapf, who supervised the routine program pictures; and young Bernard Hyman, who was in charge of a new unit making Tim McCoy westerns.

By late 1926 these four men, aided by Joe Cohn and his production department, had made MGM the new leader of the industry. Its films were consistently placing among the year's ten best, and were drawing better notices and making more money than the competition. The films were well and intelligently made (not always the same thing), the craftsmanship of the various departments giving an appetizing gloss to even the most inconsequential of tales. Cohn, working with Mayer and Thal-

The second "premiere" of *Don Juan* at the Egyptian Theatre on Hollywood Boulevard, this time utilizing the Vitaphone short subjects and recorded accompaniment. Sid Grauman had pioneered the use of searchlights for movie openings at the 1921 unveiling of *Robin Hood* at the same theatre.

Cecil B. DeMille's massive independent production of the life of Christ, *King of Kings,* was the first picture to play Grauman's Chinese Theatre, seen here being readied for the May 1927 premiere.

berg, had put together a production system that was streamlined, efficient, and designed, in Cohn's words, to "make it as easy as possible for a director to shoot his film."

The six glass-enclosed stages at the studio were in constant use. There was a stock company of thirty-eight, the largest talent pool in the industry. Scripts tailored to the images and abilities of these players were turned out by a force of twenty-seven writers, working alone or in tandem with another, fleshing out sequences for stories that had been blocked out at the supervisors' daily story conference. As a script was finished and approved by the supervisor, it was copied and sent to Cohn's five-man office, where it was routed to the twenty-five departments whose responsibility it was to see that all necessary items in the script were placed at the director's disposal. These ranged from Cedric Gibbons's art department, which could whip up a painted backdrop of a Parisian street literally overnight, to the wardrobe department, where Russian designer Romain de Tirtoff (Erté) and his seventy-seven coworkers could design a period ball gown or a sleek contemporary outfit with equal ease. The sixteen-member property department kept careful inventory of several thousand items from a mustache press to a Roman chariot. The special camera department would check the script to see what photographic effects might be needed: skies altered, landscapes and settings adapted through matte paintings, glass shots, and other closely guarded "trick" work.

These departments, plus camera, electrical, casting, carpenters, and painters, took about twenty-five days to push one project through its "on stage" phase. This was for the average film, which took roughly forty-two scenes to tell its story. The forty-two scenes were then sent to one of thirty-two film editors, who would cut them into approximately five

King of Kings was produced at the old Thomas Ince studios in Culver City. This set, representing the Temple of Jerusalem, was designed by Anton Grot and Mitchell Leisen and towered over the back lot for another thirteen years.

hundred separate "shots," the whole lasting upward of seventy minutes. From there the film went on to the titling department, where it was supplied with explanations, dialogue, captions, and anything else that might be lacking, including the necessary glossing over of any rough story spots or the addition of an occasional touch of humor.

Once all this had been previewed, pruned, and approved, the laboratory printed up 150 copies. Then one of the eighteen people in Pete Smith's publicity department would put together a "campaign" book, consisting of stories about the picture, ads, and exploitation ideas, which would be sent out to the theatres playing the film. The countrywide chain of 144 Loew's theatres was counted on to provide enough patrons at 25 cents a head to return the $150,000 cost of each film, plus a like amount in profit. By late 1926, when David Selznick went to work at MGM, the production set-up was so smooth and flexible that Selznick was hard pressed to find a way to make a suitable impression. But his background and interest in writing and literature gave him a keen story sense, and he had a sharp feel for what was commercial. He began making himself useful to Rapf by showering him with story suggestions designed to catch on to current trends:

> Why don't we make an ultra-modern society and dog story in the Alps? We could bring in the very smart Swiss hotels with skiing ... which would give great contrast with the self-sacrificing work of the monks, living alone with their marvelous dogs. A smart society girl might become lost in the snows; we might have airplanes sent out to search ... and then a St. Bernard to the rescue.

Selznick also suggested a film about schoolteachers because he felt that "a picture glorifying the schoolteacher and picturing her great personal sacrifice for the benefit of the coming generation would be very popular, and could be made very cheaply." With one eye on the box office, he felt that "a large percentage of the schoolteachers of the country could be counted on for exploitation co-operation."

And he began looking at pictures that Rapf didn't have time for, such as *A Certain Young Man.* Selznick recommended that the retakes and changes Rapf felt were necessary should not be made because they wouldn't materially improve the picture. As he put it, "There is no use spending money to make a bad picture a poor one."

Yet in the middle of this feverish commercialism Selznick was ever alert to anything new and unusual, beseeching Rapf to obtain a print of *The Armored Cruiser Potemkin* by the Russian director Sergei Eisenstein, whose films were just then beginning to be seen in America. Selznick saw the film at a private screening at the home of writer Howard Estabrook, who was an old friend of his, and was convinced that it "is unquestionably one of the greatest motion pictures ever made. It possesses a technique very new to the screen and ... it might be very advantageous to have the organization view it, in the same way that a group of artists might view and study a Rubens or a Raphael."

This combination of showmanship, drive, and idealism about movies caught the notice of both Thalberg and Mayer. At the end of the two-week trial period, Selznick was made manager of the writers' department with a weekly salary of $75; two weeks later his salary was doubled. Seven months later he had worked his way up through the writers' and story departments to full-time assistant to Harry Rapf. Finally, in April 1927, Selznick was made assistant producer under Rapf, a position of some responsibility and, to hear Selznick tell it in a letter to a friend, long, arduous hours:

> It's May, 1927, and I've wandered into the office of a director named McCarthy because it possesses a gorgeous new Electrola and I can have music while I write. Out on Stage Six my *Body and Soul* company grinds one Aileen Pringle and one Lionel Barrymore this midnight. She is furious, he is sour. Since I am neither, I duck their company. I'm advancing with incredible rapidity in this "my chosen field"; I rise every day at 6:30, take the bus to work where I work twelve or

Moviemaking at MGM, circa 1926. The caption on this still reads: "The entrance to a fashionable hotel has been constructed across the front of one of the 'stages.' ... The stars' dressing rooms are in the low frame buildings to the right."

MARCUS LOEW

His achievements in the field of entertainment are internationally known. Behind his success is the genius of the showman, the genius that is making M-G-M exhibitors rich, the genius that has built up the Rock of Gibraltar strength and stability of Metro-Goldwyn-Mayer.

One of the most beloved personalities in the motion picture industry, Mr. Loew, now celebrates his twentieth anniversary as a showman. The success of Metro-Goldwyn-Mayer is a crowning achievement in his brilliant career as a pioneer of entertainment.

NICHOLAS M. SCHENCK

The guiding personality in the executive administration of M-G-M, he typifies the kind of personnel that by reason of its practical experience and outlook on production sets M-G-M far ahead of all producers.

LOUIS B. MAYER

The mind behind the product. His career reads like fiction. His life has been spent selling entertainment to the public and he knows what it's all about. Practical leader of practical M-G-M producers at the Studio.

TO THE EXHIBITOR: In analyzing the product which you as a showman are asked to book into your theatre, your first thought must indeed be: "Who are the men behind the product?" The time has come when the choice of pictures for your theatre must be made on the basis of intelligent study of the various companies. As a showman you must look to showmen for your pictures. The men behind the M-G-M product have shown the industry that it takes practical theatre minds to create sound box-office attractions. Investigate every company in the business. You will find that Metro-Goldwyn-Mayer above all others is composed of experienced theatre minds, creating hits of which you as a showman can immediately say: "That product could only have been made by men who understand the real meaning of showmanship."

Every director on the M-G-M lot is a man of great and outstanding achievement

IT'S amazing the way the important directors in this business one by one have flocked to Metro-Goldwyn-Mayer until now at our Culver City Studio are gathered the largest number and the outstanding personalities among directors. Why do they prefer M-G-M? Because at our Studio they are in no way hampered in the making of selling-product. The boys with the eye on the box-office feel they can do their stuff best on our lot. And we want just that kind. As a result, M-G-M exhibitors can feel secure that the company they've chosen has only showman-minds making the product. And the product backs that up.

These pages are reproduced from the MGM 1926–27 product sampler. These promotional booklets were put together by the studio's publicity department twice yearly and distributed to the influential film buyers for the large theatre chains across the country. The richness and the diversity of the talent pool, on both sides of the camera, more than justified the famous catch phrase, "More stars. . . ."

More stars than there are in heaven

LILLIAN GISH: Star of Stars! Critics praise her lavishly, but it is the public that takes her close to its heart.

RAMON NOVARRO: Handsome Ben that! Great has been his public adoration, but now he leads with filmdom's favorites.

CARMEL MYERS: The irresistible siren of "Ben Hur" has a following among fans that means money at the box-office. Her name will be in M-G-M casts ("The Gay Deceiver" for one) next season.

GEORGE K. ARTHUR: Critics predict an exciting future for this talented and clever young M-G-M star who in a few screen appearances has won real popularity by virtue of youthful charm and spirit.

MARION DAVIES: Comedienne superb! Her beauty, her merry personality have won her fandom's acclaim!

JOHN GILBERT: Romantic idol of "The Big Parade!" His millions of admirers wait for his every appearance.

NORMA SHEARER: Charming Lady of the Screen! The public adores her and expresses its adoration in the theatres of the world.

METRO-GOLDWYN-MAYER STARS are the Diamonds in the sky of Filmdom! They are the Electric Light Personalities above all others to draw the record audiences today. Other Stars are waning in the film firmament. M-G-M's Great Money Names are ever building in popularity. And all the time, because we believe in Names, M-G-M is grooming the New Celebrities to delight the ever-hungry public taste.

John Gilbert, Norma Shearer — Million-dollar Names — are indications of how M-G-M fulfills your need. Other companies ask your public to pay for names whose magic is lost. M-G-M gives your public the bright lights of popular acclaim

MARCELINE DAY: A brilliant future lies ahead of this delighted young star whose work in "The Barrier" brought her fame the past year. She has a marvelous role in "The Boy Friend" for '26-'27.

LARS HANSON: M-G-M goes to the far corners of the earth to get box office material! Lars Hanson, matinee idol of Sweden, shows in his support of Lillian Gish in "The Scarlet Letter," that he's there!

ANTONIO MORENO: A favorite whose popularity grew immensely in the past year with "Beverly of Graustark" and other hits. He is the hero of "Mare Nostrum" and "Love's Blindness," for '26-'27.

LON CHANEY: Genius of Actors! The name in electric lights is guide-post to thrilling entertainment.

BUSTER KEATON: Joy-bringer! His "Battling Butler" will make him the leader of all screen comedians.

MAE MURRAY: Beautiful Merry Widow! She has intensified the fame and popularity that make her a Great Public Star.

GWEN LEE: Risen from the ranks of extra girls by her marvelous beauty, she appeared briefly in "The Secretary," "Sally, Irene and Mary," but in the coming year watch her step!

ALICE TERRY: Her role as the fascinating spy star ever had to sweep her on to the heights of popularity. Also to appear in "The Magician."

DOUGLAS GILMORE: This handsome player made a sensation as a stage-lover in "White Cargo." M-G-M saw on the alert, picked him. He will be seen in "Paris" and "Love's Blindness."

RENEE ADOREE: Her Melisande in "The Big Parade," her rare portrayals in M-G-M attractions work her as one of the industry's outstanding money-names.

ELEANOR BOARDMAN: The millions in big cities and small, love her because her beauty and appeal are typical of the best in American girlhood. Her popularity is ever growing.

LIONEL BARRYMORE: Another feather in M-G-M's cap. This great actor under exclusive contract to M-G-M. He will appear in "The Trail of '98" among others.

ROY D'ARCY: His fame as the fascinating villain of "Merry Widow" and "Beverly of Graustark" insures bigger audiences for pictures in which he appears next season.

WILLIAM HAINES: The hero of "Brown of Harvard" is sweeping forward to top most popularity. William Haines will be another M-G-M name for next season, particularly in "Tell It To The Marines."

SALLY O'NEIL: During the past year the merry girl has won her way to real fame. ("Mike" was marvelous.) Buster Keaton made her his leading lady in "Battling Butler." Another M-G-M Mariner.

LEW CODY: One of the most popular of stars, he has developed a light comedy characterization that is winning him greater stardom. Watch for "The Gay Deceiver."

OWEN MOORE: He's a good drawing card now. But with the roles that he'll get as an M-G-M star this handsome favorite is slated for top rank. He will appear in "Tin Hats" and others.

GRETA GARBO: Unquestionably the outstanding motion picture find of the past year. The public, the critics, demand stardom for her after "Ibanez' Torrent" and "Temptress." Watch!

CHARLES RAY: He showed that he could do much greater things than his roles of the past, and the public welcomed him back in "Auction Block" and "Paris."

MAE BUSCH: A great actress and a beauty of remarkable personal appeal. Her work in "The Unholy Three" in the past insures ticket-buyers wherever she appears.

JOAN CRAWFORD: Ever thinking of building the Stars of Tomorrow, M-G-M will give to adoring fans Joan Crawford roles that fulfill her promise of "Sally, Irene and Mary," "Old Clothes," "Paris."

CONRAD NAGEL: When the public sees Conrad Nagel in "There You Are" next season, they'll love him in this light comedy role (remember him in "Excuse Me!").

PAULINE STARKE: M-G-M lists the names that draw fans. This talented beauty will be seen in "Love's Blindness" and "The Trail of '98" among others.

CLAIRE WINDSOR: The public hails her as the screen's most beautiful woman. They'll like her more than ever when they see her in the cast of "Tell It To The Marines."

KARL DANE: A real find. As the "Slim" of "The Big Parade" he set the world laughing. And will continue to do so in "The Trail of '98" and other M-G-M attractions.

DOROTHY PHILLIPS: M-G-M has made sure to take advantage of this beautiful star's fan popularity by giving her a great role in "The Gay Deceiver." And in others to follow.

AILEEN PRINGLE: Her popularity ever on the upgrade, nourished by "Three Weeks," "His Hour," "Soul Mates," now finds its fulfillment in a greater popularity for the coming year.

GERTRUDE OLMSTED: The progress of this lovely screen personality in the past year has been remarkable. She was in "Dance," "Torrent" and "Monte Carlo." Among her next season's appearances is "The Gay Deceiver."

Portraits of Lillian Gish and Norma Shearer, the studio's biggest female stars of 1926.

fourteen hours a day, writing script changes, reading treatments, and it works—and my ideas work too—for my salary was given a splendid boost today . . . and yet even though I love it . . . I'm in advanced stages of decay; I don't write or read; I don't live or love; why, I scarcely think. In the months that I've been here in Hollywood I've found more friends than in years in New York . . . they're more varied, more amusing, and Hollywood or no, more intelligent. For samples: Norman Kerry and a drinking gang whose wit is sharp and whose sophistication never tires because it is natural . . . Lew Milestone, a recent comet among directors; he is Russian, and here not so many years; his mind, his manner, his humor are the nearest I've known to those of Ben Hecht. . . . Lorna Moon, a clever, brilliant, young Scot. Her stories gained her raves from Galsworthy; Thalberg employs her and I dine with her and enjoy her immensely.

MGM's supervisors now included Hunt Stromberg, a tall, good-looking fellow who had worked for Thomas Ince, and who joined MGM after Ince's death. He became second-in-command to Thalberg and oversaw most of the studio's "A" (big-budget) pictures. Harry Rapf took care of the program pictures, the bulk of the studio's output, while Selznick, still a promising small-fry, produced the Tim McCoy westerns under Harry Rapf.

Most of the studios made westerns and most of them were popular. Fox had Tom Mix, Buck Jones, and George O'Brien; Universal had popular Art Acord, Jack Hoxie, and Hoot Gibson; Harry Carey was at Pathé; and Bob Custer and Fred Thompson kept FBO solvent. About the only studio that didn't make westerns was Warner Bros., but they had Rin-Tin-Tin, which was pretty much the same thing.

Tim McCoy, Colonel, U.S. Army (Ret.), was to be MGM's only western star. With his chiseled features and steely stare, he was the archetypal silent-movie cowboy; his films were economically made, and because of his own contributions to both story and action, they were a cut above the westerns from the other studios. Within budgetary limits they were as lavish as they could be, using natural locations whenever possible, especially McCoy's home state of Wyoming. This careful attention to detail from both star and studio brought favorable notice from the trade press, if not always from the audience, which sometimes found the star just a little too steely. But the films did well, always returning their $80,000 cost plus a sizable profit.

The first two had been made under the supervision of Harry Rapf. Then Bernard Hyman took over; but he soon tired of their rigid formula, so Rapf assigned Selznick to oversee the next two. Selznick loathed westerns. Their conventional plots and standardized formula offered nothing to his imagination and he couldn't see their appeal at all, but this would be a chance actually to produce a film from start to finish. He began going over story ideas with W. S. ("Woody") Van Dyke, McCoy's director, whose films moved as fast as he talked. He and Selznick got along well; they were both young, ambitious, and knew their business. Both wanted to go on to bigger things, and the McCoy westerns were a good exercise in production, if not a chance to make a spectacular impression. It was while working on the scripts for the next two McCoy films that Selznick and Van Dyke came up with the idea of filming both stories at the same time, thereby cutting costs even more and the amount of production time involved almost in half.

McCoy was all for the scheme, and after broaching the idea to Cohn, who saw no reason why it couldn't be done, they were given the go-ahead by Thalberg. "It was a little unusual," says Cohn, "although it had been done . . . but not at MGM. Some of the quickie studios would do it, but that was out of necessity. Really all it needed was a little foresight and planning, like in the old days. You photographed Indians going up a hill, then you put Federal uniforms on them, or whatever, and they'd ride down the hill and then back up the hill, meaning that they were chasing the Indians. You could use the same people, just put different clothes on them. It didn't make any difference unless you saw the films together. Then you spotted it right away, but these were released months apart, so who could tell?"

Late in August 1927 unit manager Art Smith and a cast and crew of twenty-five left Culver City to join McCoy in Lander, Wyoming, where he had gone to use his personal influence to arrange for the use of five

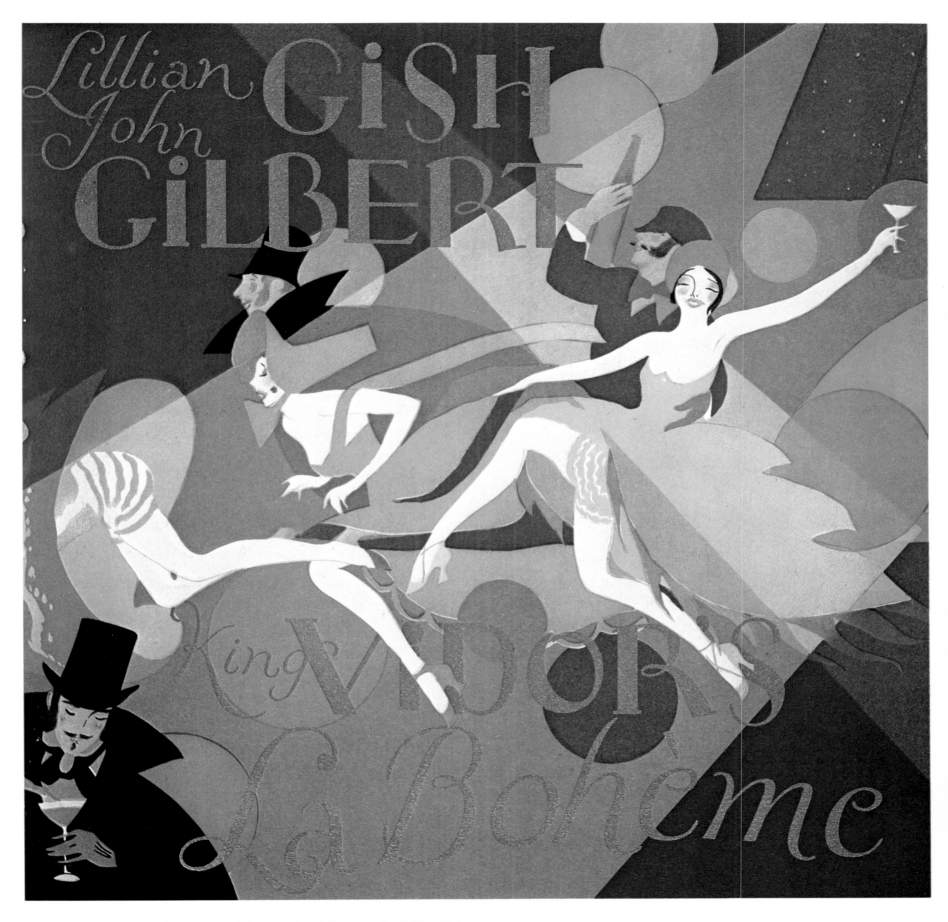

A lavish, colorful ad for a silent version of the opera *La Bohème,* starring Lillian Gish and John Gilbert. Not a commercial success, the picture was considered to be an asset to the studio's prestige.

Ben-Hur and *The Big Parade* were both still playing moneymaking engagements around the country in late 1926. *The Merry Widow,* a silent version of the operetta, turned out to be one of the studio's biggest hits and was von Stroheim's last picture for MGM. *The Mysterious Island,* in all its Technicolor glory, wasn't released for almost two years, and bore absolutely no resemblance to "Jules Verne's world famous . . . story."

hundred troops of the U.S. Army Cavalry, plus a sizable contingent of the Shoshone Indian tribe. Van Dyke took with him one finished script, *Spoilers of the West*, and an unfinished outline for a second to be called *Wyoming*. Selznick would stay at the studio, working on the second script, looking at the film as it came in, and sending out whatever else became necessary during the course of the forty-day filming schedule. The "dailies" of the exteriors, with figures silhouetted on windy hillsides and rolling Wyoming landscapes, were exciting to Selznick, who wired to Van Dyke that they were "gorgeous" and "beautiful" but that Negro actor Blue Washington "isn't black enough, and consequently not funny; better blacken him up for the close-ups."

After two hectic, grueling months away, Van Dyke brought the company back to Culver City in early November. His and Selznick's gamble had paid off. They had two complete films for a little over $100,000 instead of the $160,000 that the two films would have cost if made in the normal way.

As a reward Selznick was promoted to assistant to Hunt Stromberg, who assigned him to supervise a film version of Frederick O'Brien's best seller *White Shadows in the South Seas*, a story of native life in Tahiti. Selznick, who was "madly in love with the book," envisioned a tender love story set against a background of the destruction of the Polynesian race by white men. Nothing would do but that the film be made on location in Tahiti. Thalberg and Mayer agreed to this after being convinced by Selznick that Van Dyke would be the perfect person to direct, not only because of his talent, which Selznick thought considerable, but because of his proven ability to handle difficult location assignments. Stromberg, however, opposed this; he wanted the film directed by Robert Flaherty, the gifted documentary filmmaker who had just had a great success with a similar film for Paramount, *Moana*. His scheme was to have the film co-directed by Flaherty and Van Dyke. Selznick argued hotly that the two men couldn't possibly work together.

Stromberg refused to consider Selznick's objections, so Selznick furiously took his case to Thalberg, accosting him in the crowded MGM commissary. When Thalberg backed Stromberg, who was after all Selznick's superior, Selznick very loudly and rudely told Thalberg that he didn't know what he was doing. Thalberg stalked out amid tense silence in the crowded room. He later told Selznick he would either have to apologize or find another job. So, late in November 1927, just about the time that *The Jazz Singer* was premiering in New York City, David Selznick was once again looking for a job.

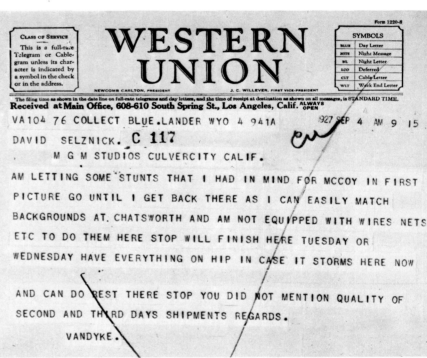

(Top) Tim McCoy on the horse, W. S. Van Dyke and cinematographer Clyde de Vinna on the platform, filming *Spoilers of the West* in Wyoming.
(Above) Telegrams were more reliable and quicker than telephones and letters in the 1920s, and location reports and other important messages were sent by this method. Van Dyke's report to Selznick indicates that production was almost finished on *Spoilers of the West*—one of the two films being made simultaneously by the location company.
(Left) Marjorie Daw, the romantic interest in *Spoilers of the West*.

'JAZZ SINGER,' WITH VITAPHONE, TRIUMPH FOR JOLSON

CHARLIE CHAPLIN TO PRODUCE 'NAPOLEON'

By Louella O. Parsons
Motion Picture Editor of Universal Service

Douglas Fairbanks

IF HENRY FORD could have looked in the backyard of the United Artists Studio, I am sure he would have been tempted to take a few photographs as Mary Pickford's new Ford car was being admired by Douglas Fairbanks, Charlie Chaplin, Joseph Schenck, Ernst Lubitsch, and four or five studio executives. Doug, as the donor of the car, was describing it in detail to Charlie, whose Rolls-Royce, standing close by, looked on jealously. No doubt Charlie was impressed. He couldn't believe it was a humble Ford, but then, neither could any of the rest of us. "Come on, some news, Charlie," I whispered between motor demonstrations.

"I am going to make 'Napoleon,'" he said.

My laugh brought Joseph Schenck to where Charlie and I were conversing.

"But he is, this time," said Mr. Schenck. "We are planning it for 1928."

Planned down, the man who made the derby hat and cane famous, said that he starts a comedy the last of February—now tentatively titled "Nowhere"—and as soon as that is finished he will begin his research work on "Napoleon."

This means that "The Suicide Club" is out. I never liked the name, anyway.

Lillian Gish

THERE were so many people at the United Artists Studio to see that I didn't get as many calls made as I expected. But I gathered up enough news to make it worth my while. David Wark Griffith will remake "The Battle of the Sexes." This story, made so many years ago by Mr. Griffith while he was kingpin at the Biograph Studio, will, of course, be entirely different in its modern form. But it should be interesting the way he now has it worked out. I have a sneaking feeling, although I could not get a single word of verification, that Lillian Gish may make her first appearance as a U. A. star in this picture. It is Mr. Griffith's next.

THERE will be no more gadding about to this and that studio for Buster Collier. When he finishes at Columbia studios he moves to Tiffany-Stahl and there he remains. That is if contracts mean anything. You see, John Stahl has signed him on a long-term contract and he will appear exclusively for Mr. Stahl and the company he represents. Buster Collier and Buster Keaton were having a grand time at the party given by I. E. Freud following the United Artists Theater opening. They were doing a team act that should be booked by the Orpheum circuit. Buster is at the party with Constance Talmadge. His recent matrimonial flurry seems to have blown over. I still maintain his trip to the marriage license bureau was either a publicity stunt or a practical joke. Maybe some day Buster will tell us the truth. Anyhow, Tiffany-Stahl say his work in "The Tragedy of Youth" is the reason for the new contract.

Buster Collier

DISCOVERED at the Samuel Goldwyn Studio, Andre Cheron, French actor. He is playing a part in "Leatherface," or "The Passionate Adventure." Ouch! Isn't that a title? Monsieur Cheron has been flying since 1918. He served in the war and then he came to Hollywood to act. I'm told he is an important part of Vilma Banky's cast, but that his heart is still in flying. The French colony in Hollywood is attempting to raise a fund to let him fly from New York to Paris in April. If they succeed we have every reason to believe the movies will be forgotten. It will be his first visit home in eight years.

PARAMOUNT seemed to think it was a big piece of news that Harry Cording had been signed to play the part of Stephen in "The Patriot." I suppose it is, although I couldn't get excited over it. Ernst Lubitsch, the director of "The Patriot," spent most of yesterday afternoon on the United Artists' lot. He was in conversation with Joseph Schenck, but I haven't heard that he is going to make a picture for United Artists. Even with my imagination I don't dare suggest this.

THE movies haven't interested Jack Gilbert a nickel's worth this week. He has begrudged every hour that he has spent away from home. No, it isn't a prospective bride, nor anything like that; it is a parrot, a bird that swears in six languages, and Jack is so keen over this kingpin that he hates to miss a single hour of his cussing.

John Gilbert

THE earthquake in Rome greatly disturbed one member of Hollywood's film colony. Sylvano Balboni's parents live in Rome and news of the quake made him fear for their safety. Mr. Balboni was the husband of June Mathis, whose memory is still fresh in the hearts of those who loved her.

I'VE had as little office. A rising young actor rises to ask me to handle his publicity. "You got so much in the paper," was he. "I'd like to have you for my representative."

LOVIN' TIME DUET

DORIS McMAHEN and George Grandee in "The Morning After," at the Hollywood Play House.— (Milligan photo.)

CITY BUILT FOR 'SUNRISE'

FOR the picturization of "Sunrise," now running at the Carthay Circle Theater, an entire city was constructed on the Fox lot. It included a streetcar, elevated and surface railways and every manner of office and residence building.

The picture has proved to be an excellent drawing card. The matinee and evening performances last Monday broke all previous attendance records at the Circle Theater.

It has had many capacity audiences, but never before have so many audiences for seats been turned away after the house was filled.

Film at Criterion Rich in Pathos and Interest

By Louella O. Parsons

Louella O. Parsons

THE strong protests uttered against the Vitaphone as a destroyer of the peaceful silence of motion pictures, suffered a glorious defeat last night. Without the Vitaphone "The Jazz Singer" would not have so completely won over the large audience at the Criterion Theater.

"The Jazz Singer" and the Vitaphone are affinities that do not jangle out of tune. If there had been long conversations and more attempts at vocal comedy, the effect would not have been so satisfactory. But very wisely Warner Brothers, save for a single scene between Al Jolson and his mother, eliminated the spoken words. But the singing! Think of hearing Al Jolson sing the words of his songs as a part of the screen play.

The combination exceeded this reviewer's best expectations. I have been one who has lamented the encroachment of the voice in the silent drama.

AGREEABLE SURPRISE

"The Jazz Singer," therefore, comes as an agreeable surprise. I must right here make it clear that there are few pictures that lend themselves as perfectly to the synchronization of music as "The Jazz Singer." The story is one of music—the Jewish boy whose father has ambitions for him to uphold the tradition of the family and become a cantor and who chooses to be a jazz singer. There are many natural opportunities for music. None of the songs are dragged in by the heels.

I never saw the stage play, "The Jazz Singer," so I do not know whether Alfred Cohn wrote his own story, or gave heed to the original play. Personally, I don't care. He has built a human interest story that is so well executed what matter if he added or subtracted situations?

As for Al Jolson. I don't blame him for traveling 3000 miles to see himself on the screen. If I could give a performance like he gives I would travel around the world. Mr. Jolson, of course, as an actor needs no comments, but the way he screens and his personality à la celluloid is worthy of several complimentary paragraphs.

Some of our best actors have failed to meet these camera exigencies, so Mr. Jolson can feel well pleased that he and his shadow fare so well. I suppose someone will rise up and label "The Jazz Singer" grand hokum. Too many people saw me wiping my eyes to make it advisable for me to take on such a highbrow attitude.

I did weep. I couldn't help it.

RESEMBLES JOLSON

While the story of "The Jazz Singer" is primarily one of mother love, there is a very attractive feminine interest in the person of May McAvoy. Miss McAvoy looks exceptionally pretty in a blonde wig and she adds the necessary love interest. Very wisely, Alan Crosland has refrained from the florid clinch in the end. It is right and fitting that the mother could continue the child object of interest to the boy.

Mr. Crosland, while we are on the subject, does a very nice piece of directing. Al Jolson as a boy is played by Bobby Gordon who bears an almost uncanny resemblance to Mr. Jolson. Richard Tucker as Harry Lee, producer, is adequate.

Any criticisms of the picture belong more to the story than to the production. It may tax the credulity to believe a father could be so hard-hearted to so young a boy. Yet, it has been done. Also, the sentimentality is perhaps a little Mid-Victorian for these callous days. Still, when all has been said and done, "The Jazz Singer" is Warner Brothers' best picture and one that they can be very proud to claim.

Last night, of course, brought a regular movie premiere—the crowds, the lights and the excitement. Conrad Nagel as toastmaster officiated in an able manner. Conrad's stage personality is too well known for me to essay any remarks. He introduced Eugene Besserer, May McAvoy, Otto Lederer, Warner Oland and, of course, Al Jolson. The speeches were short and snappy.

"Al himself broke down and wept," according to the opening day ad for *The Jazz Singer* in Los Angeles. It must have been a wet night, as Louella Parsons also admitted in her review to being moved to tears by the film.

The famed Marathon Avenue gate to the Hollywood studios of Paramount Pictures, designed by Ruth Morris.

Paramount and the Coming of Sound

SELZNICK WAS UNEMPLOYED for several weeks. Then, in January 1928, largely through the intercession of William Wellman, one of his close friends, he was offered a job as assistant to B. P. (Benjamin) Schulberg, production head at the venerable Famous Players-Lasky studio. Wellman, nicknamed "Wild Bill" for his short Irish temper and his penchant for taking out his frustrations with his fists, was a protégé of Schulberg's—Schulberg had arranged that he direct *Wings*, the first big aviation film. Its success made Wellman the fair-haired boy of the Famous Players-Lasky lot; his only failing was an inability to take supervision by any of the men assigned to oversee the production of films at Paramount. Wellman's agent was Myron Selznick,

David's brother; David was taken with Wellman's scrappy background, his talent, and his energy, while Wellman was impressed with David's intelligence, his training as a picturemaker, and his love of the moviemaking process. Wellman urged Schulberg to give Selznick a job, telling him that David was one of the few men Wellman thought he could work with in a supervisory capacity.

Several of Selznick's co-workers at MGM had also spoken highly of his abilities. At their urging, Schulberg sent for Selznick in mid-December 1927. As Selznick recalled it:

> Schulberg's assistant kept me waiting an entire afternoon, following my first interview with Schulberg, to tell me that I would have to

Until 1926, most Paramount pictures were made here at the old Famous Players-Lasky studios in the heart of Hollywood. Looking north, Sunset Boulevard is the tree-lined street at the bottom of the photo, and Vine Street is on the left.

(Left) Cecil B. DeMille is on the running board of the truck used to transport the cast and crew of the Lasky company's first production, *The Squaw Man,* in 1913. The star, Dustin Farnum, is the well-fed, hatless gentleman surrounded by squaws and other exotics.

In addition to its Hollywood facilities, Paramount also had studios in Astoria, Long Island (below), and at Joinville, in France (bottom).

work for less money than I had received at MGM, and that he wasn't sure they wanted me anyway. I demanded more money and walked out in a huff. It took some time for my pals to persuade Schulberg to see me again; when he did, he told me that my reputation for arrogance was well founded; then he asked me how long it would take for me to make good. I told him that I never wanted more than two weeks in any place to prove what I could do, so Schulberg put me on, saying that I would have to make an awfully good showing in those two weeks if I expected to stay on.

In 1928, Paramount Pictures, strictly speaking, did not make movies. It was only a distributor, the biggest in the business, one of several arms Adolph Zukor used in his all-encompassing embrace of the American film business. By 1928, this included an imposing new skyscraper in New York's Times Square, a nationwide chain of eleven hundred theatres, and film exchanges to service these theatres. Each theatre in the Paramount chain played an average of 175 films every year, supplemented by stage shows and short subjects. To keep the theatres supplied with films, Paramount had two studios in the United States: one in Astoria, Long Island, the other at Marathon Avenue in Hollywood. It was here at the Famous Players-Lasky studio, the oldest in Hollywood, that the bulk of Paramount's annual releases were made.

The four-block production complex was what had grown out of a trip west from New York made by Cecil B. DeMille and five others in 1913. They were the entire production forces of the newly christened Jesse L. Lasky Feature Play Company, an amalgamation of the talents of Lasky, ex–cornet player and vaudeville booker; Samuel Goldfish, ex-glove salesman; and DeMille, an indifferently successful playwright-actor-producer. The three men had pooled their resources to buy film rights to Edwin Milton Royle's successful play *The Squaw Man,* including the services of its popular star Dustin Farnum. Since it was a western, the partners agreed that it should be filmed in Arizona, until DeMille got off the train at Flagstaff, looked around, decided it looked more North African than Western, got back on the train, and went all the way to the end of the line, Los Angeles, where he'd heard that movies were being made. The Lasky forces set up headquarters in a barn 10 miles outside Los Angeles, because that's where they found a laboratory that would develop their film cheaply. The lab was two blocks south of the unpaved street that was Hollywood Boulevard; diagonally across the dusty road was the barn that DeMille, his cameraman, and actors used as a combi-

nation office, studio, and dressing room, sharing the space with two horses.

In 1913, the Goldfish-Lasky-DeMille combine was just another of the many little film companies that had begun using southern California as a base of production operations. The legend has grown up that Lasky-DeMille-Paramount was the first studio established in Hollywood, but it is inaccurate. The Nestor Film Company had been working there as early as 1911; D. W. Griffith had brought his American Biograph troupe to Los Angeles for the past two winters, and following him a handful of little outfits had sprung up in and around Hollywood. In terms of longevity, however, DeMille-Lasky was to become the oldest studio in the community, for the attrition rate among these small companies was enormous. Movie people were viewed with such suspicion that the local bank refused to handle the Lasky account; for the first few months of its existence, the firm's money was housed at the Hollywood Cash Grocery, three blocks away at Sunset and Cahuenga. The Lasky shoestring venture, however, was a success, and the account soon moved into a bank, where it grew in proportion to the studio, which in turn soon outgrew the barn. In 1915, a merger with Adolph Zukor's Famous Players in Famous Plays changed the name to Famous Players-Lasky, making films for distribution through Zukor's Paramount Pictures distributing combine.

Up to 1925, Cecil B. DeMille had been Paramount's biggest money earner and also its biggest spender, which resulted in his departure over the excessive cost of his million-dollar-plus *The Ten Commandments* (1923). The other of the early partners, Goldfish, had left in 1916, after a battle with Adolph Zukor over control of policy. Goldfish joined forces with the Selwyn theatrical empire in New York, forming the Gold-wyn Company, a name he liked so much that he kept it as his own, even after being forced out of the new firm.

By 1926, Paramount Pictures and, indirectly, Famous Players-Lasky had become the dominant forces in the film industry. Paramount's only serious rivals at the time were First National, a powerful exhibitors' group that had gone into production to ensure films for its theatres, and the new Metro-Goldwyn-Mayer, whose films were fast becoming known as the best in the business. This rankled both Zukor and Lasky, who saw a threat to Paramount's supremacy. In order to maintain a constant supply of products for his mini-monopoly, Lasky began looking for someone to take over the production duties at the Hollywood studio, thus freeing him for the ever more complicated aspects of financing and distribution. Early in 1926 Lasky hired B. P. Schulberg as an associate

(Left) Benjamin Percival Schulberg, veteran independent producer, whom Jesse Lasky hired to take charge of all production at the new Paramount-Famous-Lasky studios.

(Below) Clara Bow, Schulberg's personal discovery. She became one of Paramount's biggest stars and the quintessential twenties hot mama after being cast in a picture called *It,* which was not about playing tag.

producer; two years later Schulberg was promoted to general manager of the Famous Players-Lasky lot, from which post he would supervise all West Coast production.

Schulberg was the ideal man for this arrangement. He had started in the film business with Edwin S. Porter, of *The Great Train Robbery* fame, and gone through an early association with Adolph Zukor. Schulberg stayed with Zukor long enough to christen Mary Pickford "America's Sweetheart," then left, much against Zukor's advice, to develop an idea he had for combining Mary Pickford, Douglas Fairbanks, Charles Chaplin, and D. W. Griffith into a company to be known as United Artists. The idea was his, but by the time the corporation was formed, he had been maneuvered out of the arrangement. He then joined Louis B. Mayer at the latter's small studio in east Los Angeles, but the two strong-willed men soon had a falling out, the effects of which were so bitter and long-lasting that Schulberg was much later quoted as saying: "When I die, I want to be cremated and have my ashes blown in Louis Mayer's face."

Schulberg recommended to Zukor and Lasky that the company move to larger quarters, where the studio could be laid out along more efficient lines, with room for the inevitable expansion. They agreed and authorized him to buy the United Studios, Schulberg's old headquarters. The facility was completely demolished, and construction began on what was to be called the Paramount-Famous-Lasky studio. While this was being done, Schulberg began shopping around for some qualified people to help with the ambitious production schedule he had promised to deliver to Paramount. It was at this point that Selznick joined the staff and immediately went where his instincts and training were surest.

As he had done at MGM, Selznick started out in the writers' department, only this time he had the advantage of building a department up instead of reorganizing it. The increased production schedule called for a corresponding increase in the output of the contract writers; at Paramount, the writers' department was somewhat haphazardly run by Vivian Moses, who had been chided by the fourteen-year-old David about publicity for Clara Kimball Young. Many screenwriters at Paramount—and indeed the industry—were ex-newspapermen; the best of them knew how to tell stories quickly and in vivid images, all of them had some training in the who, what, where, why, when school of reporting, some even knew what made good dramatic scenes, and some knew how to construct a story. What Selznick found was that Moses was assigning stories and scripts to people who were strong on construction but not spending too much time on the fleshing out of individual scenes, assigning those tasks willy-nilly to the writers on the "dead list." Consequently, the scripts were constantly being reworked by the supervisors, the directors, and a new set of writers in a scattergun approach. The result was that the quality of the individual films was not as high as at MGM, where Thalberg had a much more imaginative and enlightened approach to picking writers for projects.

Selznick recognized this at once. With Schulberg's backing, working with Moses, he reorganized the department, instituting a six-month advance system that assigned writers to projects they were suited for instead of the usual practice of throwing any available writer at a story. Selznick

(Top) Director Victor Fleming and author Anne Nichols go over the film script of her play, *Abie's Irish Rose.*
(Center) Director William Wellman (in the fancy headdress) staging a scene with Wallace Beery for *Beggars of Life,* in early 1928.
(Bottom) Rowland V. Lee directing Gary Cooper during the making of *A Man From Wyoming.*

personally took over the training of newcomers, forming what he called the Author's Council, which involved seven or eight writers being instructed in the studio's story needs, and especially the necessity of coming up with original stories that could be shaped and adapted to the personalities of the stars. Others in the council were taught how to write a script so that a story could be told visually. Within a month of Selznick's changes, the output and efficiency of the writers' department had increased considerably.

Paramount had fifteen "stars" in their spring 1928 product offering, and each of these stars would appear in three or four films every season. Featured players were just that: performers who appeared in specific pictures, but whose appeal was not yet that of a star. Fan mail and box-office grosses were the prime barometers of a player's appeal; fan mail especially was subjected to a close analysis as to the player's appearance and the fans' attitude toward him or her. A sudden increase or decrease in mail was carefully noted: "A lot of birthday cards for Nancy Carroll this month boosts her total considerably above last month's." The collection and dissemination of all these ponderables was the publicity department's responsibility; every month they would prepare an elaborate breakdown that would be sent to Lasky, Schulberg, Selznick, and the other executives on the lot. It was only after careful consideration of such factors that a performer would be awarded star status.

Among the forty-six featured players at Paramount in early 1928 was Fay Wray, the twenty-year-old beauty who had been picked by Erich von Stroheim as his romantic interest in *The Wedding March,* which Paramount was releasing. The film had been in production for so long that Pat Powers, its principal backer, had sold out his share to Paramount; the deal included Fay Wray's contract. The young actress had come to the States from Canada when she was three years old and arrived in Los Angeles at fourteen. School was the first consideration, but during vacations she got some bit parts and even one or two leads in short films at the Fox and Century Comedy studios. After her sophomore year at Hollywood High, she decided she wanted to work on a continuing basis. Having met a man named Richard Jones, husband of the famous designer Irene, she went to see him at the Hal Roach studios, where he was head of production. As she recalled:

In those days it was all so extraordinarily simple to do that, to walk in, to get an appointment with him, say I'd like to work, and for him to say, "Well, I think we can give you a six-month contract." After that I went to Universal; I had a long-term contract there at $75 a week doing leading ladies in two-reel westerns. From there I went on to do *The Wedding March,* which was considered the most exciting project of the year, because whatever von Stroheim did was distinguished.... I never worked with another director who had such beautiful emotional energy; it just flowed from him to anyone who was receptive. There was a rapport between us, a kind of chemistry that made it so easy to work with him.... Then when Paramount took over the distribution of *The Wedding March,* they took up my contract and the first thing I did there was a film called *The Legion of the Condemned.* It was with Gary Cooper; he'd had a bit in *Wings* which attracted a great deal of

(Right) On location at Wrigley Field in Los Angeles. Cameramen Edward Cronjager and Archie Stout are behind the protective net used during filming of scenes for the Richard Dix baseball picture *Warming Up*.
(Below) Paramount's wardrobe department maintained a staff of frantic seamstresses as well as a shoe fetishist's paradise.

41

attention for him. He was very quiet, quite shy. There was a curious thing about Gary, he dozed a lot, he had the capacity to fall asleep in between shots. I think that *Legion of the Condemned* was his first leading role. William Wellman directed that; he had good energy, good drive. He loved his work and therefore he was exciting to work for. Everyone liked the film, so Paramount began to focus on Gary and me as a team. It was team time: Charlie Farrell and Janet Gaynor were at Fox, Garbo and Gilbert at MGM, so they decided that we would be "Paramount's Glorious Young Lovers." Now, my style was to underplay and Gary's style was to underplay, so in retrospect I see why it didn't work. I needed someone more aggressive to work with and at that time Gary responded more to aggressive women, in his personal life, too. So it was not the best chemistry.

Then I was cast in a picture called *Pointed Heels*. It was a role that didn't bring out the qualities that were best for me. I was a chorus girl, a sharp little New York dame. Now, I had no business being in a chorus line without any training; you just learned a few steps fast, that sort of thing ... it was unreal sometimes. You really had no control over what they did to you. There was no one in the studio who would speak up for me, or help me out in these situations, I was really very much by myself. ... I remember I was cast in a film called *The Street of Sin,* a silent film that was started by Mauritz Stiller. He didn't speak English very well, so his directions to me were often rather amusing because he couldn't express himself very well in English. On that picture I learned about star power. Emil Jannings was the star, he was at that time the biggest star Paramount had. This was the story of a Salvation Army girl and a man who was kind of a bum. I was excited about doing it because I had a death scene, and along about midway in production, they rewrote the script to give a death scene to Jannings, also, and that changed everything on that picture for me. ... Working with Jannings was fascinating, he was such a wonderful actor, larger than life really, yet he was able to achieve a very intimate feeling; the total effect was in his face and the expression and in the inner feeling that could be realized without words, and then when words became terribly important, they seemed to get in the way.

Fay Wray as a Paramount starlet in a 1927 studio fashion photo by John Engstead. The dress is by Travis Banton.

The panic of sound films didn't hit Hollywood until mid-March of 1928. Although everyone in town was conscious of Warners and their Vitaphone, it was still considered a gimmick that probably would go the way of the hundreds of other sound experiments that had popped up over the past thirty years. Edison had been the first to have a talking picture, as far back as 1898, but dropped it when pictures alone proved more profitable. Griffith had used recorded dialogue in his 1921 film *Dream Street.* Since then, there had been sporadic experiments; the synchronizing of sound and picture had been accomplished successfully years before, but the one insurmountable obstacle to the commercial success of movies with sound had been the inability of its various promoters to make the sound loud enough for everyone in a theatre to hear it. The development of the vacuum tube by Lee De Forest in 1907 radically altered the field of electric experimentation; it made possible all subsequent developments in electronic communications.

By 1923, De Forest had developed a sound-on-film system, which he called Phonofilm. The sound was photographed in a narrow pattern along the edge of the film, simultaneously with the picture, thereby solving all problems of synchronization. The sounds were reproduced through an electronic amplification system of De Forest's own design and were capable of filling New York's enormous Rivoli Theatre, where the films played. Concurrent with De Forest's successes, the Bell Telephone Laboratories were synchronizing moving pictures to large phonograph discs, which they played back through their own amplifiers and equipment. At the same time Theodore Case, an ex-associate of De Forest's, was showing William Fox a sound film system of his own that Fox enthusiastically took up and named Movietone. But it was the four Warner brothers who eventually grabbed public attention with their splashy introduction of the Vitaphone, which is what the Bell Laboratories—Western Electric disc system turned into. The heavily ballyhooed premiere of *Don Juan* in late 1926 coincided with the feverish rise in the popularity of radio. A year later, in October 1927, 50 million people in the United States listened at the same time to a broadcast of the Demp-

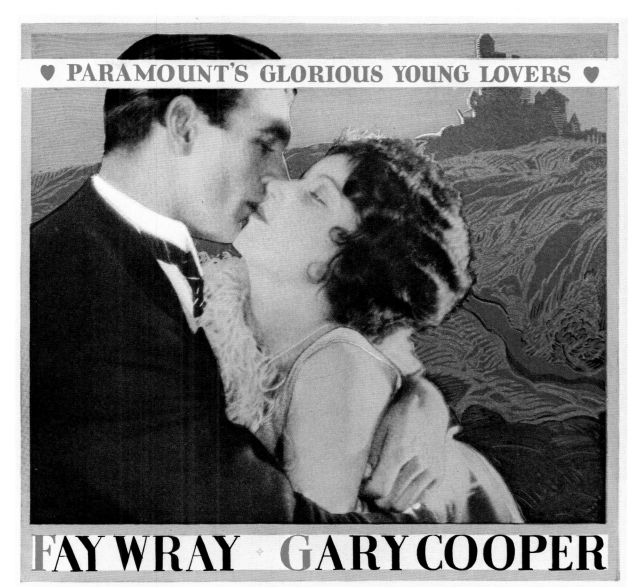

♥ PARAMOUNT'S GLORIOUS YOUNG LOVERS ♥

FAY WRAY · GARY COOPER

A new and brilliant starring combination with box-office plus

Fay Wray, heroine of "The Wedding March" and "Legion of the Condemned." Gary Cooper, hero of "Legion of the Condemned."

Three lavishly produced love dramas starring Fay Wray and Gary Cooper are coming in 1928-9

"THE FIRST KISS"

℄ Radiant youth and romance glow in these twin stars. Already famous with the public due to successes in previous pictures. 1928-9's great box-office pair of screen lovers. ℄ Their first co-starring picture, an elaborate production of a popular Saturday Evening Post (circulation, 3,200,000) serial love story by Tristram Tupper. ℄ The drama of a youth who turns picturesque river bandit for the honor of his family. And the beautiful heiress who braves scandal and death in her great love for him. ℄ Strong pictures of this type are in high favor with modern audiences. • • • • • • •

sey-Tunney prizefight; during a description of the celebrated "long count" by announcer Graham McNamee, seven people across the country dropped dead from the excitement, an achievement no film had ever laid claim to. In that same week the world's first Radio Fair was attracting thousands of New Yorkers, who were also being bombarded by ads and announcements telling them that at the Warner Theatre in two weeks they could "see and hear Al Jolson in *The Jazz Singer.*" They responded with an enthusiasm that startled even Warner Bros., and one that was carefully noted by the rest of the industry.

Big business films were numerous that winter. MGM had *Love,* with Greta Garbo and John Gilbert; Mary Pickford and Charles ("Buddy") Rogers were in *My Best Girl;* Cecil B. DeMille's *The King of Kings* was being road-shown across the country; Lewis Milestone had another success with *Two Arabian Knights* for Howard Hughes; Fox was showing *Seventh Heaven* with Movietone musical accompaniment. Paramount's share of the market was dominated by the success of Josef von Sternberg's *The Last Command* and William Wellman's aviation blockbuster, *Wings.* Film business overall, however, was in a slump. The movies had

become, in the words of one critic: "A mental transom through which the public is half-tired of peeking." Charles Lindbergh's flight to Mexico City from New York was in the headlines most of December and January, along with Henry Ford's introduction of the Model A. The film industry's attention was focused on the controversial Brookhart bill in the U.S. Senate—one of the government's first attempts to break up the trade policy known as "block-booking." While marshaling all its considerable clout to defeat the bill, which it did, the film industry as a whole had not been paying close attention to what was in the air.

And what was in the air was Jolson's voice in *The Jazz Singer.* He not only sang from the screen, but in one unexpected, delightful sequence audibly teased his mother, adding depth and humanity to the character. The audience responded overwhelmingly. In 1927, there were only 160 theatres that could show *The Jazz Singer.* Even so, by the time it opened at the Los Angeles Criterion Theatre in December 1927, many in the industry had noticed that this inexpensive melodrama was outgrossing some of the biggest pictures of the season, playing for months at a time in theatres where a run of three weeks was considered outstanding. This

D. W. Griffith, Carl Laemmle, Jr., and Sid Grauman posing with the Fox Movietone device, which made a photographic record of the sound along the edge of the film, thus ensuring self-contained synchronization.

spectacular performance was repeated all across the country in the winter of 1927–28 as more movie theatres installed sound equipment. Most of the industry leaders shrugged or were envious of the success of the film, attributing it to the star power of Al Jolson, with the Vitaphone only a clever bit of novelty showmanship.

At Paramount, both Zukor and Lasky had seen demonstrations of the Vitaphone and Fox's Movietone system; neither had been particularly impressed. Only after the money began pouring in to Warner Bros. from *Don Juan, The Jazz Singer,* and the other Vitaphone programs did the executives at Paramount and the rest of the industry begin to look into the matter of sound. Early in 1928, at the annual production meetings held at Paramount's home office in New York, Zukor, Lasky, and Schulberg decided that the sound fad was too lucrative to pass up. It was agreed that Paramount would release several of its films with sound accompaniment to cash in on the phenomenon, and see where it went from there.

At the studio, putting things on a "sound" basis was left largely in the hands of Schulberg and Roy Pomeroy, head of the technical department. Selznick and the other supervisors carried on pretty much as usual in the first months of 1928, with Selznick, now Schulberg's chief assistant, following up on the plans for the Paramount spring program. Five supervisors worked under Schulberg, with Selznick serving as their liaison. Under these men twenty films were in various stages of production, twelve of which were star vehicles. The balance were either "programmers" or "specials," where the emphasis was not on stars but on a background or an idea. Thus *Wings* was being followed up with plans for *Dirigible* as a special, and *Beau Geste* was inspiring plans for an expensive version of *The Four Feathers*. While Selznick actively watched over all this, he, as well as everyone else in the studio, was extremely curious about what was going on in the small special effects studio that had been soundproofed and equipped for recording under the control of Roy Pomeroy, the only man at Paramount and practically the entire industry outside of Warners who knew anything about the intricate perils of adding sound to movies. He had previously used a G.E. device called the Kinegraphone to synchronize the sounds of machine guns and airplane motors in *Wings;* when Lasky and Schulberg decided to try sound, they sent Pomeroy east to study the available systems. On his return, he advised that Paramount use the Fox Movietone method, and this recommendation was subsequently followed by the other major studios as well.

In early March, Pomeroy barred everyone from the vicinity of his stage, while behind its locked and insulated doors he began painstakingly adding music and sound effects to the studio's first scheduled sound release, a Richard Dix film called, appropriately enough, *Warming Up*. The studio had no sound editing equipment as yet; Pomeroy worked with two projectors running in synchronization—one for picture, one for sound. The actual cutting and matching of picture and sound was done with a stopwatch, a metronome, and the mathematical certainty that the Movietone sound image was twenty frames ahead of the picture. *Warming Up* was a baseball story. The crowd roars and music were relatively simple to add, but the split-second timing needed to coordinate the sound of a bat hitting a ball was evidently beyond any of Pomeroy's primitive means, for when the film was finally ready for its August 1928 opening, the crack of bat against ball was always before or after the hit, never exactly synchronized. In spite of this, Schulberg made Pomeroy the head of the newly created sound department, where he would oversee the training of sound recording personnel, the installation of equipment, and plans for the new mammoth sound stages, as well as supervise the addition of talking sequences to films already in production. Pomeroy had an engineer's caution. He had been taught that the microphone must not be moved, that footsteps could be easily picked up, as would any extraneous sounds such as the rustle of fabric, the clank of jewelry, the squeak of shoes. If the stage was not properly insulated, sound, especially voices, could easily distort, becoming alternately strident, hollow, sibilant, or inaudible, especially if the person speaking did not stand in a direct line with the microphone. Warner Bros. and Fox had a year's headstart in the problems of sound; Paramount was trying to catch up to them overnight, and the burden of it all fell on Pomeroy, who, not surprisingly, developed an attitude of testy intransigence.

Selznick's memories of Pomeroy were vivid: "He insisted on handling everything himself, which included the direction of a scene. One day I told him that we had cast a certain actor in the next sound picture and he curtly told me that the sooner we executives realized that there would be no casting in sound pictures without his approval the better off we would be." Fay Wray recalls another side of Pomeroy: "I had been called in to do a voice test . . . I was rather nervous. . . . I stood near the microphone and did something from *Alice in Wonderland:* 'You are old, Father William, the young man said. . . .' I remember Mr. Pomeroy being very

concerned about this test, he wanted it to go very well for me. I thought he was very sweet."

As well as testing the vocal equipment of Paramount's players, Pomeroy was continuing to add music and other sounds to several of the studio's bigger silent films, especially Erich von Stroheim's *The Wedding March* and Ernst Lubitsch's *The Patriot* with Emil Jannings. The addition of music was fine, but the gratuitous insistence on sound effects, and two brief instances of speech in *The Patriot*, proved jarring, breaking the carefully constructed mood of the film. It was clear that talking sequences would have to be carefully considered; even Warner Bros. wasn't always sure of what would work. In March 1928 they released a melodrama called *Tenderloin* that had three sequences in which the characters spoke. In the last of these, a police grilling scene, the dialogue and delivery were so flagrantly and melodramatically inept that the scene was hooted off the screen at its Manhattan premiere. Three days later Warner Bros. removed the dialogue, substituting titles to bridge the gaps, and the picture did extraordinary business. It was the sound era's first case of burnt fingers. At Paramount, Schulberg, noting the excitement generated by actors speaking, decided that films just completed or still in production should now have dialogue sequences added whenever possible. These grafting jobs were to be known irreverently in the industry as "goat glands," after the famous rejuvenation operations of the early twenties. For the film business, these "part talkers" were a form of whistling in the dark, valuable to both performers and directors as a baptism of fire. The first dialogue scenes at Paramount were done in mid-June 1928, for the already completed William Wellman film *Beggars of Life* starring Wallace Beery—a grim story about contemporary hoboes. Selznick and Wellman were unenthusiastic at the idea of having voices

A quartet of Paramount executives play host to the visiting head of the company's London office, Ollie Traggardh. (Clockwise, from upper right) David Selznick, executive assistant to B. P. Schulberg; Traggardh; Albert Kaufman, executive assistant to Jesse Lasky; Mike Levee, studio manager; and director Ernst Lubitsch.

"THE CRIME OF INTERFERENCE"

¶From the tremendous stage success "Interference," by Ronald Pertwee and Harold Dearden. ¶The legitimate smash hit of London and New York! To be produced on a spectacular scale by a special director and a cast loaded with favorites. ¶Sensational drama of a society scandal that threatens to engulf an innocent woman and how a "bad man" out of her past commits a crime to save her. The most powerful woman picture of the year.

A Paramount Picture

Opened October 18, 1927 at the Lyceum Theatre, New York, and still playing to S.R.O.

A
William Wellman
PRODUCTION

John Monk Saunders
DIRECTOR AND AUTHOR
OF "WINGS"

DIRIGIBLE

¶ "1928 will be a dirigible year," say the experts. The big ocean liners of the air will flash into the limelight as brilliantly as did Lindbergh in 1927. ¶ Paramount, ever first to sense box office, presents the first spectacular special with dirigibles as a thrilling background. ¶ Made by the producer and author of "Wings" and "Legion of the Condemned." • • •

POLA NEGRI

"LOVES OF AN ACTRESS"

Big as "Barbed Wire" and produced by the same director, Rowland V. Lee. With Nils Asther and all-star cast. Story by Ernest Vajda, author of "Service for Ladies." The poignant drama of Paris's greatest actress, whose lovers were the gallants and powers of the world. Toying with men, then hurling away fame and fortune for her first and only true love, and losing him! "The greatest picture I have ever made," says Miss Negri. It's true!

Pola in the perfect role the world has been waiting to see her portray!

A second Negri release to come.

THE STAR OF "UNDERWORLD" IN 4 STRONG DRAMAS

Public demand made George Bancroft a star. The taste of the day is for strong, red-meat film fare. Bancroft supplies it ideally. The same virility, big casts and elaborate production value will surround Bancroft pictures in 1928-9. Star pictures in the special class!

GEORGE BANCROFT

"THE DOCKS OF NEW YORK." Josef von Sternberg production, director of "Underworld." By John Monk Saunders, author of "Wings" and "Legion of the Condemned." Bancroft as a tough stevedore.

"SWAG." Winner of $15,000 Paramount-Photoplay Magazine Idea Contest, in which 40,000 picture fans entered. By Rena Vale. *And two more to be announced.*

Paramount Pictures

(Opposite) Ads from the Paramount product booklet for 1928–29, announcing its upcoming attractions. *Dirigible* was planned as a follow-up to *Wings,* but the project was abandoned and ultimately sold to Columbia Pictures. *Loves of an Actress* was one of Pola Negri's last pictures. For several years a top star at Paramount, Negri's heavy accent destroyed her image and her career almost overnight. These product books combined vivid, modern images and designs with elaborate use of four-color process and tints.

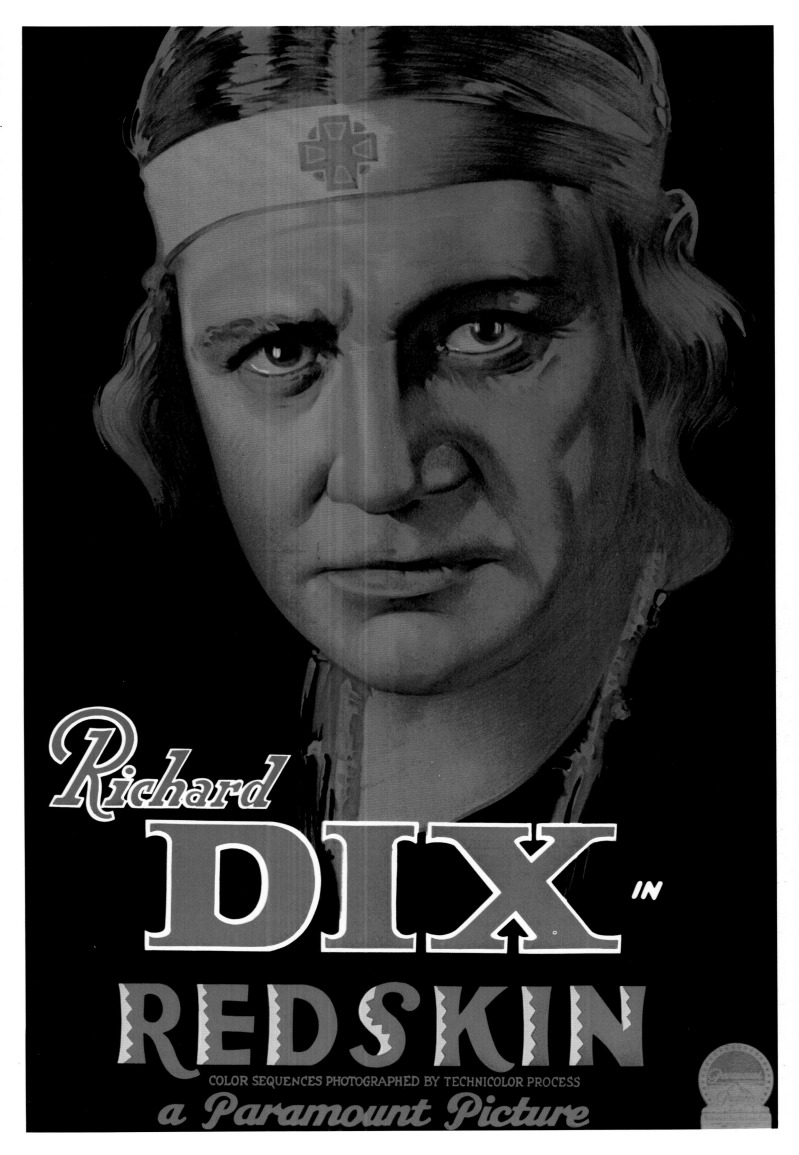

Richard DIX in REDSKIN

COLOR SEQUENCES PHOTOGRAPHED BY TECHNICOLOR PROCESS

a Paramount Picture

suddenly jump out of the picture. They decided instead to add a scene to the introduction of Beery's hobo king character, showing him walking along a country road singing. The scene would be directed by the harassed Pomeroy, under Wellman's curious eye.

The two men were soon in a heated dispute over Pomeroy's insistence that Beery had to stand perfectly still while singing; if the actor moved, the microphone wouldn't be able to pick up his voice. Pomeroy's adamant refusal to consider moving the microphone angered Wellman, who wanted some movement in the otherwise static scene. Schulberg and Selznick were called, and Pomeroy for once was overruled. Wellman hung the microphone from the end of a broom handle, moving it over Beery's head as the actor slowly ambled along and sang the first words recorded for a Paramount feature:

In the back room
Of a bum saloon,
That's where she sits all day.
Hark the bells!

In the back room
Of a bum saloon,
That's where she sits all day;
I wonder where she sits all night.

One "goat gland" case early on did prove to be a decided asset, and that was the celebrated *Abie's Irish Rose*, the second film at Paramount to

have sound grafted onto it. Getting the rights to this phenomenally successful stage comedy by Anne Nichols had been considered somewhat of a coup for the studio. Victor Fleming had directed a script carefully faithful to the play, the humor of which unfortunately depended on lengthy and numerous subtitles. The film had opened in New York as a $2 special in April 1928, where, with a running time of more than two hours, it had proved slow-moving and feeble. The reviews had been unanimously poor and business fell off immediately as word of mouth spread. At the completion of its single run the film was put back into production. In late July, Nancy Carroll and Buddy Rogers, the juvenile leads, reported to Pomeroy's stage, where they filmed and recorded a sequence showing the two of them entertaining a tentful of soldiers. Two other dialogue sequences were added, using the ethnic humor of the play; the film was trimmed by almost an hour and equipped with a synchronized score. Fortified by its sound additions, and encouraged by a new set of favorable reviews, *Abie's Irish Rose* did extremely well as a Christmas release, proving that sound, carefully and judiciously used, could be an asset above and beyond its novelty appeal.

In late July 1928, Warner Bros. had released what they advertised as the "first 100% all-talking motion picture," *The Lights of New York,* which did extraordinary business. This success, plus the experience gained with the goat gland and other sound-equipped films, convinced Lasky and Schulberg that the time had come for Famous Players-Lasky to make an all-talking film. MGM, United Artists, and Universal were still installing their equipment and waiting for their new stages to be

built; Paramount could steal a march on most of their competitors, if they worked fast and carefully. The studio had just bought the story rights to the successful stage melodrama *Interference*. It was suspenseful, had a small cast, and only three main sets, which could be easily contained within the confines of Pomeroy's experimental stage.

The film went into production early in September 1928, with William Powell, Evelyn Brent, and the English actor Clive Brook, who later that month described for *The New York Times* the tensions surrounding this first Paramount talkie:

> I found that the microphone is more difficult to face than the most hardened audience; I was conscious of a metallic little instrument hanging like a sword of Damocles over my head . . . my voice sounded unfamiliar to my ears, every word was oddly muffled; there was no echo, no resonance. Two ominous, tank-like objects were focused on me. Faces peered at me from the darkness inside these caverns. I caught the reflection of camera lenses in the plate-glass windows that form the front walls of these "tanks." Cameras were grinding, but the sound of their mechanism had been silenced. Not even the familiar splutter of the klieg lights could be heard for they had been supplanted by huge banks of incandescent lamps. The director cannot even tell us when to start; we must watch a monitor man who waves his hand for us to begin.
>
> I find myself starting off in the declamatory fashion of the stage. I was not thinking in terms of microphone sensitivity or the tremendous amplification of the apparatus. When I had finished, technicians turned on the record they had just made; I heard a deep, strange voice come booming out of the loudspeakers. It was not, I told myself, Clive Brook. It alternately faded into nothingness and then rang out in a thunderous crescendo. Pomeroy smiled at me. "Was that my voice?" I asked. "Yes, but you couldn't recognize it, could you? Try it again," he said, "and this time speak just as you would in a small room at home. Don't think of playing to the gallery; you don't have to project; the gallery doesn't exist here." After I did it the next time, I heard the voice in the loudspeakers again. This time it was unmistakably my

For Jean Arthur in 1929 a starlet's life at Paramount ranged from posing for "art" photos (opposite) to commemorating Easter with Doris Hill (above), to showing off some of the latest designs from Paramount's wardrobe department (below).

See! Hear! **RIALTO**
[DATES]
Paramount's ALL-TALKING *Picture*

INTERFERENCE

With
EVELYN BRENT
CLIVE BROOK
DORIS KENYON
WILLIAM POWELL

own. Although it was not loud, somehow it seemed to fill every corner of the huge room. I had learned my first lesson in microphone recording.

By the end of 1928, it was evident that what had started out as a novelty adjunct had quickly become first a fad, then a sensation, as amazed moviegoers discovered whole new areas of perception, of identification, of the sheer excitement of hearing sounds. It wasn't just the musical accompaniment; films had always had that, and they usually sounded better live. Nor was it just the sound effects, for those too had always been available for the first-run theatres. Rather, it was the human element: voices, expression, the emotional charge out of hearing a good actor give meaning to a line. No matter that actors had been doing that for generations on stage—this was the movies. It was as if overnight a beloved relative, dumb from birth, had sat down one morning at the breakfast table and started speaking.

At Paramount the decision was made early in 1929 to go completely to sound. For Schulberg and Selznick this meant long, grueling days and nights of work; the studio had no sound stages completed, so it was decided that all sound work would be done at night, when noise was at a minimum. An elaborate system of warning whistles was devised so that when a company was shooting sound, everything in the studio streets came to a complete standstill. This state of affairs lasted until the first of the huge new sound stages was ready in mid-1929. *Interference* had been co-directed by Pomeroy and staff director Lothar Mendes, and it was the

success of this experiment that convinced Schulberg that, for the time being at least, sound films would need the services of two directors: one for the action and one for the dialogue. In line with this he began raiding the Broadway stage for men who could handle dialogue and staging for the new technique of sound pictures.

Back in April 1928 actor-director John Cromwell had appeared in downtown Los Angeles with Edward G. Robinson in the touring New York hit *The Racket*, the first realistic stage drama about gangsters. The forty-year-old Cromwell had a long and impressive background in the New York theatre. Tall, lean, and reserved, with a fairly stern look about him, Cromwell had an air of quiet authority that was a combination of his military school upbringing and a dry, blunt wit that overlaid a practical, sensitive approach to everything he did. Two days after *The Racket* opened in Los Angeles, Cromwell had an offer from Schulberg to talk about going to work for Paramount. Until the advent of sound, Cromwell had viewed the movies with the prevailing theatrical attitude of bemused contempt. At the start, what attracted him to Schulberg's offer was the money: "The most I'd ever had in the theatre was $500 a week, that was tops; when I decided to go to Paramount, I was to start at $1,500 a week on a seven-year contract. . . . I never saw such a contract in my life; they really thought that I was the cat's, I guess because of my background. It let me do anything. I could act, or write, or direct, or all three. . . . When I reported to Paramount, Ben Schulberg, a very intelligent man, refined, unlike the usual conception of a mogul, called me in for a talk, and asked me what I wanted to do; I said I wanted to go into the cutting room, I was curious as to what made pictures work. I spent three months in the cutting room; I could have spent a year there profitably."

Cromwell's curiosity served him well in his first months at Paramount; he learned quickly how to tell a story on film, watching as the individual shots were put together both dramatically and visually. He then spent a month on the sets of several films in production, watching and absorbing the methods used in getting the scenes onto film. Cromwell had very little experience as a moviegoer; after seeing as many films as he could, he was surprised and disappointed at the vapidity of the stories being told by the movies: "Most of them came under the category of trash." It was true; at Paramount, and throughout most of the studios, the story emphasis was on accepted virtues of the day: love at first sight, loyalty, self-sacrifice. These themes were dealt with in the simplest and most melodramatic of terms; the ideas, such as they were, were illustrated as quickly and as economically as possible, utilizing the classic three-act play structure of exposition, development, and resolution, all leading to the inevitable happy ending.

By his own choice, Cromwell's first film work at Paramount was as an actor. He wanted to see the problems of sound film from the performer's standpoint, so he took a role in a talking version of the play *The Dummy* with two of Paramount's newest players, stage actors Ruth Chatterton and Fredric March. While acting in this, he began spending time in the story department, looking for something to direct. It was here that Cromwell first became aware of Selznick: "I thought at first he was a college graduate like Walter Wanger [head of production at Paramount's Long Island studio]. Wanger had graduated from Dartmouth; all the big brass at the other studios were self-made, there wasn't one college graduate among any of them; they were a whole different species. Although David did not have a college degree both he and Wanger were highly trained, literate, tasteful men, with a more or less sophisticated intelligence as opposed to the native intelligence of the pioneers, and that made a difference in working with them."

Cromwell's search through the story department turned up a piece called *Close Harmony*, which he felt was simple, sprightly, and lent itself to sound, being the story of a college orchestra. Schulberg suggested that he have a silent-picture director work with him. Cromwell agreed, and the veteran comedy director Edward Sutherland was assigned to the project. The technical problems of these early sound films were enormously complicated, not just because of the newness of the technique but also because of the limitations imposed by the equipment. On *Close Harmony,* Cromwell recalls,

There were three cameras set up in three separate boxes on rollers;

(Above, left) Preparing the corner of Paramount's temporary experimental sound stage for a "talking" test. (Above, right) Jean Arthur does a voice and speaking test under the supervision of dapper Roy Pomeroy, head of Paramount's sound department. Pomeroy was unchallenged at Paramount during the changeover, but his high-handedness and ambitions soon led to his downfall. After co-directing several pictures at Paramount, and one at RKO in 1931, he faded from the Hollywood scene. (Below) The Paramount studio projectionists prepare for a playback of a talking picture test, using the Vitaphone method of synchronized discs.

enormous things they were, must have weighed about two tons, they had to be moved by a crew of six men. There were three men in these booths, the operator, his assistant, plus a film loader. The cameramen shot through the glass window; a shot was regulated by how long a cameraman could last before he fainted, since there wasn't any ventilation. We considered ourselves lucky if we got a three-minute take. But this didn't last long. The technical strides that they made in those first days of sound were enormous. First the camera was taken out of the box and blanketed so that there was no noise. I worked with the most extraordinary cameraman, Roy Hunt. I fell in love with him; he'd been brought up in the business, and he had the most enormously inventive mind. He devised all sorts of things to get the camera moving, the carryalls and the crab dolly which would go through doorways and around corners. This was going on all the time; these improvements were almost daily occurrences.

At this point Selznick was heavily involved in the making of *The Dance of Life,* the film version of the Broadway success *Burlesque.* He worked closely with Cromwell, who had been chosen to direct, on the necessary script additions, and even chose a new title from the story files when *Burlesque* proved too misleading for theatre marquees. Ironically, the substitution was from Havelock Ellis's 1923 study of sex, which the studio had purchased just for the title. *The Dance of Life* was Selznick's first chance actually to produce one of the studio "specials." He was given a large budget and the opportunity to be as lavish as necessary; one of the numerous musical numbers even used the two-color Technicolor process, which Cromwell described as "a pain in the neck": "The color was good for its limitations, but very primitive; we had a man there telling us what colors we could use, and what they'd look like. The heat from all the additional lights was fierce ... we didn't use it too often." Barbara Stanwyck, who had starred in the play on Broadway, was not available for the film, so Selznick suggested that Nancy Carroll, one of the contract players, be given the feminine lead opposite Hal Skelly, the play's other star. Carroll was an attractive young redhead, hardworking; she could sing and dance well and act passably. But although *Burlesque* had been softened for films, some of its more serious moments were difficult for the uncomplicated youngster. Cromwell remembers:

> Carroll had a big emotional scene, where she had to break down and cry. I worked as hard as I could with her, but it wasn't very good. Then Eddie Sutherland, who was co-directing with me, said, "Let me try." He told me that when he gave the signal, I should start the camera. He talked to her and the signal came and he stepped aside and there she was crying. Afterwards, I asked him how he did it, and he told me, "I said to her, Nancy, you've got your little daughter by the hand and you're crossing the street, and a great big truck comes slashing around the corner and blap, knocks her down and runs over her and you see all this blood gushing out of her face," and he described this awful mess, and that's how he'd got her crying. It was something he'd learned working with Chaplin.

While Cromwell was coping with fainting cameramen and intractable microphones, Selznick and William Wellman were trying an experiment of another kind in *Chinatown Nights,* the Wallace Beery film that had been made as a silent. The film was edited and scored as a silent film with a synchronized score and then put back into production to add talking sequences to it. What was unique about this was the careful preparation and imagination that the two men put into the integration of the sound sequences with the rest of the film. Instead of having long sections of unrelieved dialogue, the talking was broken up into little bits strategically placed at crucial dramatic moments, which were then carefully and ingeniously filmed using unsynchronized sound and "voice-over," so that the fluidity and pacing of the original silent concept was preserved. The silent sections were accompanied by the synchronized

A performer's-eye view of a dance band set for *Close Harmony* (1928), John Cromwell's first directorial effort. Note the double-decker camera "tanks," one for close shots, the other for long shots.

The elegant Florence Vidor, ex-wife of King, was co-starred with Wallace Beery in the silent *Chinatown Nights.* When the picture was converted to sound, Miss Vidor declined to be involved, preferring instead to retire to private life as Mrs. Jascha Heifetz. She did this with such prompt finality that for some of her scenes, Selznick and Wellman were forced to hire another actress to do what they called "voice doubling" for Miss Vidor, a practice and a term that evolved into "dubbing." The gown is by Travis Banton.

Wallace Beery as the gangster object of Florence Vidor's affections in *Chinatown Nights.*

Here is Miss Vidor in the depths of her degradation as Wallace Beery's "love slave." It may have been this part, more than sound, that convinced her that she and the movies should part company. The lighting was by Henry Gerrard, the art direction by Wiard Ihnen.

Nancy Carroll and Hal Skelly in one of the burlesque sequences from *The Dance of Life*. The costumes were by Travis Banton, the art direction by Wiard Ihnen, and the choreography, such as it was, by Earl Lindsay.

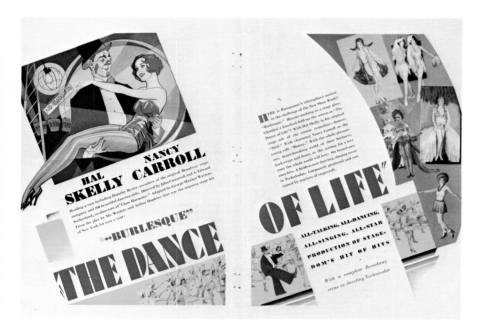

score, which was carried through even the dialogue sections. Thus the film had a unified texture and smoothness to it. The dialogue sequences were short, staccato, and unforced, talking scenes overlapped with silent action scenes, while music, sound effects, and speech were used impressionistically over montages and bridging scenes. The film emerged as a remarkably sophisticated use of sound and silence. Unfortunately, all this technique was wasted on a melodramatic and undeveloped story of a tong war and a society woman who goes to the dogs in Chinatown. However, it was the first attempt at Paramount, or anywhere else in Hollywood, consciously to merge the best of silent film technique with the stylistic opportunities of the new sound medium.

In theatres, the initial amazement of hearing people talk from the screen was rapidly giving way to a fascination with what was being said; and then—more quickly than anyone expected—to a demand by the public that what was being said be presented as imaginatively as possible, both aurally and visually. Literally within a year, the entire syntax and style of storytelling that had been built up and refined over the past thirty years was refashioned and the movies regained the hold they once had on the public imagination. When sound, dialogue, and movement were fused properly, the result was the heightened emotional awareness and response that denotes a work of art.

But silent pictures continued to be made. In early 1929 there were still 14,000 theatres in America that couldn't show sound films; they needed products to sell to the faithful. At Paramount, one of the last of these silents was an adaptation of the old melodrama *Heliotrope Harry,* to which Selznick devoted much of his attention. The somewhat lurid material, about an ex-convict who dies to save his unknowing daughter the shame of having such a father, appealed to Selznick. He retitled it *Forgotten Faces,* spent a lot of time on updating the script, and even worked actively on the editing, a procedure unusual for any supervisor producer at Paramount, or anywhere else for that matter. Selznick was putting the finishing touches to this in July 1928 when Schulberg asked him to assist Merian C. Cooper and Ernest B. Schoedsack, two "naturalist" moviemakers who had just come to Hollywood from Africa, where they had spent several months filming action and spectacle scenes for a version of A. E. W. Mason's novel *The Four Feathers.*

Cooper and Schoedsack were both fascinating figures in the Hollywood of the time. Schoedsack was an imposing, lanky giant, blessed with a wry and ironic wit, which he largely kept under wraps. An ex–Mack Sennett cameraman turned Signal Corps photographer, he had an intuitive knack for composition and lighting. He loved nature photography; his sharp sensitivity gave him an uncanny ability to capture the mood and essence of a particular place or event. His quiet, off-hand personality perfectly complemented that of Merian Cooper, whose explosive enthusiasm belied a cool, penetrating intellect that was alternately blunt and wildly imaginative. Cooper was an articulate and interesting talker, with a soft, drawling manner that was part Yankee and part Dixie. At the core of his personality was a charming ebullience that underlay an innate kindness and a poetic sensitivity to intangibles that made him equally popular with both men and women. Cooper came from a long line of Southern aristocrats, ex-slaveowners, raised to believe in the concepts of duty, honor, and loyalty. He was brought up to think that "once you gave your word on something, so help you God, you lived by that or died by it." His great-uncle, whom he was named after, gave the six-year-old Cooper a copy of *Explorations and Adventures in Equatorial Africa,* written in 1861 by Paul du Chaillu, one of the first people to explore the Dark Continent, as it was then known. Cooper read with fascination of the packs of giant apes that terrorized the native villages, in some instances even carrying off screaming women into the jungle. It was the most exciting book he had ever read, which at six is not surprising, and as Cooper recollected later: "I made up my mind right then that I wanted to be an explorer, but I knew that you had to be tough, so I concentrated on doing that ... eventually, I was able to swim the St. Johns River, which had drowned two other boys my age, and later, when I went to the Naval Academy, I became a boxing and wrestling champion." His adventurous nature led to his resigning from Annapolis, as he freely admitted, "for taking too many chances and having too many demerits. I was wild then, and I loved excitement." It was at the Naval Academy that Cooper began his lifelong involvement with planes and flying, later becoming one of the pioneers of civil aviation. After leaving the Academy, Cooper began to study at the American Geographical Society in New York, learning mapmaking and survival techniques.

When war broke out in Europe, Cooper shipped aboard a merchant freighter carrying supplies to England, hoping to enlist in the British forces. Arriving without papers or passport, he was sent back to the United States, where he eventually became a reporter on the Minneapolis *Star-Dispatch.* When America finally entered the war, Cooper immediately enlisted in the Aviation Section of the Army Signal Corps. During an air battle overseas, he was shot down in flames behind German lines. He finished out the war in a German hospital recovering from severe burns. After being decorated for his services, Cooper served with Herbert Hoover's peacetime War Relief Commission, then joined the Polish army fighting against the Bolsheviks. Captured in Russia, he led a revolt in the prison camp, escaped across Siberia, rejoined the Polish forces, and emerged from that war as a lieutenant colonel with four decorations and a street named after him in Warsaw. He also gained a partner, for it was on the train taking him to enlist in the Polish army that Cooper first met Ernest Schoedsack, assigned to cover the Polish civil war for the U.S. Army Signal Corps. The two men, widely dissimilar in nature, took an immediate liking to each other.

After the war this friendship would result in their 1925 film, *Grass.* Together with Robert Flaherty's earlier *Nanook of the North* (1921), *Grass* was an attempt to broaden the scope and power of the motion

Ernest Beaumont Schoedsack (left) and Merian Coldwell Cooper in a Paramount publicity still taken shortly after they had finished filming *Chang* in the jungles of Siam.

A frame enlargement showing the spectacular elephant stampede that served as the climax to *Chang.*

picture by using it to document other lifestyles. Cooper and Schoedsack, spurred by Cooper's early studies at the American Geographical Society, had gone to Persia to film an epic account of the twice-yearly migration of thousands of Bakhtiari tribesmen in search of food for their flocks. The two men traveled with the fierce tribes on their twenty-six-day trek, dramatically photographing the 150,000 people and their half-million animals as they forded rivers, fought off hostile tribes, and scaled the unbelievably steep, snow-covered peaks of central Persia until they reached grazing lands on the other side.

Grass was a great success on the lucrative lecture circuit, where it caught the attention of Jesse Lasky, who bought it for distribution by Paramount. Its success as a theatrical attraction led to Lasky's giving Cooper and Schoedsack carte blanche for their next film, *Chang,* a realistic account of life in the jungles of Siam. In telling the story of one man's efforts to protect his family from the savage jungle, Cooper and Schoedsack made use of marauding tigers and other wild animals. For the climax of the film—an elephant stampede—the two men and their native helpers corralled close to three hundred of the huge beasts, then turned them loose and photographed the ensuing rampage as the stampeding giants totally destroyed a mock native village that had been specially built for the scene. When the film opened at the Criterion Theatre in New York in late 1927, the climactic stampede became even more thrilling, for the screen, via Paramount's new Magnascope process,

opened up to twice its size, while the special musical score was augmented by twenty men behind the screen pounding 6-foot native thunder drums. Glowing reviews from the critics acclaimed the film's pictorial beauty and the dramatic effects, while standing-room-only crowds made it one of the biggest hits on Broadway.

Cooper and Schoedsack next went to central Africa, with Lasky's blessing and a script from A. E. W. Mason's *The Four Feathers.* Cooper had read the book while in the Russian prison camp; its story of military cowardice and redemption in Victorian England had struck a responsive chord in him. Paramount's success with *Beau Geste* (1926) had convinced Lasky that *The Four Feathers,* as envisioned by Cooper and Schoedsack, would be a worthy follow-up to *Chang,* with spectacular battle scenes between the native tribes and the British army, and another stampede, this time by hippos and baboons. They planned to photograph all these action scenes on location in Africa, then return to the United States and film the story sequences in a studio and on a desert location, carefully matching the previously filmed African sequences.

Selznick was assigned to help the two men complete the film when they arrived back in Hollywood in mid-July 1928. One of the first problems confronting them was casting the story sections of the film. Selznick recommended young Richard Arlen for the central part of Lieutenant Harry Faversham, who receives four white feathers from his friends and fiancée for refusing to go with his troop to quell a native uprising. The fiancée would be played by Fay Wray, who knew Cooper through her husband, John Monk Saunders, the original author of *Wings.* The two partners were quite naturally cautious when Schulberg urged that they consider Selznick as their associate producer. Cooper

Cooper and Schoedsack (above) on location in Africa during the making of *The Four Feathers,* and (below) on top of the iron camera bridge used in filming additional location scenes in the desert near Cathedral City, California.

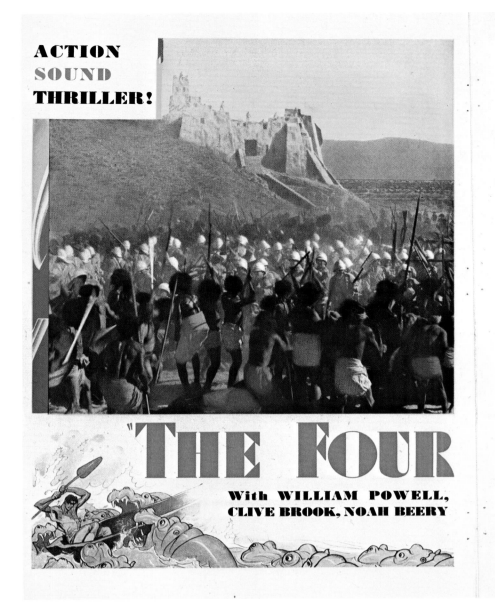

ACTION
SOUND
THRILLER!

"THE FOUR FEATHERS"

With WILLIAM POWELL,
CLIVE BROOK, NOAH BEERY

ALL THE GALLANT COURAGE OF "BEAU GESTE" ... AND THE VITAL FORCE OF "CHANG"!

Two years in the making! With "locations" extending from Hollywood to the dark jungles and burning deserts of Africa. Now comes this mighty $2-calibre action-melodrama. With marvelous musical accompaniment and original sound effects.

Imagine "Beau Geste" and "Chang" with sound! You have them both, and more, in "The Four Feathers." Your audiences will HEAR as well as SEE the fierce battle between white soldiers and native "Fuzzy Wuzzies" for the lonely desert fort. They'll HEAR as well as SEE the attack of maddened jungle beasts (actually filmed in darkest Africa).

And they'll HEAR and SEE one of the most popular stories of love and high courage ever written. Produced by the two adventurer-showmen who made "Chang." AN OUTSTANDING SCREEN ACHIEVEMENT OF 1929-30!

A Cooper-Schoedsack Production

Suggested by A. E. W. Mason's famous novel. Adapted by Hope Loring. Screen play by Howard Estabrook. B. P. Schulberg, General Manager, West Coast Productions.

RICHARD ARLEN, FAY WRAY,
and a cast of 1,000 players

---

recalls, "Schulberg told us that Selznick would help us in any way we needed. I said, 'Fine, but don't let him come on the set and bother us.' David was very young at the time, and, as I soon found out, quite brilliant. I must say this for David, he never came on the set once, he never made one suggestion. We had built a big fort out at Cathedral City near Palm Springs and we put a big sign up outside our camp on the road: WOMEN AND PRODUCERS KEEP OUT."

It was here that the African battle scenes were completed, with the "Fuzzy-Wuzzies" played by black extras from Los Angeles outfitted with suitable wigs. To add movement and excitement to the charge scenes, Schoedsack talked the studio into building a large iron camera bridge, which swept over the battlefield with either end resting on a flatbed truck. The large fort that had been built among the rocks for these sequences was ordered destroyed by Cooper to keep it from being used in other films, a move that infuriated Lasky and Schulberg. Cooper was equally angry, but for another reason. "I was furious with Paramount for not letting us finish the picture with sound. I felt sure that it would be easy, a lead pipe cinch to make *The Four Feathers* quickly into the first big outdoor sound picture. When we finished the film, I took off for New York and put all the money I made on *Chang* into civil aviation."

Selznick was left to cope with the problems of the film, which, after its first preview, appeared considerable. Audience interest seemed to go downhill after the spectacular sequences, the bulk of which were spotted in the middle of the film. The tying up of the main plot elements took up the last forty minutes of the film, which seemed an anticlimax, and Selznick recommended to Schulberg that extensive re-editing and some retakes would be necessary to reconstruct the film without dead spots.

This posed a problem since the Cooper-Schoedsack contract forbade any changes or additions without their approval. Cooper recalls:

Lasky called from Hollywood three times, so I told him that if he personally desired it it was all right to put another director on the few scenes which he (and I presumed Schulberg and Selznick) also wanted retaken. Schoedsack was by then in Sumatra, where he had persuaded Lasky to let him take a crack at a picture by himself—*Rango*—so I took responsibility for both of us and told Lasky to go ahead and put Lothar Mendes on the job, and also, if Lasky wished, to give Mendes some screen credit.

When I ran the picture over, I was horrified that Selznick, or Schulberg, had injected into our Fuzzy-Wuzzy and British Square sequence some of the most sickeningly over-grandiloquent titles I had ever seen. I went to the laboratory, and without consulting anyone, quietly cut out of the negative of the finished picture the worst of these godawful titles and let the picture ride. I thought Selznick had made a big error in his recutting of the film, but the two big action sequences were so good in themselves that I thought the picture would be a big success even though it was silent.

At the Broadway premiere at the Criterion Theatre, the audience applauded the big sequences shot in Africa but sat listless and uninterested through the interiors, and the picture never did do the kind of business Cooper thought it would. "At any rate, I made up my mind as I came out of the theatre that I wouldn't make another picture until I could be the boss."

George Cukor at the time of his arrival at Paramount Pictures, 1930.

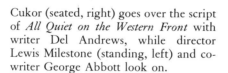

Cukor (seated, right) goes over the script of *All Quiet on the Western Front* with writer Del Andrews, while director Lewis Milestone (standing, left) and co-writer George Abbott look on.

The train from New York continually brought new talent west to Paramount-Famous-Lasky, as the studio had been renamed in 1929. These newcomers were on both sides of the camera, from established stage stars Ruth Chatterton and Ina Claire to a new contract director from New York, George Cukor, who came to Paramount early in February 1929. Selznick remembered that "Cukor arrived at the studio in a black overcoat and a black fedora hat, which he persisted in wearing for the first several weeks. . . . He assisted one or two screen directors without making much of an impression. Through this period, I became very friendly with him, and I sold my friend Lewis Milestone, who had never had any association with the theatre, on using Cukor as the dialogue director on *All Quiet on the Western Front.* Then I sold Schulberg on the great value to Cukor of learning screen technique from as great a silent director as Milestone."

Cukor's background was very similar to Selznick's. He came from a middle-class Hungarian-American family, and, raised in an atmosphere of culture, fell in love with the theatre in his teens. After graduating rather ingloriously from high school, he began getting jobs, first as a stage manager, then as a director, running his own summer stock theatre in Rochester, New York, where he directed stars of the caliber of Billie Burke and Elsie Ferguson. Cukor remarked later about this period of his life: "Nothing threw me at all. I would do a musical comedy one week and then do something else the next week. I really worked goddamned hard. Great preparation for Hollywood."

Like everyone else in the theatre, Cukor was rather snooty about the movies; this did not keep his curiosity down, however, and he was a regular if not avid moviegoer at the 68th Street Playhouse in Manhattan, liking Griffith and not much else. It wasn't until 1928 that Cukor began

to take movies seriously. It was sound pictures that did it. *The Jazz Singer* piqued his interest, but it was *In Old Arizona,* with its naturalistic use of sound, that made him sit up and think, "Aha, this is the wave of the future." Since he was fairly well known in theatrical circles, he was inevitably offered a contract by Schulberg's New York scouts. Feeling that he would be lucky, Cukor went to Hollywood and, as he put it: "I just took to it immediately; I quickly fell in love with the film medium, with Hollywood. I never wanted to go back to the theatre."

Selznick and Cukor became close friends. Selznick was amused by Cukor's fast, sophisticated sense of humor, his acerbic forthrightness, and his drollness as a storyteller. Cukor's innate taste, his sense and concern for the textures, the feel of surfaces, were all reinforced by his insistence on and appreciation of the civilized veneer of manners and attitudes that denoted breeding. His ability to make emotions and reactions understandable through use of character and environment were gifts that Selznick recognized and responded to both personally and professionally. As for Cukor, he recalls Selznick as being "very idealistic, but he wasn't pompous—the joyousness of our friendship, well, we just enjoyed each other tremendously. We always had an amusing time together, we laughed at the same things, he had regard for my work and I for his, and that is a very good basis for a friendship."

But despite their close friendship, the two did not work together at Paramount. Selznick's most frequent collaborators at this time were William Wellman and John Cromwell. Stylistically, the two men were diametrically opposed. Wellman's films were vigorous, blunt, and realistic, with a swift sureness in the storytelling and a hard-edged tenderness in dealing with character. Cromwell had a low-key, deliberate approach to his work, letting actors and characters do most of the work, seldom

The flexibility of sound developed quickly, as these photos show. By mid-1929 outdoor location work was possible, as in this production shot (top, left) from *The Studio Murder Mystery*. Star Neil Hamilton stands in front of the camera, still enclosed in its booth. Then the camera was given its own soundproofed box, which restored mobility (above). Finally a form-fitting "blimp" silencer was devised (left), and by 1930 even the most difficult of locations could be used—as in this shot (below) of George Cukor's *Grumpy* company at work outside Los Angeles.

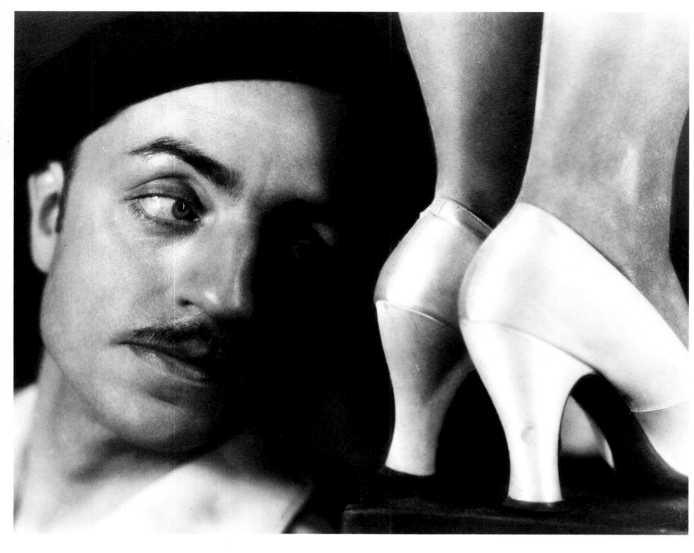

In 1930, studio photographer John Engstead did these two portraits of William Powell, whose career at Paramount was given new impetus through the coming of sound. This included posing with a pair of sharp shoes for his latest, *Pointed Heels*.

using the camera as anything other than an observer or a useful tool to focus attention on story points; there was an air of reserved detachment, of good manners and good taste, about his direction that was as revealing as it was discreet. Wellman's and Cromwell's attitudes and sensibilities complemented the two sides of Selznick's character perfectly. The aggressive restlessness of his own shrewd American business sense was offset by a quiet and reflective side, the side that wrote verse and was respectful of tradition and idealistic about women, marriage, loyalty, and honor. It was Cromwell who directed what Selznick later referred to as "my first really personal film, one I really worked on and cared about."

The film was *Street of Chance*, a story about honor among gamblers. Gamblers were among the most popular of screen topics during the twenties and thirties, right behind cowboys, marriage, infidelity, and blackmail. Most moviemen, by nature, were gamblers, otherwise they wouldn't have been in the business. Selznick came from a long line of high stakes players; even his mother was known as one of the best poker players in town, so he had a natural affinity for the subject. *Street of Chance* was rife with the built-in tragedy inherent in the unwritten code of the gambler. The ending of the story had the hero die as a result of living up to his code: he sacrifices his life so that his brother may live. It was a climax that appealed to Selznick, and he fought mightily against efforts by the sales department to impose a happy ending on the film. He argued with Cromwell about the casting, insisting that he use Kay Francis and the young ingénue Jean Arthur, with whom Selznick, so the word went, was infatuated. For the lead role of "Natural Davis," the anti-hero, Selznick and Cromwell both agreed on William Powell, who up to that time had mostly been playing stock villains and seducers. Sound films opened up a whole other area of Powell's talents. His urbane sophistication began to be noticed favorably by his bosses at Paramount and, more important, by the public.

Street of Chance was one of forty-five pictures that Selznick supervised while Schulberg was away on a six-month tour around the world. In his absence, from June through November 1929, Selznick not only watched over the production schedule but oversaw the myriad other details that went into the operation of the studio. This included working on the

PARAMOUNT POSTERS AND AD SALES

BIG talking, singing productions. Big new personalities. They must be sold big to the public if your theatre is to profit 100% from them. Paramount provides the material with which to do it. Posters, heralds, newspaper ad cuts, roto sections, novelties, etc.—all of the same high quality and box-office pulling power as Paramount Pictures. Ask the ad sales manager at your Paramount exchange.

Guide Posts to the New Show World

An Important Message for Exhibitors with Houses not yet Wired for Sound

•

PARAMOUNT QUALITY
SILENT PICTURES
for 1929-30 release

•

Of the audible feature productions in Paramount's 1929-30 program, the great majority will also be produced and released as quality silent pictures. These silent productions will stand on their own as 100% quality entertainment. Fully up to the high standards which have made Paramount the undisputed leader of the industry for eighteen years.

In addition, Paramount Silent News, with two issues weekly, will be available.

A Minimum of 40 Good Silent Productions
Complete details of titles, etc., soon

"POINTED HEELS"

WILLIAM POWELL

•

ESTHER RALSTON
HELEN KANE
"SKEETS" GALLAGHER
and others

•

From Charles Brackett's College Humor serial story of New York back-stage and society life. Directed by Edward Sutherland, co-director of "Close Harmony." Adaptation by Florence Ryerson. Dialog by John V. A. Weaver.

100% TALKING, SONG ROMANCE OF BROADWAY

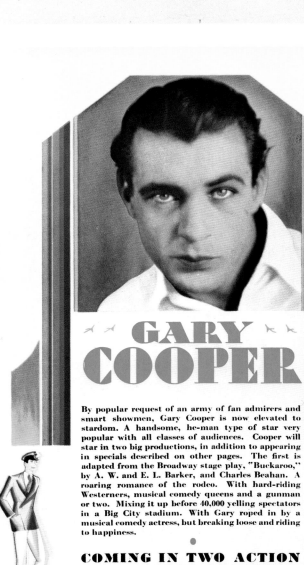

GARY COOPER

By popular request of an army of fan admirers and smart showmen, Gary Cooper is now elevated to stardom. A handsome, he-man type of star very popular with all classes of audiences. Cooper will star in two big productions, in addition to appearing in specials described on other pages. The first is adapted from the Broadway stage play, "Buckaroo," by A. W. and E. L. Barker, and Charles Beahan. A roaring romance of the rodeo. With hard-riding Westerners, musical comedy queens and a gunman or two. Mixing it up before 40,000 yelling spectators in a Big City stadium. With Gary roped in by a musical comedy actress, but breaking loose and riding to happiness.

COMING IN TWO ACTION ALL-TALKING PICTURES

Street of Chance: This set for a New York street shows the meticulous detail that went into the art direction of Paramount films. Paramount followed industry practice in crediting all art direction to the head of the department, in this case Hans Dreier. The setting above was probably by Wiard Ihnen.

silent versions of sound pictures with Julian Josephson of the title department; approving the hiring of new writers and performers; and making arrangements to bring Sergei Eisenstein to the United States to work on an adaptation of *Sutter's Gold.* Another import Selznick was involved with was bringing the German star Marlene Dietrich, whom Josef von Sternberg had just cast opposite Emil Jannings in *The Blue Angel,* a co-production of Paramount and UFA, Germany's largest film production company. In late October, while *Street of Chance* was on the stages, the stock market suddenly and spectacularly collapsed. Several of Selznick's friends were wiped out; in a memo to the New York home office late in November, Selznick made cryptic reference to "several suicides here at the studio" without going into any details. As with sound, no one at first grasped the long-range implications of the crash, except on a personal level. Several of the executives of Paramount were heavily involved in the stock market, as were millions of other Americans playing the "buy on margin—sell when it's high" game that indirectly caused the débâcle.

Schulberg came back to the studio in November to be greeted by a sixty-page memo from the nervous Selznick detailing everything that had been going on in his absence and listing all the work in progress at the time. The problems Selznick had had to deal with were indicated by his comments to Schulberg:

I have lain awake nights, for the first time in my life, wondering how you were going to react to the various moves we were making. Believe me, this has not been made more easy by the kibbitzing of what Lothar [Mendes] so aptly calls "our group of suppressed producers"— executives who yearn to be supervisors and who believe that the destructive criticisms they have made occasionally, that have been acted upon, automatically makes [sic] them producers. . . . The mental hazards they created are to me the most difficult of all obstacles to better pictures. . . .

Selznick's worries were considerably allayed by a hefty bonus check and a congratulatory telegram from Jesse Lasky, complimenting him on the "soundness of judgment, tact, common sense and courage which you used to such excellent advantage in carrying on during Ben's absence."

Considerably fortified by these affirmations of confidence, and by his own belief in his ability to make good pictures under the stresses and strains of a large studio, Selznick, who up to this time had been a fairly popular bachelor about town, decided to marry Irene Mayer, the dark-eyed younger daughter of Louis B. Mayer.

The quiet wedding took place in April 1930. After a two-month honeymoon, Selznick returned to the studio and settled down into a routine of making sound pictures—a routine that by now, after the initial few months' panic, had become as standardized and factory-like as the production of silent pictures had been. Over 12,000 theatres in the United States were now wired for sound, and every week in 1930 more than 90 million moviegoers across the country paid an average of 40 cents admission to see and hear some of the 150 pictures that Paramount released that year. The result of all this was an income of $31 million, an increase of 200 percent over the previous year. The euphoria that all this money generated at Paramount was such that the studio geared up for and announced 150 films for the following year, at least a third of them to be made in Hollywood, and Selznick would be in charge of making sure most of these were completed. Schulberg, evidently as a result of his heavy losses in the stock market and the pressures of the production schedule at the studio, was drinking heavily and gambling a great deal, impairing his effectiveness as the "fine factory foreman" that Selznick thought him to be. This situation quickly came to the attention of Zukor and Lasky, the latter confidentially asking Selznick if he would take over Schulberg's job. Selznick felt that he could not do anything that would seem underhanded or treacherous to the man who had given him his first big opportunity, so he talked to Schulberg about it. "He was very angry," Selznick later recalled, "and I said that in that case, he should forget it, since I would not consider taking the job of the man who had brought me in, and I so notified Lasky. Schulberg, from that point on, would not even see me and wouldn't talk to me."

The situation deteriorated to such a point that by late 1931 Selznick was anxious to leave the studio and set up his own independent production company with director Lewis Milestone. In a memo to Schulberg, Selznick decried the practice that allowed Schulberg to

carry in [your] mind the plans for seventy pictures yearly, plus the enormous amount of material from which these are to be made, plus the executive work involved in the management of a large studio. I see no hope for changing this system . . . we have the players, the directors, the writers—a staff comprised of people of enormous talent and great ambition, however thwarted, cynical and indifferent they may at the moment be. The system that turns these people into automatons is obviously what is wrong.

Aggravating this system was the messy financial situation prevailing at Paramount because of the crash. In spite of the record grosses of 1930–31, the complicated financing that Zukor had arranged for the acquisition of theatres and conversion of the company to sound drained all the huge profits that had poured in. Cash flow was a problem, and costs were cut ruthlessly. In late 1931, in an unprecedented move for a major studio, the entire list of featured players were released from their contracts. The unpleasant task of notifying them was given by Schulberg to Selznick, and, as Fay Wray remembers: "It was the first time I had an actual meeting with David in the studio. It was painful for him, but he was very nice about it; he had a certain charm that made you feel that it wasn't as bad as it appeared. I remember thinking after I spoke to him that it was the best thing that could possibly happen to me. I think most all of the contract people were let go. Bill Powell came to the house afterwards and we celebrated . . . we were so joyful that we were free from this big corporation that was using us as though we were commodities."

Meanwhile, the quality of the films being made was going considerably downhill, as Selznick had indicated. John Cromwell relates:

In the hallway at Paramount, I met Ben Schulberg, and he asked me to come watch a picture with him, and we went into the projection room and ran this picture and it was just terrible, one of those run-of-the-mill things. . . . The picture finished and Ben turned to me and said, "What do you think?" and I said, "Do you really want me to tell you what I think?" and he said, "Yes, by all means," so I said, "I can't understand why you're doing such a picture. In five minutes, I knew what the story was about, I could have gone on and finished the damn thing and told you exactly what was going to happen without seeing the rest of it, and I'm afraid that's the way your audience is going to react when they see it; they've seen this story so often. . . ." He chewed on his cigar and said, "Yeah, well, that's what happens when you have to turn out a picture a week for fifty-two weeks."

The straw that broke Selznick's back came in mid-1931 when all the Paramount executives were asked to take a voluntary salary cut. Selznick wrote a long, discouraged letter to Schulberg in which he refused to consider this, saying: "I do not feel that I am responsible in any way for the current depression in the firm's business. On the contrary, I think that the average of my contributions has been substantially profit mak-

ing. For the major mistakes of others, I feel in no way obligated to pay." Realizing that his refusal would probably aggravate an already difficult situation for him at Paramount, Selznick offered to resign, adding:

I should like [you] to know that in tendering my resignation, I have not sought or received any other offers . . . that I have no other job lined up or in prospect; that my only ambition at the moment is to attempt the organization of an independent unit—for I believe most strongly the best way out of the pit of bad and costly pictures in which we are now sunk is through breaking up production, in whole or in part, into smaller units that, however they may be controlled, will achieve a degree of independence from overhead, from formulas, prejudices and unsound influences. I recognize the difficulties at this time of my starting anything of my own, the industry condition being what it is, and the money situation being what it is. In spite of this, I am anxious to take my chances, rather than longer take part in anything in which I have lost enthusiasm, faith, confidence and even interest. I feel that in leaving, the most I can lose is money.

After having spent two and a half years shepherding Paramount Pictures through the intricacies of the sound revolution, becoming a married man and a respected picturemaker, David Selznick was once again out of a job.

THE Hollywood REPORTER

Vol. V. No. 28. Price 10c.　　　　TODAY'S FILM NEWS TODAY　　　　Friday, July 17, 1931

HITS FOR LONG RUNS

TRADEVIEWS
by W. R. Wilkerson

◆ THE NEWS that David Selznick was leaving Paramount was expected by very few. It came as a great surprise to his most intimate associates. He had no difficulties at Paramount other than those that would naturally come into the path of any executive of his standing with a studio as important as Paramount. There was no fight with Ben Schulberg.

Selznick was dissatisfied at Paramount because the production of pictures to meet release dates did not fit in with his ideas for the proper making of good pictures. He feels he could do better things as an independent producer, and he probably will.

•

This young production executive has ideas. Plenty of them. He knows a lot about pictures. He has the admiration and best wishes of every individual who ever worked for and with him. He is looked on as a highly intelligent producer. He can say yes and no and give you the reason for either answer.

•

Selznick is going to launch two or three independent production units. One is said to be headed by Milestone, and maybe others, around individuals who stand at the top of the production heap. Seemingly he is not worrying about releases, being satisfied that if the product is right the release is a cinch. If the pictures are bad, then the whole set-up is wrong. But guided by a hand as experienced as his, the successes will far outnumber the flops.

•

We have an idea that one or more production executives will soon follow in Selznick's footsteps. The market is wide open for good product, distributors and exhibitors are pleading for shows—hits—GOOD pictures. The industry must have them if it is to survive and it is our judgment that our business will rise or fall as a direct result of product made independently of the major studios.

•

Take any major as an instance. It is impossible for an organization to turn out 50, 60 or 70 pictures during a twelve-month period that will click at the box-office with sufficient force to show a good profit in the theatre. Good pictures require a lot of effort, more than any one major

(Continued on Page 6)

Height of Tact

With the studio gates closed to the press, a major studio caused some surprise yesterday by entertaining six Chicago gangsters on the set of one of their big productions.

Selznick Post Abolished At Para

With the resignation of David O. Selznick from the Paramount Hollywood studios, the post of executive assistant to B. P. Schulberg, managing director of West Coast production has been abolished. This statement was made by Schulberg yesterday when he was asked the name of Selznick's successor. The duties will be divided up among other studio production executives.

Selznick recently requested and obtained his release from his contract, so that he may enter the independent producing field.

Fox, Loew Dividends

New York.—Fox yesterday paid a quarterly dividend of sixty-two and one-half cents on Class A and B stock. Loew's Theatres paid semi-annual dividend of $3.50 on preferred stock, and Loew's Inc., declared its regular quarterly dividend of $1.62½ on its preferred stock, payable August 15.

RKO Loss Expected; Pathe Cost $6,000,000

New York.—RKO is expected to show a small loss for its second quarter this year. Company figures theatre attendance five per cent below that of a year ago. Six million dollars were borrowed to finance the acquisition of Pathe Exchange, Inc., and its assets.

Complaints and More Complaints

The story appearing in these columns yesterday headed "Feds in Hollywood" caused an avalanche of complaints to be registered at this office from actors, writers and directors who felt they had a grievance at the manner in which they were being tossed around by producers in some of the major studios. If just a few of the complaints are true—some producers are in for a little trouble.

Entire Booking Structure of Deluxe House May Be Changed To Take Theatres Out of Red

With shortage of box-office product, the major problem of de luxe houses for the coming year, circuit operators are considering radical changes in bookings of features that would change entire structure of sales and exhibition.

Present outlook for good product to supply the de luxe houses is chief worry of circuit execs. They can see certain hits, but cannot see where their houses can keep out of the red with the string of program attractions that must be played between the hits where weekly change rules.

Idea under consideration would reserve the hits and big pictures for the large houses. Latter would hold

(Continued on Page 6)

Barbara Stanwyck Walks On Columbia

Barbara Stanwyck has failed to put in an appearance at the Columbia studio for the production of "Forbidden," which was to have been directed by Frank Capra. Miss Stanwyck is said to be demanding three times the amount of the salary her contract calls for, with Harry Cohn insisting she carry through on the original ticket. As it stands now, "Forbidden" has been laid aside and Miss Stanwyck claims screen retirement.

Wurtzel To Europe

Sol Wurtzel will vacation in Europe for two or three months, leaving Hollywood immediately on the return of W. R. Sheehan. It is understood that Al Lewis will assume the Wurtzel duties while he is gone.

Holmes In 'Man I Killed'

Paramount has picked Phillips Holmes for the lead of Ernst Lubitsch's next picture, "The Man I Killed."

Tiff Announces Thirty

New York.—Tiffany's program for 1931-32 will be thirty features. Eight of these will be Ken Maynard westerns.

Dix With Radio For Two Pictures

A deal will be signed today between Richard Dix and Radio Pictures, whereby Dix will star in two productions, "Frontier" and "Marcheta." The deal was made with William LeBaron, production executive at RKO and will dovetail into the star's current contract.

Mexico Jumps Film Tax From $1.60 to $10-$15

Mexico City.—Mexican Government has raised film import taxes for sound-on-film pictures in English from one dollar-sixty to fifteen dollars. Disc picture goes up to ten dollars per kilo.

Hays Puts Bee On 'Once In A Lifetime'?

New York.—Rumor persists on Broadway that Universal will not produce "Once In A Lifetime," due to objections from the Hays office. No verification from either end.

Leo Settles With Fox

New York.—Joe Leo yesterday obtained satisfactory settlement of his Fox contract. All set now to organize independent theatre circuit with Jack Leo.

Czar Plans Vacation

New York.—Will H. Hays is leaving in the near future for a two-weeks' vacation at Cody, Wyo.

RKO

ALL DURING THE SUMMER OF 1931, while Selznick was in New York trying to finance his independent set-up, back in Hollywood, down the street and around the corner from Paramount's Marathon gate, the RKO studio was having production problems. William LeBaron, the man in charge of making pictures, was unhappy. He liked making individual films that interested him, not gearing up and overseeing the number of movies needed to fill RKO's 250 theatres every week. RKO was only three years old, the first studio to be formed directly as a result of the sound revolution, springing fullblown from the heads of its creators, primarily David Sarnoff of RCA and Joseph Kennedy, the Boston, New York, and lately Hollywood, Wall Street speculator. Sarnoff was the man who had instituted and commercialized the infant radio industry, being one of the guiding forces behind the 1919 formation of the Radio Corporation of America—an amalgamation of the radio patents of General Electric, Westinghouse Electric, and the American Telephone and Telegraph Company.

Sarnoff's next step was the linking up of a number of transmitting stations around the country in what was to become the National Broadcasting Company, which began operations in September 1926, the month after Warner Bros. had premiered the Vitaphone on Broadway. Sarnoff's goal was to make RCA the "General Motors of the electrical entertainment industry," but the rapid changeover of the movie industry to sound pictures, with its virtual domination by the Western Electric-Vitaphone-Movietone triumvirate, had caught Sarnoff off guard. As he saw it, sound pictures were something that RCA must have a hand in. The Kinegraphone, a joint RCA-G.E. device that Roy Pomeroy had used to synchronize the airplane effects in *Wings*, was seen by Sarnoff as RCA's entry into the sound film sweepstakes. Rechristened RCA Photophone, it was offered as a late starter in the sound-on-film field. Western Electric had pretty well sewn up Hollywood as far as sound was concerned; there was nothing left for Sarnoff and RCA except some of the smaller independent studios around town. Accordingly, Photophone was licensed to five of these in July 1928. But Sarnoff knew that if he was to make RCA a force in the industry, he would have to have a major studio connection, one that produced, distributed, and showed its own films in its own theatres.

There may have been another reason for Sarnoff's stubbornness about injecting RCA into the film business, and that was his commitment of RCA to the developing and marketing of the new television device. Although TV was still largely in the primitive laboratory stage, Sarnoff was convinced that it was only a matter of time before the technical drawbacks were ironed out and television transmission could begin on a regular basis. When that time came, Sarnoff wanted to be able to offer the public something to see as well as hear, and that meant, in those days, vaudeville and movies. The majors were obviously out; their agreements with Western Electric certainly precluded RCA using their films, and what about the thousands of theatres that were the source of the industry's wealth? Another solution would have to be found, one that, he hoped, involved a big role for Photophone. Perhaps the answer lay in the five companies that were using the RCA system. It did—in the name of Joseph P. Kennedy.

In the days before presidential and senatorial sons conferred a reflected dignity upon him, Kennedy was an ebullient, direct shark, a man whose Irish grin disarmed while it devoured. He was one of the advance guard of Wall Street bankers and manipulators who had bought their way into the film business on the flood tide of mid-twenties prosperity.

(Opposite) The Film Booking Office studio, located at 780 Gower Street in Hollywood, as it looked in late 1926. Originally the headquarters for Robertson-Cole, a British-backed firm of the early twenties, the studio went through several changes of ownership during the decade, eventually winding up as one of Joseph Kennedy's lucrative film investments, known familiarly in the trade as FBO.

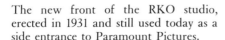

The new front of the RKO studio, erected in 1931 and still used today as a side entrance to Paramount Pictures.

Through his various wheelings and dealings he had acquired substantial holdings in the venerable Pathé Exchange, the Keith-Albee-Orpheum circuit of vaudeville theatres, and the Film Booking Office (FBO), a small production outfit on Gower Street in Hollywood specializing in westerns and action films. He once remarked to a friend, "Look at that bunch of pants pressers in Hollywood, making themselves millionaires. I could take the whole business away from them if I wanted to." Evidently he never wanted to, for aside from a few stabs at First National, he went no further than FBO, Pathé, and the KAO theatre circuit. Tough, sharp, and somewhat ruthless, Joseph Kennedy, with his considerable film-related holdings and his financial acumen, seemed to be just the person who might forge the links in David Sarnoff's scheme to put RCA into the film business in a big way. Through mutual business acquaintances, a meeting was arranged between the two men.

Sarnoff talked, Kennedy listened. RCA wanted control of FBO. Kennedy and his partner, Guy Currier, were offered $500,000 for their stock in the company; RCA also wanted to purchase Kennedy's holdings in the Keith-Albee-Orpheum circuit, plus whatever additional shares he could round up. Sarnoff then wanted Kennedy to use his ingenuity to create a single interlocking corporation merging the FBO studio and the theatre chain, into which RCA would put its holdings in the Photophone process. For doing this Kennedy and his partner would split close to $6 million cash and hold a large block of stock in the new company, control of which would be maintained by RCA. If he arranged the deal, Kennedy would get a bonus of $150,000, plus a seat on the new board of directors. Kennedy snapped up the offer so fast he didn't even have time to tell his partner until the deal had been made. Kennedy and Sarnoff formalized the pact in October 1928 while standing at the Grand Central Oyster Bar in midtown Manhattan.

In one respect, Kennedy was the perfect choice to organize the package. He would get it done, no matter how difficult the task was. On another level, however, he couldn't have been a worse choice. For all his know-how and manipulative abilities, there was no long-range thought as to future problems inherent in his method of "getting things done." The package he delivered to Sarnoff in late 1928 was considered to be a complex, fragile, yet decidedly innovative one, even at that time of widespread mergers in the film business. It called for the formation of a holding company to be called the Radio-Keith-Orpheum Corporation, the $80 million assets of which would include the FBO Hollywood studio, the talent-booking offices, and 250 theatres of the KAO circuit, licensing rights to the RCA Photophone process, and the film exchanges of FBO and Pathé. To all outward appearances, this was an "instant major," a functioning production-distribution-exhibition combine, and thus a force of some concern to the entrenched majors, who watched to see what Radio could and would do.

They needn't have worried. For the overriding problem with RKO, as it was known, was its corporate structure. It was a subsidiary of RCA, yet RCA itself was not a single entity but a jointly owned corporation of the electrical giants, the executives of which had their fingers in all of RCA's corporate pies, now including the new stepchild RKO with its glamorous film and theatre holdings. Additionally, Kennedy's package was largely a paper deal, with not too much transfer of actual cash, except to Kennedy. Its financial base rested on the assumption of an expanding, or at least a stabilized, economy. In the boom times of the biggest bull market in history, such optimism seemed safe. Exactly one year after the formation of RKO, when the stock market laid its famous egg, the weaknesses of Kennedy's cross-collateralization approach proved almost fatal to RKO, and in fact drained its resources for the entire life of the company.

Once the merger had taken place, Kennedy bowed out from both RKO and the film business, cashing in his blue chips and retiring from his filmic poker game with about $5 million more than he had come in with. RCA began equipping the newly named RKO theatres with Photophone sound equipment, while Sarnoff, as chairman of the board of RKO, changed the name of the FBO studio to the RKO studio, where "Radio Pictures" would be made. This would be in the hands of studio head Joseph Schnitzer and his head of production William LeBaron, both carryovers from the FBO-Kennedy régime. Sarnoff told them what he wanted: a series of sound films that would show off the Photophone process and put RKO on an equal footing with the existing majors in terms of quality output. LeBaron, a literate and sophisticated man from the New York theatre world, immediately put into the works a film production of the Ziegfeld musical stage hit *Rio Rita,* which it was felt would show off the new system to its fullest advantage. The film, partly shot in the then prevalent two-color Technicolor process, was in production along with another Radio Picture, director Wesley Ruggles's *Street Girl.* Both were made under adverse conditions, with the new sound stages not yet finished, and only one sound unit available for both films. *Street Girl,* being a less complex production, was finished and into the theatres first and met with fair success. But *Rio Rita,* costing $675,000, was a hit of gigantic proportions, grossing $2,335,000 in the fall and winter of 1929–30 before the impact of the stock market crash began to be seriously felt. Sarnoff and the RKO board were delighted, and signed LeBaron to a three-year contract, during which time he would be "in complete charge of production at the RKO Studio, subject to the instructions of the Board of Directors."

If LeBaron saw anything ominous in that last phrase, he never commented on it. Instead, knowing Sarnoff's desire for prestige, he began production on a mammoth film version of Edna Ferber's novel *Cimarron,* a sprawling generational saga about the state of Oklahoma. Voted best production of the year 1930 by the three-year-old Academy of Motion Picture Arts and Sciences, the film gave RKO the status of a major production company. Sarnoff and the RKO board were very happy until they saw the price tag for all this success. *Cimarron* had cost nearly $1.5 million, but it grossed only $1.38 million. Now that the company had been established, LeBaron was told, he must concentrate on maintaining the high quality without the high cost, at the same time keeping up a consistent production flow for the distribution and theatrical arms of the company. Added to his problems was the fact that RKO had just bought the Pathé organization, which included its Culver City studio, the Pathé newsreel, and the firm's network of film exchanges, hungry for pictures, the production of which now became LeBaron's responsibility. LeBaron had neither the ability nor the desire to take on

The RKO studio, at the corner of Melrose and Gower, circa 1935.

all this added work, especially in view of RKO's worsening financial condition. He declined politely, saying that he wanted to continue in a limited capacity, making one or two films a year, without being responsible for the company's entire output.

Sarnoff, as chairman of the board, was very much concerned over the health of his ailing foundling. His plans for it now included a major part in RCA's impending occupancy of the new Rockefeller Center in midtown Manhattan, dubbed "Radio City" because of RCA's involvement. RKO had taken on the responsibility for the RKO Building and the RKO Roxy Theatre, both under construction and both putting an additional drain on the parent company's dwindling resources. If RKO was to be the force in the electrical entertainment industry that Sarnoff hoped, it would need someone to take complete charge of, and clean up, its filmmaking operations.

While Sarnoff was preoccupied with RKO's future, David Selznick was spending most of the hot summer of 1931 in New York trying vainly to find the money to back his plan for an independent production that now included Lewis Milestone. He was being helped in this by Merian Cooper, for the two men had stayed in touch and on friendly terms despite their disagreement over *The Four Feathers.* Cooper was by this time quite a mover in the New York financial world, and it was he to whom Selznick turned when he found his independent idea being blocked by the major distributors. As Selznick later discovered, "My father-in-law, Louis B. Mayer, had called a meeting of all the companies to say that I must not be given a release, because [then] every producer and director would want his own unit and the studios would break up."

Cooper had found Selznick's idea "interesting," but, as he put it in a letter written in June 1931,

it is the hardest thing in the world to raise money for any industry that is not doing well, especially in times of deep depression as the present.

Nevertheless, I went around to the one man who is sort of a sport that way and might be interested in the thing for the fun of it ... he received the idea much better than I thought he would ... but wanted to know why, if you thought it was such a good proposition, you all didn't back it with your own money. I said you probably would if you had the money, but that everyone in Hollywood lived on a fairly extravagant scale and did not save much.

The "sport" Cooper was referring to was just that: Cornelius Vanderbilt Whitney, socialite, polo-playing heir to the Whitney-Vanderbilt fortunes, and a friend of Cooper's. Whitney's interest was encouraging to Selznick, but before anything substantial developed, Milestone dropped out to take an offer from United Artists. With one of the biggest names in the package gone, the project had collapsed by late August and Selznick was left high and dry.

To his rescue again came Cooper. Through his various connections in the big money worlds, he knew of Sarnoff's difficulty with RKO, and in the back of Cooper's mind an idea took shape. He had wanted for some time now to make another film; he had mentioned it to Selznick in the same letter in 1931: "I have a really great idea for making a gorilla picture, and to tell you the truth, that is what I am particularly anxious to do." The idea stemmed from his observations of the colony of baboons on the African location for *The Four Feathers,* and from his having heard of a tribe of giant apes that lived on the west coast of Africa. Another of Cooper's close friends at the time was Douglas Burden, the naturalist-adventurer, who had captured two 9-foot "dragon lizards" on the remote Pacific island of Komodo and brought them back to the Bronx Zoo, where they died. All of these elements had fused in Cooper's mind; he was convinced that they contained the germ of a movie that would, as he put it, "combine the sweep and excitement of the best of silent picture technique with the dramatic possibilities of sound." He had pitched the

The search for a suitable trademark for the new company evolved two distinct and completely opposed images. The first, the RKO shield (above, center), placed at the end of each film, was developed from the original Keith-Albee-Orpheum theatre insignia (above, left); the triangle was stood on end, bisected with an electrical bolt, and the name Radio Pictures placed on top just in case anyone didn't get the message. After the merger of the parent company with Radio Pictures in 1937, the three RKO letters were added to the design (above, right). The second and more famous of the two trademarks was the rotating globe surmounted by a giant radio tower that beeped out the phrase "A Radio Picture" in Morse code. A first and somewhat clunky version (below, left), was used on the first three Radio pictures, and then the tower was replaced by the more

graceful final model (bottom, right), patterned after the Eiffel Tower, which subsequently had the ubiquitous RKO added to its call letters. After RKO took over the Pathé studio, and before it absorbed it completely, this insignia (bottom, left), with the familiar Pathé rooster, flapping and crowing, was used for a time, but the juxtaposition of the bird and the world didn't take, being greeted by audience giggles on the several occasions it was used. (Below, right) Filming the tower trademark: Linwood Dunn, of the Radio Pictures special effects department, is to the left of the tower; Paul Detlefsen, the artist who painted the clouds on the sheets of plate glass, is on the right, and the unidentified technicians were used to move the glass panes, giving the illusion of passing clouds. The lightning bolts and the call letters were added later by animation.

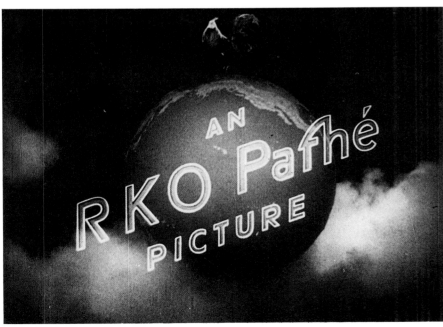 

idea to Zukor and Lasky at Paramount, but they couldn't see the appeal of it and frankly doubted that it could be made. The Fox executives were even more negative than Paramount's, and Cooper had put the idea on the back burner, knowing, as he said, that "I wouldn't be able to make this picture unless I was my own boss all the way down the line, with no interference from executives or front offices." He had told Selznick and his brother Myron about it; they were both enthusiastic, as was another close friend of Cooper's, David K. E. Bruce, financier, gentleman farmer, and later ambassador to the Court of St. James.

It was Bruce to whom Cooper suggested the idea of having David Selznick take over the foundering RKO. Cooper felt that with Selznick in charge of the studio, he would be able to make his gorilla picture the way he wanted. So, after a round robin at the highest levels of finance, Sarnoff finally contacted Selznick in late August 1931. Selznick's own version is that he personally went to Sarnoff, "because he was the only man I knew who would not be swayed by the [film] group; after many discussions, I sold him on the idea of putting me in charge not only of production at RKO but also of his own rival production unit, Pathé. In October of 1931, I signed a contract to take over both studios and merge them."

The contract gave Selznick a salary of $2,500 weekly, the title of "Vice President in Charge of Production" at the RKO studio, and made him a vice-president of RKO-Pathé. The credit "Produced by David O. Selznick" or "A David O. Selznick Production" would also be on all the pictures he personally supervised. But, try as he might, Selznick could not shake himself of the contract's stipulation that all production decisions would be subject to the authority of the board of directors, the chairman of the board, or the president of RKO. With Sarnoff's personal assurance that this would not hinder him in the least, Selznick left for Hollywood late in October, this time as the boss of two separate studios, with authority to do virtually anything he wanted with them short of burning them down.

As Selznick headed west on the train that autumn, the nation was heading toward the depths of the depression. The shock of the stock market crash had radiated waves that rippled slowly across the economic face of the country, closing factories, throwing millions out of jobs and onto welfare rolls. In 1930, 90 million Americans had gone to the movies every week, attracted by sound, color, excitement, and the chance to escape from the fears of a suddenly disordered world. By 1931, these fears had largely become reality, and as the novelty of sound wore off, attendance fell to 75 million a week, a hard fiscal blow to the film companies that had hocked themselves into near financial oblivion in order to equip for sound. MGM was still solvent, but it stood alone in the sea of reorganizations, near bankruptcies, and losses of millions. By November 5, 1931, RKO stock had dropped to a new low of 75 cents a share, and it was at this point that Selznick arrived at the studio to find a situation more chaotic than he had expected. Money was being spent in all directions without too much thought being given to films in the works. The recent merger of the RKO and the Culver City–based Pathé studios had further complicated organizational matters. Added to these problems was the William LeBaron contract, which specified that LeBaron was answerable only to the board of directors. The wording was modified so that he became subservient to Selznick, but LeBaron was

used to having his own way, and the compromise did not work out. Selznick solved this by arranging for LeBaron to take his unit around the corner to Paramount, which LeBaron did gratefully, and with no hard feelings.

The week prior to Selznick's arrival, notices had been sent to all the RKO staff writers, directors, and associate producers that their services "might not be required at the end of a 60-day period. This does not necessarily mean that your association with RKO-Pathé will be terminated within 60 days." What it did mean was that everyone was on a sixty-day trial period, at the end of which Selznick would decide who stayed, who went, and which pictures would be filmed and which scrapped. Before he left New York, Selznick had been warned that there was much deadwood and rampant nepotism on the payrolls, and he intended to be ruthless in weeding it out.

One of the people at RKO who stood to be most affected by this was twenty-six-year-old Pandro Berman, an associate producer whose father had been one of the founders of FBO; he was also cousin to Joseph Schnitzer, the president of the studio, all of which seemingly made him an ideal target for Selznick's ax-wielding. But Berman was no dilettante playing at being an executive. His background in the movie business, while not as extensive as Selznick's, was very similar. As a child, he had listened to the tales his father told about publicity stunts and deal-making; many of his relatives were in film sales and distribution, and when young Berman first considered a film career, they all told him the same thing: "Don't become a film salesman. If you want to make money in this business, go to Hollywood and learn to make pictures, because that is the only place you will ever make any money." Selznick, instead of firing Berman as he had been advised to, decided that he would be valuable as his assistant, a position Berman accepted gratefully. He soon found that Selznick was as hardworking and as dedicated as he wanted his employees to be. Berman recalls that Selznick was "a very fastidious fellow . . . he would come in in the morning with a hundred notes from which he would write memos. He had a roll of paper by his bed at night and would scribble things down when he'd get an idea. He was very meticulous, and didn't care too much about cost; he was more interested in quality. He really swept the studio out."

One of the scripts that Berman had been overseeing when Selznick took over was an adaptation of an original short story by Fannie Hurst called "Night Bell." She was the author of *Back Street, Imitation of Life,* and other popular successes of the time. Her subjects were women who usually suffered at the hands of a man, and all of whom found regeneration or success either through their moral fortitude or their dogged determination not to be got down. She shared with Edna Ferber, to whom she was sometimes favorably compared, a fondness for spinning stories over decades, bringing social attitudes and racial problems into her work.

"Night Bell" told the story of the marriage of a young Jewish doctor; set in contemporary Manhattan, the story was rich in ethnic humor and attitudes. In those days Jews, along with blacks and Orientals, were considered fair game for humor. Weber and Fields, Amos 'n' Andy, and other dialect acts were all based on stereotypical humor, broadly caricatured but seldom vicious. This was not true, however, of many sections of the popular press, nor of the general public's attitude at the time.

Irene Dunne and Ann Harding, two of RKO's biggest female attractions, circa 1932.

An 11 × 14-inch "lobby card" used by theatres playing *Rio Rita*. The stars were John Boles, Bebe Daniels, and the popular comedy team of Bert Wheeler and Robert Woolsey. The set was by Max Ree, the distinguished art director, and the costumes were by Walter Plunkett, who had been working for FBO and who really got a chance to show what he could do on this, his first big picture.

RKO's biggest success, both commercially and artistically, was *Cimarron,* with spectacular land-rush sequences filmed near Bakersfield, California. (Below, right) The picture won Academy Awards for art director Max Ree (second from right) and scenarist Howard Estabrook (left of Ree), who adapted Edna Ferber's novel, and the Best Picture of the Year award was presented to producer William LeBaron (far left), thereby pushing Radio Pictures into major studio status.

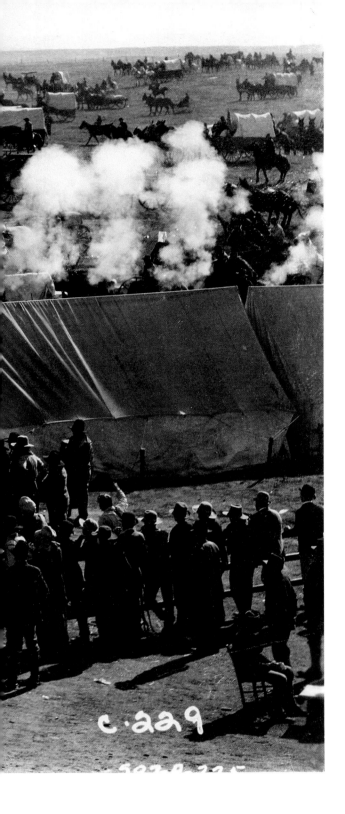

There was a strong, accepted strain of anti-Semitism to be found everywhere, from restricted hotels and restaurants to the political world, where presidential candidate Franklin Roosevelt was sneeringly referred to in some quarters as Franklin Rosenfeld. *Time* magazine, in a piece on Selznick's takeover of RKO, had referred to "the crafty and extraordinary methods of one-time fur peddlers, garment dealers and second-hand jewelers ... Jews ... who padded their payrolls with relatives, settled their biggest deals over all-night poker games and ... discussed the picture business in comic strip dialect." Selznick was described as being "a member of Hollywood's highest, smallest, most ridiculed caste, a scion of the peculiar hierarchy which has always controlled the cinema industry, and now, it seems, always will." The article, carefully preserved by Selznick with the offending passages circled, must have been an affront to his pride, especially the reference to "second-hand jewelers." Although he didn't consider himself first and foremost a Jew, Selznick was ever mindful of his heritage and background, and the article may have triggered a conscious resolve to depict Jews as more than just stereotyped comics, to present Jewish traditions and attitudes sympathetically, something that had been done only infrequently by Hollywood, notably in *The Jazz Singer* and *Abie's Irish Rose.* When Selznick took over RKO, he began systematically going over all projects slated for filming; among these was *Night Bell,* which under Berman's supervision had been turned into a screenplay by two staff writers. In comparing the original short story with the screenplay, Selznick found references to the doctor's childhood on the Lower East Side and some scenes involving his early family life that had been jettisoned, and he pointed out that the script could be made richer by including a prologue dealing with this period of the doctor's life, emphasizing the closeness and humorous affection of the family.

It was Berman's first chance to show Selznick what he could do as a producer. It was also, as he later recalled,

> my first opportunity to work with a really talented director, Gregory LaCava, who was, at that time, somewhat in disfavor in the industry as a result of having been a little too much of a drinker ... but David gave him this chance to come back, and LaCava took full advantage of it, and he did some wonderful work from then on. LaCava's method of making films was to use the script as a kind of a guideline, a framework on which he could hang his scenes; we'd start production and he'd always be amazed and delighted that the people we hired to put in his pictures were talented people and had great personalities. He would decide what he wanted to do with the picture through working with the actors on the set. He would find their personality, then he would sit down every morning and rewrite the day's work himself while they were rehearsing; and after lunch he would start shooting this new scene that he had written in the morning. And the scenes were always filled with exactly the right things for the actors to say and do according to their personalities. I remember one of his favorite expressions was, "Don't worry about the dialogue—I can always spit that out at the last minute." ... He made people do things that nobody had ever expected they were able to do.

Extra care was taken with the casting of *Night Bell.* Berman was dissatisfied with the quality of actors available in Hollywood and cabled RKO's New York representative Katherine Brown: "We need your help in finding some real character [actors] for the parts of the mother and father. This picture is really dependent upon complete reality in the characterizations ... one false note in the conception of the Jewish characters will destroy it completely." The best that was available to RKO was an actor from the Yiddish theatre, Gregory Ratoff, who was brought out to Hollywood on a short-term contract; Irene Dunne, who had become a star with *Cimarron,* was assigned the part of the wife of the doctor; and Anna Appel, another New York performer, was sent out to play the mother. The pivotal role of Felix, the young doctor, was assigned to Ricardo Cortez, whose Latin stage name hid his real identity as Jake Kranz. The film was made between January 14 and February 21, 1932; the title of the story had been changed to *Symphony of Six Million,* which Selznick felt was much more dramatic and dignified. It also tied in with an idea Selznick wanted to try, an outgrowth of his work with *Chinatown Nights* at Paramount. He felt that the near constant use of

Pandro S. Berman in 1932, when he was one of David O. Selznick's two assistants at RKO. Subsequently he became head of production at the studio, making most of the Astaire-Rogers pictures, and just about every other great film that the studio made until 1939, when he resigned to go to MGM.

music in that film had greatly enhanced its emotional qualities. The idea had not been pursued with any enthusiasm by most musical directors in the early sound years. Films up to 1932 generally opened with a burst of credit music, had one or two isolated instances of "incidental" music, and then closed with a quick fanfare. In *Symphony of Six Million* Selznick wanted to add what he called "symphonic underscoring" to the entire film; the script had been rewritten with this approach in mind, including notes that "the next sequence has our Symphonic Music Underscoring accompanying a series of impressionistic shots dissolving from one into the other showing life in the Ghetto." To provide this musical underpinning, Selznick turned to the head of RKO's music department, Max Steiner, a small, round Viennese with a puckish sense of humor and an effably romantic soul. Raised in the shadow and under the influence of Wagner, Strauss, and Mahler, Steiner had written an operetta when he was thirteen. However, conflicts with his father, a theatrical producer, over his vocation convinced him to leave Austria for England, where he started at the bottom of the musical world, playing rehearsal piano for musical comedies. He worked himself up to become one of the foremost conductors and orchestrators. When World War I broke out, he was about to be deported as an enemy alien when he emigrated to the United States, starting his musical career all over again in New York. He later said of this period:

> I almost starved to death, but then I began to get some jobs ... and pretty soon I was doing very well. In the winter of 1929 I was conducting a musical comedy called *Sons o' Guns* when Bill LeBaron, who was in the audience, asked me if I'd like to come to work for RKO. He made me a fairly good offer and two weeks later I packed up and came out.
>
> The first picture I actually wrote any music for was *Cimarron*. I didn't get any credit, but after the premiere downtown at the Orpheum everybody was saying, "It's a great picture, but who did the music, why didn't he get any credit?" So after that they made me music director. But I didn't really get a chance to do anything much until David came to RKO. I knew him because his father and I were great friends. His folks had just come out to Hollywood, and his mother and father took a terrific liking to me; we used to play 10-cent poker every Saturday night and that's how I met David. You know, I have a saying, "A motion picture producer is a man who knows everything but can't think of it." Well, David wasn't like that. ... He

knew exactly what he wanted ... he was tough, not a son of a bitch, just very intelligent. He told me what he wanted and then left me alone.

Steiner began composing for *Symphony of Six Million* while the film was still on the stages, looking at the daily rushes of scenes with Berman and the editor, getting ideas for the music, then waiting until the scenes were finally edited before finishing the composing, orchestrating, and recording, the last of which had to be done down to the second. As he explained in a letter to a friend: "I've used some original Jewish melodies, but all of these have been rearranged and reorchestrated by me and you can't tell where the originals leave off and my own stuff comes in."

Symphony of Six Million finally opened in New York at RKO's Mayfair Theatre on Broadway in April 1932, where it was greeted with good notices for LaCava's direction and the performance of Gregory Ratoff. None of the reviews mentioned the music, which is not surprising; critics seldom commented on the technical aspects of films. The picture did very well financially, returning a larger than normal profit on its $250,000 cost. Berman recalls it as being "my first good movie," and Selznick too was pleased, feeling that he had been instrumental in presenting a realistic view of Jewish family life and tradition. It was a film that he always put on his list of pictures he was proudest of.

By early 1932 the merger of the RKO and Pathé units was functioning smoothly. Selznick began sifting through the projects then in the works. *The Lost Squadron,* a Richard Dix film that had Erich von Stroheim in a major role, was on location in the San Fernando Valley for flying sequences, and director George Archainbaud was having nothing but problems. Not with the illustrious co-star; von Stroheim was subdued and cooperative. Instead, as actress Dorothy Jordan recalls: "Poor Mr. Archainbaud had a terrible time with the stunt pilots. They would get very bored just waiting around for the next set-up and they started flying all over the place, diving, flying through barns. It was quite impressive, but Mr. Archainbaud was really quite put out about it." *The Lost Squadron* had been in production when Selznick took over, and he had let it continue until he had time to review it. The incident with the flyers focused his attention on its filming; he read the script, then promptly borrowed Norman McLeod from Paramount to revise Herman Mankiewicz's screenplay, and replaced Archainbaud with Paul Sloane, to punch up the action and flying scenes. The finished film wavered uncomfortably between pretentious drama, low comedy, and a murder mystery ending that was confused and disappointing.

Another of the problems facing Selznick that winter was a project intriguingly called *Creation* that had run up close to $120,000 in development costs. In reading the script, Selznick found that it was a fantasy adventure drama about the crew of a submarine who discover a lost world under the continent of South America, replete with prehistoric animals, volcanic eruptions, earthquakes, and other expensive-sounding plot devices. The whole thing smacked very much of the 1925 silent *The Lost World,* and indeed, the man who had brought the project to Bill LeBaron was Willis O'Brien, who had been responsible for the sensa-

A composite ad art still for *Symphony of Six Million,* starring Irene Dunne and Ricardo Cortez, and featuring, as the foreword title put it, a symphony of "six million human hearts."

(Above) An 11 × 14-inch tinted lobby card. Erich von Stroheim is on top of one of the RKO sound trucks, re-christened for the occasion.

(Left) Joel McCrea and Dorothy Jordan, the young romantic leads of *The Lost Squadron.* Soon after this, Miss Jordan, a young lady of exceptional charm and great spirit, became the wife of Merian C. Cooper, returning to the screen only on rare occasions, most notably in John Ford's *The Searchers* (1956).

tional special effects in that film. O'Brien was a cartoonist and animator who years before had developed and refined the technique of "stop motion animation" in which inanimate objects were made to perform by photographing successive stages of the movement one frame at a time. Half a reel of tests on *Creation* had already been filmed using this technique, and some miscellaneous views of dinosaurs and other prehistoric beasts romping in the jungle; one long tracking shot of a man being chased by a great horned beast stood out as particularly exciting. But the picture and the whole idea were completely alien to Selznick. The script was plodding and had no drama at all, being largely a loose collection of episodes in the lost jungle. He just didn't know what to make of it; yet the heavy investment, plus O'Brien's contract, would render it too expensive to scrap, and so Selznick was stumped. The need for immediate decisions on this and a hundred other matters was causing Selznick and Berman to work the kind of hours that Berman described as "hard slugging work days. I would get in early in the morning and stay till ten or eleven at night. It was just a constant succession of problems." Overseeing details of pictures in the making, preparing scripts, and handling business matters was taking up more time than the two men had. What was needed was someone whose judgment was at least as good as Selznick's, someone who had an organizational mind, knew how to make good pictures, and how to do so cheaply and quickly.

Back in New York, Merian Cooper was laboring by day in the executive offices of Western Air Express and Pan American Airways, and at night living the life of a Manhattan bachelor. His friend "Jock" Whitney had backed a successful Broadway revue called *The Band Wagon,* starring the brother-and-sister dance team of Fred and Adele Astaire. Cooper was very impressed, believing them to be "the greatest dancers in the world at the time. Adele had more of a personality than Fred, but he was the best, he was a helluva dancer, there just wasn't anybody in his class. I saw *The Band Wagon* four or five times, just to see them dance. I remember thinking that they would be very big in the movies and that somebody ought to sign them up."

When he wasn't socializing or working at the airline offices in midtown, Cooper occupied himself with dreaming up a story line for his gorilla picture. His original idea was to capture three gorillas in West Africa and take them to the island of Komodo that his friend Douglas Burden had written about, where the gorillas would fight a battle with the huge dragon lizards that inhabited the island. He had many conversations with Burden about this in the winter of 1929–30. Burden remembers that Cooper "especially liked the strength of words beginning with K, such as Kodiak Island and Komodo, and it was then, I believe, that he came up with the word 'Kong' for a possible gorilla picture. I remember telling him that I liked very much the sound of the word 'Kong,' as in gong." The fact that the dragon lizards Burden had brought to New York couldn't live in civilization also intrigued Cooper: "You know," he said, "I've always believed that over-civilization destroys people. All of Schoedsack's and my pictures have had one basic theme: that of man's fight against nature for survival. So that idea and the death of the dragon lizards I thought might work in the gorilla picture."

One rule of picturemaking that Cooper hewed to was what he called his "three-d's: distance, danger, and difficulty." The gorilla picture had all these in varying degrees, but Cooper realized that the dramatic thread necessary to tie the "three d's" together and sustain a whole film was still eluding him. Then he recalled Burden's account of taking his young wife to the islands, where she was alternately fascinated and repelled by the giant lizards. Conjured up in Cooper's mind was the childhood image of the giant ape carrying off a screaming woman into the jungle, and a slow transformation began to take place in his imagination. Over a period of some weeks, he devised a story that involved an expedition to a remote volcanic island looking for animals for a circus. The leader of the expedition, a P. T. Barnum type, takes along his niece; once on the island, she is abducted by a giant ape, described in Cooper's original draft as

resembling a gorilla, only where a gorilla stands a scant seven feet in height, Kong towers 20 feet above the ground. His hands and feet have the size and strength of steam shovels; his girth is that of a steam boiler. This is a monster with the strength of a hundred men. But more terrifying is the head—a nightmare head with bloodshot eyes and jagged teeth set under a thick mat of hair, a face half-beast half-human.

Cooper inserted into this story his scene showing the beast fighting one of the dragon lizards; the problem of making them of sufficient stature, he felt sure, could be solved by using a variation of Paramount's Magnascope process and other trick effects. During the winter of 1929–30, Cooper developed a story along these lines that involved bringing the gorilla back to New York, and by building special scaled sets, allowing him to run amok in the city.

But this concept looked to be expensive and difficult with a real gorilla, because by now the gorilla had transmogrified into a beast in love with beauty—in this case the young girl he kidnaps. In the course of all this, in Cooper's words, "the beast goes soft, he loses his brutishness, and civilization gets him. So I wrote a foreword to the script in the form of an old Arabian proverb, which never existed, but which pretty well summed up the story: 'And lo! the Beast looked upon the face of beauty, and it stayed its hand from killing. And from that day, it was as one dead.'"

It was after writing this prologue that Cooper knew a real gorilla was out of the question. He felt that there would have to be a subtle, poetic quality to Kong himself, and that no real gorilla would do; neither would a man in an ape suit. Cooper also realized that the story, as it was constructed up to that point, lacked what he called "a chariot race," one scene that the audience would always remember. In *Ben-Hur*, of course, it was the chariot race, hence the phrase. In *Chang*, it was the elephant stampede; and in *The Four Feathers* it was the charge of the hippos and baboons. He still needed a chariot race for *Kong*. Then, late one afternoon in February 1930 as he was leaving his office in midtown Manhat-

tan, he heard the sound of an airplane motor and looked up instinctively just as the sun glinted off the wings of a plane flying extremely close to the tallest building in the city, the New York Life Insurance Building. "Without any conscious effort of thought," Cooper recalled later, "I immediately saw in my mind's eye a giant gorilla on top of the building, and I thought to myself, 'If I can get that gorilla logically on top of the mightiest building in the world and then have him shot down by the most modern of weapons, the airplane, then no matter how giant he was in size, and how fierce, that gorilla was doomed by civilization,' and I remember saying aloud to myself, 'Well, if that isn't a chariot race, then I don't know what is!'"

This was the story that Cooper outlined to David and Myron Selznick in August 1931. It was the possibility of filming it that made Cooper jump at David's offer, three months later, to come out to RKO and be his other assistant. Wasting no time, Cooper flew across the country on one of Western Air Express's new three-day New York to Los Angeles flights. He showed up at the RKO lot on November 26, the same day that Selznick had King Vidor in his office trying to convince him to direct a movie version of the old play *The Bird of Paradise*. Vidor was one of MGM's top directors; in the thirteen years since he'd started in the business, he'd made thirty films. His critical reputation had been secured

Merian C. Cooper in a posed publicity still, "dreaming up" *King Kong*. The animals are all models that had been constructed for the film.

with *The Big Parade* in 1925; after that, *The Crowd* and *Show People* had capped his silent years. Vidor had daringly turned to the taboo subject of Negro life for his first sound film, *Hallelujah!*, which MGM had reluctantly released in 1929; his next picture, *Billy the Kid*, was filmed in an early 70 mm process that MGM called Realife; then, for Samuel Goldwyn, he made *Street Scene*, which took place entirely on one set.

Vidor was considered to be a hard-edged, romantic stylist, with an independent, offbeat sense of what made good movies. When Selznick called him about *Bird of Paradise*, Vidor was thirty-seven years old, a soft-spoken Texan nearing the end of his third contract with MGM. He was taking his time about renewing it because, in his own words:

I tried to avoid the feeling that I was an employee of MGM. . . . I was always afraid of "the old nest" and "Mama MGM" and all that. . . . I didn't go for that because I always wanted to be free enough to leave. Once you became one of the company boys, you'd fall into the rut of just making what they wanted you to . . . so I would make a deal for a couple of pictures, and then the contract would end, and I'd not be on salary with MGM and I could take one or two outside pictures, then go back to MGM. So *Bird of Paradise* came during one of these in-between periods. I had just finished *The Champ* when David sent for me. . . . I went over and he gave me the script and I took it home and tried reading it and I just couldn't read it. I got past the first act and I called David and said, "I can't read it and what's more, if I read any more I'm not only not gonna make the film, but I'll go around telling everybody how bad it's going to be."

Still anxious to make the kind of picture he thought *White Shadows in the South Seas* could have been, Selznick kept after Vidor to do *Bird of Paradise*, telling him that he would be able to do anything he wanted

with the story, "as long as I gave him," recalls Vidor, "three wonderful love scenes and had Dolores Del Rio jump in a volcano at the end." Finally, Vidor agreed. Selznick's disdain for the plot was due to more than just its lurid melodrama. The play had also been the basis of a near successful plagiarism lawsuit. When the property was bought by RKO, the New York legal department warned the studio that

the plaintiffs had tasted blood in obtaining a judgment . . . which they missed collecting by a scant margin. They are out to get all they can and will pounce upon everything which might constitute an infringement. You should instruct whoever is working on the script to get a copy of [the plaintiffs'] play and make sure that nothing from it is interpolated in the script.

Dolores Del Rio, who was to be the bird of the title, was contracted to start no later than January 23, 1932, so time was pressing for the script revisions. In early December, Selznick and Vidor had decided that they should photograph the exteriors in actual locations, instead of trying to make do with Catalina Island and Laguna Beach. Based on photographs and travel folders, the Hawaiian Islands were chosen. They were exotic, and fairly close—five days by a steamer that left once a week; there was shortwave and even telephone communication. Vidor recalls:

I remember we got some sort of information that January was a good month, and the whole caravan of us took the train up to San Francisco and then the ship from there. We still didn't have a finished script, so [we] decided that we would write the rest of it on the way over. Well, it was terribly rough all the way across; we couldn't even walk around, we had trouble eating. I never got seasick, but you just couldn't write, you were being knocked around, tossed around.

The grandest romance ever written . . . most famous of all American plays sweeps to the screen a flaming pageant of a forbidden love. White man . . . brown girl . . . caught in the volcanic drama of life . . . on the moon drenched shores of a magic isle . . . where blood runs hot and the heart is free and man holds in fierce embrace the alluring image of elemental woman as the jealous God in the Mountain of Fire sunders the earth and splits the skies and hurls the sea to a bottomless pit because she broke the savage Taboo!

King Vidor in 1932, when he made *Bird of Paradise* at RKO.

Joel McCrea and David Selznick at Santa Monica in 1932. According to McCrea, it was here that Selznick asked the young actor to teach him to ride a surfboard, promising him a part in a picture if he succeeded. Selznick never learned, but McCrea was soon cast in *Bird of Paradise,* with Selznick commenting to him, "I always keep my word."

We arrived in Honolulu in pretty bad shape. We only had a week before the rest of the crew came over; in that time we had to finish the script and pick all the locations, because once the crew arrived we only had two weeks to do all our exteriors. I had in my mind that when the company arrived, we would have an absolutely mobile unit, where you could ride around or go to another island and if you saw something that looked good, you just stop and shoot there. Well, that idea got blasted when the company arrived, and they started unloading trucks, sound trucks, camera cars, and so much equipment—we had eleven trucks before they were through; it was like moving a circus. All our beautiful, undisturbed locations were ruined by the time we moved in; the equipment just tore everything up and knocked things down. I remember one of the location photos we'd looked at had shown a yacht at anchor in this beautiful lagoon, surrounded by palm trees. We had wired ahead to use the yacht in the picture; it was just what we needed for the story. When we went looking for the lagoon, we found that it had been a composite photo. The lagoon was too shallow for the yacht and there were no palm trees; so we borrowed some of the trucks the telephone company used for hauling poles, and we moved coconut trees from an inland grove to a beach that was deep enough for the yacht to maneuver and anchor.

On the second day of filming, it started to rain, with heavy winds blowing down all the carefully anchored palm trees, and for the next two weeks it rained and stormed almost continuously. Vidor recalls that "it turned out to be the worst storm of the century, or something. We were there for a month to six weeks, and we had about two or three full good days without blowing winds and rains, we had Dolores and Joel McCrea playing love scenes in the mud, so we decided to come back to California. I figured if we were going to have to put up our own palm trees and nail palm fronds to them, we may as well do it in Catalina." Selznick had okayed the company to stay an extra three weeks in the hope that they would be able to complete their work, but finally he, too, gave up; it was costing RKO $3,000 a day to work in Hawaii, and after thirty-five days, they had only accomplished half of what they needed.

Back in Hollywood, a native village was built on the back lot of the RKO-Pathé studio in Culver City. While it was under construction, Vidor filmed the balance of the exteriors on Catalina Island, then went out to the First National studios in Burbank to use their water tank for underwater shots of Dolores Del Rio as the supposedly nude princess when she first encounters McCrea, who plays the young American with whom she falls in love. Then the company spent a week on the native village set, where dance director Busby Berkeley had been working with a contingent of chorus girls in staging the wedding and other ceremonial dances. "It was David's philosophy," recalls Vidor, "to get the best for everything, and Berkeley had a reputation then. He hadn't done his big Warners pictures yet, but he had done some good work for Goldwyn, and he knew his business."

By mid-June, when the shooting was finished, the cost of *Bird of Paradise* had escalated to $732,000, making it the most expensive RKO film since *Cimarron.* This total would be increased by $20,000, which was the cost of having Max Steiner write an appropriate musical score. Steiner labored over this during the last two weeks of June, putting music to almost all of the picture's eighty-five minutes. To underline the exotic, languorous feeling of the visuals, he wrote original material, weaving it in and out of his own arrangements of traditional Hawaiian melodies. His use of the vibraphone, marimbas, ukeleles, and the steel guitar created an ambience of the South Seas that was so popular it would soon become a cliché. But in its first usage here, the swaying, strumming romanticism of the music suffuses the story with a palpable sensuality that drugs the hearer into the willing suspension of disbelief the film required. The erotic impact is greatly heightened by the redolent quality of the music, notably in the moonlit underwater sequence, the wedding procession and love scene that followed, and especially in the final moments of the story, done in complete silence except for the music, which makes palatable and believable the young princess's decision to give up her American lover.

He is lying wounded and delirious on his yacht. She knows she will never see him again, that indeed she goes to her death when she leaves him. The two are alone. He moans for water; she finds an orange and, sucking the juice out of it, lets it trickle from her mouth to his in a series of nibbling kisses shot in extreme close-up. The throbbing arrangement of ukeleles and harps is joined by the off-screen voices of the natives as they begin intoning the death chant. It grows more insistent, drowning out the love theme, drawing her away, off the boat and back to the island, where, in a series of dissolves, she is robed and prepared for her immolation. As she starts out ceremonially on her final journey, silhouetted against the skyline, the chanting voices are joined by a high clear Hawaiian tenor voice that carries the melodic line while the camera, in another series of dissolves, gives us the princess's point of view. When she approaches the fiery top, the single voice rings out above the others, and while the picture dissolves into the fire of the pit, the voice holds a long, vaulting, solo note until the screen fades slowly into blackness with a final, majestic two-note phrase from the full orchestra.

As the film neared its August release date, the trade press was rife with accounts of its production problems; the amount of money spent by RKO was rumored to be well over $1 million. Selznick was concerned that this gossip would have an adverse effect on his efforts to cut down production costs, remarking in a letter to B. B. Kahane, studio president: "We should not permit to go unchecked the grossly exaggerated stories concerning the cost. . . . I am fearful that this may have the wrong effect in certain quarters . . . especially since it didn't cost any more than many of the greatly inferior pictures of MGM and United Artists, among others. . . ." In reply, Kahane reassured Selznick: "Regarding your concern . . . I doubt if any of the Board of Directors read the trade papers, except possibly Mr. Herbert Swope . . . as for the stories themselves . . . it is to our advantage if exhibitors are looking forward to a picture that costs well over a million dollars to produce."

The picture, exploited heavily, was drawing big crowds in its runs, but didn't return its cost; even with the European gross, it still lost, according to the RKO bookkeeping method, $240,000. This peculiar system tacked on an "overhead" fee of 31 percent of the final production figure to the

cost of any film to represent the price of all the behind-the-scenes support departments, as well as legal, staff, and other indirect costs. Selznick fought constantly against these arbitrary "overheads," trying to eliminate them whenever possible. It irked him also that the RKO sales department in New York sold the pictures to its theatres for no more than 20 percent of the gross, when MGM and Paramount were constantly getting 40 and 50 percent from their theatres. Finding a way out of these inflated, enervating, unreal costs was a job that Selznick had entrusted to Merian Cooper when he arrived in November 1931. The problem of the RKO overhead was very simple to Cooper: "Make more pictures. A studio was a factory, you know, everything was there, the cost of it depended on how much you used it. If you made twice as many pictures, you reduced your 30 percent overhead to 15 percent and had twice as many pictures to bring in money. The same with distribution; the more pictures you pushed through, the more your costs fell."

Selznick, however, did not want to make more pictures, feeling it would be a repetition of the situation he had fought against at Paramount. Instead, he, Cooper, and Berman instituted a series of economies, firing excess personnel and rigidly checking costs all down the production line, so that by the time the new production schedule for the 1932–33 program was drawn up, the combined RKO and Pathé studios would be making forty-seven features and thirty shorts for a little over $11 million, instead of the $16 million it had cost the previous year to make forty-eight features and sixty-five shorts—a saving of close to $5 million.

Selznick had earlier assigned to Cooper the task of sifting through the mass of material awaiting production decisions, including the expensive, troublesome *Creation,* which had gone into hiatus until Selznick could figure out what to do about it. In the first week of December 1931, Cooper looked at the half-reel of test footage that had been shot on *Creation.* He recalled: "I looked at the test and was all for throwing that in the ashcan. It was simply a few shots, strung together, some of actual

These frame enlargements from *Bird of Paradise* give an indication of the sensuality of the picture. The moonlit underwater swim of the hero and heroine was done largely by McCrea in a bathing suit and Miss Del Rio supposedly in her birthday suit. The close-up love scenes in the picture were shot by Vidor in a manner that was erotic, yet tasteful.

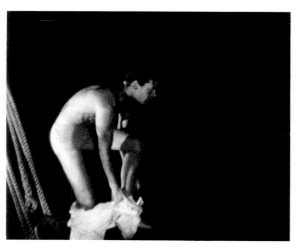  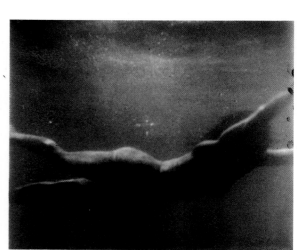

ALLURING
as a glimpse of Paradise.
There he found her
. . . bathed by the Golden
Fountain of the Sun . . . the wild girl, adored
by all the creatures of the forest. Radiant,
beautiful . . . nude as a nymph, her song
filled the woodland 'til man found the way!

DOLORES DEL RIO
JOEL McCREA
IN W. H. HUDSON'S STARTLING NOVEL
OF ROMANCE AND ADVENTURE . . .

"Green Mansions"

Bringing back the stars of "The BIRD
OF PARADISE" in another idyll of
mystic beauty . . . with nature in
majestic pageantry and love beyond the reach of sin.

SENSATIONALLY GLORIOUS

Green Mansions was planned as a follow-up to *Bird of Paradise,* re-teaming the two stars, but the failure of *Bird* to return a profit caused the project to be canceled.

animals, others of animated prehistoric monsters. Then I read the script, and I was all for throwing that in the ashcan, too; it wasn't worth a damn, dramatically or commercially." What was worth a damn, as far as Cooper was concerned, was Willis O'Brien. O'Brien was, in Cooper's words: "A true genius. The only way he could communicate an idea was by sketching it out. He could sketch animals, particularly prehistoric animals, better than any man who ever lived. He was certainly the most brilliant trick and special effects man that Hollywood had ever seen; not only that, he was as good an animation sculptor as Walt Disney was an animation cartoonist."

Cooper was not only impressed with O'Brien, but also with the small crew of artists, sculptors, and modelmakers who were working with O'Brien on *Creation.* After seeing the handiwork of his co-workers, especially of Marcel Delgado, a modelmaker, and three artists—Mario Larrinaga, Byron Crabbe, and Ernest Smythe—who were laying out the continuity of the story in a series of detailed drawings, Cooper realized that here, ready-made, was the perfect technical crew to enable him to make *Kong* exactly as he had envisioned it up to that time. In order to see how far the technical effects could be pushed, O'Brien designed and Cooper set up a short test combining an already filmed sequence of two animated beasts fighting, with a newly photographed sequence of two live action men watching and reacting to the battle. This was accomplished using the Dunning process—an ingenious photographic method that allowed the different pieces of film to be photographed and printed as one. Through a complex chemical bleaching and developing process (hence the term "process shot"), the two separate images were combined, with none of the photographic differences that were so irritating when using straight background projection. The results of this test convinced Cooper that by careful, painstaking exploitation of the various

technical and mechanical effects then in use in the industry, the production of *Kong* would be not only feasible but practical. In a memo to Selznick written on December 18, Cooper urged that the *Creation* project be scrapped, emphasizing that

the present story construction and the use of animals is entirely wrong. The whole secret of successful productions of this type is startling, unusual sensation, but that sensation must be new and have character. My idea is to not only use the prehistoric animals for their novelty value . . . but instead of having them just big beasts running around . . . make them into ferocious menaces. The most important thing, however, is that one animal should have a really big character part in the picture. I suggest a prehistoric Giant Gorilla, fifty times as strong as man—a creature of nightmare horror and drama.

Cooper then had O'Brien and his artists prepare a dozen large sketches to illustrate some of the more spectacular scenes of the story. The first sketch was the most important—it showed Kong on top of a skyscraper, being attacked by airplanes as he held a screaming woman in one hand. Cooper assured Selznick that

these scenes can be made just as drawn in the pictures . . . by using an animated figure against a projection background all played against a Dunning foreground with closeup work of full-sized head mask, hands and feet. So far as I know, this method has never been done on the screen and should prove sensational.

Knowing that Selznick would have a tough time convincing the RKO management to try anything so speculative, Cooper suggested that he be allowed to make a longer, ten-minute test, this time using the gorilla in one of the story sequences, to prove that it could be done. He estimated

AND
KING KONG
(THE EIGHTH WONDER OF THE WORLD)

The original sketch that Cooper had Willis O'Brien draw to convince Selznick and the executives of RKO of the potential of his *King Kong* idea. The gorilla was drawn by O'Brien, the skies by Mario Larrinaga, and the city by Byron Crabbe.

An engraving by Gustave Doré for John Milton's *Paradise Lost.*

that it would cost $10,000 to do this, and offered to put up half the cost himself, just to show his faith in the idea. While Selznick took the matter up with New York, Cooper had O'Brien begin work on a miniature gorilla, telling him that it "should be half-ape, half-human." O'Brien took him literally, and the resulting hybrid was described by Cooper as "the funniest thing I'd ever seen. It was a cross between a monkey and a man with long hair." Cooper then wired Harry Raven of the Museum of Natural History in New York for the skeletal dimensions of a large male gorilla. From this information, Cooper relates, "O'Brien built a miniature steel framework of a gorilla that had joints that could be locked into position so that you could get smooth movement when you animated." Over this framework Marcel Delgado fashioned rubber muscles that stretched and flexed realistically. The skeleton was then stuffed with cotton that was molded into the basic form of the animal, giving it shape and detail, and this was covered with pruned rabbit fur. Each finger had individually articulated joints, and the face had a movable mouth, lips, nose, eyes, and eyebrows. The completed model stood 18 inches high and weighed a little over 10 pounds.

While waiting for the approval to come through for the test reel, Cooper began work in earnest on fashioning a screenplay from his original treatment. Edgar Wallace, the noted English writer of plays and mystery stories, had been put under RKO contract by the previous administration, and Selznick was anxious to use him on something. He prevailed on Cooper to take Wallace as his collaborator, which Cooper did. But to Cooper's dismay he discovered that "Wallace didn't have the least conception of what I was doing. He read my treatments, at least my last treatment, then threw away all my ideas and did a horrible script of his own about some convicts escaping from Devil's Island, taking a nurse with them and finding Kong's island. He was the fastest writer in the

world, but he wrote for the ear, not for the eye, so his picture stuff never came off. He hadn't the slightest idea how to write for the screen. I recognized the publicity value of his name, especially in England, and I agreed with him over dinner one night that he could write the book version of *Kong* to be published under our joint names and that I would give him co-screen credit."

The draft of Wallace's screenplay in the RKO files, entitled *The Beast,* is not so bad as Cooper remembered, containing most of the spectacular scenes that had been in Cooper's original. Wallace, trying to use as much of Cooper's plot as possible and still salvage his own author's pride, kept cutting back and forth between his escaped convicts plot and the wild animal expedition of Cooper's treatment. His Kong has a gentler, more childlike feeling about him that completely loses the brute fierceness of Cooper's concept. There is none of the mystery, the larger-than-life quality of the character, and no sense at all of Kong being the "king of his world." Even Kong's final stand atop the tallest building in New York is given a ludicrous beginning by having him put the girl in his mouth as he climbs up to the top; and his death scene is robbed of its grandeur, being played with him lying down on the parapet of the building. According to Wallace's script, "We have a close shot of Kong with his head against the wall. He opens his eyes, picks the girl up, holds her to his breast like a doll, closes his eyes and drops his head."

Two weeks after finishing this first treatment, Edgar Wallace was dead, a victim of pneumonia; but Cooper felt bound to give Wallace co-author credit, stating, "My word was as good to a dead man as it was to a live one."

While Cooper struggled with getting a workable script, O'Brien and his crew were preparing the other miniature monsters to inhabit Kong's island. Four of these had originally been built for use in *Creation:* a flying reptile, an allosaurus, a stegosaurus, and a brontosaurus. Cooper wanted the jungle scenes on the island to have the sense of mystery and menace that was so characteristic of the jungles he and Schoedsack were familiar with. But, as with the character of Kong himself, Cooper wanted the jungle to be realistically unreal: it had to have a dawn-of-creation feeling, and for this he insisted that O'Brien and his men should copy Gustave Doré's steel engravings for Milton's *Paradise Lost.* Recalls Cooper:

> The lighting, the jungle, the foliage we stole direct from Doré. But we had great difficulty getting a sense of depth on the miniature jungle; it just didn't have the quality of receding mystery to it that jungles have, the semi-darkness, the shadows, and the sense of hidden dangers. Now I'm a genius at only one thing and that's selecting the right people. O'Brien was the kind of genius who would eventually come up with a solution for every technical dream of mine. Between the two of us we devised what we called "aerial perspective," whereby the jungle sets were built on three large tables. On those tables were a series of plate-glass panes on which Larrinaga and Crabbe painted sections of the jungle and skies, all copied directly from Doré.

Interspersed with these glass paintings were miniature trees constructed of clay, wood, and wire. The foliage for them was cut out of thin copper sheeting and mixed in with live shrubs and succulents. Properly lit, these tiny settings, when photographed, gave Cooper and O'Brien exactly what they were looking for, a lush yet chilling, ominous sense of the primeval jungle.

In mid-January 1932 the board of directors gave its approval for the filming of the test reel, and Cooper, working from his original outline, began shooting scenes on specially constructed jungle sets, carefully built to match exactly the table-top miniatures. To keep costs down, Cooper wanted to make sure that the footage from the test reel would be usable in the final film, so he decided to utilize an entire sequence from his latest treatment, opening in the jungle with the expedition in pursuit of Kong, who has captured the girl. This included their battle with a prehistoric stegosaurus; the crossing of a fog-shrouded lake on a raft where they are attacked by a dinosaur, and the ensuing chase and eating alive of some of the crew by the beast; a battle with Kong on a huge log across a deep ravine, in which most of the men are killed as Kong shakes them off the log; and the sequence ending with Kong's fighting and killing an allosaurus that has been menacing the girl. Staged in a forest

E. B. "Buzz" Gibson, a member of the technical staff, puts the finishing touches on one of the six miniature Kongs.

Two of the eighteen-inch models of Kong used in the film. Contrary to several erroneous published reports, every scene in *King Kong* was made using these models or the full-sized head, hand, or leg. At no time was a man in a gorilla suit ever used for the film—a point on which both Cooper and Schoedsack were adamant.

A drawing by O'Brien and Byron Crabbe for a sequence in *Kong,* showing their use of Doré's skies, lighting, and vegetation.

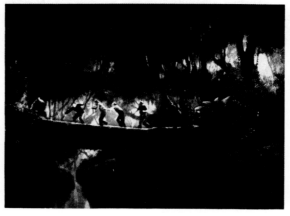

(Left) The controlling sketch by O'Brien and Crabbe used by the animators and the photographers in setting up the sequence where Kong rolls his pursuers off a log and into a terrifying chasm.

(Above) Marcel Delgado constructing the miniature log for this sequence.

(Top) The sequence as it appeared in the finished print. Left to right: The miniature Kong, holding a stand-in doll, crosses the miniature log. The background is a combination of painted glass and miniature foliage. Denham's men, pursued by a brontosaurus, run onto the log. The men and the log are full-sized. The jungle and the ravine are miniature sets, carefully matched and printed together. Kong shakes the men off the log: Kong is on a separate piece of film, the men and the log are being lifted and rolled by a chain-hoist device that matches Kong's previously filmed action, and the pieces are then put together in the optical printer.

glade, the fight is a *tour de force* of O'Brien's animating skills, as the two monsters thrust, punch, parry, gouge, and bite at each other, with Kong emerging triumphant after ripping apart the meat-eater's jaws. Cooper remembers:

> I directed the scene. O'Brien animated the gorilla and Buzz Gibson, whom he taught to animate, he did the allosaurus. It was a helluva thing to direct, harder to do than directing people, because you have to get the movements over to the animators. I'd been a pretty good wrestler in school, and a boxer, too, so I worked a lot of those feints and holds into the scene. The only way I could do it was to get up in front of the animators and act the whole thing out, first in regular speed, man-speed, then do it again in slow, slow motion for them while they were animating. Then I'd step aside until they'd done 10 feet or so, then I'd go on and do the rest. I played the gorilla, and I played the allosaurus, and I tried to give them both a certain human quality, which was hard; the ape wasn't too bad, I got that down pretty good, but I sure as hell don't look like a dinosaur.

While O'Brien continued working on the exacting and time-consuming animation for the test reel, Cooper was working with staff writer James Creelman, who began putting Cooper's ideas into an orderly story form. By late March he had completed a first draft script utilizing all of

Cooper's set pieces, including a controversial and tricky sequence where the ape peels off the heroine's clothes piece by piece, sniffing at the unusual female scent on his fingers, much as Cooper had observed the baboons in Africa doing with unfamiliar objects. Creelman's script had the slow, careful build-up that Cooper felt was so necessary to make the location of the island intriguing. Wallace's escaped convict plot was jettisoned, and the wild animal expedition became a motion picture company on the hunt for something "mysterious, all powerful, a beast God, something those little yellow mothers have been frightening their children with for generations; an animal that lives in the jungles of Skull Island."

This new script gave the giant ape his dramatic death scene exactly as Cooper had originally envisioned it, with one exception: as the skyscraper mania had altered the Manhattan skyline in the early thirties, Cooper had moved Kong's ultimate stand from atop the New York Life Building to the Chrysler Building, then finally put him on top of the tallest structure in the world, the new Empire State Building at 34th Street and Fifth Avenue.

Cooper now had a script that made dramatic sense, but he still wasn't happy with it. "It needed a fairy-tale quality in the dialogue that Creelman just couldn't seem to give it." More important, it lacked a punch to the introduction of Kong. Creelman's script still had him making his first appearance by just walking out of the jungle while one of the crew members is trying to attack the heroine, a device left over from Wallace's first draft. Creelman's description of the scene was a near carbon copy of the earlier version:

INTERIOR TENT—DAY

Ann is sleeping. Louis creeps in by her side. She wakes. He grabs her in his arms; half-demented he says: "There is death here, my little girl, but there is also love."

ANN   Let me go, you beast!

LOUIS   Tomorrow I may be dead—let me be a loving beast today!

The sound of Kong close by.

Ann and Louis in the tent struggling.

EXTERIOR CAMP—DAY

Noise of Kong. The screen of trees is drawn aside and Kong appears, stands for a second, then comes forward. He hears the noise of the struggle, goes over to the tent and picks it up.

CLOSE SHOT

Louis in the tent, looking up in terror as a big hand comes down and grabs him.

Both the situation and the dialogue of this scene displeased Cooper, who wanted, as he puts it, "a simple storybook style, especially in the character of the girl. She had to be innocent, and brave—I wanted her to be what I call 'a Woo,' a beautiful young girl who dresses in a very feminine way, puts bows in her hair and looks up at a man, accompanying everything he says with 'Woo, woo, woo.'" So *Kong* had to have one of Cooper's "Woo's" in it.

By now O'Brien had finished the test reel and it had been shipped off to New York for showing to the New York executives. Cooper was confident that when they saw the footage and looked at the sketches of the rest of the story, they would wholeheartedly approve the project. He began seriously to search for a girl to play his heroine at the same time

that he continued to work on the script and help Selznick and Berman keep RKO on an orderly release schedule.

The biggest problem confronting Selznick and Berman in meeting this orderly release schedule, apart from not having enough money, was, in Berman's words, "getting the writing done. RKO was never a rich company; we had to buy cheap stories and create originals. We couldn't compete with the Thalbergs and the Warners, who were buying great thick books and Broadway plays and making movies out of them. We were making ours out of spit and paper; that was the hardest part of making pictures, finding stories and people who could write." Hollywood by now was teeming with would-be writers; there were almost as many unemployed writers in the town as there were actors. The writers were largely unpretentious types, people who wrote for magazines and newspapers, and sometimes aspiring playwrights. There were few geniuses in the group. Some were what can be called hacks, but mostly they were competent craftsmen, people with a knack for telling interesting stories, some with an eye for revealing detail, others with an ear for dialogue that was believable and could be spoken easily. Talking pictures were only three years old, but the skills of writing and staging dialogue scenes had already advanced to a technique that was to dominate films for the rest of the decade. Borrowed almost completely from the stage, it was built on the effectiveness—visually, verbally, and dramatically—of the screenplay. The people who were writing these in Hollywood in the early thirties came primarily from New York and Chicago, the centers of the new journalism, the fast-paced, wise-cracking, melodramatic style of the tabloids, where what was said had to be concise, catchy, and easily understood.

Even so, good writers were still hard to find, and capable—even journeyman—directors were scarcer. In an effort to transfuse some new blood into the studio's rather anemic directing staff, Selznick borrowed William Wellman from Warner Bros. to direct Richard Dix and Ann Harding in *The Conquerors,* a turgid follow-up to *Cimarron.* Wellman was hamstrung by a pedestrian script by Howard Estabrook, about the winning of the West. It was the only film Wellman made with Selznick at RKO; it was an expensive failure and the two did not work together

Cooper's original idea of having Kong fight one of the giant dragon lizards, as it finally emerged on screen with Kong and a tyrannosaurus fighting it out in a jungle glade for Fay Wray, whom Kong has placed in a treetop for safekeeping. O'Brien and Cooper,

both expert wrestlers and boxers, worked for weeks on this sequence, and it is the highlight of the early part of the film as well as a classic piece of action staging; in fact, Disney copied it almost frame for frame seven years later in *Fantasia.*

again for nearly five years. Selznick had much better luck at RKO with George Cukor, obtaining him from Paramount where he had been unhappy because of a disagreement over credit on the Ernst Lubitsch film *One Hour with You,* which Cukor had directed for about two weeks. "I told Schulberg I was going to sue," says Cukor, "because they had taken my name off the picture. And I did. David had already gone over to RKO and I wanted to go with him, and Schulberg, out of sheer deviltry, wouldn't let me go. It was the only time I was aware of politicking, face to face. So I sued, and part of the settlement was that I be permitted to go to RKO. The unfortunate part of it was that RKO just took over my contract, so I didn't get a rise in salary. But the important thing was that I got to work with David on a project that was very dear to his heart, *What Price Hollywood?*"

An idea for a story about Hollywood had been growing in Selznick's mind since he had first proposed it at MGM in 1927. At Paramount, he had tried to interest Schulberg in doing a Hollywood story with Clara Bow, but Schulberg had become disenchanted with Bow and wasn't interested in it. Selznick, however, liked Bow, and early in March 1932 he tried to push through the idea of reviving her lagging career with a story called *The Truth About Hollywood,* by Adela Rogers St. John, a leading women's magazine writer and occasional screenwriter. The RKO sales department, which had considerable influence on what kind of pictures got the go-ahead from the New York office, was opposed to *The Truth About Hollywood* for two reasons: one, Clara Bow was considered to be through; and two, "Hollywood stories do unfavorable business," as the wire from the sales department put it.

Selznick reluctantly accepted the first reason, but considered the second to be no argument against the making of the film, because, as he said, "All the pictures that had been made about Hollywood burlesqued it; made everybody into fools or clowns and were not grounded in any kind of realism." Selznick wanted to show the ambience of Hollywood as a place to work; the excitement and glamour of attractive men and women living lives of pressure and responsibility. His love for the movies, the way they were made, the place where they were made; the developing mythology of Hollywood, with its ruined careers due to

Constance Bennett and David Selznick during the making of *What Price Hollywood?*

The iconography of Hollywood begins in this stylized rendering of the city at night by the Radio art department for the opening sequences of *What Price Hollywood?*

(Above) The opening frames from *What Price Hollywood?* showing the pervasive fan magazine influence of the time, and its effect on the heroine, a waitress at the Brown Derby restaurant on Wilshire Boulevard. (Left) Walter Plunkett's costume sketches for Constance Bennett were used as publicity in the style sections of many newspapers.

scandal, drunkenness, or irresponsibility; the tremendous impact of success and creative demands; and the triumphs and tragedies that these stories embodied—these were the elements Selznick wanted to put into a film about Hollywood, and it was these inarticulated feelings of his own that made him confident that a picture treating Hollywood in this way would be successful. Adela Rogers St. John's original had traces of this in its story of a waitress in the Wilshire Boulevard Brown Derby who is befriended by a successful director after she saves him from being fired by his producer for drunkenness. He promises to make her a star and keeps his promise. But thereafter the story had very little to do with Hollywood, concerning itself with the love affairs of the heroine and her snubbing at the hands of Hollywood's élite due to a blackmail scandal.

It was this later, more melodramatic and unreal part of the story that Selznick didn't like. He handed the project to Berman, giving him Cukor to direct it, Constance Bennett to star in it, and suggestions on how the second half of the story could be improved. As Berman recalls:

Constance Bennett was a fairly good star, as those things went in those days. She and Ann Harding and Helen Twelvetrees were the three stars at the old Pathé studio when RKO merged with it, and we inherited those three girls along with Bill Boyd. Those, of course, were the days of stars; Bebe Daniels, Richard Dix, we had these people under contract or on salary so we had to get properties and put them to work. That's why all those damned originals were being written, get something to put our stars in. I worked with Connie on a couple of pictures. She was okay, a woman with opinions of her own; she was terribly aggressive in her money dealings. She was the first woman to make some terrific deal with Warner Bros. [Myron Selznick was her agent] and got what was then an unheard-of salary, I don't remember exactly, maybe $30,000 for six weeks, it was sort of a breathtaking thing in the industry that she managed to get so much money.

Bennett's success was due largely to the glamorous fashion in which she managed her career and her private life. She was, to audiences of that time, one of the women who epitomized what a movie star should be:

Four sequences from *What Price Hollywood?*:

A story conference around the star's pool, actively attended by her producer, Gregory Ratoff (standing), her director, Lowell Sherman (lying), and her bored husband, Neil Hamilton (sitting, on sofa).

The star's wedding (filmed at the First Methodist Church at Franklin and Highland), which turns into a rout because of the enthusiasm of her fans.

At the Chinese Theatre, the waitress, not yet a star, assumes an English air for the microphone.

The waitress, now a star, bails her benefactor out of the drunk tank.

sophisticated, sleek, with expensive tastes in clothes and men. She had followed more or less in Gloria Swanson's footsteps in her pursuit of a career, even marrying Swanson's ex-husband, the Marquis de la Falaise de Coudray, getting a title as well as whatever else the marquis had to offer. In addition to her not inconsiderable good looks, she was a passable actress with a flair for light romantic comedy. With Bennett as the star, the sales department had no objection to the story, reminding Selznick only that the next Bennett film had to be ready for a mid-July release. It was already late in March, which meant that the picture would have to be put into production almost immediately, so Berman began a marathon round of script revisions to incorporate the elements that he, Selznick, and Cukor had agreed upon. Recalls Berman:

> We decided to make it a picture about a guy like Marshall (Mickey) Neilan, who's a big-shot director and an alcoholic, and a little girl he picks up who's a waitress and as he makes her a star, he becomes a has-been. That was our concept, so, based on this idea and Adela's original, Jane Murfin came on and wrote a screenplay which was professional but pedestrian, not funny enough or sharp enough, as her usual stuff was. So then we put Ben Markson on it with her; they finished their revisions on April 6. But David, George, and I felt it still wasn't right, so we scrapped everything except the basic outline and I got two crazy men, Gene Fowler and Rowland Brown, to come in on it. We were already in production, so we were forced to rewrite the day before to shoot the next day ... the sets were already built so we had a certain pattern we had to follow. ... Brown was a gag man and Fowler was a dialogue writer, and they contributed an awful lot of good comedy touches, some of which were based on actual incidents.

Even though Bennett's part was the lead, the character of the director, Max Carey, was the real star of the story and another rendering of Selznick's favorite type, the fatally flawed, gifted individual who, whether through irresponsibility, lack of discipline, or just hubris, manages to bring about his own destruction. His father's massive humiliation was part of this, so were all the heroes he had read about during his childhood. The death in 1920 of Olive Thomas, one of his father's early stars and a particular favorite of David's, followed by the Wallace Reid dope scandal and Valentino's death and funeral, all affected him personally. The mythology of Hollywood, with its stories of directors whose flights of fancy and creativity expensively disrupted the economics of the film business, resulting in their own downfall and the institution of the producer system, also shaped Selznick's attitude about Hollywood and its traditions. According to George Cukor:

> David didn't like cheap jibes about Hollywood or its people, he had a romantic idea that the whole world loved Hollywood ... and he didn't want to make anything bitchy or sour. So he wouldn't let *What Price Hollywood?* become cynical. It was exuberant and a little larger than life; it was a romantic story of a decent girl, and of a fellow who did her a good deed, they weren't in love with each other, they were friends, and she was grateful and in spite of her success she was always mindful of him and had compassion for him. She never lost respect for him, they had a wonderful relationship; he was, in a sense, a father figure. It was a very difficult story to write—it was a balancing act, awkward, funny, touching, and a very human story, different and very interesting. I think that's why it's been remade so many times.

(Opposite) Lowell Sherman directs Constance Bennett in a fictitious film, while a dress extra looks on.

(Opposite) Slavko Vorkapich's montage sequence showing, left to right, the suicide of Max Carey, the director, in the home of star Mary Evans, after his release from jail into her custody. Done with quick flash cuts, distorted angles, deliberate printing distortion, building up to a slow-motion, full-length fall, the sequence is accompanied on the sound track by a whirring noise that grows in intensity as the character's mental torment finds release in death.

One of the newspaper ads designed in the slick modern style by the Radio advertising department.

St. John's original story, she has stated, was based on the actual case of Colleen Moore, a youngster who was discovered by producer John McCormick. They married, she became a star, his alcoholism ended his career, and they divorced. It was the hints of tragedy about this character that intrigued Selznick, and decided him to change the direction of the story, expanding and refining the part of Carey to the point where his eventual suicide serves as the dramatic climax of the film. The part required charm, delicacy, and a particularly light touch. For this pivotal role, Berman and Cukor cast Lowell Sherman, a director himself and a sometime actor. His career dated back to 1920, when he had worked with Griffith in *Way Down East,* playing Lillian Gish's seducer. Berman remembers that "he was married to Helene Costello, John Barrymore's sister-in-law, and I think he modeled a great deal of the character of the director in *What Price Hollywood?* on John's behavior."

Gene Fowler, reworking the screenplay, was also a close friend of Barrymore's, and lines such as: "What this country needs is light wines and beer," or his riposte: "Two things that will never last—my liver and a Hollywood marriage," were echoes of Barrymore's pronouncements, delivered by Sherman in a rasping, biting voice with overtones of the Barrymore flourish.

One of the more prominent characters in the film was the producer, who in St. Johns's original was named Sam Wynne, described as "at heart, a gentle idealistic childish person, with real feelings for art and a strong belief in motion pictures." The parallel with Sam Goldwyn was considered too obvious, so the character's name was changed to Julius Saxe, and he was redesigned by Brown and Fowler to be played largely for laughs. This tendency became even more pronounced when Gregory Ratoff was cast in the role. He was an actor with a broad comedic range, and his manglings of the English language in the film were a result of his own accent and his observations of Sam Goldwyn; almost every utterance was capped by an exuberant "Eet's tereefeec!" In a sequence involving plans for a Hollywood wedding, the Saxe/Ratoff character expounds: "Gentlemen, go into an immediate conference and develop me some ideas for an outstanding wedding, something tereefic, and if we don't gross a million on her next picture, I'll buy every one of you ... well, never mind. I'll forget it by that time anyway."

Selznick, while acknowledging the need for comedy in the film, was once again opposed to presenting Jewish stereotypes and in a memo to Berman on April 13 cautioned him that "we should be careful concerning the characterization of Saxe. ... I have no objections to drawing him with humor, provided it is kept within reasonable limits. ... I'm sure you will hold this down, for the sake of the prestige of our own position as producers, if for nothing else." He also cautioned Berman not to show the director drinking at the studio, fearful that this would confirm the

distorted image many people had of Hollywood as a haven for tipplers and alcoholics.

Given the problems of the script, filming proceeded swiftly, and the picture was virtually completed by May 10. The one sequence left to be done was the crucial suicide of Max Carey. The scene had to rapidly build up to and make convincing Carey's decision to kill himself, as well as presenting the actual deed acceptably and dramatically. To achieve this, Selznick assigned Slavko Vorkapich to work with Cukor in developing an imaginatively stylistic approach to the scene. Vorkapich, a Yugoslavian emigrant, was dedicated to the idea that film was an art. He was the first person working in the American commercial film industry who had a completely intellectual concept about what film could and should do. This grasp of the two basic elements of film—rhythm and motion—led to his becoming the resident town genius at montages, those quick transitory images that illustrated story points, time spans, and other abstractions that needed visual stylization. Selznick made a concerted effort to use Vorkapich whenever and wherever possible to give the RKO films visual literacy and punch. The suicide in *What Price Hollywood?* was staged and photographed by Vorkapich and Cukor in a series of quick, gradually distorted flashbacks showing Carey's past life and his present degradation, leading up to a slow-motion re-creation of the suicide. Cukor states: "We needed the sound of turmoil, the feeling that this man's brain was bursting, and someone in the sound department devised a kind of whirring noise, that became louder and louder until it just overwhelmed him and he gave in to this destructive urge." The man in charge of achieving this was Murray Spivack, head of the sound department, who recalls:

"I knew that they needed some sort of sound effect to carry this and I thought, 'I've gotta get something unusual, that isn't familiar,' something that sounded like a brainstorm to me—it had to whir, a kind of crazy thing, and it had to increase in speed, so I got a cigar box, tore off the lid, put some rubber bands around it, tied it to a string, and swung it around in a circle faster and faster, and when it was recorded, it sounded just fine."

The final cost of *What Price Hollywood?* was $435,662. It opened at the Mayfair Theatre in New York on July 13, 1932. Critically and financially, the film was successful, making a substantial profit and getting George Cukor his first serious recognition as a director of consequence. Both Selznick and Berman were happy with the results, although Selznick had some misgivings about the overall concept, feeling that the story contrivances diminished its potential as an accurate representation of the Hollywood he wanted to show the world.

George Cukor, Billie Burke, and John Barrymore on the set of *A Bill of Divorcement* (1932). Cameraman Sid Hickox is sitting in the canvas chair. The set is by Carroll Clark.

At RKO, as at every other major studio at the time, the release schedule was built around star vehicles. But, unlike the other studios, RKO had few major stars; its biggest box-office draw was Richard Dix, a carryover from the silent days, potent in action dramas, but beginning to slide. Amos 'n' Andy, played in blackface by their creators Freeman Gosden and Charles Correll, had been novelty sensations in the 1930–31 season, but they declined to make another film; instead, a series of cartoons using their voices was made by the Van Beuran Corporation, released through RKO. Selznick, in an effort to bolster the studio star list, was, according to an interview he gave to columnist Eileen Creelman, "hoping to build into real box-office bets such newcomers as Joel McCrea, Arline Judge of *Are These Our Children?,* and Laurence Olivier."

Selznick continued to be on the lookout for new talent, especially from the New York stage. He authorized screen tests for two stage performers, dancer Fred Astaire and twenty-one-year-old Katharine Hepburn, who had made something of a name for herself as an Amazon in the Broadway play *The Warrior's Husband*. One of the projects Merian Cooper had in the works was a story called *Three Came Unarmed,* about a girl who just came out of the jungle with her brother and a monkey. As Cooper put it,

These three come unarmed to civilization; it's a wonderful story, but it needed a wild type for the girl. I was sent a picture of Hepburn in

FORM E-3 40M 2-32 O.P.

R K O STUDIOS, Inc.
LOS ANGELES
INTER-DEPARTMENT CORRESPONDENCE

Mr. Richards: Date **July 6** 193 **2**
          assign
Please ~~engage~~   Katherine Hepburn

For the role of _____ Sydney

In the picture to be known as BILL OF DIVORCEMENT

Term to commence on ~~EXPIRING~~ July 7 1932 Salary $1250.00 Per.Wk.

Number of weeks guaranteed ____ 3 week Guarantee

                                        previous picture work
Budget $1250.00 ___ Per Wk.-Last Salary $ No ___ Per Wk. Studio ____

Screen Credit Have not been advised as to the billing clause

     in Miss Hepburn's contract.

Approved: _____   Signed: _____
          Exec. Vice President   Associate Producer.

The interstudio memo assigning the new player Katharine Hepburn to her first motion picture role.

Merian Cooper had become a convert to the new three-color Technicolor process, and early in 1934 he planned to star Hepburn in a color version of the life of Joan of Arc. RKO, fearing the expense and trouble of color, scuttled the idea, and this test close-up of Hepburn is all that is left of the project.

the *Herald,* so I sent a memo to David, please have Hepburn tested; so he did, but I wasn't ready with *Three Came Unarmed.* I knew they were going to make *A Bill of Divorcement,* so I finally got George Cukor to look at the test, then David, and after they saw it, they signed Katie. I kept trying with *Three Came Unarmed,* though. After she came out here, I had Katie walking around the studio with a little gibbon on her shoulder, but that picture was my hoodoo picture and everybody else's too; a lot of other people tried to get it off the ground, but none of us could lick it. Anyway, that's how Hepburn came to Hollywood.

The play *A Bill of Divorcement* had made a star out of Katharine Cornell when she had done it on the stage in the mid-twenties. It had been considered shocking at the time of its initial presentation because of its treatment of the taboo subject of insanity, around which the plot revolved. Several adaptations of the play by various screenwriters had failed to solve the problem of making this theme palatable to local censorship boards, but finally Howard Estabrook managed to sidestep all the touchy issues with enough dexterity to satisfy everyone's reservations and still maintain the play's dramatic content.

The day Hepburn arrived at the studio, she had come straight from the train, and her eye was terribly inflamed from a cinder that had lodged in it. Her initial meeting with Cukor did not go well; she began by criticizing the costume sketches for the film that he showed her, and was generally condescending. Cukor gave her back some of her own, telling her, "It's not your place to criticize; what makes you think you know anything about clothes? You look perfectly ghastly." As production started and her talent emerged, she and Cukor began to form a friendship that would last for decades. She quickly picked up the technique of acting for the camera, Cukor teaching her that the smallest gesture was all that was necessary for the screen, that acting for it was

done, as he put it, "with the eyes." For all her rough edges, she was a pro from the outset. She wasn't even intimidated by acting opposite the legendary John Barrymore, who was playing her deranged father.

After a three-week shooting schedule, the film was finished and ready for its first preview. Selznick was nervous, as he later recounted:

I had taken a tremendous chance in casting Hepburn and in sticking to her despite the insistence of just about everybody in the studio except Cukor that she was impossible and would be laughed off the screen.... The world knows that startling Hepburn face now, but when she first appeared on the screen in the rushes, there was consternation.... "Ye gods, that horse face" ... was the prevalent remark. Not until the preview was the staff convinced we had a great screen personality. During the first few minutes you could sense the audience's bewilderment at this completely new type ... but very early there was a scene in which Hepburn just walked across the room, stretched her arms, and then lay out on the floor in front of the fireplace. It sounds very simple, but you could almost feel, and you could definitely hear, the excitement in the audience. In those few simple feet of film, a new star was born. It was one of the greatest experiences I've ever had.

Hepburn's initial surge of popularity was climaxed by her winning the Academy Award for *Morning Glory* (1933). Almost immediately, Selznick began plans for her to star in a version of *Little Women* to be directed by George Cukor. Selznick didn't stay to see the project through, but Merian Cooper did, and the result was one of RKO's and the industry's biggest successes, returning a profit of close to a million dollars on a cost of only $400,000 and thereby paving the way for the cycle of classic adaptations that was a Hollywood staple for the rest of the decade.

STREET & SMITH'S
PICTURE PLAY

MAY

10 CENTS

1/- IN ENGLAND

KATHARINE
HEPBURN
BY
DAN OSHER

THE RADIO
Flash
Page Four
January 7, 1933
January 7, 1933
THE RADIO
Flash
Page Five

THE ROXY OPENS MID A NATION'S PLAUDITS

FOR the second time in a single week, the social registrites, industrial leaders, city administrative officers and company officials, gathered to gaze at another of the wonders of RKO's Radio City . . . the Roxy theatre.

And through their amazement came expressions of grand tribute to this newest and most modern of the world's palaces of the cinema. The following day, newspapers throughout the nation, in syndicated articles, extended their plaudits to this great accomplishment.

Reproduced on this page are photographs of some of the important personages who were present at the auspicious opening.

(1) Vice-President Ned E. Depinet and Mrs. Depinet . . . (2) General Sales Manager Jules Levy and Mrs. Levy . . . (3) Amedee J. Van Beuren, President of the Van Beuren Corporation, whose specially produced Aesop's Fable, "Opening Night," was selected for the opening program with "Animal Kingdom" . . . (4) Hon. John P. O'Brien, Mayor of New York City, surrendering to an autograph seeker . . . (5) E. H. Griffith who directed "Animal Kingdom," and Mrs. Griffith.

(6) Courtland Smith, President of Pathe News, and Mrs. Smith . . . (7) President Nicholas Murray Butler of Columbia University, one of the leading minds of the world, also poses for the camera.

(8) David Sarnoff, Chairman of the Board of Directors, Radio-Keith-Orpheum Corporation and President of the Radio Corporation of America, and Mrs. Sarnoff . . . (9) Will Hays, President of the Motion Picture Producers and Distributors of America; Mrs. Hays; Mrs. Merlin H. Aylesworth; Mrs. S. L. "Roxy" Rothafel; and President Merlin H. Aylesworth . . . (10) Eleven o'clock in the morning after the opening of the Roxy, a line approximately two hundred feet long with cash customers standing four abreast, extended on the Forty-ninth street side of the theatre to the box-office as this photograph shows. The scene has been repeated every morning and evening since the opening. This phenomenal business is attributed in a great measure to "Animal Kingdom," the theatre's screen attraction.

(11) A striking night shot of the Sixth Avenue front of the Roxy. Giant searchlights illuminate the Indiana limestone front of the theatre. A 'class' yet flash display results.

(12) S. L. Rothafel, "Roxy," himself, the Master of all showmen, whose genius and vision encouraged the executives of Radio-Keith-Orpheum and the Rockefellers to enter upon this, the most gigantic undertaking in the history of all show business.

(Above and opposite, above) David Sarnoff, as head of RCA, dragged RKO into John D. Rockefeller's Manhattan renewal project, dubbed "Radio City" because of RCA's heavy involvement. RKO was responsible (through RCA) for the financing and construction of the lone movie theater, the RKO Roxy, for which it wooed the legendary Samuel "Roxy" Rothafel away from the original theatre of that name at Seventh Avenue and 50th Street. Rothafel would also be responsible for the operation of the titanic new Radio City Music Hall, a 6,000-seat theatre designed to showcase vaudeville and other high-class live acts. Titanic it was, for on its opening night, the show sank under the weight of the nearly six-hour performance. Two weeks later, Roxy suffered a heart attack, the Music Hall became a movie theatre, and the RKO Roxy was legally forced to drop the name Roxy, becoming the Center Theatre, alternately showing stage productions, movies, ice shows, and pioneer television programs.

The Animal Kingdom, Selznick's production of Philip Barry's sophisticated play, was the first picture at the new RKO Roxy. It starred Ann Harding and Leslie Howard (below, right) and featured a young Myrna Loy (below, left), who up to that point in her career had largely played exotics and evil temptresses. She was, according to Selznick, "a beautiful girl, who was no more a siren than I am . . . her roles had always been a joke to those who knew her [because] her natural field was comedy . . . When director Edward Griffith suggested her for *The Animal Kingdom,* I leapt at the idea . . . she was so good that we immediately cast her in a straight comedy role in *Topaze.*"

THE WORLD'S GREATEST CENTER OF AMUSEMENT!

CHRISTMAS in the 1932 year will go down in history of the RKO organization and of the entire amusement world. With the opening of the RKO theatres in Radio City, there will occur a great historical dual event. It marks at once the biggest forward step in the progress of RKO since its inception, and the inauguration of the greatest entertainment center in the world.

RADIO City Music Hall and the RKO Roxy will undoubtedly stand for many years as models and marks to shoot at, for enterprising leaders of amusement throughout the world. Their design and every phase of their equipment are so far ahead of the times, that they both tower miles above anything of a similar nature that has ever been done before.

ONLY the great vision of the master minds leading and guiding the RKO organization, made this epic achievement possible. We of the Radio Pictures family may indeed take great pride in being part of so progressive an organization.

REPRODUCED on these pages are a few views of both theatres, which will give you but a very faint idea of the splendor of these truly palaces of entertainment.

THE RKO ROXY THEATRE

(5) The Grand Lounge in the basement ... (6) Showing the stage and lighting system from the main chandelier ... (7) Main Chandelier, the largest lighting fixture of its kind ever built, weighs six and a half tons and is 30 feet in diameter ... (8) A view of Auditorium showing part of its 3,700 seats ... (9) A striking view of one of the tasteful Mezzanine Promenades.

RADIO CITY MUSIC HALL

(1) A view of the auditorium. Note the use of indirect lighting throughout ... (2) The Grand Promenade. The heroic mural on the wall of the staircase is over 200 feet in height. It was executed by Ezra Winter ... (3) The Proscenium Arch, opening to a gigantic stage 144 feet wide by 80 feet deep ... (4) A view of the Mezzanines from the orchestra floor.

Topaze, originally a French play by Marcel Pagnol, was produced on Broadway in an English adaptation by Benn Levy. Purchased by Radio, it was turned into a critical success by Selznick, screenwriter Ben Hecht, and director Harry d'Abbadie d'Arrast. (Below, left) An overhead view of a scene being photographed, and (below, right) how it looked to the camera.

(Left) Fay Wray listens as Merian Cooper explains to her that she will have "the tallest, darkest leading man in Hollywood," and relates to her the plot of *King Kong*. (Below) The three credited writers of *King Kong*.

JAMES
CREELMAN

RUTH
ROSE

EDGAR
WALLACE

While *What Price Hollywood?* was being filmed, the test reel on *Kong* had been shown to the New York executives and at the RKO sales convention. The word finally came back to Selznick and Cooper to go ahead with the project; a budget of $500,000 was authorized, and work began in earnest. By late March, Cooper's gorilla picture had become the subject of much conjecture. Word had gotten around that he was doing something about an outsize ape in love with a girl. The sets on which all this was happening were closed, and there was not much activity around them to indicate that anything at all was going on inside. The footage coming out of these stages was being looked at in the daily rushes, and according to Cooper: "To people who didn't have any imagination, *Kong* was a bunch of crap, you know, and everybody thought this was going to be the worst folly in the history of the picture business." George Cukor recalls, "I knew they were making something, I would see them making it for what seemed years and years, and we thought, dear old Coop, he's making this preposterous picture. David thought it was a camp too. He knew vaguely what it was all about, but I don't think it fascinated him at all." Selznick's lack of fascination with the project didn't keep him from believing in it, and as Cooper says: "He didn't have the slightest idea what I was doing, but he said that Schoedsack and I had only made three films and they had all been smashes, so he'd back me all the way. And he did too. He never interfered, never tried to tell me what to do."

Everybody knew that Cooper was still having trouble finding an actress to play his "Woo," the girl with whom the gorilla falls in love. Fay Wray, who had just returned from New York where she had starred in a play written by her husband, John Monk Saunders, remembers,

Cooper wanted to see me, so I went out to RKO. He was a practical joker kind of person; he told me I was going to have the tallest darkest leading man in Hollywood, and then he told me this rather fantastic idea about King Kong and it was not too appealing to me to work with this big gorilla, even though it was to be unreal, a manufactured one. I almost backed away from it, but he had the drawings and the concept in such a way and his boyish enthusiasm was so infectious, he was such a giving person that I just decided to go ahead. Also, you must remember, this was the depression, so that for an actress, just working was an essential thing.

Cooper remarked, "I was trying to find a blond Fay Wray and there wasn't one." But he picked the rest of his cast relatively simply: "We never tested anybody. Most of the time you'd see people in something, and you'd get a pretty good idea of what they could do. . . . I saw Robert Armstrong in a picture called *Is Zat So?* with Jimmy Gleason, and I thought he was pretty good, so I cast him as the leader of the expedition." The part of the young first mate in the script, Driscoll, who falls in love with and saves the girl from the beast, was given to a husky young French Canadian named Etienne Pelissier de Bujac, whom Selznick had seen working as a doorman in one of the restaurants on the Sunset Strip. Cooper liked his looks, but Selznick wanted to test him. The test was satisfactory, and he was given a contract and a new name—Bruce Cabot.

With these additions and a blond wig on Fay Wray, Cooper began filming story action for what was now called *The Eighth Wonder.* A news item in the studio bulletin stated: "Because of the highly secret methods of filming used, the picture is being made on a closed stage and admittance is strictly forbidden." Over a two-month period, Cooper used these actors on and off plus some extras, as he and O'Brien labored over the jungle scenes and the crew's pursuit of Kong. "Hollywood was wonderful then," said Cooper. "I collected my cast, and there was no Screen Actors Guild at that time; I could use them for a week or two, then let them go for four or five weeks, then recall them for a week or two . . . and I didn't have to pay them overtime. No one thought it unusual, no one expected any extra pay. Overtime, golden time . . . whoever heard of such nonsense? This was the bottom of the depression and everyone was glad to be working and eating."

What with his duties with Selznick, and directing the beginnings of the story, Cooper still was concerned about his script. One story point was having trouble with the RKO hierarchy: When Kong is brought to New York, Cooper had him exhibited in the new Radio City Music Hall, then being built, and it was that area that suffered most of his rampage. But Selznick, in explaining the need for a change to Cooper, pointed out, "We're going to get in a jam with Mr. Aylesworth and the other Radio City executives by the circus nature of the stunt we place there, by contrast with the dignified efforts they are making." Cooper reluctantly changed Kong's New York debut to the Polo Grounds, and then turned his attention to Kong's other entrance, the more undramatic one on Skull Island. Kong needed a build-up, he couldn't just walk on without some kind of introduction; there needed to be some forceful example of Kong's imaginative power, a dramatic visual demonstration of his hold over his world. While mulling this over, Cooper had been out at the Pathé lot in Culver City where Busby Berkeley was staging the dances for *Bird of Paradise.* On his way through the 40-acre back lot, Cooper had been struck by the remnants of the enormous sets from DeMille's *King of Kings.* The Temple of Jerusalem, with its crumbling columns and massive entrance, had especially stuck in his mind. The *Bird of Paradise* troupe was working on an exterior set of native huts, and the nighttime dances that Berkeley was filming, plus Max Steiner's rhythmic native music, gave Cooper the clue for a newer, bigger, more spectacular introduction for Kong. He would be the center of an entire religion, with ceremonial sacrifices and mysterious rituals, a source of wonder and terror to the natives who lived dangerously on his island.

(Above) Double jeopardy for Fay Wray, here being protected by Joel McCrea in a scene from *The Most Dangerous Game.* The swamp setting is by Carroll Clark and was used extensively in *King Kong,* in production at the same time. (Below) Marcel Delgado and his brother Victor constructing the framework for the full-sized hand of Kong. (Bottom) The unfinished hand of Kong being tested on Cooper's secretary, Zoe Porter.

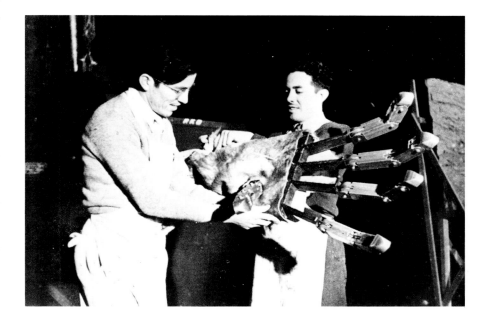

Merian C. Cooper, Fay Wray, Ernest Schoedsack, and Willis O'Brien (foreground) with extras on the native village set on the back lot of RKO-Pathé.

Kong now had a tangible legend as being "something monstrous, all powerful, still alive, still holding that island in a grip of deadly fear." The girl could be kidnapped by the natives and offered as a sacrifice to Kong. This would give Cooper the chance to add some spectacular suspense to the sacrifice, as the natives performed their frenzied rites in front of a massive wall and bolted gate "built thousands of years ago . . . but kept in repair . . . those natives need that wall . . . there's something on the other side . . . something they fear." The native village also had the advantage of lending itself to total destruction in Kong's furious attempts to recapture the girl. The new sequence would cost the studio about $15,000 more. Selznick said later that "the greatest gamble I ever took at RKO was squeezing money out of other budgets so Cooper could finish *Kong*." Screenwriter James Creelman, however, balked at the sudden introduction of what he called "the intrusion of the native village, human sacrifice angle. . . . I can't seem to build to this and the prehistoric monsters at the same time. There is certainly such a thing as reaching the limit to the number of elements a story can contain and make sense. I well understand why you want the native village and agree it would be great if there were a way to introduce it. Unfortunately, by the time my sluggish imagination manages to effect a solution . . . we may be in a jam on time."

Faced with finding a writer who could finish up the story the way he wanted, Cooper found his problem inadvertently solved by the return to Hollywood of his partner Ernest Schoedsack with his wife, Ruth Rose. They had been in India working on Paramount's aborted version of *The Lives of a Bengal Lancer,* and their return delighted Cooper, who said, "I couldn't dream of making *Kong* without Schoedsack. He wasn't working so the first thing I did was to get him to come to work at RKO." He gleefully filled the Schoedsacks in on the status of *Kong,* going on about his script problems. Schoedsack's wife was a writer. Cooper says:

I had read the stuff she wrote when she was on expedition to South America; she wrote simply and descriptively and I liked it. I had no way of telling whether she could write a script or not, but I gave her all the outlines and drafts and asked her if she could combine all the things I liked from each one. Well, she quickly showed she could write scripts like nobody's business. She changed the characters; she made Denham and Driscoll very much like Schoedsack and myself, and most importantly, she rewrote all the dialogue. I asked her to keep hitting the Beauty and Beast theme again and again, before we saw Kong, which she did brilliantly and nonchalantly. I don't think another human being in the world could have given me the simple, direct, fairy-tale dialogue that she did. It was just what I wanted.

While Mrs. Schoedsack spent three weeks revising the script, Cooper and Schoedsack began work on what would be their fourth film together, an adaptation of Richard Connell's classic short story, "The Most Dangerous Game." "We needed a project while the script was rewritten and while the animation for Kong was being done," recalls Cooper,

so I picked up this short story and got Jimmy Creelman to write the script. The title means when man hunts man, instead of animals, and I thought Monty [Schoedsack] and I could introduce all those things that we used in *Chang*—the traps and the dead falls, and all those things. None of them are in the original story, neither was the love story. . . . *The Most Dangerous Game* was a cheap picture to make—it only cost about $150,000. We saved money by using Fay Wray and Robert Armstrong in between sessions on *Kong*. Since both films were laid in the jungle, we were able to use the same sets for both, switching back and forth; I'd be shooting *Kong,* then Monty would move in and do *The Most Dangerous Game*. There's a shot in *The Most Dangerous Game* where you see Leslie Banks, the villain, running through the fog; as soon as Schoedsack did that shot, I moved in and took the same set and did the shot in *Kong* where the sailor is being chased by the dinosaur. The same thing where *Kong* shakes the men off the log; when I was through doing the live action, Monty came in and shot a scene for *Dangerous Game* showing Fay and Joel McCrea, playing the hero, crossing the log trying to escape from the madman. We had a lot of fun, and the picture was a hit, and it's been remade several times, but each time the people who did it used our concept, the traps and the love story and all.

(Right) Carl Denham and crew tempt fate by trying to photograph a native religious ceremonial taking place in front of the huge wall and bolted gate that had been "built by a higher civilization . . . to keep out something on the other side . . . something they fear. . . ." If so, then one wonders why they built a gate at all. However, the illogic of the movies being what it is, the wall and the gate were built, and on the remnants of another religious edifice (below, left), the Temple of Jerusalem from De-Mille's *King of Kings*. The native huts were left over from *Bird of Paradise*. (Below, right) The native chieftain, played by Noble Johnson, and the intended bride of Kong, played by Frances Curry. After seeing Fay Wray, however, the chief changed his mind, exclaiming, "Malem ma pakeno," which translates to "Look at the golden woman," giving rise to Denham's retort, "Yeah, blondes *are* scarce around here."

With all this leapfrogging and economical use of sets, Cooper was still being deviled by the production office to come up with a budget breakdown on *Kong* so that the various departments could plan their work and cost schedules. In a long memo to B. B. Kahane, the financial watchdog at the studio, Cooper explained:

Because of the enormous technical difficulties of this picture ... and because it is so different from any other picture ever made ... it has been impossible to make an accurate budget until the following things could be established:

1. Time of animation ... which could only be done experimentally, as it was an unknown quantity.

2. Time necessary to combine Williams, Dunning and Projection processes, as these combinations had never been used before; as you know it is only because *Kong* has these unusual and entirely new series of trick processes that it is possible to make such an unusual picture.

3. Definite working out of a script, each item of which would be practical for this unusual combination of trick shots. Schoedsack and myself and the production departments have spent the last several weeks going over each item of the script and every trick shot in detail and have eliminated everything except what was absolutely necessary, and as far as our combined opinion is concerned have brought the picture costs down to bedrock for this script. As you know, I have been fighting costs on this picture more than any other in the studio, and will continue to do so.

In order to achieve a realistic blending of the various effects used, Cooper and O'Brien devised what Cooper called "miniature projection." He explained it:

I would shoot my live actors going through the motions of reacting to the beasts or Kong, or whatever, then these scenes would be projected on small-scaled screens that Obie [O'Brien] had in his miniature sets. We would project a frame at a time, and Obie would animate the miniature action to match the live action. Nobody had ever tried anything like this before; Obie had never thought of it. If you look at *The Lost World* [1925], you see there's a matte line, with the animals above the line and the people below it. Well, I wanted the people and the animals to interreact in the same shot and in the same sets, so we got a fellow named Harry Cunningham to build three miniature projection machines so that we could use three different areas of live

action in the animated scenes. I would get these ideas of something that had never been done before, not because I wanted to do a new thing, but because I wanted to do something dramatic, and the only way I could see to do it dramatically was to come up with a new combination of processes. O'Brien was a genius.... *Kong* is as much his picture as it is mine. There was never anybody in his class as far as special effects went, there never was and there probably never will be.

It soon became obvious that for certain sequences full-sized sections of the ape would have to be built for use in close-ups. Marcel Delgado and his brother Victor constructed a full-sized bust and head of Kong, which Cooper describes as being one of "O'Brien's mechanical marvels. It took three men inside the head to operate it; one to work the eyes, another the rest of the face, and a third, the ears." The construction team also built a full-sized leg and foot, together with the all-important full-sized hand that would clutch Fay Wray in close-up throughout much of the story.

The relationships of scale between the miniature Kong and the full-sized sections were carefully worked out by O'Brien and his crew but, to their disgust, Cooper kept doing sleight-of-hand tricks with Kong and his environments. The six miniature gorillas that had been built all stood 18 inches high, and O'Brien and the other technicians scaled everything in the jungles and the Manhattan settings an inch to a foot, so that Kong was always 18 feet tall. Cooper disagreed with this:

I was a great believer in constantly changing Kong's height to fit the settings and the illusions. He's different in almost every shot; sometimes he's 18 feet tall and sometimes 60 feet high or larger. This broke every rule that Obie and his animators had ever worked with, but I felt confident that if the scenes moved with excitement and beauty, the audience would accept any height that fitted into the scene. For example, if Kong had been only 18 feet high on the top of the Empire State Building, he would have been lost, like a little bug; I constantly juggled the height of trees and dozens of other things. The one essential thing was to make the audience enthralled with the character of Kong so that they wouldn't notice or care that he was 18 feet high or 40, just as long as he fitted the mystery and excitement of the scenes and action.

Work proceeded slowly all through the spring and the hot summer months. Working on the stifling-hot special effects stage, with its closed-in, airless area, was extremely trying in those non–air-conditioned days. At one point, O'Brien's hand became infected from working with the moldy hides and chemicals and he developed gangrene. While recovering from that, during the fall, he came down with the flu, so Cooper was forced to work on much of the animation himself. To Fay Wray, the

The first views of Skull Island, legendary home of Kong, which took its name from "the mountain shaped like a skull" and its topography and location "way west of Sumatra" from Douglas Burden's description of the volcanic Komodo Island. The water is real, but the island itself is a Byron Crabbe and Mario Larrinaga painting, first seen through the ship's rigging to the ominous strains of Max Steiner's music.

making of *Kong* was "just doing little bits and pieces all the way through that whole year; when I was at Warner Bros. doing *The Mystery of the Wax Museum,* Cooper would wait for me, so I'd go over to RKO and work on a weekend. It was kind of a paradox; here it was the middle of the depression, and it seems in retrospect that for me, it was a period of an enormous amount of work." In one marathon session, Cooper worked the actress for twenty-four hours straight.

Selznick, who was preoccupied with the rest of the studio, was recruited by Cooper to help with something that was largely out of Cooper's hands—the publicity on *Kong* that had started to roll out of the New York office. A page had been devoted to the film in the RKO product book for the upcoming season, calling the film *Kong* and using one of the drawings showing the ape picking the clothes off the girl. When Cooper saw it, "I just raised hell. I said to David, 'It ain't *Kong,* it's *King Kong.*' I didn't want any advertising until the picture came out; I didn't want to give the secret away. I was just scared to death that somebody would put a man in an ape suit and try to beat us to it. And a lot of the ads that they made, well, Kong's not a gorilla in them. I don't know what he is, but he's no gorilla. I just raised bloody hell about this."

(Top) The full-sized head of Kong under construction. Made of wooden strips, cloth, wire, and metal, it was used for close-ups, and a large man could fit, uncomfortably, in the mouth, as shown.
(Above) Covered with bearskin, the head was mounted on a movable platform; a series of levers enabled three men to operate the eyes, mouth, lips, nose, ears, and eyebrows, all of which were activated by compressed air.
(Right) Merian Cooper contemplating the bust of Kong outside a studio sound stage.

Filming the night sacrifice of Fay Wray to Kong. On the camera platform Schoedsack is hatless in the sports coat.

Frame enlargements showing the abduction of Fay Wray by Kong (left to right across spread): The natives prepare to close and bolt the gate after tying the "golden woman" to the sacrificial altar. On top of the wall, the chief gives the signal to summon Kong by striking the massive gong. The wall is a miniature, the natives being photographed on the roof of one of the Pathé sound stages, then combined with the miniature wall and the full-sized altar with Fay Wray. The giant head of Kong in its first appearance, and Fay Wray's immediate and classic reaction to what she sees. The problem of having the miniature Kong pick up the full-sized actress in one shot was solved by having him loosen her bonds, whereupon she falls to the ground, out of sight, and when he picks her up, it is a miniature figure he is smitten with and carries off to his jungle lair.

(Left) Max Steiner conducting the augmented RKO orchestra in his landmark score for *King Kong*.

(Below) Murray Spivack, with some of the devices used to simulate sounds in the early days of film recording: the plumber's helpers, when cranked, gave an accurate enough rendition of horses' hooves, while the large circular device was used to provide the rise and fall of wind.

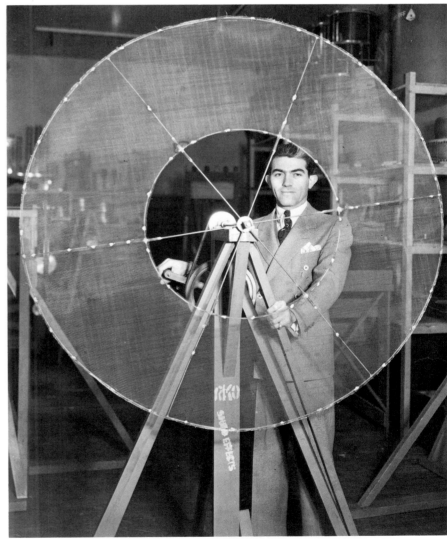

(Opposite) For the Hollywood premiere of *King Kong* at Grauman's Chinese Theatre, a special insert was published by Billy Wilkerson's *Hollywood Reporter,* which included these copper pages, with the design motif by RKO graphic artist Keye Luke. The expense of this kind of lavish promotion was the subject of intense controversy within the RKO hierarchy until it was discovered that the pages had been printed on copper sheeting left over from the production of the picture.

On page 85 is the sketch of Kong pulling the clothes from the terrified heroine. Here is the sequence as it finally appeared. The miniature Kong had been previously filmed performing all the action of picking off the girl's clothing and tickling her to make her squirm, then curiously smelling the female scent on his fingers. This had been done without the girl. When the time came to film the live action with Fay Wray, the full-sized hand and arm were used to hold the actress; portions of her costume were held together by single threads. These portions had nearly invisible strings attached to them. Cooper, off to one side, was watching the previously filmed miniature action on a Movieola. As Kong made the appropriate pulling gestures on the Movieola, Cooper would yell "now" and an off-scene stagehand would yank on the strings, pulling away another piece of clothing from the actress clutched in the full-sized paw. The two pieces of film were then combined in the optical printer. (This sequence was removed at the time of the picture's 1938 reissue, and not restored until 1969.)

him to record them, but those damned gorillas, they just ate bananas and belched all day, so that didn't turn out at all." Instead, Spivack sent a recorder out to the old Selig Zoo in east Los Angeles, and recorded the lions and tigers at feeding time. These noises were then lowered an octave, broadening them and giving the sound volume and resonance. Several of these were spliced together and played backward to give Kong his fearsome bellow. The great beast's chest-pounding was simulated by Spivack's putting a microphone on his assistant's back and hitting his chest with a bass drum mallet, the microphone picking up the pounding as it resonated throughout his body. When Kong wasn't roaring or pounding his chest, he was emitting strange sounds of simian curiosity as he toyed with his human captive. Spivack had to concoct something for what he called "Kong's love grunts." "I thought, well, he should sort of rumble, so I took a megaphone and made little grunts into a microphone and then we lowered these and that became the love grunts." For the giant ape's massive footsteps, two toilet plungers were covered with sponge rubber and tromped across a section of gravel. Spivack also recorded about twenty minutes' worth of miscellaneous screams from Fay Wray, which could be cut into the picture as needed.

He had little contact with either Cooper or Schoedsack at this point. It wasn't until mid-January, when the last of the composite scenes were coming from the lab, that he began to see Cooper with any regularity. Kong's destruction of the New York elevated railway was a scene that Spivack had worked on all night trying to finish so that it could be scored the next day. The film had to leave the studio within a week in order to be in New York in time for prints to be made for the opening. Recalls Spivack:

In those days it was nothing to see the sun come up because you're in the midst of a job, and you've gotta get it done. So I'd been up the whole bloody night working on this thing, and it came back from the lab and I waited around to show it to Cooper. I haven't had any sleep and I'm sitting there with him watching Kong tear down the elevated and thinking it wasn't bad, all the sounds and everything, and all of a sudden Coop sees this little car go by on screen and he says, "That car should have a horn," and I said, "Why, why should it have a horn?" He says, "Cars going by, you gotta have a horn." And I said, "Well, for heaven's sake, Coop, the animal's tearing down the whole Third Avenue elevated structure, all hell is breaking loose, people are getting killed, why the hell do I want to call the audience's attention to a car that's going by blowing the horn? What the hell has the car got to do with it?" And suddenly we're arguing like mad, and I haven't had any sleep and I'm exasperated with all this—my God, what does he want from my life? And I said, "You realize I gotta do this whole goddam thing over again to put your lousy automobile horn in there which has nothing to do with the scene?" and he's screaming and I'm screaming and I looked at him—Coop was kinda bald, and his forehead was a fiery beet red—and I started laughing and he said, "What are you laughing at, you silly idiot?" and I said, "Jesus, Coop, when you get mad, your goddam forehead turns fiery red," and that broke the tension, and he said, "You crazy son of a bitch, go on home and get some sleep." He was a terrifically nice guy, he spoke his piece and usually got what he wanted. Coop had a lot of class.

The size and complexity of the score was sometimes more than the RKO sound department could handle. Steiner's and Kaun's arrangements expanded the orchestra from an average thirty-five pieces to as many as forty-two, augmenting this number with extra drummers for the sacrificial ceremony and the opening credit music. While the orchestra never completely destroyed the recording system, the sheer volume of sound overwhelmed it to the point where sections had to be redone several times before the equipment could handle it. Spivack's concern for the balance of the music and sound effects was heightened when he heard the first portions of Steiner's score. "Max was imitating action with his music, we used to call it Mickey Mousing, whereby every movement had a corresponding musical figure. Well, he had all this music, it was really massive, and I had all these sound effects, and I thought, 'This is going to drive people out of the theater, all this sound,' so I began to pitch my sound effects in the same key as Max's music, so that you couldn't tell where one left off and the other began, and I carried this further whenever it would do us any good." Spivack's innovative approach to the overall concept of the sound and music gave the finished film a stylistic unity that is equal in importance to the other creative elements in the film. His sensitivity to the demands of the music and the limitations of the recording medium resulted in a sound track that is one of the masterpieces of the early sound era. With his trained musician's ear, Spivack carefully nurtures Steiner's score while it heaves, rumbles, and shrieks its way through the film, adding emotion, suspense, and terror to what is happening on screen. A grunt from an animal was immediately picked up by a corresponding growl from the orchestra, while Fay Wray's screams were echoed and intensified constantly by the strings. Music like this had never been heard in a film before. There had never been a score so ambitious and so perfectly attuned to the visuals; Steiner's music for *King Kong* was and is a landmark of film scoring, as much responsible for the success of the film as Cooper's imagination and O'Brien's gifted animation.

In the last week of January, Cooper told Selznick that the film was ready for preview. Selznick, who had seen only bits and pieces of it, was as eager as everyone else in the studio to see what Cooper had wrought, and he immediately set up a preview in San Bernardino, hurrying back from a planned weekend in the mountains. At the preview, the picture played exactly as Cooper thought it would, with one exception. As Kong shook his pursuers off the log and into the chasm below, they were set upon by huge slimy insects and snakes and graphically eaten alive. The screaming on screen was matched, in this case, by the screaming of the audience in the packed theatre, a great many of whom left; those who

stayed kept up a buzz of conversation for the next few minutes, making it difficult to keep up with the continuing story. "It stopped the picture cold," said Cooper, "so the next day at the studio, I took it out myself. O'Brien was heartbroken; he thought it was the best work he'd done, and it was, but it worked against the picture, so out it came." After the preview, Cooper relates, "David begged me to take out the scene on the boat where I had Fay do the 'scream for your life' thing; he said it would ruin the picture, but I told him that it was one of the most important things in the film, and he didn't press the point, so I was able to have *Kong* exactly the way I wanted it. Vidor was at the preview with David, and afterwards, he asked if I had to do it over again would I change anything, and I said absolutely not, it's the best I know how to do."

The world premiere of *King Kong* took place on Thursday, March 2, 1933, at both the new Radio City Music Hall and the new RKO Roxy Theatre, with a combined seating capacity of nearly ten thousand. The day before, the severity of the deepening depression had forced the closure of all the banks in New York State, but in spite of this, or perhaps because of it, spurred by a massive pre-opening publicity campaign, by the end of that week close to 180,000 moviegoers had paid more than $100,000 to see Kong lay waste to the city—ironically enough while Roosevelt was reassuring the country in his inaugural speech that "the only thing we have to fear is fear itself." Indeed, in a sense the film was equally reassuring subliminally, for the audiences who flocked to *King Kong* in the next several months saw a graphic demonstration of how modern science and technology could overcome the most destructive and fearsome of forces. The absolute chaos and economic standstill

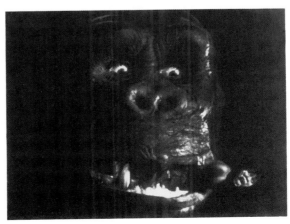

Frame enlargements showing Kong furiously battering through the gate in an attempt to recapture the girl, who has escaped his clutches. The wall here is constructed of a mixture of sand, glue, and cornmeal. After Kong breaks through, the sequence, patterned after the elephant stampede from *Chang,* becomes a mixture of full-scale action, miniature action, split screen, rear projection, matte work, and double printing as the enraged ape lays waste to the native village, stomping natives underfoot, chewing and biting their heads off in his frenzied search for the girl. The native woman holding the baby is equipped with the latest in savage fashion, a brassiere made of what appear to be coconut shells.

(Below) Three test shots for the New York theatre sequence as Kong is readied for his Manhattan debut. (Left) The matte in the camera obscuring the upper part of the platform. (Center) The miniature Kong placed in register to the live action. (Right) The scene as shown in the picture. (Bottom) Kong, enraged by the photographers' flashbulbs, breaks loose from his bonds, throwing the theatre into an uproar. This large shot is a specially prepared publicity still by studio photographer Ernest Bachrach, and has been carefully retouched to eliminate all matte lines and other telltale special effects.

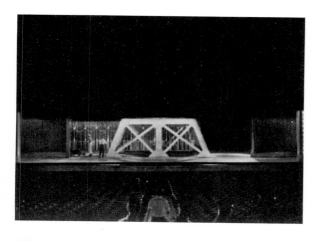  

(Above, center) Kong rips out the wall of the theatre, which is actually made of thin copper sheeting, so that it will maintain its shape. Kong's rampage in Manhattan originally involved the eating of several humans, one of whom is seen here (above, right) and all of whom were removed for the 1938 reissue. (Below) Perhaps the most famous of all these censored sequences is the "wrong woman" scene. Kong, searching for Ann Darrow, sees a blond woman in bed, reaches through the window and snatches her, upside down, from the room. Looking at her, he realizes his mistake and, in disgust, drops her screaming to the pavement twenty stories below. The woman's fall was photographed from Kong's point of view, and her single-shot drop was accomplished by photographing a stunt woman in a vertical fall onto a concealed mattress, then combining the shot with the background action.

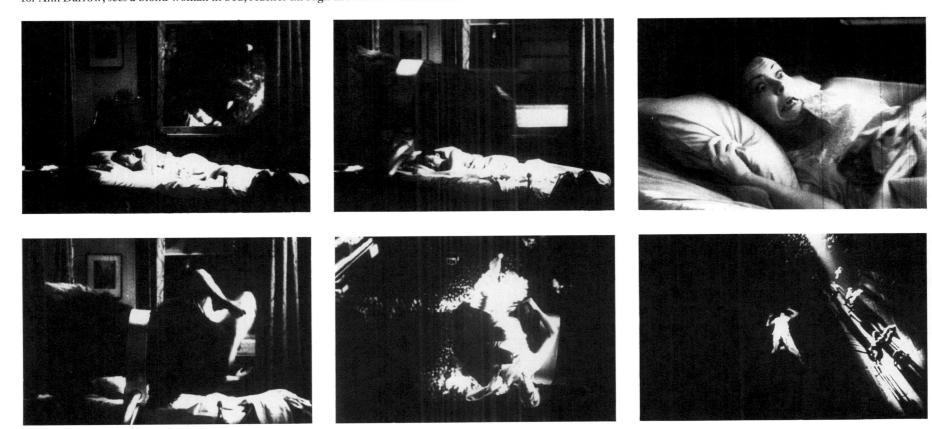

Cooper deleted the famed "spider pit" sequence from the film before its release; all that remains is this original key drawing by Ernest Smythe and Byron Crabbe (left) and this test frame showing one of the slimy monsters that inhabited the bottom of the ravine and feasted on most of the crew of the S.S. *Venture* (right).

that paralyzed the country in those bitter winter months had a metaphorical counterpart in the frenzy and destruction caused by the giant ape. His eventual destruction on and by the symbols of economic and technological progress reinforced audiences' subconscious sense that even the worst things imaginable could and would be overcome.

Two weeks later, on March 16, the Hollywood debut of *Kong* was staged by Sid Grauman at his Chinese Theatre on Hollywood Boulevard. Cooper took his new fiancée, actress Dorothy Jordan, to this special preview-premiere showing, but as he later recalled, "She liked me better than she liked my picture." When the picture finally opened to the public at the same Chinese Theatre one week later, Sid Grauman wired Cooper, " . . . never saw greater enthusiasm for any picture in my experience of presenting premieres. First time in history of any picture where applause was so frequent and spontaneous . . . audience applauded at least 20 times. . . . Every person leaving theatre tonight will be a human 24 sheet."*

The financial success of *King Kong* as it played throughout the country in the next few months vindicated Cooper's belief in the project and Selznick's faith in backing him. Costing $672,000, the picture took in almost $2 million during its first release in 1933, giving RKO a profit of more than $690,000 at a time when it seemed faced with certain bankruptcy. The durability of the film was proven over the years by numerous reissues. *King Kong* was one of the first films to be truly "brought back by popular demand," although for the 1938 revival, the Production Code Administration, which had not been in existence in 1933, forced RKO to eliminate some of Kong's more violent and provocative actions. Gone were the stompings and chewings of the humans; his methodical peeling off of Fay Wray's clothes; and his callous disposal of the "wrong woman" in New York. These changes infuriated Cooper when he learned of them years later, and justifiably, for the deletions completely change the tenor and complexity of the characterization of Kong, giving him a softer, safer quality, removing the graphic, nightmarish aspects of his mutilation and sometimes gleeful destruction of individuals. It was during these later years that *Kong* also began to be subjected to intense critical analyses. Serious discussion was given to various theories that the film was unconsciously racist, overtly sexual, with elaborate analogies explaining Kong's climbing the Empire State Building as a blatant form of phallic symbolism. Cooper, not a Freudian, firmly rejected any subconscious motivational approach, and was alternately amused, outraged, and disgusted by these ideas. To the end of his life, he maintained that "*King Kong* was never intended to be anything more than the best damned adventure picture ever made. Which it is; and that's all it is."

Schoedsack developed a much more detached, ironic view of the emergence of the *Kong* cult over the years, being resigned and occasionally irritated by the reappearance of Kong as a constant factor in his life. In a latter-day bit of doggerel, he complained:

All that lamentable noise,
Disturbs an adult's poise—
'Tis beloved by little boys
. . . Of all ages.
Fay Wray's terrifying screams,
Give them pleasure, so it seems,
In the form of awful dreams,
Of Kong's rages.

Subtle truth there, for most little girls and women do not like the film *King Kong*. They may feel sorry for the big ape, true, but the violence and identification with the heroine are too strong for the picture to be anything but an unpleasant experience for the average female moviegoer. It was years before Fay Wray understood, as she put it, "why the film made its place in cinema history. I was shocked and amazed in 1933 when I saw the enthusiasm of the original reviews. I was perhaps lacking in understanding . . . the tragedy of Kong is that his is a completely one-sided interest. There is nobody to like Kong. He just liked this little creature . . . and I think it is some fundamental thing of the imagination . . . something extraordinary just in the way the animal looked at the human creature and it made him a thinking, sensitive, soulful entity.

(Opposite, left to right) The climactic and spectacular finale atop the Empire State Building. The building itself is part miniature and part painted on glass; Kong's ascent was photographed separately in miniature, then printed in registration onto the side of the tower. Schoedsack went to New York to film real footage of the planes in attack formation; this was combined with miniature aircraft, one of which was snatched by Kong from the air and hurled to the ground in flames. Cooper and Schoedsack can be seen in the third picture in the second row as they deliver the *coup de grace* to the bleeding, bewildered giant. His final, drooping farewell to the woman he loves is played against the vast cityscape of Manhattan, actually a painting done by Larrinaga and Crabbe on glass, as projected backgrounds didn't look realistic enough. Kong's fall was photographed by a specially modified camera, running at eight times normal speed, so that the necessary slow-motion effect could be achieved. The impressiveness of the giant ape's final downfall is made the more realistic by having his body bounce off the edge of one of the upper stories before continuing its epic plunge to the street, while the terrified but courageous Miss Wray is comforted by a tuxedoed Bruce Cabot.

* The largest advertising poster then in use, seen most often on highways and the tops of buildings. See illustration, page 119.

Certainly it has felt strange to become part of a legend. Sometimes I've almost . . . But it's better not to try turning away from it but to realize that there was something lovely about it."

With its landmark mixture of sound, music, and imagery, in its energy, pace, and excitement and its unmatched ability to stimulate and involve an audience, *King Kong* stands as eloquent testimony to the accomplishments of Cooper and his co-workers. By virtue of imagination and craftsmanship they achieved the truly remarkable feat of turning an 18-inch toy gorilla into one of the mythical figures of twentieth-century civilization.

In November 1932, while coping with the problems of producing pictures on a shoestring, Selznick had received a copy of a confidential memo from David Sarnoff to the newly elected president of RKO, Merlin Aylesworth, in which Sarnoff detailed the fiscal crisis that was about to engulf the company. The worsening economic condition of the country had drained RCA's resources, and, as Sarnoff pointed out,

> The next fiscal crisis that RKO faces will come in about five weeks' time, when you will be required to meet payments in excess of $2,000,000 . . . due to the sterility of the financial markets as they are today . . . and the loss of $650,000 by RKO in the last month . . . plus the fact that all of the tangible assets of the company are pledged for loans, which heretofore have been guaranteed by RCA. . . . I must now tell you that RKO can no longer call upon the electric companies for money, and that henceforth, you must rely upon the results of your operations for the future life of RKO. The improved product coming from our Hollywood studios . . . is offset by diminishing theatre attendance. . . . I would recommend a careful examination of the overhead of the studio as a whole and the elimination of personnel and expenses as are not absolutely vital . . . it is only this result and not the method by which it is accomplished with which you and I are concerned here.

To Selznick, this was devastating. The financial crunch under which he was operating would be getting worse instead of better, and this news, coupled with Aylesworth's insistence on having final authority in production matters, demoralized him to the point of considering resigning. He had just turned down a strong offer from his father-in-law, Louis B. Mayer, at MGM, to come to work there. Mayer was frantically trying to reorganize the production ranks at the studio after a heart attack had

temporarily incapacitated Irving Thalberg. Mayer's inducements to Selznick included MGM's financial security. They had not suffered greatly from the effects of the depression; Selznick would be given his own production unit and would be free to make films the way he wanted, unhampered by financial or technical limitations. Selznick had turned him down gracefully, explaining:

> If I went to work at MGM, I would be a relative—an in-law, what's worse, of the company's head. . . . I could not face the prospect of this . . . without cringing and without a subsequent loss of self-respect. Moreover . . . I feel that I owe RKO my allegiance. They gambled and gambled heavily on me . . . allowing me to spend millions of dollars as I see fit . . . and in the face of their generosity . . . faith, I feel, should be returned with faith.

The fact that Sarnoff had sent Selznick a copy of the confidential memo to Aylesworth indicated he was letting Selznick know that Aylesworth was his hand-picked man, and that Selznick himself could no longer count on Sarnoff's unquestioned backing. His initial contract with RKO was about to expire, and the lengthy negotiations regarding the new one dragged on all during the winter of 1932–33. With Aylesworth's ascension to the presidency, the contract underwent another series of revisions, taking away much of Selznick's hard-won authority. By late January 1933, with the RKO financial picture as bleak as it was, and faced with the Aylesworth demand for approval of every script and every budget, Selznick began having second thoughts about accepting the offer from Mayer. Added to his other problems was the fact that he was no longer a free agent. He had a wife and an infant son to consider, and if the matter with RKO came to the wrong kind of head, which it seemed to be doing, he might be forced to resign out of principle.

The turmoil all this caused Selznick was brought to a sudden climax in late January, when his father died. The young Selznick, grief-stricken by his father's death, decided finally to resign from RKO and accept his father-in-law's offer to become a vice-president at the biggest studio in the world, with Mayer's assurance that he would be subordinate to no one except Mayer himself. On February 16, 1933, he moved across town to start making pictures at the same Culver City studios where he had first gone to work in 1926—but he returned to RKO just long enough to finish editing his last three productions and to see Merian C. Cooper installed as the new head of production.

The *RKO Flash,* the weekly house publication of the sales department, lavished considerable space on the efforts to sell *King Kong* to New Yorkers in March 1933.

BREATH-TAKING! STAGGERING! POWERFUL!

Here Are the Sensational Posters for The Greatest Sensation of the Age!

YOU HAVE had smash posters before those of you who recall CIMARRON, AMOS 'N' ANDY, THE CONQUERORS and others, will attest to that . . . . but never before have the in-

genuity, daring and talents of our advertising executives been called upon to describe on paper the tremendous magnitude of a show as they have been in the case of KING KONG.

They faced the task with every ingenious device at their command, and they have mastered it in the true fashion of able showmen, as the illustrations on this page will attest.

Bob Sisk and Barret McCormick, who with the able assistance of Art Director David Strumpf and his staff who accomplished the task of matching the magnitude of the show in the paper, deserve three cheers for a job well done.

If this paper won't drag them into the theatres, then nothing ever will. Of course, we don't mean the paper on the shelves, but up on the boards, all over town, where it belongs. And so, we say, if you salesmen and accessory clerks don't sell more paper on KING KONG, than on any show we have ever handled before, you just don't know your jobs, and in fairness to yourselves and your company, you ought to ask to be "wised-up" by someone who knows.

Because KING KONG is the most spectacular piece of film merchandise we, or anybody

else has ever handled, everything about it must be SPECTACULAR to measure up to it. SALES must be SPECTACULAR! COLLECTIONS must be SPECTACULAR! POSTER and ACCESSORY SALES must be SPECTACULAR! And those of us who don't measure up to the tremendous proportions of the show in putting it over, may consider ourselves spectacular flops!

THIS 6-SHEET WILL PULL MANY A DOLLAR

The three-sheet illustrated in the lower right hand corner of the opposite page, has been prepared especially for cut-out purposes. The same illustration has been utilized for a special cut-out poster which will stand ten feet high and about three feet wide when mounted and cut out. Imagine that giant ape standing ten feet high in a lobby!

BREATH-TAKING ONES (Above and below)

THE MOST SENSATIONAL 24-SHEETS THAT A BILL-POSTER EVER MESSED UP!

This cartoon caricature, published in the *Flash,* shows Merian Cooper presiding over the Radio Pictures family banquet after the departure of David Selznick.

'Tom Brown Option Taken Up, Will Make 'Forgotten Boy'

'The Handshake' to Be Next Will Rogers Production; Jane Storm Adapting It

By Louella O. Parsons
Motion Picture Editor, Universal Service

TOM BROWN

Wonder if Tom Brown understands the problems of a boy who cannot get a job and becomes a vagrant? He has had his third option taken up by Universal at an increased salary, and now he is being asked to make "The Forgotten Boy," featuring a jobless youth.

John Huston, who authored this noble attempt, tells the story of a boy with ideals who, through the present economic crisis, becomes a bum. I will say for young Mr. Laemmle that his idea is timely. The country is filled with roaming boys. We have them out here in California, strong, fine looking lads, whose favorite theme song is, "Mister, Can You Spare a Dime?"

William Wyler directs and he has a great opportunity to make an important picture.

Will Rogers' unwillingness to feature the shortcomings of the last Administration kept from making one of his best pictures of "If ...

the Jeanette MacDonald company to direct her and Herbert Marshall. J. K. McGuinness celebrated Inauguration Day by moving into the Metro-Goldwyn-Mayer Studios. Jim is sticking with the movies although once upon a time he was one of New York's most widely read columnists. Columbia expects to lead Donald Cook to stardom. Harry Cohn gets hunches and Cook is one of them. He had a hunch when he put Barbara Stanwyck into a picture, and he had a hunch when Constance Cummings was brought in after a series of disappointments at other studios. Donald's first for Columbia is "Tampico" and his next "Rules for Wives" Regis Toomey, who is also a Columbia recruit, having been signed for "Soldiers of the Storm" is that busy. He is moving into a new home in Beverly Hills.

Snapshots of Hollywood collected at random: Fifty guests at the Henry Kings', listening to Dr. A. H. Giannini's bank holiday speech on the radio, Doctor Giannini arriving later, received congratulations. All recipients of the Kings' hospitality cashed checks ...

Raymond Paige 'Lion Man' Gershwin Music Ellis Club Tom Douglas

By Florence Lawrence

There's verve and spontaneity in Raymond Paige's orchestral conducting, and his speedy tempos and well-accentuated rhythm win him immediate popularity with his audiences. Yesterday Mr. Paige conducted his second concert with the Philharmonic Orchestra. As on the former occasion of his appearance, he attracted an especially youthful audience.

One of the outstanding groups in yesterday's program was the three dances, which included "Natchez on the Hill," American, by John Powell; a "Gopak" dance from Moussorgsky's "The Fair of Sorotchinsk," Russian, and Grainger's "Shepherds Hey," English. These were given with fine appreciation of their national characteristics, and tone colorings and dynamics were well varied.

A talented young cello player, Helen Vaughn Gilbert, made a pleasing appearance in Lalo's Concerto for cello and orchestra in D minor. Miss Gilbert has a smooth and velvety tone and a brilliant technic. Mr. ...

Capitan soon ...
will ...

'KING KONG' OPENING DELAYED UNTIL MARCH 16

Thursday, March 16, will be the date of the world premiere of "King Kong," RHO-Radio's sensational jungle production, instead of Friday, March 10, as previously announced. The super thriller will have a spectacular Sid Grauman opening in Grauman's Chinese Theater.

Postponement of the scheduled date for the world premiere was made necessary by Sid Grauman's decision to elaborate the atmospheric jungle prologue spectacle far beyond his original plans. Additional time will be required to construct the ornate stage settings planned and to rehearse the augmented cast.

Filmed by Merian C. Cooper and Ernest B. Schoedsack, producers of "Grass" and "Chang," "King Kong" is hailed as outstanding among picture productions of recent years ...

DICK POWELL and BEBE DANIELS opening Thursday at Warners Hollywood and Downtown in "42nd Street."

M-G-M PREPARING TO START WORK ON 11 MORE FILMS

By James E. Mitchell

With eleven pictures being readied for immediate production, nine others in various stages of completion and five being edited and prepared for showing, Metro-Goldwyn Mayer studios are among the most active in the industry.

Productions which will be before the camera within the next few days are: "When Ladies Meet," "Tarzan and His Mate," "Harbor," "I Married an Angel," "The Great Western Sun," "Rhapsody," "Dancing Lady," "Bombshell," "The Late Christopher Bean," "Night Flight," comedy featuring ...
which C ...

Invest Your Dollars in Your Country—BUY AMERICAN

Los Angeles Examiner
AN AMERICAN PAPER FOR THE AMERICAN PEOPLE
CHARACTER • QUALITY • AMERICA FIRST • ENTERPRISE • ACCURACY
THE GREAT NEWSPAPER OF THE GREAT SOUTHWEST

PRICE FIVE CENTS

Two Sections—Part One CCC

LOS ANGELES, MONDAY, MARCH 6, 1933

VOL. XXX—NO. 85

For Complete Weather Reports
See Page 5, Part II

Today
Now Comes the Scrip Era
Some Questions Come With It
Roosevelt's Fine Beginning
Good Times Will Return

By Arthur Brisbane
(Copyright, 1933, King Features Service, Inc.)

LOS ANGELES, March 5.—Short of active calamity, the most unpleasant thing is UNCERTAINTY. A missionary held by cannibal islanders wants to know what decision the cannibal cook will reach. Today, owners of all banks closed by official order, in tens of thousands, big business men and little ones, today men would like to know what will happen.

We should be grateful, for we at least know how that the depression has run its course, at least on the surface. We are like the little boy who has swallowed castor oil and is glad that it has gone down.

Money will be provided, scrip in some states, clearing house certificates in others. And business will go on with some kind of money and good money. Ya, while the national coin will reach silver dollar will look like something. And money will be treasured. But all money is only somebody's promise to pay, a government's, a bank's or an individual's. Money is better than the name on it, or better than the credit that money, better that "worth" is much ...

used cars are ...
You'll find lowest prices of these cars daily, in the "Automobiles" columns of Examiner Want Ads.

DOCTORS GIVE UP HOPE FOR CERMAK'S LIFE

Chicago Mayor in Coma, Expected to Survive Only a Few Hours, Says Bulletin

Members of Family Summoned to Bedside as Assassination Victim Grows Much Weaker

BULLETIN
MIAMI, Fla., March 6.—(P)—At 2:30 a. m. physicians an ...

German Election Won by Hitler; Gets 272 Seats

Nation Well on Way to Fascist Dictatorship After Confidence Vote

BERLIN, March 6 (Monday).—(P)—Seventeen million voters out of 39,000,000 manifested their confidence in Chancellor Adolf Hitler in yesterday's Reichstag election, and demonstrated to President von Hindenburg that he sensed the desires of the German people rightly when he asked the chief of the Nazi Brown shirts to take the helm of the ship of state.

Preliminary allotment of Reichstag seats on the basis of yesterday's election showed early today a majority for the combined National ...

Roosevelt Declares 4-Day Bank Holiday Over Nation; Embargo on Gold; Congress Meets Thursday

SCRIP CERTAIN HERE; RULING BY U.S. AWAITED

Text of President's Bank Proclamation

WASHINGTON, March 5.—(Universal Service.)—The President's bank holiday proclamation follows:

BY THE PRESIDENT OF THE UNITED STATES OF AMERICA A ...

Scrip All Over U.S. Authorized; Postal Savings Closed

EXCEPTIONS

Treasury Head ...

Business Goes On Today as Usual in Los Angeles

Business will go on as usual in Los Angeles today ...

Hollywood—1933

FOR A TIME, especially during the peak income years of 1930 and 1931, the Hollywood film industry had been considered "depression-proof." Surprisingly, as the spreading infection slowly covered the land, money still kept coming into the theatre box offices, not in the volume of preceding years, to be sure, but on a steady, reassuring level. Having swallowed whole the threat of radio and given birth to the talkies, the movies now seemed invulnerable to the effects of the depression. In the three years prior to 1933, the major companies had all enlarged their theatre holdings; by that year there were only sixty-two out of the nineteen thousand theatres in the country that couldn't play sound movies. Warner Bros., on the crest of its Vitaphone bonanza, had bought the prestigious First National company, with its network of theatres and film exchanges and its very modern studio in Burbank, just north of Universal. As the depression deepened in the winter of 1932–33, the industry's seeming immunity proved illusory, but film companies, in spite of bankruptcies, reorganizations, and the loss of millions, still maintained their monopolistic hold on the production and distribution of films. Movies evidently were one of the necessities of American life, along with food and Amos 'n' Andy. Around the country one week in March 1933, first-run movies offered up such escapist fare as *She Done Him Wrong,* written by and starring Mae West ("Say, tall, dark, and handsome, you can be had")—the film that was directly responsible later that year for the formation of the Catholic Legion of Decency. Warner Bros.' *42nd Street* was bringing money into the box offices and new life to the musical genre, largely due to its innovative production numbers by Busby Berkeley. *King of the Jungle* offered the debut of Olympic swimming champion Buster Crabbe as an

ersatz Tarzan, and the three Barrymores were starring together for the first and only time in MGM's *Rasputin and the Empress.* Mary Pickford was appearing in *Secrets* with Leslie Howard, and shortly after its release she announced her retirement from moviemaking. DeMille's spectacular *The Sign of the Cross* had marked his return to Paramount as well as to box-office success, and Paramount was also offering the four Marx Brothers in *Horse Feathers.* These last two films were available in the second-run houses across the country, usually with Disney's *Three Little Pigs,* which was so popular that many theatres billed it above the main feature. The newsreels had stories from Germany of the new chancellor, Adolf Hitler, who most people thought looked a great deal like Charlie Chaplin. The movie theatres were comforting refuges for the 13 million people who were either homeless or unemployed.

In Hollywood in 1933, there were roughly 3,500 skilled craftsmen; this included actors, directors, film editors, cameramen, writers, and the new sound technicians. Added to these were another 27,000 workers involved in behind-the-scenes support services: secretaries, laborers, and publicity staff. The Hollywood film studios were pumping $1.5 million weekly in salaries into the Los Angeles area, with an average wage of around $50 a week. After the first expenses of sound installations, film production had been stabilized at a cost of about $200,000 per feature, with some specials going as high as $1.5 million. Cautiously optimistic that conditions would improve, the five major studios and the larger independents announced a total of 550 features for 1933–34, an increase of 50 over 1932, this in spite of the considerable drop in box-office attendance (which had been almost halved from the 1931 high of 100 million) and income.

The jobless rate in the film industry work force had gone up sharply immediately after the crash, but that had largely been as a result of overreaction by many of the studios. After the first wave of panic firings in 1929–30, the producers shrewdly realized that they had cut their costs without impairing their product. The workers were still there, only now the studios weren't liable for the costs of weekly salaries, but instead could pick and choose; it was a buyer's market as far as jobs went. Many executives capitalized on the fears of the depression, using it as an excuse to cut salaries and increase working hours. The few unions that existed in Hollywood were largely craft unions, offshoots of the other labor organizations around the country. The painters', carpenters', and other labor unions were all signatories to the Studio Basic Agreement, which had been the standard labor relations contract since its adoption by the major producing companies in 1927. A watchdog committee from both sides made sure the average studio wage was kept to around $1.50 an hour, with some skilled craftsmen, notably the scenic artists, getting as high as $2.25, while day laborers could be hired for 60 cents an hour.

In 1933 labor relations for the rest of the industry—the writers, actors, and white-collar workers—were largely handled through the Academy of Motion Picture Arts and Sciences, which served as a supposedly neutral arbitrating area for the producers to deal with their employees. There had been various sporadic attempts to organize both the actors and the writers in Hollywood over the twenty years since 1913, but the studio heads had managed to ward off any strong union takeover of their creative people. The standard practice in hiring writers was to pay the rate they had on their last job, or higher if the writer could negotiate it personally. It was only as recently as March 1932 that the writers had finally managed to get their names prominent screen credit, instead of being listed as just other craftsmen. Actors' Equity had made several unsuccessful tries at taking film performers under its jurisdiction, but the producers managed to sidestep these efforts by recognizing the Academy as their forum for cooperation, maintaining that "it was the intention of the founders of the Academy that the entire force of the organization be directed toward the friendly adjustment of differences rather than the rendering of formal decisions." In the actor's case, this "friendly adjustment of differences" meant being paid an average of $75 for a fifty-four-hour work week. Secretaries and other clerical workers were getting less than $50 a week, which was standard for the country as well. For the first few years of the Academy's existence, its agreements functioned pretty much to the satisfaction of both sides, but especially to the producers, who were maintaining a profitable status quo.

By late 1932, however, as conditions worsened and grosses fell, the producers, struggling to keep their costs in line with income, began a series of layoffs and salary cuts. By March 1933, more than 2,000 workers had joined the 400,000 unemployed on the streets of Los Angeles. In that same month, Roosevelt's closing of the banks and his taking the country off the gold standard proved to be the catalyst that set off an industry-wide panic. Universal immediately suspended all contracts by invoking the "national emergency" clause, and at Fox, employees were told that they wouldn't be paid until the banks reopened. Columbia and United Artists both shut down, while Paramount and Warner Bros. went on a part-time basis. At RKO, Merian Cooper kept the studio running despite orders from New York to close it down, while at MGM, Louis B. Mayer asked all his employees to take a "voluntary" 50 percent salary cut in order to keep the studio operating. It was a tactic he recommended should be used throughout the industry, and for one turbulent week in March, the industry was torn apart by the producers on the one hand, who advocated a salary waiver period, and the employees on the other, who protested that they couldn't exist without some income. The Academy stepped in at this point, trying to be conciliatory and recommending a 50 percent wage cut all down the line, which resulted in another outcry from the rank-and-file workers.

To get some kind of consensus as to how to cope with the crisis, Mayer and the other studio heads began a series of not-so-secret meetings on the top floor of the Hollywood Roosevelt Hotel. Their meeting room contained a large round table, the necessary number of chairs, and a massive wheeled safe that dominated one corner of the room. All through the week of March 6, proposals and counterproposals were argued back and forth, while outside in the studios, salaries weren't being paid because in those days everybody was paid in cash and there wasn't any cash. The craft unions were adamant in their refusal to consider a 50 percent pay cut, threatening to strike if their wages were tampered with. All of these problems were supposed to be dealt with by the producers at their daily meetings, some of which turned into screaming matches between Mayer, B. P. Schulberg, Harry Cohn, and Merian Cooper. Cooper especially opposed the cutting of anyone making less than $50 a week, in which he was adamantly backed by Harry Cohn, whose reputation as a "tough son of a bitch" covered up some of his better points.

The final meeting was scheduled for Friday, March 10. As Cooper relates: "It was late in the afternoon, and Mayer and Warner were both mad at Harry Cohn and me because we didn't want to make the cuts. Zanuck was there too and he was yelling, we were all yelling, and suddenly the entire room started to shake like hell, it was bouncing around, and if you looked out the window the palm trees were all bent double. Well, we just all shut up and stood there for a second and then this big safe starts to shoot across the room at us all, and it just missed Mayer and Jack Warner and went right through the wall. I was scared . . . all of us were scared; we got out of there quick."

The epicenter of the earthquake was 40 miles south, in Long Beach, which was almost totally destroyed, with hundreds of people killed. In the Los Angeles area the effects were not so drastic, and in the studios there was more fright than damage. At Paramount, Eddie Sutherland was putting W. C. Fields and Peggy Hopkins Joyce through a scene for *International House* when the props suddenly began falling off the tables and lamp stands fell backward. The camera and the sound equipment were left running while the cast and crew, led by a nervously muttering Fields, made a swift and jumpy exit. Out at Warner Bros. in Burbank, Busby Berkeley was photographing one hundred chorus girls playing one hundred neon-lit violins for *Gold Diggers of 1933*. Except for the light from the violins, the stage was in blackness when the quake hit, many of the girls were high up in the rafters, and in the ensuing panic, several of them were painfully short-circuited. None fell, however, for they all obeyed Berkeley when he yelled at them to keep calm and sit down, which they did, riding out the undulations in the dark, while below, amid the crashing, creaking, and screaming, the technicians tried to get the lights back on. At MGM, 20 miles southwest of Burbank, George Cukor was in David Selznick's new offices discussing their film *Dinner at Eight* when, Cukor recalls, "this extraordinary thing happened . . . I'd never been in an earthquake and I thought, 'What's going on here?' People were yelling at us to stand in the door jamb, so we both stood in the doorway, and the columns on the front of the studio were waving like spaghetti."

The quake proved to be the safety valve for more than just seismic strains, for on the following Monday—all passion spent, and sobered by the weekend's events—the producers and the unions agreed on a compromise solution whereby all employees except those making under $50 weekly would accept a 50 percent salary cut for eight weeks. Some of the craft unions' members still wouldn't accept and wildcat strikes plagued the studios for several weeks until the union leaders talked their men around. Shortly after this, the writers and actors, dissatisfied with the manner in which the Academy had handled the situation, broke away from its protective coverage and formed their own unions. The Screen Writers Guild and the Screen Actors Guild both soon became powerful bargaining forces in the ongoing battle with the studios. In the ensuing weeks, as Roosevelt shook out the banks and began his transformation of the economic and governmental structure of the nation, optimism slowly returned, and all across the nation the song "Brother, Can You Spare a Dime?" gave way to "Who's Afraid of the Big Bad Wolf?"

The MGM studio as it looked in late 1932, about the time David Selznick went back to work there. This view looks northeast from the intersection of Washington Boulevard and Overland Avenue in Culver City, showing the back lot with its profusion of standing sets.

MGM

ON THE DAY OF THE EARTHQUAKE, David Selznick had been at MGM a little less than a month, and, much as he had feared, his coming to the studio had aroused envy and resentment on the part of many of the MGM personnel. To some, he was trying to take the place of their beloved Irving Thalberg; to others, he was an opportunist riding on the coattails of his father-in-law, while still others felt that Mayer was trying to use him to reduce the ailing Thalberg's authority. The week of the earthquake, a trade paper, *The Hollywood Spectator,* in an editorial called "The Son-in-Law Also Rises," had referred to Selznick as "the industry's outstanding case of nepotism." Selznick's own feelings in his first week at MGM veered from energetic enthusiasm to moods of deep despondency, in which he was convinced that "all [my] past accomplishment . . . is wiped out . . . any appreciation of the future . . . is impossible because I am not an executive here . . . by right of six or seven years of struggle . . . but a relative here by right of marriage." He implored Mayer to release him from his contract, but Mayer was very carefully hedging his bets against the day that something truly damaging might happen to Thalberg's fragile health.

In 1932, when Thalberg suffered his first heart attack, Mayer had realized that it was unrealistic to expect that he would be able to continue as before, so while Thalberg was away on an extended vacation,

Mayer restructured the production hierarchy, putting himself in overall charge of the studio, with a staff of nine supervisors under him, who now would be directly responsible for their own films. And for the first time, supervisors would receive screen credit and a change in title; henceforth they were "producers," and foremost among them was David Selznick, whom Mayer was counting on to deliver the kind of prestige films that Thalberg had made. He very politely but firmly turned down Selznick's request to leave; David, faced with an intractable situation, and urged on by his wife Irene, decided to make the best of things: "I saw no alternative except to try to make some fine pictures that would, in part, regain for me the position in the industry I had lost through joining MGM."

He hurled himself into the details of setting up his production schedule, hoping to make ten pictures in the coming year. Mayer had assured him that he could have anyone and anything he wanted in the way of talent and facilities, so the first thing Selznick asked was to have George Cukor brought to MGM. This was proposed to Merian Cooper at RKO, who agreed, with the stipulation that MGM lend RKO the services of Lionel Barrymore, Myrna Loy, and Karen Morley, and further, that Cukor return to RKO in early May to direct Katharine Hepburn in *Little Women,* which had been a Selznick project before he left the studio. Cukor's arrival boosted Selznick's spirits immensely; their affectionate friendship helped David cope with the snubbings and other rudenesses he had been subjected to at the studio, and the two men began to pour their energies into the preparation of their first picture for MGM. For Selznick this first film was important. It would have to be a big enough success to gain the grudging respect of his detractors; more, it had to be good enough to restore his battered ego and self-confidence, both of which had suffered greatly since his arrival at MGM. Complicating matters was Cukor's *Little Women* deadline, only two months away. Whatever they were going to do had to be done carefully and quickly.

The first order of business was, of course, to find a story. In the regular weekly summary of available material sent to his office by Kate Corbaley of the story department, Selznick spotted the title *Dinner at Eight,* a play that had been one of the hits of the previous Broadway season. A comedy-drama of the behind-the-scenes events leading up to a posh Manhattan society dinner, the play told several interlocking stories in a trenchant, witty manner that was the special style of the authors, George S. Kaufman and Edna Ferber. Selznick had seen the play at the Biltmore Theatre in Los Angeles earlier that year, and noticed that it tended to go downhill in the second act, the ending being lugubrious and negative. Both he and Cukor felt, however, that with a little work the property could be turned into an ideal multi-star vehicle, along the lines of Thalberg's hit of the previous year, *Grand Hotel.* It also had the virtue of being extremely well written (aside from the ending) and was pretty much a "pre-sold" property in terms of audience familiarity.

Pre-sold it was, in more ways than that, for the screen rights had been purchased by Joseph Schenck at United Artists. But when he could not cast it properly, he sold it to his brother Nicholas at MGM for a round $100,000, making a very tidy profit. Selznick immediately requested that the story be turned over to him and then tried to interest Kaufman and Ferber in coming to Hollywood to write the screenplay. They declined, so he turned it over to Frances Marion and Herman Mankiewicz, two of the best writers on the lot. Parts were to be tailored specifically for ten of MGM's top stars, led by Wallace Beery, Marie Dressler, John Barrymore,

The most famous movie insignia in the world. In 1917, Howard Dietz, a recent graduate of Columbia University and an aspiring lyric writer, was working in a New York advertising agency. To him fell the task of coming up with a suitable trademark for the new Samuel Goldwyn Pictures Company. Since Pathé used a rooster and the Bison Company had a buffalo, Dietz decided that the King of the Beasts should represent Goldwyn Pictures. Not so coincidentally, the lion was also the symbol of his alma mater. The original Dietz concept was basically the one shown on page 123 and was used on all the Goldwyn films. The Latin motto ("Art for the sake of Art") was an afterthought. The actual design and drawing of the filmic frame and the lettering were done by a commercial artist named Morris Rosenbaum. In 1924, when the Goldwyn company, Metro Pictures, and the Mayer interests merged, Dietz adapted the roaring lion motif. Dietz later got around to writing for the Broadway stage and in one of his more bemused moments he wrote a song called "Triplets," in which he memorialized his creation in the following couplet: "MGM has got a Leo/But ma-ma has got a trio. . . ."

David O. Selznick in his new office at MGM, early 1933. Photograph by Clarence Sinclair Bull.

1933

At RAINBOW'S END you'll always find METRO GOLDWYN MAYER

MARION DAVIES

NORMA SHEARER

GRETA GARBO

CLARK GABLE

Howard Dietz coined the phrase "More stars than there are in heaven" and here they are circa 1933. Laurel and Hardy were not, strictly speaking, MGM stars, but were included in the line-up because MGM released the Hal Roach product. Jean Harlow and Myrna Loy were still featured players and Hedda Hopper hadn't yet turned gossip columnist.

STAR POWER

JOAN CRAWFORD

MARIE DRESSLER

WALLACE BEERY

JOHN BARRYMORE

METRO-GOLDWYN-MAYER STAR POWER

ETHEL BARRYMORE

LIONEL BARRYMORE

JIMMY DURANTE

BUSTER KEATON

RAMON NOVARRO

JOHN GILBERT

LAUREL & HARDY

HELEN HAYES

METRO-GOLDWYN-MAYER STAR POWER

 Mary Carlyle
 Helen Coburn
 Claire DuBrey
 Muriel Evans

 Neil Hamilton
 Louise Closser Hale
 Jean Harlow
 Leila Hyams

 Joan Marsh
 Una Merkel
 Gertrude Michael
 John Miljan

 Maureen O'Sullivan
 Anita Page
 Kane Richmond
 May Robson

 Verree Teasdale
John Weissmuller
 Diana Wynyard
Hedda Hopper

 Nils Asther
 William Bakewell
Helene Barclay
 Virginia Bruce

 Wallace Ford
 Lawrence Grant
 Ralph Graves
Nora Gregor

 Jean Hersholt
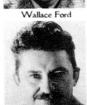 Walter Huston
 Dorothy Jordan
Myrna Loy

 Polly Moran
Karen Morley
 Conrad Nagel
 David Newell

 Ruth Selwyn
 Lewis Stone
Diane Sinclair
 Robert Young

and Clark Gable. On this last piece of casting, Selznick ran into his first stumbling block; Mayer did not want to put the highly popular Gable into the film, feeling the rugged young man would not fit into the brittle high drama of the story, especially since he was to play a doctor. Mayer was obviously remembering the unfortunate results of casting Gable as an introspective doctor in the previous year's adaptation of the Eugene O'Neill tragedy *Strange Interlude*. The picture had been a hit, but Gable's fans had complained about seeing him in that kind of a role. After the phenomenal success of *Red Dust* that winter, Mayer was carefully watching what the actor was put into, and he didn't feel that the part of the passive seducer in *Dinner at Eight* was right. Selznick acquiesced in this, and Cukor suggested the role be played by Edmund Lowe, a smooth, low-key actor of considerable charm, perfectly suited to the assignment. For the comic part of the wife of the *nouveau riche,* unscrupulous millionaire Wallace Beery, Cukor wanted Jean Harlow, who had just become a full-fledged star with *Red Dust.* Cukor had seen her in *Hell's Angels,* her first role, and he recalls that "she was so bad the whole audience laughed . . . the trouble was that she wasn't a vamp, she was a comedienne . . . she didn't seem to know all the implications of the lines she was saying . . . but she quickly developed a wonderful skill at comedy. In *Dinner at Eight* she never missed a laugh." The play offered another variation on the theme of the washed-up alcoholic actor, this time an aging, egocentric, unsympathetic type who could not face up to the realities of his lost fame and his addiction. Selznick and Cukor both agreed that John Barrymore would be perfect. "Barrymore had absolutely no vanity," says Cukor. "He played this broken-down actor mercilessly. At one point, he was supposed to say, 'I can play Ibsen,' and Jack

struck a completely inappropriate pose and recited the last few lines from *Ghosts.* Even his suicide is messed up. He tries to make a dramatic final march across the floor of his hotel room and he trips on something and ends up in this awful middle-aged sprawl."

"For years," Cukor later recalled, "people kept asking me, 'How could you ever cope with all those stars?' I had to insist I didn't have much trouble; stars are usually easier to cope with than less important people." Under Cukor's no-nonsense guidance, the filming proceeded swiftly, being marred only by the personal tragedy that faced actress Billie Burke. She had appeared in films off and on since 1916, usually as a romantic lead, and had worked for both Cukor and Selznick in her first sound film, *A Bill of Divorcement.* In *Dinner at Eight,* she was playing the first of the many roles she would be faced with for the rest of her career, the slightly daffy, silly society woman who bursts into tears when she finds that the aspic is ruined. She was the wife of Florenz Ziegfeld, the legendary producer of the Follies, *Show Boat,* and other landmark Broadway shows, whose career had foundered on the shoals of the depression and on his own free-spending ways. His health declined along with his fortunes, and his wife had been forced to work increasingly in films to bring in money. She had brought Ziegfeld out to Hollywood in the hope that his spirits and health would revive, but he continued to deteriorate. "Billie was undergoing a terrific strain," says Cukor, "because Flo Ziegfeld was dying. Indeed he died while we were shooting, but Billie insisted on continuing with the part and would not let me make anything easier for her. She was a very strong woman."

Near the end of shooting, on March 28, something happened that received almost no notice except for a small item in the Los Angeles

Marie Dressler as Carlotta Vance, *Dinner at Eight*'s aging, feisty grande dame of the American theatre, whose dog has evidently done something to incur the lady's displeasure. (The dog's name was changed by the script writers from "Mussolini" in the original play to "Tarzan" for the movie, as much from fear of political censorship as to publicize the MGM jungle tale.) Miss Dressler's film career dated back to 1914 and *Tillie's Punctured Romance.* After a long eclipse, she made a brilliant character comeback in support of Greta Garbo in *Anna Christie* (1930). From that time until her death in 1934, she was one of MGM's biggest star attractions.

(Opposite) Photographer Clarence Sinclair Bull did a series of photographs of Jean Harlow on the set of *Dinner at Eight;* the famous companion piece to this picture was used on the cover of *Time* magazine, where it attested to Harlow's sudden emergence as a full-fledged MGM star. The gown is by Adrian and the setting by either Hobe Erwin or Frederic Hope. (Below) Billie Burke as society matron Millicent Jordan, whose dinner party precipitates the dramatic action of the story. The setting is by Hobe Erwin, the gown by Adrian, and the photograph by Clarence Sinclair Bull.

Jean Hersholt, Lee Tracy, and John Barrymore in a scene from *Dinner at Eight*.

George Bernard Shaw visits the set of *Dinner at Eight*. Directly behind Shaw, partially obscured, in the hat, is publicity man Barrett Kiesling; to the right of Shaw are columnist Eileen Percy, David O. Selznick, and Marion Davies, who is either meditating or playing blind man's bluff.

Times, which mentioned that KHJ, the Don Lee radio station in Hollywood, had transmitted the motion picture *The Crooked Circle* to a television set placed in the window of Barker Bros. department store on Hollywood Boulevard across from Grauman's Chinese Theatre. "A crowd of interested spectators gathered to look at this first experimental transmission, and many voiced wonder at how it was done," concluded the article. This harbinger of things to come was, however, overshadowed by the arrival in Hollywood of the redoubtable Irish playwright George Bernard Shaw. Shaw, a spry, seventy-seven-year-old curmudgeon, was making a much-publicized trip to the United States, and at the invitation of publisher William Randolph Hearst, he had decided to visit Los Angeles. He flew to Los Angeles for a tour of the MGM studios, which, not so coincidentally, was where Marion Davies, Hearst's longtime companion, made her films, backed substantially by Hearst's money. Miss Davies was to host a large luncheon for Shaw in the thirteen-room "bungalow dressing room" that Hearst had built for her just outside the studio wall. Then Barrett Kiesling from the publicity department was to shepherd Shaw through the sound stage tour, including a lengthy stay on the *Dinner at Eight* set. Cukor was just beginning a rehearsal of a scene with Barrymore, as the washed-up actor, being told off by his agent, played by Lee Tracy, when Kiesling ushered in Shaw, Davies, Charlie Chaplin, and a beaming David Selznick. "We were all very self-conscious," says Cukor. "I think Jack knew Bernard Shaw, and while we rehearsed they sat there, and Jack Barrymore said to me, 'I'll do it up for you,' and I said, 'What does that mean?' He said, 'I'll be rather stupid and you can show me what you want, and they can see you directing.'" After the scene had been filmed, Shaw remarked that he had been more impressed with another scene of Barrymore's which he had played "amidst the popping of champagne corks."

Shaw's visit to the set of *Dinner at Eight* was covered by reporters from the local papers, whose reports were filed on the wire services that crisscrossed the country, with the result that the story and sometimes a photo appeared in thousands of newspapers nationally and overseas. As an attention-getter it was one of the luckier accidents, which made the work of MGM's publicity department easier. Pete Smith had originally set up the studio publicity department in line with Mayer's policy of wanting only the best of everything. When Smith proved more valuable as a producer of comedy shorts, the department was handed over to the cool, unflappable Howard Strickling, whose slight stutter gave him an endearing quality that immediately made people take to him. "In earlier days," recalls Strickling,

everything had been done in New York. At the studio, we made the stills and wrote the stories, but then it was all sent to New York and they would put it together and decide how to use it. There was no such thing as a campaign, theatres were responsible for their own ads and sometimes even made up their own posters, but then we began making up posters to send to the theatres through the exchanges, and we had a pressbook for each picture that contained stories, ads, and ideas on how to get attention for the picture, but all this was made up after the picture was finished. It wasn't until Mr. Mayer came and they had the merger that he and Thalberg hired Pete Smith because they felt you had to start the campaign at the very beginning, while the picture was being made.

When Selznick had arrived on the MGM lot, Strickling assigned Barrett Kiesling (who for many years had worked with Cecil B. DeMille) to work with his unit, developing items, stories, and other coverage on the Selznick projects. Working on *Dinner at Eight,* Kiesling's week began with a staff meeting in Howard Strickling's office. Everybody in the publicity department attended; all were free to make suggestions for stories, offer ideas for publicity. After going over what he considered the shortcomings of the previous week's efforts, Strickling would outline new projects for the coming week, and give fresh assignments to the staff. After this, Kiesling relates,

I would go down to the set first thing every morning, have a cup of coffee with the director if he was available, and keep in touch with the cast for any new breaking story or incident. I'd assign the still photog-

An All-Star Rebound to Normal
Between Camera Shots of "Dinner at Eight"

*Metro-Goldwyn-Mayer's brilliant all-star production. Left to right: Standing—*EDMUND LOWE (*Dr. Talbot*)...GEORGE CUKOR, *Director*...LIONEL BARRYMORE (*Oliver Jordan*) JEAN HARLOW (*Kitty Packard*)...PHILLIPS HOLMES (*Ernest*). *Sitting—*MADGE EVANS (*Paula Jordan*)...LOUISE CLOSSER HALE (*Hattie Loomis*)...BILLIE BURKE (*Millicent Jordan*)...MARIE DRESSLER (*Carlotta Vance*) ... KAREN MORLEY (*Lucy Talbot*)...GRANT MITCHELL (*Ed Loomis*)...A DAVID O. SELZNICK PRODUCTION.

In Hollywood, you see it every day in the making of pictures — *the pause that refreshes* with ice-cold Coca-Cola. It breaks the stress and strain of shooting scenes over and over. It is cooling relief from the hot kleig lights. It banishes drowsy yawns and hot, thirsty faces. It's the way to snap back to normal and be alert... Because, an ice-cold Coca-Cola is more than just a drink. It combines those pleasant, wholesome substances which foremost scientists say do most to restore you to your normal self. Really delicious, it invites a pause, a pause that will refresh you.

Coca-Cola was one of the first companies to tie its product to the movies, and especially to movie stars. Here it is used to help the cast and director of *Dinner at Eight* "rebound to normal," a not so veiled pep-up phrase designed to combat the depression. This shot was one of the first on-set color photos taken anywhere. Conspicuous by his absence is John Barrymore, who evidently didn't care for this kind of "pause that refreshes."

rapher to stay with the production. I'd do a lot of listening sometimes just to get one or two good ideas for stories, but that was just second nature. You're a salesman trying to get a salable idea. Now David was a great believer in local publicity; he especially liked to have coverage in the rotogravure section of the Sunday L.A. *Times.* Rotogravure was a very classy method of printing photos used in those days; all the major newspapers had them and it was considered quite a coup to get a picture in the roto, because of course you'd be competing with all the other studios for space, but I remember we managed to get a whole page for *Dinner at Eight* just as it was being released, and this was considered to be quite an accomplishment.

As *Dinner at Eight* neared completion, Selznick was still dissatisfied with the ending, feeling that one last bit of rewriting was necessary to make the picture end on a light note—something that would bring down the curtain and the house. What writer Donald Ogden Stewart evolved for this was a sort of coda delivered as a colloquy between the Jean Harlow and Marie Dressler characters as they walk into the dining room. Cukor directed this in one medium close traveling shot, allowing the spectator to overhear Kitty Packard (Harlow) say to Carlotta Vance (Dressler): "I was reading a book the other day," at which point Marie

Dressler does a sort of stumbling doubletake and exclaims dumbfounded, "A book??" "Yes, a nutty kind of a book," chatters Harlow. "Do you know the guy says that machinery is going to take the place of every profession?" And Dressler, with a lifetime of experience honing her timing to the sharpest edge, looks her up and down and without missing a beat or a footstep replies, "Oh my dear, that's something you need never worry about," and they walk together through the doors, which close slowly behind them.

From start to finish, *Dinner at Eight* was in production for just twenty-four days, and cost only $387,000, two facts that amazed everyone in the industry and that were commented on incredulously in all the reviews when the picture finally opened at the Chinese Theatre in late August. At that premiere, Selznick was quoted as saying, "We have, I think, achieved the ideal of *Cavalcade,* one of the finest pictures ever made... in that *Dinner at Eight* is adult, intelligent, and at the same time has an extremely wide mass and 'down to earth' appeal." Just how wide an appeal was apparent over the next several months as the picture, spurred by overwhelmingly excellent reviews and corresponding word of mouth, brought more than $3 million in rentals to MGM. It also catapulted George Cukor into his reputation as one of the top directors in the business.

Pete Smith, the famous short-subject producer, who had originally started the MGM studio publicity department in 1924; Howard Dietz, the head of Eastern publicity, a classy gentleman who had started with the old Goldwyn company, then stayed with MGM while simultaneously becoming one of the Broadway theatre's cleverest lyricists; Stuart Dunlap, the MGM representative in South America; and Howard Strickling, who took over operation of the studio publicity department from Pete Smith and kept it operating efficiently, discreetly, and imaginatively for close to forty years. A light moment—circa 1938.

A high-powered confab on the sidewalks of MGM—1933: David Selznick, Ben Hecht (back to camera with cigar), Ernst Lubitsch (with cigar), King Vidor (back to camera; he may have a cigar, it's hard to tell), and George Cukor (definitely no cigar).

At MGM, the success of *Dinner at Eight* raised not only Selznick's prestige at the studio but, more important, his self-esteem. The backbiting and viciousness he had been subjected to in his first weeks now gave way to a kind of grudging respect on the part of the other executives, all of whom were, under Mayer's new system, now so busy competing and jockeying with each other for stars and stories that they didn't have time to bait David, being too preoccupied trying to keep up with him. Another factor easing the situation was the return of Irving Thalberg to the studio in late August 1933. Selznick had been nervous about this, not knowing what Thalberg's attitude would be about his purported "replacement." The two men had a quiet meeting in Thalberg's office and David was gratified to find that Thalberg, being intelligent and sensitive, bore him no ill will but instead sympathized with him completely about what he had undergone at the hands of some of his colleagues. Thereafter, Thalberg went out of his way not only to indicate his liking for Selznick personally but also to be enthusiastic about his production projects, commenting at a meeting that David's idea for Wallace Beery to star in a film about Pancho Villa "sounds like big box office to me."

Selznick was fascinated by the duality of the Villa that the American press and newsreels had created in the early years of the twentieth century: a swaggering, lawless, bloodthirsty villain, who nonetheless was considered to be the "Mexican Robin Hood"; an illiterate, idealistic savage who had led the peons in revolt and by his death became a legendary national hero. Selznick's romantic streak was attracted by the sense of irony, fate, and myth in Villa's story, and his fight against corruption and oppression strongly appealed to Selznick's liberal sensibilities. The recent success of Warner Bros. biographies of Alexander Hamilton and Disraeli convinced Selznick that the life of Villa would be a fit subject for the scope, sweep, and grandeur that the movies could give it. This idea had planted itself in Selznick's mind after MGM had bought the rights to a biography of Villa by Edgcumb Pinchon and Odo Stade, *Viva Villa!* Selznick was excited about the project, not only from the commercial standpoint but also from the sheer production challenge of getting a good dramatic script out of the flamboyant prose of the original. The book itself had aroused considerable controversy in Mexico because of its treatment of Villa and the revolution, and MGM's purchase was made contingent upon approval of the project by the Mexican government.

While these negotiations were being carried out by Mayer, Selznick was devoting his attention and energies to finishing his second project,

an adaptation of Antoine de Saint-Exupéry's prize-winning aviation novel, *Night Flight.* Selznick had visions of its being somewhat of a high-adventure tale of pioneering airmail pilots in the Andes, with spectacular air sequences that would rival Howard Hughes's 1930 *Hell's Angels.* The trouble with this approach was that it didn't fit the material; Saint-Exupéry was an ironic philosophical writer whose works were characterized by internal musings and lack of exterior dramatic conflicts. Getting a suitable script from this had been the task first of Oliver H. P. Garrett, whom Selznick had brought over from Paramount. After Ben Hecht, Garrett was Selznick's favorite collaborator, almost his alter ego. He spent weeks with Selznick going over the novel, trying to find a dramatic path through Saint-Exupéry's metaphorical ponderings. After reading the script, Selznick was a bit taken aback to discover that the bulk of his spectacular air adventure took place on the ground, in offices and bedrooms. To correct this, he hired John Monk Saunders, aviation authority par excellence, who had written *The Dawn Patrol.* Saunders managed to flesh out the flying sequences, beefing up the role of the pilot who is trying to cross the Andes so that it would be suitable for Clark Gable, whom Selznick still had not been able to cast in one of his pictures. Gable's phenomenal rise to popularity had been comet-like from his first notice in *A Free Soul* (1931), in which he had manhandled Norma Shearer, MGM's queen, an act that set him completely apart from the herd of young leading men. His subsequent torrid teaming with Jean Harlow in *Red Dust* had further developed his blatant sexual image, and had turned him into just about the only surefire box-office attraction in the studio. Out of the seventeen films he had made in the past three years, only one had lost money, the Hearst production of *Polly of the Circus* in which he had played a minister to Marion Davies's Polly. Competition for his services among the producers on the lot was fierce. In the beginning he had been cast in a wide variety of roles to see where his appeal lay; it turned out he was at his best projecting a rugged, down-to-earth, sexy masculinity, something that Mayer and Thalberg had difficulty in coming to terms with. MGM as a studio had been heavily slanted toward female stars; its few leading men were smooth, romantic, charming, and sophisticated. Gable was new, raw in his musky sexuality, and Mayer and Thalberg were uncomfortable in dealing with his overwhelming erotic impact, trying to disguise it with a veneer of upper-class romantic attitudes until it became obvious to them that taking Gable out of his rough-tough middle-class milieu was detrimental to his soaring popularity.

Gable's last released MGM film had been *The White Sister,* a remake of a silent melodrama, in which he had co-starred with Helen Hayes, one of the studio's newest stars; the teaming had resulted in a gross of close to $2 million. Selznick felt that lightning could strike twice, so he cast Helen Hayes in *Night Flight* as the wife of the pilot flying the mail across the mountains, and then made a bid for Gable to play the pilot, which Mayer resisted, saying that the part was not strong enough. Selznick pleaded, and Mayer finally put the matter up to Nicholas Schenck, who approved. Selznick, delighted to have Gable at last, stated: "He had that God-given thing: a theatrical personality, the ability to communicate with an audience, which all the training in the world can't give you. Experience helps, but without this other quality there is no such thing as the star personality. It is an indefinable something which I like to think I can spot immediately in a person. The public caught it in Gable the first time he walked on the screen." With the cast now complete and the revised script nearing completion, Selznick asked for Clarence Brown to direct. Brown, whose career dated back to 1920, had a fine pictorial sense; he was a seasoned pilot and his love of flying made him seem the perfect choice to direct the film. A careful, methodical, low-key director, Brown was not bowled over by the various scripts, so Selznick brought in his favorite script fixer, Wells Root, and while Root worked away, Selznick readied the picture for a production start of April 12, 1933, with location work on the flying sequences scheduled for Denver, Colorado (the Rocky Mountains would stand in for the Andes). Problems developed almost immediately. Script action called for Gable's character to make a parachute jump from his plane into the snow-covered Rockies; stuntman Ivan Unger would make the leap as soon as the plane was high enough for the parachute to open and still float down in time to be photographed, which was estimated to be about 25,000 feet up. Unfortunately, Unger, who was not used to such extreme heights, passed out at 20,000 feet, so the shot was never taken, but was faked back at the studio with rear screen projection and miniatures, which detracted considerably from the scene's credibility.

Selznick's attention was not completely concentrated on *Night Flight;* he was also juggling the script details of *Viva Villa!* and a new Joan Crawford film that Mayer had asked him to take over, and his concern with these two temporarily blinded him to the defects of *Night Flight.* To film editor Hal Kern, however, trying to give the sequences some sort of dramatic cohesiveness, the film was emerging as a talky, erratic mélange, with no center or focus. "About halfway through production," recalls Kern, "I went to David's office and told him that we ought to copy Walt Disney. He didn't know what I was talking about and I said that in all Disney's films, there was something to root for right from the beginning." Selznick ran all the assembled material and then reread the script, and realized that in his determination to do justice to Saint-Exupéry's diffuse novel, he had inadvertently brought forth a baby turkey. In an effort to stave off impending disaster, Selznick ordered the picture completely rewritten, adding two subplots, one of which concerned a typhoid epidemic in Rio de Janeiro to which Gable's character is rushing a load of serum across the Andes. This prolonged the production schedule by almost three weeks and made Gable unhappy. He had been promised a long vacation after the film was finished, his first in almost a year, and the lengthy retakes were eating up the time. Gable was a hardworking, strict disciplinarian; work started for him at eight and ended at seven; he liked everything around him to be totally professional, and most of his experience at MGM had been just that. *Night Flight* was his first taste of a production in trouble, and to the insecure young actor, whose role was being rewritten and refilmed daily, it was unsettling. A quiet, almost reclusive man, Gable was, in Selznick's words, "a naturally suspicious person; it took nothing at all for Clark to start thinking that someone was out to do him in." In the case of *Night Flight,* Selznick was the newcomer, the boss's son-in-law, and the panic that surrounded the hasty revisions evidently left Gable with more than a slight contempt for Selznick's much-vaunted production abilities, something that was to have a long-term deleterious effect on the professional relationship between the two men. *Night Flight* was completed in late May, and was cut by Selznick and Hal Kern from a first preview of over two hours down to a ponderous eighty minutes.

When it was finally released in October 1933, *Night Flight* had run up production costs of $500,000, and critical and public indifference turned

David Selznick (back to camera) waiting for Irving Thalberg to complete his serve at somebody's Santa Monica beach house—1933.

Helen Hayes, at the peak of her MGM success in *Night Flight,* gazes wistfully at the studio's hottest male star in a pose that could have inspired the song "Dear Mr. Gable."

Outlining his plans for the next year, Selznick listed the projects he was actively working on, including a version of *The Forsyte Saga* to star the three Barrymores; a biography of the recently deceased Florenz Ziegfeld; a sound remake of *The Garden of Allah,* which had been made profitably by MGM in 1927; and a story called *Barbary Coast* about some lively doings in old San Francisco, ending with the 1906 earthquake and fire. At the same time he was continuing to work on the problematical *Viva Villa!* The Mexican government had approved a concept that would make the story "not strictly a historical document, but romantic entertainment with only some thread of historical truth." Some Mexican higher-ups had fought against Villa in the revolution and were not kindly disposed to the idea of glorifying a man many of them considered to be an ignorant bandit. Selznick set to work with Ben Hecht to try to get a script that would satisfy everybody and make Villa acceptable both dramatically and diplomatically. In the early summer of 1933, actor Ramon Novarro's brother Carlos was secretly sent to Mexico with a copy of the first-draft script. Novarro had friends in the Mexican political world and managed to get the screenplay approved with the promise of some minor changes, especially in the character of Villa, making him more of a brutal, groveling peasant, taking away some of the mythos with which Hecht, Selznick, and Pinchon had invested him. With the assurance that this would be done, the project was approved by the official government and most importantly by its strongman Plutarco Calles, an old enemy of Villa's. Once that particular hurdle was cleared, Selznick put Hecht on the screenplay full-time, paying him $10,000 for the job, plus a bonus of $5,000 "if the job is completed to my entire satisfaction within fifteen days. . . ." About this last, Selznick commented in a note to Mayer:

> It may seem like a short space of time for a man to do a complete script, but Hecht is famous for his speed; for quality, Hecht's ability will take care of that. . . . I do not think we should take into consideration the fact that we are paying him a seemingly large amount of money for two weeks' work . . . as this would be merely penalizing him for doing what would take a lesser man at least six or eight weeks, with infinitely poorer results.

Mayer accepted the reasoning, and Selznick, director Howard Hawks, and the art and production departments began breaking down and estimating cost and production problems brought on by the decision to film on location in Mexico. While they waited for Wallace Beery to return from a European vacation, Selznick gave the bulk of his time over to a troublesome stepchild he had been handed by Mayer, Joan Crawford's next picture, *Dancing Lady.*

it into the lowest-grossing Gable film since *Polly of the Circus.* In spite of all the picture's problems, Selznick was proud of it, defending it in a letter to MGM head Nicholas Schenck, saying, "I thought it was a fine picture when I made it and I still think it's a good picture." For years afterward, he kept it on his own personal "ten best" list.

The vicissitudes and near failure of *Night Flight* bothered Selznick not at all. He shrugged them off and immersed himself not only in his own projects but in the internal workings of the studio as well. In late May, as *Night Flight* was winding up, Selznick dictated a long letter to Nicholas Schenck, telling him:

> I believe that it is the destiny of MGM to acquire top talent whenever it develops, with the other companies serving as minor leagues developing this talent with MGM prepared for the best talent. In the production of the type of pictures that we want, it is the mediocre talent . . . that swells cost and reduces quality. We have a magnificent stock company of players that should be weeded somewhat . . . notably we are lacking in leading men and in the writing staff, we are woefully weak . . . we would be better off with twenty men getting high salaries writing the bulk of our program than we are with a staff of seventy-five, not ten of whom are worth their salt. We have a group of superb staff directors . . . but we would be better off with fewer supervisors and more producing directors for with a staff that comprised eighty percent of the ranking writing and directing brains of the world we would need fewer producers . . . they would get in the way for their creative ability is not comparable.

(Opposite) One of cinematographer Elmer Dyers's spectacular aerial shots from *Night Flight,* photographed over the Rockies, which were substituting for the Andes. According to the studio publicity files, this was the first time that infrared film was used in commercial motion picture photography.

Writer Allen Rivkin, associate producer John Considine, and co-writer P. J. ("Pinky") Wolfson in a story conference for *Dancing Lady*.

Crawford about to make an entrance in *Dancing Lady*.

Dancing Lady had been bouncing around the studio from producer to producer ever since the James Warner Bellah novel had been purchased in April of 1932. The title and the action of the story, one of those twenty-year sagas of a young girl's rise from poverty to fame, riches, unhappiness, and ultimately poverty and happiness, had seemingly made it perfect material for a Joan Crawford vehicle. The synopsis had been put in the file of plots considered suitable for the actress, with the notation that it was "nothing unusual. . . . There is some lively dialogue, some production value opportunities and a certain gallantry to the story." The story had much in common with Crawford's own background: a lonely, arid childhood in rural Oklahoma, living with her older brother and her twice-divorced mother. She worked her way through school and several cities, housecleaning, toiling in a laundry, and taking other odd and menial jobs, until she finally broke free from this and on her own enrolled at Stephens College in Missouri, supporting herself as a waitress while entertaining herself with any number of young sheiks doing a frantic knockabout Charleston, exhausting partners and winning contests. The lure of bigger things made her give up school to join a traveling nightclub show, where her combination of looks and aggressiveness ultimately landed her in the chorus of a New York musical called, appropriately enough, *Laughing Eyes,* in which she stood out enough to catch the attention of Harry Rapf on a talent-scouting spree from MGM. This hunt for fresh faces was carried on largely by the intuitive process, and Harry Rapf's male intuition told him that the big-eyed twenty-one-year-old had that little something extra that made men notice her even in the fourth row of the chorus. What she had was a driving ambition, a supple, tough sexuality, and an eagerness that made her suitable material for a screen test. Along with eighteen other girls from shows around town, Lucille LeSueur, as she was known, went through the exciting ritual of an MGM screen test, and evidently impressed Mayer and Thalberg, for two weeks later she was on the long train ride to California with a six-month contract at $75 a week.

She arrived at the studio in January 1925, when MGM was not quite a year old and films were still silent. Her rise to stardom had been quick: from her first notice in a blond wig in *Pretty Ladies* (1925) to her emergence as the apotheosis of 1920s flaming youth in *Our Dancing Daughters* (1928), she was completely a creation of the movies and of her own ambition. Even her name, "Joan Crawford," was the result of a stunt dreamed up by Pete Smith of the studio publicity department to find a "simple euphonious name for an energetic, ambitious and typically American girl." In the eight years between her arrival and 1933 she had made thirty-four films, in thirty of which she was either featured or starred. Her pursuit of stardom was singleminded and relentless; according to the studio, she answered all of her fan mail herself, no mean feat considering she averaged about two thousand letters a week, a figure that grew considerably after her 1929 marriage to the crown prince of Hollywood, Douglas Fairbanks, Jr.—a match strongly disapproved of by her stepmother-in-law Mary Pickford, who reportedly referred to her as "that Charleston queen." By the time of *Grand Hotel* in 1932, Crawford had solidified her position as a dramatic actress of some ability. At her own request, she was loaned out to United Artists for Lewis Milestone's *Rain,* a sound remake of W. Somerset Maugham's *Sadie Thompson,* which had been made with Gloria Swanson in 1928 and was a twice-told tale as far as audiences were concerned, being a talky saga of sin and redemption that offered depression audiences nothing they wanted. Its failure, followed by the flop of her next MGM film, *Today We Live,* worried Crawford; her next picture had to be a success or her career could be seriously damaged. Compounding her unhappiness was the recent break-up of her marriage to Fairbanks. The consequent unpleasant publicity brought out all of Crawford's instincts for self-preservation, and she took her fears to Mayer.

Normally Thalberg handled all matters pertaining to MGM's major players, but Crawford felt she would not get an entirely sympathetic reaction from him. She and Norma Shearer had both started within two years of each other at MGM; their rise had been parallel until, in what Crawford considered a shrewd move, Norma had married Thalberg, thereby assuring herself first call on all the best in the studio. Crawford felt that this was extremely unfair, and in her present situation she felt the wisest course was to go directly to Mayer. She knew his weakness for

MGM was one of the more adventurous of the studios in trying new ideas in graphics.
This rendering of Joan Crawford and Clark Gable by an artist named Birnbaum breaks
completely with the literal tradition of star portraits. It was commissioned "in the
modern style," as the order put it, in late 1933, around the time of *Dancing Lady,* but
was at first considered too unusual and was not used until *Love on the Run* in 1936.
Birnbaum did another solo sketch of Crawford that was used by the studio off and on
over the years—and that eventually formed the basis of the ad campaign for her return
to the studio in *Torch Song* (1953).

Some of the Adrian costume designs for *Dancing Lady*:
(Above, left) Joan Crawford in a stripper's outfit being hauled away by the law.
(Above, right) A deleted sequence from the musical number "That's the Rhythm of the Day" showing the heroine wed to a robot who turns out to be a singer, Art Jarrett, who earlier got to sing the big hit of the picture, "Everything I Have Is Yours." (Below, left to right) A bizarre contrivance of wire was the predicted fashion for sometime in the future (this outfit is supposed to have inspired the creator of the "Slinky Jim" children's toy). A black wool suit with the obligatory gardenias and a broad-brimmed Empress Eugénie hat angled over one eye marks the rise of Janie Barlow from chorus girl to "top spot." Crawford's gown is of bugle beads with a diamond pin and a black velvet collar. Another of Adrian's futuristic fantasies, unfortunately deleted before the film's release. Note Crawford's carefully retouched hips.

138

Joan Crawford in her penultimate moment as star Janie Barlow wearing an Adrian creation of spangled white chiffon. Created specifically for the musical finale of the picture, the gown cost $5,000 and was on screen for all of ten seconds.

The set designs for *Dancing Lady* were by Merrill Pye, who had first attracted attention with his work on Crawford's first starring vehicle, the silent *Our Dancing Daughters*. Pye was thirty-one when he did *Dancing Lady*; his background included architecture and furniture design. Pye's attraction to clean curves and crisp articulation was tempered by his love of theatricality, as these settings from *Dancing Lady* show: glossy, streamlined designs that typified what was starting to be called Moderne.

flattery, for the feeling that his "family" was seeking his advice; ̣ lso felt safe with him, for as she candidly remarked years later: "He never touched my boobs or pinched my butt. He was a gentleman." As for Mayer, he liked Crawford's level-headedness and her dedication to her career. Consequently, when she went to him, put her arms around his neck, and entreated him to "Help me, L. B.," he began to give the matter of her next picture more than his usual amount of attention. Feeling that her career might be helped by a change in producers, and in line with his policy of building up the executive ranks, Mayer assigned the task of finding a suitable story for the actress to John Considine, Jr. His selection of *Dancing Lady* met with Mayer's approval. He liked the story with its show business background, and gave Considine the go-ahead. Considine did not have a strong story sense, and the script prepared under his direction by Allen Rivkin and P. J. Wolfson followed the basic outline of the Bellah novel, telescoping the twelve-year period of the original down to a tight three years; as such it was episodic and downbeat, and Considine made the mistake of showing it to Crawford for her opinion. She didn't like it and told Considine so in no uncertain terms, and Mayer too, when he asked her.

Just at this point, Selznick joined the studio, and Mayer asked him to look at the script of *Dancing Lady*. Selznick spotted one immediate weakness: the title *Dancing Lady* implied music, but there was very little dancing or music inherent in the story. Selznick himself did not much care for musicals; they ranked just above westerns in appeal as far as he was concerned. Although he had had great success with *The Dance of Life* at Paramount, he felt that musicals were much too artificial; the musical numbers stopped the flow of whatever story was being told. He also had very little appreciation for music, except for certain classical pieces; popular music was a distraction to him, but he rarely listened to the radio either for pleasure or relaxation; nor was he much of a dancer, preferring to work, talk, or gamble. But although he had very little interest in the possibilities of the screen musical, he certainly appreciated the commercial potential of the genre. Indeed, he had just seen Warner Bros.' new film, *42nd Street*, and for the first time had been excited by the new techniques of visual and sound dynamics of Busby Berkeley's musical numbers. Selznick knew that Warner Bros. had another musical film in the works, and he also had kept abreast of Merian Cooper's plans to put Fred Astaire into an RKO musical called *Flying Down to Rio.* Selznick shrewdly judged that with a musical cycle in the offing, Crawford's chances of a box-office success would be greatly enhanced by casting her in this type of picture; and of course, a successful vehicle for Crawford could only be to his credit.

At Mayer's request, Selznick put *Dancing Lady* on his schedule to go into production in early June, with Considine as associate producer. Crawford was still not enthusiastic, thinking the script could not be improved much, but since it had all been done at Mayer's instigation in response to her pleadings, she said little and adopted a watchful attitude. Selznick was well aware of her reluctance, as Allen Rivkin relates: "We were having conferences in David's office, and Crawford was there to go over the script for the first time; she was a little loath to play it, we all knew that, so David throws a curve at her, he says, 'Joan, I don't know if you can play this part, it's kind of tarty. I think it's more Jean Harlow's style.' Well, Joan kind of bristles at this and she says, 'Look, Mr. Selznick, I was playing hookers before Harlow knew what they were, so let's not hear any talk about style because I know more about that than she ever will.' Well, we all broke apart, and she decided that she'd do it."

Selznick put the costume design for the picture into the hands of Gilbert Adrian Rosenberg, known simply as Adrian and probably the most famous of all designers then working in Hollywood. A native of Connecticut, he was the product of various U.S. art schools and of formal training at the Paris branch of the Parsons School of Applied Arts. At MGM, Adrian had first attracted fashion attention with his design for a hat worn by Greta Garbo in *Romance* (1930). This Empress Eugénie style, worn angled over one eye, made such an impression that it dominated the tops of women's heads for the next decade. But it was for Joan Crawford in the 1932 *Letty Lynton* that Adrian had made a dramatic impact on the emerging fashion consciousness of the American woman. Crawford was difficult to dress, being big-hipped and broad-shouldered. Rather than try to minimize her shoulders as other designers had done,

Adrian, with padding and puffed sleeves, emphasized them, creating a look that was immediately picked up by women everywhere, and like the Eugénie hat before, would reign supreme throughout most of the thirties and well into the forties. Adrian once remarked, "I never thought my career would rest on Joan Crawford's shoulders." Selznick gave Adrian pretty much of a free hand on *Dancing Lady,* as long as Crawford was happy with his designs.

To direct, Selznick and Considine chose the veteran Robert Z. Leonard, whose reputation for quietly turning out respectable, moneymaking pictures on time with a minimum of fuss had impressed them. Leonard's fairly bloodless approach to directing lent itself perfectly to the MGM style of doing things as efficiently and as lavishly as possible. He believed implicitly in the autonomy of each department, never interfering, never demanding, preferring to concentrate on the performance and the physical blocking, leaving the visuals in the hands of his cameraman and art director.

Production meetings went on in Selznick's offices, and were now joined by art director Merrill Pye, who would be responsible, along with the director and cameraman, for the overall look and feel of the picture, his forty-eighth for MGM. Pye too had seen *42nd Street* and felt, as did Selznick, that the picture was lacking glamour and lavishness, two ingredients they both believed were absolutely necessary for the success of *Dancing Lady.* Pye subscribed to the theories of Robert Mallet-Stevens, the French architect/designer who is credited with laying down the rules governing the use of modern architecture: "Smooth surfaces, crisp articulation, clean curves, polished materials, right angles; clarity, order." Pye's attraction to clean curves and crisp articulation was, however, tempered by his love of theatricality. This tasteful and imaginative blending of these two influences was immediately apparent in the sketches for *Dancing Lady* that he began submitting for Selznick's approval. The settings for the earlier part of the story were realistic without being gritty; almost stylized, making their impact through a dramatic use of contrasting areas of light and shadow on flat, neutral surfaces. For the later sections of the tale, Pye created a series of glossy, streamlined designs that typified what was just coming to be called Moderne. Devoid of all ornamentation, Moderne impressed aesthetically because of its clean, direct, flowing lines. It was a look that was at once luxurious, spare, functional, and pleasing in its simplicity; a look that was to be embraced wholeheartedly by a nation subconsciously demanding change from the literally bankrupt past. Within the space of half a decade, Moderne changed the shape of virtually everything in the American home, including the home itself—and at MGM, Merrill Pye was one of its earliest and most influential advocates. As art director, he would be able to introduce this new style to the approximately 40 million Americans who went to the movies each week in 1933.

In early June, Selznick began to search for the songs the picture needed. The script had spots for six songs, three of which would be full-scale production numbers, including the title song, one torchy love song to be sung by Crawford, and one incidental song that would be used in the opening sequences. In the script, the director of the stage show keeps insisting to his writers and composers that he wants something with jazz, something up to date for the big production number. This would be the finale of the film as well as the number in the show that makes Janie Barlow a star and the show a success. What Selznick wanted for this was a song that would be an immediate hit and would also lend itself to a lavish production number. Richard Rodgers and Lorenz Hart had just been signed to a year's contract at MGM, and Selznick asked them to write a song for *Dancing Lady.* After laboring for several days, the two men came up with a thirty-two-bar effusion called "That's the Rhythm of the Day." The song was received enthusiastically at first hearing, with Selznick telling Rodgers, "It's just what we need for the finale," but the next day Selznick evidently had second thoughts, because according to Richard Rodgers he called the composer to ask, "Could you make it a little better?" To Selznick, it was not an unusual request; writing was writing, whether it was dialogue or music, and if one could be improved by rewriting, why not the other? Rodgers explained to Selznick that songs could not be "made a little better," they were either good or bad, and had to be taken as they were, but could not be "fixed up." They would be happy to write another song, but there

A camera rehearsal on the set of *Dancing Lady*. Cinematographer Oliver T. Marsh, photographing his seventh Joan Crawford film, is at the upper left in the sweater and slacks, sizing up Fred Astaire, Crawford, and Clark Gable. Director Robert Z. Leonard is in the camp chair at the right, and dance director Sammy Lee is in the light sweater below and to the right of Leonard. In the upper left section of the photograph, grouped around the piano, are Ted Healy and his Stooges, Moe Howard, Jerry Howard, and Larry Fine, three of MGM's lesser contributions to the concept of "Art for the sake of Art."

wasn't much they could do to improve an already existing entity. A bit nonplussed, Selznick thanked him and told him there was no problem; the song would be used as it was. However, Selznick confided to Allen Rivkin that he considered the song "monotonous" and had reluctantly decided not to ask Rodgers and Hart for other contributions to the score.

Still needed were the additional production numbers for the actual on-stage play and the "torchy ballad" for Crawford. One night during this pre-production phase, Rivkin was at a party at the home of Leonard Spiegelgass, then a story editor for Fox. At the piano, noodling out various things, was a young composer named Burton Lane. Late in the evening, he played a song that he and his lyricist partner Harold Adamson had just written, a slow, sensuous, romantic ballad they called "Everything I Have Is Yours." The next day, Rivkin told Selznick, who called the two young men in, heard the song, and agreed with Rivkin that it was exactly right for the film. He liked it so much that he asked Lane and Adamson if they had anything else that might be suitable for the two missing production numbers. They came up with two songs, one called "Let's Go Bavarian" and the other "Heigh-Ho, the Gang's All Here." To properly showcase these songs, Selznick counted on Lou Silvers of the music department, who had supervised the score to the very first musical, Warner Bros.' *The Jazz Singer*. It was Silvers who pointed out to Selznick that because of Crawford's limited vocal range it would be impossible for her to sing "Everything I Have Is Yours" as had been planned. This necessitated a last-minute script change so that the song was now sung by a male singer at a penthouse party, with Crawford dancing by and humming a two-bar break in the lyric. This way it could still be said that she "sang" the song in the publicity for the film.

Now that the musical aspects of the production were under way, Selznick turned his attention to the all-important business of casting the two male leads opposite Crawford. For the part of Tod Hunter, the Long Island millionaire, Selznick wanted Robert Montgomery; but he would not be available until after the film had gone into production, so at Crawford's urging, he cast Franchot Tone, with whom Crawford was reportedly romantically involved at the time. For Patch Gallagher, Crawford wanted Clark Gable, and Selznick agreed with her, remembering that the combination of the two had proved to be a potent attraction in three films: 1931's *Laughing Sinners*, *Possessed*, and *Dance, Fools, Dance*. During production of *Possessed*, the two were rumored to have indulged in a somewhat torrid romance, but pressure from Mayer and Gable's wife, the socialite Rhea Langham, a wealthy older woman, soon brought the affair to an end. Crawford, however, still had a "case on Gable," as she later admitted. Coupled with this was her shrewd realization that she and Gable were good box office, and she was determined to have him in the film. Gable, however, had other ideas. His unease about Selznick was deepening. Selznick's forcing him into a role he felt unsuited for in *Night Flight* did not help, and Selznick's personality irked Gable. His almost arrogant self-assurance, his riding rough-shod over people until he got his own way, his manner of speaking, with the theatrical use of the word "darling" when addressing women, his pursuit and cultivation of the rich and famous, his easy charm and soft lifestyle, all of these irritated the probably envious Gable to the point where his distrust of Selznick became active dislike. At first, he refused point-blank to do *Dancing Lady*, feeling that the part of Patch Gallagher was nothing he had anything in common with. Gallagher was a man who could discuss period costumes, dance routines, musical styles, things that Gable, ignoring his own theatrical background, complained he had no interest in or knowledge of. As far as he was concerned, from an actor's standpoint, the character went nowhere and did nothing, being subservient in every way to the leading lady. But after Crawford pleaded with him, and Mayer and Selznick tactfully pressured him, he reluctantly gave in, having again been promised a vacation following the film's completion.

An example of matte work in action. (Top) The Bavarian beer garden set as photographed on stage. (Middle) The matte painting, done on large cardboard sheets; the irregular bottom outline of the painting has been specially drawn to match precisely the trees and foliage of the original set. (Bottom) The scene after the two elements were combined in the laboratory.

With Gable definitely set, the film was scheduled to begin photography on Monday, June 10. Production work now began in earnest as the film moved out of the offices and onto the stages. By 7:00 A.M. that day, Crawford was in the makeup department where her hair was washed, given a henna rinse to make it darker and more manageable, and then combed into an attractive softer style, with a part on one side. At 9:15, she was on the set, going over her lines, movements, and reactions for the first scene to be photographed, that of Janie and her fellow strippers being hauled in front of a judge for giving a supposedly obscene performance. Wrapped in a blanket that covered what was left of her stripper's costume, Crawford defiantly made a speech to the judge, defending her dancing as the only thing she knew how to do, insisting that she was hungry and took the job of stripper because it was the only dancing work she could find. Crawford liked to think of herself as a dancer, but everything she did other than ballroom dancing looked exactly like a variation of the Charleston. Her dancing always came off as graceless and studied, and in the case of her supposed "audition" number for Gable, her flailing arms and stomping feet made her look even more ungainly.

Gable was due to join the company on June 12, after a quick three-day hunting trip. However, the night before he was to report for work, he was running a high temperature, and he remained under a doctor's care for several days; his teeth and gums had become infected, causing a toxic condition in his body. By the 13th, it looked serious enough for his doctors to suggest that he might be out for three or four months. The value of the Crawford and Gable pairing made Selznick loath to rush into any panic replacement casting; he gambled on a quicker recovery. Gable's doctors sent him off for a two-week rest while he was treated for infection. Production was progressing, the rushes looked good; Selznick decided to postpone any decision until after the Fourth of July holidays. Instead, he concentrated his efforts on trying to obtain a good dancer, or, he hoped, a big name, to dance with Crawford in the finale. Fred Astaire had been signed by RKO, but he had not yet made a picture for them; even though Selznick's relations were still cordial with everyone at RKO, he didn't think they'd let a new star (they hoped) of their own make his debut in another studio's film. But Astaire's contract didn't start until August 1; there still might be time to persuade him to come to Hollywood to do a few days' work in *Dancing Lady.*

After a week of negotiations, an agreement was reached for Astaire to report to the studio on July 15 to work for two weeks. He would play himself, and it was understood that he would be given star status and would be able to do his own dance direction. Astaire and his sister Adele had just broken up their very successful stage career, Adele to marry into the English aristocracy, leaving Fred to carry on as a single. Astaire, in his own words, was "getting nervous about the stage" and "looking for a change and a chance to prove something brand-new" for himself professionally. Now, at Selznick's urging, he would be making his film debut in the best of company: MGM, Gable, Crawford, Rodgers and Hart. These were the inducements that Selznick dangled; Astaire couldn't refuse them. His new show, *The Gay Divorce,* had closed at the beginning of the summer and Astaire was to be married on July 12. He and his future wife were prevailed upon to take their honeymoon in California at the studio's expense. Immediately after the wedding, the Astaires flew to the West Coast in one of the new Ford Tri-Motor passenger planes, which seated eighteen people, traveled 150 miles an hour, and took twenty-six hours and six stopovers to arrive in Los Angeles.

Dancing in films at that time was still in the grip of the Broadway stage show style, largely variations of the old, military formation, rigidly controlled jazz-tap format, where a precision group of high steppers would go through a series of routines based on simple movements in time to the music. When it came time to film this type of show in the early days of sound, the camera, immobilized as it was, usually photographed the dances head-on, with occasional cuts to different angles, making for a very static presentation of what might have been exciting on stage. It was Busby Berkeley who instinctively rebelled against this, and began to break up his cinematic dance numbers with visual dynamics, giving his work a pace, vitality, and imagination that only partially derived from the dancing. The other studios tried to copy his style, but the people they hired to do it just didn't understand what Berkeley was

up to. Selznick didn't, and neither did dance director Sammy Lee; what they saw was dancing chorus girls, lavish settings, and lots of stunning effects. None of them saw the design behind it, or if they did, they didn't care. So with *Dancing Lady,* work went ahead on the dance numbers with a minimum of imagination and a maximum of expense and gloss. While all of this was being prepared, Lee and Merrill Pye began staging Astaire's and Crawford's numbers. This was fairly easy, as the routines were simple and the sets not complicated. What was complicating things was the fact that *Dancing Lady* still did not have a leading man. In the script, Gable's character was supposed to introduce Crawford to Fred Astaire; whoever was going to play the part would have to be cast no later than July 30, as that was the last day Astaire would be able to film.

In consultation with Gable's doctors, it was decided that Gable would come into the studio for two hours on July 30 and film his scene with Astaire and Crawford, then the production would continue to shoot around him until he was well enough to return. Gable did this, but on returning home from the studio, he was stricken with appendicitis and was rushed to Cedars of Lebanon Hospital, where he underwent an emergency operation. This put an entirely different perspective on the solution to his *Dancing Lady* role. If Selznick still wanted to wait for Gable, it would mean closing down the production until he was ready; a serious decision, rarely taken at MGM or any of the studios. Selznick put the matter up to Mayer, who, after conferring with MGM president Nicholas Schenck in New York, gave Selznick the okay to close down. In Schenck's words, it was "too important to Crawford's future that we have a fine picture and have Gable with her." Now that the decision had been made, there was nothing to do except film everything they could and then wait.

On August 25, production on *Dancing Lady* was suspended indefinitely, with the hope that it would not be more than two weeks. Gable and his doctors were now under some pressure themselves; it was no easy knowledge realizing that you were holding up a big-budget picture. Besides, Gable had been suspended without pay since June 20, a situation intolerable to his frugal nature. With his doctors' reluctant consent, he returned to the studio on August 29, ready to work. But this proved too much for him; after half a day his strength gave out and his doctors ordered him home, where it was determined that he would have to have complete rest for at least another week. Once again, the film went into hiatus. For Crawford, whose energy was at full steam when making a film, the situation was frustrating. She too was anxious to finish, knowing what it would mean to miss a Christmas release. She was as aware as any of the executives of the importance of good timing in the release of a film—probably even more since she had much more at stake. She threw herself into every related activity she could find: posing for stills, attending conferences for her next pictures.

By mid-August, "Everything I Have Is Yours" was already a hit on the radio and in record shops, giving the picture some welcome advance publicity. Based on Selznick's assurances that it would be ready in time, the sales department booked the film into New York and other large cities for the lucrative Christmas trade. Now the pressure was on to get it finished. Finally, on September 8, Gable, fully recovered, went to work with Crawford, Tone, Robert Benchley, and the rest of the cast, who had been idle for more than thirteen days. Everyone worked smoothly and efficiently at their jobs, and on October 20, the last take was made, a medium close two-shot of Gable and Crawford in their one and only kiss in the film; coincidentally, it was also the last scene. *Dancing Lady* had been in production sixty-five shooting days, fifteen days over schedule, and its "cost to complete" rounded out at $923,000.

Four days after the last shot had been taken, the film was put into final enough form for a preview to be held. Rather than go all the way out of town, as was usually the procedure, Selznick decided to hold the preview at the Fox Theatre on Wilshire Boulevard near La Cienega, in the middle of the new "Miracle Mile" business district. The theatre had been picked because it was playing a musical, Paramount's *Too Much Harmony,* starring Bing Crosby, so the crowd would be receptive.

Clark Gable and Joan Crawford in their one and only love scene in the picture, the fadeout clinch.

(Top) *Meet the Baron,* written by Herman Mankiewicz and Norman Krasna and directed by Walter Lang, was, in Selznick's own words, "a horror that I made . . . starring Jack Pearl. . . . MGM had decided to capitalize on the popularity of radio stars and Pearl was one of the biggest of the time. . . . I have never been a devotee of radio comics and only made the picture as a personal favor to Harry Rapf, who had given me my first job at MGM. I made the picture with a loathing for it and it was a terrible flop. . . . I learned then never to tackle a subject . . . for which I had not a personal liking." Pearl is in front, Jimmy Durante is behind him. The still gives no indication of the abysmal lack of humor in the film.
(Above) Helen Hayes, wife of playwright Charles MacArthur and the new first lady of the American theatre; she had been a star at MGM since her appearance in *The Sin of Madelon Claudet* (1932). Here, two years later, she is starring with Robert Montgomery in Selznick's production of Hugh Walpole's novel *Vanessa.* According to Selznick: "I took it over after the resignation of Walter Wanger . . . after working on the script . . . I realized that its production would be a complete mistake . . . whatever punch there was in the story had been deleted by the Hays office . . . but I was told to go ahead with it and not to worry about it." Hugh Walpole worked on the adaptation along with Lenore Coffee, and William K. Howard directed. The picture was such a fiasco that it halted Helen Hayes's screen career for the next twenty-two years.

To make sure of a full house in the middle of the week, the manager turned on his "preview beacon" located in the 70-foot-tall tower of the theatre. This flashed in a slow circular motion over the flatlands of central Los Angeles, letting everyone know that there would be an unannounced feature that night, and by 8:30 the two-thousand-seat theatre was nearly full. The picture was greeted with applause as the cast and credits came on the screen, and to Selznick's great relief and satisfaction, it played with very few slow spots or other bumps. The preview cards all generally praised the film. Several people commented on how much they liked the dancer who appeared with Miss Crawford. Gable had not come off well in the cards; people found him too "skinny looking" and "surly," and "How come he only kissed her once?" Selznick also had noticed how worn and drawn Gable looked in some of the close shots that had been taken the day he collapsed. The day after the preview he ordered him back to the studio for a day of retakes of those particular scenes.

After its running time was shortened by ten minutes, the film was ready to be shipped to New York for its scheduled December 1, 1933, opening at the Capitol Theatre, the first stop on its tour of the 135 theatres throughout the country controlled by Loew's, Inc. Helped along by word of mouth and good notices, not to mention the heightened air of optimism in the first winter of Roosevelt's administration, the film was exactly the kind of smash that everyone wanted it to be, bringing in a $744,000 profit over and above its cost. Selznick was happy; he had two hits to his credit, this and *Dinner at Eight.* Crawford was happy; she had only wanted one big hit and now she had it. She would end up staying at MGM for the next ten years. The sales department was happy; in fact, for about fifteen years afterward, *Dancing Lady* was used by the Loew's sales force as a barometer in measuring the "100% commercial picture." Even Mayer was happy; his faith in his son-in-law was once again vindicated for all to see, and one of his biggest stars had been saved by virtue of his and Selznick's efforts. The only irritant at this point in Mayer's life was Clark Gable, but he solved that by lending out the delinquent actor to do a picture on poverty row at Columbia. Gable, he felt, would be only too happy to come back to the security and comfort of MGM after the harassment and indignity of making a quickie like *It Happened One Night.*

Prior to all this success, however, back in early November before the film had opened, Selznick and Thalberg had moved into their new quarters in the matching bungalows that had been built for them behind the main building. Thalberg's side was quiet, restful, done in Early American; Selznick's half was starkly modern, all functional and up to date. It also housed the writers working on Selznick's pictures, including Ben Hecht and his partner, playwright Charles MacArthur, who in addition to their other talents, were rowdy, iconoclastic, and inveterate leg-pullers.

According to legend, Selznick and Thalberg were having Mayer over to visit on the afternoon of their first day in the new building. Selznick had entreated both Hecht and MacArthur not to be loafing when he brought Mayer around—they should please act industrious, give the impression of serious labor for his, Selznick's, sake. At the appointed time, when Selznick opened the door of their office and ushered Mayer in, the two men were deeply engrossed in their work. MacArthur was busily pacing the room, intent in thought, while Hecht was giving dictation to a completely nude secretary who was nonchalantly filing her nails. Hecht looked up at the entry of Mayer and Selznick, greeted them both, then went back to his chores. The secretary never wavered from her task. Mayer's face betrayed his surprise and ultimately his outrage. Not saying a word, he turned, glared at Selznick, and immediately left the building. The next day, November 10, the trade papers carried an item which told that Hecht and MacArthur had been relieved of their secretary, "who was receiving $30.00 a week for taking no dictation, answering no calls and making no appointments, a situation which was unfair to the other clerical personnel."

Considerably buoyed by the anticipated success of *Dancing Lady,* Selznick strode confidently into *Viva Villa!* By late September, the script that he and Hecht had prepared was so long that serious consideration was given to making the picture in two parts, detailing Villa's rise in the first half and tracing his downfall through the second. It was, everyone at

1934—And to the sales department, almost nothing was sacred.

MGM's trade ads prepared specifically for industry publications were much superior to their theatre and billboard advertising. This announcement ad for *Viva Villa!* is obvious but striking, and manages to impress with its strong use of bold colors, stylizations, and the somewhat bizarre juxtaposition of the lady and the sombrero.

MGM conceded, a novel stunt, but after toying with the idea for some weeks, it was decided to make one film tell the whole story.

Howard Hawks, a rugged, taciturn young director at home with simple action, was assigned to direct. On October 10, 1933, he led a caravan of some twenty trucks into the wilds of Mexico to film the early sequences of Villa's first notoriety. The plan was to set all exterior scenes in real locations all over Mexico, and to use the Mexican Army and peasants as extras in the large-scale battle scenes, which would be photographed against the spectacular beauty of the Mexican landscape. All of this had to be carefully coordinated with the Mexican government, with special attention being paid to local customs and sensibilities. After the bulk of these scenes had been completed, Wallace Beery joined the troupe on October 20, and a week later the company was joined by Lee Tracy, the fast-talking, nasal-voiced New York stage actor. Tracy's forte was delivering glib dialogue in a nonstop, high-pressure manner, which was pretty much a reflection of the man himself. He was an extremely colorful talker, with a pugnacious attitude, especially when drinking, which he did with great regularity. In fact, Tracy was one of the great lushes of the time, along with John Barrymore, Gene Fowler, and W. C.

Fields. He had come across very well in both *Dinner at Eight* and *Bombshell* with Jean Harlow; in *Viva Villa!* he would be playing the part of the cynical, wisecracking American reporter who forges Villa's image in the newspapers and newsreels, and is with him to the end, even composing Villa's death speech for him. After Tracy's arrival, the company filmed for the better part of the next month, moving all over Mexico, a country that was a publicity man's nightmare, as described by unit man Don Eddy: "This country has absolutely no semblance of modern news coverage; it's days before news gets from one city to the next; the AP and UP wire services are in El Paso and Brownsville; telephone service is next to nonexistent." Living conditions were almost as primitive as the communication system. The company was living in a train with a kitchen coach attached; the cook was Mexican and, of course, so was the food, which was just terrible. The grind and the inconvenience were getting to Wallace Beery, who began leaving the location early as often as he could and flying his own plane to El Paso, where he would stay the night. Tracy and the others couldn't go out at night, as cinematographer James Wong Howe recalled, "because there were bandits, so we had to sit in the train and play cards or chew the

149

rag." In the last three weeks of shooting, Hawks was directing the huge masses of extras in the spectacular battle scenes at Chihuahua and Parral, and photographing a complicated sequence showing the training of Villa's army. Through these weeks, the making of *Viva Villa!* had become a subject of intense political debate in Mexico, with one newspaper, the rabidly anti-government *El Universal,* branding the picture an insult to the country, claiming that Villa was being caricatured, and insisting the government kick MGM out. "It was," in the words of Don Eddy, "page-one stuff every day. We were sitting on a powder keg."

In Mexico, Sunday, November 19, was a national holiday; the entire country celebrated the revolution, and most of the *Viva Villa!* troupe, which had moved to Mexico City, joined in the festivities, only too glad to let loose after the weeks away from civilization. The powder keg that Don Eddy referred to was ignited a little after noon on the Sunday of the parade. "I was having lunch downstairs in our hotel," related Eddy,

when one of the lads from the Associated Press came rushing in and said Lee Tracy was standing on the balcony overlooking the Avenida Juarez, the main drag, absolutely naked, shouting obscenities and making bawdy gestures at the crowds who were out to see this miles-long parade. I got there just in time to see him urinating on the cadets from Chapultepec, the West Point boys of Mexico. The crowds in the street were in an uproar and the cadets were on the verge of coming after Tracy en masse. By the time I got to his room, he had just thrown out the first cop who went after him and then suddenly every cop in Mexico began to arrive. We were holding all these cops in the hall,

they all wanted to beat Lee to a pulp. By this time Lee had passed out cold in his room, which was a blessing as we were able to convince them that he couldn't be moved.

The next morning Tracy was arrested and thrown into jail, while Eddy worked feverishly trying to get him released and out of the country before matters got any worse. An appeal to the U.S. Embassy resulted in Tracy's being released by noon, and Eddy had him packed and ready to leave on the 8:15 train to El Paso, but at 7:00 P.M. he was rearrested. Carlos Novarro, pulling some political strings through his numerous relatives, managed to get the actor sprung once more. Tracy then promptly disappeared. Don Eddy found him in a barroom, regaling some newspapermen with an account of his activities. Eddy appealed to the men not to file any stories over their wire services until he got Tracy out of the country. At 6:30 the next morning, Tracy was bundled into a specially chartered three-seater airplane, which took off hastily in the direction of Texas.

At the studio, word of Tracy's escapade was received over the wire services, together with the devastating news that a plane loaded with the negative for the last three weeks' work had crashed and burned outside of El Paso. Selznick, Strickling, and production manager J. J. Cohn met in an emergency session to discuss the best way to handle the Tracy episode and try to assess the damage from the plane crash. All of the material had to be refilmed, and most, if not all, featured Tracy in some way. Most of the equipment and props had been packed and was on a train back to the United States. Cohn called Frank Messenger, the pro-

Henry B. Walthall had been the star of D. W. Griffith's 1915 epic, *The Birth of a Nation,* on which *Viva Villa!* was obviously patterned. Slavko Vorkapich had come from RKO with Selznick, and his unique ideas and theories on motion and image gave vitality and imagination to many of MGM's pictures. James Wong Howe evidently had a sense of humor, as seen by his credit shot. Herbert Stothart was in charge of MGM's

music department for close to twenty years. His scoring was, with few exceptions, one of the least impressive aspects of MGM films, the music being a gooey pastiche of musical fragments and filler that meandered through the films, with none of the pace, vitality, and excitement of the scores that Warner Bros. and RKO films possessed.

duction manager in Mexico City, and told him to have the train brought back, that the material would be re-shot in Mexico. As for Tracy, Selznick drafted a statement to go out over Mayer's signature, which was designed to calm, as much as possible, the unruly atmosphere in Mexico City. Addressing it as a telegram to the president of Mexico, Mayer apologized "for the wretched conduct of one of [MGM's] employees . . . and for the insult offered by this actor to the Mexican Cadet Corps. The Metro-Goldwyn-Mayer organization is as shocked and embarrassed by this episode as are the Mexican people against whom the indignity was visited. As a result of Mr. Tracy's behavior, MGM has removed him not only from the film *Viva Villa!* but has dismissed him entirely from its employ and has cancelled his long-term contract."

In Hollywood, the news of the incident was the subject of some amusement, but out in Culver City the atmosphere was anything but humorous as the extent of the damage became apparent. More than half the picture would have to be put back into work, requiring at least another two months. This necessitated almost completely recasting the picture, as most of the actors had other commitments. For Tracy's role Selznick settled on Stuart Erwin, a bumbling comedian who didn't have the cynical bite that the part needed. The aristocratic Mexican girl whom Villa brutalizes in the story had been played by Mona Maris; she was now replaced by Fay Wray. Director Howard Hawks abruptly quit the production and was replaced by veteran action director Jack Conway, who began filming from scratch in the mountains around Chatsworth 50 miles outside Los Angeles. A second unit had been left in Mexico under the direction of Richard Rosson, and they continued working all through the winter right into March of 1934, tempting fate on their last day by filming another parade, this time of 1,400 troops from the Military Academy. While all this was going on without incident, Selznick and Hecht were engaged in transcontinental rewrites of portions of the script, including retakes on thirty of the script's sixty-odd scenes. Hecht had gone back to his home in Nyack, New York, and his correspondence with Selznick at this point is revealing of the way the two men worked. Referring to a poignantly written scene showing the death of a bugle boy, Hecht remonstrated:

> If you shoot this like some 1890 death scene on the battlefield with the army stopping and everybody making faces, you are all wrong. The boy should be shot while blowing the bugle. . . . Villa picks him up and slings him across his saddle while the boy dies, but the charge must never cease. Villa must continue riding. This scene will be effective as hell if you take a little time and do it my way instead of turning it into some idiotic Tableau Vivant like the white powdered human statue in the Ringling Circus.

The cost of *Viva Villa!* had now risen close to the million-dollar mark; caution had to be exercised with the final cutting of the film to make it acceptable to all the factions in Mexico, as the rentals to be taken out of that country could make the difference between profit and loss. Most of the demands of the government had been met, but now suddenly in early March 1934, as the picture was being readied for the lab, Mrs. Villa, Pancho's widow, was heard from. Or rather, a lawyer and the newspapers were heard from, announcing that Mrs. Villa was greatly displeased with what she had heard about the film—namely, that her husband was pictured as a groveling brute. Selznick promptly offered to bring her to California to see the picture, promising to change anything that she found offensive. In the first week of May, Mrs. Villa, a charming, well-educated, middle-aged woman, was suddenly the focus of much solicitude and attention as the studio gave her a tour, lunch in the commissary, and a screening of *Viva Villa!*, after which an interpreter voiced her reservations to Selznick, who acted on them. That final hurdle cleared, the picture was shown to the trade press, then given an expensive road show presentation in New York at the Criterion Theatre, where it received uniformly good reviews, with, as Selznick anticipated, many comments about its brutality and violence. The MGM sales force squeezed every cent it could get from the theatres around the country in the next year, returning the picture's cost and a modest profit of $80,000. About this, Selznick defensively pointed out in a letter to Nicholas Schenck, ". . . Cost high, due to the gods and Mexico. Can you point to Beery success, before or since, without a co-star?" (As for Lee Tracy, after

being let go by MGM he was signed by 20th Century Pictures and cast as a cynical newspaper columnist in *Advice to the Lovelorn,* a loose adaptation of Nathanael West's novel *Miss Lonelyhearts;* thereafter, his film career never regained its momentum, although he did work sporadically throughout the next two decades, finally coming into his own as an actor in the 1960s in the play and the movie of Gore Vidal's *The Best Man.*)

The release of *Viva Villa!* in April 1934 marked Selznick's first anniversary with MGM; his position in the studio and in the industry had brought him a measure of personal satisfaction. The critical recognition he was receiving, and the fact that the name Selznick once again stood for a kind of specific and intelligent quality, made him slightly edgy, chafing under what he called "the easy life, and a very high-priced mess of pottage." Voicing his dissatisfaction in a letter to Nicholas Schenck, Selznick felt that he had

> matured considerably, and with this . . . has come an acceptance . . . that has made me into a completely different person . . . a person that I do not like very much. . . . I want very much to get back to the ambitious, vital and even erratic, but at least free person that I was. True, I am free from financial worry and have the liberty of expression in making pictures and doing things in a fine way which I undoubtedly would not have to the same extent elsewhere . . . the salary I am making is futile in the face of my definite and unshakeable philosophy that money may abet happiness, but under no circumstances can it be the source of it.

The source of Selznick's dissatisfaction was his sublimated desire to be independent; to be, as he put it, "absolute master of my instincts, my whims, my occasional desire to loaf, and especially to be master of my time and my destiny."

As he pointed out, though, he couldn't have had it better, not even on his own. In early 1934, MGM, and indeed the rest of the country, was starting the long steady climb upward out of the depths of the depression, and MGM itself was entering an era of munificence that amazed Selznick. It was the one studio in Hollywood that operated without stringent production budgets. To Selznick, who had been trained to work on a budget, to respect budgets, and who prided himself on keeping within budgets, this absence of fiscal restraint was shocking. But Mayer's and Thalberg's philosophy was to spend as much as necessary to do it right. This lordly disregard for money was one of the things that made picturemaking at MGM such an obsession with the people who worked there during its years of greatness. The feeling that pervaded the studio was that MGM was absolutely the best, and at the midway point in his contract, even Selznick had become an avid booster of the studio, commenting in a letter to Schenck that

> we are in splendid shape, we're quite well off on story material and on completed scripts and the organization of the studio is functioning amazingly well, although I have not changed my conviction that a single centralized production head having a dictatorship over all the production and editorial activities of the studio is the soundest plan of operation. No system of dual or triple control can . . . be very effective in the elimination of waste and the reduction of costs.

MGM's costs were now averaging about $400,000 per picture, but it had the best sales force in the business, and its pictures were always sold at terms considerably higher than the industry average. Concern for its image as "The Friendly Company" caused MGM to be more than fair with exhibitors outside its own theatre chain; if a picture did less than anticipated, the company would adjust the terms of the contract, keeping everybody happy. To maintain its reputation as a purveyor of quality merchandise, each of its forty-two United States film exchanges was sent, along with the prints of the films, a detailed "cutting synopsis" that had each scene numbered in order and broken down into footage measurements, so that if any part of a print was damaged, replacement sections could be ordered from the studio lab in Culver City. This concern for quality all along the line, for the insistence on a certain standard of excellence, had by 1934 made MGM the undisputed leader of the industry, the only company that had never missed paying a dividend on its stock, even during the worst of the depression.

An elaborate banquet set by art director Harry Oliver, with set decoration by Edwin Willis, giving some idea of the range of items that had to be available on a day's notice from the prop, casting, and "greens" departments, the set and construction depart-

ments, and of course the costume department. Director Jack Conway, wearing the light hat, is in front of the camera, and thirty-four-year-old cinematographer James Wong Howe, in the vest, is seated behind the camera.

In the aftermath of the Lee Tracy incident, Fay Wray replaced Mona Maris as the wealthy Spanish aristocrat who is the recipient of some of Pancho Villa's more unwelcome attention, including, originally, a shadowy but vocal flogging. This scene and several others depicting Villa as a drunken, brawling coward caused considerable controversy in Mexican political circles, finally gaining the attention of Villa's widow. At

Selznick's invitation she journeyed to Culver City, looked at the film, and requested that some scenes be altered to conform with the historical fact of Villa being a teetotaler, while others showing some of his more outrageous bits of invented boorishness were deleted outright, including the flogging.

153

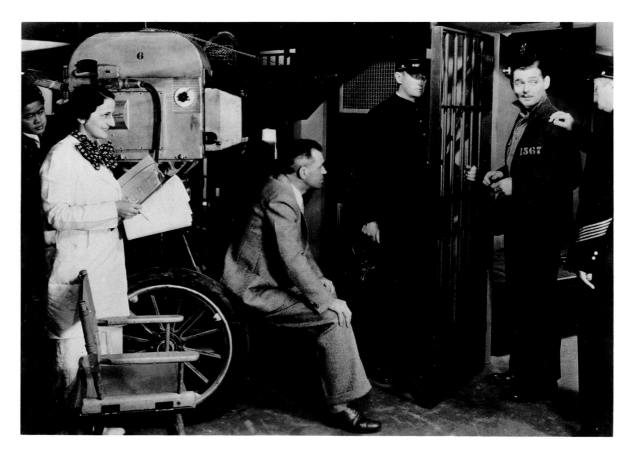

Arthur Caesar wrote a story called "East Side" about two childhood chums who grow up on opposite sides of the law. Oliver Garrett, Rowland Brown, Joseph Mankiewicz, and Pete Smith rewrote the story into *Manhattan Melodrama*, which achieved a degree of fame chiefly because of its inadvertent involvement in the death of the notorious John Dillinger, who was gunned down upon leaving the Biograph Theatre in Chicago, where he had furtively viewed the film. Directed by Selznick's first collaborator, W. S. Van Dyke, the picture had been made by MGM as a Cosmopolitan Production, which was William Randolph Hearst's company; after the notoriety of the Dillinger affair, Hearst gave orders that all references and credits to the picture being a Cosmopolitan Production be deleted. Arthur Caesar won an Academy Award for his original story. The picture marked the debut of Mickey Rooney as an MGM contract player: Selznick had seen the thirteen-year-old show biz veteran playing Ping-Pong at a party, and was impressed enough to cast him as the young version of the Gable character.

Shirley Ross in *Manhattan Melodrama* singing "The Bad in Every Man" by Richard Rodgers and Lorenz Hart. The song achieved no popularity until Hart changed the lyrics and the title to "Blue Moon" five years later. The lighting and photography are by James Wong Howe, and the costume is by Dolly Tree. The setting, MGM's idea of the Cotton Club in Harlem, is by Joseph Wright.

Reckless started life as an original story by David Selznick (under the pseudonym Oliver Jeffries) and Victor Fleming titled "A Woman Called Cheap." Arthur Sheekman did a screenplay that was planned to star Joan Crawford in a follow-up to the successful *Dancing Lady*. The story dealt with a famous Broadway star whose husband commits suicide; the plot was based on the recent Libby Holman–Smith Reynolds case. Either Mayer or Schenck decided to replace Crawford with Jean Harlow, much against Selznick's wishes, because of the recent parallels in Harlow's own life. (Above, right) Harlow is seen here with Jerome Kern, who composed one of the songs for the picture, and director Victor Fleming. Harlow couldn't sing so her voice was dubbed. The costume is by Adrian and the setting by Merrill Pye. Harlow and her co-star William Powell later became romantically involved and were on the verge of marrying when she died suddenly in 1937. (Right) A production scene from *Reckless.* Victor Fleming is seated, leaning back, near the edge of the platform; cinematographer George Folsey is wearing the white visor. The large hornlike object in the bottom center was used for music playback purposes.

"I HAVE IN MY HEART OF HEARTS A FAVORITE CHILD...HIS NAME IS DAVID COPPERFIELD"

Preface to the year 1850 Edition of David Copperfield, by the author CHARLES DICKENS.

Reprinted from N. Y. Times July 12, 1934.

NOTED PICTURE FOLK

David O. Selznick, Metro-Goldwyn-Mayer producer, will arrive in New York today on the Ile de France, accompanied by the staff which has been working on "David Copperfield" in England. Hugh Walpole, the British novelist, who was engaged abroad to assist in the adaptation of the Dickens novel, is a member of the party.

Blunderstone Rookery, where David was born. Just one of many beloved landmarks that come to life on the screen.

M-G-M Production Staff in England inspects *Aunt Betsey Trotwood's* cottage, faithfully reproduced in every detail on the screen.

"David Copperfield" Produced by METRO-GOLDWYN-MAYER will be the Most Memorable Motion Picture Event of 1935.

David O. Selznick, Metro-Goldwyn-Mayer producer, accompanied by *George Cukor* and *Hugh Walpole,* arrives in New York after months of research on "David Copperfield" in England.

The publicity department sent this announcement booklet to every newspaper and magazine in the country.

In November 1933, RKO had released the Merian Cooper/George Cukor production of *Little Women* with Katharine Hepburn, which had turned into a bonanza, outgrossing just about every film in release. The success of the picture had vindicated Selznick's long-held belief that, contrary to industry tradition, classics were not taboo screen material, but could, with proper care and intelligent handling, be turned into artistic and commercial smashes. He now began an intensive campaign to convince Louis Mayer to let him make a picture out of *David Copperfield,* another of his childhood obsessions, and Selznick asked George Cukor, who had returned to MGM from RKO, if he would like to direct it. Cukor relates: "We approached L. B. Mayer and he was dubious about the whole thing, but we pointed to the great success of *Little Women* and the fact that the story could be had for nothing and we finally won him over. Mayer thought it would be a great vehicle for Jackie Cooper, whom he was especially fond of, but David and I looked at each other and we both said, 'Oh no, absolutely not,' and we argued and won him over. That was one great strength of Mayer's; he would listen to intelligent reasoning and if he had confidence in you, he could be swayed."

Both Selznick and Cukor, with their strong-minded affection for the Dickens novel, were determined to make as accurate a translation of the book as their resources and their zeal would permit. And they needed all the help they could get. Very few people at MGM were enthusiastic about the project; the executives and the New York sales force were wary of the whole undertaking. Two recent Dickens stories, *Great Expectations* and *The Mystery of Edwin Drood,* had both been flops as talking pictures, and nobody looked beyond that: Dickens was not hot. Not only that, but he was difficult to adapt. The novel had no single plot line but was built on the cumulative effect of the individual scenes and characters. Trying to keep as many of these as possible and still make a picture that would be commercial seemed almost an insurmountable task.

In the interest of accuracy, Selznick and Cukor convinced Mayer to let them go to England, not only to investigate the actual locations but also to look into the possibility of making the picture there. MGM had a lot of money in England, its pictures were even more popular there than they were in America, and the burgeoning British film industry was beginning to show signs of serious competition on its home ground. And most important, they hoped the trip would turn up a child actor who could successfully manage the part of the young David; the success of the whole project rested on this. With Mayer's blessing, the Selznicks, including Myron, George Cukor, and writer Howard Estabrook left the United States on April 18, 1934, on a highly publicized trip. The day after their arrival, Selznick assured journalists in a heavily attended press conference that "we are out to please the English public first in this presentation of an English story, and we hope to attract the American public as well."

The two men were deluged with thousands of photographs from all over the country; within four weeks of their stay, they saw more than 2,500 actors and photographically tested more than 100 of these in an effort to find the talent they needed. They found it in unexpected ways and places, and not only for *David Copperfield.* On a weekend jaunt to Paris to relax, Selznick met Fritz Lang, one of Germany's outstanding directors, who had recently fled the growing terrorism and anti-Semitism of the ruling Nazi Party. Selznick, much impressed with Lang's work, immediately signed him to a contract with MGM, commenting that "Germany's loss is our gain."

Everywhere that Selznick went, he half-superstitiously and half-sentimentally carried with him the old-fashioned red leather copy of *David Copperfield* that his father had given him years before. As an added investment in the fidelity of the adaptation, Selznick convinced the prestigious English novelist and Dickens expert Hugh Walpole to come back to Hollywood to help them on the script. In London Cukor remarked to an interviewer, "I have no one really in mind for David, I still think we'll need an unknown; he must be a good-looking, educated lad." Then, suddenly, they found their David in ten-year-old Freddie Bartholomew, whom both men thought perfectly suited for the part. He had been submitted by his aunt, and after talking to him both Selznick and Cukor were impressed with the boy's naturalness and his charming manners, but much to their surprise and chagrin, the boy's parents proved completely uncooperative, refusing to even consider allowing the child to test for the part. Reluctantly, the two men wound up their trip and came back to the United States to start work on the picture. This matter of young David was a considerable concern to Cukor: "Just finding children with British accents in this country is impossible," he said. "I suppose we'll have to go up to Boston; that's the closest thing we have in America." With this, Selznick dispatched two talent scouts to various parts of the country in June and July of 1934. One of them, Billy Grady, from MGM's New York office, after several weeks of effort, wired Selznick: "Have seen nearly thousand kids, selected 14 prospects; have looked at so many brats of all types that if I see an expectant mother on the street I will probably throw rocks at her."

Back at Culver City, Cukor and Selznick continued to cast the picture, drawing on the large contingent of British actors then in Hollywood, and reaching as far east as the Broadway stage for Basil Rathbone, a romantic leading man, to play David's cruel stepfather, Mr. Murdstone, and bringing Frank Lawton out to play the adult David. For the part of Micawber, Selznick briefly considered comedian Oliver Hardy, but was persuaded by Cukor that Charles Laughton would be better suited for

the role. Now getting desperate for a David, Selznick wired frantically to the New York office: "Copperfield child situation serious. Must have child who looks charming and speaks beautifully, but must have sufficient ability to learn difficult part and carry more than half picture. If have to do without English accent, just have to face issue and get child who speaks well." For the slimy Uriah Heep, Cukor finally cast Roland Young, a fastidious, middle-aged British light comedian; and for the small but memorable part of Dan Peggotty, Cukor reluctantly went along with Selznick's casting of Lionel Barrymore. By now it was a week away from the starting date, but the absence of a child caused Selznick to postpone the start of filming. As he later related,

The nightmare of casting that part right was ferocious. There were practically no English boy actors over here, and if we brought one over we would be breaking a strict English law about importing child performers. That had been the problem with Freddie Bartholomew, in addition to his parents, and I was about at the end of my rope when suddenly Freddie's aunt, who was a very resourceful woman, turned up in Hollywood with Freddie. I could have kissed her with pleasure.

Selznick and Cukor made a conscious effort to capture as much of the authentic Dickens flavor as possible in their version of *David Copperfield*. This church setting (with Hugh Walpole in the vicar's box) is copied exactly from one of the famous illustrations by "Phiz" that accompanied the first edition of the novel. Art direction was by Merrill Pye and set decoration was by Edwin Willis.

Much of the cast of *David Copperfield* is in this publicity photo: Lewis Stone as Mr. Wickfield, Madge Evans as Agnes, Edna May Oliver as Aunt Betsey, Roland Young as Uriah Heep, Lennox Pawle as Mr. Dick, Frank Lawton as the adult David Copperfield, W. C. Fields as Mr. Micawber, Jean Cadell as Mrs. Micawber, and director George Cukor. (Missing are Lionel Barrymore as Dan Peggotty, Basil Rathbone as Mr. Murdstone, Maureen O'Sullivan as Dora, and Freddie Bartholomew as the child David.)

Since he was here we thought that would take care of the English regulations, but then his father gave out reports to the English press that we had signed him for the part before we left England, which wasn't true, but put us in the position of violating English law. It was very frustrating, because the child was so perfect, but it seemed there was nothing for it but that Freddie would have to go back to England. He was on his way across the country to New York, when Zoë Akins, a writer friend of mine, suggested that she might wire to a London friend who was close to the British Home Office. The answer came back that Freddie was out of their jurisdiction, that it was entirely a matter for the American Labor Department and not theirs. Well, we managed to drag Freddie off the boat in New York just before he was to sail. That was a close one and I still breathe hard when I think about it.

In the last week of September 1934, the long-awaited first day of shooting on *David Copperfield* finally arrived. The production was budgeted at a little under $1 million, a considerable sum, even for MGM, the responsibility for which now rested squarely on Selznick's shoulders. No matter that Mayer was his boss, and had okayed it, as had Nicholas Schenck in New York; the failure of the picture would be nobody's fault but his. The concept, the script, the director, the cast, and the art direction all had his wholehearted approval; if it didn't come off it wouldn't ruin his career, but it would be a serious setback as well as an extreme personal disappointment, so the tension on the first day was higher than usual. It was stretched nearly to the breaking point when ten-year-old Freddie Bartholomew arrived at the studio minus his front tooth, which he had lost over the weekend. His scenes were postponed while he was rushed to a dentist and hastily fitted out with a false tooth. After the damage had been repaired, George Cukor directed the first shots on *David Copperfield* on September 27, and the picture started moving smoothly along the well-oiled tracks of MGM's production assembly line.

In mid-October, Charles Laughton reported to the studio to begin his scenes as Micawber, a role which, as Cukor reiterates, "he didn't want to do, but had been persuaded. He came to the set and he had a most

marvelous makeup, he'd shaved his head and he looked perfect for it. We shot for three or four days and then Laughton withdrew." This was not entirely unexpected on Selznick's part, for he had been unhappy with the dailies of Laughton's work, agreeing with Hal Kern, who said that "Laughton looked as if he was going to molest the child." As soon as his unsuitability became apparent, Selznick had asked MGM's New York office for an opinion as to "how much difference commercially would there be having W. C. Fields instead of Laughton? Fields would probably make a better Micawber, but we've always felt we required the one important name in the cast in Laughton." After being assured that the difference was negligible, negotiations were begun to bring Fields over from Paramount to play the part. As Cukor states: "He was a wonderful combination of the personality and the part; he was born for it."

The picture finished filming the day before Thanksgiving, and immediately thereafter Selznick, Cukor, and film editor Robert J. Kern (brother of Hal Kern) began the painstaking task of combing the edited material, trying to get the story down to a manageable length for its first preview. They finally whacked it down to two and a half hours, but it was obvious that, at that length, audience interest kept drifting. Cukor recalls: "Someone came up to me and said that the second half wasn't as good as the first, and I had to reply that the second half of the book wasn't as good as the first." The three men began another round of cutting, some rewriting, and retakes of several scenes. Selznick later remembered: "The entire studio thought we were going to go on our noses. Even at the second preview, some of the executives consoled me with the opinion that it might do well in England." (In mid-December the second preview had been held, in Bakersfield, with much more encouraging results.) After this, it was shortened even more, and the picture was taken to Santa Ana for one more trial, and this time Nicholas Schenck was present. After the picture had run and the audience comments were being gathered, Selznick, Cukor, and Schenck were discussing the reaction in the lobby of the theatre and Selznick was somewhat nervous. "I asked Mr. Schenck," Selznick related, "what was the maximum length we could release it in and he gave me a reply that I have never forgotten: 'What do you mean, how long can you make it?' he

THE BEST-LOVED
MOTION PICTURE OF 1935

Prepare your heart for an experience never to be forgotten! The world has waited for this great motion picture. For two years it has been in production, the mightiest undertaking of Metro-Goldwyn-Mayer. Highest praise has preceded it, but your own tear-dimmed eyes, your own thrilled heart will tell you best how wonderful, how exciting, how tenderly moving it is! Directed by George Cukor, whose previous film success was "Little Women". A Star Cast of 65 players, bringing to life each immortal character. Its gayety and its heart-stabbing drama await you ... exactly as Charles Dickens might have wished for his greatest story.

Produced by
DAVID O. SELZNICK

Directed by
GEORGE CUKOR

A
Metro-Goldwyn-Mayer
PICTURE

"Farewell!" Touching scenes between mother and son that you will never forget.

"Barkis is willin'!" You'll enjoy the love-lorn Barkis, too timid to pop the question.

Agnes' heart almost stopped beating as David announced to Aunt Betsy Trotwood his forthcoming marriage to Dora.

The villainous Uriah Heep little suspected the trap being set for him.

David feels the wrath of his cruel step-father, Murdstone.

"Something will turn up!" There are laughs and tears in the lovable characterization of W. C. Fields, as Micawber.

The love of David for Dora is one of the sweetest romances of all your picture days.

Charles Dickens
DAVID
COPPERFIELD

with W. C. FIELDS · LIONEL BARRYMORE · MADGE EVANS
MAUREEN O'SULLIVAN · EDNA MAY OLIVER · FRANK LAWTON
LEWIS STONE · FREDDIE BARTHOLOMEW · ELIZABETH ALLAN · ROLAND YOUNG

159

A deleted montage sequence from *David Copperfield* by Slavko Vorkapich showing the adult David's growing infatuation with the childlike Dora (Maureen O'Sullivan). Starting with a close shot of Frank Lawton daydreaming, the sequence proceeds (left to right) with a slow-motion romp in the woods, continuing as the two figures rise into the heavens, the whole ending with David's vision of the stars forming his love's name.

asked. 'How long is it good?' " Hearing this, Selznick decided not to worry about the length, but to go on his instincts of what was right. He finally got the film down to two hours and nine minutes, an hour longer than the average feature of 1934.

When the picture finally opened at the Capitol Theatre in New York in January 1935, it turned out to be the biggest success MGM had had in years, which was more than just a blessing as the picture had to recover its production cost of $1,069,225 as well as the money spent on a truly massive advertising publicity campaign. Even after it began its astounding run in New York, Selznick recalled, "it was thought that perhaps it would not repeat its success throughout the country—that there might have been just enough lovers of Dickens in New York to support the run at the Capitol." By the end of the summer, the picture had grossed a phenomenal $3.5 million in the United States. Equally important was the British reception of the film; when it opened in March at the Palace Theatre in London, the critics spoke of "triumph," "a classic from a classic," and "the most gracious work of film art that America has yet sent us."

A side benefit to MGM from the production of *David Copperfield* was the decision by Mayer and Schenck, prodded by Selznick's enthusiasm, to establish an MGM studio in England, which was done in early 1938 and

which lasted for almost thirty years. For Selznick, of course, the hosannas greeting *David Copperfield,* and the immense prestige accorded to him as its producer, were literally the fulfillment of a lifelong dream.

It has been said, rather simplistically, that suddenly, in 1933, audiences wanted a return to "clean pictures," as if the movies had been on a real pornography binge. In truth, there was nothing particularly objectionable about the stories that were being told from the screens of the early thirties; they did, however, deal fairly realistically with the seamy underside of the times: the depression, gangsters, corruption, and rather courageously—some of them anyway—with the hopelessness of life as it was lived at that time. What was missing from this welter of unreal reality, at least to moviegoers, was the sense of striving for good, for nobility, and the subconscious quest for the positive aspects of human behavior—literally for heroes. So the great success of both *Little Women* and *David Copperfield* was not just a lucky hunch of Selznick's, nor a shrewd manipulation of public fancies, but a spontaneous and intuitive reaction on the part of both Cukor and Selznick. Out of the confluence of these two men's talents and their sensibilities emerged two acknowledged classics, *David Copperfield* and *Dinner at Eight,* and a charcoal sketch (*What Price Hollywood?*) of a subject that each man would later develop into his own individual masterpiece.

W. C. Fields and Freddie Bartholomew in a classic moment; costumes by Dolly Tree.

Director George Cukor rehearses a scene with Lennox Pawle, Freddie Bartholomew, and Edna May Oliver.

A crane shot from *Anna Karenina*, with director of photography William Daniels behind the camera operator on the boom.

One of the lures Mayer had used originally to persuade Selznick to return to MGM was the promise of producing a Garbo picture. This was a privilege that had heretofore been reserved exclusively for Thalberg; under his watchful eye, the career and legend of the reclusive Garbo had been carefully nurtured and developed until by 1935 she was the most famous and respected film star in the entire world; her following in Europe was even larger than in the United States. Her last two appearances, in *Queen Christina* and an adaptation of Somerset Maugham's *The Painted Veil*, while successful in both markets, had not been particularly distinguished. In asking Selznick to produce her next vehicle, Mayer hoped that he would do what he had done for Joan Crawford: provide Garbo with a vehicle that would not only restore her to favor with her public but also provide the kind of handsomely produced film that would enhance her prestige—as the foremost tragedienne of her time—and incidentally provide MGM with a substantial financial success. This was not an easy assignment; Garbo was an extremely strong-willed lady, whose sense of what was right and wrong for her sometimes led to the likes of *Susan Lennox: Her Fall and Rise*, in which even her talent had been submerged in a sea of soap. Late in 1934, while finishing *David Copperfield*, Selznick began the search for a story that would properly show off the actress's extraordinary gifts while at the same time satisfying her demands for script, cast, and director approval. Story editor Kate Corbaley sent him a long list of suggestions that had been stockpiled for Garbo, including an as yet unproduced play called *Dark Victory*, which was about to be done on Broadway with Tallulah

Bankhead in the role of a doomed young heiress. It was this story, with its modern setting, that Selznick and Cukor both felt would be best for Garbo, Selznick going so far as to relay to the actress his opinion that "this is the best modern woman's vehicle I've read since *A Bill of Divorcement*, and which I think has the makings of a strikingly fine film." But Garbo had other ideas; she wanted to do a new version of *Anna Karenina*, which she had already filmed once, in 1927, coyly disguised under the title *Love* and fitted out with an obligatory Hollywood happy ending. She let Selznick and Cukor know this; their enthusiasm for the idea matched Garbo's for *Dark Victory*, and Selznick felt compelled to write to her: "I personally feel that audiences are waiting to see you in a smart modern picture and that to do a heavy Russian drama on the heels of so many ponderous similar films . . . would prove to be a mistake." Garbo, through her intimate friend and trusted intermediary, writer Salka Viertel, let them know that she was adamant about *Anna Karenina*. Selznick reluctantly accepted; but Cukor, weary at the prospect of another period costume picture, declined, returning to RKO where (disastrously) he made *Sylvia Scarlett* with Katharine Hepburn.

Selznick meanwhile was resignedly confronting the enormous mass of material in the Tolstoy novel; further complicating his task was the newly instituted Production Code, which forbade any overt discussion or depiction of infidelity on the screen. To do the initial adaptation of the work, Selznick hired Clemence Dane (whose play *A Bill of Divorcement* he thought so highly of) because, as he related, "of her celebrated ability at portraying the dramatic lives of women, and her skill at editing."

Continued Selznick, "[When] Miss Dane arrived in Hollywood, she was aghast that there should be any circumstances that permitted classification of such a classic as *Anna Karenina* with the cheap sex dramas that had caused [the formation of a censorship board]. We finally persuaded her to work with us and I assigned a collaborator to her, the very competent Salka Viertel." Viertel was an expatriate European and a woman of great erudition and passionate liberal beliefs. Her recollections of the scripting of *Anna Karenina,* and especially of working with Clemence Dane, were recounted in her autobiography, *The Kindness of Strangers:* "Clemence Dane's real name was Winifred Ashton and she wore long, trailing chiffon dresses, had never been married and told me that she had never had a love affair. 'So we shall rely on YOUR experience, my dear Salka,' she announced when we began work on the script. 'I have very little understanding for Anna Karenina. What DOES she want? Her husband is a perfect gentleman; she has a social position, an adorable child, but of course, the poor thing is Russian!' "

In early morning story conferences, the two women and Selznick decided to eliminate everything from their treatment that did not involve Anna and her ill-fated love affair with the dashing officer, Count Vronsky. In so doing, they retained only fragments from the several stories that serve as subplots and counterpoint in the original novel, constructing a sort of four-pointed triangle, with Anna torn between her love affair, her duty to her husband, and her fierce, almost consuming passion for her child. The screenplay that Viertel and Dane delivered was found by Selznick to be much too lengthy, with a flatness to the dialogue and an overall moroseness to the telling that he found just a trifle *too* doom-laden. Playwright S. N. Behrman was brought in to continue the collaboration with Salka Viertel, Miss Dane being anxious to get back to London where she had a play rehearsing.

The script was next given to staff writer/gag man Ted Shane, whose ideas and comments had some merit and a certain wry charm in the expression of the difficulties inherent in the project:

> To my mind, the scene in which Vronsky and Alexei Karenin meet over the delirious bed of their common wench Anna can ill afford to be left out of the present version. I find it one of the most dramatic incidents in the book ... it would give Garbo the opportunity to do the work of a lifetime.... I suggest this in full cognizance of the fact that the Vronsky baby cannot be born in the time of Breen [the censor]. However, I am sure it can be so perfumed, edited and tied with a ribbon that the scene will come out purely as a sickness episode.... Anna can collapse at the races or something like that and be thrown into a high fever.... Maybe Garbo should do it again in ten years and have the illegitimate baby.... Maybe she could have it in this one; if the music is loud enough, nobody will notice.

Selznick was amused, but the censors, having no sense of humor, refused to allow Anna's additional baby, even with music.

One of the greatest difficulties in the preparation of the picture was the quest for authenticity. The Communist rulers of Russia were determined to wipe out all traces of the czarist era, and would not cooperate in any depiction of these times, leaving MGM's research department to cope for themselves as best they could. To lend more authenticity to the surroundings and to the overall look and feel of the picture, Selznick asked the legendary Erich von Stroheim to look at the script. Von Stroheim's presence on the MGM lot was an ironic reminder of the fickleness of film fame, for his early days of greatness had been at Metro Goldwyn, with Mayer and Thalberg, for whom he made his magnum opus, the nine-hour *Greed,* which the two men reduced to a more commercial two hours, and *The Merry Widow,* one of the silent era's biggest hits. Von Stroheim's Prussian arrogance, his old-world sophistication, his fascination with the perverse and the darker side of human nature and events, and especially his lordly disdain for the realities of commercial moviemaking, all these made him anathema to Mayer. It was an indication of the paradoxes of Mayer's nature that in spite of his personal dislike for the man, he continued to employ him. For *Anna Karenina,* von Stroheim wrote twenty-one pages of single-spaced criticism and suggestions that dealt largely with military customs and matters, most of which Selznick rejected, replying:

Everybody contributed to the success of the MGM films, as this thoughtful memo from Basil Rathbone to Selznick attests. (The check marks are Selznick's, indicating that he has read the contents.) Selznick welcomed any and all contributions and ideas from everyone working on a picture, giving them careful consideration and using the best of them.

I met with the Karenina unit today on your suggestions and I am sorry to say that by the time I finished reading your memoranda I myself reached the decision which the others shared, against the proposed changes ... we will however make one or two of the minor changes you recommended. I am very grateful for your interest; you have, as you know, my very best wishes for the most successful writing career in the studio.

Actual photography of *Anna Karenina* began in mid-March 1935 with the script still incomplete. To direct, Selznick had chosen veteran Clarence Brown, ex-auto mechanic and engineer, whose film career stretched back to 1915. A solid craftsman as well as the best "women's director" on the lot, the forty-two-year-old Brown was considered to be the man who best could handle Garbo. He had directed her first major success, *Flesh and the Devil* (1927), and had guided her through the perils of her first talking picture, *Anna Christie; Anna Karenina* would be the fifth film the two would make together. "I had a special way with her," Brown confided,

> I never gave her direction in anything louder than a whisper. We stood around discussing a scene and no one ever knew what we were saying. She liked that. She was very shy, and nervous in front of strangers. In the early days, we had so much light on the sets, she couldn't see beyond the rows of lamps; as film got faster and faster, we began to use less light and she could see visitors plainly and she would stop dead, close up like a clam. "When people are watching," she said, "I am just a woman making faces at a camera." We got around that finally by putting black flats all around her and I sometimes found myself directing her through the cracks in these flats. What she had, it was something in her eyes, something that could reach out and tell the audience what she was thinking. I couldn't see it with the naked eye—not even looking through the camera, close-up. I'd shoot a scene over and over; then move on to the next one thinking I'd not gotten what I wanted. But when I saw the scene on the screen, I realized it had been there all along.

In spite of the unfinished screenplay, the filming of *Anna Karenina,* under Brown's carefully organized direction, moved along swiftly, helped by Garbo's extreme professionalism. She was serious-minded and thorough in her approach to her work, arriving promptly on the set at nine in the morning, letter perfect, not only in her own lines but in everyone else's, too. "She knew just what she had to do, and how she was going to do it," says Brown. "She would listen respectfully if I suggested changes, sometimes disagreeing, but always quietly and intelligently. She wanted to always give the best she had. Everything was for the sake of the picture." This extreme concentration on details and the emotional demands made on her by her roles wearied her to the point where she had it written into her contract that she would automatically quit working at 5:00 P.M. every day, regardless. When her maid Ursula handed her a cup of tea, it was quitting time; it created quite a sensation when, on *Anna Karenina,* she continued working on a complicated scene until 5:30; it was considered so noteworthy that the Associated Press sent out a worldwide news flash on it, much to the delight of Selznick and Howard Strickling.

As the picture neared completion in late April, Selznick began concentrating on the editing of the finished sequences and the publicity, of which he felt there had not been enough. In a memo to both Howard Dietz and Strickling in early May, Selznick said, "The picture looks excellent; Garbo herself thinks it's far and away her best work, so I hope you are not going to dish it out as if it were another *Christina* or *Painted Veil.*" On the strength of two previews, Selznick also felt that MGM was passing up a terrific chance to capitalize on the appearance in the picture of Freddie Bartholomew, who was playing Anna's son. This was his first film since *David Copperfield,* and Selznick peppered both Dietz and Strickling with memos "begging, urging and pleading that we do something about Freddie Bartholomew; we can add an additional $500,000 gross to *Anna Karenina* if Bartholomew is properly publicized. To my mind, he is on his way to being as big a child star as Shirley Temple; wherever I go I hear him referred to as 'that magnificent child from *David Copperfield,*' and for us not to capitalize on this in the publicity is sheer waste."

Greta Garbo as the doomed Anna and Fredric March as her lover Vronsky in one of their more sun-dappled moments. Setting by Frederic Hope, costumes by Adrian.

The Smart Screen Magazine

SCREENLAND

November

15c
20c in Canada

Greta Garbo

Enter Freddie Bartholomew's Contest and Begin His "Life and Adventures"

Del Rio and Connie Bennett Talk about Each Other!

Basil Rathbone as the stern, unrelenting Karenin, seen here with Greta Garbo and Freddie Bartholomew. Rathbone had been a romantic leading man on the English and Broadway stages until Selznick turned him into a character villain in *David Copperfield*, much against the will of Rathbone, who feared that the part would "type" him. A correct assumption, for Selznick immediately rushed him into *Anna Karenina*; from that point on he was MGM's resident expert in smooth, suave, slightly sadistic villainy.

The picture opened at the Capitol Theatre in New York on August 31, and the reviews were laudatory, with critics all agreeing that Garbo's performance was her best in years, and infinitely superior to her 1927 effort. The picture had cost well over $1 million, but returned a hefty profit of close to half a million dollars, making it Garbo's biggest success in years. She herself was extremely pleased with the result, and according to Selznick, "asked me to produce all her pictures, but by that time I was getting ready to leave MGM and in spite of the honor, I had my own ambitions."

Selznick was referring to his decision, reached early in 1935, not to renew his MGM contract, but to strike out on his own, in his long-standing desire to be an independent producer. This urge had been with him ever since 1931 and his Guild Pictures plan with Lewis Milestone. In the depths of the depression, times were not exactly propitious for going it alone, even backed by the Whitney millions, and Selznick instead had opted for the security of first RKO, then MGM. By 1935, however, business conditions were much better, Selznick had reached the end of his salaried tether at MGM, and after his series of spectacular successes, Jock Whitney was even more eager to back Selznick in his desire for autonomy. Whitney had made him a strong offer just before Selznick joined MGM, and in fact, was present at the signing of Selznick's original contract with the studio. He had turned up again late in 1934, and he and Selznick had reached an agreement in principle for the formation of a company to be known as Selznick Pictures, which would be incorporated as soon as Selznick was legally free of his obligations to MGM. When Selznick informed Mayer, Schenck, and Thalberg of his decision, they all tried, as he put it,

to talk me out of it, but I explained to each one personally that this was my last opportunity to try the things I have wanted to do all my life, and whatever the cost to me, I must have my fling or regret it all my life. Starting my own company has always been an obsession of mine, unquestionably inherited from my father, an obsession shared by my brother Myron—that there be no interference with our work. Thalberg was especially supportive of this after I explained my feelings to him, and he became my first official investor in the new company. He said to me, "Have you raised your money?" and I said, "Not a dollar." He said, "Norma [Shearer] and I would feel very pleased if you would let us be your first stockholders," and they put in $200,000. So I went east in the summer of 1935 to finance my own company with their money and $200,000 from my brother Myron.

Officially, Selznick resigned from MGM on June 27, but in a separately negotiated arrangement he was paid $20,000 to continue with his services as producer of *Anna Karenina* and what would turn out to be his last film for MGM, an adaptation of Dickens's *A Tale of Two Cities*.

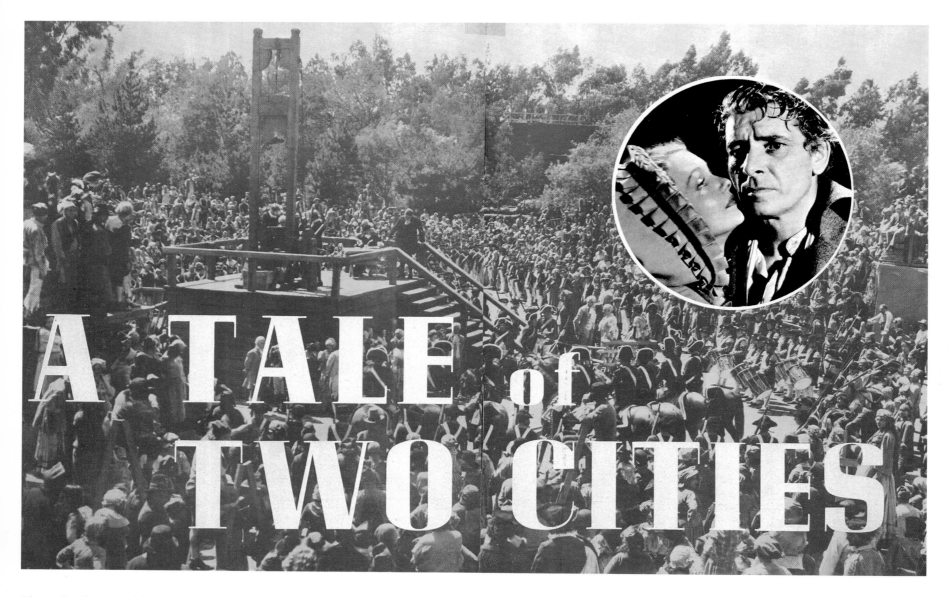

A TALE of TWO CITIES

The trade ad prepared for *A Tale of Two Cities*; it gives a close-up look at the actual guillotine set on the back lot; compare this with the shots on page 171.

If *David Copperfield* was Selznick's childhood favorite, then *A Tale of Two Cities* was the book that most affected his adolescence; he had read it first in his early teens. The story of a doomed love, with a man giving up his life out of love for someone else, and an unrequited love at that, had instilled in Selznick a lifelong fascination with thwarted romance and unhappy endings. This would be Selznick's fourth major picture to make use of the theme, and it was something he would return to throughout the rest of his career, reaching a delirious apex in his *Duel in the Sun* (1946).

After negotiating with Ronald Colman for the lead, Selznick chose as director veteran Jack Conway, who had done yeoman service on *Viva Villa!* on a moment's notice. "Since the picture is basically melodrama," Selznick wrote, "it must have pace and 'pack a wallop' and Conway can give us this. . . . I also think he has a knack for bringing people to life on the screen." To Joe Cohn of the production department, Jack Conway was "a good director, not a great director . . . he had a sense of the dramatic. . . . Jack came from that tough school . . . he used to direct cowboy star Art Acord and the two of them would have fist fights just to see who could lick each other."

Cohn was meeting with both Selznick and Conway, going over the art department's plans for the picture that had been drawn up by Frederic Hope and Edwin Willis under Cedric Gibbons's supervision. Because of the elaborate nature of the production itself, the art department would have to coordinate the various settings. The spectacular vistas of Paris would be made up partly of sets, partly glass and matte shots, and partly miniatures. Because of the need for a careful blending of all these elements, the director was forced to work closer with the art directors than usual. Sometimes, because of the script requirements, a set would be built that would satisfy everyone but still pose problems for the other

technical people. Oliver Marsh, who was director of photography, recalls:

every scene in *A Tale of Two Cities* was a problem . . . David wanted one scene with Colman lit only by candlelight . . . it was a close-up of Colman and we got it by using the fastest film available and opening up the aperture all the way . . . the most difficult scenes I think were the interior of Defarge's wine shop, shooting out through the windows and showing action taking place inside and outside simultaneously. Only twice before in my experience has this problem come up . . . we usually try not to do it because of photographic difficulties . . . but we solved it by having ten different sets of window glass of amber shades, ranging from pale straw to deep orange, and changing them as the outside light changed during the day's work.

Production had started on *A Tale of Two Cities* on April 11, and considering the size and complexities of the story, it was moving along swiftly. Selznick, meanwhile, had assigned a new writer, young Val Lewton, to oversee the research and the writing of a separate script for the Revolutionary sequences, which were being held up until after principal photography was finished. Lewton was the nephew of Alla Nazimova, one of Lewis J. Selznick's early stars, and the young man was extremely literate, intelligent—and shy. He loved research and writing, as evidenced by the fifteen-page narrative chronology on the storming of the Bastille that he delivered to Selznick. It was a concise, telling, and clear explanation of the causes of the Revolution as well as a detailed rendering of bits of action and other vignettes that would be helpful to the second unit director who would stage these sequences. The second unit was so named because it usually utilized a second director, plus a second technical and camera crew, and it usually filmed at the same time that the primary unit was working, although in a different location.

Because of the complicated nature of the special effects in the picture, no previews were held until early October, when it was taken to Long Beach and shown to, as Selznick phrased it, "an audience of rowdy sailors and their dates. It was way overlength but they loved it." Immediately after the showing, Selznick and editor Conrad Nervig began slicing away at the three-hour mass of footage. But Selznick, preoccupied as he was with setting up his own company, did not give his usual close attention to details in the picture, resulting in some near ludicrous touches. During the storming of the Bastille, the stunt men who jumped onto the drawbridge were costumed as women, which fooled no one, as their movements and action gave away their gender. In a scene between Miss Pross, Lucie's protector, and the evil Madame Defarge, the two actresses Edna May Oliver and Blanche Yurka were doubled by two stunt men for their climactic fight scene, and as they wrestled over tables, chairs, and around a room with the action speeded up in the camera, the result brought guffaws and hoots from the preview audiences and derogatory comments from the reviewers after the picture opened.

Selznick, as a parting gesture, wrote Nicholas Schenck a long letter, detailing his hopes for the picture and lamenting the fact that no one in the publicity department had paid any attention to it while it was in production:

It is not so hard for me to understand this indifference; I have had to meet it on every picture, without exception, that I have made for the company.... I write you this because I will not be here to fight the battles of *A Tale of Two Cities*.... I appeal to you for the company's

sake to do something about ... making sure that it is handled properly by the sales and advertising departments.... I think it is an outrage that there has not been a word about the picture in either the trade or lay press for months and months.... I regard this as typical of the entire company's attitude.... I hate to make my valedictory to the company a letter of bitter complaint ... many of the men in the publicity department will be very annoyed I am sure but I feel I owe it to the company to see that it gets its rewards for what looks like a very successful investment, and my pride in the completed production is such that I would hate to see it treated as just another output of the machine.

He sent copies of this broadside to every member of the executive staff at MGM.

"David was a gooser," says Howard Strickling; "he thought he knew more about publicity than anybody else, so we were always getting these notes from him ... he'd press everybody...." In this particular case, the pressure was a little too strong. Howard Dietz, who took few things seriously except his lyric writing for the Broadway stage, promptly responded with a short, stinging note:

Thank you for the copy of the letter ... complaining about the publicity treatment you've received while at MGM.... I have tried to figure out why you've been so ignored and decided it was that shy, shrinking personality of yours ... no one knew your name very much in the early days and now they are even conscious of your middle

(Below) Director Jack Conway, Edna May Oliver, and Elizabeth Allan in a relaxed moment between scenes. (Bottom) Female extras on the back lot waiting to be made up and fitted for the storming of the Bastille.

(Below) Two members of the makeup department spraying the extras with paint to age and dirty their costumes. (Bottom) A lunch break on the back lot during the storming of the Bastille; the French Army costumes are from the wardrobe department and the men's shoes evidently from Florsheim.

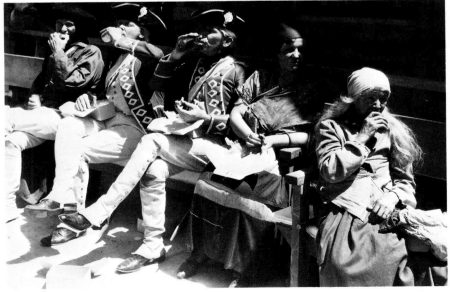

initial. Rest assured I will never reveal that the "O" stands for just—
"O." You remind me of the bisexual Marquis who, when asked which
he preferred—men or women, replied, "I like them both but there
ought to be something better."

Copies of this were addressed to all the executives who had received
Selznick's letter. After reading it, Selznick hit the ceiling, firing off a
telegram to Nicholas Schenck complaining of "the boorish and insulting
letter Howard Dietz sent to me," and demanding that Schenck chastise
Dietz. Schenck, however, had been equally furious, without Dietz's mischievous humor, for on the same day that Selznick sent the telegram he
received a long, critical letter from Schenck:

> I do not understand how you could write such a letter ... you have
> been spoiled by too easy accessibility to money and people for pro-
> duction ... had your road been a little harder you would be less quick
> to make these selfish and egotistical observations ... your parting
> remarks to MGM should be of gratitude for the success we helped you
> to achieve ... had you just written this to me without broadcasting
> copies to all our executives, I would simply have called you on the
> phone and proved to you how wrong you were, but you have placed
> me in a position where I have had to answer you by letter, sending
> copies to the very same executives. ... I regret having to write such a
> letter for I have always had the greatest affection for you.

Selznick was absolutely surprised at this. He had not anticipated that his
letter would do anything other than "pick the organization out of the
apathy it had regarding this property." Indeed, after his initial outrage at
Dietz had worn off, the two men, as Selznick related, "talked the matter
over and wound up with some laughs and a mutual understanding."
Selznick's concern for Schenck's reply was, however, deep and worrisome. His first reaction was to dictate a long, defensive reply, saying: "I
never thought for a moment that you were so thin-skinned as to be upset
by a criticism of any department ... as for its being about my personal
publicity, this is a fantastic misinterpretation ... if your familiarity with
my character could not stop you from writing such a letter, I am very,
very sorry indeed." But, cautioned by his wife Irene, and on the advice of
Mayer, Selznick decided not to send this. Instead, he wrote a conciliatory
reply, telling Schenck

> how badly I feel that I should have offended you so ... by a letter that
> you apparently misunderstood. Please believe that I have gratitude for
> all the kindness shown me by you ... my final letter to you was going
> to be about the wonderful time I had at MGM, after my first trying
> months. ... I feel simply wretched that I seem to have wiped out all
> the good with one stroke. ... I am considering demolishing the type-
> writer ... as I would rather stop dictating forever than intentionally
> show dis-respect for you or the organization. ... I hope this will clear
> the unfortunate impression that I so unintentionally ... created.

Tempers cooled, apologies made and accepted, David Selznick, thirty-
three years old and near the top of his profession, left MGM and moved a
half-mile east on Washington Boulevard to the white-columned, colonial
mansion façade of the old Thomas Ince studios. From there he intended
"to put my family's name on a trademark and restore it to its former
importance in the movie world ... by making artistic pictures that are
commercial successes."

(Opposite) Ronald Colman as Sydney Carton.

The final scenes of *A Tale of Two Cities:*
The long shot of the Paris square is a combination of
glass painting and matte work—the two men at the right
edge of the platform are busy throwing a headless corpse
into the cart. Next, Colman as Carton begins his final
climb and the guillotine is readied (note the blood on the
stock). As the camera moves in closer, Carton's voice is
heard soliloquizing "... it is a far, far better thing I do
than I have ever done ... it is a far better rest I go to than
I have ever known ..." and the camera rises slowly past
the bloodstained blade and into the sky over Paris while
a chorus invokes the 23rd Psalm.

David O. Selznick, John Hay Whitney, Loyd Wright (attorney for United Artists), and Katharine Brown at the time of the formation of Selznick International.

Hollywood—1935

BY THE SPRING of 1935, the tidal wave of the depression had begun to recede, the number of jobholders was up even if wages were not, and more than 80 million Americans—15 percent more than in 1934—paid an average of 25 cents twice a week to get into the 13,386 movie theatres. The ubiquitous "double bill" ("two features for the price of one"), which had been introduced during the worst of the depression, was now an accepted and demanded form of moviegoing, as were Tootsie Rolls, popcorn, Mickey Mouse, and assorted give-aways. Except in the first-run downtown theatres, the average neighborhood "show" changed double bills twice weekly and had a special matinee on Saturdays for children, offering a fifteen-minute episode from an action serial, a cartoon, a comedy short, and a feature, usually a western, all for 10 cents. The content of all films was now watched over not only by the Will Hays organization but also by the indignantly righteous National Legion of Decency, the film classification arm of the Catholic Church, which successfully prohibited anything on screen that smacked of moral honesty.

In the film industry itself, bankruptcies, mergers, consolidations, and reorganizations had changed little of the Hollywood profile. The post-depression industry was dominated by MGM, Warner Bros., Paramount, RKO, Universal, and United Artists. Columbia Pictures, once the lowliest of the low, through the combined efforts of Harry Cohn, its crusty owner, and Frank Capra, its young hotshot director, had upgraded its product considerably and was now considered a "major." Gone was the once mighty First National, now part of the name of the Warner Bros. studio out in Burbank; the Famous Players-Lasky name had disappeared almost completely, being replaced by the dominant Paramount Pictures, while the two studios of William Fox, one in Hollywood and the new Movietone City out in Beverly Hills, now bore the name 20th Century-Fox, the result of an amalgamation with the Darryl Zanuck–Joseph Schenck independent operation, which, before the merger, had been one of the mainstays of United Artists. Since its founding in 1919 to distribute the pictures of D. W. Griffith, Charlie Chaplin, Douglas Fairbanks, and Mary Pickford, United Artists had been under the collective thumbs of its founding partners; its expensive network of film exchanges and theatres in some key cities could not maintain the costs of distributing and exhibiting the few pictures made by the four United Artists. Artists they were; shrewd business executives they weren't. Despite their skill at dealmaking, the partners could not understand why their distribution company never brought them the expected returns on their high-grossing films.

In 1921 the four had hired Joseph Schenck, brother of MGM's Nicholas, to head the company; under his ingenious management the firm, by taking on outside product to release, actually began to prosper. Griffith had dropped out of the business when his last picture, *The Struggle* (1931), had proved a fiasco, and the interminable wranglings with the remaining three volatile partners finally became too much for Schenck. He and young Darryl Zanuck, with whom he had formed 20th Century Pictures, releasing through UA, quietly and suddenly merged their outfit with Fox. Having no further use for UA, Schenck abruptly resigned, leaving not only a vacancy in the executive office but a gap in UA's very weak release schedule. The presidency was filled by Al Lichtman, sales manager for the company and a former associate of David Selznick's from the Paramount days. The two had stayed in touch professionally and socially, and Lichtman knew of Selznick's desire to go on his own. When Lichtman took over UA after Schenck left in May 1935, he began assiduously wooing Selznick to sign a releasing contract with the company. While the other studios were releasing close to fifty pictures a year, UA never had more than twenty, and the defection of Zanuck-20th Century, with its six pictures yearly, left the company in anemic condition.

But Selznick was in no hurry to make a deal. He considered offers from RKO and Paramount, and for a time even toyed with the idea of setting up his own distribution arm, in partnership with his brother Myron, who in the past five years had become the most powerful agent in the business. Armed with his $400,000 from Myron and the Thalbergs, David had gone outside the industry for the rest of his financing, as he did not want entrenched "picture money" second-guessing whatever it was he might want to do. Instead, he took up the Whitney offer, which amounted to some $2.4 million, divided between John Hay ("Jock") Whitney and his sister, Mrs. Charles Payson, and cousin, Cornelius ("Sonny") Whitney. And, not wanting his basket full of only Whitney eggs, he obtained another $300,000 from New York bankers Robert and Arthur Lehman and taxicab magnate John Hertz. Backed by approximately $3 million of independent money and with a board of directors made up largely of sharp young minds dedicated to the same standards of quality as his own, Selznick became impatient to start his own production. Late in May, he suddenly decided to accept Lichtman's offer of a United Artists release, signing a contract that called for the delivery of ten pictures in the next two years.

Having successfully negotiated the deal, Lichtman almost immediately resigned his post, and, retracing David's footsteps, joined MGM as head of its sales department. In another of the inbred round-robin movements so beloved of the industry, Dr. Attilio Giannini, younger brother of the founder of the Bank of America and a member of Selznick's board, took over as president of United Artists, giving Selznick the twin blessings of a banker on the board and a president in the closet. David had invested no money of his own, but his time and talent were considered enough to make him president as well as owner of more than half the new company, which he grandly christened Selznick International Pictures.

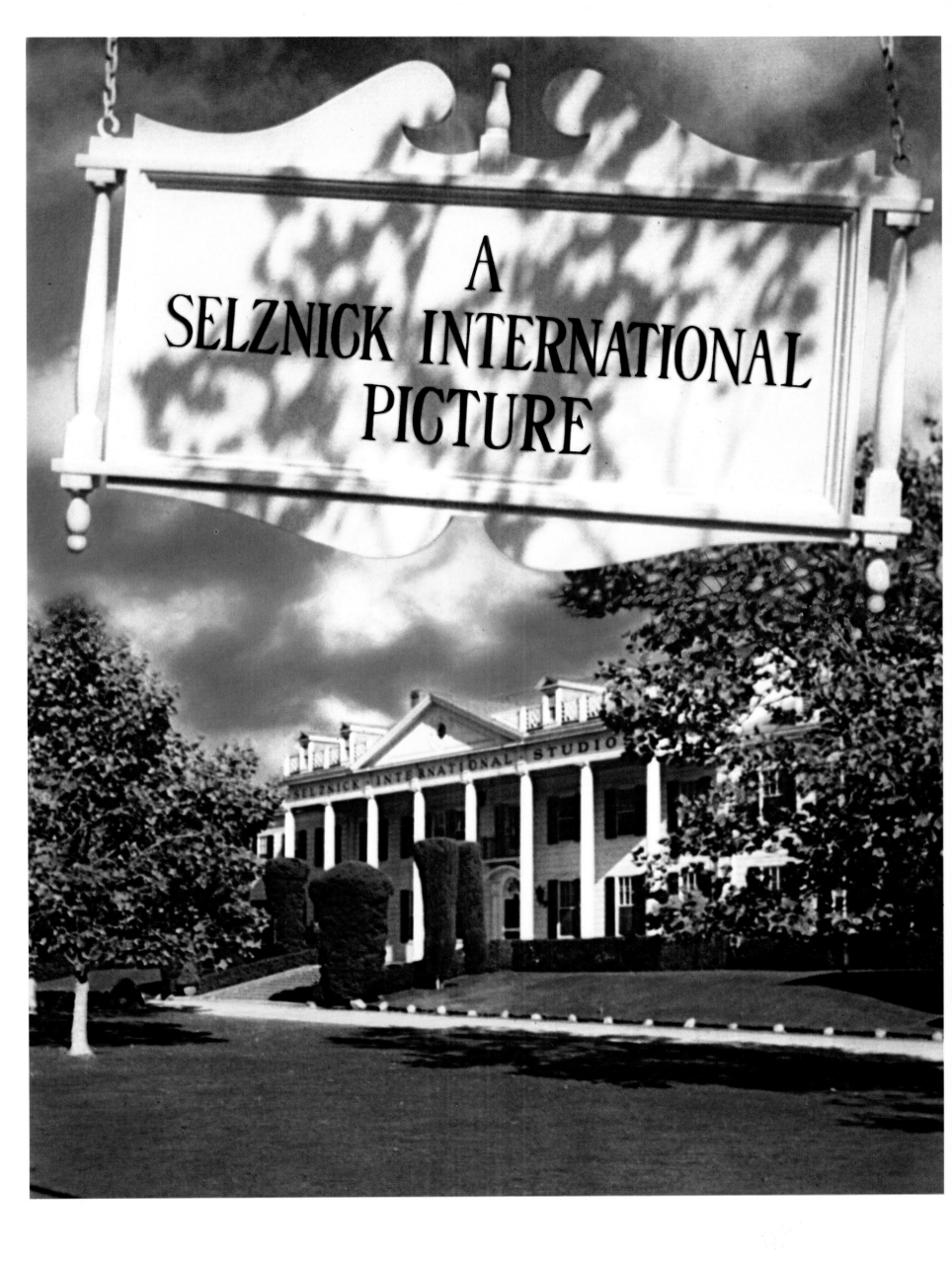

Selznick International

IN OCTOBER 1935, David Selznick was ruminating to a group of reporters on his hopes and plans for Selznick International: "The day of mass production has ended ... it has become, in the making of good pictures, so essential for a producer to collaborate on every inch of script, to be available for every conference and go over all details of production that it is physically impossible for him to give his best efforts to more than a limited number of pictures." Then, in a moment of unpretentious candor, he told them that "it never has been nor ever should be the function of motion picture producers consciously to educate; our mission is to discover the nature of the demand and meet it as best we can," going on to point out what he considered a notable trend in the past few years: "Audiences are smarter than we give them credit for, and they have become much more selective in their choice of pictures they will pay to see.... They don't like being 'played down to' so our new company ... will 'play up to' our prospective audiences. My object as a producer has always been to make the finer things, and to leave the trash to the other fellows. I firmly believe that the future of pictures lies in producing stories of high caliber."

Having publicly issued his "declaration of principles," Selznick now set about implementing them, cautiously and with the aid of a hand-picked staff largely recruited from his last year at MGM. These were people who had impressed him with their ability to think along the same lines he did, and who strove through interminable hours to give him the results he wanted. His secretary, Marcella Bannett, had been with him since his RKO days. She had an extremely keen, analytical mind, and could cope with the most outlandish and erratic of David's work habits, quietly and efficiently organizing his business life so that as much of his time as possible was devoted to the particular project at hand. While she looked after the organization of Selznick's activities, he set about the task of structuring a functioning production set-up. From MGM came George Cukor, who would join Selznick as soon as he finished directing

Irving Thalberg's very prestigious *Romeo and Juliet;* also from MGM came film editor Hal Kern, who had started his career in 1915 with Thomas Ince, and was in a sense coming full circle, as the Selznick headquarters were in Ince's old studio. He was a quiet, straightforward man, with a methodical, devoted concern to the details of picturemaking that caught Selznick's attention at once. "I first worked with David at MGM," Kern says, "and we got along very, very well, and after a while he began to rely on me for certain things and I sort of became his assistant. I used to carry around little three by five cards and I would write things down on them to remind myself, and I remember David said to me years later, 'Hal, you know what first attracted me to you? You came in here one day and I asked you to do something and you pulled out a little package of cards and wrote everything down as we talked and I knew right then that it would be done and nobody would forget anything.' "

The one individual who was evidently forced upon Selznick was the Bank of America's watchdog, Henry Ginsberg, who was given the job of general manager of the studio operation. He was a close friend of Joseph Rosenberg, the Bank of America man in charge of motion picture loans, so the B of A was watching after its investment with both Giannini and Rosenberg. Val Lewton was brought over from MGM to head the all-important department that would find the "stories of high caliber" Selznick intended to make.

The New York office was to be headed by Katharine Brown, the young woman whom Selznick had first met at RKO. A peppy, no-nonsense redhead with a sharp mind for story values, she could be alternately as charming and as cold as Selznick when closing a deal. In giving control of his New York affairs to a woman, Selznick was alone in the industry, for women in films were seldom given the chance to be anything but stenographers or stars; in the craft unions, they were largely frozen out by male dominance and there were no female executives as

The imposing front of the studio had originally been built as a set for Thomas Ince's 1924 production of *Barbara Fritchie*. When Cecil B. DeMille took over in 1925 for Producers Distributing Corporation, he converted the set to an administration building. Pathé took it over after DeMille folded; Pathé then merged with RKO, and Selznick subsequently leased the entire lot. He kept offices there for the next thirty years.

such in the business. Kay Brown surrounded herself with some of the best and brightest of the new emerging career women, well-educated girls who had to go to work to survive and wanted to put their new liberal arts degrees to good use. Selznick's pictures and indeed those of the entire industry were designed to appeal to women—they decided what was read, what was seen, what was listened to, and sometimes even what was talked about, and the money that passed through their control was heavily competed for in magazine publishing, over the radio, in newspapers, and by the movies—especially the movies. Selznick intuitively responded to many of the same things that appealed to modern women: the tactile feel and look of a fabric or a style, the heady emotionalism and glossy romance of stories that women responded to more than men. Whether by design or just through intuition, Selznick and Kay Brown both realized the value of surrounding themselves with intelligent, articulate women, and it was the values and interests of these women that began to be seen in movies throughout the thirties and forties.

The prime job of the New York office was to hunt for story material, to read books, magazines, and newspapers, and to go to out-of-town tryouts of plays in the hope of turning up something that might be filmable. While Kay Brown and her staff went about organizing this process for Selznick, he announced that the first Selznick International picture would be another of his childhood favorites, *Little Lord Fauntleroy,* Frances Hodgson Burnett's Victorian era classic about the little American boy who became a British lord. The book had been popular for years, and Mary Pickford had starred in a silent version, playing both the young lord Cedric, "Ceddie," and his mother, "Dearest." The picture had been one of her biggest successes, and it was with some reluctance that she allowed Selznick to remake it, but being gracious to her new associate at United Artists, she sold him the rights. The announcement of the project caused Ben Hecht to send Selznick a telegram: "The trouble

with you, David, is that you did all your reading before you were twelve."

Hecht was not the only one dubious about the idea. The story was considered to be a chestnut, with the popular image of Fauntleroy having evolved into that of a stereotyped sissy: a young boy with long flowing curls and a languid air, dressed in a velvet suit. About the curls Selznick made publicity hay, asking the public through newspaper releases how they felt about Fauntleroy's long hair. While the results of this audience sampling were being tabulated, Selznick borrowed Hugh Walpole from MGM to do the screen adaptation, and the two of them, collaborating with another writer, Richard Schayer, worked all through the late summer months of 1935, while Selznick simultaneously carried on negotiations with MGM to borrow Freddie Bartholomew to play the lead. And as the first step on the long road toward building his own stars, Selznick signed Dolores Costello, one of the ex–Mrs. John Barrymores, for the part of "Dearest."

Selznick's expressed hope was to build up his own roster of stock players, either by using established freelancers or by finding unknowns who could be potential star material, and lending out both to other studios. "I feel that working at different studios can only be beneficial to both the studios and the players." On this principle, he had convinced Ronald Colman to sign a long-term contract with his new company, and then promptly loaned him to Columbia for one picture, which turned out to be Frank Capra's version of the James Hilton best seller *Lost Horizon.* Selznick intended the same policy for his directors, and his contract with George Cukor specifically called for "loan outs" to other studios, a clause that worked to everyone's advantage as MGM obtained Cukor to direct the planned Garbo vehicle *Camille* in return for lending Bartholomew.

Now that Selznick had his script and a cast for *Fauntleroy,* he began considering directors, and at his brother Myron's urging, he hired John

Cromwell, one of Myron's clients. Cromwell was just winding up a three-year stint at RKO, where he had made several excellent pictures, including a critically acclaimed version of Somerset Maugham's *Of Human Bondage* with Leslie Howard and the Warner Bros. ingénue Bette Davis. Remembering their past association with pleasure, Cromwell accepted Selznick's offer, mainly, as he put it, "to see what he had in the back of his mind as to how he would handle this ... it appeared to me that the story was so old-fashioned and dated that it could be dangerous material. Now David was as aware of this as I was, and I watched him as he tried to translate what was good in the original story into something acceptable for modern audiences."

The picture was in production for two smooth months and the final cost was a little over $500,000, a figure that was higher than the industry average at that time. When Selznick was called on this by John Wharton, the treasurer installed by the Whitneys, he replied that it was his observation that

> there are only two kinds of merchandise that can be made profitably in this business—either the very cheap or the very expensive pictures ... if we hope to get grosses over a million dollars on all our pictures we will have to be prepared to spend the money to get these ... if we don't deliver really top-notch product ... we are going to take a terrible beating after the first few pictures.... There is no alternative open to us but to attempt to compete with the very best ... which I thought to be our intention all along.... From my standpoint I wish we could have five pictures a year for which chances of success were as high as for *Fauntleroy,* at the same cost....

Selznick's instincts proved right, for when *Little Lord Fauntleroy* opened at the Radio City Music Hall as the 1936 Easter attraction, police had to be called out to control the crowds who flocked to see what the critics were so enthusiastic about. The picture turned a nice profit and earned a medal from the League of Nations. The new company, it seemed, was off to an auspicious start.

Selznick International was not the Whitneys' only film investment. Since 1933, the two cousins had been heavy investors in a new process for making full color pictures developed by the Technicolor company, something they had been introduced to by Merian C. Cooper, who was an enthusiastic advocate of this new system. It was a sophisticated and complex method of solving one of the oldest problems in motion pictures—how to put realistic-looking color on a screen.

Before the turn of the century, the French firm of Pathé Frères had evolved a method of hand stenciling color onto short films, something that exhausted the hundreds of young women who did it with magnifying glasses and camel's hair brushes. But this color was not "natural," not derived from the original. The only way to do this had been discovered as far back as 1861 by the Scottish physicist James Clerk Maxwell, who proved that all colors were made up of a combination of three "primaries"—red, blue, and green—and that by using colored filters in front of the camera and projector, black-and-white photographs could be made to appear to be in color. Early experiments were hampered by the mechanical limitations of trying to get three separate but simultaneous black-and-white filtered images that could then have the color added to them by being projected through the appropriate filters. The 1909 Brit-

(Top) Freddie Bartholomew, Mickey Rooney, and director John Cromwell on the set of *Little Lord Fauntleroy* (1935). (Left) Freddie Bartholomew making his mark in the cement forecourt of Grauman's Chinese Theatre. The gentleman hovering over him is Jean W. Klossner, who inspired in Grauman the idea of the cement ritual. Klossner's family had been masons as far back as the building of Notre Dame, and he had been taught that the signature of a mason is a handprint. After completing the cement work on the Chinese Theatre, Klossner was in the process of leaving his mark when Grauman asked him what he was doing. Showman that he was, Grauman realized immediately the beauty of the idea and appropriated it, with embellishments, for the forecourt. Klossner jealously guarded the recipe he devised for the cement that gave it the right consistency for the handprints and footprints ceremony. Three days were necessary for the preparation of the chemicals, and on the night of the event, Klossner would arrive in a flowing robe and artist's beret to vie with Grauman for the spotlight.

PRODUCED BY DAVID O. SELZNICK . . . .

(Top, left) A hand-colored frame from the 1903 block-buster *The Great Train Robbery*.

(Top, right) This 1915 Technicolor image was colored by floating the positive print one side at a time, first on a red chemical solution and then on a blue-green bath.

(Middle, left) By 1926 Technicolor had devised a method of two-color printing that involved dyeing two separate pieces of positive film and then cementing them back-to-back, as in this shot of Gloria Swanson in *Stage Struck*.

(Middle, right) This close-up of Fay Wray from *Mystery of the Wax Museum* (1933) gives a good indication of how far the company had pushed the limitations of the two-color process. All the color was now being applied to one side of the film by a unique dye transfer process using two small matrices similar to rubber stamps, which printed the red-orange and blue-green images one on top of the other on a single strip of blank film.

(Bottom, left) Technicolor's new process added a pure blue record to the red and green records, and the result was the first successful three-color process for taking and printing motion pictures. Here is Mary Pickford in a test scene from a proposed version of *Alice in Wonderland* to be made with Walt Disney. The project never got off the ground.

(Bottom, right) Miriam Hopkins and Nigel Bruce in *Becky Sharp* (1935), the first full-length feature production using the new Technicolor process. The color design was by Robert Edmond Jones, who worked closely with director Rouben Mamoulian in stylizing the color and using it to make dramatic points.

ish process called Kinemacolor was the first commercially successful method of doing this, but its color was not completely true to life, as it compromised on the primaries by using a red-orange and blue-green combination; and the finished product resulted in poor definition and considerable eyestrain. In 1912 three graduates of the Massachusetts Institute of Technology, Herbert Kalmus, Daniel Comstock, and Burton Westcott, started an engineering firm in Boston; they specialized in physics and chemistry, and one of the problems dropped into their laps was how to take the flicker out of motion pictures. Somehow in the process of taking the flicker out, they became interested in how to put color in. The upshot was the appearance in 1915 of the Technicolor Motion Picture Company, named after their alma mater, but substituting an "i" for an "o" in the second syllable, thereby sparing themselves years of bad jokes. The three men, after an abortive experiment with the rotating filter method, decided that to be commercially successful, the color in their process would have to be contained on the film itself. Working with the same two-color compromise that Kinemacolor had devised, they began a long and expensive series of experiments throughout the early and mid-twenties, eventually devising a special camera that used a prism to break the image down into the black-and-white records of the individual colors. The negatives of these were then turned into tiny "matrices" similar to rubber stamps; each matrix was dyed with the appropriate color and brought into contact with a single blank film that "imbibed" both dyes. This "imbibition" (or dye transfer process) was unique to Technicolor, and over the years it was refined and improved

until, with careful control, the two-color process could deliver results that were exquisite if not accurate.

The first surge of enthusiasm for Technicolor occurred between 1928 and 1930, as the producers added color to sound in an effort to make pictures as attractive as possible. Kalmus and his associates had deliberately kept Technicolor small during its formative years in order to maintain quality control, and the sudden demand for the process caught them unprepared, but not unwilling—they began renting out the cameras and processing the film as fast as the producers could put up the money. The result was a series of garishly tinted pictures that did Technicolor more harm than good, and by 1931 the color boom had turned into a depression bust. Kalmus, seeing fifteen years and several million dollars' worth of work and experimentation about to be wiped out, decided on one last herculean effort to overcome Technicolor's basic shortcoming, the lack of a three-color image. A new camera was designed and a third strip of film was added to the original two, this to record the all-important blue component.

Merian Cooper, when he first went to work at RKO in March 1932, saw an early demonstration of this new method and gave an enthusiastic recommendation to Selznick, who tried to interest the RKO board in taking it up, but they declined. Walt Disney had also been impressed with the process and began using it in his cartoons, the success of which convinced Cooper to become a heavy investor in Technicolor, and he persuaded the Whitneys to join forces with him in a company called Pioneer to make and market feature films in the new process. Very

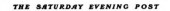
This ad for the old two-color process is misleading, as it could not deliver true yellows or blues.

The legendary Natalie Kalmus, whose name appeared as color director on every Technicolor film up to the late 1940s. There is considerable controversy over exactly what her function was. Her husband had originally given her the task of overseeing which colors could be used in the old two-color process, and she carefully supervised these productions, side-stepping the garish combinations that the two-color compromise was capable of producing. When the new three-color process was introduced, she insisted that the colors be muted pastels, a dictum that drove art directors and costume designers to distraction. Her bland grip on Technicolor was soon loosened by the combined efforts of Merian Cooper, Robert Edmond Jones, and Walt Disney.

Herbert T. Kalmus, the ambitious force behind Technicolor. It was he who kept encouraging his associates Daniel Comstock and Burton Westcott in their experiments, raising considerable amounts of money for research and experimentation and keeping his eye on the long-range goal of making the process commercially feasible.

The Technicolor process at work on Pioneer Pictures' *La Cucaracha* (1934), the first live-action short subject to use the new three-color method. Lloyd Corrigan directs Steffi Duna and Don Alvarado in a dance number while cinematographer Ray Rennahan, behind Corrigan, photographs the sequence. The camera exposed three strips of black-and-white film simultaneously, using a patented beam-splitting prism to direct the image to the proper film emulsion. The red and the blue images were recorded on a bi-pack (two negatives sandwiched together) traveling at right angles to the lens, the red being recorded on the front emulsion while the blue was passed through to the rear emulsion. The green went straight through the lens and the prism and was recorded in the normal manner. These black-and-white negatives were then separated and printing plates, or matrices, made from them. These were dyed the negative, or complementary, colors of yellow (for the blue record), cyan (for the red record), and magenta (for the green record). Each of these separate complementary color images was printed one on top of the other on a single strip of blank film that imbibed the separate dyes, the combination of which resulted in a full-color picture. This method of printing, similar to lithography, gave the Technicolor process a range and latitude that was never achieved by any other process and kept Technicolor pre-eminent in the field of motion-picture color until the introduction of Eastmancolor in the early 1950s.

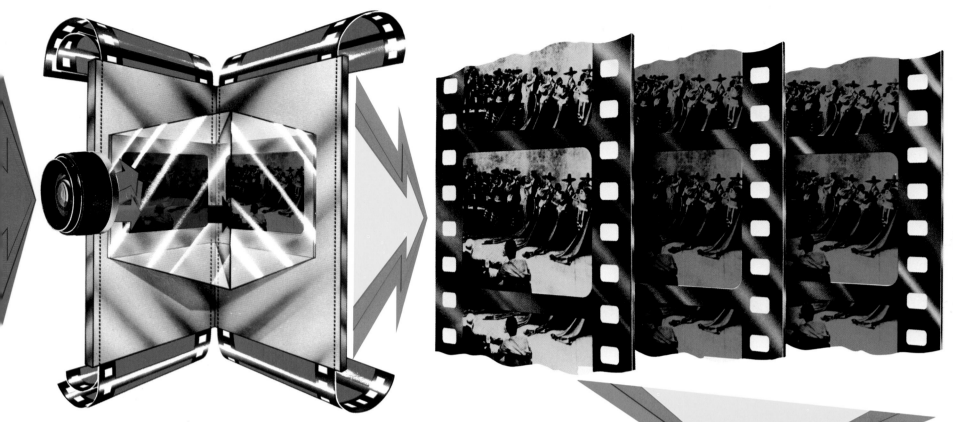

Ernest Dryden (top, right) designed the costumes for *The Garden of Allah*, including these two for Marlene Dietrich. (Right) This evening gown made of muted yellow silk was one of thirteen outfits that the heroine, Domini Enfilden, took with her on her trek into the wilds of the Sahara. (Above) Her wardrobe also included this chiffon creation, which helped Domini in her search for spiritual truth and true love. Dietrich's penchant for trudging through the desert in high heels had been started in *Morocco* (1930), at the end of which she followed her lover, Gary Cooper, into the Sahara in a pair of high-heeled ankle straps.

slowly, their efforts and Disney's successes developed a new industry curiosity about Technicolor, but this time Kalmus and company were not caught unprepared. An ironclad contract went with every Technicolor deal; the company supplied everything—camera, cameraman, film, color control, and processing—all rented for a specific time period. After the day's shooting, the camera was taken back to the new Technicolor plant and the film processed by the complex and highly secret printing system. The color that emerged from this fortress-like building was carefully controlled, well focused, and rich—color that was light years ahead of the many smaller competitive processes then in use. When Whitney backed Selznick, it was with the understanding that Technicolor pictures would be a major part of the new company's production plans. True to his word, at Whitney's urging, Selznick announced in early February 1936 that the second Selznick International picture would be *Dark Victory,* a play owned by Jock Whitney, which would be made with Technicolor and would star Merle Oberon, Alexander Korda's English discovery. Waxing enthusiastic on the subject of color, Selznick commented to an interviewer that "the importance of color in the future scheme of things cannot be overemphasized. The only danger with it is the possibility of producers relying upon it too much . . . color will enhance the presentation of the story but as with acting and directing, photography must always remain a secondary and subservient element in creating the finished product."

Just as he gave out this statement, *The Trail of the Lonesome Pine*—made in Technicolor—was released by Paramount, attracting large audiences and receiving much favorable comment on the beautiful outdoor color photography. Its success evidently prompted David to have second thoughts on the choice of material for his first color film. *Dark Victory,* a somber modern drama about a dying heiress, was deemed unsuitable; in its place Selznick announced another choice from his seemingly inexhaustible supply of classics, the desert romance *The Garden of Allah,* written in 1907 by Robert Hichens and also to star Merle Oberon. It told the story of Domini Enfilden, a young, wealthy, religious European woman who goes to the Sahara (which the Bedouins call the Garden of Allah) in search of spiritual peace. Instead, she finds love and tragedy in the person of Boris Androvsky, a Trappist monk who has run away from his monastery and is tortured by guilt as a result. All this was told with a sort of purple lassitude and anguished soul-searching, suffused with mysticism and the regenerative powers of love and the desert. By 1911 it had been enough of a success as a play to have been revived twice, and it had twice been filmed, most recently by MGM in 1927.

While at MGM, Selznick had intended remaking *The Garden of Allah* as a talkie with Greta Garbo. Now he bought the rights from them for $62,000 and immediately began to whack away at the languorous prose of the novel, trying to breathe some life into the somewhat dated material. Pioneer Pictures had made only two features, *Becky Sharp* and *The Dancing Pirate,* neither of which had been completely successful as movies, marred by poor direction, miscasting, and uninspired writing. But Selznick, Whitney felt, would be able to make a Technicolor picture that would be dramatically compelling, superlatively cast, and well written and directed. If that happened, it would help put Technicolor over, thus increasing the value of Whitney's stock in the company, so David was told to go ahead and spend what was necessary, and a budget estimate of $1.2 million was arrived at. The bulk of this would be spent on a month's location filming in the Arizona desert at a spot called Buttercup Valley, 60 miles outside Yuma.

With the scope and the budget so enlarged, Selznick began having reservations about Merle Oberon as Domini. Her color tests were fine and she was giving good readings of the script, but she was not a major star, nor did she possess the necessary mystique. With the picture scheduled to go before the cameras within weeks, Selznick began mulling over the final casting, not only of Domini but also of the male lead, Androvsky. Then quite unexpectedly in late March he solved both his casting problems at one blow by hiring Charles Boyer and Marlene Dietrich for the leads. The two had suddenly become available after they had both walked off the Paramount picture *Hotel Imperial* in a dispute over the firing of director Ernst Lubitsch. Boyer was just exotic and romantic enough for the part of the Trappist monk, added to which he was new enough in Hollywood not to have been seen to death, and he

Merle Oberon and Gilbert Roland in a color test for *The Garden of Allah.* Selznick had signed Oberon for the lead, and the sudden availability of Dietrich necessitated his paying Oberon $25,000 to cancel her contract.

David O. Selznick, Marlene Dietrich, and Charles Boyer looking cool and dapper in the 105-degree heat of Buttercup Valley, Arizona.

Black Dietrich

Dietrich in red

Red-and-yellow Dietrich

Dietrich in red, yellow, and blue

The portrait on the opposite page was taken in late 1936 by the celebrated photographer Anton Bruehl. It had been commissioned by *Cinema Arts,* an expensive, high-quality film magazine modeled after *Vogue* and *Fortune.* J. S. Selden, the art director of *Cinema Arts,* broke the image down into its color components, as shown above, all of which taken together not only yield stunning interpretations of Marlene Dietrich but also give a good idea of how she looked in each stage of Technicolor printing.

(Overleaf) Filming *The Garden of Allah* 60 miles outside of Yuma, Arizona, in the Mojave Desert, April 1936. A complete tent city was constructed to house the sixty people making the film, including director Richard Boleslawski (right, seated under the Technicolor camera). W. Howard Greene, who, along with Hal Rosson, photographed the picture, is peering through the viewfinder on the camera at Marlene Dietrich and Charles Boyer. The reflecting pool was designed by art director Lyle Wheeler and constructed in the desert by a gang of twenty laborers and grips, who also brought in the palm trees. They had to do this three times, as windstorms kept filling the pool with sand and knocking down the trees.

These frames from a Technicolor print of *The Garden of Allah* give a good approximation of the creamy texture and subtlety of the colorings used. The scene of Dietrich and Boyer in the desert was the work of W. Howard Greene; the caravan was filmed by the second unit cameraman, John Waters, who had been borrowed from MGM. Below is a rather self-conscious attempt to achieve the look of the old masters: "A monastery near a certain capital of Europe." The lighting on the crucifix was painted on the wall, while the vaulted ceiling and the sun's rays were painted (by Jack Cosgrove) on a plate of sheet glass, which was placed in front of the camera and photographed simultaneously with the real action.

was receiving a terrific build-up as a new Continental lover. Selznick considered Dietrich to be a true movie star, one who was being mishandled at Paramount where she was given roles that were artificial and remote. But, while appreciative of Dietrich as a star attraction, he was also concerned about her star temperament, cautioning her that the budget for the picture was already extraordinarily high and that her $200,000 fee was adding to it greatly; he hoped she would not cause any delays between takes, messing about with her makeup and her costumes. Dietrich promised the utmost cooperation, assuring Selznick that the tales of her production hold-ups were nonsense and, anyway, she had to be in London by early July for a picture, so she would certainly do everything she could.

She began working with director Richard Boleslawski, former actor, author, dancer, cavalry officer, and a fugitive member of the Moscow Art Theatre. Selznick was still stitching the script together, rereading his copy of the book for some clue about how to handle the archaic dialogue. Admitting defeat as production neared, he brought in playwright Lynn Riggs, whose Broadway career was in high gear, and the two tried to put believable words into the characters' mouths. Late in March, Boleslawski led an expedition into the Arizona wastes where temperatures were over the hundred mark and filming could only be carried on from dawn till noon. Several weeks of enforced isolation and the lengthy shooting delays due to the location forced tempers up as well as the budget. To see what was causing the trouble, Selznick dispatched Henry Ginsberg's new assistant, Raymond Klune, a young man who had just joined the production department after spending some years with D. W. Griffith and with Paramount's East Coast studios.

"I went down there," recalls Klune, "and they were so far out in the desert that they were all eating, drinking, and breathing sand. There were about sixty people and there were all these internal feuds; people were getting sick from sunstroke and it just was not a very efficient way to make a picture." Klune relayed this opinion to Selznick, recommending that the company be brought back, but Selznick held on for a while longer, hoping that the company could achieve its objective of getting some spectacular desert views to serve as a background for the rather turgid plot. He sent Lyle Wheeler down to the location to work with Boleslawski on getting as many of the exterior scenes done as quickly as possible. The interiors would be done on their return to Culver City. In anticipation of this the art director, Sturges Carne, was having built on Stage 14 the interior of a desert chapel that was unintentionally turning into a cathedral. Ray Klune was horrified to find the set being built of real adobe bricks a foot thick. When he said to Carne and the construction foreman, Harold Fenton, "It's none of my business, but what the hell are you doing this for? The stage will collapse," Carne answered him by saying, "You're right, it is none of your business." The following week, as the chapel neared completion, the floor did collapse, sending the entire set into the basement, whereupon Carne was fired and Wheeler took over for the balance of the film.

Nevertheless, by July 7 shooting was finished. Dietrich left immediately for London, and David and Hal Kern began picking out the photographic takes and angles that would make up the final negative. They did so hampered by the fact that they were using black-and-white work prints, as Technicolor took several days to process and deliver color dailies. Once the picture had been assembled, they began the long and delicate process of balancing the color, which varied not only from scene to scene but from shot to shot. However, the beauty of the Technicolor processing method lay in its correction control. Each scene was adjusted in accordance with the wishes of the art director, the cameraman, the Technicolor advisers, and Selznick. When the disagreements began between the Technicolor people who said something shouldn't be done and Selznick's staff who wanted it done, Merian Cooper from Pioneer would step in and act as peacemaker. Cooper had studied painting and how the old masters used color composition, and it was he who persuaded the Kalmuses that the color look of Technicolor should be modeled after the Dutch and Flemish painters of the sixteenth and seventeenth centuries, with their rich, rounded pastels and their use of color to draw attention to detail. His influence was strongly opposed by Kalmus's wife, Natalie, who was in charge of all color matters for the company and who wanted everything bright and clear and almost monochromatic.

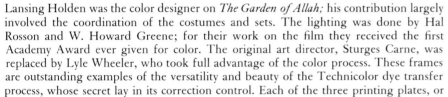

Lansing Holden was the color designer on *The Garden of Allah;* his contribution largely involved the coordination of the costumes and sets. The lighting was done by Hal Rosson and W. Howard Greene; for their work on the film they received the first Academy Award ever given for color. The original art director, Sturges Carne, was replaced by Lyle Wheeler, who took full advantage of the color process. These frames are outstanding examples of the versatility and beauty of the Technicolor dye transfer process, whose secret lay in its correction control. Each of the three printing plates, or matrices, could be made to absorb different amounts of the color dyes, which gave an enormous range to the hue and intensity of any color. These dyes were laid down separately on the film over a faint black-and-white key image, which sharpened the definition and gave the colors their characteristic richness. (Above, left and right, and bottom, right) Charles Boyer and Marlene Dietrich. (Below, left) Viennese dancing star Tilly Losch is the seductive dancing girl. (Below, right) Joseph Schildkraut in a red fez. (Bottom, left) Basil Rathbone holds hands with Dietrich.

Cooper prevailed, however, and *The Garden of Allah* was given a sumptuous, luminous look by the Technicolor laboratories, which now began the slow, exacting process of turning out completed prints of the film.

In early summer, while this was being done, Selznick and his wife (they now had two children) took off for a much-needed two weeks in Hawaii. On his return he began tinkering with the picture again, ordering so many changes that Technicolor had to put on an emergency crew to have the picture ready for the invitational preview at Grauman's Chinese Theatre on October 30. Just before this, he confided to Jock Whitney that "everybody here seems to be quite pepped up about the picture in its present form and I certainly hope they are right. Personally, I am goddam sick of it and wish that I could stop getting ideas on ways to improve it. . . ." When it finally premiered at the Chinese Theatre in a glamorous and highly visible preview, the cost had skyrocketed to an astronomical $1,447,760, and while it received respectable notices, the picture never returned its cost, being the first failure Selznick had had since *Vanessa: Her Love Story* (1935) at MGM. But Whitney and Selznick, looking at the film as a Technicolor showcase, considered that the money had been well spent. For in its original dye transfer form, *The Garden of Allah,* with its extravagant, robust, and exquisitely controlled color, turned out to be one of the visual masterpieces of 1930s picture-making and of incalculable benefit in the prestige it brought to both Technicolor and Selznick International.

The problems in producing *The Garden of Allah,* the enormous overruns on the cost and the disorganized state of its making, proved that Selznick International was not yet a smoothly functioning production outfit. Part of the trouble was the new staff's lack of familiarity with each other's operating methods, which caused misunderstandings and confusion. As *The Garden of Allah* neared completion, Selznick began working out the logistics of setting up a studio that would be able to adapt itself to his working habits—which now, without the entrenched discipline of MGM or Paramount, had begun to take on a more self-indulgent, erratic form—in order to allow him to operate in what was for him the most productive if not the most efficient manner. To do this, Henry Ginsberg had organized a loose confederation of departments, all of which were to be instantly responsive to Selznick's every production whim. Central to this was the job of production manager, and Selznick had gone through three in the first year: Phil Ryan, Ray Flynn, and Ted Butcher, all industry veterans who just could not quite adapt to David's high-pressure, almost improvisatory methods. To find someone who could do the job to his satisfaction now became an imperative, for in late 1936 Whitney, Selznick, and the other directors of the company had decided to go all out in their plans for Selznick International. Whitney in particular was anxious to streamline his film interests, and in the interest of efficiency a merger was effected between Selznick International and Pioneer Pictures, with Merian Cooper joining the company as a vice-president and executive producer.

After a series of board meetings in November 1936, it was announced that Selznick International would make twelve pictures in the coming year, four of them in Technicolor, at a total cost of $9 million, upping the Whitney family investment to close to $12 million. "It is our hope," said Whitney, "to take the commanding position in the independent

THEY LOVED EACH OTHER WITH THE FIERCENESS OF THOSE WHO HAVE BEEN DENIED LOVE!

Nothing else mattered. As they faced each other, time stopped in its flight...The memory of barren, bitter years fell away...nothing remained except the tropic stars, the silent desert night and the tumultuous beat of their singing hearts!

Selznick International Presents

Marlene DIETRICH
CHARLES BOYER

THE GARDEN OF ALLAH
IN TECHNICOLOR
Produced by DAVID O. SELZNICK
From the book by ROBERT HICHENS • Directed by RICHARD BOLESLAWSKI • Released thru UNITED ARTISTS

field, and to be the first independent company operating on a large scale to concentrate solely on high-quality pictures. We have no intention of adding to the industry's burden of cheap product." This new schedule would require more studio space; the company had been leasing space at the RKO-Pathé studios, but now arrangements were made to take over the entire lot, rename it Selznick International Studios, and operate the entire plant as a rental facility. To make all this run smoothly and at maximum efficiency would require a production manager who was intelligent and unflappable enough to cope with all the crises that Selznick's pictures seemed heir to.

Selznick had been very impressed with Ray Klune's handling of the various problems on *Allah*, especially his ability to anticipate a problem and to see it through to its quickest and most sensible conclusion. After a final bit of exasperation with Ted Butcher, Selznick asked Klune to take the job. Klune accepted, not without some trepidation, for as he stated, "With David, there were days when you weren't even sure what you were going to do tomorrow, and in motion pictures any time lost is a hell of a lot of money lost. And with the plans for the expansion, taking over the whole studio, and with outside producers coming in, we would have more activity than the majors had at the time. Being an independent operation meant you had to organize for each individual project." Klune assumed his new post just as David, through his brother Myron's agency, was closing a deal with William Wellman to make two pictures for the year-old Selznick International.

William Wellman's career had been rushing along at a pell-mell pace, which was characteristic of both him and his pictures. After leaving Paramount in 1930, he had gone to Warner Bros.-First National, where he had startled the nation with *The Public Enemy* (1931), a trenchant, honest, and quite brutal picture about gangsters. In the years following, he had turned out thirty-five films, including two minor masterpieces, *Heroes for Sale* and *Wild Boys of the Road*. He and Selznick had collaborated with not such happy results on *The Conquerors* at RKO; then he had toiled awhile in MGM's vineyards, stamping out no vintage and arousing the wrath of Mayer in the process. Wellman's Irish temperament, his background as an aviator in the Lafayette Flying Corps during World War I, and his friendship with Douglas Fairbanks, Sr., were all factors that led to his becoming first an actor, then a director, and sometimes out of necessity a writer. The forty-year-old Wellman was tough, as any number of adversaries could testify; he had a wide circle of acquaintances and was fiercely loyal to his close friends, a circle that included Selznick. When angered, he could jump into a fray as quickly and as dangerously as any of his on-screen heroes. His view of the world, as expressed in his pictures, was a kind of hard-boiled romantic gallantry, an appreciation of the ironies of life and a romantic's view of the foibles of human nature. Like so many of his contemporaries in the business, he had a reputation for being a hell-raiser, but a line he wrote for a character in one of his Selznick scripts best sums him up: "In private life I'm a, well, you know! But whatever I do, I still love beauty . . . and I respect lovely things." The script was called *It Happened in Hollywood*, and it was one of two properties that Wellman brought with him when he came over from MGM.

The metamorphosis of *It Happened in Hollywood* into its final form as *A Star Is Born* is a shadowy, difficult-to-follow, but fascinating trip through the myths, gossip, and emotional verities of the village that the Hollywood movie colony really was. The people who inhabited it were concentrated close to each other and confronted with themselves and their work every single day, on the screen, in the papers, and on the radio. The lore of the town was rife with successes, has-beens, comebacks, ruined marriages, and tragic deaths, and after years and years of retelling and being gossiped about and clucked over, these events and people took on a kind of romantic patina, becoming the authentic legends of Hollywood, making winners out of losers and giving some of them an immortality that transcended anything they might actually have done in pictures. *A Star Is Born* is the closest thing we have to an ideal of the movies: what they meant to the people who worked in them and to the people who went to see them. It is a particularly vigorous chunk of Hollywood lore—noble, tragic, romantic, idealistic, but with a firm sense of the rueful ironies of life as it should be lived. All of this came about through the meshing of the Selznick-Wellman personalities and sen-

David Selznick clowning aboard the S.S. *Invader* sometime in 1937. The gentleman on the right is screenwriter Wells Root, with whom he worked on several projects, including *The Prisoner of Zenda*.

SELZNICKS EXPECTING NEW HEIR

Picture Producer and Wife Look Forward to Arrival of Second Child in Spring

A second child is expected in a few months by the David O. Selznicks.

Mrs. Selznick, the former Irene Mayer, youngest daughter of Louis

Mrs. David O. Selznick

B. Mayer, said last night she expected the child late in the spring.

"We're very happy," said the proud father-to-be, film producer and member of one of Hollywood's best known families.

Their first child, Jeffrey, was born in 1932. Mr. and Mrs. Selznick were married in 1930. They made last night's announcement at the home of Cedric Gibbons, director.

William Wellman (seated in front of camera) and some of the crew filming *A Star Is Born* (1937). Cameraman W. Howard Greene, one of the best of the Technicolor photographers, is leaning on the massive camera. Chief grip Fred Williams is directly behind him, and assistant director Eric Stacey is to the right of Wellman (in sweater and tie).

sibilities. Their ideas are so inextricably melded into the writing and texture of the story, the production and attitude of the picture, that the two men had difficulties determining who was responsible for what. Selznick has stated, "It was really a concept of my own, to tell the story of a rising star and a falling star . . . the original idea, the story line and the vast majority of scenes are my own," points which Wellman does not concede: ". . . Like hell! It was a story I wrote with a young writer named Bob Carson . . . based on things that happened . . . things from memory."

All that survives of Wellman and Carson's original story is a thirty-two-page rough draft of the first third, plus an outline for the rest of the story. Opening in a small movie theatre in the Canadian hinterlands, it introduces star-struck young Esther Victoria Blodgett watching Norman Maine in a tropical melodrama called *It Happened in Tahiti*. She lives in a farmhouse with her aunt, uncle, and grandmother. She is young, romantic, and yearning to make something of herself; only her grandmother gives her any understanding and encouragement, telling Esther after one particularly nasty battle with her aunt that the blood of the pioneers is in her veins, that her family has always stood up to adversity and overcome it; they conquered the wilderness: "We did it even though it broke our hearts. Because for every dream of yours that comes true, you pay the price in heartbreak . . . but if you're my granddaughter—if you've got any of my blood, you'll go out to that Hollywood you're always mooning about . . . maybe it's your wilderness; your frontier." With that, Granny gives her life savings to the girl and Esther is off to Los Angeles, where, while standing bewildered in front of the Brown Derby, she is caught up in a crowd that suddenly surrounds drunken matinee idol Norman Maine as he and his inamorata have a pitched verbal battle, which ends with the woman sweeping away while Maine signs autographs for the crowd. He scrawls his name across Esther's newspaper, and drives off leaving the girl open-mouthed in awe on the sidewalk.

From this point on, the original story was in outline form only, indicating forty-three more scenes that would tell the rest of Esther's adventures in Hollywood, her struggles to find film work, the people she

meets, including again Norman Maine, with whom she becomes romantically involved, and the comic-relief producer Joseph Grantham, who gives in to Maine's urgings to take a chance on Esther, whom he renames "Mona Lester" because he has a copy of the Mona Lisa in his office. As Mona's star rises, Maine's falls, his alcoholic hijinks coming to a head when he arrives drunk at the Academy Awards where Mona, now his wife, is receiving an award, interrupts her speech to make one of his own, and tells off the gathering for being hypocrites. After this he goes on another bender and is humiliated at a racetrack by getting into a brawl with his ex-publicity man. Arrested, he is remanded to the custody of Mona, who tells Grantham that she is giving up her career to care for her husband. Grantham tries to dissuade her, saying that there's nothing left of Norman to take care of; but she is adamant. Norman, overhearing this and not wanting to be responsible for the ruin of Mona's career, commits suicide by swimming into the Malibu sunset. At his funeral, Mona is set upon by her fans. Having had enough of Hollywood, she returns to Canada and her grandmother.

This was the story line that Wellman and Carson delivered to Selznick and, according to Wellman, "David said he was sorry, but he didn't like it. I thought it was a hell of a good story and I told it to his wife Irene, just before they went off on their Hawaiian vacation, and she went crazy over it. When they came back, David called me and said he had decided that he wanted to do the story." What Selznick had disliked about the original story was the attitude of its telling. It was satiric to the point of caricature in its treatment of Hollywood as a place, with all sorts of visual sight gags running through it about the process of moviemaking; the characters, except for the two leads, were either comic or vicious, and the look and feel of Hollywood the town came off as crazy, corrosive, bitter, and spirit-crushing. But once again, Selznick's romantic inclinations were stirred by the potential of the idea. The nagging dissatisfaction he had felt about *What Price Hollywood?*, the disappointment at what the story could have been with more time and thought—these factors evidently convinced him that *It Happened in Hollywood* could be turned into

192

something very close to what he felt about the place and the people.

The appeal of the eternal Cinderella story, a nobody who becomes somebody, crossed with elements of the Pygmalion legend and a bittersweet love story—the possibilities began to excite Selznick. Added to this were the phantoms, the ghosts of all the Hollywood tragedies, and his own personal memories of his father's failure, his mother's strength and loyalty, the Valentino funeral, and other examples of how the pressures of Hollywood could destroy the weak and reckless. Most recently, the case of John Gilbert came to mind. One of the great stars of the silent screen, Gilbert's career had been destroyed overnight, it seemed, in the changeover from silence to sound. Supposedly it was his voice, and that may at first have been a contributing factor; but what it really was was the revelation that the character he was presenting, the virile, flashing-eyed, romantic seducer, had been rendered unbelievable by sound. This almost instant rejection completely destroyed Gilbert's confidence and he never recovered. He had married a young actress, Virginia Bruce; while her career went full speed ahead, his skidded to a stop. He became an alcoholic, she divorced him, and soon after he was dead of a heart attack at the age of thirty-six. Selznick's Paramount mentor, B. P. Schulberg, had been brought down by booze, and the continuing tragedy of John Barrymore was evident to all who knew him or worked with him. Fragments of these stories and events were floating loosely in Selznick's imagination; the magnetism of the Wellman-Carson idea began pulling all these forces into a recognizable dramatic form, and on July 30 Selznick dictated his suggestions for changes in the story. Esther's farm was moved to North Dakota and she now sees Norman Maine for the first time as he drunkenly disrupts a concert at the Hollywood Bowl. The romance between the two, said Selznick,

> needs more development, more humor and perhaps some gentle comedy. Suggest looking at what we did in *What Price Hollywood?* with the Bennett character and her husband. We must be awfully careful that the fall of the star won't seem to have started with his marriage.

We should plant his faults very early and try getting over the idea that Esther feels she can help him if they married. More importantly, after the death of her husband, we should keep the idea that she is through, she won't go on, the producer pleads with her to no avail, but then at the very end, we can have some sort of tremendous lift with the grandmother telling her that there are a few people in the world made for more important things—giving her a pep talk on her career and stardom, etc.

Wellman and Carson delivered the second draft, incorporating the suggested changes, but Selznick found this version to be "much too straight now . . . you've taken out all the comedy. . . . I don't want to go over into burlesque as the first draft did . . . but some things can be used for laughs . . . the weird things seen on the streets of Hollywood . . . strange costumes, etc. We need at least one, maybe two comedy characters to run throughout the picture . . . you should put to the test every line and bit of business because if they are not entertaining or unusual the material is going to be awfully dull."

Then, very suddenly during this preparation phase, an event took place that stunned Hollywood and deeply affected David's whole concept of the Hollywood story. Over the Labor Day weekend Irving Thalberg died, completely unexpectedly. Not only was he one of Selznick's closest friends, but also someone whom he considered to be "the man who did more to raise the standards of motion picture production . . . giving all of us ideals of consistency . . . of uninterrupted integrity of endeavor." His death and the events surrounding his funeral at the Wilshire Boulevard Temple, with Thalberg's widow, Norma Shearer, and the other celebrated mourners being besieged by fans, evoked unpleasant echoes of the Valentino circus. Once again Selznick was forcibly reminded of the tawdriness of the moviegoers' world, where even death was considered to be just another chance to ogle the stars. The uncanny parallels between his Hollywood story and Norma Shearer's bereavement made Selznick extremely apprehensive about the wisdom of pro-

The title frame from *A Star Is Born,* photographed at night with the sky and lettering added later by Jack Cosgrove. Looking northeast across Hollywood proper, the building at the lower right is the First Methodist Church at Franklin and Highland. It served many purposes in many films, including the location for Constance Bennett's wedding in *What Price Hollywood?* and Norman Maine's funeral in *A Star Is Born.*

The iconography of Hollywood and the appeal of its excitement and glamour were given a sumptuous presentation in *A Star Is Born*, from the opening montage panning across the sky and hills through the impact of the converging planes, trains, and buses zooming into the camera. The views of the movie colony playgrounds included (above, left) the swimming pool at the Ambassador Hotel and (above, right) the opening day of the Santa Anita Racetrack (December 26, 1936).

(Opposite) These frames showing the arrival of star-struck Esther Blodgett at Grauman's Chinese Theatre were made from a Technicolor print of the film, which explains the strange shape of the theatre. The camera tilted down from the turret and panned over to the front of the theatre in an arc, leaving out a portion of the forecourt, but it was such a beautiful shot that we decided to piece it together here so that you could see the world's most famous theatre in its Technicolor heyday. Like thousands of tourists before her, Esther Blodgett can't resist trying a star's footprints on for size. The theatre's current attraction, for those with sharp eyes, is *The Garden of Allah*.

ceeding with the project, but after his emotional confusion settled down, he decided to go ahead, with one important change: the comic-relief producer, Joe Grantham, now became Oliver Niles, a paragon of dignity, taste, patience, and loyalty, who is concerned about his two stars on a personal level rather than on a strictly-business, exploitative basis as implied in the early drafts. To take up some of the comic slack left by this change, Wellman and Carson invented the character of Matt Libby, demon press agent, whose whirlwind of ideas and nonstop press release dialogue was patterned after Russell Birdwell, the head of Selznick's publicity office. The character of Libby proved valuable in that he became Norman Maine's nemesis, the repository of all that was crass and vengeful in Hollywood.

Once past his uncertainty about the story, Selznick began to be edgy about the title, wiring Kay Brown in New York that "feeling here is that 'Hollywood' has become identified with cheap quickie pictures such as *Hollywood Boulevard* . . . also Warners is making *Hollywood Hotel* which will be released before our picture. Anxious to get a romantic title which would link with two stars we hope to get for the picture . . . what is your reaction personally and Mr. Whitney to title *The Stars Below* which fits picture?" She wired back Whitney's reply: "Don't think *Stars Below* is clear . . . if poetic title is being thought of what about earlier suggestion of mine . . . *A Star Is Born?*" Selznick responded: "Tell the Chairman of the Board that we are enthusiastic about his suggestion and are delighted and astonished at the source. Please clear and register it immediately."

Now having a title and half a script, the legal department began the arduous search for any prior conflicts over the title, the names of the characters, and more important in this case, the story points that were based to some extent on actual situations. The first was relatively simple: the title had been used by P. G. Wodehouse for a short story; he was working at MGM and turned out to be very gracious about it, releasing the title for no fee. Finding the real-life counterparts of the characters was much more time-consuming. The legal department subscribed to a service that had offices in every major city in the country. Upon request, these legal research services would check through all the major city directories, telephone books, and other sources to turn up names that might be similar, the reason for this being the many invasion of privacy suits that could be brought against the studio for unwarranted use of a person's name. Finally, on the subject of story similarities, the legal office made up a twenty-page brief, listing similarities in situations and incidents between the story and some of the more well-known real-life parallels, including the John Gilbert affair and the Frank Fay–Barbara Stanwyck marriage—he a major star, she a struggling unknown, until they got on the Hollywood seesaw.

Wellman said the familiar incidents were "just things that happened," sometimes to himself, as in the dramatic courtroom scene where Maine is verbally assaulted by the judge, which had happened word for word to Wellman when he was up on a drunk driving charge. Maine's drunken speech to the Academy was lifted in spirit from an earlier Wellman-Selznick collaboration, Paramount's 1929 *The Man I Love,* for which writer Herman Mankiewicz devised a scene where Richard Arlen as a drunken, has-been fighter tells off a bunch of society snobs, while his cast-aside wife watches tearfully. And one sequence in particular was written into the picture several weeks before shooting began. Wellman and Selznick were going over scenes in the script when George Cukor joined them late in the afternoon. He had been, he told them, "to see Jack Barrymore about playing a part in *Camille* . . . he had put himself into some kind of home in Culver City to stop drinking. He was a friend of mine and I went to take the script to him. It was an old frame house that called itself a rest home. I went into some dreary, depressing room . . . and I noticed something that always strikes me as very shabby . . . they hadn't changed the tablecloths. Then Jack came in with a sort of an aide called Kelly, and Jack said, 'Can we sit in here, Kelly? Nobody's going to come through and disturb us by pretending he's Napoleon?' They liked the scene so much," says Cukor, "that they put it into the script." But most of the dialogue was rough, as was the overall feel of the scene, so it was sent for rewriting accompanied by a blue memo page of instructions addressed to "Parker and Campbell." Parker and Campbell were Dorothy and Alan, husband and wife, she of the famous Algonquin round table, author of ironic, strong short stories and reams of epigrams

and short verses of which the most famous was "Men seldom make passes/At girls who wear glasses." He was her husband, good-looking, younger than she, very professional and workman-like in his writing. Intimates of Lillian Hellman, Robert Benchley, and other literary lights of the time, they were flown in from New York at $1,750 a week for the two of them to write the final adaptation, especially the dialogue, and to punch up characterizations.

Selznick was unhappy about Esther Blodgett's stage name, Mona; it was almost a caricature. At one of the story conferences Carson suggested changing it to Vicki, short for Victoria. This arbitrary choosing of names was neatly and sharply skewered in the final picture in a scene in which Oliver Niles and his publicity man, Matt Libby, run down all the various combinations that might fit, in alphabetical order: "Esther Lester—keep the Lester, drop the Esther. . . . Vicki, Vicki, pronounced Vicki Vicki, rhymes with sicky . . . very nice." The new name is then tried out on any number of secretaries, assistants, and everybody within earshot, before being conferred on the new Galatea.

What bothered Selznick even more than Esther's name was the ending: Esther/Vicki's giving up the movies and returning to her grandmother in North Dakota. This was remedied by following Selznick's suggested change of bringing the grandmother out to Hollywood of her own accord after Maine's publicized death, because, as she puts it, "I know when I'm needed." She convinces Esther to stay and return to the movies, and Esther goes to the premiere of her latest picture at Grauman's Chinese, where she sees Norman Maine's footprints in the cement with the words "Good luck." Fortified by this, she makes a gracious little speech to her fans, telling them how glad she is that they want her back, then, as this draft of the script had it, "Her eyes welling with tears, and looking off into some far-off place of her own, she goes into the theatre as the music builds to a tremendous crescendo and we FADE OUT."

Preparation now went ahead in earnest to make this Selznick International's third picture, even though it was legally a Pioneer picture. Pioneer had the Technicolor contract, whereby it was committed to make a certain number of pictures in the process by certain dates because of the scarcity of Technicolor cameras; there were only five in Hollywood, and their use was scheduled very tightly. Consequently, *A Star Is Born* would have to start filming no later than October 31. With that date set, the rough script was sent to Henry Ginsberg's office, which routed a copy to the heads of each of the several departments that for the next few months would occupy themselves with getting the story on the screen. One of these was a recent and experimental addition to the staff of artisans/craftsmen who put a picture together—color designer. Ostensibly, this job was done by Natalie Kalmus at Technicolor, but Selznick International, with its fairly heavy color schedule, needed someone on the premises at all times to work out the kinks and rough spots in the color scripts and schemes. This somewhat innovative task was put under the supervising eye of Lansing C. Holden, architect, illustrator, flier in World War I, and a close friend of Merian Cooper. Holden's script for *A Star Is Born* broke the story down into master scenes, and an overall color choice was made to fit the mood of each scene. Holden commented:

Every color designer must recognize that the one key color present in every scene is the color of the face of the actor. The background should be kept a cool, neutral color so that it will retreat behind the face, which is always warm. The designer must know the type of lighting used in every scene. . . . Color should be used like music to heighten the emotional impact of a scene and it is the job of the color designer to plan so that the lighting and costumes and the backgrounds are all harmonious . . . because in a dark theatre, surrounded with a jet black frame, colors on the screen are increased in contrast; this concentration makes them seem even brighter than they are.

With all this to be concerned about, Holden began making color sketches of the scenes as he saw them from the script, then submitting them to Lyle Wheeler, the art director of Selznick International and a man with his own ideas about form, design, and especially color. Wheeler too had an architect's training, as well as being an illustrator; the depression had pushed him into the movies, because, as he put it, "Architecture took a dive . . . and I knew some people in the picture

(Above) Lyle Wheeler, artist, illustrator, and architect, is seen here with four of the set models for *A Star Is Born.* These models were used by the director and the cameramen to work out camera angles, lighting, and blocking. Two of Wheeler's set designs for *A Star Is Born* are shown below. He was one of the first art directors to use glass brick extensively in his designs, as in this room (below) in the home of Norman Maine's director, Casey Burke. The Malibu beach house of Norman Maine and Vicki Lester (bottom) is a model of conservative late-thirties design, with its brick walls, slatted doors, and early American furniture—a combination that dominated American interior decorating for the next decade. Set decoration was by Edward Boyle.

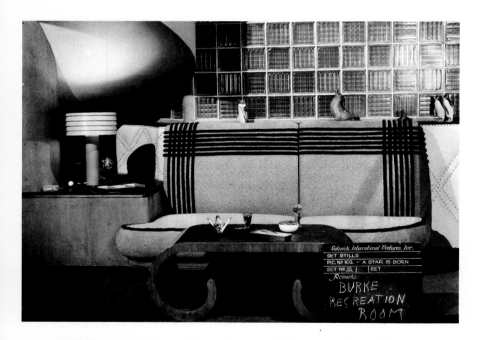

business and they often said, 'Come on, go to work.'" He did so, becoming an assistant art director at MGM on *David Copperfield,* and impressing Selznick with his taste, imagination, and the brisk, efficient manner in which he got across his ideas both on paper and on the screen. Wheeler was one of the key people Selznick had brought with him from MGM. He has said: "David was one of the first producers who loved color . . . and we both felt that in *A Star Is Born* the color should not be noticeable, that it should not get in the way of the story; we tried to lose the gaudiness and not emphasize the fact that there was a beautiful blue sky with white clouds because then your story point is right out the window."

The problems confronting Wheeler on *A Star Is Born* were compounded by the fact that Selznick wanted to make the picture as realistic as possible in its depiction of Hollywood, and the reality, as Wheeler pointed out to him in one case, simply was not attractive:

David and I had an absolutely huge argument about the set for the studio commissary. He wanted the original MGM commissary to be used the way it used to be, a really junky place. I said that no one in the world really knows what it looks like; I said it's a mistake to show that piece of junk that we ate our breakfast and lunch in. He said no, that was the feeling he wanted, and I wouldn't give in, and he said, "You do it the way I want it." So I did, and the day before we were to shoot he came down and said, "You're right, build the other one." So I had already designed it, it was based on the new one that Cedric Gibbons had designed at MGM, so I used that as the model and used a lot of glass brick, which was just then coming in, and big circle windows so that you could see people going by . . . we tore the old one down in ten minutes and you'd never believe the number of people we had in the crew that built the new one. We worked all night but we had it up and dressed the next day, ready for shooting.

With sets being built and the script nearing a semblance of finality, the very delicate matter of casting began to occupy all of Selznick's and Wellman's attention. The role of Norman Maine was almost schizophrenic as written, with sudden shifts back and forth between his drunken binges and the smooth, easy charm of a romantic leading man. There were not many actors of any stature who could play the part; adding to the difficulty was the character's suicide, a gamble dramatically, for the on-screen suicide of a leading romantic character, especially in a modern original, was something of a calculated risk. To make Norman Maine believable would require a performer who had the looks of a matinee idol and the talent to portray the character's self-destructive impulses, and combined these with enough charm to win the audience's sympathy and liking. If it had been five years earlier, John Barrymore would have been perfect, but his own problem kept him from being seriously considered. David turned to one of his brother Myron's stable of clients, offering the part to Fredric March, whose film career had begun at Paramount at the same time Selznick's had. In seven years he had become one of the most sought-after leading men on the American screen, with a versatility that could embrace everything from the sophisticated repartee of *Design for Living* to the ghoulish terrors of *Dr. Jekyll and Mr. Hyde,* for which he received an Academy Award. He had an air of quiet authority about him and there was an underlying sensitivity and good-humored melancholy to the best of his work that had not been used to its fullest advantage in Selznick's *Anna Karenina.* He had just finished playing the title role in the Warner Bros. epic *Anthony Adverse,* based on the year's phenomenal best seller. It had been the ninth in a row of costume pictures for the actor, and part of the appeal of *A Star Is Born* as pitched to him by David was that it would be a modern role, in Technicolor; as Selznick argued persuasively, it would

return you to the gay, swashbuckling modern type of romantic role in which you were so successful early in your career in pictures like *Laughter* and *The Royal Family.* . . . The latter, which you always liked, has many things in common with Norman Maine. When you read the script, please bear in mind it's unfinished and if you have any strong feelings about any of it we can discuss this and consider changes.

(Above) The bedroom of a bachelor movie star as designed by Lyle Wheeler and furnished by Edward Boyle. Wheeler's use of massive blond walls and indirect recessed lighting set a style trend throughout the country. The man in the bed and the one bent over the book at the right are both Fredric March, as we pieced this picture together from two separate shots in the film. (Below, left) A studio commissary, by Wheeler out of Gibbons, circa 1937. (Below, right) Starlet Vicki Lester is given a voice lesson by actor Edwin Maxwell in an office designed by Wheeler, decorated by Boyle, and color coordinated by Lansing Holden.

March read it and agreed to take the part, with only a few reservations about the dialogue, which Selznick assured him was being rewritten.

Now that he had his male star, Selznick began searching for an actress who was also a star and could play the part, making palatable the combination of sweet innocence and unswerving ambition that the role called for and still managing the transition to the tragic heroine of the final scenes. He vacillated for a time between the Austrian actress Elisabeth Bergner and Hollywood's Margaret Sullavan before something made him take up the idea of Janet Gaynor. She had been one of the sweethearts of American films in the years immediately preceding the changeover to sound and had won the first Academy Award given to an actress, in 1929, for her performances in *Sunrise, Seventh Heaven,* and *Street Angel.* During the early years of the depression, her sweet wholesomeness and ingénue's charm had kept her career going at a steady pace, but after the appearance of Mae West, Marlene Dietrich, and other exotics of the 1934–35 period, her popularity had declined until she was seriously considering giving up acting. Her last film, *Small Town Girl,* made for MGM, had been directed by William Wellman, and while the stories of their differences on the set were well known, Wellman did not raise serious objections to Selznick's suggestion that they consider her for the part of Esther Blodgett/Vicki Lester. She was, after all, a star; she

was intelligent, hardworking, and a good actress, with just the right combination of sweetness and spunk that the part called for. Selznick offered her the role, and she accepted it immediately.

After several days of makeup and costume tests, the *Star Is Born* company got down to serious dramatic business on the October 31 Technicolor deadline. It was a Saturday and the cast call had been for 9:30—dressed, made up, and on the set, which was the interior of Esther's Hollywood boardinghouse. After Wellman had run through two blocking and camera movement and line rehearsals, the first shot was taken at 9:55. Work continued at this swift pace until they had done six of the script scenes that took place in this set and covered three pages of dialogue with sixteen different camera positions. When they all quit at 7:00 P.M., they had photographed approximately three minutes of the finished picture. This pace was typical of Wellman; he was one of the fastest shooters in town, and drove himself as relentlessly as he drove his cast and crew.

For the next eight weeks, the company worked on the forty-two sets Lyle Wheeler had designed, ranging from the interior of a streamlined camper to the forecourt of the Chinese Theatre on Hollywood Boulevard. While Wellman directed the main action with the principals, a second crew, under assistant director Richard Rosson, was leapfrogging

all over Hollywood, photographing landmarks, street scenes, and other bits and pieces that would be used in the various montages and for background process plates, especially important in a color picture. This second unit, taking along special effects man Jack Cosgrove, on November 18 journeyed down the coast to Huntington Beach where they photographed the coastline and vistas of the ocean at various times of the day to be used as backgrounds for Maine's suicide, getting what they considered to be a spectacular sunset effect at 5:00 P.M. The next day, in an eerie pre-echo of the picture's final scenes, the body of actor John Bowers was washed ashore about a mile from where the company had been working. Despondent over his inability to get work and the break-up of his marriage, he had set out alone in a sailboat two days earlier, telling friends that "he was going to sail off into the sunset and never come back."

According to the production department, by the first week of December the company had already shot 122 minutes of footage and the picture was only three-quarters complete. This was forcibly brought to Selznick's attention by Hal Kern, who had assembled what they had up to that point. The average running time for a feature was 90 to 100 minutes, so this posed a problem, as Selznick was still contemplating adding scenes to the story. Instead, faced with Kern's rather startling information, he began dropping scenes that had not yet been filmed, and for a week considered eliminating completely the prologue in North Dakota and the character of the grandmother, switching her "chin up" speech to the producer, Oliver Niles. When Kern heard this he was aghast, telling David: "The grandmother is one of the wonderful characters of this picture . . . she's the one that really sends this little girl to Hollywood . . . if we take her out, we lose her great speech about the pioneers and all and we lose an important understanding of what Esther is about, where she comes from." Selznick had a high regard for Kern's opinion and since he was adamant about it, the grandmother stayed in the picture; to make room for her, several sequences showing behind-the-scenes activity in the studios were dropped, as well as a long honeymoon montage, and a montage of Vicki's rising fame. These eliminations and revisions left roughly two weeks' more work for Wellman and the principals, but on December 8, Wellman became sick with the flu. Rather than shut down the company for however long he would be ill, Selznick borrowed Jack Conway from MGM, who continued working the company without a break. When Wellman recovered, he looked at the Conway material, didn't like it, and he and Selznick agreed that he could reshoot it. The

picture was completed on December 28, with the filming of the scene on a set of the forecourt of Grauman's Chinese Theatre, where the widowed Vicki sees Norman's footprints but goes bravely on into the theatre.

After spending a month on editing and finishing up the bits and pieces of bridging material, Selznick arranged to preview the picture in Pomona, a little town set in the middle of the orange groves that surrounded Los Angeles. It was an unnerving experience, for according to Wellman, "About a half an hour into the picture most of the audience got up and left. I thought to myself, Jesus, they hate it, we're dead, but Bob Carson ran out to ask them what they didn't like. It turned out that they liked it fine but many of them worked in the orange groves and it was a bad winter and the smudge pots had to be kept going or the crops would wither." The ones who stayed had been attentive, laughing in all the right places, and the preview cards had been enthusiastic, but there had been too much laughter in the early part, which suddenly stopped as the story moved into tragedy. It was not, as Selznick observed, a smooth transition, and the ending lacked the emotional lift he had felt was so necessary to keep the story from ending on a depressing note. The picture was so close to being what he wanted it to be, but it needed more work, more brushing up of some of the details; there were a handful of scenes he felt could be measurably improved by rewriting and restaging: "I find that there is a reaction of uncertainty that March has committed suicide," he wrote Wellman. ". . . We lose a strong point if it is not clear to the audience that he has done so, and that Gaynor does not know he has. As it is, even when the audience learns that it is so, it is too much for them to grasp at this minute, the fact that she thinks it is an accidental death."

By now Parker and Campbell had left the project, so David turned the rewrites over to two junior writers he had been grooming. Ring Lardner, Jr., was the son of the famous writer, and Budd Schulberg was the son of David's ex-boss. To them fell the chore of rewriting material they were not completely familiar with, and they bogged down. Selznick now turned to MGM, borrowing one of their hottest young writers, John Lee Mahin, who'd been brought to Hollywood by Ben Hecht. "David wasn't sure about the balance of the comedy and the build-up to the tragedy," says Mahin. "It wasn't coming together. After I looked at the picture I told him that he shouldn't think about making it into more of a comedy. The handwriting is on the wall when the girl first sees him drunk at the Hollywood Bowl. It has to be a tragedy." Mahin wrote several additional scenes for the picture, and it was he who came

A Star Is Born used some of the best character actors in Hollywood for the subsidiary roles. In the photo at the left, set in the North Dakota farmhouse of the Blodgett family, are J. C. Nugent as Esther's uncle, child actor A. W. Sweatt as her teasing cousin, and Clara Blandick as her impatient Aunt Mattie. Directly behind Janet Gaynor is actress May Robson as Granny, who gives Esther the money to go to Hollywood and who turns

up again at the end of the story to encourage Vicki to stay a star. (Right) Adolphe Menjou as the aristocratic, kindly producer Oliver Niles; Lionel Stander as demon press agent Matt Libby, Norman Maine's nemesis. The cast also included Edgar Kennedy, Franklin Pangborn, Guinn Williams, Peggy Wood, and Marshall ("Mickey") Neilan playing a director.

up with the "tremendous lift" for the ending that so far had eluded Selznick, Wellman, and all the other writers. Mahin had been struck by a line of dialogue written by Parker and Campbell and delivered by Oliver Niles after Vicki tells him she will not make any more pictures. As he leaves her he says, "Goodbye, Vicki Lester, you were a grand girl—and good luck, Mrs. Norman Maine." Mahin suggested to Selznick that they retake the scene at the Chinese Theatre, changing it so that Vicki, on her way to the microphone, is momentarily halted by seeing Maine's footprints. "Simply retake the reaction to the footprints, more or less as it is," recommended Mahin, "then she pulls herself together and the announcer asks her if she will say a few words, Gaynor advancing with all the pride in the world, throwing her head back, and with tears in her eyes saying, 'Hello everybody, this is Mrs. Norman Maine,'" thereby giving the picture its long-sought-after perfect ending on a note of triumph, a line so right that it became an instant classic and is one of the few phrases to exist apart from its source as the essence of Hollywood romanticism.

After the necessary changes were made, a second preview was held on March 9 in Long Beach, and this time, with the new ending, the picture received loud and sustained applause at the end, and the preview comment cards were all highly complimentary. Selznick was now being pressed by his distributor, United Artists, to stop fiddling with the picture and tell them when they could announce it for release. Hal Kern, Henry Ginsberg, and Selznick figured that the picture could be made ready for a preview premiere at the Chinese on April 18, with the New York opening following after that. The United Artists people managed to get the picture booked into the Radio City Music Hall as the Easter attraction. Because of the length of time it took to get the Technicolor prints made, the studio went on double time in order to finish the credits, inserts, color balancing, and all the other details that Selznick loved to lavish his attention on. One of these areas was the music, which was in the hands of Max Steiner, whom Selznick had brought over from RKO when he went independent. Steiner had scored the first two Selznick International pictures, and he and Selznick had worked harmoniously on both films, but on *A Star Is Born* they clashed repeatedly. Selznick ordered new bits and pieces of music, seemingly arbitrarily, for various scenes; switched music tracks around because he thought they fit certain scenes better than others; and otherwise interfered in what Steiner rightfully believed to be his province. Because of Selznick's constant changes and interference, the score was such a mess when it came time to put it to the picture that David ordered a complete new recording of it done literally overnight.

Steiner's anger and the pressure were factors that worked to the picture's advantage, for his score to *A Star Is Born* is one of the delights of the film, giving a syncopated excitement and full-bodied glamour to the depiction of Hollywood; his use of muted trombones and trumpets with echoing tinkly pianos against lush strings established once and for all the sophisticated-sounding romantic ambience of the town in the thirties. By the time Steiner had reworked it, Selznick was greatly pleased with all of the score, and he continually reused portions of it in his pictures for the next ten years. Steiner, however, was so irritated by the whole experience that he asked Selznick to release him from his contract so that he could take an offer with Warner Bros. Selznick, not wanting to lose him entirely, worked out a split contract with Warner Bros. whereby he had the right to use Steiner on four films within the next two years.

As the release date neared, Selznick began to be concerned about the selling of the picture; based on the campaigns put on for *Fauntleroy* and *The Garden of Allah,* he was not impressed with the way United Artists sold his pictures, and he began urging Whitney in New York to convince UA to have several advertising agencies prepare ideas for a campaign, rather than the usual United Artists custom of doing it in-house. Yet selling the picture would have to take place in spite of several obstacles from Selznick: he refused to allow a synopsis of the picture to be published, and he ordered Russell Birdwell's publicity department "not to go in for any copy that gives the story away or, conversely, is too sophisticated as the picture is directed very largely at the fan magazine audience, even though I have attempted to make it appeal also to the higher type audience."

Selznick was a shrewd judge of different publicity approaches, as evidenced in a long memo he sent to Whitney, Birdwell, and George Schaeffer, the new president of United Artists:

> There is no sense in spending money for ads in national magazines on a picture that does not have simultaneous openings all over the country ... while I assume that the interest in Hollywood is world-wide and that March and Gaynor are popular everywhere, I still feel that we should spend more on *A Star Is Born* than on *Allah,* which had a naturally foreign appeal, and *Fauntleroy,* which had a natural English appeal. To this end I think we should spend upwards of $50,000 domestically and $25,000 overseas to properly exploit the picture.

As part of the publicity, the Mutual Broadcasting Company would hook up a coast-to-coast program from Grauman's Chinese the night of the premiere, an event that took place on April 20 with massed searchlights,

The Hollywood home of Mr. and Mrs. Norman Maine. These sequences were photographed on the grounds of the Beverly Hills estate of Harold Janss. The Janss family

was prominent in southern California real estate; their investment company owned most of the Westwood area and had earlier donated 200 acres of land to UCLA.

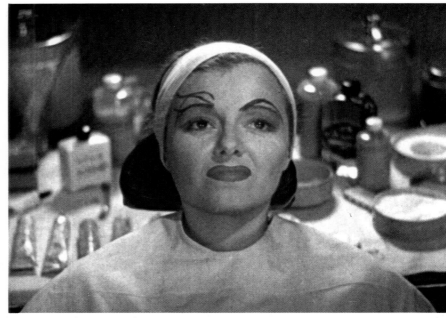

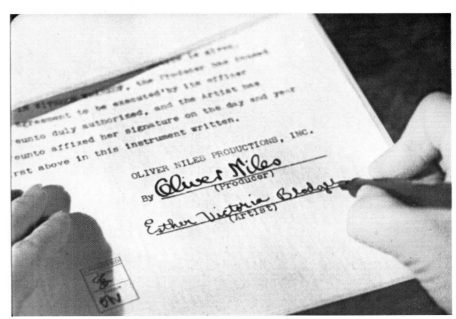

Cinderella meets the fairy godmother: Esther Blodgett's screen test with Norman Maine, the biggest star in Hollywood. (Top, left) Studio makeup artists (Adrien Rosely and Arthur Hoyt) try to turn her into some variation of the reigning screen queens: eyebrows courtesy of Dietrich, Lombard, and Harlow; mouth *à la* Crawford. Giving it up as a bad job ("Does she always have to look surprised?" one of them mutters), Esther's natural look is allowed to come through ("Tastes change," explains Oliver Niles, "and like eyebrows, I think tastes are coming back to the natural."). On the set (middle, left), Esther is prepared for the camera by being energetically de-bugged (by Billy Dooley), while the director and his crew (middle, right) wait. Playing the part of

the director (with hand on chin) is Owen Moore, former star of the silent screen, whose alcoholism ruined both his career as a performer and his marriage to Mary Pickford (he was her first husband). Moore was a client of Myron Selznick and was given this part as a favor by David. Standing behind Moore in this scene is Andy Devine, playing the comic-relief role of an assistant director and Esther's best friend in Hollywood. Directly in front of the camera is Carleton Griffith, and the actor to the right of the camera is Charles Williams, a familiar character face all during the 1930s and 1940s. Esther's test with Maine (bottom, left) is a success, and she is signed to a contract by Oliver Niles (signature by David O. Selznick).

203

The quintessence of Hollywood tragedy—the peak of Vicki Lester's film fame and the most humiliating moment of her life. At the Academy Awards ceremony in the Biltmore Bowl (first row, center—a combination live set and Cosgrove painting), Vicki Lester wins the Award for her performance in *Dream Without End*. As she makes her acceptance speech, a drunken Norman Maine arrives and interrupts, demanding two awards for the worst performances of the year. As he gesticulates wildly, he accidently slaps Vicki, bringing a gasp from the stunned crowd. Instantly contrite, he accompanies her to her table while the orchestra strikes up dance music, and, still in an alcoholic stupor, he orders another drink as the golden Oscar silently mocks him.

Death and Transfiguration:
After bailing Norman out of night court on a drunk charge, Vicki decides to give up her career to care for her alcoholic husband. Telling this to a sympathetic Oliver Niles, Vicki is overheard by a supposedly sleeping Norman Maine, who listens as Niles tells her that her husband is a mere shell, "a man with nothing left." Her mind is made up, and Niles acquiesces, saying, "Goodbye, Vicki Lester, you were a grand girl—and good luck, Mrs. Norman Maine." Distraught because of what he feels he has done to the woman he loves, Maine decides to commit suicide and embraces her before taking his fatal swim. As he goes out the door he turns and calls to her; she looks back questioningly. "I just wanted to take one more look," he says, and swims out into the Pacific sunset. The sunset effect seen through the doorway is a background projection, and the sun on the horizon as Maine plunges into the ocean is a painting by Jack Cosgrove.

  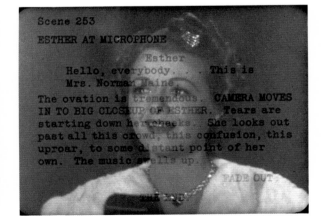

Vicki, talked out of giving up her career by her grandmother, goes to the premiere of her latest film at Grauman's Chinese Theatre. When she sees Norman's footprints, she is almost overcome but pulls herself together to give one of the most memorable curtain lines in movie history. The long shot of the premiere (top, left) is actual footage from the gala preview night of *The Garden of Allah* at the Chinese Theatre, with Vicki Lester's name added through Cosgrove's wizardry. The costumes are by Omar Kiam.

massed fans, and massed celebrities, the last group responding to the picture as if they themselves had made it.

In a town notorious for its easy compliments and back-slapping enthusiasm, the picture was honestly praised from all sides and by everybody in the industry, from technicians on up to the highest executives. One who was not so pleased, however, was Samuel Briskin, the new president of RKO; he considered suing Selznick for infringement of copyright on the earlier *What Price Hollywood?* The suit was never carried through, partly because Selznick convinced Briskin not to, and partly because the company's lawyers could not find strong enough evidence that plagiarism had in fact occurred. Nevertheless, many people over the years have held that *A Star Is Born* is a remake of the earlier film. This is not so. Aside from the basic idea, which is a standard, there are few similarities between the two pictures. In treatment, characterization, and outlook they are completely dissimilar except for one bit of dialogue that Selznick had evidently liked in *What Price Hollywood?* in which the director, just before his suicide, says to the departing girl: "Hey." She turns: "Yes?" He: "Nothing. I just wanted to take one more look." The line had been used twice in that picture. It was used three times in *A Star Is Born,* the last most poignantly just before Maine's fatal swim. It's the kind of gimmicky, self-conscious dramatics that pictures could get away with then and that sometimes, as here, transcend the cliché and become honestly moving.

In the vernacular of the time, "There wasn't a dry eye in the house" when the film ended opening night; the reception around the country in the following months was the same. The picture made Janet Gaynor popular all over again, this time on a much more mature level, more in keeping with the actress's own personality—humorous, gracious, and intelligent. And the part of Norman Maine became one of Fredric March's classic portrayals, the kind that thirty years later people would still be congratulating him for. He was nominated for an Academy Award for best performance of the year, as was Janet Gaynor, and William Wellman was nominated for his direction. The picture itself was nominated as one of the best of the year, receiving also a nomination for best screenplay and one for original story, which is the only award it won in a ceremony held at the Biltmore Bowl on March 10, 1938. Wellman, as one of the co-authors of the story, allegedly took his Oscar over to David's table and said, either sarcastically or honestly, "Here, you deserve this, you wrote more of it than I did."

During its first year of release the picture did tremendous business—it became Selznick International's biggest moneymaker, returning $2,550,000 on a cost of $1,221,382. But Selznick was still disappointed with the way United Artists had handled the picture. They took only 45 percent of the theatre gross, returning 30 percent of that to the producer, which in the case of *A Star Is Born* meant a profit of only $448,000. Selznick was positive that the picture had more money in it and constantly badgered the United Artists people to keep selling it for higher terms, which they did not do, letting the second-run theatres have it for a flat rate, usually $300 per engagement. In mid-1939, after the picture had been out of circulation for a year, Selznick urged that Murray Silverstone, sales manager at United Artists, reissue it, saying,

> Is there nothing you can do to convince your men . . . to make up in some measure what they failed to give us on *A Star Is Born?* . . . If not we must arrive at the conclusion that it is futile to put the time, money and effort into a picture that was necessary for *A Star Is Born,* because if a picture like this can make as little profit as it did, I can't conceive what hope there is for our other products, bearing in mind that a picture like *A Star Is Born* comes along very rarely indeed.

Profit and loss aside, the picture is one of Selznick's finest, and Wellman notwithstanding, it is an early example of the producer as auteur, a personal film down to the tiny fact of Selznick's handwriting being used for the Oliver Niles signature in the close-up of the Vicki/Esther contract. David Selznick was thirty-four when he made *A Star Is Born,* and so, practically, were the movies. The particular springlike freshness of the picture is due not only to its unmistakable craftsmanship but also to the sentiments lying just under the healthy glowing surface, a sense of love, that second burst of emotional awareness that takes a person from adolescence into young adulthood, still idealistic, optimistic, and full of

potential not untinged with a little irony at the changes wrought by time. In *A Star Is Born,* Hollywood—the time, the place, and the attitude—was flawlessly presented as conceived by its audience. The picture was made near the zenith of this romantic age of filmmaking, and the way it projects the positive aspects of the town, the people that it so carefully presents and preserves, can only evoke regret for the passing of a frame of reference, of beliefs, that existed solely in and at the movies. It is the essence of the American movie industry and of David Selznick at their peak—charming, energetic, intelligent, tasteful, a little sad, and full of a sense of self.

A Star Is Born has one other distinction: it was the first picture to use the Selznick International trademark, something that was intended as a temporary solution to a problem that had been bothering Selznick since the company began. "For some time I have been trying to get a trademark," he wrote in late 1935,

> which would immediately identify our pictures as the lion does on MGM and the radio tower on RKO . . . to date I have not been able to get anything that really is outstanding, the best idea so far is an eagle, preferably in flight . . . or perhaps perched on a rock and maybe moving its darling little head. . . . I think it should be an actual shot of something rather than anything drawn or it is very likely to look as crummy as does that 20th Century Pictures trademark.

Nobody could come up with anything that pleased him, and the search went on for the better part of a year; a prize of $150 was offered to anyone who could suggest an idea. From Kay Brown in New York came two suggestions that she had "from a twenty-year-old kid who is a friend of my hairdresser . . . he has sold insignias to Hearst . . . I told him that the essential thing was dignity . . . and noise, as there is no insignia today that beats Leo the Lion . . . he suggests Mt. Vesuvius erupting the name of the company . . . the next one is a bee that flies through a rainbow spelling out the name . . . and the last is to have a seal in motion, bouncing a ball on its nose, spelling out the letters as it does." Selznick replied, "I have gone over your suggestions for a trademark—and I think we still need a trademark. Tell the kid that Paramount has been using a volcano for the last 25 years, the bee belongs in a tree, and the seal in the zoo."

Both *Little Lord Fauntleroy* and *The Garden of Allah* had been released with an announcement line at the beginning saying "Selznick International Presents," moving Selznick to remark, "It is a shame to be wasting so many good opportunities to build up trademark value." He was also convinced that the trademark should have a distinctive sound to identify it—like the lion's roar, the RKO beeping tower, and the 20th Century-Fox fanfare. As time drew near for *A Star Is Born* to be released, Hal Kern drove to work early one morning and for some reason went through the curving front entrance past the graceful knurled wooden signs that had hung at the entrance to the studio since its Ince days. It was a particularly lovely spring day, as he recalls: "There were some beautiful white billowy clouds behind the building, the lawns were a bright green, and the building itself was very imposing. So I thought we should photograph this and use it until we got a permanent trademark. So I got Duke [Howard] Greene, the Technicolor cameraman, and we took the camera out just a little after noon and photographed the sign close up and then swung down for a long shot of the building, and just as we did a flock of birds flew over the main building and some guy came out the front door, but we used it anyway because of the birds." Selznick continued searching for a permanent trademark for the next several years, but finally gave up and settled for the one that Kern had temporarily thrown together. The last bit of necessary "identifying sound" was supplied by Alfred Newman, the music director for United Artists studios, who took over Selznick's music chores after Steiner had left. Two years before, Newman had scored the second Pioneer Technicolor picture, a musical called *The Dancing Pirate.* In it he had used a Javanese gamelan orchestra which played a musical fragment that had stayed in his mind. When the time came to put music to the Selznick trademark, Newman composed a five-second variation on this phrase, announced by chimes and echoed by a full orchestra; this musical badge was added as an afterthought in late 1937 during the scoring of the company's fourth picture, *The Prisoner of Zenda.*

THE IMMORTAL LOVERS
ALL THE WORLD LOVES!

David O. Selznick, who gave you DAVID COPPERFIELD
and A STAR IS BORN, presents a thrilling, modern romance of exciting intrigue and high adventure.

SELZNICK INTERNATIONAL

presents

RONALD COLMAN
IN
THE PRISONER OF ZENDA

WITH

MADELEINE CARROLL · MARY ASTOR · RAYMOND MASSEY · DAVID NIVEN

C. AUBREY SMITH

DOUGLAS FAIRBANKS, JR.
as Rupert of Hentzau

Produced by DAVID O. SELZNICK
Directed by John Cromwell
Based on Edward Rose's dramatization of Anthony Hope's novel
RELEASED THRU UNITED ARTISTS

(Top) Designer Walter Plunkett working on costume sketches. (Above) A gown and other garments being constructed in the costume department. (Below) Ronald Colman shows David Selznick how old he looks in the special rubber mask devised by Jack Dawn for the original prologue and epilogue of *The Prisoner of Zenda*.

The story of *The Prisoner of Zenda* had been a staple of stage and films ever since its publication in 1894. Its central location, the mythical kingdom of Ruritania, had come to symbolize all the escapist romantic fiction that had sprung up in its wake. The subtitle of the book, "Being the history of three months in the life of an English gentleman," gives no hint of the action of the tale; and its central idea, that of an identical double masquerading as the king of a tiny country while the real king is held prisoner in the castle of Zenda, was implausible in the extreme, but was presented in such a wry, detached manner that it kept the tale popular for years, along with its central characters: Rudolf Rassendyll, the Englishman pressed into service to save a kingdom; the villainous Black Michael, the king's brother, whose designs on the throne set the plot in action; and his charming, unscrupulous associate, the dashing Rupert of Hentzau, all of whom were after the golden, virginal Princess Flavia, the king's intended. The novel by Anthony Hope had been dramatized in the early part of the century, and the play had toured successfully around the country for years, finally ending up, in 1913, as the very first of Adolph Zukor's "Famous Players in Famous Plays." Since then it had been filmed once more (1922), in a lavish silent version directed by Rex Ingram for Metro Pictures. Selznick had wanted to remake the picture with sound while he was at MGM, and had several different scripts prepared, but never got started. His interest in it was reawakened by two factors. The first was the publicity surrounding the abdication of King Edward VIII in December 1936; Selznick noted that "the case had made very topical an old problem—that of king and commoner and queen and commoner." The second factor was Ronald Colman's contract. "I frankly would not have purchased the material from MGM if I hadn't had Colman and if I hadn't determined in advance that Colman would play the role. One of the thousand and one functions of the producer is to make sure the star is happy with his assignment or risk losing him when the contract expires." The biggest drawback to Colman's acceptance of the part was that it was one of those dreaded "dual roles" he disliked so much and that had almost kept him from doing *A Tale of Two Cities.* "We were able to avoid the issue on that picture," Selznick related, "but in *Zenda* . . . it was obviously impossible for anything but the dual performance as it was necessary for the entire kingdom to be fooled, including the King's brother and his fiancée. Colman and I talked at great length about the picture, about its drawbacks, about what I saw in it and his fears concerning it."

While the script was being polished, Colman tested for various make-ups and costumes, and the special effects involving the double roles worked out, it became imperative to cast the rest of the picture, especially the part of Princess Flavia. This was not a great acting role, having only one good scene, but it was important to the success of the story because the part was a traditional symbol of purity and nobility. "She had to be divinely beautiful," said Selznick, "regal, virginal, blonde and young . . . on the other hand not so young as to make Colman look old. We went through lists of girls by the hour and by the week . . . and with a star as important as Colman, not only does he have to be satisfied, I have to be satisfied; the woman engaged has to be satisfied, her agent has to be satisfied and probably her mother and father and a lot of other people have to be satisfied." One of these was the director John Cromwell, whom Selznick felt had "the sensitivity and judgment which are so necessary in respect to the sensibilities of audiences, particularly in England, which are sensitive about the behavior of royalty."

The two men continued to search for the right actress to play Princess Flavia, while casting the other parts for the picture—taking advantage of the ever larger pool of British talent coming to Hollywood. Raymond Massey was given the role of the treacherously resentful Black Michael. A recent addition to the town was a graduate of the British Army, young David Niven, a carefree charmer who had decided to try a career in Hollywood at the urging of his friend, actor Nigel Bruce. He was able to extend his charm into the reading he did for Cromwell, and was given the small but meaty role of one of the king's aides, with C. Aubrey Smith playing his superior. Mary Astor, an actress whose career seldom did her talent justice, would play the mysterious lady in black, Antoinette de Mauban, in unrequited love with Black Michael. The choice part of the rascally Rupert of Hentzau went to a new Selznick contract player, Douglas Fairbanks, Jr., who was, like Selznick, second-generation Hollywood royalty.

With the bulk of the major casting completed, the search for a Princess Flavia now intensified. "We tested several girls for the part," said Selznick. "I was very impressed with Anita Louise, she was very beautiful, and sincere, but John felt that she lacked the regal quality that the part needed, then my brother Myron suggested we try Madeleine Carroll, and she turned out to be perfect." Well, almost perfect. "I did have one problem with her at the beginning," said Selznick, "which was a complete change of makeup for her. She had been using basically the same makeup since she had started in pictures with a great deal of success, and it's pretty hard to get a woman to change her style especially when she is regarded internationally as a great beauty ... but I felt that for the Princess there should be no trace of artifice, no makeup visible and we had a number of arguments about reducing the amount she used on her mouth, her eyebrows; we even took the polish off her nails so that she would seem like a princess of the 1880's instead of a movie star of today ... which we achieved throughout the picture ... although every now and then she would sneak something in when we weren't looking."

The costuming proved more of a problem than usual because of the large number of uniforms needed. The accidental copying of a uniform used by any European or South American country could lead to the picture being banned in that country; hundreds of sketches were made and then checked against every single uniform in the world, a time-consuming process.

On March 8, 1937, John Cromwell directed the first scenes in the picture, a contemporary prologue and epilogue, showing Rassendyll in old age. To achieve the proper aged look, Colman wore a new kind of makeup devised by Universal's Jack Dawn, not so much a makeup as a thin rubber mask, with openings for the eyes and mouth, which slipped right over his head. After two weeks of shooting, Selznick grew increasingly dissatisfied with the visual look of the picture and replaced Bert Glennon with James Wong Howe, whom he had previously worked with on *Viva Villa!* and *Manhattan Melodrama.* Howe, the only Chinese cameraman in Hollywood, had to put up with a great deal of condescending prejudice in the first twenty years of his career, but the quality of his work, his uncanny ability to get right to the photographic essence of a scene, and his cheerful, enthusiastic use of new and innovative approaches to the lighting and movement of his photography had brought him to the top of his profession.

He took over after lunch on March 22, completely relighting and reworking the photography of the spectacular and suspenseful sequence of the false king's coronation. An anonymous reporter visited the set that afternoon, and his observations provide an accurate vignette of several hours' activity on Stage 11 at Selznick International:

... the huge set represents a European cathedral ... which has at least 400 people on it, dress extras and bit players.... John Cromwell directs this crowd by issuing his instructions to his assistant Fred Spencer who delivers them through a public address system.... The action calls for Ronald Colman to walk the length of the cathedral to a platform below the altar where he will be crowned King ... the camera is on a dolly and will follow him as he walks through a lane formed by the King's household guard. The guard is composed of professional movie soldiers under the command of Captain Richard von Opel, late of the Austrian army, who has organized a private army of 100 men between 22 and 27 which he rents to producers for just such scenes as this, with his guarantee that his soldiers are all trained in the manuals of sidearms, rifle and saber of all foreign countries. James Wong Howe ... sounds twice on his klaxon horn mounted on the dolly indicating that he is ready for a rehearsal. The trumpeters blow, the massive doors open and Colman begins the march to the coronation platform. One more rehearsal and Cromwell decides on a take ... the makeup and wardrobe assistants buzz around Colman, fix a stray lock of hair, brush and rearrange his uniform, check on his medals and decorations ... the policeman on guard at the set gives one long whistle inside the stage, and another outside which means that absolute quiet within the vicinity of the set has been ordered. The assistant director cries, "Roll 'em," the blimp on the camera is snapped shut and the director says in a soft monotone, "Camera?" ... The scene is shot three times; Cromwell finally gives it an okay and a new

Madeleine Carroll poses for artist James Montgomery Flagg; the portrait was to be used for publicity on *The Prisoner of Zenda.*

Madeleine Carroll utilizing the slant board—a device that allowed actresses to rest between takes without wrinkling their costumes. Her gown and all of the other designs for *The Prisoner of Zenda* were by Ernest Dryden.

(Above) Cinematographer James Wong Howe devised an overhead track for this pullback shot in *The Prisoner of Zenda* that allowed the camera to retreat farther and farther back from the figures of Ronald Colman and Madeleine Carroll as they descend a marble staircase to greet their courtiers. (Opposite) The problem of having Colman perform a dual role was solved in a number of ingenious ways by Howe and the optical department. (Top) The king and his look-alike cousin first encounter each other in a forest glade. A simple split screen was used here; the demarcation line is obvious, directly in front of Colman, standing at left. (Second from top) Colman shakes hands with himself. Colman actually shook hands with a double (the figure on the right). The

set-up is ordered ... while the electricians and the grips are moving the equipment in preparation for the next scene, Colman's fencing instructor, Ralph Faulkner, twice American Olympics champion, takes him to an open space on the stage and the two go through a routine until it is time for Colman to go back to the set.... The stand-ins for the actors take their places and the electricians and the cameraman begin working out the lighting effects ... as Howe suggests changes in the lights, Jimmy Potevin, the chief electrician, calls them out to the crew working on the catwalk above.... They are just about ready to take the scene when the assistant director notices a wristwatch on one of the extras within camera range ... another is discovered wearing glasses and Cromwell wants to know if he was wearing them in the scenes already taken ... nobody seems to know for sure but the actor is quite positive he has been, so he is allowed to keep them after Ivar Enhorning, the technical director, okays them as being in existence during the period of the story.... The extras are again cautioned about chewing gum during the scene ... finally the scene is lighted and ready ... the scene is shot three times and Cromwell says, "Print the first and last" ... by now it is six o'clock and the assistant director hollers, "Wrap it up," ending 8 hours' work which will only run a few minutes on the screen.

What this reporter didn't and couldn't observe was the tension and sometimes friction that existed between members of the company. Cromwell had problems with young Fairbanks, commenting that

he had been overly indulged ... and cared more for the privilege of enjoying life than the application required to learn a profession.... I don't know which annoyed me most, Fairbanks's indifference or Colman's laziness ... he never knew his lines ... he had probably read them over the night before ... so precious minutes were wasted before each shot ... all of which adds up to a tidy sum.... Colman also had a "bad side" photographically.... I was able to plan all of the action with this in mind ... but then Miss Carroll caught on that he was being favored and she decided that she had a bad side too. I yessed her and got to Jimmie Howe and asked if this was true ... he said she couldn't be faulted from any angle ... so I went to her and asked her which side was bad ... unfortunately she picked the same side as Colman.... I pointed out to her that it would be impossible to do any scenes with the two of them as they would both have to face in the same direction ... she pouted for a day or two ... wouldn't speak to me and then gave in.

Even though the company had finished their work on the stages by six, in the front office the evening's work was just beginning for Selznick and his staff of secretaries and stenographers, one of whom, Lydia Schiller, had just joined the studio. An independent, efficient, level-headed young lady, she was one of the new generation of middle-class children who had grown up on the movies. She had come to Hollywood from Detroit with a burning desire to get into the picture business, not in front of the camera, but behind it, to be one of the people who wrote all the action. "My mother wanted me to be able to take care of myself ... so I took a good business course—shorthand, typing—then enrolled in a correspondence course that taught me how to write.... I learned about scenarios.... Finally I decided to come to Hollywood." She arrived in 1929, applied for a job in the MGM stenographic pool, and was immediately hired as a script girl, the person who sat on the set and noted every movement of the actors, the camera, which lens was used, details of costumes, props, and all the other infinitesimal details that go into the matching of different scenes. In 1936 she went to work at Selznick International:

In those days, everybody painted the picture of Mr. Selznick as such a fearful monster ... everybody was afraid of him ... don't do this, don't do that, don't speak up ... so for the first few days I was there I would practice my shorthand.... I sat out in the front office with two other girls, I'd be there at nine o'clock in the morning waiting all day long and far into the night.... I waited and waited and the longer I waited the more panicked I'd get.... This went on for days and finally I was ready to have my first view of the inner sanctum and be put to the test.... Most of the time at least two of the girls would go

in for dictation ... one would take notes while the other rested, often they both took the same thing so they would cover each other.... He was terrible at dictation ... he wouldn't change his voice, he walked around chairs and mumbled a great deal.... During *The Prisoner of Zenda* he was having conferences with the writer Donald Ogden Stewart ... I think it was around two or three in the morning, the conference broke up, but we couldn't go home, he wanted to do some dictating.... He was so dead tired that he practically didn't know what he was saying.... My share of that whole day's work was a two-line memo....

I went out to my desk, I was really angry, and he came out with his hat on the back of his head. It must have been close to four in the morning, and he saw that I was angry and asked what the matter was ... he was basically a very kind man, soft spoken, very gentlemanly ... and after I found that out I wasn't afraid of him so I just spoke up and said, "Mr. Selznick, I've been here all these hours and look at this thing I've got here ... I can't see that there's anything to this secretarial work, this kind of nonsense is not for me, I just can't do it." He looked down at me almost with amusement and said, "Lydia, I'm not going to change my way of working, I'm not going to change my hours." ... We looked at each other and I said, "There's only one thing for me to do, I'm quitting." ... I don't think he believed me ... he just looked at me and walked out. So the next day I went in to quit, but thanks to Bobbie Keon, who'd hired me in the first place, I was reassigned, and after a while I began to admire Mr. Selznick ... he was such a perfectionist.... Those of us who lasted stayed because we did appreciate that about him ... he demanded the best in us.... It was a challenge, just trying to keep up with him, and if you lasted with him, he allowed you to participate, he would listen to you, consider what you said ... sometimes accept it, sometimes not.... There weren't many executives who did that, and it was a rare opportunity for a worker and what finally endeared him to so many of us.

After two relatively uneventful months of filming, the picture, running two hours and fifteen minutes, was taken out for its first preview in late May 1937, after which Selznick decided that the pacing of some scenes was too slow, the writing could be improved, and the picture generally made much better. Accordingly, he ordered the retaking of thirty-one separate shots, out of a preview total of 420. This sometimes involved the re-doing of an entire scene. The renunciation scene was rewritten by playwright Sidney Howard, working in the studio on another project, and George Cukor redirected and reshot the scene in early July. After a second preview that month, it was decided to eliminate the framing device, saving some five minutes of footage and telling the story straight. This done, another two months were spent in perfecting the "trick" shots, recutting, and musical scoring, this time by Alfred Newman, who was just beginning to develop into a background composer of consequence. He gave *Zenda* a virile brassy sound, softened by his characteristic high, massed strings, which gave a yearning poignancy to the music, especially in the graceful ascending love theme for Rassendyll and Flavia. Image and sound reached a remarkable fusion in the troublesome renunciation scene. The camera pulls back swiftly in a wide, arcing movement on the final tableau of Flavia with her hands laid tenderly on the kneeling Rassendyll's head, while shafts of sunlight stream in through the window imparting a benedictive effect, enhanced by the music, which holds a gradually softening long-line threnodial version of the love theme as the scene quietly and slowly fades out.

The final cost of *The Prisoner of Zenda,* including making four hundred prints of the picture, was $1.3 million; it grossed $2.8 million, making it the company's biggest success but with a profit margin of only $665,000. This was one of the continuing problems of the studio; whatever profits came in were eaten up by the overhead and Selznick's insistence on spending money until everything was perfect, which meant that the stockholders had not received a dividend on their money. They were all fairly wealthy, so it would not seem to matter very much, but business, after all, is business, and the poor showing of the Selznick stock prompted Jock Whitney's sister Joan Payson to comment, "Everyone says that Mr. Selznick's pictures are of the best, but I've yet to see a nickel of return on my investment." This bothered Selznick, who rather than

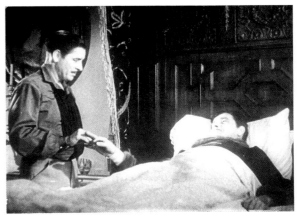

camera shot through a plate of sheet glass that had been taped to cover the area of the double's head and shoulders. After exposing the action, the film was rewound in the camera, the plate glass was retaped to cover everything *except* the area of the double's head and shoulders, and Colman changed costumes and stood in the exact spot that the double had stood in. Colman's head and shoulders were then photographed in perfect register with the double's body. (Third from top) The two Colmans drinking together was accomplished by double exposure. (Bottom) Colman seemingly puts a ring on his own finger. The hand and arm belong to a double—once again a variation of the taped-glass approach was used.

(Above) Douglas Fairbanks, Jr., as Rupert of Hentzau and Ronald Colman as Rudolf Rassendyll are put through their fencing paces by John Cromwell (left of camera with pipe). James Wong Howe is on the camera cart (in hat). Selznick was dissatisfied with the tempo and excitement of this sequence and called in W. S. Van Dyke from MGM to re-do it.

(Below) These two stills from *The Prisoner of Zenda,* taken on a roll of color film by still photographer Fred Parrish, are interesting when contrasted with the black-and-white world in which the picture existed. (Left) Madeleine Carroll and C. Aubrey Smith stroll through a dimly lit garden setting. Her pink gown would photograph white in the final sequence. (Right) Colman as Rudolf Rassendyll is crowned king, standing in for the vanished monarch, who is a prisoner in the castle of Zenda. On either side of him behind the throne are David Niven and C. Aubrey Smith.

cutting his costs, and therefore his quality, kept after United Artists to be more aggressive in selling the picture, especially for higher terms in the initial engagements.

The financial situation was about to be adversely affected by events that were largely beyond the control of Selznick or United Artists, for just as *The Prisoner of Zenda* was being released, the economic health of the country, which had been improving steadily since 1933, suffered a sharp and unexpected relapse with stock prices tumbling and the unemployment rolls rising by some 2 million workers. The bulk of Hollywood's output in 1937–38 consisted of outdoor adventures and historical romances, usually dealing with some aspect of the country's past and designed, as Selznick commented,

> to appeal to youth, for the motion picture business belongs to youth … all the great social and political movements of this or any age are the activities of youth … it is far more impressionable than maturity. Since we build our pictures on the emotions of the younger generation … we must be very concerned with the lessons we teach with our stories. The pictures we put on the screen are glamorized ideals with which even the most rational and well presented idea finds it difficult to compete. Girls on six continents argue that they should be allowed to behave differently than their mothers because of the screen behavior of Loretta Young and Janet Gaynor. If Clark Gable buys a particular car, sales of it go up … the fact we must face is that the great entertainment, propaganda and social weapon of the motion picture is the weapon of youth, the weapon by which youth increasingly will bludgeon its elders into thinking *its* way.

The accuracy of his observations was not lost on his contemporaries in the business, and from late 1934 to the early 1940s the industry was in the somewhat sticky grip of Shirley Temple, Mickey Rooney, and a gang of frolicking, aggressive semi–juvenile delinquents called the Dead End Kids, from the Broadway play that had introduced them. All of these moppets, in one guise or another, fought for truth, justice, and the American way. Their innocence, self-sufficiency, and ultimate respect for

authority were reassuring to the older members of the audience, and as Selznick pointed out, very influential on the younger viewers, which in part accounts for the largely homogeneous look and attitude of the middle classes of the next couple of generations. Selznick did his own considerable bit in this area by bringing Mickey Rooney to MGM to join the already popular Jackie Cooper, and by pushing Freddie Bartholomew into prominence. As the end of 1937 approached, Selznick decided to do still more by remaking Mark Twain's *The Adventures of Tom Sawyer* as a lavish Technicolor paean to the wonders of American adolescence in the nineteenth century.

Selznick considered the Twain classic to be "the closest thing we have to an American *David Copperfield*," and originally it was intended to be the first Selznick International picture, but in 1930 Paramount had made a sound version, which John Cromwell had directed with Jackie Coogan. Paramount's registration of the title with the Motion Picture Association gave it protection until 1938, during which period no other major company could use the property—a gentlemen's agreement that kept the studios from stepping on each other's titular toes. To complicate this situation further, *The Adventures of Tom Sawyer* was in the public domain, meaning anyone could use the story without paying the author's estate anything; in this case, however, the heirs of Samuel Clemens had copyrighted their father's pen name, so that if Selznick wanted to advertise it as "Mark Twain's Tom Sawyer," he would still have to pay the estate a hefty $50,000. He did this in mid-1936, then discovered to his fury that the Clemens estate had also just licensed Paramount to make the sequel, *Tom Sawyer, Detective,* which they planned to film immediately as a "quickie," a low-budget program picture that would definitely take the edge off the major production Selznick planned.

Little Lord Fauntleroy had been substituted, and Selznick began negotiating with Paramount. He wanted one of two things from them: to sell him their story rights to *Tom Sawyer, Detective,* or to delay its release until his *Tom Sawyer* was produced and had played off its U.S. theatrical engagements; the latter might take as long as two years. Paramount agreed to this on condition that Selznick buy from them the screenplay to

The renunciation scene, staged first by John Cromwell, then by George Cukor, and played against one of Lyle Wheeler's massively theatrical settings. Set decoration was by Edward Boyle.

William Wellman in a strait jacket during the filming of *Nothing Sacred.* The stunt photo was dreamed up by the fellow smirking at the left, Russell Birdwell, Selznick's irrepressible publicity chief. An ex–Hearst journalist, Birdwell's manic and inventive mind conjured up such space-grabbing stunts as having the entire village of Zenda, Canada (population thirty), flown to the New York premiere of *The Prisoner of Zenda.*

Fredric March, Walter Connolly, and Ben Hecht on the set of *Nothing Sacred.*

their 1930 version, which Selznick reluctantly did, paying out another $10,000 and getting the right to use all the material written for that version. Selznick now tried to interest King Vidor in directing the picture, to no avail. After returning from his Hawaiian vacation, Selznick lined up William Wyler. The two men spent several days in the Sacramento region looking for locations that would pass for the Mississippi, but casting the picture properly took so long that Wyler withdrew. Then it was to be William Wellman's next picture after *A Star Is Born;* instead, that turned out to be *Nothing Sacred.*

When Wellman first joined Selznick International, he had brought with him two projects, one of which became *A Star Is Born.* The other was a sequel to his 1931 Warner Bros. hit, *The Public Enemy,* which he called *Another Public Enemy,* written by him and Robert Carson. This went into pre-production with the finishing of *A Star Is Born;* it was to star Fredric March and would be in Technicolor. Warner Bros., of course, objected to the use of a title similar to its copyrighted picture, so *Another Public Enemy* became *Let Me Live.* With the script ready, sets designed, and casting under way, Selznick, in late April 1937, had an abrupt change of heart about the whole project, later telling writer Quentin Reynolds that he stopped it because, "although it was a sure-fire money-maker . . . it didn't have the dignity and good taste that I want my name associated with." So he sold it to MGM, where it emerged later that year under the title *The Last Gangster.* Jock Whitney, meanwhile, had been after Selznick to make a comedy—not a pratfall, Laurel and Hardy slapstick type, nor a brittle upper-class comedy of manners such as *Private Lives* and *Dinner at Eight,* but rather a new form that had emerged in 1934 with *It Happened One Night.* These "screwball" comedies, as they had come to be known, were slightly anarchic in their comedic approach, disregarding probabilities, going beyond farce and approaching burlesque as they satirized manners, morals, pretensions, and just about every other sacred cow existing in the United States in the mid-thirties.

When Jock Whitney brought up the subject of a comedy as the next Selznick International picture, Selznick was at first unenthusiastic. Whitney was pleasantly persistent, however, and Selznick decided that if Whitney's will be done, then Ben Hecht would have to do it—a neat bit of backhanding on Selznick's part, as Whitney and Hecht, while not exactly detesting each other, did not like to be in the same room together. David put the idea of Hecht up to Whitney, who grumbled somewhat, wiring Selznick: "If you're absolutely convinced that there is no one else who can do the job, then go ahead and hire him." Whitney was under the spell of Universal's *My Man Godfrey,* a classic example of this new type of "cockeyed comedy," which had been directed by Gregory LaCava and starred William Powell and Carole Lombard, and at Whitney's urging, Selznick made a concerted effort to hire Lombard for whatever comedy could be concocted. This had to be done through his brother Myron, who handled the actress's career. It was under Myron's aegis and largely through his astute guidance that her career had zoomed from the early days as a Mack Sennett bathing beauty to her present prominence as the epitome of movie star glamour of the thirties. She was flip, cynical, tomboyish, extremely modern in her attitudes and manner of playing; a natural, unforced spontaneity jumped out of her performances, giving her a quality of good-humored honesty that, coupled with her unselfconscious sensuality and offbeat beauty, had by 1937 turned her into one of the biggest-drawing stars in the business. This fact was shrewdly capitalized on by Myron, who demanded and received top fees for her performances.

Lombard was now one of the highest paid actresses in town, earning $465,000 in 1937, a highly publicized figure she neatly turned to her own advantage by announcing that 85 percent of it had gone in taxes to the government, stating that she enjoyed living in a free country, and adding, "I don't need all that money for myself . . . so why not give what I don't need for the government to improve the country?"—a sentiment that received public thanks from President Roosevelt. She was one of the delights of the Hollywood social scene, her irreverence and sense of humor making her as much sought after socially as professionally. David had known her for some years, since they were both struggling at Paramount, and considered her to be worth the $18,750 a week that Myron demanded he pay her. Lombard's schedule made it imperative

THIS IS NEW YORK
Skyscraper Champion of
the World . . .

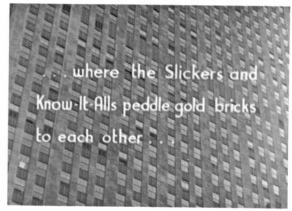

. . . where the Slickers and
Know-It-Alls peddle gold bricks
to each other . . .

(Bottom) Times Square as caught by the Technicolor camera in 1937 for the opening sequences of *Nothing Sacred*. (Left) Ben Hecht's foreword to the picture is set against a background of Rockefeller Center skyscrapers and Times Square at night. Some idea of the cynical attitude of the film can be gained from the frame at the lower right.

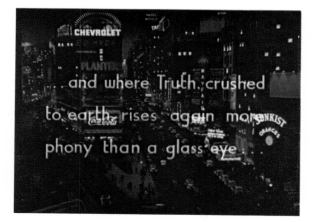

. . . and where Truth, crushed
to earth, rises again more
phony than a glass eye . . .

MISS
HAZEL FLAGG
LUNCHED HERE
TO-DAY

ALL KINDS OF
CHEESE AND BOLOGNA
OUR SPECIALTY

For *Nothing Sacred,* Walter Plunkett designed these costumes for "The Heroines of History—A Salute to Hazel Flagg." The night club setting is by Lyle Wheeler, with ceiling by Jack Cosgrove. The girls—alas!—are anonymous, but their characterizations are straight out of Minsky: Lady Godiva (could you have guessed?); Pocahontas, looking apprehensive; Catherine of Russia; and Katinka, showing the audience the finger she stuck in the dike, thereby saving Holland (and you thought it was a boy).

that Selznick start whatever he was going to do with her no later than mid-June. This was early April, and David put in an urgent appeal for Ben Hecht to come up with a quick original comedy that would be suitable for Lombard, March, Wellman, and Technicolor. Hecht at this period was one of the busiest and most prolific writers in the business, writing, rewriting, and ghostwriting scripts at the highest possible fees. Late in April, he sent Selznick a partial outline for an untitled comedy that opened in a sleazy Havana night club with a group of eight men and women travelers "who belong to a special class—a cult whose God is a combination of swank, superiority and emptiness ... devoid of all human problems, with neither ideals nor morals ... these people are sincerely unimpressed by everything, including themselves." It went on to tell the story of how one of them falls for the singer in the night club, pursuing her all over Havana, through a house of ill repute "where the girls dance for them, and the colorful natives sing, turning the scene into one of a thousand delights." He finally takes her back to New York, where she becomes his mistress until his finances fall apart; then he decides that she should marry one of his well-heeled friends. "In the last three months she has become a very well-dressed and presentable young lady ... he'll fix her up with a history of family connections and if it's the last thing he does, he'll put her over." Hecht's outline abruptly ended here, but it already had several problems as far as Selznick was concerned. Its assortment of very wealthy types was presented in an extremely unattractive light, and David was mindful of the sensibilities of his circle of moneyed friends; the girl was the mistress of the hero, which was forbidden by the motion picture Code; and the story's unfinished state would make it impossible to meet the Lombard deadline.

Selznick, meanwhile, had taken an option on a short story by writer James H. Street that was soon to be published in Hearst's *Cosmopolitan* magazine. Called "Letter to the Editor," it related a pithy little tale of a small-town spinster, Adele Morris, who writes to the editor of a large New York newspaper offering to sell a story of her imminent demise as a victim of radium poisoning. The editor immediately snaps up the offer, after confirming by wire with the woman's doctor that she is actually dying. He brings her to New York, assigning his reporters to take her

around the city: "Show this dame the town ... each of you birds write me a story of your experiences as the escort of a dying woman ... keep your traps closed ... don't hurt her feelings and we'll use the stories after she croaks. It'll be a sensation." It turns out that she is a fraud, that she and the doctor are the same person, and the reason for her deception is that she had been in love with a young man who jilted her after he had come to New York and gone to work for the editor's newspaper, which had turned him into a bleary-eyed alcoholic, and she wanted revenge. The twist at the end was that the editor, instead of being outraged, decides to expose the hoax in his own paper, "about how New York, city of rackets, got outsmarted by a dame from Mount Ida, Arkansas. My God, what a story."

And indeed it was. Selznick, after ascertaining that Hecht liked it, bought it for $2,500, paying Hecht $30,000 for writing an acceptable screenplay with the provision that it be done to his satisfaction within thirty days. Hecht was not only prolific, he was *fast*. The bulk of the screenplay he called *Nothing Sacred* was written during a four-day cross-country trip on the Super-Chief. He changed the focus to show what a cynical, phony town New York was, making the spinster a young girl from Warsaw, Vermont, who is mistakenly diagnosed by her small-town doctor to be dying of the original radium poisoning. Her supposed illness comes to the attention of an ace reporter on the *New York Morning Star,* who convinces his cynical managing editor that it is the stuff of which circulation hay is made. He goes off to Vermont to bring the girl to New York. As he arrives, the girl is being told by her doctor that he made a mistake and she isn't going to die. She is disappointed: "It's kind of startling to be brought to life twice—and each time in Warsaw." The reporter appears, makes his offer, and the girl, unable to resist the thought of getting out of Warsaw and going to New York "dead or alive," swears the doctor to secrecy and goes to the big city, vowing to have fun and "not go to bed until I have convulsions and my teeth start falling out." The reporter falls in love with the girl, and is delighted at the end when the hoax is discovered and his editor assigns him to write the story of the "greatest betrayal since the days of Judas Iscariot."

The name of the heroine was changed to Hazel Flagg, her last name

being lifted from one of Selznick's secretaries, Harriet Flagg, and the script was delivered to Selznick in late May. Selznick found certain difficulties with it, the most glaring being its treatment of the editor and publisher of the *Morning Star,* which Selznick felt might insult his friends in publishing. Selznick asked Hecht to tone down the editor's antics, making him more of a long-suffering victim of the reporter, who became the chief cynic and troublemaker, one whom "the hand of God, reaching down into the mire, couldn't elevate to the depths of degradation." Hecht did as requested, but balked at Selznick's request to change the ending so that the editor wasn't a willing, even gleeful accomplice to the exposure of the hoax. The ending was too good, Hecht argued, and there was nothing he could come up with that would be as effective; stating that he had lived up to his end of the bargain, Hecht left Selznick to contend with three-quarters of a comedy and no ending.

He was now faced with several problems: a suitable finish, the Lombard deadline, another one for Fredric March, plus the inability to postpone starting the picture because of the Technicolor schedule. He and Wellman decided to put the picture into the works as scheduled, using the script as it was while Selznick assigned Ring Lardner, Jr., and young Budd Schulberg to devise an ending that would get them out of the corner Ben Hecht had written them into. The best they could come up with was Hazel and the reporter on board a cruise ship in the tropics receiving a telegram from the editor describing the lovely funeral service that had been given the girl, thereby keeping the integrity of the newspaper intact as well as saving face for the editor. It was an ending that satisfied no one, but it went by so quickly, and Wellman had directed the rest of the script with such iconoclastic relish, that no one seemed to mind the letdown of the last couple of minutes. Completed on schedule at a cost of $1.3 million, the picture opened at the Radio City Music Hall in time for the Thanksgiving holiday, where it proved to be no turkey by filling the huge theatre for each of its six daily showings. But because of high distribution and advertising costs it lost $4,000 in its first year of release. However, due to its attitude, playing, and direction, it came to be regarded as a classic example of the whole school of wacky, hard-boiled, and sarcastic comedies that its title represents. When the picture went into production, Selznick had wired Whitney: "You wanted comedy, boy are you going to get it; after this, I am either the new Mack Sennett or I return to Dr. Eliot [the editor of the Harvard classics]." In spite of the critical success of the picture, Selznick decided not to follow it up with another like it and did in fact "return to Dr. Eliot" and *The Adventures of Tom Sawyer.*

Carole Lombard in three close-ups from *Nothing Sacred,* photographed by W. Howard Greene. In the shot at the left she has just passed out from drinking too much champagne at a party in her honor, but the entire congregation is convinced that the moment has finally come for Hazel Flagg, the poor doomed girl dying from radiation poisoning. Her gown is by Travis Banton.

Lombard in an early Kodachrome taken by John Engstead, her favorite photographer.

(Above) William Cameron Menzies's sketches for the sequences showing the children lost in the caves were carefully outlined to indicate the live action and the matte paintings. (Opposite) The sequence as it finally emerged on screen. (From left to right) The townsfolk, headed by Aunt Polly, pray outside the caves, while inside a search party tries to find Tom and Becky. Tom tries to find his way out of the labyrinth using a string in case he gets lost. He is pursued by the villainous Injun Joe (Victor Jory), who has been hiding in the caves because of Tom's testimony, which convicted him of the murder of one of the graverobbers. Becky watches, terrified, as Tom is cornered by Joe; Tom throws his lucky horseshoe at Joe, who loses his balance and falls into the gorge below. Calming the hysterical Becky, Tom follows a beam of light that leads the two of them to a cleft in the mountain, through which they escape. The exterior shot of the townsfolk and the long shots of the children in the cave and Joe's fall are all combinations of live action and Cosgrove paintings.

Selznick finally had a script that satisfied him. As written by John V. A. Weaver, it maintained a delicate balance between the episodic nature of the original novel and the more dramatic structure of the 1930 Paramount version, with the climax built around Tom and Becky Thatcher being lost in a cave and pursued by the villainous "Injun Joe," who had earlier been convicted of murder based on testimony from Tom and his friend Huckleberry Finn. Ben Hecht, while trying to come up with a new ending for *Nothing Sacred,* did some work on the structure of several scenes and polished the dialogue, trying to keep the flavor of the original while making it more "speakable." Selznick had earlier instructed Kay Brown of his New York office to start looking for "untrained children. . . . I feel that the greatest publicity story in the history of the business would be our finding Tom Sawyer or Huck Finn in an orphan asylum . . . which would arouse such a warm public feeling that it would add enormously to the gross of the picture."

Months of searching through orphanages, reformatories, and public schools finally turned up Tommy Kelly, the twelve-year-old son of an unemployed Bronx fireman, whose lack of training gave him a refreshing naturalness that made up for his inexperience. A series of tests done in Culver City in early June saw him winning out over professional children for the part of Tom. Both Huck Finn and Becky Thatcher were cast from the ranks of Hollywood children, Jackie Moran to play Huck and eleven-year-old Ann Gillis, who had previously worked for Selznick in a small part in *The Garden of Allah,* as Becky. Because of the long delays in getting the script ready and finding the children, Selznick had to relinquish his Technicolor commitment, and the picture, with Henry C. Potter directing and James Wong Howe photographing in black and white, began filming on the Paramount ranch in the San Fernando Valley region. A replica of a small Mississippi town had been constructed under Lyle Wheeler's direction. The company had been filming there for close to two weeks when, due to a cancellation, a Technicolor unit suddenly became available. Selznick closed the production down for three days, while makeup, costume, and lighting tests were undertaken, then started the picture over from the beginning.

The change in schedule necessitated a change in directors: Potter was replaced by Norman Taurog, an expert with children, whose work with Jackie Cooper in *Skippy* (1931) had been responsible in large part for the child actor's subsequently becoming a star at MGM. The sudden switch to Technicolor created a problem in that the sets, which had all been designed for black and white, had to be adapted overnight, with the result that color was deliberately avoided except in the costumes. Most of the sets were repainted a carefully neutral beige, gray, and white, with the occasional dab of color supplied by flowers and other accessories. This was James Wong Howe's first color picture, and he tried, as he later recounted, "to keep the major part of any scene's coloring confined to the players . . . the only difficulty that was constant was the necessity to use twice as much light as we would for a black-and-white picture. Some cinematographers favor very flat Technicolor lighting, but personally I favor a soft lighting for color. . . . Those of us who have studied painting have noticed that the old masters achieved their effects, not by the direct sunlight approach that corresponds to our spotlighting, but by using what might be termed a 'directed' north light for the modeling light."

When the picture was previewed, in what was becoming a Selznick tradition, it went back before the cameras for two additional weeks of retakes, this time with George Cukor directing. These involved all the scenes of the children in the schoolhouse, partial reshooting of Tom's and Huck Finn's adventures on Jackson Island, and a complete redoing of the "tag," finishing up with May Robson whacking whiny Cousin Sid for the end of the picture.

Filming of the retakes, inserts, and other miscellaneous bits was completed on December 31, 1937, and the picture was rushed through Technicolor processing in time to make its Radio City Music Hall release date of February 11, 1938. Its hefty production cost of almost $1.5 million kept it from being a financial success. But pleased with the two children, Tommy Kelly and Ann Gillis, Selznick announced plans to re-team them in a picture called *Heartbreak Town,* a sort of junior version of *A Star Is Born* that had been written by Marshall ("Mickey") Neilan, but this was never done. Instead, Tommy Kelly was loaned to Sol Lesser for a picture called *Peck's Bad Boy with the Circus* and Ann Gillis did several unremarkable low-budget pictures before they both retired in the early forties.

As for *The Adventures of Tom Sawyer,* in spite of all Selznick's time and effort, it turned out a disappointment, artistically as well as financially. Selznick was hoping for another *David Copperfield,* and instead came up with another *Garden of Allah:* tasteful, reverential, with one or two good moments, but basically old-fashioned and slightly dull. It marked the end of his long cycle of adaptations of his childhood favorites. From this time on, he directed his efforts toward building up his roster of stars and directors.

An ultramodern, ultrachic night club setting by Lyle Wheeler—this time for one of Selznick International's best but least-known films, *The Young in Heart*.

By early 1938, as *The Adventures of Tom Sawyer* went into release, Selznick International had delivered to United Artists only six of its scheduled twelve pictures for the two-year releasing contract, and those had not been delivered on time, primarily because of Selznick's obsession with perfecting every detail. It had originally been his hope to hire directors who could also produce, such as Gregory LaCava and Frank Capra, so that they would be able to make pictures without strong supervision from him; but as he began to be more and more absorbed in overseeing everything that went into the making of the company's pictures, this became more and more a forlorn hope.

Letting a director function unhampered by him from start to finish on a project was something that he never considered, nor did most anyone else in the business except Columbia's Harry Cohn with Frank Capra, and Merian Cooper with John Ford at RKO. The function of a director at the time was summed up by Selznick:

> At most studios, his job is solely to get out on the stage and direct the actors, put them through the paces that are called for in the script . . . he is handed a script, sets, staff, everything else, all the tools and he goes out and directs. I don't think it's a very sound process because . . . the man who is directing the individual scenes should have some conception of what was intended in the preparation of the picture and so I always have my director . . . in on the script as far in advance as possible . . . and he's in on the cutting with me right up to the time the picture is finished. . . . I do this even though it isn't obligatory, nor is it the custom in most of the larger studios.

It was this paternalistic attitude that kept many a good man from working with Selznick; unless he was very strong-willed and aggressive, a high-caliber director, one who really initiated and carried through his own projects, would not stand for Selznick's constant changes and other interferences in what he would consider his rightful domain. George Cukor, who had been under contract to Selznick International since early 1937, had yet to make a film for the company. The independent movement of directors was becoming stronger throughout the industry as the more competent, gifted craftsmen began to chafe under the restraints of the producer-dominated studios. And in late 1937 this particular core group of Hollywood professionals, emboldened by the 1935 National Labor Relations Act (the so-called Wagner Act), banded together to form the Screen Directors Guild "for their mutual aid and protection . . . to bargain collectively . . . free from the domination or control of their employers." Selznick argued with an additional statement in the platform of this new group that said, "In the making of motion pictures . . . the director has been and is the central creative force controlling and coordinating . . . the brains and talent that goes into . . . the final product on the screen." In a ghostwritten reply on behalf of the producers, he told the Guild that

> we have no objection . . . to dealing with any labor group . . . or in complying with the provisions of the Wagner Act . . . but we must frankly refuse to deal with any group intending to wrest control of production from those men who have been authorized by . . . thousands of stockholders of our several companies to manage this production of motion pictures. . . . We feel very strongly that the Wagner Act was not intended to include a group of individual creators whose working conditions could not possibly be standardized and who actually have always resented and opposed any spasmodic attempt at standardization and who we can say with safety are the highest salaried group of individuals . . . men whose working conditions have no parallel in American industry in their ease, and in the days, hours, weeks and even months of idleness during which most of them receive their unequalled and even unapproached high salaries, and until we receive a determination from the government that the Wagner Act does in fact include this group under its concept we must refuse to accede to any peremptory demands on the part of your group.

This letter was signed by Darryl Zanuck, Jack Warner, and Eddie Mannix representing the producers and was sent to the executive committee of the Screen Directors Guild, made up of Howard Hawks, Edward Sutherland, and John Ford. Within a very short time, the Roosevelt administration had made it very clear that the Wagner Act did indeed take in directors and assistant directors under its provisions, and the producers, Selznick included, reluctantly bowed to the inevitable and watched as the Screen Directors Guild began the slow erosion of the omnipotent producer.

This bloodless but painful defeat was doubly unsettling to Selznick as John Ford was contracted, through Cooper and Pioneer, to make two pictures for Selznick International, and Ford, who didn't care for Selznick anyway, was a particularly strong-willed man, who seldom forgot or forgave a slight. His contract with Pioneer had been taken over by Selznick with the merger of the two companies. Merian Cooper recalls:

> I thought Jack Ford was the very best director alive, so when Jock Whitney and I formed Pioneer, one of the first things I did was to make a deal with Ford to direct two pictures at $85,000 a picture, which aroused the ire of every studio head in Hollywood, including David, as Ford's last picture, *Mary of Scotland,* only paid him $45,000, and I was told that I was ruining the price of the directors as no other director was getting that kind of money. In the deal I made with David and Jock Whitney, I was to be a vice-president of Selznick International. I was to pick my own pictures and have full authority for producing them, with David to have veto power of any picture I picked if he thought it would be a money loser, but with nothing to say once the picture was agreed to. Now about this time, Ford had read a short story in *Collier's* magazine called "Stage to Lordsburg," which he bought the rights to and told me he wanted to make a picture of. . . . Ford wanted John Wayne for the lead; I didn't know Wayne, but I ran several pictures in which he appeared, *The Big Trail* and a couple of *The Three Mesquiteers* pictures he'd done at Republic, and I agreed with Ford that he was perfect. I knew Claire Trevor, and Ford and I settled on her for the girl, and I told Ford to go ahead and verbally commit for both Wayne and Trevor, and then we went up to David Selznick's house for dinner to tell him about the picture, which we called *Stagecoach.*
>
> To my surprise, David was not impressed. First he said we had no big name stars and secondly "it was just another western." He said we'd do a lot better if we did a classic. . . . Ford and I both jumped David hard on this. Jack Ford can state a case as well as anybody who ever lived when he wants to take the time to do it; I'm not too bad myself, and over coffee, we argued that this was a *classic* western with *classic* characters and we finally convinced him and got the go ahead. But the very next morning, David called and asked us to come in and see him and the very first thing he says was that he had given our "western" "deep thought" and it was his studied conclusion that the picture would not "get its print costs back" unless we put stars into the two leads. . . . He thought we would be highly pleased when he told us that he could get Gary Cooper and Marlene Dietrich instead of Wayne and Trevor. I was dumbfounded. . . . Besides the fact that they were bad casting, they were both too old, and I had given my word to both Wayne and Claire Trevor through Ford that we would use them. . . . We argued all morning, but I couldn't shake him and he couldn't move me, so right then and there I resigned . . . it cost me plenty, too. . . . The company owed me $64,000 in salary which I had decided not to take until I actually started production, I was vice-president of both companies and owned a piece of each, but I threw the cash and the long-term contracts overboard on what was to me a point of honor. After I left, Jack told David that he'd made a contract with me personally to make *Stagecoach* regardless of what company made the picture, so he left too.

Selznick's reaction to this contretemps was alternately defensive and outraged:

> I don't think we should be chumps about this . . . if Ford actually has a commitment with us I see no reason for releasing him. . . . I feel very strongly that we must select the story and sell it to Ford instead of him picking some uncommercial pet of his. . . . I see no justification for making any story just because it is liked by a man who, I am willing to concede, is one of the greatest directors in the world but whose record commercially is far from good. I feel that Ford is no more sure-fire than is Cukor. Both are great . . . but both need to have their stories selected and guided for them. [In Ford's case] I am somewhat

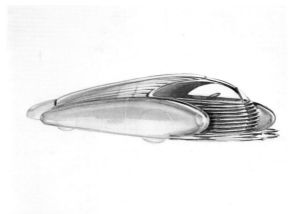
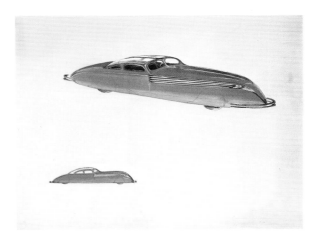

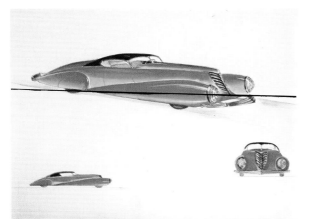
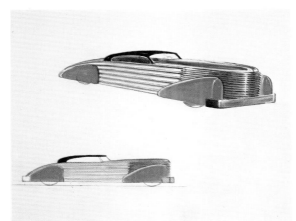

Early sketches by Lyle Wheeler for the Flying Wombat, a futuristic automobile that figured prominently in the plot of *The Young in Heart*. The design that was finally used was a composite of elements from all these sketches. The car itself was custom built on the chassis of a Chrysler that belonged to the son of H. J. Heinz, the pickle king. (Below) The Wombat, ready for filming.

The Young in Heart was an adaptation of I. A. R. Wylie's novella *The Gay Banditti,* about a family of rogues who are reformed through their contact with a kindly little old lady known as Miss Fortune. Selznick wanted Maude Adams (top) to play the part; she tested for it but decided not to do it. Next he went after Laurette Taylor (above). She too tested and she too declined, and the part finally went to Minnie Dupree, veteran stage performer, seen here (below) with Billie Burke, Roland Young, and Janet Gaynor as most of the nefarious family.

wounded, as this is the first time in my career that someone has said that he did not want to work for me . . . and I have no particular desire to have him here if he doesn't want to stay. . . . He is an excellent man, but there is no point in treating him as a god and if he doesn't want to be here I'd just as soon have some other good director.

The departure of Merian Cooper and John Ford aggravated the problem of Selznick International's trying to live up to its releasing deal with United Artists, for Cooper, as head of Pioneer, was supposed to deliver four pictures during the two years of the contract. When Cooper left, Pioneer Pictures ceased to exist except as a legal caretaker of the company's assets: *Becky Sharp* and the other Technicolor features, including two made by Selznick International, *A Star Is Born* and *Nothing Sacred.* Cooper and Ford formed Argosy Pictures, a unique little holding company whose only assets were the talents of its two partners. Ford convinced Walter Wanger to contract with Argosy to film *Stagecoach* and with Cooper's blessing and Wanger's money Ford went off to Monument Valley to film the western that Selznick was convinced would be a total failure. Cooper meanwhile also made a deal to go over to MGM, where he did an uncharacteristic and mildly successful picture called *The Toy Wife,* while Selznick, with whom he maintained a close personal friendship, looked around for something to fill the void left by Cooper's departure.

In December 1937, Elsa Neuberger, a young lady in the Selznick Eastern story office, whose intellectual curiosity led her all over New York in search of new developments in plays, art, and pictures, dropped in to the tiny Cinéma de Paris Theatre. She was prompted by a review in *The New York Times* stating that "*Intermezzo,* the new Swedish picture, shows that even the most timeworn material can be made interesting; the sincerity of the acting, especially on the part of the young charming Ingrid Bergman, confirms the good opinions she has won at home and abroad in former pictures."

These sentiments were echoed by Elsa Neuberger in her report to Kay Brown, who forwarded to Selznick the favorable opinion, along with the critics' reviews, a packet of still photographs, and a print of the film. Selznick, who was swamped with work, asked some of his staff to take a look. Ray Klune remarks that "a group of us ran the picture. We didn't know precisely what we were looking at but we were fascinated with it, even though it was all in Swedish with English subtitles, it was sort of a romantic soap opera type of thing . . . but we were all impressed with Ingrid Bergman and we told him that we all thought she was great, sensational, let's get her by all means. He said, 'Well, I thought you were looking at it to see whether we should remake the story,' and we said, 'Oh yes, by all means remake it with her in English.' "

Such enthusiasm was not lost on Selznick, who was ever on the alert to build up his roster of performers, especially with new faces, having the double advantage of being fresh to the public eye and relatively inexpensive to put under contract. So he cabled Kay Brown, first to buy the American rights to the story and then to leave as soon as possible for Europe to see if she could interest the Swedish actress in coming to Hollywood to make a picture. When Kay Brown arrived in Stockholm, she was a bit disconcerted to discover that Bergman was married to a rather austere doctor, and was the mother of an infant daughter.

The twenty-three-year-old actress's parents had both died by the time she was twelve, leaving her homeless; she was sent to live with her elderly uncle, who had five older children. Shy and lonely, she was teased unmercifully about her size and her awkwardness. She said later: "I retreated more and more into myself, withdrawing into a dream world with creatures of fantasy who were less oppressive than the people around me. I determined more than ever to become an actress because in the make-believe world was the sanctuary where I could submerge all my inhibitions and play act at being things I was not." By 1934 she was not only enrolled in the Royal Dramatic Theatre School but had made the first of several films that eventually brought Kay Brown to her door. Of this first meeting Bergman later said: "I wanted very much to go to Hollywood, but I was worried about my daughter, who was too tiny to take on such a long journey . . . my husband was working hard at his medical studies and I wanted nothing to interfere with them . . . and

226

The Young in Heart was light, scintillating, and heartwarming, due mainly to the screenplay of Charles Bennett and Paul Osborn, the direction of Richard Wallace, and the playing of the cast, which included (above, left) Janet Gaynor, Roland Young, Billie Burke, and Douglas Fairbanks, Jr., as the somnolent Carleton family, about to be ridden out of Monte Carlo on a rail, and (above, right) Paulette Goddard, who had just been placed under contract to Selznick. The picture also marked the debut of Richard Carlson, a young actor from Yale who, on the strength of his appearance in this film, went on to a thirty-year career in films and television.

(Below) The technical staff of Selznick International Pictures. Among those in this group photo are: (sitting) cameraman Leon Shamroy (with hat in hand), director Richard Wallace (in plaid jacket), assistant director Eric Stacey (in striped tie); (standing) Hal Kern (behind Shamroy), Jack Cosgrove (in light suit, with hand in pocket), William Cameron Menzies (next to Cosgrove, in striped suit), second assistant director Ridgeway Callow (behind and between Cosgrove and Menzies), and production manager Raymond Klune (behind and left of Cosgrove). Mike Kelly, studio cop and father of Tommy Kelly, is standing at far right.

Ingrid Bergman, as she looked in the Swedish version of *Intermezzo* (top, left), and in four shots from her Technicolor screen test for the Selznick remake.

when Kay talked about a seven-year contract, I was terrified.... I just couldn't imagine it.... Stockholm was the only home I'd ever known and I felt secure there.... But worse than that I was scared to death that Hollywood would not like me."

In a cabled message, Kay Brown told Selznick of Bergman's misgivings, and of the fact that she had several contractual commitments in Sweden that would keep her from signing any sort of contract immediately. Replying to this, Selznick said: "Would still be interested even if she does not start till next year ... would like to know about her commitments as we might want to get her out of some ... in connection with terms for her I might point out that she was not starred in Sweden, since the main title of *Intermezzo* stars Gosta Ekman and Inga Tidblad. A cold shudder has just run through me on the realization that maybe we are dealing for the wrong girl. Maybe the one we want is Inga Tidblad ... you had better check on this." After much persuasion by Kay Brown, Bergman agreed to sign a contract for one picture, and it was with the assurance that this picture would be a remake of *Intermezzo* that she consented to come to Hollywood in the spring of 1939. Selznick, however, was not positive that he wanted to use her in the story, trying instead to interest Loretta Young in playing the Bergman role, that of a young concert pianist who falls in love with a married violinist.

"One of the principal reasons for buying foreign pictures to remake," he commented, "is that when they are good they save a very large part of the agonies of creative preparation and a large part of the cost as well. By actually duplicating, as much as possible, the original edited film, we will save weeks in shooting and a fortune in unnecessary angles and extra takes, as the camera work on the original *Intermezzo* was very good, and there is no reason at all to vary it ... and we must get a director who is willing to do such a duplicating job." Leslie Howard, the suave English matinee idol who was working in the studio on another project, was decided upon for the violinist. As the time drew near for the picture to

begin photography, Selznick was forced into a decision about which actress would play the pivotal role of the violinist's inamorata, and he took the plunge and sent for Ingrid Bergman. But he instructed his publicity department:

I don't think we ought to go into any big publicity campaign in advance of her appearance ... because build-ups on foreign importations have reached a point where the American public resents the players when they do appear. I think that the best thing to do would be to import her quietly into the studio, go about our business of making the picture ... and then feed an important and favorable public reaction of her when the picture is finished.... With this in mind I think we should avoid interviews with her at the boat and should let her arrive in Los Angeles very quietly which will give us the opportunity to discuss a change of name with her when she arrives.

Bergman presented herself at the studio the day after her arrival, not without some trepidation, for as she candidly remarked:

I was very worried to come over because I'd seen many examples of actresses coming over and they changed them completely and then sent them back home again ... so I went to the studio and saw this great producer and these were his first words, he looked up at me and said, "Would you take your shoes off please," so I realized that the first thing was that he thought I was too tall, and I was very unhappy, but I had to tell the truth, no use taking the shoes off because my heels were so low ... this was my height. Then we started to discuss my name, he said, "You know that name is impossible because nobody can pronounce it, and Bergman is German and in these days we don't want anybody to think you are German." The following day he took me to the makeup department to discuss what they should do with my face and makeup and hair and I started to think, oh this is terrible, now they're going to change everything ... and then he got an idea, he was going to make me the first natural girl. He said, "Nothing is going to be changed, you're going to be exactly the way that you were in Sweden." In those days actresses looked more or less alike, and he got this idea that I was going to be different ... which relieved me. But I fought about my name, I said, "It's my name, isn't it?" but what was in the back of my mind was that my contract was for one picture, *Intermezzo*, and then I was going to go back to Sweden, so I refused to change my name, thinking that if the picture failed I would be going back home having accomplished nothing but a change of name, and I didn't want to be a phoney with a new name in Sweden.

Production finally got under way on the American version of *Intermezzo* on May 24, 1939, with William Wyler directing and Harry Stradling doing the photography. Five days into the shooting, Selznick became alarmed at Wyler's lack of speed, and after a long discussion with Wyler, Selznick removed him. The director finally decided upon was Gregory Ratoff. In spite of his mangled English, delivered in a thick Russian-Yiddish accent, he had a certain sensitivity under his blustering comic manner that managed to bring out the best in the pedestrian

script, and he did it quickly and efficiently, much to Selznick's satisfaction. Shooting began under his direction on June 5. Five days later Selznick was again dissatisfied, this time with the photography of Harry Stradling, telling him that "there is no single thing about the physical production of the picture that compares in importance with the photography of Miss Bergman. The curious charm that she had in the Swedish version—the combination of exciting beauty and fresh purity—certainly ought to be within our abilities to capture. Unless we can bring off the photography so that she really looks divine, the whole picture can fall apart from the standpoint of audience effectiveness."

Selznick pulled Stradling off the picture, replacing him with Gregg Toland, whom he borrowed from Samuel Goldwyn, a move that prompted much concern from his new star who, according to Selznick, "had tears in her eyes and she wanted to know whether it would hurt Stradling's standing, because after all he was a very good cameraman— and it didn't matter if she was photographed a little worse—she would rather have this than hurt him." Toland's initial work on the picture met with Selznick's relieved approval: "He has found the most important thing of all is in the proper shading of her face and in going for effect

(Overleaf) Filming the Selznick version of *Intermezzo: A Love Story* on the back lot. Cameraman Gregg Toland stands to the right of the dollying camera as it photographs a scene with Leslie Howard and Ingrid Bergman. Director Gregory Ratoff is striding forward (upper right) with arm outstretched, gesticulating to assistant director Eric Stacey. The set, representing a French port, was by Lyle Wheeler. The large serpentine device at the upper left is a wind tunnel that silently emitted a strong breeze ruffling the water's surface. Milton Gold was the still photographer on this production.

(Below) Leslie Howard and Ingrid Bergman in a scene from *Intermezzo: A Love Story,* as the Selznick remake was called. Art direction was by Lyle Wheeler, set decoration by Casey Roberts, and costumes by Travis Banton for Bergman and Irene for Howard. His violin playing in the film was actually done by Toscha Seidel, while Bergman's piano efforts were dubbed by Norma Drury.

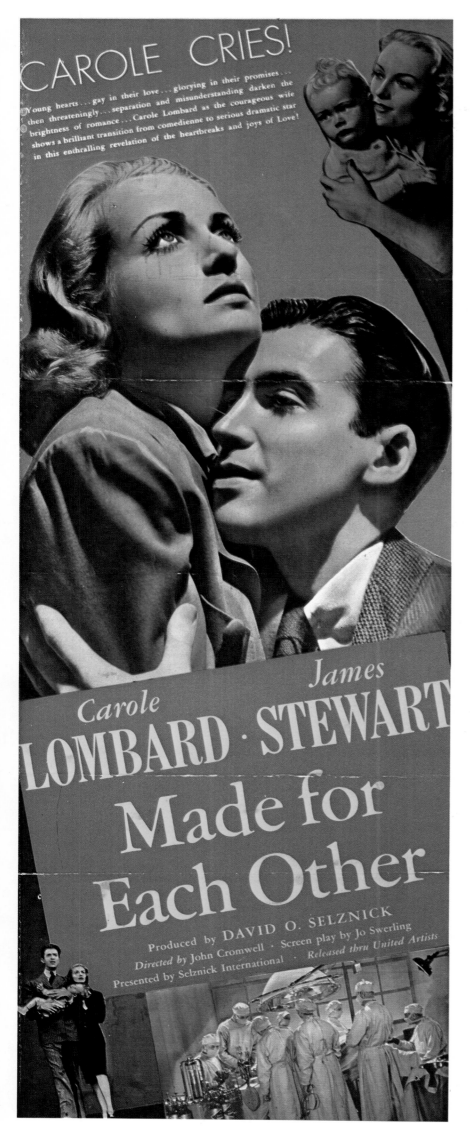

CAROLE CRIES!

Young hearts...gay in their love...glorying in their promises...
then threateningly...separation and misunderstanding darken the
brightness of romance...Carole Lombard as the courageous wife
shows a brilliant transition from comedienne to serious dramatic star
in this enthralling revelation of the heartbreaks and joys of Love!

Carole
LOMBARD · STEWART
James

Made for
Each Other

Produced by DAVID O. SELZNICK
Directed by John Cromwell · Screen play by Jo Swerling
Presented by Selznick International · Released thru United Artists

Made for Each Other was an original screenplay by Jo Swerling about the problems of a young married couple. It was Selznick's penultimate picture on his original United Artists contract and was a conscious effort to change Carole Lombard's image from that of a hoydenish comedienne to a dramatic actress. After previews revealed a lack of dramatic intensity, Selznick had the ending of the script re-written to incorporate a suspenseful section involving an airplane rushing serum to the couple's ailing child, something he lifted directly from *Night Flight,* which in turn had derived the device from an actual incident involving Selznick's brother Myron. In spite of everybody's efforts, the picture emerged as little more than an above-average domestic drama, disappointing both Lombard and James Stewart, her co-star, who had been borrowed from MGM.

lightings on her; this sort of careful attention to lighting effects I regard as equally important as the dialogue and the performances if we are to get the artistic gem that we hope out of our simple little story."

Production went smoothly for another month; the problem of Leslie Howard's being unable to handle the violin convincingly was solved by using a combination of two methods, one suggested by Bergman that had been used in the original Swedish version, which involved having two violinists stand on either side of the leading man, whose arms were held closely at his side; one violinist had his arm outstretched and did the fingering, and the other did the bowing. This worked fine in close shots. For longer, full-length shots a split-screen process was used. The violin music played in the film was dubbed by Toscha Seidel, and the constant use of the main theme, "Intermezzo," which had been carried over from the Swedish version, prompted Selznick to remark that the piece was "magnificent, we should not try to better it since it haunts everyone who sees the picture; however I do think we should get in some other famous concert pieces such as 'Humoresque' etc., to get the full showmanship value of solo violin pieces that audiences are always screaming for and to avoid the curious impression that one gets that the violinist plays nothing but 'Intermezzo.' "

Principal photography was completed in late July; a preview in Huntington Park ran 103 minutes, much too long, but the audience seemed to like it in spite of the slow spots, and the preview cards all raved over Bergman. A week of retakes, two more weeks of cutting, then the picture was taken for a second preview on August 17 in Santa Barbara. This time the picture ran eighty minutes and elicited a much more enthusiastic response, and once again the preview cards were ecstatic over the new actress. She was now most anxious to return home to Sweden, as the international situation was growing grimmer by the day, with Nazi Germany threatening to plunge Europe into war unless a strip of land known as the Polish Corridor was turned over. Selznick decided that the picture could be completed without keeping her in Hollywood any longer, and she returned to Sweden at the end of the month, remarking years later: "I prayed that I had done well and that David would want me back. I loved working in Hollywood and I loved the people I had worked with. I wanted so much to come back, but I missed terribly my husband and my child."

The final preview of *Intermezzo* was held in Pomona at the Fox Theatre on August 31, 1939. This time at a lean seventy minutes, it played with no dead spots and the audience was unequivocally enthusiastic; the minor repairs necessary to finish it for release could be done within a matter of weeks.

Intermezzo opened in Hollywood in October, and both the critics and the public acclaimed Bergman as a new star. Selznick telephoned her to let her know that he was taking up her option for two more pictures and calling her back to Hollywood. "I cried all that day," the actress recalled. "When we were making the picture, David and Gregory Ratoff and other people said I was good, but I didn't trust them. It was wicked to feel that way, but when I learned that audiences were pleased, then, and then only was I convinced and satisfied."

While the war in Europe built up its devastating momentum, David Selznick turned to the completion of a project that had for the past three years occupied not only his attention but that of most of the literate population of the United States, his film version of the phenomenal best-selling novel, Margaret Mitchell's *Gone With The Wind.*

233

Margaret Mitchell Marsh, the Atlanta housewife and thirty-five-year-old author of the
most popular American novel ever written.

GONE WITH THE WIND

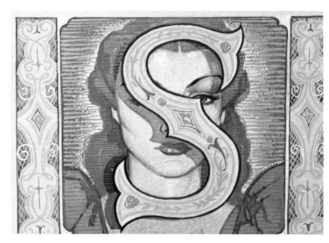

These sketches illustrate the traditional Hollywood treatment of classic or best-selling books. As originally conceived, *Gone With The Wind* was to begin with a shot of the book, showing its distinctive jacket; the cover opens, the pages turn, and the camera moves in to a close shot of the first line of the novel: "Scarlett O'Hara was not beautiful, but men seldom realized it when caught by her charm as the Tarleton twins were...." The line dissolves into a close-up of Scarlett, and the story is under way.

Gone With The Wind

ACCORDING TO David Selznick's daily activity log for May 20, 1936, at 1:28 P.M. he was in a projection room looking at edited sequences from *The Garden of Allah* when the teletype in his office clattered out a message from Kay Brown in New York: "... have just airmailed detailed synopsis of *Gone With The Wind* by Margaret Mitchell, also copy of book.... This is an absolutely magnificent story ... a great literary property and we must have it.... The book is 1,000 pages long and I have only gotten through half of it, it is one of the most lush things I ever read.... I am absolutely off my nut about this book.... I beg, urge, coax and plead with you to read it at once.... I know that after you do you will drop everything and buy it."

The novel she was so enthusiastic about had been the talk of the New York publishing world for the last two months; executives of the Macmillan Company, one of the oldest and most respected firms in the business, had let it be known that they felt they had something extraordinary in this first novel by a thirty-five-year-old Atlanta housewife and ex-feature writer for the Atlanta *Journal*. In 1926, largely to amuse herself while recuperating from a broken ankle, she had begun to write the story "of a girl who was somewhat like Atlanta, part of the old South, part of the new South; how she rose with Atlanta and fell with it and rose again; what Atlanta did to her, what she did to Atlanta and the man who was more than a match for her. I took them and put them against a background which I knew as well as my own background." Off and on for the next several years she continued to "hit the story a few licks," as she put it, through the last years of the twenties, the crash and depression of the early thirties, finally, in 1935, bringing her pile of unfinished manuscript out of the storage closet to which she had consigned it and, in a self-confessed weak moment, turning it over to Harold Latham, a Macmillan editor who was scouring the South for publishable material. By the time the story was ready for publication in early 1936, it ran to 1,037 pages covering twelve years in the life of its heroine, Scarlett O'Hara—spoiled, prideful, willful, and resilient—set against a meticu-

lously detailed background of the last of the plantation days, the Civil War, and Reconstruction as lived in Atlanta during that whole turbulent period of social and economic change.

Because of the high cost of printing, the book would carry a $3.00 price tag on its scheduled May 5 publication date, 50 cents higher than usual for fiction. Ten thousand copies of the book was the first print order from Macmillan, but then a sudden and unexpected acceptance of the novel for its July 1936 selection by the Book-of-the-Month Club (then ten years old) boosted the original print order by 40,000 copies, forcing Macmillan to move the official publication date to June, but also allowing it to send actual bound books instead of galley proofs, as was the usual custom, to the story departments of the various motion picture companies. Each received the 2½-pound volume in mid-May from the publisher's agent, Annie Laurie Williams, who sent along a note stating that the asking price would be $100,000, quite a sum for a first novel by an unknown author, but one that the shrewd Miss Williams reckoned would get everybody's attention, automatically giving an aura of importance to the book.

Katharine Brown at Selznick International was only one of the women in the New York motion picture world who went "off their nut" over the fortunes of Scarlett O'Hara. At Universal, Elsa Neuberger, before she left to join the Selznick forces, was highly vocal in her praise of the book to the new head of the company, Charles Rogers, who wired her back: "I told you no costume pictures." In the Burbank, California, studios of Warner Bros., Jack Warner had been briefed on the synopsis and the opinions of the New York people that the book would be big; he dangled the role in front of his recalcitrant young star Bette Davis, who turned up her nose and decamped hastily for England to try to break her contract. When she went, so did Warner Bros.' interest in the book, narrowing Annie Laurie's potential field down considerably. There was MGM, where she hoped Irving Thalberg might be intrigued with it as a vehicle for his wife, Norma Shearer. Paramount was already out of the

1936—David O. Selznick in his office, engrossed in something that could very well be *Gone With The Wind.*

running; it was their disastrous picture version of *So Red the Rose* the previous year that was cited as evidence that the Civil War was not to be messed with. RKO noted the "unsympathetic nature of the heroine," and felt that "so many involvements of plot and background ... the censorable material ... and the period in which it is laid would make it prohibitively expensive." So RKO dropped out, but not before the studio's biggest female star, Katharine Hepburn, read the book and immediately began badgering the heads of the company to reconsider. Darryl Zanuck of 20th Century-Fox, after reading the synopsis, seriously considered making an offer, but was put off by Annie Laurie's asking price.

Meanwhile, in Kay Brown's office at Selznick International, a young woman named Franclein Macconnel had promptly begun the delicate task of synopsizing the massive story. In four days she had finished a fifty-seven-page condensation that managed to convey much of the strength of the plot and characters. It was this that Kay Brown sent to David Selznick on May 20, paving the way with her strongly worded teletype message. Both the synopsis and the book arrived at the Culver City studio on May 22. But Selznick, preoccupied as he was with the troublesome *Garden of Allah,* did not have time to read even the synopsis, prompting the anxious Kay Brown to send a copy of the book to Jock Whitney in the hope of getting faster action from him. So far the only nibble had come from Zanuck, who had offered $35,000, which Annie Laurie disdainfully turned down, much to Kay Brown's relief and Margaret Mitchell's shock. Kay Brown bombarded Selznick with daily telegrams, teletypes, and memos, exhorting him to "just pick up the book and read from chapter 21 to 26 ... it is something that would 'tear the heart out of a body' ... I am going to try to do everything in my power to keep this from being sold until you make up your mind.... I know Mr. Whitney will let me spend the money for this book if you will." "The money" had now come down considerably, from $100,000 to $65,000. Finally moved by her incessant badgering, Selznick read the synopsis on May 24 and wired her: "Have carefully thought about *Gone With The*

Wind ... think it is fine story and understand your feeling about it. If we had under contract a woman ideally suited to the lead I would probably be more inclined to buy it than I am today ... feel that its only showmanship values would be in either such star casting or in a tremendous sale of the book.... I do not feel we can take such a gamble ... therefore most sorry to have to say no in the face of your evident enthusiasm."

Selznick had not reckoned with Kay Brown's determination, however. If she couldn't convince him head on, she would outflank him, and for this tactic she enlisted Jock Whitney, who was reading the book and whose enthusiasm was becoming as rabid as hers. While she worked on Whitney, Selznick was having second thoughts, for he wired her the next day: "... feel there is excellent picture in it ... suggest you call this to Cooper and Whitney's attention for possible Pioneer color picture, especially if they can sell the very colorful man's role to Gary Cooper.... Were I with MGM ... I would buy it now for ... such combination as Gable and Joan Crawford." So far, Selznick had heard only from Kay Brown and knew the story only from the synopsis. By now his own interest began to be piqued, and he re-read the synopsis, this time with an eye to buying the story as a vehicle for Ronald Colman, with whom he had one more picture to make. Throughout most of June, Selznick vacillated between interest in the story and concern over the cost and the casting resources necessary to make it properly. While he waffled, Katharine Hepburn, who had finished the book, intensified her efforts to get RKO to buy it for her, and negotiations were tentatively reopened by studio chief Sam Briskin, which Annie Laurie dutifully reported to Kay Brown. Frantically, she brought up her big guns, beseeching Jock Whitney to convince David. Whitney needed no additional prodding from her; he had finished the book. According to Selznick, "Jock wired me that if I was nervous about paying the price, that he would personally buy the book and hold it for the company, if we decided we wanted it.... I couldn't risk letting him have the last laugh on me...." So he instructed Kay Brown to make a firm final offer of $50,000 for the rights, saying: "I cannot see my way clear to paying any more. . . ." RKO's last offer had been for $45,000. Annie Laurie decided the $50,000 would probably be the best she could get and advised Miss Mitchell accordingly. Mitchell quickly accepted, much to Kay Brown's relief.

By late June laudatory reviews of the book were beginning to appear in growing numbers, climaxed by front-page notices in the book review sections of *The New York Times* and the *Herald Tribune.* The effect of all this was to start a stampede by the picture companies to Annie Laurie's door. RKO was now determined to get the property for Hepburn, and on Miss Mitchell's arrival in Manhattan on July 29, the studio hierarchy spent several hours trying to persuade her to change her mind and accept their offer of $55,000. But she came from a long line of people who believed that once you gave your word, you kept it, and she turned them down flat. The next day, Miss Mitchell met with Kay Brown and the other "Selznickers," as she called them, and warned them that she was selling the book against her better judgment as she was positive that it would be impossible to make a picture out of it, saying: "It had taken me ten years to weave it as tight as a silk pocket handkerchief. If one thread is broken or pulled when they begin cutting, they will have technical problems they never dreamed of." With that warning she signed her contract, giving Selznick International Pictures the right to "the exclusive, complete and entire motion picture and broadcasting rights, including television, in the property known as *Gone With The Wind* . . . [furthermore] the owner shall not be responsible for any additions, adaptations, substitutions or other changes the purchaser may make, or for any words or any delineation or interpretation of character different than that contained in the property."

By July, bookstores could not keep up with demand; they began reordering in huge numbers. In mid-August, two printing plants were working on the book in three eight-hour shifts a day, and entire freight cars were filled with copies to be delivered all over the country; the book was selling an average of 3,700 copies a day. By the end of September, over 330,000 copies had been sold. Nothing like this had ever happened in the publishing world before. The book began to be joked about on the radio, editorialized about in newspapers, used as the basis for sermons, becoming one of the first popular-culture media events, a massive, spontaneous demonstration of word-of-mouth advertising as men and especially women took the story for their own. For this Scarlett O'Hara and her saga were something new in American fiction: a vital, determined, courageous, and dominating heroine who used every resource at her command to meet adversity and beat it on its own terms. To a generation of women, *Gone With The Wind* represented the first time that a twentieth-century woman's voice had spoken to them about their lives and their beliefs, giving them a sense of themselves and their place in American society.

While the gale force of the novel's popularity began to build, Selznick, off on vacation in Honolulu, finally read the book and was alternately ecstatic and apprehensive about what he had gotten himself into. The synopsis had given some indication of the scope and relationships of the story, but nothing had prepared him for the pictures conjured up in his mind by Miss Mitchell's prose, nor for the absorbing and detailed characterizations and their complex interworkings. He hadn't been so excited by a project since *David Copperfield,* but he realized at once the enormous problems inherent in undertaking something of this magnitude. Months, perhaps years of careful, meticulous planning would be needed; the mass of material contained in the novel would have to be condensed, much of it eliminated, if it were to be brought into manageable proportions. This was made even more obvious when Selznick returned to Culver City in August and found the stacks of mail from readers all over the country, imploring him not to change the story "like the movies always do," and giving him the first hints of the controversy that would surround the casting of the central roles. Lydia Schiller was given charge of organizing this correspondence, keeping track of who the favorites were. She kept them in a file marked "Scarlett Letters," and the names seemed to change on a monthly basis. "The first few months had Miriam Hopkins and Margaret Sullavan leading the suggestions," she recalls, "with many people very strong for Ronald Colman as Rhett." As October approached, sackfuls of mail continued to plague Selznick with vociferous suggestions and demands about most of the central characters, but always

about Scarlett, and it wasn't just the public that had joined Kay Brown in going "off their nut" over the story. In Hollywood, seemingly every female performer between the ages of Shirley Temple and May Robson decided she must have the part, and the Selznick studio offices on both coasts were inundated with photos, letters, telegrams, and phone calls from anxious agents and ambitious actresses—a situation the studio press chief Russell Birdwell gleefully reported to the trade and national press, building a publicity campaign out of the unprecedented interest that was beginning to astound even the most hardened veterans of the Hollywood press corps.

All this fuss was gratifying to Selznick, but it was very premature because he had still not settled on a writer to do the script. After his return from Hawaii he had tossed the choice back and forth in his mind between Ben Hecht and Sidney Howard, and finally decided to offer the assignment to Sidney Howard because "he is the best constructionist around right now." The distinguished Mr. Howard had won the Pulitzer Prize in 1924 for his play *They Knew What They Wanted,* and he had subsequently added to his reputation with *The Silver Cord* and stage versions of *Yellow Jack* and Sinclair Lewis's *Dodsworth* (just adapted by him to the screen for William Wyler and Sam Goldwyn). Howard was an old friend of Merian Cooper's, the two had flown together during the war, and Selznick asked Cooper to help Kay Brown in convincing Howard to take the job. Cooper gladly did so, as he too was under the spell of the book; he commented in a letter that it was "the story of a bitch and a bastard . . . and the most supreme book written on courage in the English language." Cooper's persuasiveness and his own perusal of the book convinced Howard to take on the job, which he did in mid-October 1936. Selznick immediately began a campaign to have Howard come to Culver City to do the script, telling Kay Brown: "I have never had much success with leaving a writer alone to do a script without almost daily collaboration with myself and [the director]." Howard, however, preferred to work on his farm in Massachusetts, free from conferences, distractions, and the endless discussions he knew would go on with Selznick.

Frustrated at having Howard out of immediate earshot, but dashing off instructions by mail, Selznick was also beginning a series of daily conferences with George Cukor, who had just come from MGM where he had directed Greta Garbo in *Camille,* following on the heels of his work on the prestigious Thalberg production of *Romeo and Juliet.* They had both been large, complex projects, two of MGM's biggest pictures of the year; *Gone With The Wind* would be his first picture for Selznick International. Cukor had read the book just as it began its phenomenal climb to popularity and he candidly admitted years later, "I didn't think it was the second coming of Christ. . . . It was an effective, slightly crappola thing, but a damn good story with some very original things in it. . . . In spite of its faults it had vitality and was a very picturesque, good rich book." Cukor's favorite for Scarlett was Hepburn, who was furious with RKO for not buying the property for her. She and Cukor were now close friends and they waged a heavy campaign to convince Selznick that she was perfect casting, but he didn't agree. In his mind, and that of the by now millions of readers, Scarlett O'Hara was an extremely feminine, seductive girl-woman, shrewd but not bright, and despite Margaret Mitchell's opening disclaimer, she had to have the kind of beauty and sex appeal that would make Rhett Butler's twelve-year pursuit of her convincing to moviegoers. Hepburn could play all these things, indeed *had* played all these things before, but that, as far as Selznick was concerned, was the basic problem with casting her or any other leading actress in the part: the pre-identification that they would bring to the role, whether it be Hepburn, Margaret Sullavan, Bette Davis, or Miriam Hopkins. Casting any one of these would alienate too many of the potential audience, and ultimately relegate the picture to the status of a star vehicle rather than giving it the fresh new feeling he wanted it to have. This meant a talent search, and, as Selznick wrote to Kay Brown, "an entire cast of new faces . . . *Copperfield* and *Tom Sawyer* have been child's play by comparison. You had better get yourself prepared accordingly."

To do this, Brown organized a three-prong reconnoitering operation: casting director Charles Morrison was to cover the Western states; one of Selznick's assistants, Oscar Serlin, would cover the Northern half of the country, while Brown herself led an expedition through the deep South, searching through high school and college drama departments and the hundreds of local little theatres. In Atlanta, they auditioned five hundred people in one day, and Miss Mitchell, in spite of her efforts to keep her distance, was so intrigued that she seriously considered disguising herself and watching the proceedings. Some idea of the pressure that Kay Brown and her small crew operated under can be gained from her wire to Selznick: "We are in Atlanta, barricaded in our rooms. The belles turned out in droves. For the most part they were all healthy mothers who should have stayed at home; the rich debutantes are all offering to pay us to play Scarlett, and all the mammys in the South want to play Mammy. I feel like Moses in the Wilderness. . . . I need a drink and Georgia is a dry state."

While the search went on, the board of directors of Selznick International was holding its annual meeting and contemplating how best to deal with the problems entailed by its prize property, not the least of which was the expense of producing it properly. The company had a fluctuating working capital of only about $3 million. It was obvious to both Selznick and Cooper, the only two picturemakers on the board, that the production problems of script, length, design, and special effects would boost the cost of the picture considerably beyond the company's present resources—to upwards of $2 million, a staggering sum in the uncertain days immediately following the depression. Considerable discussion and argument took place at the November 1936 board meeting about the wisdom of the company's tackling the project at all, with Henry Ginsberg trying to persuade Selznick and Whitney to accept one of the lucrative offers that were coming in for the rights to the book (the last offer had been for $1 million) and take a hefty profit. Selznick persuasively argued against this, saying that "making *Gone With The Wind* was exactly the kind of challenge I had been searching for since *David Copperfield,* and I was determined that our little company . . . should take this story that would strain the resources of the largest of the studios and . . . try to make it the biggest picture of all time."

It was suggested that they could use just half the book, as Warner Bros. had recently done with *Anthony Adverse,* but Jock Whitney was adamant in backing Selznick's desire to follow the whole story from beginning to end, or as much as could be strung together dramatically. Selznick said later of Whitney's involvement in the project: "He was probably more active in connection with the production of *Gone With The Wind* than any man in his executive position as head of the company has ever been before. Throughout all the time we were preparing it his faith never wavered; never for a moment did he have any doubts about the outcome, or worry about its cost, assuring the members of our Board that he was confident of the final result and that he would share responsibility with me for it." Putting his money where his mouth was, Whitney and his immediate family ponied up another $5 million, some of it coming from Pioneer, for it was at this meeting that the two companies were formally merged and the decision made to take over the entire RKO-Pathé studio, not only because of the expanded production schedule but also because of the looming necessities of *Gone With The Wind.*

On December 14, 1936, Selznick received from Sidney Howard a fifty-page memorandum entitled "Preliminary Notes on a Screen Treatment of *Gone With The Wind.*" Not a script, not even a treatment, it was Howard musing his way through the dramatic pathways of the book. He broke the story down into seven main sequences, following the structure of the novel very closely, using the "warm, simple opening scene, fading in on the . . . Tarleton twins . . . as they visit Scarlett on the porch at Tara." Howard eliminated all of Miss Mitchell's detailed backgrounding of the subsidiary characters, the flashbacks involving Scarlett's parents, the parallel between Scarlett and Atlanta being the same age and the same type—young, vigorous, and pushy—but kept the emphasis on Scarlett's Irish heritage, her "love of the land," as her father puts it. The twin love stories of Scarlett-Rhett, Ashley-Melanie were developed throughout the outline just as they had been in the novel. In his treatment of Rhett Butler, Howard found himself "troubled throughout the war section of the book by the lack of both variety and invention in what Rhett does as he makes various appearances . . . perhaps we should show him doing his stuff as a blockade runner . . . we should take this liberty because it is vitally important to dramatize Rhett's activities very clearly and at once." To work in the war background, Howard suggested a series of six

These three pictures were taken by a research photographer who accompanied director George Cukor and Hobe Erwin, the film's original interior decorator, on their trip through the Clayton County section of north Georgia in mid-1937. Margaret Mitchell conducted them on a tour of the area, pointing out portions of the territory where she had placed the fictional plantations of Tara and Twelve Oaks. Remnants of the plantation era were still to be found, including (top) this modest ante-bellum dwelling. The clapboard house (middle) is very similar to Margaret Mitchell's childhood home and is probably much closer to her description of Tara in the novel than what finally emerged in the film—in character, at least, if not in design. The cotton fields (above) were typical of this section of the country.

Oct. 19, 1938

Mr. David O. Selznick
Selznick International Pictures, Inc.,
9336 W. Washington Blvd.,
Culver City, Calif.

Dear Mr. Selznick:

Mr. Neville Reay, of your
publicity department, has asked me to write
you, giving the results of our "Scarlett O'Hara"
contest.

Unfortunately, no exact
tabulation was made, but the following information will give you what you want, I believe.

Out of approximately 70,000
letters, Bette Davis, the favorite, polled close
to half the votes. Katharine Hepburn was second,
with approximately 13,000. Miriam Hopkins ran
third - Margaret Sullavan, fourth - Joan Crawford,
fifth - Barbara Stanwyck, sixth. A great number
of people voted for an unknown actress to play
the role of "Scarlett," and a handful mentioned
Carole Lombard.

Best regards,

Sincerely,

Jimmie Fidler

Dear Sirs—

Please don't spoil "Gone
With the Wind" by putting
Cary Grant in it as Rhett
Butler. What about Frederic
March?

Yours sincerely—
Sue James

A sampling of the thousands of letters that deluged the studio immediately after it became known that Selznick had purchased the motion picture rights to *Gone With The Wind*. Jimmie Fidler was a gossip columnist whose radio show was popular nationwide.

---

different montages illustrating the declining fortunes of the South, with vignettes of food and medical scarcities in Atlanta, battle scenes, and the eventual collapse of the Confederacy, with Scarlett midwifing Melanie's baby in a hot, dry, deserted Atlanta, after having run to Dr. Meade for help, only to find him surrounded by the dying remnants of the Confederate Army. Howard ended the first half of his outline with Scarlett returning to Tara, finding her mother dead, her father half mad, and the once verdant land almost totally destroyed. Here he suggested a seventeen-scene montage showing the hazards and back-breaking toil and constant foraging for food endured during the final days of the war by Scarlett and her family and those of the servants left, with her vowing quietly to herself that "as God is my witness, we're going to live through this and when this war is over I'm never going to be hungry again," whereupon she immediately kills a marauding Yankee cavalryman, saying afterwards, "Now we've got a horse and some money and we can get something to eat and some cotton seed to plant." Following the intermission, Howard found himself "seriously troubled with laying out the material of the second half.... Our chief difficulty will come from the lack of organization of the material ... something Miss Mitchell herself is only partially successful at concealing.... In making this Reconstruction part of the picture as vivid as I should like ... the introduction of the Ku Klux Klan is [especially difficult].... Because of the lynching problems we have on our hands these days, I hate to indulge in anything which makes the lynching of a Negro in any sense sympathetic." Scarlett's return to Atlanta for the tax money to save Tara, her rejection by an imprisoned Rhett, her marriage to Frank Kennedy and his death, and Rhett's proposal were all covered quickly and efficiently by Howard. For the final sequence, he wrote that

unfortunately for our purposes, the novel at this point has nearly two hundred pages of disjointed incident covering some five years and the marriages of Scarlett and Rhett ... the birth and death of Bonnie, the death of Melanie and Scarlett's realization of her imaginary love for Ashley, and her learning that Rhett is through with her ... I have tried my utmost to avoid this doubling of deaths at the end by omitting Bonnie ... but I use her because Rhett's explanation on Page 1031 of the book has, I think, something very like tragic profundity: "... I liked to think that Bonnie was you, a little girl again, before the war and poverty had done things to you. She was so like you, so willful, so brave and gay and full of high spirits, and I could pet her and spoil her—just as I wanted to pet you. But she wasn't like you—she loved me. It was a blessing that I could take the love you didn't want and give it to her ... when she went, she took everything."

Selznick spent most of the Christmas season and the first week of 1937 going over these notes, comparing them with his breakdown of the novel and discussing them with Cukor, replying to Howard on January 6, telling him:

I am very happy over your approach to the story, rough as it is.... I recognize, perhaps even more than you, the problem of length. I am prepared for a picture that will be extremely long ... as much as 2½ hours . . . but even getting down to this length is going to be tough.... We must prepare to make drastic cuts and these must include some of the characters.... One of the problems we have in *GWTW* is that it is so fresh in people's minds.... I urge you very strongly indeed against making minor changes ... which may give us slight improvements, but there will be five or ten million readers on our heads for them; where for the most part, they will recognize the obvious necessity of our making drastic cuts. I am embarrassed to say this to you who have been so outstandingly successful in your adaptations, but I find myself a producer charged with recreating [the] best-beloved book of our time, and I don't think any of us have ever tackled anything that is really comparable to the love that people have for it.... I certainly urge most strongly against including any sequences in which Rhett is shown "doing his stuff" as a blockade runner. We will be forgiven cuts if we do not invent sequences.... The fact that the book and the picture may be somewhat out of balance in stressing Scarlett for two thirds and Rhett through the last third doesn't worry me.

What was worrying Selznick was the financial investment that seemed to be mushrooming. Howard's preliminary notes had brought home the realization that the unofficial estimate of $2 million might miss the mark by a wide margin.

While waiting for Howard to deliver his first draft, Selznick and his staff were preoccupied with the preparation and production of the next three pictures on the release schedule: *A Star Is Born, The Adventures of Tom Sawyer,* and *The Prisoner of Zenda.* As these moved out of the offices, onto the stages, and finally into the theatres, work proceeded simultaneously on several aspects of *Gone With The Wind.* Barbara Keon, Selznick's script secretary, Lydia Schiller, and several of the other women in the office began breaking the novel down, indexing every major event and action, cross-indexing this for time periods, seasonal changes, the historical background, and then making separate indexes for characterizations, dialogue topics, character relationships, clothing, descriptions of interior and exterior sets, so that even before there was an official script, there were ten detailed reference scripts that could be used as guides in the extensive pre-production work that was obviously going to be necessary. This was still late 1936, and the production department had not yet shaken down into the smooth efficient operation that Selznick hoped it would become. The location problems and the cost overruns on *The Garden of Allah* had frightened Selznick into the realization that the making of *Gone With The Wind* could be a fiasco without a production manager who was considerably more than merely capable. It was early in 1937 that Selznick first began thinking seriously of offering the job to Ray Klune. Klune too had read the book and, "It scared the hell out of me.... There were so many characters, all those relatives and Scarlett had all those kids, you know. But then after I got over my initial shock, and David assured me that they were going to eliminate a lot of the people, I settled down and read it again.... Now I knew we were going to make the picture, nobody, not even David, seemed to know exactly when . . . which I was glad for, because I began thinking about the various methods we could use to get it done and I realized that it was just a vast job of preparation."

In trying to arrive at a reasonable approximation of a budget without a script, Selznick asked each of the department heads to go through the book and break it down into what they considered to be the absolute minimum needed for sets, costumes, and performers. As head of the art department, Lyle Wheeler, with his architectural and illustrative background, not only made a budget for his department but also began working with the illustrators in sketching his ideas for the sets. Over at RKO, Walter Plunkett, with whom Selznick had worked on the beginnings of *Little Women,* was busy on the costumes for *Mary of Scotland* with Katharine Hepburn; at her urging, he had read the book when word filtered out that Selznick had bought it. Plunkett, as he later recalled, "wrote [Selznick] a note begging for the costuming job. An immediate reply asked me to sign a contract, and as soon as I did, Selznick said right at the beginning that I was to work only with him. He didn't want anyone to see the sketches I was going to do. I read the book two more times, making notations of every line and passage containing a reference to clothes or related subjects. Then my secretary read the book to catch any items I might have missed, then we made a script of these notes, and it worked out that there would be almost 5,500 separate items, all of which would have to be made from scratch." Complicating Plunkett's task further was the fact that styles of clothing in the book, especially women's fashion, underwent two visible metamorphoses, from the prewar plantation days with their distinctive billowing hoop skirts, through the improvised look of the impoverished war years, to the bustles of the Reconstruction era. Plunkett's initial breakdown of the story, added to Wheeler's estimate for settings and Klune's projections of the manpower involved in front of and behind the camera, added up to a rough total of $2.5 million—or the entire year's production budget for Selznick International. The figure gave Selznick momentary pause, and he immediately discussed it with Jock Whitney, who bolstered him up by reiterating what he had told him earlier: "The important job we have to do is to make the picture properly and in accordance with public expectation."

According to the publicity fact sheet for the completed picture, "The first script prepared at Selznick International was finished February 20, 1937." But there is no trace of this first draft screenplay in any of the

Val Lewton, Selznick's story editor and the nephew of actress Alla Nazimova. A cultured, literate man, his opinion of the studio's prize property is almost visible in the carefully masked expression on his face: he remarked to several of his associates that the book was "ponderous trash" and thought Selznick was making the biggest mistake of his career. Lewton later went on to greater fame as the producer of *The Cat People* and *I Walked with a Zombie* (which sound like trash but aren't).

Director George Cukor and Sidney Howard, the Pulitzer Prize–winning dramatist to whom Selznick gave the seemingly impossible task of wresting a filmable script from the 1,037 pages of Miss Mitchell's novel. This photo was taken in mid-1937, when Howard was in Culver City working on the third draft of his adaptation with Selznick and Cukor. Howard ended up making three separate trips to Culver City to work on revisions. As late as April 1939, while the film was in production, he was called in by Selznick to work on the construction and dialogue of the second half of the film.

G A B L E · A S · R H E T T

PHOTOPLAY THROWS ITS HAT IN THE RING

Herewith we enter the Great Casting Battle of "Gone with the Wind," because to our mind there is but one Rhett—Clark Gable. So sure were we of our choice that we had Vincentini paint this portrait of Clark as we see him in the rôle: cool, impertinent, utterly charming. We like all the other handsome actors mentioned as Rhett—only we don't want them as Rhett. We want Gable and we're going to stick to that regardless

Drawings by Vincentini

Selznick files; the earliest script in the collection is dated August 1937, and it is probably as close to Howard's original as there is. This "first completed version" follows the story from the opening with sixteen-year-old Scarlett and the Tarleton twins at Tara to the ending twelve years later in Atlanta with Rhett leaving Scarlett after telling her: "I wish I cared what happens to you, but I don't." Scarlett then turns for comfort to Mammy, who assures her, "He'll come back . . . ain' I always been right before?"; and Scarlett tells Mammy, "We'll go home to Tara, Mammy . . . I'll get strength from Tara and I'll think of some way to get him back. After all, tomorrow is . . . another day." It was largely a straightforward literal rendering of the book. The scenes were primarily dialogue sequences, with the dialogue usually taken from Miss Mitchell's original. As a dramatist, Howard did not care for the large gesture or heavily dramatic moments, and the script is largely a succession of almost polite conversations and understated drama—an interesting, intimate, and spare version of the story, but to Selznick, not theatrical enough; he felt it missed the high emotionalism and heady romanticism that permeated the novel. An even greater problem was discovered after Hal Kern had broken the script down scene by scene, timing these individually: when added up, the estimated running time of the picture was almost five and a half hours.

But in spite of its shortcomings, this script was a beginning and Selznick liked enough of it to know that at least they were on the right track. As with every other one of his projects it needed, he felt, extensive rewriting, eliminating some sequences and some of the seventy-nine separate speaking roles that Howard had written in. Conversely, although he was pleased with Howard's handling of the main narrative line for Scarlett, Melanie, Rhett, and Ashley, Selznick was disappointed with the lack of impact in the war scenes in and around Atlanta. Howard's penchant for throwing away drama and avoiding ringing climaxes

of any kind is nowhere more evident in this script than in the scenes of Scarlett's return to Tara to find her mother dead, her father crazy, her sisters near death, and the plantation devastated. Howard illustrated all this by having Scarlett ask her father, "Where's Mother?" Her father replies, "We buried your mother yesterday." This was followed by an immediate dissolve to Mammy and Pork, the two remaining house servants. As Mammy strokes Scarlett's hands and notices the calluses, she lectures her on the fact "dat you can allus tell a lady by her han's." Whereupon Scarlett lashes out with:

> Fiddledee-dee! What good are ladies now? What good are gentleness and breeding? I came home for Ma's comfort and guidance and she isn't here to give them, and nothing she ever taught me will help me now. Better I'd learned to pick cotton like a darky. Mother was wrong! We were all wrong, Mammy! We've all got to work now! And plow and sow and weed and pick cotton like field hands. . . . Anyone who won't work here can go with the Yankees! Tara's all I've got left and I'm going to keep it . . . if I have to break every back on the place! It's like my Pa once said to me—after all, land *is* the only thing that lasts!

Here the sequence faded out, Howard having jettisoned his first choice of Scarlett's vow in favor of this more subdued climax.

This bothered Selznick greatly, for he felt that the whole core of Scarlett's character and her transformation lay in these sequences, and that if they did not match up to the indelible impression left by the novel, then no matter how much effort they put into every other aspect, the picture was doomed to failure. It was imperative, he felt, to capture the essence of the twenty-eight pages that it took Miss Mitchell to describe, in some of the best writing in the book, the hopelessness of Scarlett's situation, which begins with her absolute, pathetic defeat at finding

> Tara . . . acres desolate, barns ruined, like a body bleeding under her eyes. . . . This was the end of the road, quivering old age, sickness, hungry mouths, helpless hands plucking at her skirts. And at the end of this road, there was nothing—nothing but Scarlett O'Hara Hamilton, nineteen years old, a widow with a little child. . . . She was seeing things with new eyes for, somewhere along the long road to Tara, she had left her girlhood behind her. She was no longer plastic clay, yielding imprint to each new experience. The clay had hardened, some time in this indeterminate day which had lasted a thousand years. . . . She was a woman now and youth was gone. . . . When she arose at last and saw again the black ruins . . . her head was raised high and something that was youth and beauty and potential tenderness had gone out of her face forever. What was past was past. . . . There was no going back and she was going forward. . . .

The scene ends with Scarlett saying: "As God is my witness . . . the Yankees aren't going to lick me. I'm going to live through this, and when it's over, I'm never going to be hungry again. No, nor any of my folks. If I have to steal or kill—as God is my witness, I'm never going to be hungry again."

It was this sense of futility, of change and determination and courage writ in romantic theatrical images, that Selznick felt was missing not only in this crucial section but throughout the entire screenplay, and he was determined to keep working with Howard until all these elements were somehow captured. So Howard reluctantly made the trip westward to Culver City, spending most of the spring and summer of 1937 in daily sessions with Selznick as the two men struggled to reconcile their opposing styles and to merge the best of their dramatic instincts.

As Howard traveled west, George Cukor was swinging in a wide arc through the South retracing Kay Brown's trail, looking at promising potential Scarletts and Melanies and spending several days in Atlanta, where Margaret Mitchell took him on a tour of the various locales of the story in and around the city. Cukor's passion for research and atmosphere was well served by Miss Mitchell, who spent several days showing him and his two assistants the distinctive red earth of Clayton County and some of the old homes that had been built before Sherman marched through Georgia, giving them a tour of the area outside Jonesboro to the approximate locations of both Tara and Twelve Oaks.

Cukor was accompanied on this trip by Hobe Erwin, one of the leading interior decorators in the country, who had a respected, prosperous business in New York. Erwin dabbled in motion pictures; he had worked with Cukor on *Little Women* and had gained his confidence and respect. After a period of protracted negotiations, Erwin was signed to an unusual contract that gave Selznick "the right to consult with [Erwin] in the East between now and the date we designate for starting [production] without compensation. After start of production we will guarantee him $5,000 for ten weeks work," his salaried services to commence "not earlier than August 1, 1937, and no later than July 15, 1938," a clause that indicates when Selznick hoped to start and finish the production. Cukor and Erwin, through the efforts of Miss Mitchell, were given access to some of the more outstanding houses in Atlanta. But after touring them through the outlying regions of the city, Miss Mitchell commented in a letter to Kay Brown:

> I am sure they were dreadfully disappointed... for they had been expecting architecture such as appeared in the screen version of *So Red the Rose* . . . and this section of North Georgia was new and crude compared with other sections of the South, and white columns are the exception rather than the rule. I besought them to please leave Tara ugly, sprawling, columnless and they agreed. I imagine, however, that when it comes to Twelve Oaks they will put columns all around the house and make it as large as our new city auditorium.

As Cukor wound up his tour, Walter Plunkett began his. If Cukor had an appreciation for research, Plunkett had a perfectionist's devotion to it. He loved discovering the details of craftsmanship, the look and feel of the past as expressed by the styles, the fabrics of clothing and its accessories. Selznick knew of Plunkett's mania for perfection and had not been above taking advantage of this zeal. The contract he negotiated with Plunkett called for the designer to work on the research and designs for three months with no compensation, and after production started, to work for $750 weekly. Plunkett's trip to Atlanta was entirely at his own expense and on his own initiative; he took along his notes on costumes and discussed them at great length with Margaret Mitchell and, as he recalled, "she was very amused when I showed her that she had described almost every dress of Scarlett's as green." Miss Mitchell arranged meetings for him with some of the more notable dowagers of Atlanta society, a number of whom had trunks full of clothing of the pre- and post–Civil War periods. Plunkett was in his element, "handling and sketching these museum pieces"; he was even allowed to clip sample swatches from the seams of the garments so that the fabric could be reproduced for use in the picture. "One woman in Charleston," recalls Plunkett, "even sent her children out to gather a box full of thorns from a tree native to that area . . . because during the blockade days of the war, there were no metal pins and clothing was held together by these thorns."

As Plunkett completed his research and left the South, word came in May 1937 that Margaret Mitchell had been awarded the Pulitzer Prize for fiction. This, coupled with an earlier announcement that *Gone With The Wind* had been selected as the most distinguished novel of 1936 by the American Booksellers Association, created a second stampede to the bookstores, so that by the middle of 1937, one year after publication, sales of the novel had reached the astonishing figure of 1,375,000, with no let-up in sight, confirming the book's unofficial status as a modern classic. In mid-1937 Selznick noticed an increasing number of demands that the part of Rhett Butler should be played by Clark Gable. Earlier, there had of course been the calls for Ronald Colman, some for Fredric March, and surprisingly even for Basil Rathbone, whom numerous Southerners, according to Margaret Mitchell, considered perfect for the part. (Miss Mitchell, who managed to maintain a sense of humor about this national mania, commented privately that she personally would like to see Rhett played by either Groucho Marx or Donald Duck.) But it was Gable who began to dominate the daily flood of mail throughout 1937, especially after the widespread success of *San Francisco* in which his character of Blackie Norton had much the same appeal as that of Rhett Butler—a proud, iconoclastic outcast; rough, tough, but with a touch of class about him and a final vulnerability that allowed him to be humbled by his love for a woman. MGM had Gable tightly locked under contract; when Selznick first approached Louis B. Mayer to investigate the possi-

Drawings by Vincentini

IS THIS SCARLETT?

Again Vincentini scores—with this picture of Scarlett, as Photoplay conceived her. The prime requisite was, we told him, that Scarlett must be in Gable's arms, for, you see, we still insist on Clark as Rhett. For the rest, she must have the fire of Paulette Goddard; the acting ability of Shearer; the voice of Alicia Rhett, Southern girl candidate, whose name is really identical with the hero's. The artist, we believe, has endowed her with all these qualities, and a few individual charms of her own, for isn't she still Scarlett O'Hara, Miss Unknown? Now turn the page and read her story

bilities of Gable playing the part, he was told it could be arranged in one of two ways: Selznick could come to MGM and make the picture as an MGM production; or MGM would loan Gable to Selznick and put up half the estimated $2.5 million cost of the film in return for distribution rights and 50 percent of the net proceeds for seven years. Neither of these options was particularly appealing to Selznick, although the second proposal was not absolutely out of the question. But he was under contractual obligation to release his pictures through United Artists until 1939, which meant a delay of almost two years if he wanted Gable badly enough. Warner Bros. offered to give him Errol Flynn, Bette Davis, and Olivia de Havilland for the principal parts, asking only 25 percent of the profits, but this was not given more than momentary consideration by Selznick. Bette Davis was not Scarlett O'Hara by any stretch of his imagination, and he remarked to intimates that he would give the part to Katharine Hepburn before he'd give it to Davis. The only other real possibility for Rhett was Gary Cooper, and that might be arranged, as Cooper was under contract to Sam Goldwyn, who in addition to being a close friend of Selznick's was also tied up in the United Artists fold. As to the differences in suitability of Gable and Cooper for the part, Selznick later commented: "They were the two great symbols of their time... they each had different appeals. Clark was the great sex image, as well as having an extremely virile appeal... whereas Gary was the symbol of America. The extraordinary thing about both was that men liked them as well as women, so there was no resentment by the men at women in the audience falling in love with them.... And more importantly, at least as far as the underlying character of Rhett Butler was concerned, both Gable and Cooper were always gentlemen in the true sense of the word." So Selznick, and ultimately Jock Whitney, began working on Goldwyn to let them have Gary Cooper. But Goldwyn, for reasons that have never

These costume sketches by Walter Plunkett were done in early 1938 on the basis of his several readings of the novel and the first Sidney Howard script. Plunkett's attention to detail is evident not only in the design of the costumes but in his careful renderings of the personalities of the various characters as described by Miss Mitchell, and they probably influenced Selznick's ideas of what the performers should look like. Almost all of these designs were used in the final picture.

been made clear, was opposed to the idea and let the negotiations die of neglect, leaving Selznick with no choice but to try to make a more equitable deal with Mayer and MGM.

One of the schizophrenic aspects of Hollywood has always been the way in which the closest of friends, even blood relations, would give no quarter in their business dealings with each other. These men were completely unsentimental, using personal knowledge of each other's affairs and misfortunes to try to get the upper hand and squeeze every single possible benefit and concession to themselves out of their deal-making. Selznick, no slouch when it came time to be ruthless, found himself outmatched by the intractability of Mayer's terms. As Merian Cooper explained it: "We couldn't make the picture and satisfy the public without Gable.... The Whitneys didn't need Metro's money and we didn't need their distribution . . . but because of Gable, we were forced into making a deal with them." Cooper errs in stating that they didn't need MGM's distribution; next to Gable, it was the most attractive and ultimately valuable aspect of the eventual MGM contract. United Artists, because of poor organization, insufficient manpower and resources, never did have the kind of selling organization that inspired Selznick's confidence. If he and Whitney were going to risk several millions of their dollars, their reputations, and years of their lives, then a deal with MGM at least would minimize the possibilities of not collecting all the money there was to be had in the movie marketplace. So in mid-1938, after months of negotiations, soul-searching, and debates back and forth with Whitney and the other executives, Selznick resignedly chose to take MGM's offer, deciding that Gable, half the production costs, and the distribution set-up might be worth 50 percent of the profits.

All during 1937 and well into 1938, Selznick and Sidney Howard had labored together and separately, in Culver City and New York, over the second, third, and fourth drafts of Howard's original, with the avowed intent of getting it down to filmable proportions. In an effort to gain another perspective, Selznick asked Hal Kern to go over the latest version and recommend where cuts might be made. Kern recalls that

"David asked me to do this . . . and he had Metro's script department do an estimate too. Timing scripts is a process involving taking the shooting script, sitting down with a stopwatch, and conjuring up the action and reading the dialogue out loud, much as you'd visualize it being done from what you know of pace and speed in the staging. On *Gone With The Wind,* the script David gave me in mid-1938 I estimated would run about 26,000 feet, or something like four hours and twenty minutes. MGM's estimate was 29,000 feet, and David asked me why theirs was so different from ours, and I had to tell him that they were timing at what they knew to be Cukor's tempo, which was invariably slower than most, while I was just timing at what I thought would be the ideal tempo, one that allowed us to do a picture without too much drag in it. He wanted to know if there was anything I felt we could cut, and I told him that I had spent hours at home going over it, trying to come up with something that I could tell him was too long." Kern felt the cuts would have to come in the subsidiary characters, and the background events of the Civil War. This latter was covered by six montages in the latest script, put in largely at Selznick's insistence to illustrate the worsening fortunes of the South, its defeat and surrender, Lincoln's assassination, and the subsequent arrival in the South of the perils of the Carpetbaggers, the military occupation, and the humiliation of Reconstruction.

The biggest problem with making these suggestions was the confusion they caused Selznick: he truly did not want to drop anything that was already in the script; he just wanted to tighten and improve it, and especially the dialogue, insisting that Howard not invent new dialogue but use Miss Mitchell's whenever possible. When Howard demurred, Selznick would put it in himself, and Howard, finally wearying of the mess of day-long conferences, constant changes of mind and approach by Selznick, fled disgustedly to New York in October. Selznick followed him to Manhattan, where he insisted the two continue working while Howard rehearsed his new play, *The Ghost of Yankee Doodle.*

In Culver City, keeping track of the permutations of the various drafts and alternate versions of scenes became the task of Lydia Schiller, who recalls

being more and more roped into the enormous detail of things . . . following one character throughout the book, sitting in on story conferences, taking notes. Then I was assigned as script girl and moved into George Cukor's office and worked with him on pre-production, and worked with Eric Stacey, the assistant director, on breaking down the script, laying all the sequences out on a production board, and all those thousands of details. As time passed, we were all amazed at how the thing kept mushrooming. David's ideas were very costly . . . what he planned to do, it seemed, would absolutely break the company. . . . He didn't have the backing of any of his executives . . . they all called it Selznick's folly. . . . Whitney gave him support and his wife Irene, he leaned a great deal on her opinions . . . but everybody else, I think even Danny O'Shea [Selznick's attorney] thought that this was the greatest mistake he'd ever made.

Selznick too was very aware that one false and unconsidered move could result in the kind of mistake that Lydia Schiller talks about. After the script, the casting remained the most troublesome aspect, especially insofar as his announced decision to "give the American public a new girl, if possible. To this end," said Selznick, "I have spent close to $50,000. . . . Between George Cukor and myself we have seen practically every bit player and young actress that was even remotely a possibility . . . as well as hundreds and even thousands that were not. . . . We have had readings, we have made tests, we have trained girls who looked right, but whose talent was uncertain. Not only that but we have had the cooperation of every other studio in town trying to find a new girl, since I promised . . . that if they succeeded in finding me a girl they could have an occasional picture with her. . . ." In June 1938, evidently weakening in his own resolve, Selznick sent up a trial balloon announcing to the press that Clark Gable and Norma Shearer would be playing the leads in the picture. The reaction was much worse than he anticipated: Shearer, said the letters and columnists, was too old, she was too reserved and ladylike, too much the screen *grande dame* to play the part. Shearer listened to her fans and turned down Selznick's tentative offer, saying, "Scarlett is a

thankless role; the one I'd like to play is Rhett." Terrified lest the publicity backfire and turn public opinion against the project, Selznick gave orders that no more information was to be sent out on the picture, "not one single word . . . that is not an official and final announcement."

All during the spring and summer of 1938, while he was spending five hours a day with Howard working on the script, and wrestling with the Gable-MGM decision, Selznick was still actively occupied with the two pictures he had in production, *The Young in Heart* and *Made for Each Other.* Both were relatively simple to make in that, being fairly economical modern stories, they did not demand the hours of attention that he was devoting to *Gone With The Wind.* Selznick had Lyle Wheeler and his illustrators begin roughing out sketches not only of the sets, but also of the lighting compositions and the camera angles, in the belief that this would save time and money. The idea had come to Selznick when he had heard Merian Cooper relate what Walt Disney was doing on his feature-length cartoon *Snow White and the Seven Dwarfs.* Cooper had been impressed with Disney's "story-boarding" technique and remembered having done somewhat the same thing with *King Kong.* Selznick's decision to have a live-action feature script done completely in sketch form was innovative, although the approach had been used for years on individual sequences and on musical numbers or other scenes that needed careful organization and special effects.

Selznick now began looking for someone who could take over the coordination of the composition and color design of the entire picture. He found him in mid-1937 in the person of William Cameron Menzies, one of the industry's pioneer art directors, who had designed the silent Fairbanks fantasy *The Thief of Bagdad,* and had gone on to become one of the most influential visual talents working in the American film industry. Selznick detailed his plans for Menzies in a memo to Jock Whitney in September 1937:

I feel we need a man of Menzies' talent and enormous experience on the sets of this picture and on its physical production. . . . What I want on *Gone With The Wind* and what has been done only a few times in picture history (and these times mostly by Menzies) is a complete script in sketch form. . . . This is a mammoth job that Menzies will have to work on very closely with Cukor. I also want him to design and lay out and in large degree actually direct the montage sequences. In short, it is my plan to have the whole physical side of the picture . . . personally handled by one man, and that man Menzies . . . who may turn out to be one of the most valuable factors in properly producing this picture.

Selznick was also deep in discussion with Henry Ginsberg and Ray Klune about the limitations of their present studio set-up. The company was still leasing production space from RKO-Pathé on a picture-by-picture basis, but after they took over Pioneer's commitments, it was obvious that this arrangement would be inadequate. Accordingly, Selznick International leased the entire studio for one year beginning in mid-1937. A year later, regardless of a $33,000 loss from this operation, the agreement was renewed over the opposition of Sonny Whitney and other board members who wanted to go back to the old, less expensive arrangement. Selznick, however, contended that "it would be impossible to produce *Gone With The Wind* under the old basis because of the size of the picture and the inadequacy of the equipment of the Pathé studio. Accordingly, I think we should exercise our option on the studio for another year . . . and proceed to build up our key personnel and purchase essential equipment with the view to having sufficient capable people and equipment to tackle a picture of the magnitude of *Gone With The Wind.*"

One of these "key" people Selznick was referring to was Jack Cosgrove of the small but vitally important "special effects," or—as it was usually referred to in the industry—"trick" department. Every major studio of the time had one, and it was their existence that made possible much of the scope and grandeur of pictures of that era. By use of paintings, glass shots, double exposures, process backgrounds, and a whole range of other technical tricks, they made it possible for just about anything that could be dreamed up by a writer and director to be put onto film convincingly—the most celebrated case of this being *King*

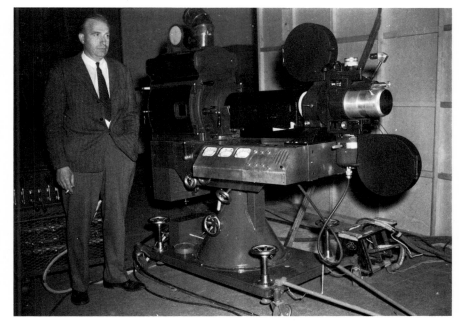

(Top, right) Production manager Raymond Klune, Daniel T. O'Shea, David Selznick, and his executive secretary, Betty Baldwin, in one of their few nonfrantic moments, going over still another draft of the script. (Above) Jack Cosgrove, the special effects wizard to whom fell most of the task of supplying *Gone With The Wind* with its epic production values, shown here with one of the two specially built machines that enabled him to accomplish this. This modified 35 mm projector had a light source several times more powerful than any projector then in existence, allowing him to beam the image from one machine directly into the lens of another and making possible the copying of color process plates and matte paintings with no appreciable loss of color. (Top, left) Art director Lyle Wheeler and David Selznick going over some of the sketches drawn by Wheeler and his staff. (Above, left) Wheeler and William Cameron Menzies, the guiding genius behind the dramatic Technicolor look of *Gone With The Wind.* It was Menzies who gave the film its carefully stylized visuals, tying the disparate sequences together with his eye for color and composition. His sketches indicating color mood and lighting design were gone over carefully by Lyle Wheeler, who turned them into workable master drawings, adding to them his detailed renderings of both exterior and interior set designs. (Left) Wilbur Kurtz, a walking encyclopedia on the Civil War in north Georgia. He was also a close friend of Margaret Mitchell and at her suggestion had been hired by Selznick International to oversee the details not only of the history but also of the sets. He gave Selznick, Wheeler, and Cukor detailed descriptions and drawings of the city of Atlanta, farm implements, and household items; among other things, he wrote a 32-page description of a typical Southern barbecue of the pre–Civil War era. It was Kurtz who supplied the studio construction staff with the blueprints for the distinctive barrel-vaulted Atlanta train station. A skilled architect and illustrator, Kurtz is seen here with one of his renderings, a painting of Twelve Oaks, which he did not design but whose conception benefited from his suggestions.

Twelve of the 1,500 production sketches made to guide the director and cinematographers in obtaining the proper look and feel of *Gone With The Wind*. (First row) Menzies sketched this version of the opening scene, showing Scarlett and the Tarleton twins on the porch of Tara; Gerald O'Hara's evening gallop home from Twelve Oaks and the family at prayer were done by J. McMillan Johnson. (Second row) Scarlett eavesdropping on the staircase at Twelve Oaks was done by Dorothea Holt; it underwent considerable revision before it was used in the film. The waltzing couples at the Atlanta bazaar and Scarlett trying on the green bonnet given to her by Rhett are both the work of Dorothea Holt. (Third row) The population of Atlanta waiting in front of the telegraph office for news from Gettysburg and the sketch of the battlefield through which Scarlett travels on her way back to Tara are by Johnson. Scarlett being greeted by her half-crazed father is by Menzies. (Fourth row) Scarlett and Melanie hovering over the body of the Yankee cavalryman Scarlett has just shot is also by Menzies. The sketch of Rhett and Scarlett's Atlanta home under construction is by Johnson, and Scarlett's ornate, garish bedroom in the house is the work of Dorothea Holt.

Kong. As Selznick grew more deeply immersed in the production aspects of *Gone With The Wind,* it became apparent to him that "I could not even hope to put the picture on the screen properly without an even more extensive use of special effects than had ever before been attempted in the business.... In the preparation of the script... I made it part of my business to look for and to conceive opportunities for furthering the spectacle values and improve [*sic*] the production design of the picture.... I calculate that there will be over one hundred trick shots in *Gone With The Wind*... so we had better be prepared to invest substantial amounts of money to upgrade our equipment in this department."

While, at Selznick's urging, Cosgrove was experimenting with ways of extending the effectiveness of Technicolor trick work, Ray Klune and Lyle Wheeler looked for ways to economically accomplish the production of the hundreds of sketches that were coming out of the Menzies department. Wheeler recalls that the Menzies sketches "were difficult technically . . . they were very stylized . . . but we strove to keep that feeling . . . and still make it real enough so that you thought you were there.... David was very particular because he had certain scenes that were in his mind, certain color feelings, shadows, realistic or unrealistic, that he wanted . . . so we did an awful lot of tests just to see how these color and lighting effects would work out."

One of the biggest hurdles faced by the art department was in locating accurate photos and other visual evidence of Atlanta's past, since so much had been destroyed by the fire of November 1864. The research department of Selznick International was headed by a woman named Lillian Deighton, who was diligent and exhaustive in her labors, but the material was just not there. For help, Selznick turned to Miss Mitchell, who despite her desire not to become involved was nevertheless anxious to do everything she could to help make the picture as historically accurate as possible. She had remarked that she "didn't care what they do to the story, I just hope [they] don't distort the history.... Southerners are indignant when our history is portrayed improperly." So when Selznick's request reached her, she responded by saying she could be of no help herself but strongly recommended that Selznick get hold of Wilbur Kurtz of Atlanta, whom she considered the greatest authority on the Civil War in the area, and who also had a fine collection of early Atlanta pictures. Kurtz was brought out to the studio in January 1938 and stayed for several weeks, helping Menzies and Wheeler with the visual layouts of Atlanta and the fictional plantations. In his diaries, Kurtz relates, "As to Tara . . . Mr. Cukor, who had seen Clayton County . . . knew that plantation houses down there at best were nothing wonderful, but since Tara was also fictional... they both indicated that the house should be 'warmed up' a bit. 'After all,' said Mr. Selznick, 'the Atlanta and Clayton County audiences are a very small percentage.' This indicated . . . to me . . . that he was taking the larger view of things and playing up—or down—somewhat to the general . . . preconceived ideas of the world-at-large about things Southern. Maybe he's right. . . ."

The two sketches above show different versions of the staircase in the postwar Atlanta house of Rhett and Scarlett and give a good example of Selznick's and Wheeler's insistence on re-doing the drawings until each was satisfied. The final version (below) was modeled by Lyle Wheeler after a grand staircase from a mansion in the Nob Hill section of San Francisco, possibly the Flood or Crocker home. Dramatically compelling, it became the focus of much of the action of the last third of the film. (Property man Arden Cripe is on the staircase with Vivien Leigh, Cammie King, and Hattie McDaniel.)

By now almost two years had elapsed since Selznick had bought the book, and while he had been active on other projects, George Cukor had not made a picture since *Camille.* Through most of this period, he had been occupied with preparations for *Gone With The Wind*—an expensive layoff, for Cukor had been on salary at Selznick International all that time at the rate of $4,000 a week, making it likely, as Selznick pointed out, that

> we are in danger of paying him about $300,000 for his services on *Gone With The Wind.* . . . Regardless of his great abilities . . . I am fearful that he is [becoming] an expensive luxury. . . . George's statement is that this is not his fault . . . that he could have done pictures . . . but we have not forced him to do pictures. . . . When I first tackled *A Star Is Born,* I spoke to George about doing it and he didn't feel that he wanted to do a Hollywood picture . . . when we took H. C. Potter off *Tom Sawyer* . . . George didn't want to do it . . . when we needed him for another picture he preferred to direct Garbo. . . . I think the biggest black mark against our management to date is the Cukor situation and we can no longer be sentimental about it. . . . We are a business concern and not patrons of the arts. . . .

What Selznick failed to mention here was his own constant reiteration

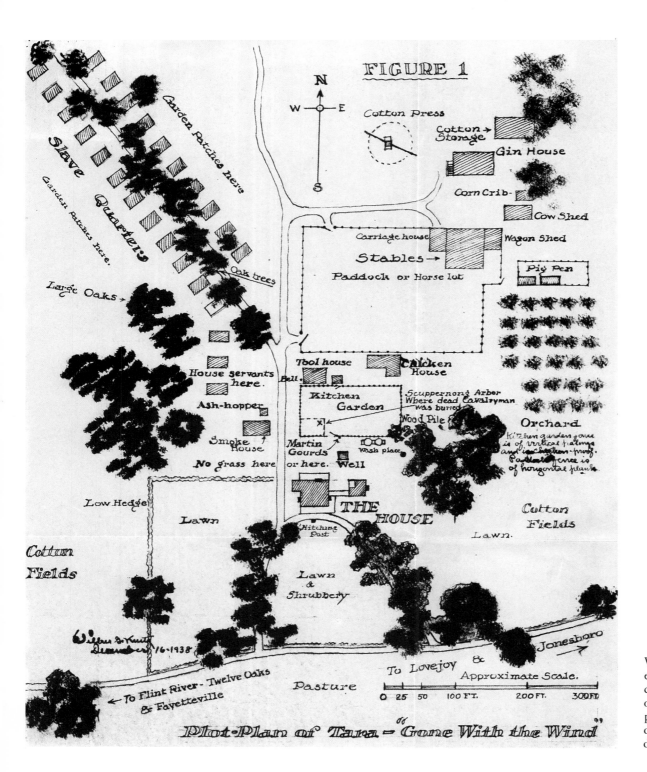

FIGURE 1

Plot-Plan of Tara - "Gone With the Wind"

Wilbur Kurtz drew up this plot plan of Tara and its environs from descriptions provided by Margaret Mitchell. It played an important part in giving a proper sense of direction in the staging of all of the scenes at the plantation, keeping the art director and cameramen and directors consistent in their use of sunlight, arrivals and departures, and camera angles.

that *Gone With The Wind* was to go into production "shortly," and his reluctance to let Cukor take on any outside projects that might conflict with the somewhat vague starting date. As the winter of 1937–38 gave way to spring and Selznick still did not have a satisfactory script or even a hint of a Scarlett O'Hara, he resolved part of his financial worries about Cukor by lending him to Columbia Pictures to direct Katharine Hepburn and Cary Grant in an adaptation of Philip Barry's play *Holiday*.

While Cukor was off at Columbia, Selznick was suddenly confronted with a long-simmering, potentially unpleasant controversy concerning *Gone With The Wind*—both the book and the picture to be made from it. Around the studio this was euphemistically referred to as "the Negro problem," and it had its origins in the feelings of many blacks about the way in which their history and sensibilities had been portrayed in the novel. As early as April 1937, Selznick had started receiving clippings from the many Negro newspapers and magazines of the time, which were not exactly hospitable to the work. One criticism from Dora Popel in *The Journal of Negro Life* commented that "the general outline of the history is true ... but Miss Mitchell's presentation of Civil War and Reconstruction problems is unwarrantedly biased.... In her array of 'Mammies,' 'Cookies,' 'Porks,' and 'Sams' one sees only ebony black Negroes ... who had been docile and childlike as slaves become suddenly impudent and vicious as 'free issue' Negroes." Another reviewer,

L. D. Reddick in *The Journal of Negro History,* stated: "This book no doubt is honestly written ... but at the same time ... it is written with a passionate sectional and racial bias. It is almost painfully weak in the handling of the larger social forces implicit in the materials." Selznick and Howard had gone out of their way to see that in the picture, at least, "Negroes come out on the right side of the ledger," removing the Ku Klux Klan and any other scenes that could be remotely construed as anti-Negro propaganda. Unfortunately, however, the script that they had prepared made use of the anathematic term "nigger" in the dialogue scenes, and the few readings that had been held to cast Mammy and the other black character parts had quietly enraged the performers who had been forced to utter the term. Their outrage had been transmitted to the headquarters of the National Association for the Advancement of Colored People, which promptly launched a campaign against both the picture and Selznick, with editorials in all the leading black papers exhorting their readers to boycott the picture and to write letters demanding that all the black characters in the picture be removed. This was not quite the tempest that it would be today, for at that time blacks were at the very bottom of the economic and social spectrum, except for the privileged few who made good in the entertainment and educational worlds and were considered "a credit to their race."

Selznick was certainly no bigot, but he did subscribe to the prevailing liberal ethic of the time, which treated blacks with "dignity" yet kept them in their place. When the first wave of letters and editorial protests broke over his head, he was surprised, bewildered, and a little angry—and also a little fearful. He had a long memory of the race riots over *The Birth of a Nation,* and the thought of any such controversy surrounding *Gone With The Wind* caused him anguish on both a personal and a corporate level. "I feel this particularly keenly," he wrote to Jock Whitney,

because it might have repercussions not simply on the picture and not simply upon the company and upon me personally, but on the Jews of America as a whole among the Negro race.... I think these are no times in which to offend any race or people.... I feel so keenly about what is happening to the Jews of the world that I cannot help but sympathize with the Negroes in their fears, however unjustified they may be, about material which they regard as insulting or damaging. I personally think it most important that we should go after prominent space in all the Negro journals, both local and national, to not merely obviate the possibility of further trouble and resentment but contradict and cure any impression that presently exists... that the picture will be derogatory.... We must explain how sympathetic we are and that the only Negro characters in the picture... are treated with great dignity... and that the only liberties we have taken with the book... is [*sic*] to improve the Negro position in the picture... that we have not characterized any of the Negroes as mean or bad and that they have nothing to worry about as far as a pro-slave angle is concerned or anything else and that we have the greatest friendship toward them and their cause. *I am most anxious to remove any impression (which I am sure is very wide-spread) that Gone With The Wind, this company and I personally are enemies of the Negroes* [Selznick's emphasis].

A number of influential black reporters were brought out to the studio and personally assured by Selznick that all offensive terms would be removed from the script; he hedged a bit on their suggestion that he hire a black technical adviser because, as he remarked in a memo to Whitney, "we're surrounded now on all sides by advisers... one more will only confuse us... and such a person would probably want to remove what comedy we have built around the Negroes... no matter how lovable we have made them." The reporters left the studio extolling their treatment and assuring Selznick that the 3 million readers of the Negro papers would "give us their blessings and pray for us nightly." For the time being, at least, as Selznick remarked, "the situation seems to be well in hand."

Cukor, having finished *Holiday* quickly, reported back to the studio and immediately began an intensive round of screen tests trying to find the elusive Scarlett. These tests were valuable for two reasons: first, Cukor's direction of them was his own sort of homework/rehearsal, to see how the scenes played, how they could be blocked and staged, which portions of the script would work and which needed further refinement. They were also helpful in that they gave Selznick and Hal Kern an indication of the tempo and pacing that the picture would be played in, and in this respect Selznick was greatly worried, for as he pointed out to George, "I hope you will realize more fully than you do, just how far I have to go in cutting the script and just how far you have to go with tempo.... I am frantic to learn that the latest test of the Scarlett-Ashley paddock scene is not shorter than the last time you did it... but actually is twenty feet longer." Pace and tempo aside, however, the most important aspect of these tests was still to turn up an actress who was young enough, fresh enough, and talented enough to play the part. So far, Selznick felt that

the failure to find a new girl is the greatest failure of my entire career.... It would be shocking if the starting date rolls around and we have found neither a Scarlett nor a Melanie nor an Ashley and have to resort to people that have been dug up from high schools and God knows where else.... Certainly I would give anything if we had Olivia de Havilland under contract to us so that we could cast her for Melanie.... It is a long time since George has seen her sister Joan Fontaine... she certainly should have readings.... Our best Melanie

to date is, I think, Dorothy Jordan. I am . . . depressed about the Ashley situation and I feel our snobbish attitude about newcomers may have cost us a great performance by a great star.... I suppose our best possibilities, depressing as it seems, are Leslie Howard and Melvyn Douglas.... All we have to do is line up a complete cast of such people... and we can have a lovely picture for release eight years ago. Concerning Scarlett, I think our best possibilities at the moment are Jean Arthur, Loretta Young, Doris Jordan, Katharine Hepburn and Paulette Goddard.

This was written in late July 1938, and Paulette Goddard was just finishing her first major role for Selznick in *The Young in Heart,* her only other part of any importance prior to this having been in Chaplin's 1936 *Modern Times.* She and Chaplin were living together, supposedly as man and wife, a situation that no one looked into too closely. She was attractive, intelligent, with a kind of sparkling insouciance about her personality that carried over into her screen appearances. In her tests, she was the most appealing of all the women they had tested so far, and both Cukor and Selznick felt that with considerable coaching she might make a credible Scarlett. Around the studio, she was considered by most of the staff to be the probable choice. But not everybody was delighted with this idea. Russell Birdwell, in particular, had harsh words about the choice:

Strictly from a publicity standpoint, I can not go too strongly on record in opposing the proposed selection of Paulette Goddard for the role of Scarlett O'Hara.... I must warn you of the tremendous avalanche of criticism which will befall us and the picture should Paulette be given this part.... It will throw us under the shadow of such a resentful press that all of our good public relations work of the past will be completely dissipated. I have never known a woman, intent on a career dependent upon her popularity with masses, to hold and live such an insane and absurd attitude toward the press and her fellow man as does Paulette Goddard.... The girl who gets the part... must be prepared to have her life laid bare in cold black type. This, Goddard is neither willing nor able to do. Briefly, I think she is dynamite which will explode in our very faces if she is given the part.

If Selznick vacillated and felt like a failure over Scarlett, he was at least positive about Rhett Butler, and in August 1938 he announced at a very formal contract signing that he had arranged with MGM to borrow Clark Gable for the part. On the day of the signing he sent a special memo to every department at the studio, assuring them that "the contracts that have been signed with Loew's, Inc. for the release of *Gone With The Wind* in no way affect its identity as a Selznick International picture or its production on this lot. You will, accordingly, please continue uninterruptedly on your work on this picture, which will definitely start production between November 15 and January 15." Separately, in a small handwritten note to Cukor, Selznick advised him to "Please call Clark Gable on your own, and tell him how happy you are, etc. Start that relationship!"

Gable's contract stipulated that Selznick pay him $4,500 per week plus a bonus of $16,666. Gable had not wanted the part, commenting that

everybody had their own idea of what Rhett should be like.... It was annoying to have people look painfully surprised when I said that I hadn't read [the book]. When I finally did read it, I saw very clearly what I was in for... and I was scared stiff.... Miss Mitchell had etched Rhett into the minds of millions of people... it would be impossible to satisfy them all.... The public interest in my playing Rhett puzzled me.... I was the only one, apparently, who didn't take it for granted I was going to play the part.... I knew what was coming the day that David called me.... He put his cards on the table... he was going to try to get me from MGM if he could... but I like to pick my spots and now found myself trapped by a series of circumstances over which I had no control... it was a funny feeling.... I think I know now how a fly must react after being caught in a spider web.... Rhett was simply too big an order.... I didn't want any part of him.

As an actor Gable was, in spite of his phenomenal fame, still extremely insecure. It was only after being persuaded by Carole Lombard, with whom he was romantically involved, and MGM's lure of the large

August 24, 1938—Louis B. Mayer and David Selznick sign the contract by which MGM gave Selznick $1.25 million and the services of Clark Gable for the role of Rhett Butler. In return MGM obtained the distribution rights to the picture for five years plus 50 percent of the profits, while Loew's, Inc., MGM's parent company, got 15 percent of the gross receipts for distributing the picture. Al Lichtman, who negotiated the deal, smilingly hovers over Mayer. Gable received his salary of $4,500 weekly plus a $50,000 bonus for signing, which he used in divorcing his second wife so that he could marry Carole Lombard. MGM insisted that Selznick pay one-third of the bonus in addition to Gable's salary.

bonus and the promise to assist him in his divorce proceedings with his wife, that he decided to take on the role. Once the deal was made, however, Gable said no more and resigned himself to the inevitable. He had to finish one more picture for MGM, *Idiot's Delight,* after which he would take his six-week vacation and report to Selznick International, according to the contract, "not later than January 5, 1939 . . . for a period reasonably necessary to complete the role."

This setting of the start date by MGM forced Selznick into the realization that he had only four months to resolve all the details that were still unsettled, and that the time had now come when he would have to make all the postponed decisions regarding the settings, the costumes, and the casting, both in front of and behind the camera. The many postponements had already cost him the services of Hobe Erwin, who had agreed to extension after extension, until finally, in October 1938, he wrote Selznick, "I think we should terminate the contract now . . . the postponements have cost me more than I could possibly make on the picture." Erwin suggested a replacement, Joseph Platt, decorating consultant for the prestigious *House & Garden* magazine, a man who was, in Erwin's words, "not only my peer, but in lots of ways exceeds me. . . . He is a great designer, illustrator, painter . . . and will be able to handle the assignment beautifully." Meanwhile, Klune, Menzies, and Wheeler were wrestling with one of the biggest headaches in the script, what was called "the burning of Atlanta" although, as Wilbur Kurtz pointed out to them and Selznick, "Scarlett left Atlanta on September 1st, and the city wasn't burned by Sherman until November 14th or 15th." However, Miss Mitchell had spent four paragraphs describing the destruction of the Confederate munitions warehouses, and it was this that Selznick and Howard had written into the script, expanding the conflagration beyond all recognition of what was described in the novel until it took on the proportions of a burning city. Lyle Wheeler, meanwhile, had been spending a great deal of time on the 40-acre back lot, going over the plans for the transformation of the standing sets into the streets of Atlanta.

In order to build Tara and the Atlanta railroad station, the area in front of the standing sets had to be cleared of a number of leftover settings, and the area directly behind these street sets was still dominated by the huge wall that had been re-dressed for *King Kong,* in front of which stood the remnants of the native village from the same picture. Wheeler got the idea that it might be easier to burn those sets down than to bulldoze them. He reasoned that if they gathered all the sets they wanted to get rid of, put false fronts on them, built a shell to suggest the railway station and the freight yards, and then burned them, it would probably work very well for the fire scenes. The idea was brought up at the next production meeting; Selznick was dubious, but Wheeler, Menzies, and Klune were all for it and persuaded him that it should be tried, that the area had to be cleared anyway and this was one way of doing it. Selznick reluctantly gave approval while he now came to grips with his most pressing problem other than finding a Scarlett: the script. In all the months of preparations, he had not exactly lost sight of the fact that the script was not complete. Indeed, he'd continued to work on it almost daily, first with Sidney Howard, until he quit in disgust, then with Barbara Keon, reworking each scene countless times until the only way that order could be brought out of the chaos was to start a separate file for each sequence, circling the bits that he liked from each version in red pencil. This formless mass of revisions took up almost an entire four-drawer file cabinet, and by October, Selznick realized he would now, somehow, have to wrest a workable script out of this mess. To do this at the studio, with its continual distractions, was obviously impossible, so Selznick decided to take four packing cases full of the various drafts and go to Bermuda, a trip he hoped he could "talk Margaret Mitchell into taking at our expense . . . such a trip might not frighten her as much as one to Hollywood." She wasn't frightened, she just wasn't interested. So Selznick took Jo Swerling, who had just finished revising the script of *Made for Each Other,* with him to Bermuda. They labored for almost two months, and when they returned to New York, the script was in no more manageable shape than when they had left, something that Selznick attributed to Swerling's inability to come to terms with the material. From Bermuda, he wired Kay Brown that he would need a new writer as

(Above) William Cameron Menzies's sketches for the burning of the Atlanta munitions warehouses, vividly described by Miss Mitchell in four paragraphs in the novel. Selznick turned this incident into one of the most spectacular and dramatic scenes in the film, as Scarlett, Rhett, Melanie and her newborn baby, and the slave girl Prissy escape besieged Atlanta by fleeing through the burning railroad yards. The sequence had originally been designed to be shown on a screen twice normal width; it was filmed using a special double-mounted camera, and tests were made on a 60-foot wide screen at one of the studio sound stages. But Whitney and MGM both convinced Selznick that the picture didn't need this gimmick, and the plan was dropped. Some idea of the scope of Selznick's approach can be gained from the drawing at the bottom, which shows the approximate proportion of the enlarged-screen idea.

(Right) The Selznick International back lot, called "Forty Acres," looking north toward Washington Boulevard with the Santa Monica mountains in the background, in early 1938. The towering structure in the foreground is what was left of DeMille's *King of Kings* set and *King Kong*'s wall and gate. This and all of the surrounding sets were equipped with false fronts and stood in for the burning munitions warehouses in *Gone With The Wind*.

Filming the burning of the Atlanta munitions depot, Saturday night, December 10, 1938. Twenty-seven cameramen operated seven Technicolor cameras, three of which are under the corrugated sheeting in the center. The fellow with his hand in his pocket wearing the topcoat, hat, and sweater directly in front of these makeshift sheds is art director Lyle Wheeler. At the extreme left, wearing a dark hat and holding a microphone in front of his mouth, is William Cameron Menzies, who directed the sequence. This shot was taken during a lull in the proceedings. Director George Cukor, wearing a white scarf, is above Menzies, talking to Daniel O'Shea. In the circle is Selznick, standing next to Vivien Leigh, to whom he had been introduced earlier in the evening by his brother Myron. Laurence Olivier, wearing a scarf and a dark topcoat, is standing slightly ahead of them with his hands in his pockets.

soon as he arrived in New York: "Not interested Sidney Howard, but understand Oliver Garrett's play is a terrible flop so we should be able to get him cheaply ... want him to do continuity certain sequences, maybe throughout picture if price right ... would want him familiarize himself with book and script and prepare work en route home and at studio." In New York, in addition to Oliver H. P. Garrett, the growing company of Gone With The Winders was joined by Atlanta historian Wilbur Kurtz, who would later be going out to the studio to oversee all the historical details of time and place. While they were conferring on the new screenplay in New York, the question of Ashley's Christmas leave in Atlanta came up: Was it before or after Gettysburg? Kurtz said it was before; Selznick said no, it was the Christmas after. Relates Kurtz, "I insisted I was right and David countered with a bet of ten cents! I took him up and he looked through the pages. ... I was weakening before he turned to the marked page—but he was getting too much fun out of it. Finally he found the page and triumphantly told me that I owed him a dime. 'No one can ever accuse me of not having read the book,' he declared."

The Selznick party left New York on November 28, on board the Super-Chief bound for Los Angeles. Oliver Garrett spent most of the trip in his stateroom, pounding away at the sixth revision of the script. While the train roared westward across the wintry landscape, Ray Klune and his staff in Culver City were hard at work on the final preparations for the spectacular fire sequences. Klune realized that it would be impossible to keep the flames burning for more than forty minutes. During that time, they would have to photograph the action of the escaping Rhett and Scarlett, with several dramatic bits of business that were called for by the script. And they would have to catch the fire from every conceivable angle, using as many cameras as possible. Since Technicolor had only seven cameras at the time, the work would have to be scheduled for a day when all of them were available; the earliest date was Saturday, December 10, which gave them approximately two weeks to work out the logistics of the sequence. "We planned the whole thing sort of as a football rehearsal," recalls Klune. "We built a miniature of the whole damned thing and kept it under lock and key, because it was an expensive one and we didn't want anyone messing around with it. ... We rehearsed for about ten days, every move, every camera position—we decided during these rehearsals that instead of changing lenses on the cameras, which was a brute of a job on those Technicolor things, we'd move the cameras instead. We'd move the camera from position one to position five—different lenses on each camera because we wanted to get a medium shot, a long shot, and a close shot from almost every position. So we had all the camera positions indicated on the model, and the camera crews." Klune wanted as much control as possible over every aspect of the scene; he knew how dubious David was about the whole idea, and he was determined that every detail of the potentially hazardous venture would be gone over minutely to minimize the chance of the operation becoming a useless fiasco and, even more important, of the fire itself getting out of control. The studio was surrounded by the Culver City suburbs, and the height of the main set plus the age of the material caused him to worry that flying fragments could cause a major disaster. The Culver City Fire Department had been alerted, but they had only two pieces of equipment, and Klune wanted the entire area ringed with fire trucks, including the section behind the main set facing the Baldwin Hills. The cooperation of the Los Angeles Fire Department was enlisted, and they promised thirty-four pieces of equipment for the night, which eased his mind a bit on that score. But Klune was still concerned about

The end result of all the pyrotechnics: Yakima Canutt, the stunt man for Rhett Butler, leads a wagon through the inferno with Dorothy Fargo, one of the two doubles used for Scarlett O'Hara.

the length of time needed to move each camera from one position to the next, set it up, and start photography, all of which would be going on while the fire raged; and it could only rage for so long. He began trying to find some way to control the actual fire, so that it would perform on demand. To achieve this, he brought in Lee Zavits, "the best special effects man in the business," as Klune called him. Zavits devised an ingenious and unprecedented method of solving the problem. Behind the false fronts of each of the sets, they constructed an intricate double network of pipes, one of which would carry a mixture of kerosene and coal oil, and the other, larger one, water. The two would be force-fed from two main pumps set off to one side, each manned by two men. The pipes with the oil mixture were equipped with electric valves to shut off the fuel, at which point the water pumps would take over and douse the flames, giving Klune the control he wanted.

Selznick and the rest of his party arrived back in Culver City on December 2, one week before the big event. But when Klune briefed him on what they'd been doing and took him on a tour of the back lot, showing him the false fronts and elaborate piping, and running through the planned camera moves, Selznick suddenly got cold feet. "Are you sure that this is the best way to do this?" Klune recalls him asking. He

reassured him; but several days later, Selznick was at him again. "He was very nervous about it. He said, 'You're positive everything is ready?' I told him, 'David, we're as ready as we're ever going to be. Another day and we'll be overtrained. We've got everything scheduled for tomorrow night, we've got all the fire companies we can get, insurance is covering everything; everybody is keyed up to a fever pitch. If we postpone it, we might as well not do it, we could never crank up our enthusiasm again.' So we got the go ahead to do it as planned."

At about four o'clock on the afternoon of Saturday, December 10, the sun went down, and the temperature, which had been in the mid-seventies, dropped to 30 degrees. The last of the Technicolor cameras arrived from the studios where they were being used and were put into place. Fire tests were made on some small foreground structures, light tests were made by meters from various distances, and Klune called for one last rehearsal, with cameras, actors, and position switches. According to Wilbur Kurtz: "Property men were lugging things around and the cameramen and electricians were weaving about in a most businesslike fashion. The place swarmed with firemen . . . and fire trucks." At 6:30 there was a ninety-minute dinner break, after which everybody returned to the set and waited for Selznick to arrive. He had sent out a number of

The Temple of Jerusalem and the great gate from *King Kong* come crashing down in fiery splendor as the wagon with Rhett, Scarlett, Melanie, and Prissy crosses in front. The wagon and its occupants were added later by Jack Cosgrove, who superimposed the separately filmed action of the wagon onto the footage of the collapsing building.

invitations to friends and relatives to come watch the proceedings, the start of which was set for eight o'clock. By that time nearly everybody had arrived, including Selznick's mother. When Selznick's limousine finally arrived with him and George Cukor, there were almost two hundred people behind the ropes that Klune had set up back of the cameras. This bothered Klune, "because with all those people, it could get very confusing, if everyone got to screaming and yelling at one another. So to ensure that there would be no misunderstanding, I took the public address system and talked to all the guests, including David, and asked them to please not talk during the whole thing that was to follow, that we expected that it would be burned out within 45 minutes, and that during that time we wanted absolute quiet, because this was either going to come off or it wasn't." Everything was ready, awaiting Selznick's okay, but he asked Klune to delay a while longer; his brother Myron still had not arrived. Lydia Schiller recalls:

I was rushing from camera to camera, keeping track of which one was where, which lens they had, what angles they were shooting.... We had some buried cameras, some close to the fire ... so my work for the night was to watch the action very closely, to match the principals when we changed positions, and to watch the progression of the wagon through the fire, and make sure that [the stunt man and woman playing] Rhett and Scarlett were always in the right positions.... I was standing right with Mr. Selznick and he was very angry with Myron for being late, he held up the start of the burning because he wanted him to be there.... Finally we saw Myron coming ... he had two people with him and Mr. Selznick said, "Let 'er go, Ray," and then all his attention was focused on the action.

Klune gave the signal to Menzies, who relayed it to Lee Zavits behind the fire break to one side of the large *King Kong* gate. The grips started the pumps feeding the oil mixture through the network of pipes. Zavits had wired the sets in various strategic places so that by pressing a contact switch, sparks would ignite the gasoline; he counted sixty seconds, then pressed the switch. Instantly there was an ear-splitting whoosh as the fire ignited the oil-soaked timbers and surged upward 300 feet into the night sky. To Lydia Schiller "it was just suddenly the holocaust ... it scared all of us ... it was like a whole town suddenly going up in flames.... Just as this ferocious thing happened, up comes Myron with these two people ... all three seemed to be a few sheets to the wind and Myron said

This early sketch of Tara makes it look like a suburban home, circa 1938. It was Wilbur Kurtz who suggested replacing the slender wooden posts with whitewashed square brick columns, copied from one of the research photos.

something to Mr. Selznick but he just shook him off, he was so engrossed in the fire." A battery of huge searchlights—white and amber—were mounted on platforms; in front of some of these were asbestos tables on which fires were lit, giving out a thick black smoke, which streamed across the field of light making irregular patches of fast-moving shadow, as if a blaze were in progress in back of the cameras. As soon as the fire had started, Menzies called "action," and Rhett and Scarlett drove a wagon across the front of the inferno. The stunt man didn't really do the driving, however; on the floor of the wagon, out of camera range, was another driver who controlled the horse by two slender wires passed through a small opening in the front of the wagon and attached to the horse's bit, enabling him to control the horse's rearing and plunging. In the middle of the first take, the wagon suddenly lost its left front wheel, the horse sat down, and Klune called for Zavits to douse the flames. At this point, Lydia Schiller remembers that "Mr. Selznick turned to Myron and said, 'What did you say?' and Myron replied, 'Here's your Scarlett,' and introduced him to Vivien Leigh.... I don't think Mr. Selznick was suddenly electrified." But Selznick later remembered: "When my brother introduced her to me, the dying flames were lighting up her face.... I took one look and knew that she was right—at least right as far as her appearance went ... and right as far as my conception of how Scarlett O'Hara looked.... I'll never recover from that first look."

While this exchange had been taking place, the cameras had been moved to their secondary positions, a gang of grips had moved out the faulty wagon, and a new one had been put in its place. Klune gave the signal and the fire began again. "It went beautifully," says Klune; "instead of the three or four burns, we got six or seven." As the inferno raged, the low-hanging clouds spread the reflection of the flames over most of Culver City, and for the hour and a half that the fire continued, the phone lines in Los Angeles were jammed with anxious callers, all of whom seemed convinced that MGM was on fire. "When Selznick heard this," related Wilbur Kurtz, "he was tickled immensely." On the seventh take, Menzies gave the signal and an off-camera tractor tugged at the blazing remnants of DeMille's *King of Kings* and Cooper's *King Kong*, causing the structure to collapse spectacularly—a phoenix in reverse. Selznick, never particularly analytical about his own past, probably gave no thought to the ironies of the moment—or perhaps he did have a flashing thought of the times when he had seen these same sets as he took the bus to work during his first weeks at MGM, or of the dark days in 1932 when Cooper had come to him for the money to rebuild this set for a project that in the intervening years had been transmuted into the status of a legend. Later that night he wrote to his wife in New York: "The fire sequence was one of the greatest thrills I have had out of making pictures, first because of the scene itself, and second because of the frightening but exciting knowledge that *Gone With The Wind* was finally in work."

If it was an emotional moment for Selznick, it was even more intense for Ray Klune, who recalls: "After it was over, I just sat down exhausted.... I was sweating all over ... and shaking from the strain, and David came over to me, put his arms around me and said, 'You were right, I'm sorry. This was one of the greatest things I've ever seen. I think you're the best production manager I've ever known.'" Forty years later, the memory of that moment was still strong and vivid enough to cause Ray Klune to be moved almost to tears as he related it in a voice suddenly thick with emotion, adding quietly: "It's something I'll never forget."

The cost of the entire operation had been only $24,715, just $323 more than the allotted budget, which according to Klune, "would probably run about half a million dollars if you did it today." The ninety

258

The final version of Tara, as it was built on the back lot, doesn't quite follow Miss Mitchell's description of "a clumsy, sprawling building . . . built by slave labor"; in fact, the result was judged classy enough to be featured in the November 1939 issue of *House & Garden,* for which this Kodachrome was specially taken. The landscaping of the plantation was done by Florence Yoch, a friend of the Whitneys', who had done some work on their Long Island estates.

minutes between the start of the fire and its conclusion saw the completion of one of the most important and ultimately memorable moments of the picture. But of even more consequence was the inadvertent turning up of Vivien Leigh. The twenty-five-year-old actress was in Hollywood on a quick holiday from London to see Laurence Olivier, laboring on Goldwyn's *Wuthering Heights.* Theirs was a passionate involvement, in spite of each being married to someone else. She had journeyed halfway around the world to be with him; in five days she would have to return to England for a contracted stage performance. Her determination to be with Olivier was coupled with an equal resolve to enter herself in the O'Hara sweepstakes. She had achieved some measure of success in English theatrical circles, being considered not only beautiful but an actress of great potential. Her several appearances in British films had not escaped the attention of Selznick, who had not been impressed, but Leigh, who had studied the part of Scarlett O'Hara in England, was convinced that if she had the opportunity she could make a favorable impression. Myron, who was Olivier's American agent, was her entree to David, and accordingly she was all charm, high spirits, and vivacity in the hours immediately following her meeting with him. Olivier, who was as frenzied about her as she was about him, had remarked to Myron: "Just look at Vivien tonight! If David doesn't fall for that, I'll be very surprised."

Fall he did, for the next day Selznick confided in a letter to his wife: "Myron brought Larry Olivier and Vivien Leigh with him to the fire. Shhh: she's the Scarlett dark horse and looks damn good. Not for anybody's ear but your own: it's narrowed down to Paulette, Jean Arthur, Joan Bennett and Vivien Leigh." All this enthusiasm on the strength of one reading, for she had not yet been given a screen test. The morning following the fire, she had read through the library scene for Cukor in which Scarlett proclaims her love for Ashley Wilkes. Where most of the other actresses had played it as either coy and sentimental or arch and hysterical, Leigh had, as Cukor recalls, "a kind of indescribable wildness about her" that he found "very exciting." Her clipped British accent needed some work, which she assured him she would do. Twelve days later, Selznick abruptly canceled another test for Paulette Goddard; the actress, costumed and made up, was replaced by Vivien Leigh, who later recalled, "When I put the costume on it was still warm from the previous actress." After several days of tests and accent rehearsals, both Selznick and Cukor were convinced they had finally found the perfect Scarlett. But there was a problem: Leigh, in addition to being committed to a stage play in London, was under contract to Alexander Korda, and the negotiations involved were long and complicated. There were two other factors that had to be contended with: first, she was English, and the wrath of the South and indeed the entire country might conceivably rise up in nationalistic indignation; added to this was the moral outrage that could follow if it were learned that she and Olivier were involved in an extramarital affair. The American public liked its movie stars lusty and romantic on screen, and pristine and virtuous off. With Leigh, her acting ability and her physical rightness for the part made the risks worth taking; she was unknown in this country and her situation with Olivier could be handled discreetly and even turned into a romantic asset. All these problems whirled through Selznick's mind while the negotiations with Korda were carried on via cable and letter. Leigh, in a surge of optimism about her chances, had already freed herself of the stage commitment, then spent several days waiting for some news from Selznick. When word finally came, it was from Cukor, inviting her and Olivier to a Christmas party at his home. During cocktails, he took her aside and told her that the part of Scarlett had been cast. When she asked who had been given the part, he told her offhandedly, "I guess we're stuck with you."

GIRLS TESTED FOR THE ROLE OF SCARLETT

Name	Where From	Date Tested
Louise Platt	New York City	September 28, 1936
Talullah Bankhead	New York City	December 22, 1936
Mrs. J. H. Whitney	New York City	April 5, 1937
Lynn Merrill	New York City	May 24, 1937
Linda Watkins	New York City	June 3, 1937
Susan Fox	New York City	June 3, 1937
Adele Longmire	New Orleans; New York City	August 18, 1937
Haila Stoddard	New York City	November 9-10, 1937
Diana Forrest	New York City	November 9-10, 1937
Edith Marrener	New York City; Hollywood	Dec. 2, 1937; Dec. 6, 1937
Linda Lee	New York City	December 13, 1937
Dorothy Mathews	New York City	December 13, 1937
Ardis Ankerson	New York City	February 4, 1938
Paulette Goddard	Hollywood	February 9, 1938 Feb. 12, Feb. 19, Nov. 8-9-11, Dec. 8, Dec. 20-21, 1938
Terry Ray	Hollywood	Feb. 9-12-19, 1938
Anita Louise	Hollywood	Feb. 10, March 21-22-23, 1938
Em Bowles Locker	Richmond, Va.	Feb. 15, 1938
Margaret Tallichet	Hollywood	March 19, 21-22-23, 1938
Frances Dee	Hollywood	March 24, 1938
Nancy Coleman	Hollywood	Setp. 29, October 1, 1938
Shirley Logan	Hollywood	Sept. 29; Oct. 7, 1938

Page 2

Name	Where From	Date Tested
Doris Jordan	New York; Hollywood	October 17, 1938; Nov. 18, Nov. 29, Dec. 8, 1938
Marcella Martin	New York; Hollywood	Oct. 17, 1938; Dec. 21, 1938; Jan. 11, 1939
Fleurette DeBussy	New York City	October 17, 1938
Austine McDonnel	New York City	October 17, 1938
Mary Ray	Hollywood	Nov. 8-9, 1938
Lana Turner	Hollywood	Nov. 17-18, 1938
Dianna Barrymore	New York City	November 24, 1938
Jean Arthur	Hollywood	December 17, 1938
Joan Bennett	Hollywood	December 20, 1938
Vivien Leigh	London; Hollywood	Dec. 21-22, 1938

GIRLS SUGGESTED FOR SCARLETT BUT
WHOSE TESTS WERE GENERAL

Katharine Aldridge	New York City	October 17, 1938
Lyn Swann	New York City	Dec. 27, 1938

The official studio list of all the actresses tested for the role of Scarlett O'Hara.

(Above) Jean Arthur with Hattie McDaniel. Arthur was the first established film star to do a complete test for the role. At the time, Selznick commented in a letter to his wife, "[She] has been no end of trouble. . . . I look at her as though I had never known her before!" (She and Selznick had had a brief romance in the late twenties, when they were both at Paramount.) Miss Arthur is reputed to have burned her screen test after losing the part. (Below) Makeup artist Monty Westmore and hair stylist Hazel Rogers prepare Paulette Goddard for her color test for the role of Scarlett O'Hara. Goddard was the leading contender for the part and the only actress besides Vivien Leigh who was given a Technicolor test for the role (bottom).

(Top, left) Tallulah Bankhead was the first well-known actress to try out for the role. Her test was photographic only, as Selznick was mostly concerned about her ability to convincingly portray the sixteen-year-old Scarlett. (Top, right) Melvyn Douglas tested for the role of Ashley Wilkes opposite Lana Turner, who was trying out for Scarlett. Of Douglas as Ashley, Selznick remarked, "He gives the first intelligent reading we've had yet." Turner was physically right for the part, but her woeful inexperience dropped her out of the running early on. (Above, left) Douglass Montgomery (also known as Kent Douglass) as Ashley and Joan Bennett as Scarlett. Bennett gave one of the best readings of the role and was with Paulette Goddard one of the leading contenders for the part. Douglass Montgomery was the studio's in-house Ashley, testing with four different actresses, the last being Vivien Leigh. (Above, right) Model Edythe Marrener did several tests for Scarlett, on the strength of which she signed a contract with Paramount Pictures, changed her name to Susan Hayward, and had a very successful thirty-year career. She is seen here with Dorothy Jordan in the part of Melanie. Miss Jordan had given up a promising career to become Mrs. Merian C. Cooper and was coaxed out of retirement to test for the role of Melanie Wilkes. (Below, left and right) Vivien Leigh with Douglass Montgomery in her first screen test for the part of Scarlett O'Hara, playing the paddock scene, in which Scarlett tries to persuade Ashley to run away with her to Mexico. Cukor directed the scene and Ernest Haller photographed it.

(Top) January 14, 1939—David O. Selznick ends two and a half years of searching when he announces that Vivien Leigh, a little-known British actress, will play Scarlett O'Hara. Like the fictional heroine, Miss Leigh had an Irish-French ancestral background. At the same time Selznick finalized the casting of the two other central roles by signing the twenty-three-year-old Olivia de Havilland to play Melanie Hamilton and the forty-three-year-old British-American matinee idol Leslie Howard to play twenty-six-year-old Ashley Wilkes. Howard, considering the role foolish, had not wanted to play it, but Selznick finally persuaded the reluctant actor by promising to let him be associate producer as well as co-star of the studio's remake of the Swedish film *Intermezzo.* Olivia de Havilland, who had become one of Hollywood's leading ingénues after her appearance in the Warner Bros. 1935 success *Captain Blood,* was called by Selznick and George Cukor to read for the part of Melanie at the suggestion of her sister, Joan Fontaine. This had to be done in secrecy, as Miss de Havilland was kept on a tight acting leash by the head of her studio, Jack Warner, who didn't like his players to be too ambitious. Selznick and Cukor were impressed by the actress and approached Warner, who refused to consider lending her, his reasoning being that she would be too hard to handle after playing such a meaty role. Miss de Havilland took matters into her own capable hands and circumvented her boss by appealing to his wife, Ann, convincing her that it could only be to the studio's credit to have her play a plum role in the biggest picture of the year. Mrs. Warner agreed, and she convinced her husband. Warner loaned out de Havilland for a cash payment plus the services of James Stewart, with whom Selznick still had a one-picture commitment. Ironically, at Warner Bros. Stewart was cast as the lead in the film adaptation of *No Time for Comedy,* a role Laurence Olivier had created on Broadway. (Above) A party at Myron Selznick's home the week before filming was to start on *Gone With The Wind.* (Clockwise, from left) Vivien Leigh, Laurence Olivier, David Selznick, George Cukor, Irene Selznick, Jock Whitney, and Merle Oberon.

The final casting of the picture was formally announced on January 13, 1939, and it came as no surprise to most of the industry, as *The Hollywood Reporter* had run an article on January 5, quoting several unnamed sources to the effect that Vivien Leigh had been given the part, and that Olivia de Havilland was to be borrowed from Warner Bros. to play Melanie Wilkes, with Leslie Howard as Ashley. The expected storm of controversy over the selection of the British-born Miss Leigh turned out to be only a brief flurry, while her relationship with Laurence Olivier was discreetly cosmeticized by Selznick's insistence that the two live apart during the filming. With the public consciousness ministered to and tucked in for the duration of production, Selznick and his staff began the feverish round-the-clock activity that would finally put *Gone With The Wind* into actual work. Now that the cast was assembled, Walter Plunkett was at last able to begin constructing the more than two thousand costumes that had been designed for nonexistent actors. On the back lot, after the debris of the fire had been cleared away, the construction crew was building the shell of the Atlanta train shed in front of the already finished Atlanta streets. Behind the car shed and up on a slight grassy knoll, the foundation and the brick steps of Tara were being laid in place. On top of this the front facade only would be built, and part of the roof, the rest being added by Jack Cosgrove's special effects department. Trucks were delivering trees, bushes, and green sod to plant around the house, while a special crew was busy constructing oak trees out of telephone poles, barrel staves, chicken wire, plaster, and paint. The photographic problem of re-creating "the red earth of Tara" was ingeniously solved by the combined efforts of Menzies, Zavits, and Klune, who brainstormed into existence the use of pulverized bricks, which would be scattered not only over Tara but all of the Atlanta street sets.

In his inner sanctum, Selznick was plowing through the last series of decisions that needed to be made regarding the final technical staff. Earlier he had made up his mind that Lee Garmes would be the perfect person to photograph the picture. Garmes was a small, round, energetic man, who'd been in the business since 1916. He had pioneered the innovative "north light technique," derived from his study of the work of Rembrandt, whereby all the light sources came from one direction, giving his images a clean, luminous quality. Since 1937, he had been working in England; when he received a cablegram from Selznick asking him to come back and work on the picture, he said, "You could have knocked me over with a feather because I had been reading so much about it that I thought it was practically finished. I got my agent to accept and cut my salary almost in half to do it." By the time Garmes arrived in Hollywood, the picture was a week away from its starting date, and Garmes plunged right into work on the makeup and lighting tests of Vivien Leigh. To assist Cukor in making certain that the customs and attitudes of the story's era would be presented as accurately as possible, Selznick had brought to Culver City, at Margaret Mitchell's suggestion, Susan Myrick of Atlanta, who in addition to being a close friend of Miss Mitchell's was also an expert on everything pertaining to the manners, morals, and sensibilities of the South, past and present. Her unerring eye for details and her ear for the proper sound of Southern speech were put to good use by Cukor and Selznick in the weeks before shooting started.

As the days crept nearer to the starting date, Selznick made one more concerted effort to pummel the script into a semblance of finality, throwing writers at it like darts in the hope that one of them might hit a bull's-eye. In the two weeks preceding the January 26 target date, John Balderston, Michael Foster, Edwin Justus Mayer, John van Druten, and F. Scott Fitzgerald all tried their skills at cutting, pasting, writing, and rewriting; but on the day before the first scene was to be shot, Selznick admitted defeat in a long letter to Jock Whitney:

> Don't get panicky at the seemingly small amount of final revised script.... It is so clearly in my mind that I can tell you the picture from beginning to end, almost shot for shot.... I want to match up the best things from the book (and from the various scripts) as well as try to make cuts.... The job that remains to be done is to telescope all these into the shortest possible form.... A couple of nights ago I was sick with trepidation, but as of tonight—the night before we start shooting—I am filled with confidence ... but you will have to bear with me for the next couple of months, which will be the toughest I have ever

January 20, 1939—Cinematographers Lee Garmes, Wilfred Cline, and Karl Struss photographed these Technicolor makeup, hair, and costume tests of the performers in *GWTW*. This series of tests convinced Selznick that the color schemes for some of the costumes were too drab, that the hair styles were wrong, and that the makeup on the actresses was too light. Hazel Rogers, hair stylist at Selznick International, was assigned the lesser performers, and Sydney Guilaroff was brought over from MGM to re-design Vivien Leigh's hair; as it turned out, he did only the opening sequence of the film, and then Hazel Rogers was reinstated. Leslie Howard, after seeing his test in the Confederate uniform, remarked that he "looked like a fairy doorman at the Beverly Wilshire Hotel." Fred Crane and George Bessolo, the two actors testing for the Tarleton twins (third row, right), could not be made up to convincingly resemble each other, so it was decided that they would be the "Tarleton boys" instead. Selznick also wanted their hair

to look redder, since they were described as "carrot tops" in the book. (During the course of the production, Bessolo changed his name to George Reeves—and years later took to changing his clothes in phone booths.) Evelyn Keyes (above, left) was a young actress from Atlanta under contract to Cecil B. DeMille. She had impressed photographer Max Munn Autrey with her beauty, and he had sent a letter to Selznick suggesting that she be tested for Scarlett. Selznick didn't like her for Scarlett but thought she would be effective as Scarlett's bitchy sister Suellen. Ann Rutherford (above, center), who had achieved a certain fame as Polly Benedict in the Andy Hardy series at MGM, was borrowed for the role of Scarlett's sweet younger sister, Carreen. Five-year-old Cammie King (above, right) was given the part of Scarlett and Rhett's daughter, Bonnie, after her sister, who had been tested six months earlier, outgrew the part. Miss King was the stepdaughter of Herbert Kalmus, the president of Technicolor.

263

(Above) Lyle Wheeler and his secretary with one of the models for the exteriors of the Atlanta street scenes. This was the largest setting ever built for a movie, with fifty-three full-size buildings and two miles of streets. (Below) Harold Fenton, construction superintendent, standing in front of the blackboard on which he kept a record of the progress of all of the ninety sets used in *Gone With The Wind* on the stages and on the back lot. At the same time, Fenton and his crew of 125 men were also readying the sets used in *Intermezzo* and *Rebecca*.

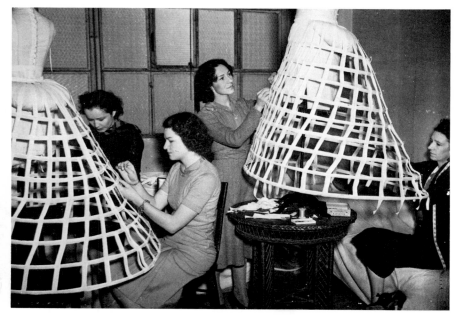

The costume department constructed the 5,500 separate items necessary to dress the performers, including the hundreds of hoop skirts, corsets, and other undergarments that were no longer in existence.

known, possibly the toughest any producer has ever known, which is the general opinion of the whole industry.... You have had faith in me to date, and I beg you to continue to have this faith until the picture is finished ... at which time if the picture isn't everything that everyone wants, I ... am willing ... and anxious to leave the whole goddam business.

The next morning, Thursday, January 26, at 8:00 A.M., on the front lawn of Selznick International, actress Mary Anderson ran the Confederate stars and bars up the flagpole, officially marking the start of filming. Vivien Leigh and the four other performers needed for the day's work had been at the studio since six, being costumed and made up. By 8:30, they were gathered on the steps of Tara on the back lot while George Cukor called for the blocking and camera rehearsal. The first scene scheduled was also the first scene of the picture, Scarlett and the Tarleton boys talking about the war and the upcoming barbecue at Twelve Oaks. It was a vital scene, for it unspooled the dramatic thread that would carry all through the story—Scarlett's discovery that Ashley, the man she loves, is to marry his cousin Melanie. The two actors playing the Tarleton boys were at worst amateurs and at best adequate. Directing them, for a perfectionist like Cukor, must have been frustrating, for his concentration was on Scarlett and her reactions to them, and also on the general air of the scene, which had to immediately conjure up a whiff of the Old South and its particular graces. Cukor had to spend an inordinate amount of time trying to bring the two actors down to the natural unforced kind of work neither of them had been trained in, and Leigh, though a gifted technician, was not above being rattled by having to stop constantly while Cukor tried to make the scene and the actors all blend together. The tension permeated the entire studio: "Everybody was nervous," recalls Ray Klune, "and it showed in the next day's rushes. George had Vivien on too high a key, way up there. David felt that she was playing it as though it were the first act of a dress rehearsal. The same thing with the boys ... they were overdoing it."

The light failed right after lunch, so Cukor and Vivien Leigh moved to the unfinished bedroom interior set, where they were joined by two seasoned actresses, Hattie McDaniel, playing Scarlett's shrewd Mammy, and Butterfly McQueen, a New York import who had been cast as the shrill, slow-witted servant girl Prissy, one of the main sources of comedy in the picture. Approximately one hundred people were jammed around the small set—carpenters, painters, grips, technicians, trying to finish it up. By 5:00 P.M. the set and the camera crew were ready. The scene involved Mammy getting the sixteen-year-old Scarlett ready for the barbecue, and it was the first good scene that Cukor had to work with. He labored over it gleefully, delicately touching up the finer points of the relationship between the two women, pulling McDaniel down from being just a little too broad and swift in her dialogue, giving the interplay between the two a richness and an honesty that resonated throughout the rest of the story.

The next day in the rushes, Selznick was disappointed with the first scene, realizing it would have to be retaken and shrugging the results off as first-day jitters. The bedroom scene was infinitely better, but Selznick was shocked to find that Cukor, without consulting him, had inserted a small bit of dialogue between Mammy and Scarlett, with Scarlett insisting that Prissy take all the food Mammy had prepared for her, "right back to the kitchen, I won't eat a bite," while Mammy insists: "Oh, yas'm, you is, you's gwine eat every mouthful." To Cukor this was necessary to smooth the way for what he felt was an abrupt and arbitrary change of mood in the script as written. He had lifted the dialogue almost verbatim from the novel, and Selznick, while realizing the value of it, was still unhappy with the fact that it had been done. In addition, Cukor's pacing of the scene bothered Selznick; it was full of pauses, glances, and reactions. He realized that it was these subtleties that made it work, but it ran one minute longer than it had in the tests, and it had needed shortening then. At the end of the first day's filming, with one and a half scenes completed out of a total of 692, the total amount of money spent on the picture was a whopping $1,081,465, out of a total budget estimate of $2,843,000.

As the first week wore on, Cukor continued to make David aware of his unhappiness with the fragmentary nature of the script. Cukor was a

The week before filming is to start, Selznick muses on the back lot, standing in the reconstructed Atlanta train station, with Tara in the background.

January 26, 1939—(Above, left) The original opening sequence as filmed by George Cukor. The Technicolor cameras turned the Tarleton boys into the aforementioned "carrot tops" to such an extent that the scene had to be re-shot because their hair was such a bright orange. (Above, right) Even though the Atlanta bazaar sequences were later extensively re-filmed by Victor Fleming, Cukor's shot of Rhett Butler's entrance remained in the final film. (Below) Cukor registering delight as he photographs the waltzing figures of Vivien Leigh and Clark Gable on a specially built camera platform that gave the illusion that the camera was moving among the dancers.

very fastidious director who relied on the script to anchor his perspective while he worked out the character variations with his actors. He found himself chained not to an anchor but to a bobbing buoy going in several directions at once, with montages of the Civil War and talky vignettes by subsidiary characters explaining the progress of the war in Georgia, all of which underwent a daily chain of revisions. Cukor, having spent the past three years with the characters, examining their relationships and their behavior, was now trying to cram this mass of detail into the actors' performances, spending what seemed to Selznick inordinate amounts of time on gestures, inflections, movements, nuances, and the hundred and one other variations of human behavior that a good actor or actress is capable of conveying. Throughout the first two weeks of filming, David kept cautioning Cukor about his tempo and speed, the need for swiftness in the pacing. He became increasingly disappointed with what he was seeing in the rushes. All the careful preparations, the hundreds of sketches for settings and art direction, were not, he felt, being captured on screen. He commented in a note to Menzies and Klune that: "the more I see of our film and compare it with other color pictures such as *Robin Hood,* the more I realize how much we are kidding ourselves in feeling that we could get really effective stuff on the back lot. . . ." By the end of the first ten days' shooting, the combination of Selznick's discontent, his rewriting, and Cukor's near-obsessive attention to detail had resulted in a total accumulated footage of twenty-three minutes, ten minutes of which were scheduled for retakes.

On January 31, Clark Gable joined the company to begin work as Rhett Butler, and the atmosphere on the set, which had begun to smooth down, began to tense up again. Selznick remarked: "Clark was nervous about the gigantic publicity campaign and whether he could live up to it . . . and also he felt that I was introducing a new woman star on his shoulders and would throw the picture to her. I assured him that if he still felt that way when the picture was finished, I would repair it in any way he felt it was necessary, so that calmed him down and he went to work." The first scenes Gable worked in were the complicated ones of the Atlanta charity bazaar, which necessitated his learning the Virginia reel and otherwise acting the dandy, something he was extremely uncomfortable doing. His edginess and insecurities about his role and his abilities were not made easier by the emotional climate on the set. Cukor, Vivien Leigh, and Olivia de Havilland had by now developed a rapport with each other, and Gable, who for years had been pampered and catered to at MGM, felt like an outsider. Because of the complexities of Scarlett's character and her relationship with Melanie, Cukor was spending a great deal of time working with the two actresses, which did little to allay Gable's fears regarding his own role. Cukor's efforts with Gable were directed mainly at loosening him up, trying to get him to give the part a kind of mocking, tongue-in-cheek elegance. But Gable was not what is known as a "quick study." His acting style was more or less an extension of his own personality; anything more than that caused him great torment, in spite of his professionalism. Also, Gable did not understand Cukor's method of working—the personalities and temperaments of the two men were poles apart. Gable was used to specific meat-and-potatoes direction from the likes of Jack Conway and Victor Fleming, men who spoke seldom and right to the point—they knew how to deal with him, how to keep him at ease; in the parlance of the time, they were "men's men," whereas Cukor was cultivated, sensitive, fussy, and maddeningly vague in his instructions. Gable was used to being told specifically what he was doing wrong and how to correct it, and he felt he was not getting this from Cukor.

To Selznick, "Gable was extremely intelligent without being intellectual. . . . He had no complicated psychological side, his mind was uncluttered. . . . If he did have problems, he didn't impose them on his performance. . . . Clark's performances were simply a reproduction of what the author created. . . . It is conceivable that another actor might have read a different dimension into Rhett, but you wouldn't have had Margaret Mitchell's Rhett. Clark brought precisely to life what she wrote, and what millions of readers wanted. . . . I don't know of any actor of the past fifty years with the exception of John Barrymore who could have played Rhett as well as Clark did. . . . If he was dissatisfied with Cukor, he never once mentioned it to me, nor did he ever criticize George." It is not surprising that he didn't mention it to Selznick, as he knew that the

two men were close friends; besides, there was Gable's own dislike of Selznick. At MGM, however, it was different. He let his unhappiness be known to several of the executives there, reportedly telling intimates, "I don't want Cukor; I'm going to have him changed." Gable may have been insecure about his abilities as an actor, but not about his power as a star. There was a clause in his loan-out contract with Selznick that absolved MGM of all responsibility "if the artist refuses to perform," and this was his ace in the hole if the situation became too unbearable for him. Gable was shrewd enough to know that word would get back to Selznick from MGM that he was displeased, and as Selznick later admitted, "I knew about it"—it was just one more straw added to the pressures of the picture. He could not afford to have Gable unhappy, he had given up too much to get him, and the picture would suffer without him. And increasingly, Selznick found himself irritated with Cukor's insistence on doing things his own way. As he felt more and more unhappy about the results of the filming, he began to place the blame on Cukor and to tighten his hold on Cukor's direction, telling him on February 8:

> Before we started this picture we had a long discussion concerning my anxiety to discuss with you in advance the points that I personally saw in each scene; this for many reasons became impossible. . . . Then we discussed seeing each scene rehearsed, and this idea was in turn lost sight of in the pressure of many things. Now the idea becomes more important than ever because we have little or no opportunity . . . to discuss each rewritten scene before you go into it. I therefore . . . would like to try to work out a system whereby I see each block scene rehearsed in full before you start the shooting on it . . . this would avoid projection room surprises for me and conceivably would be of considerable service to you.

For Cukor, this was very nerve-wracking: "David changed our whole method of working . . . he seemed to trust me less. . . . I was the director, after all . . . and the director should shoot the scene before the producer sees it. . . . That's when the producer's opinion is important, when he sees it on the screen for the first time." Just exactly what decided Selznick to replace Cukor will never be known; it was probably a combination of all of the above circumstances.

Matters came to a head on February 13, while the company was filming Rhett, Scarlett, Melanie, and Prissy leaving Aunt Pittypat's house just before the Yankees enter Atlanta. During the lunch break, Cukor went to see Selznick about rewrites for the upcoming scenes involving Ashley's Christmas leave, trying to persuade him once more to return to the Sidney Howard original instead of the more lengthy and wooden Garrett-Selznick rewrite. Cukor later related to Susan Myrick his version of what had transpired, and she in turn wrote to Margaret Mitchell:

> George said he cannot do a job unless he knows it is a good job, and he feels the present job is not right. . . . For days he has looked at the rushes and felt he was failing. He knew he was a good director and knew the actors were good ones, yet the thing did not click as it should. . . . He became more and more convinced that the script was the trouble . . . so he told David he would not work any longer if the script was not better and that he wanted the Howard script. David told George he was a director—not an author, and he (David) was the producer and the judge of what is a good script. . . . George said he was a director and a damn good one and he would not let his name go out over a lousy picture and if they did not go back to the Howard script, he, George, was through. And bullheaded David said, "Okay, get out."

Selznick's version was considerably different:

> George had reached the point where he found it impossible to accept my viewpoint on certain things. . . . There was no particular dispute or incident, it was just a day by day insistence on my view of the whole concept. . . . I had to see it through in my way in every single department. . . . I had to insist that George follow my judgment . . . but he began disagreeing with me on my concept, so I told him that if the picture was to fail, it would fail on my judgment alone. I was careful to keep George on the job until I arranged for him to take over another picture. And neither before or after I made the change did I ever have one word of discussion about the director with Gable.

The novel *Gone With The Wind* had over 150 subsidiary characters who figured prominently throughout the ten-year saga of Scarlett and the South. Selznick and his scriptwriters managed to reduce this to fifty speaking parts—a record number for any production. One of Selznick's greatest strengths was his casting instinct, and he peopled the film with a rich assortment of some of the best character actors from Hollywood and New York. (Top, left) Thomas Mitchell as Gerald O'Hara, master of Tara and father of Scarlett, who taught his daughter that "land is . . . the only thing that lasts." (Top, right) Victor Jory played the obsequious Yankee overseer Jonas Wilkerson, whose affinity for comporting with poor white trash led to his dismissal by Ellen Robillard O'Hara, Scarlett's mother, played by Barbara O'Neil. Oscar Polk was Pork, one of the O'Hara's three household servants. (Middle, left) Melanie and her Aunt "Pittypat" Hamilton.

Laura Hope Crews was cast by George Cukor after Billie Burke had been judged too young. (Middle, right) Scarlett is an unwilling aide to Dr. Meade, played by Harry Davenport, the seventy-three-year-old stage veteran whose film career had begun in 1912; the sergeant behind him is Ed Chandler, and the wounded soldier in pain is George Hackathorne. (Above, left) Carroll Nye was Frank Kennedy, Scarlett's second husband, whom she stole from her sister Suellen because he had $300 to pay the taxes on Tara. Big Sam, her father's ex-foreman, who saved her from being attacked, was played by Everett Brown. (Above, right) Butterfly McQueen, a twenty-eight-year-old New York stage actress, memorably portrayed Scarlett's shrill, dim-witted servant girl Prissy—the one role that Margaret Mitchell wished she herself could have played.

The richest characterization in the entire film was given by Hattie McDaniel as Mammy, the sly, leather-lunged, bossy Emily Post of the O'Hara family and the only person, besides Rhett Butler, who was not fooled by Scarlett's airs and tears. Miss McDaniel was forty-five years old when she played the part and had spent most of her life touring the black theatrical belt, performing in tent shows, cabarets, and vaudeville and on the legitmate stage. Her timing and her comedic and dramatic talents were taken fullest advantage of by Selznick, Cukor, Victor Fleming, and Sam Wood, all of whom gave her some of the juiciest bits in the film. A native of Wichita, Kansas, Miss McDaniel had to be taught by Susan Myrick to speak in the rich dialect of a transplanted Savannah black who had lived in the north Georgia country for twenty years. (Above, left) Mammy's stunned reaction upon hearing Scarlett tell Frank Kennedy that her sister Suellen, to whom he is engaged, "got tired of waiting, was afraid she was going to be an old maid, and is going to marry one of the county boys next month." (Above, right) " 'T'aint fittin'—it just ain't fittin' " is Mammy's disapproving retort to Rhett's declaration that he is going to buy his daughter a blue velvet riding habit.

"Twelve Oaks" This was not far from Atlanta ✝

I like this for Ashley's home.

As late as February 1939, Lyle Wheeler, William Cameron Menzies, and Wilbur Kurtz were still wrestling with the concept of Twelve Oaks, Ashley Wilkes's home. Even though she refused to become officially involved in anything to do with the film, Margaret Mitchell did send this newspaper clipping of the Covington, Georgia, home of Mrs. M. S. Turner to Kurtz, noting, "I like this for Ashley's home." (Bottom) Cosgrove's lack of success with this view of the approach to Twelve Oaks was due to the fact that the carriages were photographed in a field outside the studio and then double-printed onto a painting into which Cosgrove had put the shadows of the trees falling across the driveway. There was no time to re-shoot it so that the shadows could be made to ripple across the carriages instead of becoming transparent.

What Selznick refers to as "disagreement on concept" was really a difference of stylistic approach. Selznick and Menzies had decided on a florid theatrical look and feel for the picture, while Cukor was minutely detailing his characters, an approach that Selznick felt did not catch "the big feel, the scope and breadth of the production." In this he was partly right, but it was a moot point, as he had always intended to have someone else direct the larger spectacle scenes. Most of the work that Cukor did on the picture, however, remains in the completed film. His detailing of the O'Hara family, the complex intertwining relationships of the female characters throughout, his attention to the resonances of the time and the place suffuse the early part of the story with a strength and concern for the characters that is so strong and dense that the rest of the picture can proceed on its narrative way without concerning itself about depth of characterizations.

On Monday morning, February 13, the Hollywood film community read in both trade papers that

> George Cukor and David O. Selznick last night issued the following statement: "As a result of a series of disagreements between us over many of the individual scenes of *Gone With The Wind,* we have mutually decided that the only solution is for a new director to be selected at as early a date as is practicable. . . ." [Selznick added:] "Mr. Cukor's withdrawal . . . is the most regrettable incident of my rather long producing career, the more so because I consider Mr. Cukor one of the very finest directors it has ever been the good fortune of this business to claim. I can only hope that we will be so fortunate as to be able to replace him with a man of comparable talents."

There was nothing new or unusual about directors being replaced on pictures. It was an accepted activity in those days; Selznick himself had been doing it almost his entire career. What was surprising, and what has been made much of all these years, is his supposed ruthlessness in doing this to Cukor. To the world outside Hollywood, the event was news only insofar as everything concerning *Gone With The Wind* had taken on an air of national importance, but in the film community the reaction was one of shocked surprise. Even on Selznick's own staff, the firing was greeted with incredulity: "I never thought David would can George," says Hal Kern. "They were such great friends. . . . It really took guts to do it." In Kern's opinion, this marked Selznick's emergence as a full-fledged producer—someone to whom the picture was the overriding concern.

Selznick went to extraordinary pains to make sure that there was no misunderstanding in the town that George was being replaced because of inadequacies. He spent the next several days finding another suitable project for him so that he would continue working and not suffer the agony of enforced idleness after what was obviously a tremendous blow to his professional pride and standing. Before the news broke, he asked Louis B. Mayer to assign Cukor to the upcoming film version of *The Women,* Clare Boothe's hit play, which had a cast made up of the studio's biggest female stars. Mayer agreed, and Ernst Lubitsch, who had been scheduled for that, was instead assigned to direct Garbo in *Ninotchka,* the two pictures emerging among the best of the year. Both Selznick and Cukor were highly intelligent, civilized men, and their reactions to the situation were in keeping with their sensibilities: rueful regret, untinged with bitterness or recriminations. While they never worked together again professionally, their friendship and their personal regard for each other remained largely unchanged.

Cukor was still directing the picture, working on the scenes of the birth of Melanie's baby and events leading up to the escape from Atlanta, when news of his removal reached Vivien Leigh and Olivia de Havilland. Their immediate reaction was a hasty call on Selznick; still in their costumes, they begged him to reconsider, arguing with him for close to an hour, following him around the office in their determination to make him change his mind, until finally they cornered him on top of his window seat, while Leigh cajoled, reasoned, and pleaded. She later repeated her remarks to a reporter, telling him: "My test was directed by George. . . . I would like people to know how grateful I am for the pains George took with me when I was trying to get myself into the character of Scarlett. It was not easy; it was very hard. Or I was stupid. In any case, I've never known anyone to be so patient . . . as George was with me. He devoted himself for days at a time to teaching me mannerisms, coaching me in voice inflection, and trying to explain to me and implant in me something of the thinking and psychology that made Scarlett what she was. And no matter what happens—whether I do a good job or a bad one I shall be eternally grateful to George Cukor." But in spite of the entreaties of the two actresses, Selznick refused to reconsider. He later remarked: "I have learned that nothing matters except the final picture."

As soon as Cukor left, production was shut down "for several days" while Selznick tried to find another director. To do this, he turned once again to MGM, offering the job to King Vidor, who politely turned him down. Selznick thereupon prevailed upon Mayer to give him Victor Fleming, busy shooting the studio's expensive, troublesome musical fantasy *The Wizard of Oz*. Mayer was agreeable to this providing Fleming was. Fleming had been looking forward to taking a long, relaxing vacation; he wanted no part of the massive problems that obviously would confront him on *Gone With The Wind*. But he and Gable were extremely close friends, and he could not resist Gable's repeated entreaties to come in and help him out of his Rhett Butler predicament. The three-pronged attack of Gable, Mayer, and Selznick finally won Fleming over, and he agreed to leave the last few days of *The Wizard of Oz* to King Vidor, who finished up the picture by filming the "Over the Rainbow" musical sequence.

Saturday, February 18, Fleming spent all day and most of the night at the studio with Selznick, familiarizing himself with the script, the already filmed material, and the production methods that had been devised. "Fleming was another of that extremely masculine breed," remarked Selznick. "I didn't know him well socially.... He was one of the most attractive men, in my opinion, who ever came to Hollywood, physically and in personality.... I enjoyed working with him.... He was an expert craftsman.... He had been a cameraman and knew his cinematics thoroughly." Fleming had started his career as a director in 1920 with one of Douglas Fairbanks's biggest early successes, *When the Clouds Roll By*, which had pretty well defined the Fairbanks personality—breezy, athletic, optimistic, and wearyingly energetic. Fleming's forte seemed to be strong, rugged action, with an emphasis on masculine sensibilities and codes, but he was surprisingly gifted at dealing with the sensitivities of human nature, as proved by his 1927 *The Way of All Flesh* with Emil Jannings; and his wild, outrageous streak made Jean Harlow in *Bombshell* one of the comedic highlights of 1933.

He had not read *Gone With The Wind*, so he had no preconceived idea of the story, and after a look at the completed footage and a careful appraisal of the script itself, he bluntly and forcefully reiterated to Selznick what Cukor had been saying all along: "Your script is no fucking good." This, coming from someone as objective as Fleming, forced Selznick into acknowledging the seriousness of the situation. The immediate problem now became what to do about it, as Fleming refused to direct the script as written; each day that filming was suspended was costing $65,000, just in overhead. Selznick was frantic to find a way out of his script predicament, and as he had so many times before, he turned to Ben Hecht, who coincidentally was just finishing up a writing assignment at MGM. "David and Victor arrived at my house about 8:30 Sunday morning," recalled Hecht.

> They knew I always had an early breakfast and they told me they had arranged to borrow me from MGM to write *Gone With The Wind*. I was just about to go back to New York and I didn't want to get involved in all this, and I told David so. We haggled back and forth over coffee, and he offered me $10,000 for two weeks' work, so I thought, "Well, I'll take a chance." I hadn't read the book, I never read those kind of books, and on the way over to the studio, David was denouncing me as a stupid holdout—that I wasn't fit to call myself a writer. We got to the studio [where] we were met by John van Druten, who wrote plays well, but movies not so well. He was going to work with us, so I asked him if he'd read the book. He said, "Yessss"—he was an English boy—and I said, "What did you think of it, is it a good book, Johnnie?" "Oh yess," he said, "It's a fine book— for bellhops"; well, David got furious and fired him on the spot....

There wasn't time for me to read the whole book, so David decided he'd tell me the whole story—which I couldn't follow; it seemed to me to be what we used to call in Chicago as long as a whore's dream—and

(Above) Lyle Wheeler designed this portion of the porch of Twelve Oaks, constructed over the entrance to Stage 11, for the arrival of the guests at the barbecue. The camera followed Scarlett through the door and into the great hall, built inside the stage. (For years tour guides at MGM pointed to a Southern mansion set on the back lot as Twelve Oaks, but this was not true; only one sequence was photographed at MGM—an exterior shot of the Atlanta house showing Rhett teaching Bonnie to ride her pony.) (Below) J. McMillan Johnson's sketch for Scarlett's return to the ruined Twelve Oaks. A portion of the floor, staircase, and ruined wall was built full size; the upper sections of the staircase and the walls were photographed using a "hanging miniature": a miniature construction of the set hung several feet in front of the camera, matching the perspective of the full-sized setting. The combination—if done correctly—is undetectable.

as pointless. So I read the script that they had—it was really a humpty dumpty job—and I asked David if there wasn't a better one, and he dug up the Sidney Howard original, and it was a superb treatment, so I said I'd do the picture based on this script. Of course, I didn't know the characters, so to save time David and Victor decided that they'd act out all the major parts for me—David played Scarlett and somebody named Ashley, and Victor acted Butler and a girl named Melanie. It was very funny, but it . . . kept up till 2:00 A.M., and after a while the humor got a little vague. They'd talk about a scene, then act it out, and I would write it up. I was shrewd enough to involve David in this so there would be no comebacks or rewrites possible, and while their acting seminar went on I'd catch a few winks on the couch. David didn't sleep at all—he was the Dexedrine pioneer of Hollywood, and was getting shots to keep him awake. He was also on some kind of a diet, so we had nothing but bananas and peanuts to eat while all this nonsense was going on.

For five days and nights Hecht cut, rewrote, and straightened out the narrative focus of the story, accomplishing in that time what had eluded Selznick and all the other writers for three years—a tight, concise, visual retelling of the Howard original through the first half. It was strictly a technical job, there was no creative writing involved, and Hecht contributed nothing except the all-important ability to cut through the dense underbrush of numerous rewrites, clearing away the clutter of the minor characters' digressions and loquacity that strangled the main plot line. "On the fifth day," Hecht related, "the blood vessels in Vic Fleming's

right eye exploded and Selznick finally collapsed in what we thought was a coma but turned out to be just a deep sleep. I had finished rewriting everything up to the girl's return to her plantation, which had taken about a week; when he finally woke up David offered me another raise in salary if I stayed beyond the two weeks, but I said there wasn't enough money in the world for this kind of suicidal work—eighteen to twenty hours a day, and after the second week I got out in a hurry."

By now there was enough revised script for Selznick to give orders to restart production, which was done on March 2, after Fleming and Selznick had both recuperated. Literally starting all over, Fleming's first scene was a retake of the opening, with Scarlett once more telling the Tarleton boys that "this war talk is spoiling the fun at every party this spring." Ridgeway Callow, second assistant director, recalls that the day before shooting, "Fleming came onto the set and said to my boss Eric Stacey and myself, 'They tell me that you're supposed to be the best team in the picture business. But I'm going to put both of you in the hospital before this picture is over.'"

The week after production restarted, Selznick got rid of the last of his lingering dissatisfactions when he removed Lee Garmes as director of photography, replacing him with Ernest Haller, who shot the scenes of Scarlett's entrance to the main hall at Twelve Oaks, which Garmes had set up. Garmes commented: "It was very sad. I didn't want to leave the picture. I loved the story and I was very friendly with David, but he just didn't quite understand the softer shades and tones that we were able to get with the new faster stock, so we agreed to disagree." But Selznick had very definite ideas of what he wanted the color to look like:

Neutral colors certainly have their value, and pastel colors . . . make for lovely scenes . . . but this does not mean . . . that the longest picture on record . . . has to deal one hundred percent in these. . . . This picture . . . gives us the opportunity as in Scarlett's costumes, to throw a violent dab of color at the audience to make a dramatic point. . . . The Technicolor experts are here for the purpose of guiding us technically . . . and not for the purpose of dominating the creative side of our picture as to sets, costumes or anything else.

While Selznick fretted over the color, the costumes, and the second half of the script, Fleming took complete control of the production and it had begun to roll down the long road toward getting all the estimated 650 remaining scenes on film. He was doing this at an average rate of three script pages per day, which worked out to about two minutes of footage daily. "The camera rehearsals were what took so long," says Lydia Schiller. "The lighting, steadying the camera, just moving that Technicolor camera was a massive operation, and Mr. Selznick did like his moving camera shots . . . and you know on some of those smaller sets it was just murder to get that camera in there."

With Fleming in charge, Gable's attitude and demeanor changed completely. He relaxed and, under Fleming's careful handling, even began to enjoy the role, although as Ridgeway Callow remembers, "He worked well with everybody, but the crew didn't like him. I know at MGM they were supposed to be crazy about him, but they were not at Selznick. He was very aloof." On March 25, after completing some close-up retakes of the bazaar sequence, Gable left for six days.

Some of Lyle Wheeler's set designs for *Gone With The Wind:*
(Opposite page) Scarlett's bedroom at Tara (top, left): the fresh room of a Southern girl, the "sweet, gentle, beautiful and ornamental" young lady that Scarlett was—at least outwardly. The good taste of Ellen, Scarlett's mother, is evident in the polished floor covered with a brightly colored rug, the simple mahogany furniture, and the white ruffled tester bed. The parlor at Tara (top, right), arranged for Scarlett's wedding to Charles Hamilton. The delicate French marble mantel bespeaks Ellen's Savannah background; Gerald O'Hara's tastes are apparent in the hunting prints above it, and the room is given a rich feeling by the green velvet portieres around the windows. The entrance hall at Twelve Oaks (bottom, left), with its graceful, curved double staircase, copied from a mansion in South Carolina. The beautiful Greek Revival look of Twelve Oaks was enhanced by the series of Corinthian columns that lined the main hallway (bottom, right). Scarlett is standing in the hall leading to the library.
(This page) Rhett's bedroom in the postwar Atlanta house (top, left), dominated by the huge oil portrait of Scarlett painted by Helen Carleton. The parlor in Aunt "Pittypat" Hamilton's Atlanta home during the war (top, right) was the height of fashion with its elegant Victorian furniture and ruffled draperies, but the room, like its "pink-cheeked, fussy" owner, is crowded and overdecorated. The furnishings and other set decorations were by Edward Boyle in collaboration with Joseph Platt, the interior decoration consultant for *House & Garden.* Platt's contributions to the picture are still a subject of controversy. Scarlett's bedroom in the Atlanta house (bottom, left) is in stunning contrast to the simplicity of her room at Tara. The Atlanta house had "more of everything than the governor's mansion," bought with the postwar affluence of Rhett's blockade running. Rhett said it was "a nightmare," but the tufted satin wall and luxurious canopied French bed mirror Scarlett's violent reaction against her bitter wartime poverty. The library at Twelve Oaks (bottom, right) differed markedly from Miss Mitchell's description of "a dim room with towering walls . . . completely filled with books . . . heavy furniture . . . high-backed chairs with deep seats . . . and velvet hassocks for the women."

These twelve frames from *Gone With The Wind* contain some of the most memorable examples of Walter Plunkett's costume designs. (First row, left) Scarlett's white crinoline gown in the opening scenes was a substitution for the green-sprigged muslin that she had originally worn. Selznick felt that the white gown gave her more of a virginal, sixteen-year-old quality. (First row, center) The green-sprigged muslin creation that Scarlett wore to the Wilkes's barbecue was in turn a substitution for the green watered silk festooned with ecru lace visible in the tests on page 263. (First row, right) Scarlett's ivory silk gown for her marriage to Melanie's brother Charles was her mother's wedding dress, hurriedly re-made to fit Scarlett because of the haste with which the wedding was arranged. (Second row, center) Scarlett wore this calico dress, varied in six different ways, throughout the middle portion of the film. Melanie's nightgown in this same shot was used to wrap the bloody head of the Yankee cavalryman Scarlett has just shot. (Second row, right) The most famous costume in the picture—and probably in all motion picture history—was the dress Scarlett made from her mother's green velvet portieres, so that she could "go to Atlanta looking like a queen" in the hopes of borrowing $300 from Rhett to pay the taxes on Tara. She even went so far as to decorate the bonnet with a gilded chicken foot—all to no avail. The spectacular variety of Plunkett's designs for the female characters in *Gone With The Wind* has tended to obscure his outstanding talent for designing for men, as can be seen in several of the shots above, especially those of Rhett Butler. Plunkett's ability to indicate character and attitude through line, color, and fabric remains unsurpassed.

Ona Munson played Belle Watling, the leading madam of Atlanta's red-light district, winning the role over such actresses as Betty Compson and Marjorie Rambeau. (Below, left) Belle's scenes were brief but effective, and, for the time, quite frank in letting the audience know that she was Rhett's mistress. (Below, center) In Atlanta, Scarlett visits Rhett in jail and encounters Belle, who impudently eyes Scarlett and shocks Mammy ("Who dat? Ah ain' never see'd hair dat color in mah life. Does you know a dyed-hair woman?"). (Below, right) Miss Munson's finest moment was her scene with Melanie, in which she tells her that no matter how grateful Melanie is to her for saving Ashley's life, she must not speak to her publicly, as "that wouldn't be fittin'."

Clark Gable with his favorite director and close friend, Victor Fleming. It was Fleming who created the Gable image in the early 1930s, patterning the rather insecure actor after his own tough, honest masculinity and giving him a sense of humor that enhanced Gable's own powerful sexuality.

During his short leave, he and Carole Lombard eloped to Kingman, Arizona; his first day back on the set, there was a small celebration attended by everybody, including Selznick, who was fond of Lombard and truly wished Gable well. Then production resumed at a pace even more hectic than before. The pressure on everybody in the studio was now tremendous, not just from the immense workload but because of Selznick's erratic working habits.

"He was a hard worker," recalls Klune, "but he was not a well-organized man at all. He had great difficulty in organizing his own time properly, and consequently he could never catch up with the things that needed his attention." And the script, no matter how much work was done on it, always needed more attention, like a sick child in the night. Ben Hecht had stayed on the week after the marathon day-and-night sessions that had finally shaped the first half. His second week was spent at a much less frantic pace; he worked during the day trimming the second half down, eliminating everything except the two central stories of Scarlett and Rhett, Melanie and Ashley. He did his best to maintain a smooth narrative flow in the latter half, but the story as trimmed down by Howard lacked the strong action of the first half, and as the plot unraveled itself around Scarlett's love life, it lost much of the epic quality of the book, becoming largely a series of static dialogue sequences between the principals. These weaknesses were readily apparent to Selznick, and he labored over Hecht's work. Dialogue was written, rewritten, and changed again, sequences were altered, dropped, shifted, in a nightmare of schedule revisions and last-minute changes. Klune tried to keep up with these changes, but it was difficult and wearying: "There were days when we didn't even know what we were doing tomorrow. It was not at all uncommon for David to call me at three in the morning and ask me what we were shooting tomorrow. I'd say, 'David, you've got the schedule right there on your desk, so I know that you know.' He'd say, 'Can we change it?' I'd say, 'At this time of the morning?' This happened time and time again."

For Lyle Wheeler, these last-minute changes of Selznick's were particularly frustrating: "I'd have a set all built and ready to go for the next day and David would suddenly decide to shift the scene because it needed rewriting or it wasn't finished yet. He'd tell me, 'We're going to write all night and we need a bedroom set tomorrow morning.' . . . I had a crew that worked many many nights all night long and all day just trying to keep up. We always did, though." One thing that was not

keeping up was the money. The constant changes and long overtime hours for the gangs of laborers and other workers were wreaking havoc with the budget, and early in April Selznick realized with a shock that he wouldn't have enough money to finish the picture. Still to come were some of the most expensive scenes, all of which would require thousands of extras, hundreds of workers, and another estimated million and a half dollars. To his rescue once again came the Whitneys, at least Jock and his sister Joan Payson, who advanced some of the money. The balance was to have come from C. V. Whitney, but evidently C. V. declined, for Selznick was forced to turn to MGM for the money, showing Al Lichtman about an hour's worth of completed footage. Lichtman was enthusiastic at what he saw, jubilantly predicting: "This picture will gross nineteen million dollars." He took Selznick's request for more funds back to Mayer, who passed the buck to Nicholas Schenck, knowing that he would turn it down. It was a squeeze play of the most naked kind, for if Selznick could not raise the money, the picture would by default fall into MGM's lap. Not quite stumped, Selznick played his last trump card: Attilio Giannini of the Bank of America. A screening was arranged for him and for Joseph Rosenberg, who was in charge of motion picture loans for the bank. They too were impressed, but bankers can be impressed without being fiscally foolish. All of Selznick International's books were examined and the deficits on the last three pictures stuck out like red flags. Selznick and *Gone With The Wind* were bad risks. The only way the bank would advance the money was if it were guaranteed by the Whitneys. But in order to get the guarantee, Selznick had to give up a portion of his ownership of the company and of his share in the proceeds of *Gone With The Wind*. A straight bank loan of $1.25 million was advanced and the production continued on its seemingly interminable way, safe now from the rapacity of Nick Schenck and MGM.

As soon as the money came through, Selznick gave orders to Klune to schedule the bulk of the spectacular exterior scenes, starting with the panic-stricken populace fleeing Atlanta. The evacuation sequences were scheduled for two days' grueling shooting on April 5 and 6, involving six hundred extras dressed in period costume, carrying every conceivable kind of prop as they struggled to get out of the city while Sherman's army bombarded it. This mass of humanity, animals, props, and explosives had to be carefully organized, not just from the standpoint of the camera but also for the most efficient manner of handling the mobs of extras, getting them costumed, onto the set, and into their places, re-

April 4, 1939—For three days, in 80-degree heat, Vivien Leigh dodged and darted her way through four hundred extras and twenty pieces of horse-drawn equipment, filming the panic-stricken populace fleeing Atlanta.

hearsing their movements, and coordinating the simultaneous levels of action. This last was all-important, for as Lydia Schiller recalls,

> Because she was the center of so much of the action, we couldn't use a stunt double for Vivien Leigh. In the scene where she comes out of the hospital and sees the city going mad, she really took chances. . . . When the army was moving out and there was chaos . . . she ran in between those caissons, they were going at full speed . . . and anything could have happened. . . . There were so many narrow escapes for her. . . . I remember once she was trying to get out of the way of a speeding fire wagon and she ran smack into the path of another wagon coming in from the opposite direction. . . . She just froze, stopped dead in her tracks, and fortunately her hoop skirt flared up and frightened the horses; they reared back and stopped. . . . She took it all in stride, she was a real trouper.

The stress on the actress was not all physical. Her emotional involvement with Olivier led to one particular outburst that helped the scenes she was working in. "Laurence Olivier was leaving to go back East to do a play," says Schiller, "and she wanted to go to the airport to see him off. . . . But Mr. Selznick wouldn't let her go . . . he said it would cost too much . . . so she came in and she'd evidently been crying all night, her eyes were all red and swollen and we wondered if we'd be able to photograph her. So Mr. Selznick scheduled a crying scene for her . . . one right after the death of her first husband, when she's complaining about having to wear widow's weeds, and she threw herself on the bed and sobbed and sobbed. . . . Those were real tears."

Leigh was not the only one who was near cracking up. "We were there working our asses off for fourteen to eighteen hours a day for almost six months," recalls Ridgeway Callow. Selznick himself was going at a killing pace, being fed thyroid extract and Benzedrine to maintain his energy while he worked on the script for the remaining sequences and also on the cutting of the already filmed footage with Hal Kern. Sandwiched in between were conferences on sets and costumes still to come, looking at actors for the small roles, and overseeing the special effects shots that Jack Cosgrove was working on. These were particularly important. They were more time-consuming than anything else in the picture and more critical in terms of the exacting demands not only on Cosgrove but also on his equipment. Cosgrove's technique involved painting with oils on panes of glass 3 to 4 feet wide. "Jack was the

greatest man in the business for these paintings," recalls Hal Kern, "but he was also a pretty heavy drinker. It never affected his work, but I'd go into his workshop and he'd be up on this little platform with no railings, he'd hold on with one hand and he'd be painting with the other, hanging out over twelve feet of nothing and so drunk he didn't even know his own name. . . . Then he'd climb down and maybe fall the last foot or so and go look through the camera finder to see how the match was, and then he'd climb back up there and do it all over again. I was always amazed that he never fell and broke his neck."

One of the shots posed a completely baffling set of problems for Cosgrove. It was the first large "pullback" in the picture, showing Scarlett and her father in silhouette under a tree looking out over Tara nestled in the rolling hills of Georgia, backdropped by a flaming sunset sky. The problem arose from trying to blend the four pieces of film, all of which had been photographed at separate times, combining the live action, two different paintings, and the sunset effect. Cosgrove was going crazy trying to compute the speed of the three separate camera moves necessary to keep the pullback effect in synchronization. Finally, Ray Klune called in the mathematics department at UCLA and they figured it out, using advanced calculus.

On the sets, Vivien Leigh and Fleming were at loggerheads over the interpretation of her role; she was trying to stay as close as possible to the Cukor interpretation, while Fleming wanted her to play Scarlett tougher, making her, in Leigh's opinion, "much more of a bitch," with a consequent loss of sympathy and believability. Leigh, with no one's knowledge, was visiting Cukor on the Sundays she had off to get his help in keeping her perspective about the part, something she later discovered was also being done by Olivia de Havilland, so Cukor managed to keep his finger in the picture even in its advanced stages. Because of the fragmentary nature of the script, Leigh had begun to carry a copy of the book with her everywhere, consulting it before she did a scene to make sure of her bearings and to ascertain that nothing was left out or changed that she felt was important. Selznick began to be irritated by her insistence on consulting the book, yelling at her on several occasions to "please put that damn book away." The tension was beginning to tell on Fleming, who had been working at full steam, nonstop, for well over a year. In mid-April Selznick, alarmed, wrote to Henry Ginsberg:

We may soon have a serious worry to face . . . that may again halt

This portrait of Clark Gable and Vivien Leigh as Rhett Butler and Scarlett O'Hara was taken by Fred Parrish using the Kodachrome process. *Gone With The Wind* was one of the first productions to use color photographs extensively for publicity purposes.

278

The city of Atlanta was re-created relatively faithfully from photos and drawings supplied by Wilbur Kurtz. The train station (above, left) was built practically full scale on the back lot from blueprints of the original. This shot of troop trains arriving at Christmas was doctored by Jack Cosgrove, who added the sky and mist in the upper right-hand section of the set; he also added the smoke emerging from the stack of the engine. Only the portion of the engine seen in the shot was actually built; the side not visible to the camera was made of wooden struts and wheels mounted on a dolly. (Above) The populace of the city waiting in front of the *Examiner* office "while two nations came to death grips on the farm lands of Pennsylvania" was a split-screen shot by Cosgrove, who doubled the number of people visible by photographing two hundred extras on one side of the wagon and carriage and then having them change their costumes and stand on the opposite side, giving the impression of the square being jammed with hundreds of people. (Left) No trickery was involved in this shot of the populace fleeing the city as Sherman begins his bombardment. Six hundred extras were used in these sequences, which took three days to film.

production.... I have ... been worried that Fleming would not be able to finish the picture because of his physical condition.... He is so near the breaking point, both physically and mentally from sheer exhaustion, that it would be a miracle in my opinion if he is able to shoot another seven or eight weeks.... Since it would be impossible for any substitute director to step in without taking the time to thoroughly familiarize himself with the book and the scripts, I think we ought to start now selecting an understudy....

While Selznick kept a wary eye on Fleming's health, he decided to break the picture up into three units, one under Fleming, concentrating on the principals, and two second units, one of which, under director Chester Franklin, went to Chico, 100 miles outside of Sacramento, to get the shots of Gerald O'Hara galloping his horse across the fields of Tara, and also to photograph the background shots of Tara devastated after the war. The other unit, under travelogue director James ("as the sun sets in the West") Fitzpatrick, had been dispatched on a three-week tour of five Southern states to obtain atmospheric footage for the titles, montages, and other photographic backgrounds. In addition, William Cameron Menzies, working with Cosgrove at the studio, was occupied filming all the bridging sections, bits and pieces of action, beginnings and endings of sequences, and tying up the photographic and special effects loose ends, while simultaneously laying out and preparing to shoot the still-pending battle scenes.

The breaking point Selznick had predicted for Fleming was finally reached just as he was wrapping a delicate and time-consuming two days' shooting on Melanie's death sequence. Ironically it came when Gable refused to do a sequence in which Rhett Butler cries in Melanie's lap at Scarlett's near death from a miscarriage. Gable was embarrassed, believing that it was "unmanly" to cry; he was adamant, and no amount of persuasion from Fleming could change his mind. Gable left the set at 11:30 A.M., finished for the day, but Fleming's work was just beginning. There was a late night call for a scene between Scarlett, Melanie, and Belle Watling, making her first appearance in the story. It had been planned as an exterior night shot on the back lot set of the Atlanta street. Fleming, still upset at Gable's intransigence, was in no mood for any back talk from other cast members, and when Vivien Leigh made the mistake of arguing with him yet again, Fleming's temper gave way. According to John Lee Mahin, who was on the set, "Vic rolled up his script, threw it at her, and said, 'You can shove this up your royal British ass,'" and stormed off the set. He later confided to Mahin that on his way home to Malibu, he had seriously considered driving his car off one of the Palisades cliffs.

Selznick had not been unprepared for such a development, and when it became clear that Fleming would not return for that night's shooting, he hastily borrowed Sam Wood from MGM. Aided by Menzies, who took care of the set-ups, and armed by Selznick with a detailed description of what the scene should be, Wood began filming the scene at 1:00 A.M. "It was freezing cold that night," recalls Ridgeway Callow, "and every time that Ona Munson as Belle Watling walked over to get into her

"Scarlett O'Hara was not beautiful . . ." wrote Miss Mitchell in the opening sentence of the novel, but David Selznick obviously disagreed, as evidenced by these shots of Vivien Leigh from the film showing the many faces of Scarlett O'Hara, from the opening scene with the sixteen-year-old beauty on the steps of Tara (photographed by Hal Rosson), through war, marriage, poverty, Reconstruction, birth, death, attempted rape, miscarriage, and lost love, until the final image of the tear-stained face of the twenty-eight-year-old Scarlett, who refuses to acknowledge defeat in Rhett's rejection of her, vowing to return to Tara and to "think of some way to get him back. After all, tomorrow is another day."

Clark Gable was the quintessence of the American male movie star. Thirty-eight years old in 1939, he was at the height of his physical appeal, and *Gone With The Wind* marked the apex of his career as a sex object. He was more than a match for Scarlett O'Hara in that department—if not in the final outcome of the battle of the sexes.

May 4, 1939—Director Sam Wood, who had just finished filming *Goodbye, Mr. Chips* in England, took over on *Gone With The Wind* during Victor Fleming's "sickness." He is seen here with Leslie Howard, Vivien Leigh, and a distinguished visitor to the set: Al Smith, former governor of New York and almost president of the United States. (Middle) Susan Myrick (in riding breeches), a friend of Margaret Mitchell's and a forthright, intelligent lady, was brought in from Atlanta to oversee the accuracy of Southern customs and speech in the film and was the final arbiter in all matters pertaining to Southern decorum and manners. (Bottom) The pressure on Vivien Leigh was tremendous. Working six days a week from 7:00 A.M. sometimes until midnight, the actress appeared in almost every one of the picture's ninety sequences. Here she is getting a massage from Isabel Jewell, who played Emmy Slattery, daughter of poor white trash, who was indirectly responsible for the death of Scarlett's mother.

carriage, the horses would decide to take a leak. They must have done it fourteen times, until their bladders finally ran out and we were able to get a good take." They shot till 4:00 A.M., then were back on the set at 9:30 A.M., and Wood directed the shots of a haggard Scarlett, determined to make herself attractive to Rhett Butler, having Mammy make a dress from the green velvet curtains in the Tara parlor.

Wood was a competent, stolid director who could be counted on to put the actors through their paces efficiently and unimaginatively. By now, the performers were well into their roles, so Wood's job was more or less that of a traffic manager. The production began to take on a subdued, clenched-teeth quality, as everybody involved determined to plow through the remaining necessary scenes. But Wood lacked the driving force, the narrative emphasis, and the strong visual storytelling sense that Fleming had brought to the production. Accordingly, Selznick began a concerted campaign to woo Fleming back to work, offering him a share in the profits, to which Fleming is reported to have replied: "What do you think I am, a chump? This picture is going to be the biggest white elephant of all time," a sentiment that did not deter Selznick at all. He enlisted the aid of Gable and Vivien Leigh, and the three of them turned up one Sunday in late April at Fleming's beach home, bearing a large cage of love birds. Leigh was appropriately apologetic, Gable persuasively contrite, and Selznick convincing not only in his concern for Fleming's health but also in his proclamations of how much the picture needed his gifts. After a two-week rest, Fleming returned, Selznick having agreed to keep Wood working as an alternate first unit.

Fleming's first day back had him overseeing the first of five separate attempts to get a dramatic dawn shot of Scarlett's vow in the field of Tara to "never be hungry again." Selznick wanted this to be an affirmation of her indomitability, and her transformation from pampered spoiled child to a mature, determined woman, and it had to be thrilling enough to close the first half of the picture on a highly inspirational note. The scene was scheduled to be filmed on the barren ranchlands called Lasky Mesa near Agoura, several hours from the studio in the San Fernando Valley. To be ready at dawn, the cast and crew had to leave the studio at 1:00 A.M. "We did this several times," recalls Ray Klune,

> because each time David didn't like something about it, either the pullback or the sky or something wasn't right. Vivien and I were not on good terms when we were up there. She hated location. She had to get up so early in the morning, and we'd get out there and sometimes the sun wouldn't come out, it would be all fogged up and a couple of the trips were a waste of time. But then we finally got a good one. It was after an all-night rain, we drove out there and it was pouring and she cursed me out, but the weather prediction had indicated that it would stop before dawn and I knew if it did it would be a beautiful sunrise. Vic thought I was crazy and they were both cursing the hell out of me. But the rain stopped, and even though we were all covered with mud, we got the most wonderful shot. And later she said to me, "Ray, you were right, and I was a bitch," and I said to her, "You're right on both counts."

Klune was now immersed in preparations for the last major production problem in the picture, that of Scarlett's search for Dr. Meade among the wounded and dying soldiers surrounding the Atlanta railroad station. In the book, Margaret Mitchell had used one vivid paragraph to describe Scarlett's reaction to the sight of hundreds of men "lying in the pitiless sun, shoulder to shoulder, head to feet . . . lining the tracks, the sidewalks, stretched out in endless rows under the car shed. Some lay stiff

A harassed Victor Fleming, back at work after two weeks' rest, instructs a tense Vivien Leigh on the dramatic necessities of the scene at hand: Scarlett's search for Dr. Meade among the 1,600 dead and dying Confederate soldiers lying in the Atlanta railroad yards.

(Overleaf) A rehearsal for the massive pullback shot of the Confederate wounded lying in front of the Atlanta train station. A 60-foot construction crane was used to hold the camera, and a special concrete ramp was built for it. On the camera platform are Fleming, cameraman Ernest Haller, and his assistant, Arthur Arling. In addition to eight hundred extras, the scene was populated with eight hundred dummies, who were rocked back and forth by live actors discreetly camouflaging the fraud.

The dramatic high point of Clark Gable's performance in *Gone With The Wind* was this scene of Rhett Butler crying in Melanie's lap over Scarlett's near death from her miscarriage. Rugged leading men, especially romantic heroes, did not cry on screen in the 1930s and forties, and Gable's reluctance to do so was as much from fear of the damage to his image as from his own insecurities as an actor.

and still, but many writhed under the hot sun moaning. Everywhere, swarms of flies hovered over the men . . . everywhere was blood . . . groans, screamed curses of pain. The smell of sweat . . . of unwashed bodies, of excrement rose up in waves of blistering heat until the fetid stench almost nauseated her." Selznick wanted this scene to open on a close-up of Scarlett's horrified reaction to what she sees, then have the camera slowly pull back and up, revealing more and more, literally hundreds of wounded and dying men, with the camera finally coming to a stop on a close-up of the tattered Confederate flag waving over the entire scene. "There was no camera crane large enough to get the kind of a shot David wanted," recalled Klune.

I think that the biggest camera crane in town could only get twenty-five feet off the ground, and we estimated that to take in the expanse of scene that was pictured in the sketches, the camera would have to be about ninety feet off the ground at its highest point. So we found a company that operated the largest construction cranes in southern California, and we got one of their men out to the studio. I showed him the back lot and the scene and explained the problem to him, and he said that they could find us a crane that had an extension range of one hundred and twenty-five feet. Now the problem there is that a camera crane is a precision instrument, whereas a construction crane is anything but. . . . We found that it shook at the very beginning of the movement and at the very end, and as the truck that it was mounted on went into gear and pulled back. The arm itself was pretty smooth during its up and back extension. It was then that I came up with an idea that eliminated the need to use the engine, which was what caused the vibration. We built a concrete ramp about one hundred and fifty feet long—it had to support a piece of steel that weighed ten tons—and these were the days before fast-drying concrete and we couldn't put the damn crane on the ramp for two weeks, but when we finally did, we rehearsed it and the crane slid back down the ramp as smooth as glass while the arm raised and it worked out very smoothly.

Now that the mechanical aspects had been worked out, the sequence needed to be populated with what Klune estimated to be almost two thousand extras, which was just about all that Central Casting had on file. Casting calls usually went out to extras the night before they were needed, and there were several large-scale pictures in production at the same time. "We prepared far enough in advance, we thought," Klune said, " but Central Casting told us the most they could promise us for the next few weeks was about eight hundred people. So we decided to use the eight hundred and intersperse dummies among them, and that'd save us a lot of money. The Screen Extras Guild made a big fuss about it and tried to get us to pay for the eight hundred dummies, and I said, 'No, not one cent,' and they raised all sorts of hell, but we held firm on it and said if you can supply us with real people, we'll pay, otherwise we'll use the dummies. Well, they were only able to come up with a little over eight hundred and that killed the case completely. . . . We never heard another word about it."

Selznick now took on the task of trying to convince Gable to cry in the scene of Rhett's remorse over Scarlett's miscarriage. He was helped in this by Carole Lombard, who persuaded her dubious husband that there was nothing unmanly about an actor crying, that it would be a memorable scene, pointing out that he knew all along he was going to have to do it and couldn't back out now. Selznick relates that "Clark was violently opposed to this and said that nothing was more contemptible than self-pity, that he just could not see himself weeping over this situation. I argued with him and told him that the most universally felt emotion in the world is self-pity, that we all felt sorry for ourselves at one time or another . . . that this would bring public identity with the feeling that he too was vulnerable." Fleming diplomatically offered to film the scene with tears and without, and let Gable decide which one to use. Helped considerably by the design and mood of the scene, a blue-tinged rain-washed night, and by the sympathetic playing of Olivia de Havilland, Gable—under Fleming's sensitive handling—managed to reveal some of the inner torments of Rhett Butler, who up to that point in the film had largely been a charming, superficial cipher. After seeing the rushes, Gable reluctantly agreed that the weeping version was the better of the two, and okayed the use of it in the picture.

This was one of six color photographs taken on the sets of *Gone With The Wind* by a photographer for *House & Garden* magazine. According to Lyle Wheeler, the wallpaper in this shot was the only contribution of Joseph Platt, who is credited with the interiors. Platt, the interior decoration consultant for *House & Garden,* received much publicity in the magazine as the designer for all the film's interiors, something that infuriated Wheeler and Selznick, who immediately put a stop to it.

Olivia de Havilland as Melanie Wilkes in a studio portrait by Fred Parrish.

Leslie Howard as Ashley Wilkes in a studio portrait by Fred Parrish.

The intertwining and complex relationships among Scarlett, Ashley, and Melanie described in the novel were not changed at all in the film. Scarlett loves Ashley, who loves Melanie, who loves Scarlett, who despises Melanie. Scarlett's attitude toward Melanie softens later, for she stays through the siege of Atlanta to help Melanie have Ashley's child and then nurses her back to health at Tara. Scarlett's reluctant admiration for Melanie grows after Melanie helps Scarlett bury the marauding Yankee soldier Scarlett has killed, and on Melanie's deathbed, Scarlett finally sees that Melanie has always been her best friend—and the kind of great lady that Scarlett had wanted to be. Scarlett also realizes that she never really loved Ashley and that she in fact loves Rhett. But it's too late: Melanie dies, Rhett leaves, and Scarlett is left with nothing but Tara and a helpless Ashley, clinging to her skirts and sobbing.

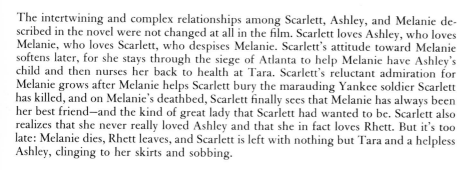

The love scenes between Scarlett and Rhett crackle with a sexual electricity that gives the picture a vibrancy that is one of its main attractions. It begins with their first stormy meeting in the library at Twelve Oaks and intensifies at the Atlanta bazaar (top, left), when Rhett shocks the Confederacy by bidding $100 ("in gold") to dance with the newly widowed Mrs. Hamilton, and Scarlett scandalizes the town by accepting. Their on-again, off-again romance differs slightly from Miss Mitchell's account in that in the film Rhett tells Scarlett several times that he loves her—something he doesn't do in the book until the end. He does try to convince her that "we belong together, being the same sort," and after they finally marry, she taunts him with the fact that "I shall always love another man," whereupon he does the only thing a frustrated husband could do—carries her up the stairs for a night of forced passion. Their scenes have an erotic tension and frankness daring for the time, especially in a costume picture, where everyone usually behaved with decorum and good manners.

Film editor Hal Kern (center) is bent over a Movieola examining a sequence from *Gone With The Wind* with his associate, James Newcom (far left), while assistant film editors Richard van Enger and Ernest Leadly and an unidentified associate editor continue trying to reduce the 160,000 feet of printed film to its final 18,000-foot length.

Production had now been going on for five months; winter had given way to spring, and spring had quickly turned to a blistering summer as the five units struggled to finish up the bulk of the principal photography. On the stages, the heat was aggravated by the huge amounts of light needed for the Technicolor photography. The stages weren't air-conditioned and according to Klune, "It was just brutal. We had great big exhaust fans, but it was still hell." But the production was driving furiously toward the finish date, with Selznick urging everyone to realize that "it is going to take the combined efforts . . . of all of us . . . to speed up the rest of the picture. . . . Quite apart from the cost factor, everybody's nerves are getting on the ragged edge and God only knows what will happen if we don't get this damn thing finished." Finally, on June 27, the last scene was filmed under Fleming's direction. It was, oddly enough, practically the last scene in the picture, Rhett's farewell to Scarlett, and Selznick had revised and rewritten the sequence the night before, bringing the new pages down to the set personally, watching carefully while Fleming set up the shot and rehearsed Vivien Leigh as Scarlett tearfully inquired of Rhett: "If you go, where shall I go, what shall I do?" And he coolly looked at her and replied: "My dear, I don't give a damn." Just before the shot was taken, Selznick added the word "frankly" to the beginning of Rhett's last line, which gave it a kind of lilting, off-handed finality and promptly became as much of a classic catchphrase as Scarlett's "I'll think about it tomorrow." (As a precautionary measure, an alternate version was shot, using the phrase "I just don't care," and this was used at the previews.)

Later that afternoon, Selznick wired Jock Whitney: "Sound the siren. Scarlett O'Hara completed her performance at noon today. Gable finishes tonight or in the morning, and we will be shooting until Friday with bit people. I am going on the boat Friday night and you can all go to the devil." Five months and one day after it had started, *Gone With The Wind* was finished . . . almost.

Now began the arduous, exhausting task of sifting through the mass of filmed material in search of a finished picture. This took up all of July and August, with Selznick running the material over and over with Hal Kern, who recalls that "Selznick was very interested in editing; he truly believed that a picture could be ruined or made great in the editing. He would talk to me for hours about the pros and cons of doing something in a certain way; he wasn't sure why a person had to keep traveling in the same direction across a screen, if you cut away from them. He thought that the camera could just turn it around and that the audience would still be able to figure it out." These editing sessions with Kern would start early in the afternoon and go on for days.

Kern and his crew had made the first rough assemblage of footage early in July, and found that what with numerous takes and angles of the same scenes, the picture ran almost six hours. All through the sweltering months of summer the editors, Selznick, Barbara Keon, and Lydia Schiller ran the material over and over again. "Every day, it would get a little shorter," recalls Lydia Schiller. "They would make the changes. Mr. Selznick would say, 'Let's not use that shot—let's go to a close-up here.' It just went on forever. We'd be making copious notes so that the cutters could work on these sequences in the morning. Then we'd get them back and he'd want to change this, take that out, put that in, calling for an alternate take or another angle. Then our next session in the projection room he would look at that version and see if he liked it. . . . We worked this way night after night, paring, changing—the night would just disappear—the work was so intense. Bobbie Keon and I would trade off and spell each other, but Mr. Selznick and Hal were at it nonstop, once I think for almost forty-eight hours."

One of the most troublesome sequences in the picture was the very ending of the story, for, as Selznick explained:

We found it impossible to get into script form even the hint that Scarlett might get Rhett back that is inferred in the book. In reaching for a satisfactory ending for motion picture purposes, we tried two or three ways . . . indicating something of the kind after she went back to Tara . . . but none of them worked . . . and I finally cooked up an ending of my own. . . . I felt that the one thing that was really open to us was to stress the Tara thought even more than Miss Mitchell did. . . . Accordingly, after Rhett leaves Scarlett, she turns from the door sobbing, "I can't let him go . . . what is there to do . . . what is there that matters?" Suddenly we hear the ghostlike voice of Gerald saying, "Land's the only thing that matters, it's the only thing that lasts. . . ." Then Ashley's voice saying: "Something you love better than me, though you may not know it. Tara." Then Rhett's voice: "It's this from which you get your strength, the red earth of Tara." The last part of each speech is repeated in turn with increasing tempo and volume . . . during this Scarlett has been emerging from her despair . . . reacting to the realization that she still has Tara . . . and as the camera moves in to a big closeup of her she says, "Home . . . I'll go home . . . and I'll think of some way to get him back. After all, tomorrow is another day." We immediately dissolve to Scarlett standing at Tara in silhouette, the camera pulls back just as it did on Gerald and Scarlett to an extreme long shot as we come to our end. . . . This seemed to give the picture a tremendous lift at the end where it was necessary and where, without something of the kind, we might have ended on a terrifically depressing note.

Working furiously, Selznick and Kern managed to get the film down to five hours by late July. But by that time the cutting continuity was so mangled with cuts, additions, and replacements that neither Selznick, nor Kern, nor any of the editors could make head or tail of it. So Lydia Schiller was assigned to sit down at a Movieola with the cut footage and construct a shot-by-shot description of what had been edited. "I worked on that for about two weeks," she recalls. "I can't remember exactly, it was all such a blur." After she had put it together, the two men spent another hectic month paring the footage down further. While working on the editing, Selznick was also obsessed with the idea of giving the picture a beginning that would live up to the subject, something that would evoke the grandeur and the majesty of the title. He told Hal Kern, "I want the biggest main title that has ever been made." So Kern went off to Pacific Title, the lettering company that specialized in trailers and other kinds of graphic design, and told them he "wanted the letter 'G' to come on and fill the screen, then the same with 'O,' and so on, until each letter had swept across individually. But we found out that the proportion was all wrong, so finally they came up with each of the words individually sweeping across; it took away a little from my first thought, but it was still very impressive, and David loved it when he saw it." To film it, a special dolly had to be borrowed from MGM. It took three men to operate as it moved across the four plate-glass sheets on which the lettering had been hand-painted.

By September 9, Selznick decided that the picture was ready for its first preview, the planning of which he left to Hal Kern, cautioning him not to let anyone know where and when it would take place.

I said to him, "David, the only person who tells about a preview is you, you're always telling all your friends." So I told him that if he didn't know where it was going to be, then he couldn't tell anybody. I told him to tell his secretary that he didn't feel well, that he was going home, and to get in his car, that the chauffeur would know where he was going but David wouldn't. He could make one stop to pick up Mrs. Selznick and Jock Whitney, and that was it. Meanwhile I had taken all the film in a car up to Riverside. . . . I had previewed up there quite a long time and had a couple of good friends who managed the big theatres. . . . So we drove up to the Golden State Theatre, and I looked in and they were playing a Richard Dix picture called *Man of Conquest* and they didn't have more than two hundred people in the place. So then we walked over to the Riverside; they were playing *Beau Geste* and had a full house. . . .

When the picture had ended, the manager stood up in front of the audience and told them there was going to be an unannounced preview, that it was going to be one of the biggest pictures of the year, and that it ran over four hours. He didn't tell them the title; in case anybody left, I didn't want them blabbing. Once some people had gone, I closed the theatre, wouldn't let anybody make phone calls or come back in after they'd left. The manager said, "This is against the law, I can't do it," so I told him I'd do it for him. I'd got hold of the local police department and had cops on every door so that nobody could come in. The manager says, "Hal, I gotta call my wife; she'll kill me if I don't let her know," so I said, "Okay, but I'm going to stand right by the phone and you tell her nothing except to come right over." Which he did. . . .

By this time the Selznicks had arrived with Whitney, and we made one more announcement that once the picture had started nobody would be allowed to make any phone calls, and that if they left, they wouldn't be allowed back in. So then the lights went down and I was sitting next to David and Mrs. Selznick, and when the curtains opened and Margaret Mitchell's name came on the screen, there was this silence for just a second and then the audience started applauding, and when the title came on and swept across the screen, why I never heard such a sound in my life. . . . The people stood up and cheered and screamed. . . . I had the remote control sound mechanism next to me and I had to turn it up full blast just so you could hear the music. Mrs. Selznick and Jock Whitney started crying like babies and so did David . . . and so did I. Oh, what a thrill it was . . . it was just thunderous, that ovation, and they just wouldn't stop. . . . To this day I still get chills when I remember it. The picture ran four hours and twenty-five minutes, and at the end, the ovation started all over again.

The preview cards unanimously and enthusiastically praised everything about the picture; the phrase that most often leapt out was the cliché "the greatest picture I've ever seen." Selznick carefully tabulated the results of these cards and on the basis of the negative reaction to the question, "Do you think any battle scenes should be added to the picture, or any fuller portrayal of the Civil War, its causes and development?" he jettisoned plans for the filming of these scenes, and decided with much relief that few or no additional scenes would be needed. About his "cooked-up" ending, Selznick remarked that "I tried this out with considerable trepidation, but to my delighted surprise . . . apparently there is no thought in the minds of anyone that this is not exactly faithful to the book, in spirit at least, even though it isn't one hundred percent book material as is true with so much of the picture. . . . Also to my great pleasure, not one preview card mentioned that they wanted to see Rhett and Scarlett together again. I think they still hope they will get together, but it leaves them something to discuss, just as the end of the book did."

For the next month, Selznick and Hal Kern, joined occasionally by Victor Fleming, tried to squeeze another hour out of the picture. They did this by removing a section showing the O'Hara family on their way to the Twelve Oaks barbecue, with Scarlett and her sisters arguing and Mammy scolding them; the dialogue from this was used in a retaken scene showing the girls at the barbecue getting ready for their afternoon naps. Also deleted was a scene showing Twelve Oaks and its guests and servants slumbering after the barbecue; and Scarlett's wedding night with Charles Hamilton, which she made him spend in a chair. The sequences showing the evacuation of Atlanta and the scenes in the hospital were all considerably shortened, as was Scarlett's search for Dr. Meade at the railway station, including her encounter with John Wilkes, Ashley's father, who dies in her arms as she tells him of his impending grandchild. Also cut was a scene of Belle Watling nursing the wounded soldiers, which was not in the novel. A conversation between Scarlett's two sisters was removed in which they discuss what the South will be like after the war with all the best men dead and no one to marry Southern girls. Also deleted was a sequence showing Belle Watling and her "girls" testifying at the inquest into Frank Kennedy's death, and a sequence between Bonnie and Scarlett the morning after Rhett's "rape."

By the second week of October, the combined efforts of the three men and a crew of assistant editors and secretaries had reduced the picture to just under four hours. While Selznick and Kern tinkered with this, Fleming directed three days of retakes and added scenes, tempting fate by directing still another version of the opening scene on Friday, October 13. This time Vivien Leigh, fresh and rested from a two-month vacation, was dressed in the high-necked white gown she wore in the later evening prayer scene, since Selznick felt that it gave her more of a virginal sixteen-year-old quality than did the original green-sprigged muslin dress. The scene went smoothly and quickly. Five days later, Hal Kern called the manager of the Arlington Theatre in Santa Barbara asking him if he could bring up *Intermezzo* to preview. The theatre had just opened *What a Life*, the picture that introduced teenager Henry Aldrich to moviegoers; it was playing with *Charlie Chan at Treasure Island*, and

Some striking examples of Jack Cosgrove's special effects work on *Gone With The Wind.* (Top, left) The shot of Scarlett and her father looking out over the fields of Tara was a combination of two matte paintings of the house and sky, a separately filmed black-and-white silhouette of the two figures, and a third matte painting of the tree. (Top, right) This view of Tara at night was done using one of the miniature models of the plantation, with the sky and surrounding trees added through matte painting. The carriage going up the drive is a miniature, photographed separately and printed onto the final composite shot. (Above) This long shot of Atlanta was a combination of the actual back lot set with the larger vista of Atlanta added through a matte painting done from sketches supplied by Wilbur Kurtz. (Above, right) Scarlett's search for Dr. Meade had her climbing over piles of rubble, with the top of the ruined building added by matte painting; the whole scene was overlaid with wisps of smoke, which were added separately. (Right) Scarlett's trek through the war-torn countryside on her way back to Tara was a combination of three different pieces of film: the wagon with its occupants was filmed on the back lot, the countryside and the clouds was a Cosgrove painting, and the rainbow was a background projection that jiggled a bit.

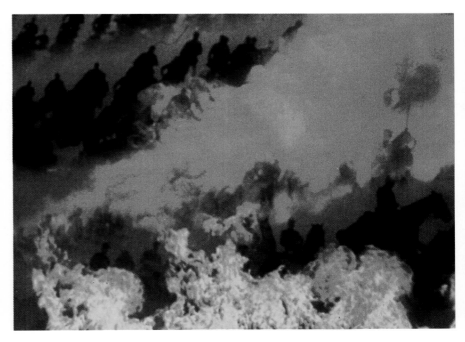

(Top, left) This shot of Atlanta during the fire was achieved by lighting the actual back lot set with red-orange reflectors and smoke pots, while the rear of the scene showing the fire over the tops of the buildings was added by Cosgrove, using process plates projected onto a miniature screen set up behind the foreground screen, on which he projected the previously filmed Atlanta street footage. The two screens were then re-photographed simultaneously using a specially adapted Technicolor camera. (Top, right) This shot of the battlefield was a combination of five separate pieces of film: the wagon and its occupants was filmed separately; the curling black smoke was another piece; the foreground and left side of the frame, with the dead soldiers, was a Cosgrove painting; the overturned canvas wagon was a separate miniature; and the sky was another painting. (Above, left) Three separate shots were necessary for this scene: the burned-out building on the left was a painting, as was the sky and some of the foreground; the water and the wagon were real, photographed separately and added later. (Above) The only special effects shot in the picture not done by Cosgrove was this swirling montage of Sherman's troops marching through Georgia, which opened the second half of the film. As production neared completion, time was running short, and Cosgrove's work load was fierce, so Hal Kern took some unused battle footage, some fire effects, and some Menzies sketches over to the MGM special effects department, where Peter Ballbusch combined them all and came up with this stunningly effective collage, which invariably drew applause when the picture was given its first press and industry screenings. (Left) Rhett and Scarlett's postwar Atlanta house was actually the entrance walk to the Selznick studio combined with a Cosgrove painting—all of which overawed Prissy and Pork, the house servants, standing with Mammy, who was not impressed: "Humph. 'Tain't quality," she sneers.

295

Gone With The Wind was innovative in many ways in the film industry: cost, length, fidelity to source, and especially the way it pushed the frontiers of Technicolor photography to their limits of excellence. With Selznick's enthusiastic encouragement, William Cameron Menzies constantly devised new visual approaches in the establishing of mood through the use of color, lighting, and composition, as seen in these five frames from the film. (Top, left) The O'Hara family at evening prayer, photographed by Lee Garmes and lit by flickering candles, which gave the scene a hushed, churchlike quality. (Top, right) Selznick originally felt that Menzies had gone too far in his theatricalism in this red-orange-drenched shot of Rhett's farewell to Scarlett on the McDonough Road. Selznick ordered it re-taken, but Fleming, Menzies, and Wheeler convinced him to keep it in the film. (Above) The green teapot, symbol of gossipy, jealous old ladies, dominates the scene in which Mrs. Meade and Mrs. Merriwether (Leona Roberts and Jane Darwell), the town dowagers, cluck disapprovingly over Scarlett's postwar conduct. (Above, right) Ernest Haller shot the delicately lit dawn scenes of Scarlett and her father in the study at Tara, when she first discovers her father has lost his mind—one of the most poignant moments in the film. (Right) Rhett proposes to Scarlett in Aunt Pittypat's parlor as the late-afternoon sun suffuses the room with a golden autumnal glow. These shots were photographed by Ernest Haller and Ray Rennahan, both of whom won Academy Awards for their work on the film. There was no precedent for what Menzies had done on *Gone With The Wind,* so in order to give him an appropriate credit, Selznick and Lyle Wheeler together devised the title of production designer. For his "outstanding achievement in the use of color for the enhancement of dramatic mood," Menzies was awarded a special plaque by the Academy of Motion Picture Arts and Sciences.

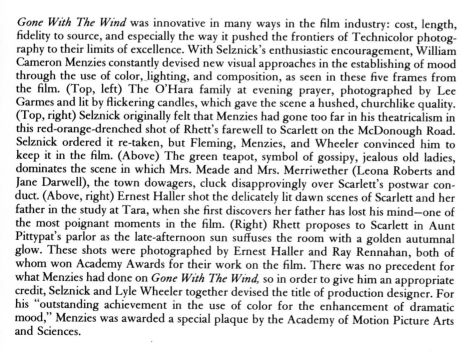

Margaret Mitchell was reportedly unhappy with Ben Hecht's foreword to the film, which described the Old South as a "land of Cavaliers and cotton fields . . . of Knights and their Ladies Fair, of Master and of Slave. . . ." "I certainly had no intention of writing about cavaliers," she wrote to a friend, feeling that the lines gave a distorted, romantic view of her book. But Selznick's concept of the story was extremely romantic, a larger-than-life depiction of a doomed civilization. These five frames from the film give a good idea of his picture-postcard approach to the idealization of the Old South, including this shot (top, right) of the Mississippi riverboat that carries Rhett and Scarlett to their honeymoon in New Orleans. The boat is a miniature printed onto footage of the river left over from *The Adventures of Tom Sawyer.* The scenes of the barbecue at Twelve Oaks (above, left) and the Atlanta bazaar (above) were the most outstanding pictorial representations of what Miss Mitchell described as a way of life that had "a glamour to it, a perfection, a symmetry like Grecian art." The barbecue was photographed at the old Busch Gardens in Pasadena, soon after converted into an Army training facility. The sequence of the wartime bazaar in the Atlanta Armory was re-done twice at Selznick's insistence: it was re-shot by Victor Fleming after Cukor's departure and the arrival of a new script (and also to eliminate Clark Gable's bogus Southern accent), then re-shot again because Selznick was dissatisfied with Jack Cosgrove's matte painting of the top of the set, which he felt made the whole thing reminiscent of an Italian wedding. (Left) The death throes of the Old South were represented vividly in this classic scene of the Confederate battle flag waving bravely over the remnants of the Army in the last, gray days of the Lost Cause.

Max Steiner (right) goes over a music sheet for *Gone With The Wind* with Lou Forbes, head of the Selznick music department and brother of Leo Forbstein, head of the Warner Bros. music department, from which Steiner was borrowed to work on the film. At the same time that he was composing for *Gone With The Wind*, Steiner was also writing the score for Warner Bros.' *Four Daughters*—and working twenty hours a day trying to finish them both. His doctor was giving him daily injections of thyroid extract and vitamin B-12 shots. With all that, Steiner almost didn't compose the score, as he kept telling Selznick that he couldn't meet the deadline. Selznick was used to hearing that from Steiner, but to ensure that the work would be done, he let it be known that he was thinking of replacing Steiner with Herbert Stothart, the head of the MGM music department. Word of this reached Steiner, who was properly furious, as Selznick knew he would be, and Steiner redoubled his efforts, composing almost all of the three hours and fifteen minutes of music that the picture needed. One of his orchestrators, Hugo Friedhofer, was pressed into service to write the music for the escape from burning Atlanta, while two fragments from Franz Waxman's score for *The Young in Heart*, as well as an ominous bit of music by David Axt from *David Copperfield*, were used for the scene in which Melanie knocks on the door of Bonnie's death chamber. Steiner's score mixes original compositions, folk tunes, and music of the Civil War period to give the film a sumptuous, romantic sound, interspersing it with slyly humorous comments on the action, as in the quotations from "Massa's in de Cold, Cold Ground" at the death of Scarlett's first two husbands.

Kern was counting on this family-oriented midweek change of bill to guarantee a decent house. "We took *Gone With The Wind* up there," recalls Kern, "and it wasn't put together yet, so it was twenty-four reels of picture and twenty-four reels of sound, and when we carried in this forty-eight reels the manager looked at me and said, 'Hal, you bastard, that's not *Intermezzo* you're bringing in here.' So I did the same thing we did at Riverside, locked the doors and all, and when the picture flashed on the screen, well, it was pandemonium all over again."

The trims and deletions from the first preview had left some scenes without beginnings and endings, while omissions had been bridged with temporary title cards. To smooth out all the rough spots and fill in the gaps, Selznick now put into the works a ten-day shooting schedule of additional scenes and still more retakes designed to fill in the missing linking sequences, and to photograph additional ones made necessary by deletions and Selznick's desire to enhance scenes that lacked dramatic punch. The most elaborate of these additions was a sequence designed to be cut into the trek to Tara, showing Scarlett, Melanie, and Prissy hiding under a bridge during a thunderstorm as a detachment of Yankee cavalry passes overhead. Adding to the filmed drama was a violent clash between Ray Klune and Victor Fleming over the methods of filming the scene. "Vic didn't want to shoot it," recalls Klune. "We were on the back lot, and it actually started to rain and he said it would make it impossible to shoot, that we wouldn't be able to light it properly. I said, 'Vic, we're here, it's supposed to be raining, we've spent the money, let's shoot the damned thing.' Well, he got so mad, he blew up and said, 'You do whatever these Jews want you to do, don't you?' And I said, 'You son of a bitch, if you feel that way, why do you take the money? I'm doing what I think is the right thing to do; I want you to shoot this scene, and if you want to bitch it up by shooting it badly, that's your prerogative, but I don't think you will.' "

Unbeknownst to Klune, Fleming's festering frustration with the whole *Gone With The Wind* production had been brought to a head earlier that day during a meeting with Selznick, who was trying to work out the screen credits. "I asked Vic Fleming," relates Selznick, "whether he would like to see us include a card crediting people who had contributed greatly to the picture ... George Cukor, among them ... Sam Wood ... who had a great many sequences in the picture.... My conversation with Vic on the subject literally didn't last thirty seconds.... He obviously, and no doubt understandably, wasn't happy about the idea, saying in so many words that he didn't think it was necessary to credit them on screen ... and without further discussion I immediately told him to forget about it, that as far as I was concerned it was a closed issue." Fleming, however, brooded over it and the incident began to assume the proportions of a major insult, especially after he saw the program that had been prepared by MGM under Howard Dietz's supervision. Dietz, in an effort to give Selznick as much credit as possible, had inserted a clause stating: "There were five directors on *Gone With The Wind*, all supervised personally by David Selznick." Fleming was enraged at this, assuming that it had been done at Selznick's insistence. No amount of persuasion or explanation by Dietz and Selznick could convince him otherwise, and the unintentional gaffe led to a breach between the two men, with Gable taking Fleming's side—his own reservations about Selznick being reinforced by what he considered to be a betrayal of his closest friend. The coolness between actor and producer turned frigid, with Carole Lombard, who genuinely liked Selznick, trying her best to reconcile them—to no avail.

Selznick was adult enough to be able to shrug off the disappointment of Gable's and Fleming's attitudes; besides, he had more important matters to worry about. One of the most worrisome of these was the Hays office's refusal to allow Rhett Butler's final line to contain the taboo word "damn." The word had not been heard on American screens since the adoption of the Code in 1933; prior to that, there had been several instances of mild profanity on screen, but the new puritanism of the rest of the decade had swept away curse words, nudity, double beds, and unpunished transgressions against the law of man and God. Selznick, however, took the bit between his teeth and, in a lengthy letter to Will Hays, argued persuasively:

The word as used in the picture ... is not an oath or a curse.... The worst that could be said for it is that it is a vulgarism, and it is so described in the Oxford English Dictionary.... Nor do I feel that in asking you to make an exception in this case ... this one sentence will open up the floodgates of [profanity]. I do believe, however, that if you were to permit our using this dramatic word in its rightfully dramatic place, it would establish a helpful precedent ... giving your office discretionary powers to allow the use of certain harmless oaths and ejaculations whenever they are ... not prejudicial to public morals. The omission of this line spoils the punch at the very end of the picture and on our very fade-out gives an impression of unfaithfulness after three hours and forty-five minutes of extreme fidelity to Miss Mitchell's work which has become ... an American Bible.

Selznick's arguments and, at his instigation, the urgings of several other industry leaders convinced Hays to overrule his own board of advisers. Upon payment of a $5000 fine for violation of a Code provision, the picture was allowed to go out equipped with both the "damn" and a Code seal, creating one more sensation in the industry.

The picture had been announced for a December 15 premiere in Atlanta, which was less than a month away, and there were still literally hundreds of production details that needed not only Selznick's constant attention but the staff's as well. Max Steiner poured himself into the completion of a score that equaled the picture's visual magnificence, composing leitmotifs for all the main characters, with a thundering, majestic keynote theme for Tara that leapt up the scale an octave and raised gooseflesh on everyone who heard it. For more than three hours his music sighed, wept, and soared its way through the story, as rich, colorful, and vivid as the Technicolor scenes themselves. Massed descending violins, echoing celeste, and fragrantly scented humming choruses lent an air of redolent nostalgia and evanescent romanticism to the picturization of a way of life that was, as Ben Hecht's title phrase described it, " ... a dream remembered; ... a civilization gone with the wind." Steiner's music for *Gone With The Wind* is one of the most superb scores ever written for any picture at any time, and countless hearings later, even apart from the film, it still has the ability to move and involve the listener. It is the summation and peak of the whole romantic movement in film scoring that Steiner himself had begun earlier in the decade with *Bird of Paradise* and *King Kong,* and it stands as a testament to his spirit as much as the picture itself does to Selznick's genius.

In the last month before the scheduled premiere in Atlanta, work was as intense as ever while everyone tried frantically to get the picture into its final form before Technicolor started making prints. "On the last weeks of *Gone With The Wind,*" relates Hal Kern, "I was working almost twenty hours a day. David just didn't want to let go of it and I would have to threaten him.... I'd say, 'David, unless you let me have this sequence to cut for the lab, we'll never make the premiere date.' I'd literally have to pull it out of his hands. I know just how he felt, though; there were at least three Cosgrove shots that I wish we'd had more time on, because they were the only things in the picture that weren't perfect."

Kern was dividing his time between the studio and the Technicolor laboratories, spending most of the days and nights at the lab, trying to get the color perfectly balanced and matched. Today this is done largely by computer, but in those days it was done by eye, by time-consuming trial and error. Kern recalls: "I told Technicolor, 'You call me at my house any time and I'll come over when you've got a scene ready.' They'd call me at three in the morning, and I'd go over and say, 'This scene is too red, take out some of the magenta, put some more yellow in here....' This went on and on.... David, who was near collapse himself, began to get very concerned about me and he wanted me to stop and rest. I told him I felt fine, that if I stopped or he stopped, we'd be another year getting the picture out, because there were things that we had to do that he wouldn't do unless he had a deadline."

If Kern was working himself to the limit of his endurance, Selznick, in an artificially stimulated state, had gone beyond him. By now he was existing on a steady diet of vitamin B-12 shots, thyroid extract, and Benzedrine, seeming to work more hours than there were in the day to prepare not only for the premiere but also the all-important press preview, now scheduled for December 12. "The man gave his life's blood on this," recalls Lydia Schiller. "He literally went gray trying to finish it in

time." The day before the preview Selznick was still making minor changes; at the last minute, he changed the punctuation of the foreword title, altering a semi-colon to a period in the line, "look for it only in books, for it is no more than a dream remembered. A civilization *Gone With The Wind.*"

As Technicolor frantically printed up this change and spliced it into the first finished print, 750 élite members of the local and national Hollywood press corps and their guests were filling the 1200 seats of the Four Star Theatre on Wilshire Boulevard for the first and one of the most important official screenings of the picture. Their reactions and what they would write about the film would determine to a large extent the attitude audiences would bring to it. The phenomenon that had been building for the last three years, the intense national interest and curiosity about everything connected with the picture, had reached the point where it was estimated that more than 56 million Americans were eagerly awaiting their chance to see *Gone With The Wind.* This was largely a positive curiosity. Everybody wanted to like the picture, hoped that it would live up to their expectations, and the previews had indicated that it probably would. But the first true test would be at the Four Star, before a gathering of individuals whose critical judgments would be shaped not only by the film itself but by the events surrounding it: by their daily exposure to the industry gossip, to the reports of bruised egos, constant changes and uncertainties, to the rumors of power plays within Selznick International and MGM, the bickering, recriminations, and the final massive outlay of money—$4,085,790, more than any picture had ever cost in the entire history of the Hollywood film industry—as well as by an intensive three-year publicity campaign that by now many in the press were convinced could not possibly be lived up to.

The screening was scheduled for noon. Five minutes beforehand an edgy David Selznick and a quiet Victor Fleming slipped into seats in the back row of the theatre. Lydia Schiller was with them, and she recalls:

We went in and sat down quietly.... Mr. Selznick and Fleming were both very nervous ... we were all very intense.... It was a full house with a very hostile attitude.... They were chattering away ... but they quieted down very early.... One thing was the beauty of it ... the scenes behind the titles and the opening scenes for that time were quite extraordinary, and you could sense the tide turning almost immediately. It got so quiet you could almost hear a pin drop, they just all got so totally absorbed, and at the intermission it was very thrilling.... The applause was not polite, it was loud, sustained, and genuinely enthusiastic, and the joy of that was quite something.... Afterwards I don't recall that we went back to the studio ... it's hard to explain that sense of loss we all felt, it sounds silly, I know, but we did ... it was out of our hands now. I remember Mr. Selznick saying that he didn't know whether he'd ever be able to get it out of his system.... He was afraid this was his peak ... not in ability, but in enthusiasm and interest.... He was like the rest of us ... we had lived with it day and night for almost two years and we just felt absolutely lost.

The main titles from *Gone With The Wind* utilized a graphic approach unusual in an era when motion picture credits were normally presented quickly and simply: titles were usually announced rapidly, with as much information as possible crammed into several frames. The majesty and excitement of the *Gone With The Wind* credits was apparent from the very first appearance of the title card that announced the cooperative venture of the two studios and the fact that the film was in Technicolor; this dissolved into a full-frame credit for Margaret Mitchell, at which point the main title boomed across the screen, each word filling the entire frame momentarily, perfectly capturing the feeling of romantic grandeur that Selznick wanted the picture to have. The backgrounds for all these titles were carefully selected for mood and beauty. Many of them had been photographed in the South by James Fitzpatrick, while the vistas of the plantations and the city of Atlanta were paintings by Wilbur Kurtz combined with Jack Cosgrove's matte work.

MARGARET MITCHELL'S
STORY OF THE OLD SOUTH

THE WIND

The Players

AT TARA
The O'Hara Plantation in Georgia

Gerald O'Hara	THOMAS MITCHELL
Ellen, *his wife*	BARBARA O'NEILL

Their Daughters:

Scarlett	VIVIEN LEIGH
Suellen	EVELYN KEYES
Carreen	ANN RUTHERFORD

Scarlett's beaux

Scarlett's beaux

Brent Tarleton	GEORGE REEVES
Stuart Tarleton	FRED CRANE

The house servants:

Mammy	HATTIE McDANIEL
Pork	OSCAR POLK
Prissy	BUTTERFLY McQUEEN

In the fields:

Jonas Wilkerson, *the overseer*	VICTOR JORY
Big Sam, *the foreman*	EVERETT BROWN

AT TWELVE OAKS
The nearby Wilkes Plantation

John Wilkes	HOWARD HICKMAN
India, *his daughter*	ALICIA RHETT
Ashley, *his son*	LESLIE HOWARD
Melanie Hamilton, *their cousin*	OLIVIA de HAVILLAND
Charles Hamilton, *her brother*	RAND BROOKS
Frank Kennedy, *a guest*	CARROLL NYE

and a visitor from Charleston

Rhett Butler	CLARK GABLE

IN ATLANTA

Aunt Pittypat Hamilton	LAURA HOPE CREWS
Uncle Peter, *her coachman*	EDDIE ANDERSON
Dr. Meade	HARRY DAVENPORT
Mrs. Meade	LEONA ROBERTS
Mrs. Merriwether	JANE DARWELL
Belle Watling	ONA MUNSON

AND

PAUL HURST	ISABEL JEWELL
CAMMIE KING	ERIC LINDEN
J. M. KERRIGAN	WARD BOND
JACKIE MORAN	CLIFF EDWARDS
L. KEMBLE-COOPER	YAKIMA CANUTT
MARCELLA MARTIN	LOUIS JEAN HEYDT
MICKEY KUHN	OLIN HOWLAND
IRVING BACON	ROBERT ELLIOTT
WILLIAM BAKEWELL	MARY ANDERSON

David Selznick liked to go to costume parties dressed as Teddy Roosevelt, and at the conclusion of production on *Gone With The Wind*, Jock Whitney sent him this oil painting as an affectionate gag gift.

The press preview of *Gone With The Wind* proved to be an inadvertent elegy to the passing of one era of Hollywood history, too, for early that same morning the news came of the sudden, unexpected death of Douglas Fairbanks, Sr., an event that cast a momentary pall over the ecstatic reviews of the picture. Victor Fleming was unable to fully appreciate the extent of the praise coming his way, for Fairbanks had been a very close personal friend—had literally given him his first chance to make a name for himself. In order to serve as a pallbearer at the funeral, Fleming absented himself from the *Gone With The Wind* festivities in Atlanta and refused to comment on anything about the picture, leaving the field completely free to Selznick, who, the night before the press preview, was glibly ambivalent in his attitude toward the film; he was quoted in *Time* magazine as saying: "At noon, I think it's divine, at midnight, I think it's lousy. Sometimes I think it's the greatest picture ever made.... But if it's only a great picture, I'll still be satisfied." With that he flew off to the Atlanta premiere.

Considerably overshadowed by the magnitude and spectacle of the Atlanta and New York openings earlier in the month, the Hollywood premiere of *Gone With The Wind* took place December 27, 1939, at the venerable and prestigious Carthay Circle Theatre out in the flatlands of the Wilshire district. It was the last great movie event of the year and of the decade, and MGM's publicity department under Howard Strickling was determined not to be outdone by the Eastern galas. Searchlights lined both sides of the street for two blocks on either side of San Vicente Boulevard, where the theatre was located, creating a spectacular, blinding display that could be seen for miles. Ten thousand spectators lined the adjacent streets, screaming and roaring their approval as two thousand of Hollywood's élite squeezed their way down the long distinctive garden forecourt and disappeared into the theatre. Inside, the auditorium was rapidly filling up, but Selznick could not understand why a large block of approximately fifty seats in the middle of the theatre remained empty. As the time drew near for the 8:30 curtain, they remained unoccupied. Selznick accosted Russell Birdwell, who had handled the studio's preparations for the opening, and asked him about the blank space, and was a bit shamefaced when Birdwell reminded him that Selznick himself had insisted on holding out a block of tickets for his own personal use. He had been so busy that it had completely slipped his mind; the tickets were still in a desk drawer at Selznick's office. A hurried conference sent several aides scurrying to homes in the neighborhood, inviting fifty startled residents to be the guests of David O. Selznick at the premiere of *Gone With The Wind,* which would start in ten minutes. And so, in the midst of the bejeweled, furred, and tuxedoed throng sat a group of fifty bewildered people in shirtsleeves, sweaters, and sports coats, wide-eyed with delight at their surroundings and this seemingly arbitrary stroke of good fortune. At exactly 8:29, an overwhelming roar from the crowd outside penetrated the inside of the theatre, announcing the arrival of Clark Gable and Carole Lombard. As they swept into the theatre and down the aisle to their seats, the overture started, the lights slowly dimmed to blackness, the curtains parted, and the Selznick International trademark flashed on the screen to a burst of applause. After three years and $4 million worth of work, David Selznick's great gamble, his "folly" and "white elephant," was finally given over to the judgment of his peers.

This was not the first time that *Gone With The Wind* had been on the screen of the Carthay Circle. Late in November, Selznick and Hal Kern had taken the nearly completed picture to the theatre for a private midnight showing to test the sound levels. Selznick was horrified to discover that "as famous a theatre as the Carthay Circle had ... such wretched sound.... The reproduction was simply awful ... the machines weren't even in balance. If this is true ... at the leading showplace of the motion picture capital ... then it is undoubtedly true of 90% of all the theatres in the country ... and it is possible that all our efforts and expense to make *Gone With The Wind* perfect . . . could be ruined through the lack of care and the sloppiness on the part of the exhibitors." To prevent this, Selznick, even while immersed in the round-the-clock details of finishing the picture, began deluging the MGM sales and distribution forces with daily memos and wires on how the picture should be advertised, how it should be sold and be presented, arguing

The Weather
Yesterday: High, 55. Low, 36.
Today: Cloudy. Low, 38.
Complete Weather Details on Page 22.

THE ATLANTA CONSTITUTION

The Constitution Leads in City Home Delivered, Total City and Trading Territory Circulation

The South's Standard Newspaper
Associated Press United Press North American Newspaper Alliance

VOL. LXXII., No. 187. ONLY MORNING NEWSPAPER PUBLISHED IN ATLANTA ATLANTA, GA., SATURDAY MORNING, DECEMBER 16, 1939. Entered at Atlanta Post Office As Second-Class Matter Single Copies: Daily, 5c; Sunday, 10c. Daily and Sunday: Weekly 25c; Monthly $1.10

'GONE WITH WIND' ENTHRALLS AUDIENCE WITH MAGNIFICENCE

Gable, Miss Mitchell Talk Alone After He Begs a Chat

PETITE ATLANTAN MEETS FILM STARS FOR THE FIRST TIME

'Isn't He Grand? Just What I Expected,' She Exclaims; Their Conversation Kept Secret.

By YOLANDE GWIN.

The man who put $4,000,000 into filming "Gone With the Wind" and the principal stars who put their hearts into it, met the author of the book for the first time yesterday afternoon.

Petite Margaret Mitchell, quiet of voice, smiling somewhat reservedly, save at rare moments, gave her hand to David O. Selznick, the producer; to Clark Gable, Vivien Leigh, Evelyn Keyes, Ann Rutherford and Laura Hope Crews, of the cast, and to Carole Lombard, Gable's glamorous wife, at a cocktail party of the Atlanta Women's Press Club.

"Isn't He Grand?"

Said Mr. Gable: "Do you suppose I could have a few words with her? After all there is a lot I want to tell her."

Said Margaret Mitchell: "Isn't he grand! Just what I expected."

Said Carole Lombard: "Clark has been dying to meet you, Miss Mitchell."

Said Miss Vivien Leigh: "I think she is perfectly marvelous."

It all took place in a room 18x11. There was another room and the bar, into which guests overflowed.

Peggy Mitchell had the spotlight and stole the scene. The greatest names of Hollywood gave it to her willingly.

Gable only wanted to talk to "Peggy" Mitchell, and Gable, as in all his movie roles, found a way to get his girl.

What Did They Say?

They disappeared into a private dining room of the club at 5:16 o'clock. The door was locked. There Gable and Miss Mitchell talked over many things. Both refused to repeat what was said. The world would like to know the things they talked about but probably never will.

Minutes slipped by, but "Peggy" and "Rhett" were still in conference. The clock showed 5:25. Most of the club members were getting a little nervous. What were they saying? Was she telling him she had him in mind for her character when she wrote the book?

When they came out Peggy joined Vivien Leigh and Laura Hope (Aunt Pittypat) Crews in the main room. She confided to them:

"If I sit up too straight, think nothing of it. Somebody jerked a chair back too far today and I sat down too hard on the floor. Now I'm wrapped in adhesive tape."

Carole Lombard slipped into a chair beside her.

Good-byes Said.

Soon Miss Mitchell's husband, John Marsh, beckoned it was time to leave.

It was nearing 6 o'clock. Louis B. Mayer slipped her coat on for her. Mrs. Mayer was there and

Continued in Page 8, Column 7.

Margaret Mitchell meets "Scarlett" and "Rhett." Here is the first picture showing the Atlanta author with the movie stars, Vivien Leigh and Clark Gable, who bring the principal characters of her "Gone With the Wind" to life on the screen. The picture was made yesterday afternoon at the party given by the Atlanta Women's Press Club for Margaret Mitchell and not for the stars. All the motion picture people gathered to meet the woman who wrote the story they enact. And it was Gable and Miss Leigh looking for the autographs this time.

Constitution Staff Photo—Bill Wilson.

EPOCHAL PICTURE MADE BY CROWD AT FIRST SHOWING

Two Brilliant Shows Presented—One Within Theater, the Other a Colorful Drama Outside

A company of ladies and gentlemen, including the city's elite, assembled in De Give's Opera House last evening for the first showing of a cinematograph film named "Gone With the Wind," whose subject matter was the experiences of this city and immediate section during the recent outrageous assault upon southern rights which is euphemistically termed in some quarters "The Civil War." The entertainment attracted the beauty and chivalry not only of our own people but those from other sections, including the north. It was received with enthusiasm. The picture, or series of pictures in motion, was based upon a book written by one of our talented young matrons, Mrs. John Marsh, nee Margaret Mitchell, who drew from our glory and tragedy a most arresting novel.

By WILLARD COPE.

Even if "Gone With the Wind" had been contemporary with the scenes it depicts, and its review had appeared as this imagined quotation from an issue of The Constitution of the '70's, it premier still would have been the greatest possible news story in Atlanta since Sherman.

In brilliance, in color, in distinction, in action and in plot the premiere last night evidenced what a quiet, bright-eyed somewhat mouselike young feminine person can do in drawing to her home city the notables of America. It was merely one aspect of her remarkable one-book literary career.

Apt Commentary.

If ever there was an apt physical commentary upon an event, it was the presence of the greatest known peacetime concentration of lights—five 800-million candlepower army searchlights—in front of the theater.

They will be talking about the premiere, and its divers eye-arresting, pulse-quickening, heart-warming details when the last small boy there, is an old, old boy indeed, biting toothlessly into his porridge.

There was build-up. There was timing. But through it all ran a comforting, kindly, pleasant, even sentimental thread, or strain. The whole brilliant scene had reality.

Held Together.

All present—in an assemblage which drew from every important region and stratum of American life—were held together by the sense of sharing in a common, and most historic, experience.

Sitting with them in seats about the theater were Miss Mitchell, the author; David O. Selznick, the producer; such stars as Gable, Leigh, de Havilland, Munson, Rutherford, Keyes and Crews; the head of the publishing house which brought out the original book, and its associate editor, Lois Dwight Cole, lifelong friend of the author, who might justly have been termed coauthor since it was she, as the story runs, who insisted that a literary scout for her firm should look up Miss Mitchell on a now historic southern trip.

It was as if two shows were being presented simultaneously—the fictional "Gone With the

Continued in Page 8, Column 2.

Opportunity Families Call to You for Help

This Is Time To Give Beautiful Christmas Gift for Whole Year.

By FRANK DRAKE.

Today marks the telling of the story of the seventh Opportunity family, Atlanta, and only two have been assured of a break in life thus far.

The fever of "Gone With the Wind" has subsided in the city this morning and the people who were tremendously excited about the visit of all the movie stars are getting back their normal blood pressure. They had a wonderful time welcoming Clark Gable and Vivien Leigh and all the rest but now the "Gone With the Wind" ball and premiere are things of the past.

It's time now, Atlantans, to really think about Christmas and the poor whom you have always aided.

You're planning a bright cheery Christmas for yourself and your family, aren't you? You and your children are looking forward to the day not so distant when everybody in the house will wake up early and shout "Christmas gift" to each other in happy, cheerful voices. Excitement will be rife.

Families in Need.

In the midst of all this merriment, stop for a moment and think about Opportunity families No. 2, No. 3, No. 4 and No. 6, whose tragedies have been told you this last week in The Constitution.

Continued in Page 11, Column 2.

Opportunity 7 Asks Chance

Mrs. Z. is 45, and a widow.

Death and the late unlamented depression makes Mrs. Z. Opportunity No. 7 in this year's Ten Opportunities campaign of The Constitution and the Family Welfare Society.

To help Mrs. Z. fit herself for a job and readjust her life following two terrific shocks, only $18 a month is needed. We believe Atlantans will want to help Mrs. Z.

For the 15 years of her married life Mrs. Z. was as happy as any woman could be. Her husband had a small business of his own and he was a good husband. Perhaps he was a better husband than a business man though. When the depression came along, it eventually wiped out his profits and he operated in the red for a while. Then he had to mortgage their home in an effort to save the business.

No profit, and time finally got the business and the house. The shock of losing everything he had, killed Mr. Z. He died less than a year ago.

Mrs. Z. has carried on as best she could, but the death of her husband and the loss of her home have taken their toll. When all of Mr. Z.'s business affairs were settled a few months ago, Mrs. Z. found that the most she could hope for was about $10 a month. And that only for a short time.

Mrs. Z. believes she has found

Continued in Page 11, Column 2.

A New Film Era

"Gone With the Wind's" Greatness Is Hailed Following Premiere

By LEE ROGERS,
Motion Picture Critic of The Constitution.

It is wonderful.

"Gone With the Wind" opens a new film era. It has everything a great picture could have. It has everything that everybody wanted.

Vivien Leigh is "Scarlett." And Clark Gable is now, more so than ever, the box office public's choice as "Rhett Butler."

All the actors and actresses were marvelously cast and were excellent, but the picture belongs to "Scarlett," just as did the book. Miss Leigh, who changed moods as swiftly as did the character she portrayed, qualifies herself for an Academy Award. Her acting deserves the highest superlatives one wishes to bestow.

Olivia de Havilland as sweet little understanding "Melanie" reached the high spot in her career, and the Gable who portrayed the "Rhett Butler" so wrapped up in his daughter "Bonnie" was completely the character.

Have no fear about the film. It follows closely the story Margaret Mitchell wrote. For three hours and 40 minutes it sticks, in the main, to the plot, situations and story. At times it drags from a motion picture standpoint, but that is overlooked as each new scene is awaited eagerly as Miss Mitchell's printed words come vividly to life.

Ranking with the greatest spectacle scenes in motion picture history is the burning of the ammunition trains, the flight to "Tara," and the wounded yelling soldiers on the tracks at the car shed. Drama is at its height many times. Among the best scenes are when "Scarlett" flies into a rage on finding "Melanie's" baby due and that the negro "Prissy" lied about knowing how to deliver it. Another to Miss Leigh's credit is the closing scene when "Scarlett" learns she loves "Rhett" but for once is unable to hold a man.

The color in the film is almost natural.

Red Cross Grants Finns $250,000

British Hurl New Air Strength Upon Nazis in North Sea Area.

By ROBERT BUNNELLE.

LONDON, Dec. 15.—(AP)—Great Britain's fast-expanding air force was disclosed tonight to have flown boldly to the attack in mass offensives against Germany's boasted air superiority, launching a big-scale war in the air.

With the cold and cloud-blown North sea as the battleground, the British pressed repeated waves of fast long-range planes, capable of both bombing and fighting, against the air and sea escort of a crippled German cruiser, and against Nazi seaplane bases at Borkum, Sylt and Norderney.

These continuing offensive patrols were Britain's answers to persistent Nazi air raids and minelaying forays on British naval anchorages and sealines.

The battle for air mastery, which already has accounted for the loss of some of Britain's and Germany's best fighting aircraft, was expected to turn the North

Continued in Page 2, Column 6.

Norman Davis Hears Finland Can Hold Out Until Spring, Then Acts.

WASHINGTON, Dec. 15.—(AP)—A prediction that Finland's tiny army could hold out until spring against the overwhelming Soviet forces came today to the American Red Cross, which immediately appropriated $250,000 for Finnish war relief.

Quoting Finnish military authorities, a cable report to the Red Cross added, "if adequate military help is forthcoming, defense can be continued for a long, long time."

The report was written by Wayne Chatfield Taylor, former assistant secretary of the treasury who is now a member of the three-man Red Cross delegation in Europe. He flew to Helsinki from Stockholm three days ago.

Ambulances Ordered.

In response to Taylor's recommendations, Norman Davis, the Red Cross chairman, appropriated $100,000 at once and announced that $150,000 more would be made available as needed.

The first order placed was for 10 light ambulances to be shipped to Finland within 30 days. A large part of the funds remaining from the $100,000, Davis said, will be placed at the disposal of the Finnish Red Cross.

The Red Cross, Davis said, also is canvassing for two doctors trained in the treatment of typhus

Continued in Page 3, Column 1.

Louisiana Politics

The pot has been brewing for many years in the Cane Belt, but the common man has had little to say. The Gallup Poll has discounted shotguns and other hindrances to bring Constitution readers a true picture of his feelings.

Read the Poll Tomorrow

In Other Pages

The premiere of *Gone With The Wind* in Atlanta on December 15, 1939, set a new level in the heights to which motion picture publicity could climb. The spectacle of the premiere, which MGM later boasted had been handled with "magnitude and dignity," was stage managed by the company's publicity head, Howard Dietz, who persuaded the governor of Georgia to declare a three-day holiday in the days before the opening; the mayor closed all the schools and public buildings on the day of the premiere. (Left) More than 300,000 people lined the streets of Atlanta to see the arrival of Laurence Olivier, Irene Selznick, Olivia de Havilland, David Selznick, and Vivien Leigh (below, left). But the biggest reception of all went to Clark Gable and Carole Lombard (below, right), who arrived in a specially chartered American Airlines plane that had "MGM'S GONE WITH THE WIND" emblazoned on the side, much to Selznick's chagrin. Gable was astounded at the hysteria of the screaming thousands who lined the parade route into the city (bottom, left). (Bottom, right) Vivien Leigh is escorted to the Junior League Ball the night before the premiere by Laurence Olivier, who, the newspapers kept insisting, "is in Atlanta on his own business." David Selznick hovers in the background behind Miss Leigh, looking somewhat nonplussed by all the madness around him. The newspaper accounts of the premiere successfully pushed the news of the European war off the front pages for two days. The day after the New York opening (opposite), MGM began calling *Gone With The Wind* "The Greatest Motion Picture Ever Made"—a label that is still appropriate over forty years later.

BROADWAY JAMMED AT TWIN PREMIERES

Thousands at Capitol and Astor to See Celebrities at 'Gone With the Wind'

300 POLICEMEN ON DUTY

Only Persons With Tickets Permitted to Walk Between 50th and 51st Streets

The varied dialects and accents of New Yorkers were commingled last night when thousands of persons impeded pedestrian and vehicular traffic as they stood packed along Broadway, gaping at the celebrities and fanfare attendant upon the premiere of Margaret Mitchell's story of the old South in Technicolor, "Gone With the Wind," at the Capitol and Astor Theatres.

For the first time since the twin premiere of "Hell's Angels," in 1930, pedestrians had to show a movie ticket to walk along a block on Broadway. More than 300 policemen finally reduced the confusion that had been brought on by two batteries of Klieg lights, a few searchlights, television sets and hundreds of bejeweled and lavishly gowned women.

Politeness toward civilians was the word that was bandied around among the uniformed men when they came on duty, shortly after 7 o'clock. But before an hour had passed they had to show more than courtesy to keep the west side of Broadway clear between Fifty-first and Fiftieth Streets, where the Capitol is located, and between Forty-sixth and Forty-fifth Streets, the site of the Astor.

Strict Regulations Set

In the former block the police refused to allow pedestrians unless they had the purple, gray or green tickets which admitted them to the Capitol. Along the latter block the police formed a line down the center of the block, forcing pedestrians to keep moving in two sluggish lanes.

Within the hour before 7 o'clock there was little excitement outside the theatres. As a deputy chief inspector described the affairs complacently: "It's just the old mahoska." One of the harried cab drivers, however, described the event a little bit differently. "And to think a rebel had to start all this," he growled.

As usual the celebrities, famous on the stage, screen and in private business, were late in arriving. This had two results. First, the "curtain" at the Capitol was forty-five minutes late and twenty minutes behind schedule at the Astor.

At the former theatre, where publicity men had gone to work with a vengeance, the early comers took advantage of the delay to examine the Confederate atmosphere. Inside the lobby were two huge portraits of Clark Gable and Vivien Leigh, who play the roles of Rhett and Scarlett.

All along the marble staircase were large vases containing poinsettias, gladioli and roses. Seven professional models, wearing the tight bodiced and hoop skirted dresses of Civil War days, stood outside the foyer distributing programs "to ladies only." An official of the theatre explained there were only 3,000 of these souvenir programs available, with a capacity audience of 5,400 arriving.

Celebrities Chatter Gayly

Finally, a half hour after the show was supposed to have begun, the celebrities began filling the lobby, chattering gayly, while their jewels reflected the huge colored lights installed especially for this occasion. The model dressed as Scarlett tossed aside her cigarette and took her station.

The movies started making history then and there; take David O. Selznick's word for it. "For three years I have been working and waiting and hoping; waiting for New York to pass judgment on my picture," he said.

Similar sentiments were uttered by James Stewart, Olivia De Havilland, Alice Faye, Constance Bennett, Will Hays and others. Clark Gable and Vivien Leigh said nothing. They were not there.

Finally, at 9 o'clock, after photographers had exploded innumerable bulbs from all parts of the lobby, and the harried theatre officials had been predicting "curtain going up in three minutes" for the tenth time, the curtain did go up.

It went up with an oriental touch that was a slight to the Confederate flags in the lobby. Brass gongs sounded five times and the heavy gold brocade curtain rose slowly. Celebrities hastened to tell their radio audiences how thrilled they were and entered the darkened theatre.

At 10:40 there was a ten-minute intermission in the four-hour movie and the audience filled the lobby and lounge, gushing in exuberance and complaining of fatigue.

UNITED ARTISTS TO FIGHT

Move by Goldwyn to Terminate to Be Resisted in Court

The move of Samuel Goldwyn to terminate his contract with United Artists will be "resisted in every legal way" by that organization, according to a statement made last night by Murray Silverstone, executive chairman of the United Artists Distributing Corporation. Mr. Goldwyn's intention was announced Monday by Max D. Steuer, his counsel.

Mr. Silverstone's statement said: "We have received this morning a letter from Samuel Goldwyn, Inc., in which it attempts to terminate its exclusive contract with us. We have not breached our contract, it is in full force and effect, and we again reiterate that we shall resist in every legal way any attempt on the part of Samuel Goldwyn, Inc., or Samuel Goldwyn to deliver pictures through any distributor other than United Artists up to and including the term of his contract which does not terminate until Sept. 2, 1945, the expiration date of our present exclusive contract. We will continue to carry out our obligations in the future as we have in the past. The matter has been referred to counsel."

Dramatic Workshop Opened

The dramatic workshop of the school for Social Research, 66 West Twelfth Street, was opened formally yesterday afternoon with a reception at the school when Dr. Alvin Johnson, director, introduced Erwin Piscator, who will head the new faculty.

THE SCREEN IN REVIEW

David Selznick's 'Gone With the Wind' Has Its Long-Awaited Premiere at Astor and Capitol, Recalling Civil War and Plantation Days of South—Seen as Treating Book With Great Fidelity

GONE WITH THE WIND, as adapted by the late Sidney Howard from Margaret Mitchell's novel; directed by Victor Fleming; musical score by Max Steiner; production designer, William Cameron Menzies; special effects by Jack Cosgrove; art scenes staged by Lee Zavitz; costumes designed by Walter Plunkett; photography by Ernest Haller, supervised for Technicolor Company by Natalie Kalmus; technical advisers, Susan Myrick and Will Price; historian, Wilbur G. Kurtz; produced by David O. Selznick and released by Metro-Goldwyn-Mayer. At the Capitol and Astor Theatres.

Scarlett O'Hara	Vivien Leigh
Rhett Butler	Clark Gable
Ashley Wilkes	Leslie Howard
Melanie Hamilton	Olivia de Havilland
Mammy	Hattie McDaniel
Gerald O'Hara	Thomas Mitchell
Ellen O'Hara	Barbara O'Neil
Frank Kennedy	Carroll Nye
Aunt Pittypat Hamilton	Laura Hope Crews
Doctor Meade	Harry Davenport
India Wilkes	Rand Brooks
Belle Watling	Ona Munson
Carreen O'Hara	Ann Rutherford
Brent Tarleton	George Reeves
Stuart Tarleton	Fred Crane
Pork	Oscar Polk
Prissy	Butterfly McQueen
Suellen O'Hara	Evelyn Keyes
Tom, a Yankee Captain	Ward Bond
Bonnie Blue Butler	Cammie King
Johnny Gallagher	J. M. Kerrigan
Emmy Slattery	Isabel Jewell
India Wilkes	Jane Darwell
Jonas Wilkerson	Victor Jory
John Wilkes	Howard Hickman
Maybelle Merriwether	Mary Anderson
A Yankee Looter	Paul Hurst
Cathleen Calvert	Marcella Martin
Beau Wilkes	Mickey Kuhn
Bonnie's Nurse	Lillian Kemble Cooper
Reminiscent Soldier	Cliff Edwards
Elijah	Zack Williams

By FRANK S. NUGENT

Understatement has its uses too, so this morning's report on the event of last night will begin with the casual notation that it was a great show. It ran, and will continue to run, for about 3 hours and 45 minutes, which still is a few days and hours less than its reading time and is a period the spine may protest sooner than the eye or ear. It is pure narrative, as the novel was, rather than great drama, as the novel was not. By that we would imply you will leave it, not with the feeling you have undergone a profound emotional experience, but with the warm and grateful remembrance of an interesting story beautifully told. Is it the greatest motion picture ever made? Probably not, although it is the greatest motion picture we have seen and the most ambitious film-making venture in Hollywood's spectacular history.

It—as you must be aware—is "Gone With the Wind," the gargantuan Selznick edition of the Margaret Mitchell novel which swept the country like Charlie McCarthy, "the Music Goes 'Round" and similar inexplicable phenomena; which created the national emergency over the selection of a Scarlett O'Hara and which, ultimately, led to the $4,000,000 production that faced the New York public on two Times Square fronts last night, the Astor and the Capitol. It is the picture for which Mr. Gallup's American Institute of Public Opinion has reported a palpitantly waiting audience of 56,500,000 persons, a few of whom may find encouragement in our opinion that they won't be disappointed in Vivien Leigh's Scarlett, Clark Gable's Rhett Butler or, for that matter, in Mr. Selznick's, Miss Mitchell's.

For, by any and all standards, Mr. Selznick's film is a handsome, scrupulous and unstinting version of the 1,037-page novel, matching it almost scene for scene with a literalness that not even Shakespeare or Dickens were accorded in Hollywood, casting it so brilliantly one would have to know the history of the production not to suspect that Miss Mitchell had written her story just to provide a vehicle for the stars already assembled under Mr. Selznick's hospitable roof. To have treated so long a book with such astonishing fidelity required courage—the courage of a producer's convictions and of his pocketbook, and yet, so great a hold has Miss Mitchell on her public, it might have taken more courage still to have changed a line or scene of it. But if Selznick has made a virtue of necessity, it does not follow, of course, that his transcription be expertly made as well. And yet, on the whole, it has been. Through stunning design, costume and peopling, his film has skillfully and absorbingly recreated Miss Mitchell's mural of the South in that bitter decade when secession, civil war and reconstruction ripped wide the graceful fabric of the plantation

Clark Gable and Vivien Leigh

age and confronted the men and women who had adorned it with the stern alternative of meeting the new era or dying with the old. It was a large panel she painted, with sections devoted to plantation life, to the siege and the burning of Atlanta, to carpetbaggers and the Ku Klux Klan and, of course, to the Scarlett O'Hara about whom all this changing world was spinning and to whom nothing was important except as it affected her.

Some parts of this extended account have suffered a little in their screen telling, just as others have profited by it. Mr. Selznick's picture-postcard Tara and Twelve Oaks, with a few-score actors posturing on the premises, is scarcely our notion of doing complete justice to an age that had "a glamour, it is perfection, a symmetry like Grecian art." The siege of Atlanta was splendid and the fire that followed magnificently pyrotechnic, but we do not endorse the superimposed melodramatics of the crates of explosives scorching in the fugitives' path; and we felt cheated, so ungrateful are we, when the battles outside Atlanta were dismissed in a subtitle and Sherman's march to the sea was summed up in a montage shot. We grin understandingly over Mr. Selznick's romantic omission of Scarlett's first two "birthings," and we regret more comic capital was not made of Rhett's scampish trick on the Old Guard of Atlanta when the army men were rounding up the Klansmen.

But if there are faults, they do not extend to the cast. Miss Leigh's Scarlett has vindicated the admired talent quest that indirectly turned her up. She is so perfectly designed for the part by art and nature that any other actress in the role would be inconceivable. Technicolor finds her beautiful, but Sidney Howard, who wrote the script, and Victor Fleming, who directed it, have found in her something more: the very embodiment of the selfish, hoydenish, slant-eyed miss who tackled life with both claws and a creamy complexion, asked no odds of any one or anything—least of all her conscience—and faced at last a defeat which, by her very unconquerability, neither she nor we can recognize as final.

Miss Leigh's Scarlett is the pivot of the picture, as she was of the novel, and it is a column of strength in a film that is part history, part spectacle and all biography. Yet there are performances around her fully as valid, for all their lesser prominence. Olivia de Havilland's Melanie is a gracious, dignified, tender gem of characterization. Mr. Gable's Rhett Butler (although there is the fine flavor of the smokehouse in a scene or two) is almost as perfect as the grandstand quarterbacks thought he would be. Leslie Howard's Ashley Wilkes is anything but a pallid characterization of a pallid character. Best of all, perhaps, next to Miss Leigh, is Hattie McDaniel's Mammy, who must be personally absolved of responsibility for that most "unfittin'" scene in which she scolds Scarlett from an upstairs window. She played even that one right, however wrong it was.

We haven't time or space for the others, beyond to wave an approving hand at Butterfly McQueen as Prissy, Thomas Mitchell as Gerald, Ona Munson and Belle Watling, Alicia Rhett as India Wilkes, Rand Brooks as Charles Hamilton, Harry Davenport as Doctor Meade, Carroll Nye as Frank Kennedy. And not so approvingly at Laura Hope Crews's Aunt Pitty, Oscar Polk's Pork (bad casting) and Eddie Anderson's Uncle Peter (oversight). Had we space we'd tell about the tragic scene at the Atlanta terminal, where the wounded are lying, about the dramatic use to which Mr. Fleming has placed his Technicolor—although we still feel that color so hard on the eyes for so long a picture—and about pictures of this length in general. Anyway, "it" has arrived at last, and we cannot get over the shock of not being disappointed; we had almost been looking forward to that.

Candlelight Concert at Center

The Rockefeller Center Choristers will usher in the season's Candlelight concerts today at 5:15 P. M. at Rockefeller Center. The group will sing carols and excerpts from Handel's "Messiah." The choristers have been selected from those who work at the Center and have been rehearsing for months under the direction of John R. Jones. The group will also be heard tomorrow at the same time.

REMEMBER
The Hundred Neediest

BEHIND THE EXCITEMENT of last night's premiere ... the conviction that "GONE WITH THE WIND" is the greatest motion picture ever made!

(See directory on this page for times of showing and price information.)

  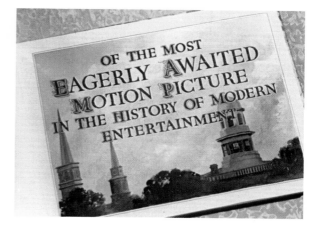

Six frames from the original Technicolor coming-attractions trailer for *Gone With The Wind,* produced by Frank Whitbeck of MGM's Culver City publicity department. It was unusual for the time in that it showed no scenes from the film itself, opting instead for a series of paintings done by Wilbur Kurtz based on stills from the film. Variations of this approach were used to sell *Gone With The Wind* for the next fifteen years; it was not until 1954 that actual scenes from the film were used in these "prevue trailers," as they were known in the industry.

heatedly against their plan to present the picture on a continuous performance basis, telling Al Lichtman of MGM:

> I think that not having reserved seats is a shortsighted policy that will kill the goose that promised to lay the golden eggs.... It means that thousands of people are going to be standing in line for a four-hour picture and the repercussions will be terrible. Such greed on the part of the Loew theatres or any other theatre operator can make money for them but hurt us terribly.... This picture represents the greatest work of my life, in the past and very likely in the future.... I am associated with it in the public mind... and I do not intend without every possible struggle to be blamed for making a miserable botch of its exhibition.

There were two factors in this plan that bothered Selznick. The first, as he pointed out, had to do with

> my cross examination of a number of people in the middle and lower middle class brackets.... One woman told me that she had been saving her money to pay $1.65 for reserved seats to see *Gone With The Wind*... and upon hearing that she would be able to buy the best seats, unreserved, for $1.10, said that she certainly would not do this... and at that low price, the picture was obviously not what it was cracked up to be ... and that she would wait until it got to the neighborhood houses at regular prices. I believe there are countless thousands of people [just like her] who will be eager to pay advanced prices... to get reserved seats... but who will be [disappointed] and even enraged at being gouged for advanced prices and forced to stand in line and scramble for seats... for something that most of them consider to be a gala event.

The second issue troubling Selznick had to do with his conviction that "everything about *Gone With The Wind* must be set up as separate and apart from any other picture that has ever been made." All motion picture theatres operated on a continuous performance basis, with patrons buying tickets and going in whenever they felt like it, even in the middle of a picture, a practice that gave rise to the phrase, "This is where

we came in." Selznick was terrified that this might happen to *Gone With The Wind,* saying:

> I don't intend to have the picture murdered by allowing any schedule that permitted a large part of the audience to see it backwards, or incomplete, or that they stand in the back of theatres for part or all of its four-hour running time waiting for seats.... We have nothing to gain by several shows a day and a great deal to lose ... since it's obvious that the picture would be ruined by seeing it backwards and the subsequent loss in word of mouth advertising can be ruinous to both Loew's and ourselves.

This ongoing dispute was left unresolved throughout the period of editing and post-production; but at the two previews in Riverside and Santa Barbara, Selznick, via the preview cards, queried the audience about their preferences regarding continuous or reserved performances. Ninety percent replied that they thought seats should be reserved, and armed with these facts, Selznick finally convinced MGM of the wisdom of his logic. After their acquiescence on this, he replied in a conciliatory vein: "Nobody on earth knows how *Gone With The Wind* should be handled, and nobody on earth can find out without experimentation, and that is my principal objection to the present plan, the lack of flexibility in both the distribution and exhibition plans." Now that he had persuaded MGM on these points, he set about to implement what he considered to be the most important aspect of the picture's exhibition: the way in which it was presented to the waiting public.

> I am anxious to do everything possible to see to it that the picture is presented with taste and with showmanship. The old David Belasco tradition of the theatre, the D. W. Griffith and the Samuel Rothafel "Roxy" method of presenting a picture as though it were a jewel have been too long lost.... As in everything else that is offered to the public, the way in which a production is presented is highly important... doubly important in this case, because I don't think that the members of the audience feel that they're getting something that is worth extra money unless the method of presenting it indicates we feel we have something extraordinary.... I hope that a presentation

FIFTEEN CENTS

DECEMBER 25, 1939

TIME

THE WEEKLY NEWSMAGAZINE

SCARLETT O'HARA

To Dave & Myron, Vivien Leigh.

(Cinema)

VOLUME XXXIV

(REG. U. S. PAT. OFF.)

NUMBER 26

plan will be worked out that will be uniform throughout the country.... The starting times of the picture should be advertised prominently.... I feel that there should be two or three minutes of music which we will supply, before the main title, which we should not permit any exhibitor to cut off.... The lights should be dimmed as the music continues and as the picture starts all the lights should be out except those required by law, as we have found through long experience that house lights ruin Technicolor... and this again is something that will have to be hammered into the heads of exhibitors.... We have found from experience at our previews that the audience is left absolutely stunned at the conclusion of the picture.... It packs a tremendous emotional wallop... and we must be very careful not to jar this mood by suddenly turning on the lights, playing any kind of inappropriate music or putting anything else on the screen.

All of these suggestions were ultimately contained in an elaborate "presentation manual" prepared by MGM and sent to each theatre in advance of the picture's engagement. Nevertheless, all of Selznick's worst fears about the handling of the picture came true in the initial week of its two Los Angeles engagements. The picture was playing the two-performance, reserved-seat policy at the Carthay Circle and four continuous performances at the downtown United Artists theatre. Both theatres were under the operation of the Skouras brothers, Charlie and Spyros, and at the UA theatre, in spite of careful instructions to the contrary from both Selznick and MGM, the Skourases insisted on running three shorts with the picture, adding forty-five minutes to the length of the show during the day. They also restricted the intermission to one minute between halves, leading one female patron to complain in a letter to Selznick, "I ask you, what can you do in a minute?" On the strength of this and other letters, Selznick sent a member of his staff, Val Lewton, down to the theatre to monitor the shows. His report gives a firsthand account not only of the presentation of the picture, but also of unguarded audience reactions to what they were seeing:

The audience reaction to the picture was as it was at the previews. There was the usual applause at the first appearance of Gable and there was slight applause for Leslie Howard. The audience took the entire first half of the picture well and they took all of the laughs. The intermission was one and one-fourth minutes at this show and pandemonium reigned. There was tremendous confusion in the lobby and aisles when the overture for the second half of the picture started. In the second half the audience really went to work, especially on what we term the rape scene. They liked to have Gable compel Scarlett to sit in the chair and listen to him, and when he picked her up and ran up the stairs with her, the applause was almost equal to that extended to Babe Ruth when he made a home run. They enjoyed the bedroom scene on the following morning immensely. They cried and they cried hard at Melanie's death, and when Rhett gave the tag line they applauded, and at the end of the picture, there was tremendous applause.... Many were crying. I spoke to the manager and he felt very keenly that four shows a day is murder to the picture, that you should not allow theatre operators any discretion as to the length of the intermission but should force them to hold to a ten-minute length. So far as I could determine, the length of the show does not hinder the audience's enjoyment... during one performance only twelve persons got up to go to the lavatories. Dozens of people sat through two showings of the picture and I spoke to one old bird who was going back in to see it a third time.

The situation at the reserved-seat Carthay Circle was even more chaotic and haphazard. The Skouras brothers very cautiously were putting seats on sale only a week in advance; as these were sold, they would put up another block of seats, completely defeating the purpose of advance sales. The confusion was added to by the fact that they had only one small box office and one telephone line, leading to frustration and anger on the part of potential patrons. One of these, a Mrs. Mildred Gregory, wrote an indignant note to Selznick detailing her husband's efforts to obtain tickets for their wedding anniversary and complaining of scalping by ticket agencies. The same sentiments were expressed in an editorial in *The Hollywood Reporter,* and Selznick frantically wired Jock Whitney:

This is our picture and it is high time we brought a few ethics into the business in our relationship with the public.... If ever there was antagonism being built up against an enterprise this is it.... Our obligation to the public must be maintained and fulfilled regardless of whether Loew's considers this interference or not.... The situation at the Carthay is getting worse by the hour and worries me tremendously as an indication of what may be happening elsewhere.

It worried Selznick on another more personal front also, for, as Frank Capra pointed out to him, "The one reason why *Gone With The Wind* might not win the various Academy Awards was because not enough people among the voters will have seen it." Academy procedures in those days were different from today. Studios did not have large private screenings of their pictures for the membership; they went to the theatres and saw them just like everybody else. In spite of the opening night at the Carthay, the bulk of the ten thousand rank-and-file Academy voters had not yet been able to see the picture. This was a potentially serious situation, since Selznick and his staff had worked themselves to exhaustion not only to meet the Atlanta premiere date but also to get the picture finished in order to meet the Academy stipulation that a picture, to be eligible for the Awards, had to open theatrically in the Los Angeles area before the end of the calendar year. After pages of transcontinental wires and letters, the situations at the two local theatres were clarified and smoothed down, with the United Artists theatre changing to two continuous shows a day and one reserved performance at night, while the Carthay Circle installed a new, larger box office, two extra telephones, and put seats on sale for two months in advance. The lessons learned from these first engagements proved extremely valuable in handling the rest of the picture's first year of release across the country, so that by the end of May 1940, *Gone With The Wind* had grossed the astounding amount of $20 million. In the entire history of the film business, no picture had even come close to this. There was some speculation that D. W. Griffith's *The Birth of a Nation* might conceivably have done as well, but it was impossible to tell as that picture had been sold outright to States Rights distributors for a flat fee, and anything that came in to them was not reported. Not until 1938 and the $8 million gross of Disney's *Snow White and the Seven Dwarfs* had any other picture taken in more than $5 million, and Disney's success had been considered an unbeatable fluke by virtue of the novelty of the cartoon form and its broad-based appeal to the family trade.

A large part of the amazing gross of *Gone With The Wind* was due to the very high admission prices; at a time when movie prices seldom went above 50 cents tops, the lowest-priced ticket for *Gone With The Wind's* first road show engagement was 70 cents. And MGM's sales force demanded and got an unprecedented 70 percent of each dollar that came into the theatre box office, so that out of the initial $20 million, the return to MGM was $13 million. After deducting production costs, advertising and distribution expenses, and the costs of each Technicolor print ($1,100), there was a profit of $8 million to be split evenly between Selznick International and MGM; and this was only from the first road show playoff in some four thousand theatres. Still to come were the "popular price" return engagements, which the picture would play beginning in January of 1941, and which promised to be nearly as lucrative as the original release. And if this pecuniary windfall were not enough, on the evening of February 29, 1940, Selznick's fears about the Academy Awards were put to rest as the picture was voted an unprecedented eight awards by the Academy membership, in almost every major category, with an honorary plaque given to William Cameron Menzies "for outstanding achievement in the use of color," and one to the Selznick studio for "pioneering in the use of co-ordinated equipment" in the production of the film. Strangely enough, the two major awards that it did not win were for two of its most important ingredients: Clark Gable's performance lost out to Robert Donat's in *Goodbye, Mr. Chips,* and Max Steiner's landmark score was passed over in favor of Herbert Stothart's rearrangement of the Harold Arlen melodies for *The Wizard of Oz.* The Awards were not the closely guarded secret they are now, and the Los Angeles *Times* had jumped the gun by publishing the winners even before the ceremony began. Because of this, the Academy subsequently instituted the showmanly gimmick of the sealed envelope.

The Academy Awards for 1939 were almost a clean sweep for *Gone With The Wind*. In addition to two honorary plaques, it received eight awards, including a posthumous one for Sidney Howard's screenplay. Tragically, Howard was killed in an accident on his farm in August 1939, just as the picture was nearing completion. (Above, left) David Selznick received the award for best production in a year that included *Stagecoach, Mr. Smith Goes to Washington,* and *Wuthering Heights.* Vivien Leigh won the award for best performance by an actress, beating out such competition as Bette Davis in *Dark Victory* and Greta Garbo in *Ninotchka.* (Above, right) Victor Fleming won the award for best direction for *Gone With The Wind,* but he wasn't at the ceremony to receive it. This shot was specially posed several days after the event. (Below, left) The most emotional moment of the evening was Hattie McDaniel's award for best performance by a supporting actress, the first time a black had ever been nominated let alone honored. Miss McDaniel's acceptance speech had been ghostwritten by someone at the studio; she carefully memorized it, and after promising to continue "being a credit to my race," she broke down in tears and left the stage. (Below, right) At the Academy Awards ceremony, Ernest Hopkins, president of Dartmouth College, presents David Selznick with the Irving G. Thalberg Memorial Award "for the most consistent high quality of production during 1939." Selznick had originally suggested to the Academy in 1937 that a production award be given in memory of Thalberg, and it was a highly emotional moment for him when he was presented with the bust of his friend.

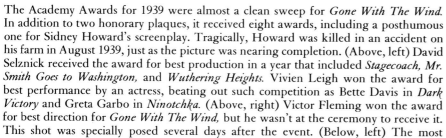

At the 1939 Academy Awards ceremony: (top) Lyle Wheeler accepting his award for art direction, and (above) Hal Kern (right) and James Newcom receiving their awards for film editing for their work on *Gone With The Wind.*

The production of *Gone With The Wind* marked the peak of Selznick's career, as he had noted, and also the high point, the full flowering of the romantic era of Hollywood's film industry. It represented not only the maturing of Selznick's powers as a creative filmmaker but the coming together of all the forces that had been shaping the look and style of the Hollywood motion picture in the decade since the advent of sound. In form and content the film embodies the virtues of an age, for embedded in *Gone With The Wind,* but close enough to the surface to be effectively perceptible, are the accumulated values, traditions, and attitudes of the first four decades of twentieth-century America—the romantic, idealistic, yet pragmatic spirit that characterized the two generations that had grown to maturity with the movies, that saw in them a reflection of themselves, of their inarticulated, shared longings, a symbol of their ability to be resilient, to bend with the gale force of the social and economic changes of the times, to take the worst that life had to offer and to overcome it by sheer willpower and determination. By invoking a consciousness of the heritage of the past, *Gone With The Wind* subliminally called up a ringing affirmation of the future of the national character. The ability of Selznick and his associates to respond to these intangibles, and to transmute them into film, is what gives the motion picture *Gone With The Wind* its particular timelessness and its capacity to continue to awaken in its audiences a powerful and positive emotional response. It does this in the best tradition of the newly emergent popular culture, using the kinetic and psychological power of movement, sound, color, humor, and sentiment to evoke in the spectator a subconscious sense of the positive virtues, the enduring nature and indestructibility of the human spirit.

The success of *Gone With The Wind,* the enormous financial and artistic awards that were showered on it and on Selznick, had a long-lasting effect on the industry, only part of which Selznick comprehended in a rather shortsighted comment he made that year to a prominent exhibitor: "... *Gone With The Wind* saved the industry, and gave it new courage to make big pictures, at exactly the right moment—the moment when it looked certain that it was going to be flooded with cheap pictures as a result of panic over the loss of the foreign market." This may have been true, but a much more accurate evaluation of the impact of *Gone With The Wind* on the Hollywood film industry came from the perceptive documentary filmmaker-turned-critic Pare Lorentz, who predicted: "Selznick and Whitney have made a picture that has given the movies enormous prestige ... and they have probably ruined the industry in that the only way that the Napoleons of the West Coast can surpass this one is to do what they did, spend money like generals, take three years and employ the best brains in the industry and cast the best actors on two continents."

It is impossible at this remove to reconstruct the impact of *Gone With The Wind,* the phenomenon that it represented to the industry and to the public. It was the first true "event" movie of the sound era, and its production and marketing set the pattern for all subsequent large-scale efforts in the picture business; the *GWTW* syndrome would dominate the industry's thinking and goals for the next thirty-five years as everybody tried to duplicate its success. Selznick himself, almost as soon as the picture was completed, began trying to follow it up. In December of 1939, he asked Kay Brown to see if Margaret Mitchell would consider either writing a sequel or selling the rights to the characters. Miss Mitchell, weary of the three-ring circus her life had become, replied in a characteristic manner to Kay Brown, who relayed her comments to Selznick:

> As to the sequel, Peggy [Miss Mitchell] said quite honestly she did not believe she would do a sequel and that she had, from her point of view, extremely good reasons for not doing it. She said actually in the book when Rhett left Scarlett he was 45 years of age, and furthermore, that she felt that Rhett's words, "I wish I could care what you do or where you go but I can't," are an indication that Rhett had finally lost interest in Scarlett and would never return to her. In the picture that line doesn't appear—but Rhett's last words, "Frankly, my dear, I don't give a damn," implies [*sic*] that this is a fight and that there's always a possibility that a fight can be made up. Therefore Peggy, from her point of view, doesn't believe that Rhett ever would return to Scarlett, and therefore she herself could not write a sequel in which the two would come back together and she believes that this is what the public would want....
>
> Now as to selling us the rights to the characters—she will not do this and she has many reasons for it, which I will outline below. She is hopeful that you can be persuaded also to give up the idea of a sequel. The first reason is that she is not sure that she would like anybody else to create the situations for the characters that she knows so well.... Second, she thinks possibly you might suffer very much if you took the characters, of course with her permission, and created a story for them, and advertised that it was by another writer—at least, she thinks, this would hold true in the South, and that you would get reverberations of absolute commercialism culminating in a lack of interest on the part of the people to go and see the picture. Third, she thinks that certain books do allow sequels, but she is afraid that *GWTW* does not.... As far as she is concerned, the story of Rhett and Scarlett is ended, and ... the story of the descendants is not a sequel, or at least not the sequel the public wants and would be prepared to receive. Now, for the last point, and what I consider the most important point ... a mediocre sequel will damage the re-make rights.... I think you can do pretty much anything in pictures, but I would hate to see even you tackle the sequel to *GWTW.* To me it's just like making a sequel to *David Copperfield* or *Les Misérables.*

And with those final words of wisdom from Kay Brown, Selznick reluctantly shrugged off any lingering hope of continuing the saga of Scarlett.

Rebecca

THE NOVEL *Rebecca* had been published in England in early 1938, becoming an immediate best seller and repeating its success later that year in the United States. Daphne du Maurier had written a modern-day *Jane Eyre,* an archetypal Gothic romance utilizing to the fullest all the elements of the genre: a shy, repressed heroine; a wealthy, moody, romantic hero; a brooding, mysterious mansion presided over by a sinister housekeeper; and the hint of a ghost story in that there is hanging over the entire tale the unseen presence and memory of the hero's first wife, dead under mysterious circumstances. The story unfolds through the narration of its unnamed heroine—a story suspenseful, compelling, and ultimately melodramatic, with settings ranging from the glamorous French Riviera to the somber Cornwall coast of England, perfect material for the movies. The indefatigable Kay Brown hurried a synopsis to David Selznick in May 1938, as soon as the English edition was released, with the comment that

> the book has good writing and some dramatic scenes let into a rather hysterical plot. The fact that it is melodrama isn't so much against it, after all, melodrama has been responsible for some box office classics—but the fact that the hero definitely murders his first wife, no matter how understandable it is in the story, makes it ... chancy from the censorship angle. Aside from this, there are good roles for Ronald Colman and Carole Lombard.

Selznick was still vainly trying to find another picture to wind up his contract with Ronald Colman, and after reading the synopsis of *Rebecca,* he was sure that it would be perfect for the actor and wired Kay Brown

to "find out price and further information as to its likely sales. . . . If it is a really big seller . . . it would be worth the effort to lick the major problem. . . . I will give further thought to the censorship problems here . . . and will await word from you . . . whether you can secure it at a reasonable price." Apart from thinking it good for Colman, Selznick, after a first reading of the complete story, was convinced that the book would have "tremendous appeal for women . . . and that it is really great box office"; his only voiced concern about the property, aside from the murder angle, was the title. "It's difficult to think of calling a picture *Rebecca,*" he commented in a letter, "unless it was made for the Palestine market," and when Kay Brown quoted a price of $50,000 for the rights, Selznick offered to give Doubleday Doran a little extra money if they would change the title for the American market. When they refused, he told Kay Brown to close for the book anyway, shrugging, "Let's forget our worries about the title and hope that the book clicks as importantly as it looks as though it's going to."

Click it did, for after its U.S. publication date in September 1938, spurred by good reviews and excellent word-of-mouth comments, *Rebecca* sold close to 200,000 copies in its first months, and if Selznick had not been spoiled by the phenomenal sales of *Gone With The Wind,* he would have been ecstatic at the book's popularity. Immersed as he was in finishing up *The Young in Heart* and *Made for Each Other,* and getting *Gone With The Wind* ready for the cameras, Selznick paid only passing attention to *Rebecca,* feeling that if the book's popularity continued to grow, it could only benefit any picture that he made from it. But Colman, for whom he had bought the story and who he was positive would be enthusiastic about it, instead developed serious reservations. "Colman told me," related Selznick in a letter to Jock Whitney,

> that years ago, when he was making five pictures a year for Sam Goldwyn, he would have welcomed *Rebecca,* but now . . . with fewer pictures and his own say about stories, he [is] very hesitant to do it. . . . He felt that the things Max de Winter is called upon to do would prejudice his public against him. . . . He is so fearful about the murder angle and also about the possibility of the picture emerging as a woman-starring vehicle that he will not do it unless he sees a treatment. . . . We then discussed at great length the alternate possibility of making the murder of Rebecca instead a suicide by Rebecca . . . and as we talked Colman grew more and more enthusiastic. . . . When I left, all that stood between Colman and us getting together was his strong feeling that Max murdered Rebecca with insufficient motivation.

Even if that were overcome, Selznick realized that there was no guarantee the quixotic Colman would in fact consent to play the part: "Waiting for him, we might find ourselves in a jam," he commented in the fall of 1938. "If we move quickly, we can sign Leslie Howard for the part, otherwise we may lose him too. . . . Bill Powell has been absolutely wild about the role and is anxious to do it, but I turned him down on the expectation of getting Colman."

As Selznick and Colman played ring-around-Rebecca, Selznick was demonstrating his producer's versatility by juggling the two completed pictures while getting *Gone With The Wind* off the ground and spending several hours a week developing a picture based on the *Titanic* disaster of 1912. He was also continuing to shop the international talent market for suitable bargains. Having found Ingrid Bergman in Sweden, he began paying serious attention to the renascent English film industry, which had begun to develop its own native talent. The names of English directors began to be heard more and more in U.S. film circles. Alexander Korda was the first; his *The Private Life of Henry VIII* gave a new respectability to the derisive term "British picture." He was followed by Victor Saville and Robert Stevenson, whose direction of *Tudor Rose* and *King Solomon's Mines* brought him to Selznick's attention. Stevenson was put under long-term contract to Selznick International, joining another of his celebrated countrymen, Alfred Hitchcock, whom Selznick had snatched up late in 1938, intending him to direct the impending *Titanic.*

Hitchcock had come a long way since his days as co-writer/art director on Myron Selznick's 1924 British production *The Passionate Adventure.* He was, by 1937, the preeminent director in the British film industry, a position he achieved with an almost unbroken series of successes beginning in 1926 with *The Lodger,* an edgy tale about a man who might be Jack the Ripper. Three years later he directed the first talking picture made in England, *Blackmail,* notable for its then innovative use of moving camera and impressionistic use of sound, including voice-overs and long, effective stretches of silence, something considered quite remarkable since the prevailing ethic was that sound pictures must use sound incessantly. After that he dabbled in several different styles of pictures, including a straight musical *(Waltzes from Vienna),* a comedy revue format *(Elstree Calling),* and a film version of Sean O'Casey's *Juno and the Paycock.*

But it was his mastery of the thriller that brought him to international prominence. From *The Man Who Knew Too Much* in 1934 through *The Lady Vanishes* in 1938, the Hitchcock style was compounded of vagaries of plot as well as of human nature, developed through a highly stylized visual method that gave the observation of seemingly irrelevant details a perverse, suspenseful fascination, constantly catching the audience off-guard, with emotional involvement developed almost entirely by the editing rather than the acting, which was often reduced to choreographed head turns and eye movements. This basic montage technique had grown out of Hitchcock's early training in engineering, mechanics, advertising, and art direction, all of which gave him an instinctive understanding of the function of design and the interplay of objects within a given context. The equivocating nature of his films, with their sudden sharp twists and their illogical logic in a world in which no one was to be trusted and in which nothing was as it appeared to be, possibly stemmed from his severe Jesuit training as a child, his loneliness and anxiety at

being confronted with implacable authoritarian figures. His parents added to this by being stern and from all accounts rather unloving: Hitchcock has related how his father, to punish him for some minor trespass, gave him a note to take to the local police station; the officer in charge read it and promptly locked up the child in a cell for five minutes, telling him, "This is what we do to bad boys."

Like many solitary individuals of the time, Hitchcock found fulfillment through the movies—first at them, then in them—obtaining a job at the age of twenty with the new English branch of Famous Players-Lasky designing title cards. Seventeen years later he had reached the very top of the heap in the British film business, and to any ambitious and serious-minded moviemaker, there was nowhere left to go except Hollywood. Hitchcock had stayed on friendly terms with Myron Selznick since their involvement in the early twenties, and at his urging in late 1938, Hitchcock said yes to David Selznick's offer of a contract that would pay him $40,000 per picture. After finishing his last British picture, which coincidentally was an adaptation of a Daphne du Maurier novel, *Jamaica Inn,* Hitchcock packed up his wife and child and left for Hollywood in late March 1939.

Hitchcock's arrival at the studio caught Selznick in the middle of overseeing the bulk of the spectacle scenes for *Gone With The Wind.* Consequently he wasn't able to devote much time to his new director beyond several brief meetings with him early in April. The *Titanic* project had largely been scuttled; Selznick's original plan had been to purchase the liner *Leviathan* and use it as a stand-in for the doomed *Titanic,* but the prohibitive costs of doing this, coupled with the lack of a finished script, caused him to reluctantly drop the idea. Instead, he and Hitchcock decided that *Rebecca* would be an ideal first project. It had an

---

DATE: 5-27-38   #3

TITLE: REBECCA
AUTHOR: Daphne Du Maurier
FORM: Novel - 630 Pp MS - To be pub Doubleday Doran Fall, 1938
TYPE: Murder Mystery Romance
LOCALE: Monte Carlo - England
SUBMITTED BY: Curtis Brown
READ BY: Dorcas Ruthenburg

THEME: A POOR BUT DELIGHTFUL YOUNG COMPANION MARRIED A DISTINGUISHED ENGLISHMAN TWICE HER AGE BUT IS COWED BY CONSCIOUSNESS OF HIS FIRST WIFE'S PERFECTIONS. GRADUALLY SHE LEARNS THAT REBECCA WAS A FIEND WHOM HER HUSBAND KILLED. HE IS FREED.

SUMMARY:

A shy young English girl is companion to a vulgar American, Mrs. Van Hopper, at Monte Carlo, when she meets Maxim de Winter, a distinguished man of forty-two, owner of a famous estate, Manderley, a widower whose beautiful wife was drowned the year before. After three weeks during which the English lass adores de Winter breathlessly, he proposes. They are married at once.

Returning to England after seven weeks, the new Mrs. de Winter is rather overawed by the lavish old house, the competent, unfriendly housekeeper, but most by the consciousness of the perfections of the first wife, Rebecca, a poised, brilliant, sophisticated creature. Her timid successor feels gauche, and is convinced that her husband is still devoted to this memory.

After several unhappy months, the first Mrs. de Winter's boat is found, containing a body. Maxim admits to his wife that it was he who murdered Rebecca, a fiend in reality. Suspicion points to Maxim during the inquest, but the verdict is returned as suicide. In spite of efforts of a blackmailer to upset it, they find that Rebecca had just learned of incipient cancer, giving a sound motive for her act. The housekeeper, convinced of her employer's guilt, burns Manderley, but Maxim and his wife are free to live unshadowed lives.

**

313

English setting, and an exciting straightforward plot that seemingly lent itself to easy adaptation. This latter chore Selznick delegated to Hitchcock, feeling secure in the knowledge that the director always collaborated closely with the writers on his scripts. Selznick, however, did not realize that Hitchcock's attitude toward any story material was to use it as a springboard for his own ideas. Selznick found out about this in a roundabout way through a message from Kay Brown, who relayed the information that Daphne du Maurier was "weeping bitter tears over what was done to *Jamaica Inn*.... She is hoping that *Rebecca* isn't going to turn out as big a disappointment." Selznick reassured her on this point, saying, "It is my intention to do *Rebecca* and not some botched up semi-original as was done with *Jamaica Inn*."

Even though Selznick had not had extensive story conferences with Hitchcock, the two men had carried on a lengthy correspondence regarding a screen treatment, including some of the problems inherent in the novel's trick of having the story narrated by the young heroine. In a rather unusual move, Selznick had given Orson Welles permission to do a radio dramatization of the novel on his "Mercury Theatre of the Air" in December 1938, a month after Welles had convinced the country that it was being invaded by Martians in his celebrated "War of the Worlds" broadcast. Selznick had two good reasons for doing this: *Rebecca* was "not receiving sufficient publicity considering its sensational success as a book, and Welles, who is very much in the public eye right now, would be able to attract enormous attention to both the book and our upcoming picture.... In particular I was intrigued to hear how he would handle the first person method of telling the story following the book in this method.... It has never to my knowledge been used in a picture except to a minor extent in a Fox picture of some years back called *The Power and the Glory*." After hearing the broadcast and reading the Welles script, Selznick urged Hitchcock to "give some thought to this idea.... We might accomplish it by having the girl start to tell the story and using her as a narrator over silent film until we slip into the picture proper...."

While Selznick was concerning himself with the problems of Scarlett O'Hara and the Civil War, Hitchcock began working with writers Joan Harrison and Philip McDonald on adapting the du Maurier novel. His difficulties became evident in a long memo to Selznick:

It is for you to decide if the girl's character should have humor or not.... This comment is prompted by the fact that the girl in the book is continually shown as an extremely sympathetic, gauche and moderately attractive young girl whose processes through the story are expressed mostly mentally.... In endeavoring to transcribe such a character to the screen something might have to be substituted for the first person style of telling ... and one thought we had was to show the girl in the Monte Carlo section to be fairly bright, attractive and amusing enough to take de Winter out of his morbid state.... This would also give us something to contrast her with on the arrival at Manderley.... At present this contrast does not exist in the book.... There is also going to be quite a problem to put over the justification for the murder. Is it sufficient to put this over verbally through de Winter's own words, or must it be done pictorially, in order to make absolutely sure that we do not lose any sympathy for him? In many ways, one feels that it may be necessary to see Rebecca in order to make certain about this.... On the other hand, there certainly is a great quality to the story in the fact that we *feel* Rebecca throughout rather than see her ... although de Winter's description of her is practically a visual one. Flashback? Ugh! ...

Answering the latter part of this quickly, Selznick referred to a letter from Daphne du Maurier:

She greatly hoped we wouldn't resurrect the dead wife.... Her conviction is that once this beautiful young woman is shown ... the contrast between her and the dull, rather plain second wife would kill the latter.... My own conviction is that there is no woman we could show who could possibly satisfy everybody's conception of what the dead wife looked like.... I am hopeful that we will accomplish what we want either with dialogue alone or with a flashback limited to Max alone.

Finally in early June, just as *Gone With The Wind* was winding up principal photography, Hitchcock delivered his first draft screenplay of *Rebecca* to Selznick. As was his custom, and indeed the custom in the entire movie industry, he had departed considerably not only from the scenes in the book but also from its attitude toward characters and settings; out of the 105 scenes in the treatment, only twenty appeared substantially as they were in the book. Selznick was horrified, and immediately fired off a ten-page, single-spaced memorandum to Hitchcock detailing his unhappiness:

I am shocked and disappointed beyond words by the treatment.... It's a distorted and vulgarized version of a provenly successful work, in which for no reason that I can discern, old fashioned movie scenes have been substituted for the captivatingly charming du Maurier scenes. We bought *Rebecca* and we intend to make *Rebecca*.... I have never been able to understand why motion picture people insist upon throwing away something of proven appeal to substitute things of their own creation. It is a form of ego which has very properly drawn upon Hollywood the wrath of the world for many years and candidly I am surprised to discover that the disease has apparently also spread to England.... I don't hold at all with the theory that the difference in medium necessitates a difference in story telling, or even a difference in scenes.... Readers of a dearly loved book will forgive omissions if there is a good reason for them but they will not forgive substitutions.... The only safe and sure way of aiming at a successful transcription of the original into motion picture form is to try as far as possible to retain the original.... This is the process that I had hoped was being engaged in on *Rebecca* ... and this is why I kept warning you to be faithful.... I have my own ego and I don't mind letting my creative instincts run wild on an original or in the adaptation of an unsuccessful work ... but it is not so great that it cannot be held in check for the adaptation of a successful work. I don't think I can create in two months or two years anything as good with the characters and situations of du Maurier's *Rebecca*, and frankly, I don't think you can either. I want this company to produce her *Rebecca*, not an original scenario based upon it.... It is my regretful conclusion that we should immediately start on a new treatment, probably with a new writing set-up.

Hitchcock had no reply to this and no choice but to do as instructed, which he did with amazing speed. By the end of June he had delivered another treatment to Selznick, this one written in collaboration with his wife, Alma Reville, and another writer named Michael Hogan. Attached to it was a note saying: "This treatment follows the exact line of the novel and contains rough dialogue by Daphne du Maurier. It will serve as a basis for discussion in order to decide what deviation may be permitted so as to remove some of the character weakness and slight static quality which I feel have emerged especially in the last scenes...." Having pulled enough good scenes out of the novel to tell the story as Selznick thought it should be told, Hitchcock and his adapters now began working these into a cohesive script form, and by the end of July had a third draft which Selznick felt lacked only a suitable dialogue writer to turn it into a finished screenplay. Fortuitously, Selznick discovered that the playwright Robert E. Sherwood would be available. He was just winding up his adaptation of his own play *Abe Lincoln in Illinois*, which John Cromwell was going to make for RKO, and Selznick immediately hired him to revise *Rebecca*'s dialogue, modeling it after du Maurier's original, paraphrasing it, and shortening it to make it more "speakable." Sherwood worked on this all during August and September, while simultaneously tidying up the messy business of Rebecca's murder by Maxim de Winter.

Selznick and Hitchcock had been struggling with this touchy point for months, trying to come up with something to satisfy both Colman's reservations and the restrictions of the motion picture Code, which forbade murderers to go unpunished. On the latter point, Selznick was losing his patience; he had just fought the battle of Rhett Butler's "damn" and was in no mood to give in to the Hays office's insistence that Max de Winter could not murder his wife. "Here is a story that has appealed to Americans by the hundreds of thousands, even millions," he wrote to Jock Whitney.

(Above) Joan Fontaine and Laurence Olivier. (Below) Three of the actresses who were given screen tests for the role of the nameless second Mrs. de Winter: Margaret Sullavan, Vivien Leigh (seen here with Laurence Olivier), and Loretta Young.

316

On the set of *Rebecca:* Alfred Hitchcock, script girl Lydia Schiller, and Joan Fontaine. Cinematographer George Barnes is at the far left. Miss Fontaine's costume was by Irene (uncredited).

A family publication like the *Ladies' Home Journal* saw fit to reprint this story without fear that it was anything immoral.... I think if we made *Rebecca* as written without adding anything censorable beyond what du Maurier wrote, and if the big theatre chains tried to gang up to stop us from showing it in their theatres because it hadn't been passed by the [Code] we would have a pretty good case of violation in restraint of trade ... which we could take to the courts—and more importantly to the press and public because I don't think Mr. Hays and his cohorts would very much relish the thing being fought out in the public prints. I could almost certainly guarantee tremendous support from the Guild groups here, actors, directors and writers.... It was bad enough trying to make pictures that would break even when we had a world market to play to, now that the foreign market is gone, the whole damned Code becomes doubly onerous.... We need at least to have something like the freedom that newspapers and magazines and book publishers and the legitimate stage have.... Instead, this short-sighted industry allows itself to be strangled by this insane, inane and outmoded Code.

In spite of Selznick's entreaties to Whitney and his fulminations, the Code emerged triumphant. At chief censor Joseph Breen's bidding, and much to Selznick's disgust, de Winter's murder of the evil Rebecca was rewritten so that it became an accident. "The whole story of *Rebecca,*" fumed Selznick, "is the story of a man who has murdered his wife, and now it becomes the story of a man who buries a wife who was killed accidentally." This latter story point needed to be glossed over carefully and quickly, which Robert Sherwood did very adroitly, inserting it into the long monologue de Winter delivers to his second wife in the very dramatic confessional scene where he tells her that he never loved Rebecca, that he hated her, that their marriage was a sham.

Selznick thought that Sherwood's begging of the issue might satisfy Ronald Colman's hesitancy about the part. Colman, however, was no longer hesitant; he just wasn't interested. His refusal forced Selznick and Hitchcock to consider other choices. The first of these was William Powell, who was still extremely eager to play the part in spite of Selznick's earlier turndown. The problem there was his MGM contract. He could be borrowed, but the price was high, and the availability not as extensive as Selznick would have liked. Instead Selznick approached Laurence Olivier. The two men had known each other since Selznick's RKO days when Olivier had been hired by the studio on the strength of his resemblance to Colman; he had made two rather lackluster pictures, then had gone back to England in disgust at the lifestyle and his lack of success. Olivier was ambitious and completely absorbed in his craft and his career. In the seven years since he had left Hollywood, he had worked in England at developing his talent both on stage and in films until his fast-growing reputation began to attract offers from America. It was his acceptance of the role of Heathcliff in Goldwyn's *Wuthering Heights* in late 1938 that brought him back to Hollywood, to be followed by Vivien Leigh—which had worked out well for everyone. Under William Wyler's careful, patient, and painstaking direction, Olivier gave a performance in the Brontë story that was dark, frenzied, tender, and brooding; the picture opened in New York in May 1939, simultaneously with the stage production of *No Time for Comedy,* in which he also starred. The extremely laudatory reviews for both picture and play—and the newspaper accounts of the crowds who were storming the front doors of the Radio City Music Hall and the stage door of the Morosco Theatre

wanting to get a look at this new matinee idol—convinced Selznick that Olivier would be a safe, even sure bet for Maxim de Winter. Accordingly, early in June 1939—with Hitchcock's approval and Myron's office arranging the contract—Selznick signed Olivier for the part and immediately opened up a hornet's nest for himself, for as soon as the contract was signed, Vivien Leigh began a concerted campaign to induce Selznick to cast her opposite Olivier in the part of the nameless heroine.

The casting of this part had been one of the problems Selznick had been mulling over ever since he bought the book. "The part was considered to be the biggest plum in years," Selznick said later, "second only to Scarlett O'Hara." Throughout the first year of script work, and while devoting his time to *Gone With The Wind*, he had been considering actresses continually. The most recurring possibility was Margaret Sullavan, the attractive, husky-voiced girl who had been a star since 1935's *The Good Fairy*, in which her sensitive, capricious quality caught the public fancy. In her favor for *Rebecca* was the fact that she had already played the part successfully in the radio broadcast with Orson Welles. After *Gone With The Wind* had started production, Selznick had been impressed with Olivia de Havilland's performance as Melanie, a part that had much in common with the second Mrs. de Winter. There was also Loretta Young, whom Selznick thought to be a "good bet.... She's a good actress and would be easy to deglamorize," and finally a new young stage actress from New York named Anne Baxter, whom Selznick tested on the strength of a recommendation from Kay Brown. He found her "touching ... a shade young ... very sincere and very difficult to photograph." Now added to these was Vivien Leigh, who, said Selznick, "is anxious to play in *Rebecca* for obvious reasons. She really thinks she could knock us dead in a [test]. It is my personal feeling that she would never be right for the girl, but God knows it would solve a lot of

problems if she was right, and I have too much respect for her ability as an actress, too much consideration for my own peace of mind during the months of August and September when a certain young man [Olivier] is going to be in these parts, and too much appreciation of how good it would be for her future with us if she were to play in *Rebecca* ... and I have ... told her she could make a test with Larry."

Leigh made a test, "hopping right from Scarlett into the part of the girl, with very little preparation," related Selznick, "and she was terrible." He promised to let her do another scene after the completion of *Gone With The Wind*, but she was in such a hurry to join Olivier in New York that she left without doing it. After the couple had returned to England that summer, another test was arranged in London, and air-expressed to Selznick in Culver City, where he looked at it and remained convinced that she was still wrong. To make sure his judgment wasn't colored by Scarlett, he asked George Cukor to come in and look at the tests of Sullavan, Baxter, and Leigh. "Bearing in mind that he is a great personal friend of Vivien's, and a great enthusiast of her [talent]," stated Selznick, " ... I was careful not to give him any prompting whatsoever, and he looked at them all very seriously and quietly except for some loud guffaws at Vivien's attempts to play it. He made the same comments that Hitchcock and I did—that she doesn't seem at all right as to sincerity or age or innocence.... He said that in his opinion the most touching was that of Anne Baxter." As for Olivia de Havilland, borrowing her from Warner Bros. had been difficult enough for *Gone With The Wind*; Jack Warner hadn't wanted to let her do it, believing that she would be spoiled by the part. After finishing as Melanie, she was scheduled to be loaned to Sam Goldwyn for another picture, which complicated matters further.

Selznick would have pursued this, had it not been for de Havilland's

(Opposite) This sketch of the ruined Manderley, which opens the story, was done by Lyle Wheeler. The handwritten description of the scene is probably Hitchcock's. (Above) The largest of the Manderley miniatures took up nearly all of one of the Selznick International stages.

sudden refusal even to test for the part when she discovered that her sister also was being considered for it. Her sister was Joan Fontaine, and it was indirectly through her that de Havilland had first been considered for Melanie Hamilton. Fontaine had been working rather listlessly in pictures since 1935, usually in small parts at RKO. Her biggest break and her greatest trial had come when she was cast as Fred Astaire's dancing partner in the first RKO picture he had made without Ginger Rogers, *A Damsel in Distress*—an apt title, for Fontaine was not up to any of the demands of the part except the charm, which she handled nicely. While at RKO she had caught George Cukor's eye, and in the fall of 1938 he had asked the young actress to come to the Selznick studio to test for the part of Melanie. She arrived dressed to the teeth, causing Cukor to exclaim: "You're too chic.... Melanie must be a plain, simple Southern girl," whereupon Fontaine suggested he test her sister Olivia de Havilland. Underneath all the chic, however, Cukor spotted a vulnerability and innocence that he remembered when he left *Gone With The Wind* and went to MGM to do *The Women*. He cast Fontaine in a small, sympathetic part in that, and was pleased enough with the results to suggest to Selznick that he consider her for *Rebecca*. While testing the other actresses, he kept bringing Fontaine back for more tests, now under Hitchcock's direction, and as late as August 1939, a month before the picture was to start production, Hitchcock was reporting to Selznick:

I showed the tests of Anne Baxter, Joan Fontaine and Margaret Sullavan to Mrs. Hitchcock and Joan Harrison.... They were both distressed about Fontaine, Mrs. Hitchcock feeling that Fontaine was too coy and simpering to a degree that it was intolerable ... and that her voice was extremely irritating.... Both felt that Anne Baxter is much more moving [but they expressed the fear that] she would not be able to play love scenes due to her age and lack of experience.... Both

agree that Margaret Sullavan is far ahead of either of them....

Based on this reaction, Selznick decided, as he related, "to forget about Fontaine for the role, since I couldn't get anybody on the staff, except Hal Kern, or anybody in the New York office to agree with me about her.... They couldn't see her for dust ... people kept calling her 'the wooden woman.'" With the physical production of *Gone With The Wind* over, the staff had begun to recuperate from the tremendous strain of the project. By contrast, *Rebecca* seemed to be almost a holiday. It was not complicated except for the forty separate settings that were required, and of these, twenty-five were interiors, primarily of the mansion Manderley.

Lyle Wheeler, who was still overseeing construction of sets for retakes on *Gone With The Wind*, recalled, "That picture went on into Thanksgiving. I had a bet with Ray Klune when we started it; I said it would go on to at least Thanksgiving, and he said it wouldn't. But the sets on *Gone With The Wind* were still up when we started *Rebecca*.... I remember we couldn't wait to strike the Twelve Oaks hallway to make room for Manderley." Manderley proved to be the biggest problem in the picture, almost as troublesome as Tara. Ray Klune remembered:

David felt that Manderley was almost as important a character in *Rebecca* as any of the people ... it was almost a living thing.... We had sent a second unit over to England to do a lot of background work.... Hitchcock knew exactly what he wanted ... but none of the mansions that our people came back with satisfied David. There were several very real problems with the mansion, at least as far as our using a real one. The first was that we had to show the exterior under many different conditions: rain, night, bleak, daytime, warm and inviting. It also had to be destroyed by fire. So Lyle and I, and I believe Hitchcock

319

(Top, left) Judith Anderson as the sinister housekeeper, Mrs. Danvers, who was in love with Rebecca and hates her successor. (Top, right) George Sanders, in the telephone booth, played Jack Favell, Rebecca's sleazy cousin, and evidently one of her lovers—another in a long line of charmingly attractive Hitchcock scoundrels. The man in the topcoat is Alfred Hitchcock, making his trademark cameo appearance in his first American film. The still is misleading; in the finished scene, Hitchcock can barely be glimpsed walking by in the background. (Above, left) Gladys Cooper and Nigel Bruce, as Maxim's sister and brother-in-law, arriving at the Manderley costume ball. (Above) Florence Bates as the *nouveau riche* American tourist Mrs. Van Hopper, who employed the future second Mrs. de Winter as a traveling companion. The character's vulgarity is beautifully captured by Hitchcock in a shot of her stubbing out her cigarette in a jar of cold cream. (Left) The menacing Mrs. Danvers conducts the second Mrs. de Winter on a tour of Rebecca's room, intimidating her with the knowledge that she can never hope to match the first Mrs. de Winter's breeding, glamour, and sex appeal. Later she tries to convince the frightened girl to throw herself from the window of Rebecca's room to the courtyard below.

by this time, we came up with the idea of several different-sized miniatures of Manderley. We figured that the only way to do it really effectively was to build probably the largest-scale miniature that had ever been built; then another miniature half that scale; and then sections of it full scale. Now we had a terrible time with David on that. He was afraid it would look phony in miniature, he didn't think we were right, but we argued long and hard for our position and he finally said to me, "You know, someday I'm going to get you ... but you were right and I was wrong on the burning of Atlanta, and I'm going to give you another chance to be wrong with this."

So he gave the go-ahead and we built the biggest miniature first.... It took up all of one of the old stages—it was just huge.... I think it cost $25,000.... It was so big and it took up so much of one of the old unsoundproofed stages that we couldn't really get far enough away from it to get a full feeling of the scale of it, so that's why we needed the smaller one, which enabled us to go way back, to show the scale of the whole estate.

When the first budget came through on the picture, Selznick was extremely displeased at the $947,000 estimate Klune's department had come up with. In one of his high-pressure lack-of-sleep moods, he criticized every single detail of the budget, saying:

I can't help but feel that our departments are trained to do things in the most expensive possible way and that nobody gives a thought to the cheaper way of doing things, even on a picture such as *Rebecca* which has a comparatively small cast, practically no physical problems and a simple wardrobe.... I think that the presentation of such an estimate as this is a disgrace and proves pretty conclusively that we need some sort of production and cost management ... that we ought to arbitrarily set a budget of $850,000 tops for *Rebecca* and so lay it out that each department is budgeted and must keep within this budget ... and that any department head that does not ... is going to be fired. Something as drastic as this is needed at this time once and for all to prove to the organization that *Gone With The Wind* is finished and that we are trying to make some pictures that will make some money.... If there is going to be any extravagance in our picture-making it is going to be indulged in by me personally to improve the quality of pictures, and I am not going to have it thrown away through sloppy management.

Several days after this diatribe, Selznick cooled down considerably after a long conference with Hitchcock, who told him that he thought he could save $40,000 on sets alone. Hitchcock was accustomed to using his art director's imagination and his engineer's training to make the most of the minimum budgets he had been working with in England—but that was when he had been left alone, to work unhampered on both script and sets, without anyone breathing down his neck. Here he had Selznick, Klune, and Wheeler all pulling him in different directions, with Selznick in particular alternately praising him and privately complaining to Klune that

Hitchcock has made a lot of grandstand speeches to me, and probably to you, about saving money on sets through revising his method of shooting various scenes.... I think he should be told by you that our method of operation with him on future pictures for which he is under contract to us is going to be dependent upon his performance on this picture.... In particular I wish you would say to him that we are going to watch very carefully the finished result to see whether we get on the screen the value of the sets that he has approved.

Having made Hitchcock's unfamiliar situation in a new country a little more uncomfortable, Selznick, at the end of August, now decided to settle his problem of the casting of the second Mrs. de Winter. He had absolutely ruled out Vivien Leigh, and his enthusiasm for Margaret Sullavan blew hot and cold. "Imagine," he remarked, "Margaret Sullavan being pushed around by Mrs. Danvers [the housekeeper] right up to the point of suicide!" As for Fontaine, Selznick related that

I told her of my feelings that she could not sustain the part and that she would be monotonous through the entire picture and that as a consequence I would be very hesitant about casting her in the role

until I saw her in some more tests.... Her answer to that was that she would be delighted to play the part but that she didn't want to make any more tests ... besides, she was getting married in a week ... so in spite of my liking for her I decided I couldn't be the only sensible person in the world and let her option drop.... The best thing to do would be to work out a deal with Anne Baxter. Then several things happened in succession—Hitchcock started swinging around to Fontaine after listening to discussions of the part by Sherwood and myself.... John Cromwell, who had directed her first test, stated that we were out of our minds not to put her in the part, and then I asked George Cukor to look again at all the tests.... He and Cromwell are the two men who in my career of producing have demonstrated the most accurate sense of casting. After looking at them, George said in his opinion that if he had to start the picture immediately he would without hesitation select Fontaine.

Over the Labor Day weekend Selznick "paced the floor ... and brooded over the fact that if the part were miscast, the whole picture would be wrong; that if I had enough nerve to cast an English girl as Scarlett O'Hara, why couldn't I have the courage of my own convictions about Fontaine? I reminded myself that she would have the benefit and guidance of Hitchcock ... so I went to the studio bright and early the next morning ... and asked her to cut her honeymoon short and come back to play the part."

Alfred Hitchcock directed the first shots of *Rebecca* on Friday, September 8, five days after England had declared itself at war with Germany. Hitchcock, Olivier, and most of the other British members of the *Rebecca* company were frantic with concern about their families, and just exactly what might be happening to their homeland. The atmosphere on the set was funereal for the first few days of shooting, as was the pace at which Hitchcock was working. The production had been budgeted for thirty-six days' shooting time, which meant that he would have to complete four pages of script each day, something he had assured Selznick he would be able to do. By the end of the second week, *Rebecca* was five days behind schedule; when Ridgeway Callow, the assistant director, pointed this out to Hitchcock, he replied: "Reggie, if I make this picture on schedule and it's a lousy picture, they will not say to me, 'The picture is lousy, but good old Hitch brought it in on schedule.' Regardless of the schedule, they'll forget about it if it's a good picture."

Hitchcock was well aware of how important this picture was to his future in America, and he was being painstaking and methodical, especially with Joan Fontaine, who was nervous and unsure of herself, traits that were only in her favor as far as her characterization went. Hitchcock did his best to intensify this by letting her know that Olivier had wanted Vivien Leigh in the part, which added to her insecurities and made the filming even slower as numerous takes were required to get an adequate performance out of her. Slowing things yet further were Hitchcock's methods of working: he would shoot only the film he needed to cut the picture together the way he thought it should be done. This "cutting in the camera," as it was known, was anathema to Selznick, who liked to cover a scene from every possible angle so that he could experiment in the cutting room. As he began seeing the dailies coming in from the *Rebecca* stages, he realized that he was not getting this, and took time off from his editing of *Gone With The Wind* to tell Hitchcock:

Reducing the number of angles is highly desirable ... but it is of no value if you are simply going to give us less film per day than a man who shoots twice as many angles.... There are things about your methods of shooting which I think you simply must correct, such things as letting the actors remain idle while the camera crew line up and the camera crew remaining idle while the actors are being rehearsed. It is just infantile not to realize that these two processes must go through simultaneously and if the noise disturbs you then rehearse them on the sidelines somewhere.... Good average time on *Rebecca* would be acceptable under normal conditions ... because of the war, and the loss of the foreign markets ... bad time on *Rebecca* [is] impossible to accept.

Hitchcock's reply was that it was taking time to work with Joan Fontaine and that the script, still in a semi-finished state, was slowing him up. "I am aware that it takes time to get a performance out of Joan Fontaine," replied Selznick,

> but every picture I have ever worked on had some such difficulty.... Miss Fontaine requires work, but so does every other girl who has been aimed at stardom ... you are fortunate in having a completely competent cast of highly expert actors.... In most of the studios you wouldn't have anything like the cast you have now.... Perhaps you can charge me with the condition of the script, but I don't feel this is a factor.... But whether you or I is responsible or we are responsible jointly (which is probably close to the truth) the fact remains ... that you have had the script many days ahead and there has been no question of it coming out at the last minute.

Hitchcock was not used to this kind of supervision, nor Selznick's insistence on having his script adhered to rigidly, but he was in no position to force the issue. Lydia Schiller was pulled off her editing duties on *Gone With The Wind* and assigned as script girl on *Rebecca,* with instructions to let Selznick know if there was the slightest deviation from the approved script. The first week of October was scheduled to be taken up with the filming of the scenes of the young wife surreptitiously investigating Rebecca's lavish bedroom, which has been preserved intact since her death by Mrs. Danvers, the housekeeper. The scene grew tense, moody, and dramatic as the heroine was confronted by the malevolent housekeeper. "Mr. Selznick wanted to open the sequence on a close-up of the embroidered 'R' on the bed and then pull back from that," recalls Lydia Schiller,

> and move around the rest of the room, as the girl discovers it. Hitchcock decided that the scene should start with the camera back. When I called his attention to it, he said, "No, I'm going to do it this way." It wasn't my place to argue, but it was such a drastic change from what I knew Mr. Selznick wanted that I called his office and told his secretary. Right away, there was a memo delivered by hand from Selznick criticizing what had just taken place. Hitchcock stopped everything and said, "Was Mr. Selznick on the set? I didn't see him.... What's going on here? I've got a memo here from him telling me not to shoot it this way.... Who's doing this reporting?" I was sitting in my camp chair ... and Hitchcock looked at the assistant director and started pressing him, accusing him.... I couldn't keep quiet, so I said, "No, Mr. Hitchcock, it wasn't Reggie [Callow], it was me."... He was just stunned, so taken aback, as if I'd done something unspeakable.... He said, "You, Lydia? I thought you were working with me, for me, instead you've been spying on me, reporting on me."

> Needless to say, I went through the baptism of fire after that. I had no peace from then on.... In his very quiet way ... as we'd sit and work over the script, he would say these things to me ... they were obscenities, I didn't even know what they meant.... It was just shattering to me ... my father and brothers never even said hell.... Two or three times I had to leave.... I finally decided that these words that he was saying to me were simply letters strung together ... they had no meaning . . . they couldn't touch me and I was finally able to overcome that feeling of revulsion I felt and continue with the work.

Geniuses are erratic in their behavior, and Hitchcock was no exception. He demanded total loyalty from his crews, and when he felt he had been betrayed he could be merciless and unyielding. Yet Fred Parrish, the still photographer, relates a story that is exactly the opposite of Lydia Schiller's: "I had noticed that when they set up the camera for an over the shoulder shot of one of the actors, that when they reversed the angle for the other actor, he was on the wrong side of the frame. I mentioned this to Mr. Hitchcock, but he told me I was mistaken and that I should just pay attention to my stills. The next day, after he'd looked at the rushes, he came on the set and called everybody together and told them what I had said and how rude he'd been to me, and that I had been right and he wanted to apologize to me in front of everybody."

Selznick meanwhile was looking carefully at the rushes and becoming concerned not just about the pacing and tempo of the scenes but also about the performances in them. He commented to Hitchcock:

> Larry's silent action and reactions become slower as his dialogue

The opening sequence, faithful to the moody, atmospheric first paragraphs of du Maurier's novel. The mansion is the smaller of the two models, around which Wheeler and Cosgrove had built a miniature forest that the camera moved through on a concealed track. The scenes of the coastline cliffs and ocean were filmed with doubles at Carmel, California, and combined through a split-screen process with studio footage of Laurence Olivier and Joan Fontaine.

becomes faster.... For God's sake speed him up, not merely in these close-ups but in the rest of the picture on his reactions which are apparently the way he plays on the stage, where it could be satisfactory.... While you're at it make sure that we know what the hell he's talking about because he still has a tendency to speed up his words and to read them in such a way that an American audience can't understand them.... I think you've handled Joan with great restraint, but I think we've got to be careful not to lose what little variety there is in the role by underplaying her in her emotional moments.... From this point on to the end I'd like to urge that you be a little more Yiddish Art Theatre in these moments, a little less English Repertory Theatre, which will make the restraint of the rest of the performance much more effective ... and will not make it seem as though Joan is simply not capable of the big moments.

Filming proceeded on *Rebecca* at the slow pace of one and a half to two pages a day until mid-November, when it abruptly ceased for three days due to Joan Fontaine's coming down with the flu. Just as she recovered, the stagehands' union called a three-day wildcat strike, making a total of six days lost. While the first unit was closed down, two second units were hard at work, one on location at Del Monte up the California coast near Monterey, filming exterior scenes of the approach to Manderley and the grounds of the estate. Here, too, there were serious problems, as the entire crew came down with a severe case of poison ivy which put them all into the hospital for three days. Another unit, under assistant director Eric Stacey, journeyed to Catalina to film the exterior beach scenes.

After Joan Fontaine recovered, the principal photography was completed on November 20, twenty-six days behind schedule. The picture then went on the shelf for more than a month while Selznick finished up *Gone With The Wind*. After coming back to Culver City from the Atlanta and New York premieres, he took *Rebecca* on December 26 to San Bernardino for its first preview. "It was in the roughest kind of assembly form," he related, "and thousands of feet overlength ... but we had a splendid audience reaction.... Judging by the enthusiasm of this preview audience and the way they applauded the main title ... it would seem that the public has been looking forward eagerly to the picture and awaits it in great numbers.... It may prove to be the most successful picture we have made with the exception of *GWTW*."

To make sure of this, Selznick ordered the picture put back into work for several days of retakes, having Hitchcock re-do more than thirty scenes in the picture, including the climactic sequence showing the burning of Manderley by the crazed Mrs. Danvers. Over the years, Hitchcock has enjoyed telling how he talked Selznick out of having the smoke from the burning Manderley form a huge R in the sky, but the script, Selznick's notes on the scene, and Lyle Wheeler, the art director, all directly refute Hitchcock's claims about this. "Nothing like that ever was brought up, except perhaps as a joke," according to Wheeler.

When Selznick looked at the rushes of this crucial sequence, he found himself

disappointed in the fire in Rebecca's room.... The lighting is extremely uninteresting.... It should be lit weirdly with an effect as though lit entirely by firelight with the shadow of the flames, etc.... We're a little slow in getting to the embroidered R.... There's no photographic effect as there should be ... of the flames rising as they devour the R to give us a natural curtain of flames as a background for our end title.... The whole thing is not nearly as good as it should be and if we can fix it at a little expense, I think we should.

Once the retakes were completed, Selznick turned the picture over to the composer Franz Waxman to supply it with a suitable atmospheric musical score, borrowing Waxman from MGM, where he was completing his work on George Cukor's sophisticated comedy *The Philadelphia Story*. Waxman was a versatile and prolific German émigré who had first gained attention in Hollywood with his eerie, impressionistic score for Universal's 1935 *The Bride of Frankenstein*. Selznick had used him previously to give *The Young in Heart* its lilting, humorous feeling, and he now counted on him to provide *Rebecca* with an appropriately ominous yet romantic atmosphere. Waxman's difficulty in doing this was twofold:

he was still working on *The Philadelphia Story,* and *Rebecca* was still in an unfinished, unedited state. Selznick, however, was eager to have the picture open as soon as possible, as he was planning on closing down the studio for several months afterward and taking a long vacation. When Waxman protested that he couldn't write a score to an unfinished picture, Selznick insisted that "the idea that music cannot be written until a picture is finally cut is so much nonsense.... There is no reason on earth why a score shouldn't be written from a rough assembly even if it involves a certain amount of rewriting when the picture is finally cut." Selznick, whose knowledge of every other aspect of film production and craftsmanship was astute, proved his ignorance of the problems of music composition by stating that "the exact timing of music has little or nothing to do with the composition of it, particularly as to the themes ... and all the musical strains regardless of whether a scene is ten feet or a hundred feet long.... I think that this ought to be hammered into Waxman ... and if he works from script without seeing the picture, he could have 90% of the score ready by the time we turn the picture over to him." Fortunately, Waxman was able to work from the first rough cut of the picture, and he rose to the occasion magnificently, giving the music a sumptuous and mysterious romanticism that perfectly matched the gleaming, opulent quality of the picture. Selznick, ever the tinkerer, didn't like portions of it after he heard it, and since Waxman was unavailable for revisions, he ordered Lou Forbes, the head of his music department, to substitute sections of Max Steiner's score for *A Star Is Born* for the offending portions, which irritated both Waxman and Steiner.

By the time *Rebecca* was ready for release in March 1940, it had reached the considerable cost of $1.28 million, some $513,000 over Selznick's hoped-for original budget. United Artists, hoping to prove to Selznick that he was wrong about their sales department, marketed the picture as forcefully as they knew how, capitalizing on the considerable prestige of *Gone With The Wind,* and eventually attaining a gross of $2.5 million for *Rebecca*'s first year of release. Selznick's gamble on Joan Fontaine paid off handsomely. She received glowing notices for her performance, and was nominated for an Academy Award, one of eleven nominations the picture received, including Hitchcock's direction and Waxman's music. The overwhelming success of *Gone With The Wind,* which was playing its second engagements around the country during early 1941, had a positive "spillover" effect on the fortunes of *Rebecca,* for on February 21, 1941, in one of those perverse manifestations that characterize so many Academy Awards ceremonies, *Rebecca* was voted the Best Picture of 1940, edging out *The Grapes of Wrath, The Great Dictator, The Long Voyage Home, The Philadelphia Story, Our Town,* and Hitchcock's second American film, *Foreign Correspondent. Rebecca*'s victory seems, in retrospect, to be Hollywood's last thumbing of its nose at the newly emergent pictures of realism and cynicism, which were just then beginning to crack through the wall of pervasive romanticism that had been the industry staple of the past decade.

The successful release of *Rebecca,* coupled with the *Gone With The Wind* phenomenon, pushed David Selznick to the very top of his profession; in the past two years he had created three new stars—Ingrid Bergman, Vivien Leigh, and Joan Fontaine—made the most overwhelmingly successful picture in the history of the business, and followed it up with another critical and financial hit. In a sense, Hollywood at the end of 1941 could truly be said to be David O. Selznick's Hollywood. It had taken him fourteen years of nonstop, obsessive devotion to his goals, but by the end of that year he had accomplished everything he had set out to do: restore his family's name to prominence, make artistic pictures that were commercial successes, and gain the respect and admiration of his contemporaries. Having reached the top, he didn't know quite what to do next. The rigors of the past two years had depleted him, and he decided to close down his studio. As he put it in a letter to his wife,

I want to loaf, play, and write and love. I don't even want to try to make money during this period ... I want to be gone 3 months, 4 months, 6 months, stay away as long as we like ... maybe London for the *Wind* premiere (King and Queen there, I believe). I want to see you curtsy.... I want to go gloriously in debt for a Great Cause ... and I'll never forgive either of us if we let *anything* interfere.

Hollywood—The War Years

THE ACADEMY AWARDS for 1940 were presented at a banquet at the Biltmore Hotel in downtown Los Angeles on February 21, 1941; the 1,400 guests who heard *Rebecca* announced as the Best Picture of the Year had earlier been treated to a 6½-minute address by President Roosevelt, inaugurated the month before for an unprecedented third term. In his speech, transmitted direct from the White House, Roosevelt paid tribute to the accomplishments of the motion picture industry. His words—the very fact of them—conferred a kind of official blessing on the movie people and their work, boosting their prestige nationally and their pride in themselves locally, not without some justification. The year 1940 had marked the fiftieth anniversary of the invention of the American motion picture. The Hollywood film industry, in the twenty-four months between January 1939 and February 1941, produced 715 features, ranging from *Andy Hardy Gets Spring Fever* to *Wuthering Heights.* Twice each week during those two years, 83 million people in the United States paid 25 cents to sample the feast that the industry spread before them. Between 1940 and 1941, moviegoers had poured a little over $2 billion into box offices, climaxing a spectacular decade of accomplishment for the film industry, in which it had refined the new technique of sound and demonstrated its mastery of method, form, and style. Roosevelt's speech on the night of the Awards paid tribute to this hard-won maturity and also to the part the movies had played in heartening the country through the vicissitudes of the past ten years. Roosevelt was one of the first modern leaders to recognize a fact of modern life: the ability of mass communication devices to manipulate people, to shape their attitudes, values, and conduct. He had been the first chief executive to appear on the rapidly developing sight and sound device called television as he officially opened the New York World's Fair on May 1, 1939. On July 1, 1941, RCA and NBC, under license from the government, began commercial television broadcasting over station WNBT to the 7,500 receiving sets in the metropolitan New York area. Transmission started at noon that day, an occasion that went unnoticed by all but the interested few. In his New York headquarters, David Selznick knew of it through his friendship with William Paley of CBS, but along with everybody else in the movie business, Selznick was not at all impressed by the event. What did impress him that afternoon was a girl, "a big-eyed girl," whom he saw waiting in his outer office.

Her name was Phyllis Walker, and she was one of the handful of young hopefuls whom Kay Brown and her staff were always on the lookout for. Since the successful launching of Ingrid Bergman, Vivien Leigh, and Joan Fontaine, Selznick had become increasingly talent-minded, concentrating on signing up promising, inexpensive young performers with the intention of developing them and lending them out to other companies. It was a strategy he had wanted to pursue during the six years of Selznick International, but the economics of picturemaking dictated that to a large degree he use known names. Now the enthusiastic public response to his last three "discoveries" convinced him to concentrate his energies on discovering and developing new talent. This was less exhausting and much less expensive than making pictures; it wasn't as

much fun, of course, but the ratio of possible return on the small investment of putting people under contract and grooming them for "loan outs" appealed to his gambler's instinct, and there was always the satisfaction to be gained from having his hunch about someone pay off handsomely. The wheeling and dealing involved was also free from the daily pressures of production, and for a compulsive worker like Selznick it was almost a rest cure; the herculean efforts of the last three years had left him creatively depleted. To an interviewer early in 1940 he had remarked: "Frankly, I think I must have been out of my mind to tackle *Gone With The Wind* ... it's the only explanation I have for even attempting something like that ... nothing will ever seem hard to me again."

Before he could rest from these labors, however, he had to oversee the breaking up of the Selznick International company. The tremendous returns on *Gone With The Wind* and *Rebecca* had boosted the company's income to such an extraordinarily high level for one year that unless it was reapportioned, most of it would go for taxes. Whitney by now had tired of playing at the movies. While he was very fond of Selznick personally, the man's unorthodox and turbulent methods of moviemaking had become extremely unsettling to a person of Whitney's orderly temperament. So in August 1940 the major stockholders of Selznick International agreed to dissolve the company. After splitting the first wave of profits from *GWTW* and *Rebecca,* Selznick and the Whitney interests ended up with close to $4 million each. In order to help them keep as much of this as possible, Walter Orr, Whitney's tax lawyer, devised a complex and innovative scheme whereby the major partners in the company sold to each other portions of the assets, something that Selznick characterized as "one of our lesser contributions to Hollywood, the introduction of capital gains." There is much less tax paid on the sale of assets, and in order to maximize the benefits of this, the tax lawyers made an agreement with the government that the dissolution would be spread out over the next three years. Selznick kept his 44 percent interest in *GWTW,* and took over the contracts of his three female stars, Bergman, Leigh, and Fontaine, those of directors Alfred Hitchcock and Robert Stevenson, and actress Hattie McDaniel. He also assumed Selznick International's commitment to deliver two more pictures for United Artists release, while the Whitney interests, in addition to keeping their 48 percent of *GWTW,* bought the negatives of the nine Selznick International productions, subsequently selling them off to a reissue company called Film Classics, which kept them in circulation all during the forties, the color films being reprinted in the garish two-color tones of Cinecolor.*

For the next few months Selznick devoted most of his efforts to the thousands of details involved in setting up his new company, David O. Selznick Productions, while at the same time investing some of his windfall in buying properties that might be turned into the two pictures

---

*Selznick almost immediately bought back *Rebecca* from the Whitneys and later made an effort to regain the rights and the negatives to every Selznick International picture. He succeeded with all but *A Star Is Born, Nothing Sacred,* and *The Young in Heart.*

(Top, left) MGM put *Gone With The Wind* into general release for the first time in December 1940, a year after its road show openings, giving the picture a gala "birthday" celebration at Loew's Grand Theatre in Atlanta. Selznick flew Vivien Leigh, Laurence Olivier (the two had married in September 1939), and Alfred Hitchcock down for the festivities, the proceeds of which were to benefit the British War Relief. Due to poor weather, the plane was grounded in Louisville, and Margaret Mitchell was prevailed upon to preside over the cake-cutting ceremonies in Atlanta. This popular-priced release grossed $9.7 million, and the picture was voted the most popular of 1940 in the *Film Daily* exhibitors poll. (Top, right) At the Academy Awards ceremonies for 1940: Ginger Rogers won the award for best actress in RKO's *Kitty Foyle;* David Selznick produced the best picture, *Rebecca;* Lynn Fontanne presented Rogers with her award; James Stewart won for best actor in *The Philadelphia Story;* and Bob Hope, in addition to being master of ceremonies, was presented with a special plaque "in recognition of his unselfish services to the motion picture industry." (Above, right) Alexander Korda, Mary Pickford, a jovial David Selznick, and a dubious Charles Chaplin on the lawns of Pickfair the day Selznick became an equal partner in United Artists. (Right) Selznick, director Robert Stevenson (partially obscured), architect William Pereira, script supervisor and production assistant Barbara Keon, and author Aldous Huxley in a 1941 production meeting on the projected Selznick version of *Jane Eyre,* for which Huxley was writing the screenplay. Selznick eventually concluded that it was too similar to *Rebecca,* and he sold the script and the services of Stevenson, Pereira, and Joan Fontaine to 20th Century-Fox, who starred Fontaine opposite Orson Welles. The painting on the wall is of David's father, Lewis J. Selznick. (Above) Selznick, his wife Irene, and their two children, circa 1941.

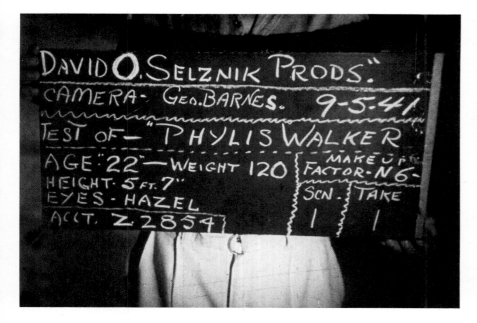

(Above) The screen test for Phyllis Isley Walker, for whom Selznick had "great enthusiasm. [I hope] that overnight she will be a star." (Below) About Gregory Peck, Selznick was less enthusiastic, wiring Kay Brown, who had suggested testing the young actor, "He photographs like Abe Lincoln. . . . If he has a great personality, I don't think it comes through in these tests." Peck, a native Californian, went to New York in 1939; after serving stints as a barker at the World's Fair, a tour guide at Rockefeller Center, and a photographer's model, he joined the Neighborhood Playhouse; within two years he was in demand as a young leading man on Broadway. Selznick evidently had second thoughts about Peck's appeal and signed the twenty-six-year-old actor to a nonexclusive contract in 1943—something of a rarity for the time, because the war had depleted the ranks of leading men and there was fierce competition among the studios for romantic leads. Peck had appeared in the low-budget RKO war melodrama *Days of Glory;* Selznick later loaned the actor to 20th Century-Fox, with the proviso that he be given the lead in the A. J. Cronin best seller *The Keys of the Kingdom,* which Fox had purchased from Selznick. As a missionary priest in China, Peck was required to age from eighteen to eighty; he did it so convincingly that he was nominated for an Academy Award in 1945—the year that saw his emergence as a full-fledged star.

his new company owed United Artists. One of these purchases was the hit Broadway play *Claudia* by Rose Franken, an affecting little comedy-drama about a young, inexperienced bride, which had made an overnight star of actress Dorothy McGuire in the title role. Selznick bought the rights, but did not immediately sign up Miss McGuire; his idea was to find a new personality to cast in the film version, who could be turned into another star in the Selznick constellation. Which was why the twenty-one-year-old Phyllis Walker was waiting in his outer office.

The daughter of Texas exhibitor Phil Isley, the young woman was shy and withdrawn. She had studied dramatics at Northwestern University and then enrolled in the American Academy of Dramatic Arts in New York, where she met and fell in love with a struggling young actor named Robert Walker. They were married in 1939, had two children, and Phyllis had even had a short-lived Hollywood career at the Republic studio out in the San Fernando Valley, home of "B" westerns and Saturday matinee serials. After appearing in *Dick Tracy's G Men,* she had decided that the movies were not yet for her and returned to New York to play small roles in smaller theatres.

Selznick, seeing her sitting in the waiting room, was immediately taken with her. After watching her test, he told Kay Brown, "I have great enthusiasm for her," and having spoken to the girl for several hours in mid-August, he decided to give her a contract, his only reservation being her husband and children: "I told her that I wouldn't want to give her a big opportunity and . . . make her a star . . . only to find that we had difficulty later about her family being [in New York]. She assured me that this would not be the case, that if we sign her, her husband is quite prepared to move to California with the two children. Incidentally, what is the husband like?"

Robert Walker was a gangly, good-looking youngster, almost as shy as his wife, but with a certain awkward charm to his manner that gave him an immensely appealing quality. Selznick considered signing him also, saying: "If we can make a brief initial deal, it might be better to do it now, and preserve his pride so that it doesn't look as though we're signing him just because of her. But . . . wouldn't it be wonderful if he turned out to be a good bet himself?" Walker did turn out to be a good bet, for he was signed up by MGM within the year, and they began using him in small roles, while Selznick deliberately kept Phyllis Walker off the screen until he could decide

whether we want to use her in *Claudia* . . . everyone connected with motion pictures who has seen her work has gone overboard about the girl. . . . I have seen her on the stage and I know the excitement she causes in audiences. . . . It is my sincere hope that she will overnight be a star. . . . Incidentally, I would like to get a new name for her. . . . Phyllis Walker is a particularly undistinguished name. . . . I don't want anything too fancy . . . I would like to get a first name that isn't carried by a dozen other girls in Hollywood. . . . I would appreciate suggestions.

While concerning himself with the future of Phyllis Walker, Selznick was also busy with David O. Selznick Productions, Inc. His success with *Gone With The Wind* had given new prestige to the independent producers, or "indies," as they were somewhat derisively known. Independents, which had been defined for years as fly-by-night, poverty-row operations, were at the bottom of the Hollywood production hierarchy. In the industry's youth, the independents had been all there was; but as the years passed, Zukor, Loew, and Carl Laemmle had formed studio complexes that slowly absorbed the small individual units. By the early thirties, the only independents operating on a level comparable with the majors were the indestructible Samuel Goldwyn; the venerable Hal Roach, who had been crafting two- and three-reel comedies since the early twenties; and, of course, Walt Disney, who was independent in the fullest sense of the word. With the advent and success of Selznick, however, others were encouraged to try their luck, and at the close of the 1930s there were twenty major independent producers working in Hollywood. Ten of these were financed and released through RKO, which had started encouraging outside producers to make pictures on its lot. RKO had also managed to woo Samuel Goldwyn away from his United Artists contracts, a loss especially damaging to UA, which had counted heavily on his sustained production schedule to fill its release calendar.

UA still had an impressive roster of producers releasing pictures through its network of twenty-six national exchanges, but with Goldwyn gone and Selznick inactive for two years, UA sorely needed product.

There were rumors that Selznick was going to release his future pictures through MGM after fulfilling his two-picture obligation to UA, and indeed the offer had been made, but Selznick was wary of retracing his steps. He was also still suspicious of UA's distribution and sales set-up and, when approached to renew his contract with the company, indicated he would do so only if he had a say in the way the company was run. This meant that he would have to become a stockholder, which seemed unlikely since it was this very request by Goldwyn that had been turned down by Pickford, Chaplin, and Fairbanks (D. W. Griffith had given up his stock in 1931). After the death of Fairbanks, however, Chaplin and Pickford were persuaded to let Selznick buy into the company. Following an involved series of negotiations, he paid $300,000 for a one-third share, with a pledge to deliver ten pictures within the next five years. In a unique form of kickback, United Artists advanced Selznick $300,000 to help him start production, and agreed to pay him $125,000 for the first four pictures that he personally produced for the company to release. He also received favorable distribution terms, along the lines of the preferential treatment given to the original owners; additionally, changes were made in the operational procedure of the company and a new management team was put in with one of Selznick's hand-picked men on the board, all of which was designed to prevent the Pickford-Chaplin duo from running the show as they had been trying to do for the last several years, with much back-and-forth acrimony.

With United Artists reorganized in a manner more acceptable to him, Selznick now created a smaller subsidiary production company called Vanguard Films, which would finance pictures not personally produced by him but made more or less under his supervision, thus fulfilling his contractual obligations. In late 1941 Selznick wrote: "I have stepped back into the role of a producer. I feel very strongly that the best contribution that the owners of United Artists can make to the company is to produce pictures." On the same day in October that Selznick made these comments, the newspapers carried headlines that the Japanese Empire had a new premier—the head of the army, Hideki Tojo—who warned President Roosevelt to stop meddling in Japan's affairs. As the Thanksgiving holiday passed, and shoppers began jamming the stores in preparation for Christmas, the main topic at the Selznick studio was the redecoration of the boss's new office. Selznick had just rejected a strong offer from Sam Goldwyn to come and set up headquarters at the Goldwyn studio, for Selznick felt at home on the RKO-Pathé lot. He had leased the smaller wing of the main building and decided it needed extensive remodeling to fit his scheduled production plans. Lyle Wheeler, who was working on the design and decoration of the interiors, recalled: "We were working on Sundays on this; it was quiet, there were no phone calls and we could concentrate. This one particular Sunday, my mind was not on working, my wife was in the hospital in Santa Monica about to have our first child. Right after lunch, Bobbie Keon, David's secretary, came in and told us that the Japanese had attacked Pearl Harbor. . . . There was a lot of fear at that time that they might be planning an attack on California.* . . . I remember going right from the studio over to the hospital. . . . There was some panic there, they wanted to get everybody out of the hospital as soon as possible."

On December 9, 1941, the day after Roosevelt asked Congress for a declaration of war, the industry's Motion Picture Committee Cooperating for National Defense, which had been in existence a little over a year, changed its name to the more concise War Activities Committee, assuring Roosevelt that it "stood ready to cope with any and all demands that the Government might make upon the trade."

After manpower, the first demand was a call for the industry to use its know-how to raise funds. An elaborate series of cross-country rallies to sell Defense Bonds and Defense Stamps was organized by the Holly-

---

* After the war, plans were found in the Japanese War Ministry for a projected invasion of the Los Angeles area. They had been drawn up by an overoptimistic Lt. General Homma (later the conqueror of Bataan and Corregidor), and one of the unique features of this project was a special task force whose instructions were to rush from the beachhead to the MGM studios in Culver City, secure a copy of *Gone With The Wind,* and send it to the general in Manila.

wood Victory Committee, sending stars all over the country to raise the necessary millions to finance the war. Five weeks after Pearl Harbor, the Hollywood community had its first taste of the carnage that was about to engulf the country: Carole Lombard was killed in a plane crash returning from a bond-selling tour. The shock of her death and the circumstances surrounding it brought the war's sobering realities to Hollywood. Selznick was particularly stunned by the tragedy; Lombard had been one of his favorite people. As his brief note to the grieving Clark Gable said:

> Words are futile—and besides you have had so many of them. Please permit me to say that in a lifetime of experience in this business, I have never met so inspiring a personality, so invariably lovable and happy-natured a person as Carole. She will be missed by all who knew her as long as we live.

Just before leaving on the tour, Lombard had called Selznick to ask for a 16 mm print of the last film she had done for him, *Made for Each Other*. Selznick and Whitney jointly sent Gable the print, with an accompanying note asking him to accept it "from the stockholders of Selznick International as a small expression of regard and of sympathy, and as a token of the affection that we all had for Carole."

These same stockholders, now reduced to Selznick, Jock and C. V. Whitney, David's brother Myron, and Merian C. Cooper, had just received the company's share of the proceeds from the third tour of *Gone With The Wind*. Playing at popular prices—25 to 30 cents—for the first time, it brought in another $1,065,835 to Selznick International. The estimate of the Whitney lawyers and tax accountants was that the public appetite for *Gone With The Wind* had been sated, that there was barely another million left in it. However, as the lawyers and tax accountants forcefully pointed out, the continued possession of the film could jeopardize the carefully worked out capital gains arrangement made with the government. Unless the assets of the company were disposed of by August 1942, the entire tax set-up might be disallowed. Selznick did not want to let go of his share of the picture, no matter how much or how little was left; but on the advice of the attorney, he made a half-hearted approach to MGM, asking $2 million for his share, and met with a flat turndown.

Jock Whitney was another matter. *GWTW* was complicating his business life, which he desperately wanted to straighten out. With the entry of America into the war, Whitney enlisted and was commissioned a major; in mid-1942, he was anxious to be off to the fighting, but even this haste did not detract from his business sense. Just before his departure he spent a weekend with the Selznicks, and it was then that the disposition of *Gone With The Wind* was decided upon. According to Selznick:

> Jock and I had a talk in my bedroom, which I deliberately made very brief as I dislike discussing business at home. I told him that I was willing to buy him out rather than sell, but Jock stated flatly that he would only sell at twice what he would buy me out for. . . . Since Jock was so reluctant to sell to me, I sold to him. . . . I felt that if anybody should make a profit out of it, it should be Jock, for nothing he could ever do to me in business, and no profits I could possibly make out of my share, could compensate for the magnificent support and help he gave me at the most crucial point in my career, and I shall never forget this.

So Whitney bought out Selznick for $400,000, and a year later, in August 1943, Whitney and his group sold their holdings to MGM for $2.4 million, giving Loew's, Inc., almost complete ownership of the picture except for two small interests held by Myron Selznick and, ironically, C. V. Whitney. At the conclusion of the dissolution, Selznick and Whitney sent a portion of their share of the proceeds to Margaret Mitchell, who replied in a most gracious letter:

> I came home from a long day at the Red Cross, too tired to take my shoes off, and . . . found your letter and the very generous check. . . . I had to read it twice before it made any sense and then it almost made me cry. You two and I and hundreds of others have been associated in the most phenomenally successful event in motion picture or theatrical

history. I have seen the picture five and a half times now and have examined it from many angles—musical score, costumes, bit players, etc., and I like it better each time. And each time the film reaches out and takes my hand to lead me down paths that seem ever new, for I forget in watching that I was the author of the book and am able to view the film with fresh eyes. At the Grand Theatre here in Atlanta, they play the theme music from *Gone With The Wind* when the last performances of the night are over. Frequently John and I and many other Atlantans remain in our seats to listen to it. . . . I never hear this music without feeling again the strange mixture of emotions that I experienced on that night nearly three years ago when I sat in the same theatre and saw the film for the first time. I doubt if I could describe those emotions, but they did not include fear that it would not be a great picture. Years before I had seen your picture *David Copperfield* and I realized that here was a producer of . . . integrity who was breaking all the Hollywood rules by producing the book the author wrote . . . adding to it his own color, firing it with his own imagination, heightening effects with his own genius. So on the night of the premiere, I knew before the film began to roll that it would be a great picture and before many minutes had passed I knew it was even greater than I could have expected. I have always thought myself fortunate that Selznick International produced *Gone With The Wind*.

Throughout this period of crisis, uncertainty, and the dislocating social and economic changes, Selznick refrained from active movie-making, continuing instead to develop and package projects that he would then sell outright. He bought the rights to A. J. Cronin's best seller *The Keys of the Kingdom*, prepared a screen treatment, then sold the material to 20th Century-Fox, along with a new contract player, Gregory Peck, whom he had discovered and tested via Kay Brown. Selznick's initial impression of Peck was not favorable. He wrote to Kay Brown: ". . . he photographs like Abe Lincoln. . . . If he has a great personality, I don't think it comes through in these tests. He must be a fine legitimate actor judging by your great interest in him . . . but I don't see what we could do with him." He was persuaded otherwise, however, and placed the twenty-six-year-old actor under long-term contract in 1943, insisting when he sold Fox the rights to *The Keys of the Kingdom* that they not only use Peck in the lead but also buy half his contract. He followed the same procedure with the dormant *Claudia* project, selling it to Fox along with the services of its star, Dorothy McGuire, whom he had finally signed to a personal contract, half of which Fox now took over.

These moves on Selznick's part infuriated his partners at United Artists, who felt that he had made personal profits on production money advanced to him by UA. Chaplin brought suit against Selznick on behalf of UA, but the action was not taken to court because in the legal opinion of Edward Raftery, the president of UA, "There does not now exist a cause . . . either at law or at equity against the Selznick Company or David O. Selznick personally." Part of Chaplin's strategy in filing the suit was to force Selznick into production; in the two years since becoming part owner of UA, Selznick had not delivered one picture for release. Selznick shrugged off the lawsuit and instead of resuming production, he continued carefully to watch the careers of both Ingrid Bergman and Joan Fontaine, lending Bergman only for pictures that he felt were right for her abilities and would increase her market value. Ironically it was a project that he was reluctant to lend her for that brought Bergman her biggest success since *Intermezzo*.

Producer Hal Wallis at Warner Bros. wanted to borrow Bergman for the romantic lead opposite Humphrey Bogart in a wartime melodrama he was making, but Selznick had high hopes of getting her cast in the screen version of Ernest Hemingway's best seller *For Whom the Bell Tolls*, which Paramount was about to make. Selznick had almost bought the book himself, feeling that "it was so right for Bergman," but he was still exhausted, and "could not face up to a job of this size, so I reluctantly passed it up, yet I was determined that Bergman should play the part of [the heroine] Maria, regardless of who bought it. . . . I got exactly nowhere with Paramount, although I convinced everybody else." Meanwhile, Wallis was after Bergman for his picture, which he called *Casablanca*. Selznick kept putting him off, hoping that Paramount would

(Above, left) Jennifer Jones accepting her award for best actress in *The Song of Bernadette* (1943), her first major film. She is flanked by veteran actors Donald Crisp (left) and Charles Coburn, who won for best supporting actor in *The More the Merrier*. (Above) David Selznick at the Awards dinner, bracketed by Ingrid Bergman, nominated for her role in *For Whom the Bell Tolls*, and winner Jennifer Jones. Bergman had also starred in *Casablanca*, which won the award for best picture. (Left) Selznick was surrounded by beautiful women at the 1943 Awards ceremony. Here he is seen with Joan Fontaine, who had won her own award in 1941 for her performance in Alfred Hitchcock's *Suspicion*, which many felt was a consolation prize because she had not won for *Rebecca*. For the 1943 Awards, the Board of Governors dispensed with the usual informal dinner party and instead the winners were announced at a gathering at Grauman's Chinese Theatre. It marked the first time that outsiders were allowed to attend the event; servicemen were admitted free, and the public could buy tickets. It was also the first time that the Awards were broadcast by radio, which was done by two local stations, KNX and KFWB, NBC having turned it down as having too little commercial appeal.

come to their senses. They didn't, casting ballerina Vera Zorina for the picture, and Selznick reluctantly gave in to Wallis's entreaties to lend Bergman for *Casablanca*, "which I liked when I heard the story." Shrewd trader that he was, Selznick let Wallis have Bergman for two pictures upon payment of a hefty fee, and in return for the right to do one picture with Olivia de Havilland, still under contract to Warner Bros. He then turned around and sold this commitment to RKO, which promptly cast the indignant actress in an unfunny comedy called *Government Girl*.

While *Casablanca* was in production, Selznick kept an anxious eye on its progress, for he knew that Paramount would soon realize its mistake with Vera Zorina and come to him for Bergman. As he described it:

The inevitable day came, when Paramount called and wanted to know if Ingrid were available, because they were thinking of making a change. . . . Fortunately *Casablanca* finished at this very time . . . and I called Ingrid and told her that she was Maria. . . . I wanted to demand a two-week hiatus in production to give her a rest between pictures . . . but she begged me to let her proceed at once, the day after she finished *Casablanca*. . . . I devoted the next three days to the supervision of her makeup tests, including particularly her haircut, which I insisted should be under my supervision. . . . Every lock was taken off under my eye . . . because I didn't want them to do with Bergman what . . . they had done with Zorina, destroying her looks with a simply murderous haircut.

Casablanca was a success at the box office, and Bergman, as Selznick had predicted, was nominated for an Academy Award for her performance in *For Whom the Bell Tolls*. She lost to another Selznick protégée, Jennifer Jones, which is the name that had finally been given to young Phyllis Walker. Selznick had shrewdly kept the girl under wraps, letting

her appear in several stage productions around the Los Angeles area to develop her self-confidence, believing that she had "the potential to be a great screen personality." He watched her progress not only professionally but socially as well: "I hope she is not being made aware of the theatrical interest in her; I wish she would stay away from producers and agents and everything connected with the [industry] as I am terribly afraid she is going to get spoiled. Already she has lost some of that eager blushing quality that made her so enchanting when we first saw her." Finally, a property came along that he thought would be perfect to introduce her to moviegoers: "When I read *The Song of Bernadette*, I personally and initially suggested her to [20th Century-Fox] for the role and offered to let her test for it, so convinced was I that she would get it. . . . My enthusiasm was shared by Henry King, who was to direct the picture, and she was signed for the role." *The Song of Bernadette* was a somber, heavily religious account of the "miracle of Lourdes," wherein a young peasant girl told of having a vision of the Virgin Mary in a grotto; a spring subsequently bubbled forth from the spot, said to have remarkable curing powers, and the area soon became a center of religious pilgrimage. Bernadette Soubirous was declared a saint in 1914, and Franz Werfel recounted her legend in the novel published in English translation in 1941. It became a popular and inspirational picture, due in no small part to Jennifer Jones, not so much for her dramatic performance, which was awkward and hesitant, but for the amazing quality of spirituality she managed to convey in the role. Her intensity, coupled with her freshness and unfamiliarity, convinced the Academy voters that she had given the best performance by an actress for 1943. With a single picture, Jennifer Jones had become one of the hottest properties in town, and along with two of the other nominees, Ingrid Bergman and Joan Fontaine, she was under contract to David O. Selznick.

753 HOLLYWOOD CANTEEN, HOLLYWOOD, CALIFORNIA

(Opposite) April 4, 1943—The Hollywood Bowl was temporarily redecorated by MGM's Cedric Gibbons when Selznick produced a massive benefit performance for the United China Relief Fund. Spencer Tracy opened the program by introducing Seaman Henry Fonda, who introduced wartime hero Dr. Corydon M. Wassell, who quoted Confucius. Taking this as their cue, twenty major female stars then took part in a pageant dedicated to the guest of honor, Madame Chiang Kai-shek. Her 36-minute speech was broadcast live nationally. The epilogue, which "sang a song of China," had a script by Harry Kronman, was directed by William Dieterle, had Walter Huston as narrator, and ended with an appearance by Edward G. Robinson as Generalissimo Chiang Kai-shek. The music for all this was written by Herbert Stothart and played by the Los Angeles Philharmonic. Selznick had the entire proceedings filmed and gave Madame Chiang, who was touring the country, a documentary record of the evening. (Left) The Hollywood Canteen, mecca of every GI who ever got near the West Coast. Located at 1450 Cahuenga Boulevard, one block south of Sunset, it was a cooperative venture between the studios and industry personnel, who raised the money to build and operate the facility, and the craft unions, whose members donated their time and labor to build the $25,000 structure designed by art director Alfred Ybarra. The stars and other performers who staffed it made it memorable for the more than 3 million servicemen who passed through its doors from opening day on October 17, 1942, to its closing late in 1945.

Since You Went Away

By the end of 1942, the United States had completely made itself over for the war effort, and on this wartime footing the movies boomed as never before. Theatres ran continuously around the clock to accommodate hordes of defense workers, who for the first time in years had money to spend and nothing to spend it on. About the only thing that wasn't rationed was the movies. They were being cranked out: an endless escapist parade of musicals, comedy, horror, and war propaganda films, all greeted with the kind of public response once reserved for the biggest pictures and the biggest stars.

Some seven thousand men from the film industry were in uniform, either drafted or enlisted, but David O. Selznick wasn't one of them. Thirty-nine years old, nearsighted and flatfooted, he had been classified 4F, but this did not keep him from trying to find a place for himself in the war effort. In a letter to Merian Cooper, who was a colonel in the Air Force, he told of his frustrations in this area:

I've made a number of stabs and many trips to Washington . . . but so far as I can see the government is convinced it can do very well without me. . . . I have sold myself on the idea that there must be hundreds like me, perhaps thousands, eager and anxious to do their part, but who haven't yet been fitted in. I was told I could have a majority . . . and maybe a little higher . . . particularly with a little training . . . and that was the part that appealed to me the most; but the work they wanted me to do—running a radio program—seemed to me ridiculous. . . . I have very strong feelings against this sort of commission . . . rightly or wrongly, at least as far as I am concerned, men in uniform should be fighting and shouldn't be doing jobs that could be done just as well in civilian clothes. . . . Things in Hollywood are not greatly changed outwardly, although the regulations are becoming more stringent every day. It has taken a war to force the companies to cut the unnecessary and ridiculous quantity of their product . . . there is now a very severe limitation on how much you can spend on sets—$5,000 per picture for new materials unless you get special dispensation . . . there is a great shortage of raw stock . . . and leading men. . . . Gable is a private in the Army, Tyrone Power is a private in the Marines, Henry Fonda is a gob . . . and every day comes news of one or two more to add to the dozens who already are in. In the words of Adolphe Menjou, if this keeps up, the women stars in pictures will be willing to work with men their own age. . . .

Apart from serving on several industry defense committees, Selznick's most notable effort in this field was his chairmanship of the Hollywood branch of the China War Relief Committee. Madame Chiang Kai-shek was touring the United States in early 1943, and at his invitation she came to Hollywood in April to be the guest of honor at a huge fund-raising benefit in the Hollywood Bowl, which Selznick successfully produced. Overseeing this event sparked his enthusiasm for picturemaking once again, and he began to look for a project that would make him feel he was contributing something worthwhile to the spirit of the times, something that would capture the feelings of unity and national purpose and would reflect and enhance the positive virtues of what the country and the people were experiencing, that sense of the continuity of American life despite the extraordinary dislocating pressures of the war. Selznick didn't want anything blatantly flag-waving or propagandistic, or mindlessly entertaining. And in keeping with his own sense of himself and his role in the film community, his movie would have to be noble and expansive, truly reflecting his vision of how the American public conceived of itself. Patriotism, in those superheated days of World War II, was a virtue to be paraded, to be demonstrated: on a cash basis by the purchase of bonds, and on a spiritual level by the sacrifice of husbands and sons. Families were given stars to hang in their windows for each person serving in the armed forces; children were growing up without fathers; mothers were breadwinners and heads of households, holding the country together till the safe return of their men.

Selznick's own abiding and deep-seated love for the country had been instilled in him by his father. This was coupled with his own growing awareness of what the war was doing to the quality of life in the United States, and it was these observations, these ideas and feelings that he wanted to put into a picture, weaving them in with a contemporary love story, which would have the war as a disruptive, pervasive background and show just how much, or in some cases how little, the war had changed everyone and everything in America. All this had to be inspirational without being mawkish or unbelievable. The problem was finding a story or at least the germ of an idea that could be developed to encompass such elements. Selznick had been quite moved by MGM's *Mrs. Miniver,* about the trials and tribulations of a typical English family during the first dark years of the war. The Academy had chosen it as the best picture of 1942 and Greer Garson as the best actress for her performance in the title role. Selznick hoped to find the American equivalent for his wartime effort.

In June 1942, several weeks after he had seen *Mrs. Miniver,* he sent a memo to his new story editor, Margaret McDonnell, asking her to start looking "for a story about the home front . . . a war story without battles . . . ask around at the other studios to see if they might have suggestions on stories they passed up." For the next nine months, the story department staff ran through an average of fifty pieces of material a week, some magazine stories, some novels. Of these, 270 were synopsized and sent to Selznick, who didn't like any of them. An item about the search for a suitable story was carried in the "chatter" column of *The Hollywood*

333

Margaret Buell Wilder, the author of the book *Since You Went Away*, and her two daughters, Brig (left) and Jan.

Shirley Temple signing the contract with David O. Selznick that brought her out of retirement at sixteen to play the part of Brig in *Since You Went Away*.

Reporter in early 1943, and it caught the eye of William Dozier, the story editor for Paramount. He had just finished reading the galley proofs of a new book "about the problems of a wife who must keep home and family intact while her husband is at war." *Since You Went Away—Letters to a Soldier from His Wife* had previously appeared in serial form in the *Ladies' Home Journal*, where it was such a success that its author, Margaret Buell Wilder, had expanded it for publication as a book. Dozier sent Selznick a synopsis with a note saying:

> The book is a series of letters by a Dayton newspaperwoman to her husband ... the details of family life on the home front are presented without self-pity or maudlin sentimentality, the characters are very real, the sacrifices and hopes understandable to thousands of American wives now going through the same ordeal. ... For your purposes the book would require considerable treatment and reconstruction.

The letters do no more than talk about the problems of an upper-middle-class housewife living on allotment checks, raising two girls named Jan and Brig, having to run the house without help, and trying to find some effective way of coping with her loneliness and feeling of ineffectuality. Selznick immediately liked the style and theme of the book, seeing it as a "modern day *Little Women*." He bought the story rights for $30,000 and brought Mrs. Wilder to Hollywood to do an adaptation of her book, working with her to put the letters into some semblance of story form. She labored during April and May from an outline supplied by Selznick, who commented that "the characters in the book are all sketchily drawn, with the exception of Anne [the wife]. ... We must give them flesh and blood, interesting character relationships and current problems of their own. ..." Once she had finished, Selznick took the basic structure and began writing the screenplay himself, under the pseudonym "Jeffrey Daniel," the first names of his two children. Into it he poured all he ever felt about families, American society, and the war's meaning to what he considered to be the average American. Lydia Schiller, who worked on this phase of preparing the script, recalls: "Mr. Selznick would have us all make lists of things we thought were important as illustrations of what the war was doing to the people; coping with shortages, slang expressions, he especially wanted to have the dialogue as accurate as possible, especially for the children. So we were all asked to ask some young people for slang expressions."

By mid-June 1943, Selznick had amassed a script that roughly followed the chronology of Mrs. Wilder's original letters from the time the wife, Anne Hilton, returns to her Midwest home after seeing her husband off to the war. It proceeded to cover in detail the year 1943 with its effect on the lives of the Hilton family and their boarder Colonel Smollett, and his strange relationship with his grandson Bill; Tony Willett, an old friend of the family, a charming, debonair sketch artist turned Navy man; Anne's bitchy divorcée friend Emily Hawkins; and a parade of other characters, some from the book, some invented by Selznick for the film. The main difference between the book and the film was this expansion of the script, having the Hilton family touched by every aspect of life in the country at the time, which resulted in a vast panorama of America in crisis and transition, teeming with harried, lonely people, civilians and military alike, thrown together briefly in crowded trains, movie theatres, overflowing cocktail bars, jammed into restaurants, churches, sweating in booming factories, and suffering in hospitals jammed with the war's results.

For a Selznick script, the preparation went remarkably fast and almost smoothly. By the time shooting began, the only changes were in the details of scenes, the bridging between sequences, and the dialogue, much of it written by Selznick himself with the help of F. Hugh Herbert, whose successful Broadway comedy *Kiss and Tell* had just introduced the teenaged charmer Corliss Archer to American culture. Selznick thought Herbert could contribute to the development of the younger daughter, Brig, the fourteen-year-old semi-tomboy with a shrewd, practical, bargaining mind, who misses her father terribly and is indefatigable in her efforts to do something about the war. Even while the script was being developed, Selznick began a concerted campaign to coax one of America's sweethearts out of a premature "retirement" to play the part. Shirley Temple, whom every moviegoer in the country had watched grow from a moppet to an awkward teenager, had not made a

Robert Walker and his estranged wife, Jennifer Jones, played Bill Smollett and Jane Hilton, the romantic leads.

Art director Mark-Lee Kirk had first caught Selznick's attention with his masterful period settings for Orson Welles's *The Magnificent Ambersons* (1942). Selznick asked him to be as realistic as possible in his settings for *Since You Went Away;* the result was a combination of American traditional, as in the kitchen and bedroom settings (above, left and right), and a more imaginative approach, as in the Paradise Cocktail Lounge (top, left). The Hilton home (top, right), the work of production designer William

Pereira, was built complete on one of the studio sound stages. Critic James Agee referred to the set as "if . . . not an average U.S. reality, . . . an average U.S. dream." Set decoration was by Victor Gangelin. (Opposite) Still photographer Marty Crail took this classic pose of Claudette Colbert reading aloud the letters from her husband in the Army to their two daughters, played by Jennifer Jones and Shirley Temple.

picture since the 1942 *Miss Annie Rooney,* in which she had tried to play an awkward teenager falling in love. The results were less than satisfactory, and the girl's parents had decided that Shirley and the movies should part company for a while. The public, however, never lost its interest in her nor its affection for what she represented. Selznick shared this appreciation, commenting that "Shirley has an enchanting adolescent personality . . . with great charm and beauty . . . and if we can get her for this . . . it will be considered something of an event." Several weeks of negotiations back and forth with her parents ended with Temple being put under exclusive contract to David O. Selznick Productions. The role of the older daughter Jane had been expanded beyond the "e" added to her name; she came to represent all the young girls in the country who were growing from adolescence to maturity through the early years of the war. Jane changed from a dreamy-eyed romantic schoolgirl with a crush on her "Uncle" Tony to a level-headed, clear-eyed young woman, largely through her tragic romance with the doomed Bill Smollett.

To Selznick, a great deal of the appeal of *Since You Went Away* was the opportunity to show off what he could do for his newest star,

Jennifer Jones. After her success as Bernadette, Selznick was determined to demonstrate her versatility by casting her as the "all-American girl next door," and his reworking of the script to enhance her role and the character's development was one of the things he continually tinkered with throughout the preparation and shooting of the picture. For the pivotal role of Bill Smollett, the colonel's shy grandson who falls in love with Jane, Selznick decided to borrow Robert Walker from MGM, where he had, as Selznick observed, "clicked in a tremendous way . . . in the picture *Bataan* . . . the reviews and the tremendous public reaction to him in *See Here, Private Hargrove,* which followed it . . . have hit in a terrific way for him." Selznick took a great risk in casting the actor opposite Jennifer Jones, for the two had just separated, and the high-strung intensity of the young actress could be adversely affected by the emotional demands not only of the part but of the added strain of playing highly romantic scenes opposite her estranged husband.

To make sure that the potentially dangerous situation would be handled with tact and restraint, Selznick brought in John Cromwell to direct. The two men had not worked together since *The Prisoner of*

Zenda six years before, but Selznick felt that Cromwell had the "innate dignity . . . and the calmness and the integrity to give me what I want from this script." The subject matter appealed greatly to Cromwell, who recalled the personal turmoil of the times:

I was fifty-seven then, and it seemed to me that there were plenty of men who were just as old as I who were going in, flying, doing things in the war. . . . I remember feeling that I was indulging myself by staying working and not doing what I might have been able to do . . . but then I realized that there wasn't a hell of a lot I *could* do. . . . So when David offered me this . . . I was very intrigued . . . it was a great challenge and I liked that. David had written the screenplay himself . . . he had a great talent for writing colloquial dialogue and I am sure that the main reason he wanted me was his awareness that I was a good check on his enthusiasms. He had a good story mind, but he had a weakness for certain emotional kinds of scenes . . . an overemphasis on emotions. . . . We had all sorts of arguments about various scenes . . . he would keep going over them, analyzing them and polishing until I finally had to say to him that he was refining the life out of it . . . and that frightened him. . . . It had its effect.

During his three-year production hiatus, Selznick had released many of his artisans and technical people. Lyle Wheeler and William Cameron Menzies had left, and Selznick found it no easy matter to replace either of these men. As the fighting dragged on, the armed forces took the bulk of professionally trained talent, and he and Ray Klune, who had stayed on as production manager, began a hunt for technical talent that resulted in Selznick's putting under contract several newcomers, including the young architect William Pereira, to whom Selznick gave the task of designing the sets and overall look of the picture. As he worked on the script of *Since You Went Away,* Selznick would have the young man sit in on meetings to absorb the ideas he wanted to get across on film. The centerpiece of the action was the two-story suburban Hilton home, and Pereira drew up a design that, while not the average American home, was at least a dream version of it. Almost a complete house went up on Stage 13, with fixed, solid walls, ceilings, an actual second floor, and a full-sized street in front with reduced-scale homes on it—all this in line with Selznick's passion to make the film as realistic as possible. His instructions to cameraman George Barnes were to keep all light sources absolutely natural; if the light from a lamp covered only a small area, then the set should be lit that way, and not filled in with other illumination as was the usual practice.

By early May, pre-production had reached the point of casting the lead roles: Anne Hilton; her husband Tim, who would appear in flashbacks; and Tony Willett, the bachelor charmer whose passion for Anne is thinly disguised under a veneer of wisecracks and badinage. For Tony, Selznick reached into his new contract bag of talent and pulled out Joseph Cotten, a good-looking, ingratiating Southerner of enormous charm and talent who had come to Hollywood with Orson Welles's Mercury Players, impressing the town with his work in *Citizen Kane* and the just-completed *The Magnificent Ambersons.* Selznick, liking Cotten personally, gave him a contract and carefully selected his appearances, building up his popularity as a leading man and lending him for such offbeat efforts as the murderer in Hitchcock's *Shadow of a Doubt.*

Earlier in May, Selznick had seen the as yet unreleased *So Proudly We Hail,* a heavy drama of Army nurses in the South Pacific, and had been impressed with Claudette Colbert's performance in it. He had known the actress well since their early Paramount days and she was a close friend of his, but he was afraid of approaching her directly to play Anne Hilton, the mother of two teenaged daughters, in a script that wasn't completely ready. But her lure at the box office was considerable, as Selznick pointed out: "Even light little comedies with her have never done under a million and a half domestic." As one of the top stars in the business, Colbert was in great demand and consequently very expensive—$250,000 a picture. Instead of asking her, Selznick chose the more roundabout way of sounding her out by having Hedda Hopper run an article in her daily column that Selznick was considering her for the part. Colbert, according to Hopper, "called me. . . . She wanted to know whatever had given me the notion that she would consider playing the mother of two teen-aged girls." Continued Hopper, "Then I went to work on her. 'David

Selznick doesn't make anything but good pictures, does he? You don't expect to be an ingenue all your life, do you?' 'Well, no,' she replied. 'Listen, Claudette, this is going to be a big picture. . . . Selznick doesn't make failures. If the part isn't right for you, it'll hurt him more than it will you. He can't afford to make anything but a success—and to do that it has to be just right for you as well as for others. Why don't you think it over?' 'All right,' she said, 'but Selznick hasn't asked me yet.' 'He will,' I replied. Two minutes later I had David on the phone. I told him Claudette was definitely interested, that he should call her. He did. A month later, she signed for the part."

Selznick had rather optimistically planned to start photography on *Since You Went Away* no later than September 8, 1943, but three weeks before the start date Ray Klune, who was the key to the whole operation, came down with pneumonia. Preparations ground to a halt while Selznick furiously injected himself into all the preparatory work that he felt no one but Klune or himself could do properly. The overriding difficulty was that Selznick had not made a picture for such a long while that it took three times as long to organize everything and get the production moving. The sets weren't ready. Wartime restrictions made it almost impossible to spend any money on dressing them properly, and Selznick, several days before filming was to begin, was bringing in furniture from his own home because of what he considered "the wretched condition of the furnishings and the overall look of the [Hilton home] set."

Still trying to finish the script, and being tugged and pulled in every direction by all the logistical demands of the picture, Selznick dashed off a seven-page memo to the ailing Klune, which began: "I'm very sorry that you've been ill, and of course, I can't blame you for this," then proceeded to blame him for everything that had gone wrong:

I always want to have the benefit of the ideas of any creative workers on the staff. . . . I want to make it clear to everybody that I want no hurdles or barriers between any of the creative personnel and myself on any picture which I personally produce and that includes camera workmen, lighting, costumes, makeup, hairdress, locations and set dressing. . . . Miss Colbert was very frank with me in expressing her displeasure at the way things were not being run. . . . Her dressing room is a mess, the gas doesn't work, the electric clock doesn't either, which will probably mean that she'll be late for all her calls and it will be nobody's fault but ours.

If Selznick was furious, Klune was outraged.

Here I was in the hospital, barely able to see straight, and he sends me this memorandum. I said, "Well, I've had it, and I'm going to quit," and I did. As soon as I got back to the studio, I went in and I told him, and he said, "Are you kidding?" and I said, "No, I'm not . . . I've had the biggest ulcers since I'm with you and when I'm in the hospital with pneumonia you write a memo that indicates that you're thoroughly displeased with me . . . and I don't like that kind of thing." He said, "I didn't mean it all . . ." and I said, "Why the hell did you write it then?" I told him I wouldn't walk out on him. . . . I had already made arrangements to go to work for 20th, but I told him that I would stay until I broke in someone new to take over the picture. He was after me for several days, trying to get me to change my mind. . . . He was very sweet to me during that whole last period . . . and when I finally did leave, he gave me a big party and a lovely watch which I treasure.

All during the latter part of August and into early September; Los Angeles was in the grip of a ferocious heat wave, and on September 8, the day filming was scheduled to start, a strange thing happened: around noon, the sun disappeared behind a brackish, greenish-brown cloud that enveloped the entire city, causing eyes to water and lungs to clog up. The large volume of smoke and chemicals pouring out of the wartime factories had been trapped by the heavy, humid air, bringing a new and permanent development to the Los Angeles area—a combination of smoke, haze, and fog known colloquially as smog. It was a condition that caused havoc to the outdoor filming schedule for the picture, with several of the exterior scenes being moved indoors.

After the first few days of confusion, production settled down into a fairly smooth routine, as Cromwell started his cast and crew down the

The centerpiece of *Since You Went Away*—the sequence that captures perfectly the innocence and vitality and romanticism of the time—was the dance at the fictional Chamberlain Field hangar. Agnes Moorehead played the bitchy hoarder Emily Hawkins, whose idea of doing her bit for the war effort was to arrange an entertainment for "those poor boys who are going off to die." With this sequence, the story moved from the light charm of the early family scenes to the dark grimness of the wartime reality. The change in mood was handled superbly by director John Cromwell and cinematographer Stanley Cortez. The sequence begins with the arrival of the teenaged hostesses and the infectious, jiving gaiety of the couples jitterbugging to "The Dipsy Doodle," while Jane (Jennifer Jones) and Bill (Robert Walker) evince their first hints of interest in each other. The music changes, and photographically the scene subtly switches from high-keyed intensity to darker tones, reflecting the jagged rhythms of the conga. Finally, the aching, nostalgic strains of "The Emperor Waltz" are heard, and the dancers, slowly and awkwardly turning, become stark, shadowed figures. Searchlights illumine the crowd as the camera pulls back to an extreme long shot of the vaulted hangar framed by a massive pair of outspread wings supporting a five-pointed star.

The opening sequence of *Since You Went Away:* Lee Garmes's camera moves through the den of the Hilton home, showing artifacts of the family's history, including the bronzed baby shoes of one of the Hilton girls (actually the shoes of Daniel, the younger of the two Selznick boys), and finally coming to rest on the family bulldog, Soda, watching Anne Hilton come home after seeing her husband, Tim, off to war. He was played by Neil Hamilton, who originally appeared in three prewar flashback sequences in the film. After the first preview, Selznick, realizing he had to cut an hour out of the picture, reduced Hamilton's role to an 8 × 10 photograph.

long 127-day schedule, which was the time allotted to film all 420 scenes in the script. Aside from the complexities of the larger scenes, the biggest problem of *Since You Went Away* was just the sheer bulk of the story, the hundreds of little scenes that had to be labored over for hours to meet Selznick's perfectionist demands. George Barnes, the cameraman, was fired after the first two weeks, as he seemed unable to photograph Jennifer Jones in a way that satisfied Selznick; he was replaced by Stanley Cortez, who had just come from working on Orson Welles's *The Magnificent Ambersons* with Joseph Cotten and Agnes Moorehead. Selznick added Moorehead to the film as Emily Hawkins, Anne Hilton's bitchy, avaricious acquaintance, symbol of all the hoarders and self-centered, shallow women Selznick had observed in Hollywood. She joined an ever-growing cast of stars and featured players that included Monty Woolley as the irascible Colonel Smollett, and Hattie McDaniel as Fidelia, the Hiltons' peacetime maid, who comes to room with them for the duration and stays to cook, fetch, carry, and get in her share of malapropisms and comic relief.

"I had very little trouble with the cast," John Cromwell recalled. "They were all very professional and level-headed. Claudette especially was wonderful to work with, very experienced, no temperament." Not to Cromwell perhaps; but her professionalism was made up in equal parts of talent and an overriding concern for the way she was photographed. In common with most of the women who had survived as stars in the Hollywood firmament, she knew exactly what was best for her and was intent on seeing that she got it, in the way of camera angles, lighting, and the other intangibles that kept her in the forefront of her profession. Selznick commented in a memo about

the delays on Miss Colbert's makeup and hairdress which I suppose we have to cope with although I think we could reduce this with a diplomatic approach and achieve more cooperation.... We should check with Paramount and find out whether they went through quite as much with her as we are going through—the makeup business, the two days off a month, the vague dates of the two days, the unwillingness to shoot important or close scenes late in the day.... We have spent a fortune on rebuilding sets and changing set-ups . . . because of her refusal to have the right side of her face photographed, on top of which we have to pay her not only a fabulous salary, but also give her (periodic) two days off a month, which works out to $5,000 every four weeks for doing absolutely nothing, and now she's demanding three days.... I think you should get with her and her agent immediately about this, explaining that we have broken our necks to accommodate her, but she is the only woman in town who gets three consecutive days off a month.... Miss Jones, for instance, gets by on *none*.... I would really appreciate it if Claudette would try to get by on one for the duration.... Tell her there's a war on and we all have to make sacrifices.

Cromwell had a much more difficult time with Jennifer Jones. "She was very unhappy in the part . . . about as unhappy as I've ever seen a girl be on the set.... She thought she was much too old . . . much too big and gawky.... It made her feel awkward . . . she couldn't reconcile herself to the part.... Most of it was her imagination . . . there was no basis for it. ... She didn't say too much about it . . . there wasn't too much she could say about it." Jones was not only uncomfortable with the part. She was also extremely uncomfortable playing the very poignant love scenes with her about-to-be-ex-husband, and on two occasions her emotional upsets caused her to flee the set in tears. Selznick had to come to her dressing room and calm her down before she could continue.

While preparing *Since You Went Away*, Selznick found he needed a multifaceted scene to move the focus from the lightness and charm of the early family scenes to the larger, darker, more impersonal tapestry of the war. What he devised was a servicemen's dance given by the local ladies' league, which served to confront the characters with hints of impending tragedies and simultaneously to give a sense of the passing of an era and of the gallantry of youth in the face of inescapable duty. The scene was designed as a spectacular evocation of a particular kind of national spirit, and Selznick labored for weeks over the preparations for it, demanding that the extras used to play the participants at the dance "look like decent high school kids in the Middle West and not like a lot of peroxided extras. . . . For the servicemen I want to see kids of all apparent ancestries . . . Scandinavian, Irish, Jewish, etc. . . . a definite cross section of America. . . . Be sure that the kids and the soldiers in all the foreground shots give us a picture of American youth that is one that we will be proud to send around the world and not one that is typical of Hollywood mob scenes. Because of the complexities of the sequence, it was scheduled for five days' work and over seven hundred local college students were hired to play the servicemen. Selznick was constantly on the set, hovering over director John Cromwell and second-guessing cinematographer Stanley Cortez about lighting and composition. After being filmed, edited, and scored completely, this became a scene that seemed to extract the essence of a common experience specific to that particular time and place. Its effectiveness works on several levels, the fusion of music, action, and mood superbly balanced by the interplay of light, shadow, camera movement, and staging, capturing perfectly a unique and innocent state of mind and sense of purpose.

Filming had been proceeding fairly swiftly, considering the number of scenes and the more than two hundred separate speaking parts, when suddenly, in rapid succession, cameraman Stanley Cortez received his draft notice, and a flu epidemic felled Claudette Colbert, Jennifer Jones, Shirley Temple, and Hattie McDaniel, plus several members of the crew simultaneously, causing a production shutdown of almost two weeks. There was nothing the frantic Selznick could do except call the insurance company and try to get the losses covered. Cortez he replaced with Lee Garmes, who was "appalled at the way that the sets were built. You couldn't move the walls; it was so realistic that you had to shoot into some rooms through the windows only. . . ."

During this down period, Selznick dispatched five separate camera crews fanning out across the United States, picking up footage of the country at war, covering the factories and foundries, the bond rallies, salvage drives, and the thousands of servicemen already in rehabilitation hospitals. Five days were spent at the Kaiser shipyards at Richmond, California, covering the plant procedures under the watchful eye of the military censor, and ultimately getting several spectacular shots of workers streaming out of the plant in late afternoon. These were to serve as the backdrop for a sequence in which Anne Hilton goes to work as a lady welder and befriends a middle-aged European immigrant whose child has been killed by the Nazis. Selznick had written what he felt was a touching scene for the two as the older woman tries to tell the younger one just what America means to her, in the course of which she recites the words engraved on the Statue of Liberty, and then says to Anne, "You are what I thought America was when I prayed with my little son that God would let us go to the fairyland across the sea." The scene, as written, had a voice-over narration by Anne Hilton as she recounts this to her husband in one of her nightly letters, and as Selznick and Cromwell both realized, it teetered dangerously on the edge of bathos. It needed an actress who could make the somewhat sticky sentiment come alive and become believable. In one of the most inspired bits of casting in the entire film, Selznick brought Alla Nazimova out of retirement to play the part. She had been one of his father's biggest early stars, and her powers as an actress had not diminished over the years. The scene was played with Nazimova sitting quietly at a lunch counter, speaking movingly of the Statue of Liberty and its inscription. Her face is suffused with a sudden beauty, and her voice and her gestures as she recites the phrase, "I lift my lamp beside the golden door," give the sequence a resonance far beyond what it had on the printed page. As the camera moves back from her face to frame the two women against the hordes of workers streaming out the shipyard gates, she tells Anne simply, "You are what I thought America was." It is one of the most telling and affecting moments in the final finished picture, aided by a subdued, hymnlike version of "America the Beautiful" on the sound track, matching perfectly the lilt, simplicity, and strength of Nazimova's performance.

As production crawled toward its completion date, beset by delays and shutdowns and retakes, Cromwell caught the same flu that had knocked out twelve members of the cast and crew, and during his two-day absence just before Christmas, Selznick decided that he would direct the sequences involving the birthday party for Colonel Smollett. He shot three and a half pages of dialogue over the next two days, but after seeing the rushes he asked Cromwell to re-do them. Regarding his

Alla Nazimova and Claudette Colbert played a moving scene in the cafeteria of the shipyards in which Anne Hilton (Colbert) has gone to work as a welder. Against the background of a huge semicircular window through which can be seen the massive crowds of factory workers streaming out at the end of the day, the camera moves in unobtrusively on Nazimova as she speaks eloquently of her dream of emigrating to America with her small son, who was killed by the Nazis before they could escape "to the fairyland across the sea." Telling Colbert of her trip to the Statue of Liberty, she recites its inscription with an almost religious fervor, giving the sequence a strength and a moving honesty that makes it one of the most memorable in the film.

341

directorial foray, Selznick later commented, "Frankly, it's easier to criticize another man's work than to direct myself. As a producer I can maintain an editorial perspective I wouldn't have as a director."

At last, on February 9, 1944, after five weary months of production, John Cromwell took the final shot, which Selznick always tried to coordinate with the last scene of the picture. The ending was a quiet, almost diminuendo tag to the dramatic climax of the main story. On Christmas Eve, her husband still missing, Anne and the family are starting a melancholy Christmas when the phone rings, bringing news that Tim is safe. After the commotion of rejoicing, the scene dissolves to Anne coming out of the house into the snowy night on her way to work. She pauses in the darkened street, while her voice on the sound track says: "I've let go of the past, Tim.... I'm not afraid to face the future now because you'll be here to share it with me ... the new world ... which we'll make better than the old." She looks up into the snowy sky, then turns and walks slowly away into the night as the scene gently fades out.

The first preview in San Bernardino ran for almost four hours, and while the comments were respectful and even laudatory, they all complained of the length. Selznick felt that the picture needed major cuts, and he began by eliminating all the flashbacks of the Hilton family's prewar life, as well as the documentary footage of the country at war. He also realized that the ending didn't work at all, being anticlimactic and almost downbeat, instead of projecting the quiet, thoughtful feeling he had hoped for. While paring the footage to under three hours, he ordered Jack Cosgrove to put together a new final sequence using the large miniature of the Hilton home that had been built for seasonal mood shots. This version had the wife, Anne, running up to the second-floor landing of the house with the news, "Pop's safe ... I just got word, he's coming home," then being surrounded by her daughters in a tableau seen through the window from the outside. Using miniature projection, the camera pulls back from the shot, keeping it in focus, and retreating swiftly back and up to take in the entire expanse of the house, over which a title is superimposed, exhorting everyone to

Be of Good Courage,
And He Shall Strengthen Your Heart
All Ye that Hope in the Lord.

To accompany this musically on the sound track, Selznick had hired the Polish composer Alexander Tansman, but after hearing his score, Selznick threw it out and instead borrowed Max Steiner from Warner Bros. Selznick implored Steiner to use three themes he liked from *A Star Is Born*, which Steiner did, but he balked at Selznick's insistence on "The Emperor Waltz" for the dance sequence. "We were at war with Germany," recalls Steiner, "and David wanted me to use a German waltz to send off American boys. I wouldn't do it.... We argued and argued; I wanted 'American Beauty Rose' and he wouldn't give up on 'The Emperor Waltz.' Finally I walked out and he got somebody else to come and finish the scene." The waltz aside, Steiner's music for the picture was magnificent, earning him his third Academy Award the next year.

The final cost of *Since You Went Away* was $2,780,000, and with a running time of two hours and fifty minutes it was the longest, most expensive film made in Hollywood since *Gone With The Wind*. Selznick was being urged by United Artists to hurry it into release, and even his friend Y. Frank Freeman at Paramount urged haste, as the picture was so solidly grounded in the year 1943 that any lengthy delay in its exhibition could seriously damage it by giving it a dated, stale quality. While the studio staff carefully put the finishing touches on it and United Artists prepared an expensive, star-studded advertising campaign, making much of the fact that this was "the producer's first picture since *Gone With The Wind* and *Rebecca*," Selznick suffered a personal tragedy. In March 1944, his brother Myron, at age forty-five, died suddenly of a portal thrombosis, a complication from his drinking, and David was saddened and depressed to the point of abandoning work on the film. After his father's death, it was the most wrenching personal tragedy he had ever had to face up to, and he was inconsolable. *Since You Went Away* stayed unfinished for almost a month while Selznick nursed his grief. He considered holding up its release a year, thinking of filming additional material to gloss over the time lapse, but he was persuaded out of this not only by his staff but by Ben Hecht, who had seen a rough cut of the picture and was

moved enough to write Selznick, "Finish it! ... You have wangled onto the screen the amiable and indestructible face of democracy ... the USA finally makes its debut on the screen.... The film rises above its story and sings out like a song of America ... and it made me cry like a fool." Thus urged on by his old friend and aware of the financial disaster that might ensue with any further delay, Selznick pulled himself together and completed the film.

Since You Went Away was given a formal premiere at the Carthay Circle in June 1944, the first gala premiere Hollywood had seen since the start of the war. The select audience was respectful and even moved to applause at the conclusion of some sequences, but it was clear that the picture was not having the effect Selznick thought it would. The everyday realities of the war were too close for too many in the audience that night, and Selznick's idealized representation of what was happening in the country struck many as false. The public, however, responded to the picture's cast and the massive advertising campaign, and favorable word of mouth spread quickly. Playing at slightly advanced prices, over the next year it grossed $4,918,412, some $500,000 of that from New York's Capitol Theatre alone.

The reviews were strangely mixed, most of them commenting on the glossinesss of the production and complaining of the length, and many dismissing it as an expensive tear-jerker. Only the very perceptive James Agee, reviewing it in *Time*, had any encouraging words:

> What makes *Since You Went Away* sure-fire is in part its homely subject matter, which has never before been so earnestly tackled in a film, in part its all-star acting [and] most of all David Selznick's extremely astute screen play and production. Selznick has given Claudette Colbert the richest, biggest role of her career. She rewards him consistently with smooth Hollywood formula acting, and sometimes—especially in collaboration with Mr. Cotten—with flashes of acting that are warmer and more mature.... Though idealized, the Selznick characterizations are authentic to a degree seldom achieved in Hollywood. [The picture is] a deft, valid blend of showmanship, humor, and yard-wide Americanism.... There are scores of ... evidences of a smart showman's eye, mind and heart.... Added up, they give the picture taste, shrewdness, superiority, life.

For Selznick, *Since You Went Away* was an extremely personal film. The picture abounds in little personal touches that remain largely unrecognized by an audience, from the use of his own child's bronzed shoes in the opening sequences to the insertion of one of his published poems, "Now We Are Three," written to commemorate the birth of his first child, shown in the Hilton memory book in Selznick's handwriting. It is as heartfelt a reflection of his idealization of America as *A Star Is Born* is of his concept of Hollywood, the difference between the two being largely a matter of the degree of public response. *A Star Is Born* dealt with a generally remote conception of what moviegoers hoped Hollywood was like, while *Since You Went Away* treated a very personal subject for millions of them in a manner that was too romanticized and symbolic to be accepted as anything other than an awkward, distorted version or reality. The underlying sentiment and the feeling of heightened emotionalism bounced off critics and moviegoers alike, and *Since You Went Away* slipped into the limbo of half-remembered films, an experience too much of its time to exist apart from it. Today, it is Selznick's least known and least appreciated film; in fact, it is the only film of his that no longer exists in its original form. Almost immediately after its initial engagements, Selznick cut the picture by twenty-five minutes, eliminating much of the detail and several of the vignettes, bits that gave the film its density and verisimilitude. It was further truncated by another fifteen minutes when Selznick re-released it in the late forties; it was this mutilated version of *Since You Went Away* that circulated in theatres for years, a choppy, dated, and confusing domestic drama with most of its symbolic, inspirational sequences gone, thereby eliminating the vitality and honesty of a picture that in its original form was an idealized, sprawling epic of a people, a country, and a sensibility.*

---

* ABC, which purchased many of the Selznick films after his death, put a newly restored full-length version of the film into theatrical circulation in 1979.

(Top) A portion of the all-star cast of *Since You Went Away,* gathered for the picture's climactic Christmas Eve sequence. (From left) Hattie McDaniel, Joseph Cotten, Keenan Wynn, Jennifer Jones, Craig Stevens, Alla Nazimova, and Monty Woolley. (Above, left) John Cromwell talks with twenty-two-year-old Robert Mosely, a Bakersfield, California, telephone lineman serving in the Coast Guard. Selznick had written a vignette sequence in the film in which Jane and Bill meet a young sailor with whom they spend an evening. Selznick wanted the bit played by an unknown, possibly a real sailor, but had not been able to find anyone to fill the bill. One of his executives, Henry Willson, while attending the "Lux Radio Theatre" broadcast of Janet Gaynor in *A Star Is Born,* spotted young Mosely in the audience. He whisked him off to Selznick, who signed him for the role that same night; two weeks later, Mosely came to Hollywood on a three-day pass and filmed his scene (above, right). Selznick was convinced that the young man had star potential, and he instructed Willson to put him under long-term contract at $100 a week, to commence upon his discharge from the service. Selznick and Willson came up with a new name for the good-looking youngster—"Guy"—for, as Selznick put it, "the guy girls would most like to meet"; his last name, Madison, was taken from a Dolly Madison cake wagon parked in front of the studio. (Left) In *Since You Went Away* Stanley Cortez made use of what he called "psychological photography," using long, stark shadows from a single light source to induce feelings of depression, sadness, and loneliness, as in this shot of Jennifer Jones standing forlorn on the train station platform after bidding a tearful farewell to the doomed Bill Smollett.

344

Spellbound

Claudette Colbert was nominated for an Academy Award for her work in *Since You Went Away*; ironically, at the Awards ceremony on March 15, 1945, she lost out to Ingrid Bergman in George Cukor's *Gaslight*. Selznick had loaned Bergman and Joseph Cotten to MGM for the film, in return for which he obtained Robert Walker for *Since You Went Away*. It was one of those circular trade-off deals that he was becoming so adept at, but that often drove his contract people crazy.

Selznick was also the proud possessor of half of the contract of Gregory Peck, the actor whom he had reluctantly signed and whose first major film, *The Keys of the Kingdom*, just being released, looked to be a substantial hit. This, plus his starring role opposite Greer Garson in MGM's unreleased *The Valley of Decision*, suggested that Peck was about to be an important new personality, and Selznick decided that the time was ripe to reap the harvest of his star-building efforts. Accordingly, he turned down all offers for Peck and Bergman in early 1944, deciding to keep them both for himself and to combine them with another of his farmed-out talents, Alfred Hitchcock. After *Rebecca*, Selznick had made himself a tidy sum by lending out the director to other studios. The practice delighted Hitchcock, offering him the opportunity to work on projects as different as *Suspicion* (for which Joan Fontaine won her Academy Award), *Foreign Correspondent, Shadow of a Doubt* (which broke industry tradition and set a precedent by being filmed almost entirely on location in the small town of Santa Rosa, California, and became one of Hitchcock's personal favorites), and *Lifeboat* (in which he experimented with the elaborate analogy of the democracies versus the dictatorships, with all the action confined to the single setting of the title). But Selznick's practice of loaning him out for high fees had its drawbacks. The cost of Hitchcock's services to Universal for *Saboteur* was so high that the budget of the film suffered accordingly, much to Hitchcock's chagrin, as the story was a pet project of his.

By late 1943, Hitchcock, freed from Selznick's inhibiting influence, had begun to loosen up, to move away from the self-conscious stylistics of his British films and into the less formal classicism of the American sound narrative, using less cutting and more camera movement and assimilating himself easily into the mainstream of commercial Hollywood filmmaking. After *Lifeboat*, Hitchcock had returned to England to make some short films for the British war effort. When he returned to Hollywood in early 1944, he brought with him an unfinished adaptation of a 1927 novel called *The House of Dr. Edwardes* by Francis Beeding. A perverse, frightening little mystery, it told of the young intern Constance Sedgewick, who goes to a remote castle in Switzerland to become an assistant to the famous mental specialist Dr. Edwardes. When she arrives, Dr. Edwardes is on vacation and the asylum is under the leadership of the strange Dr. Murchison, who reads books on Satan and flinches when the shadow of the cross falls across his body. She finds herself in a coven of devil worshippers, and barely escapes being sacrificed by Dr. Murchison, who turns out to be one of the inmates. Constance is rescued from altar duty by the timely arrival of Dr. Edwardes.

Hitchcock, with his fascination for the dark recesses of the human mind, had been working with writer Angus McPhail trying to wrest a believable script from the book, but was having very little success. He brought the project back to the United States, hoping to interest Selznick in letting him make it as his next picture. But Selznick, burdened down with the problems of *Since You Went Away*, had no enthusiasm for the story, commenting, "I don't think we should make this picture . . . in these times it is somewhat of a waste of Hitchcock, who ought to be preparing something in which we could utilize our stars and which would have more promise of being an important picture." Selznick had no alternate suggestions that Hitchcock liked any better, however, and since Peck and Bergman could only be kept for a short time before going on to their next commitments, he reluctantly gave Hitchcock the go-ahead on *The House of Dr. Edwardes*, but insisted that he use Ben Hecht to help him lick the more lurid aspects of the story, even suggesting that the supernatural ramifications could be dispensed with.

At this period Hecht was disciplining himself to work on only two pictures a year, then beat a hasty retreat to New York where he was undergoing psychoanalysis to help him through some domestic difficulties. The Freudian concepts of guilt complexes and repressed memories as the source of mental and physical ailments had been around for years,

but had only recently been taken up seriously by the upper middle classes, emerging as a new fad and achieving glamorous respectability in Moss Hart's 1941 musical play *Lady in the Dark*. It was Hecht who suggested changing the focus of *The House of Dr. Edwardes* from devil worship to a murder mystery solved through elements of psychology. "He turned out to be a very fortunate choice," remarked Hitchcock, "for he was very keen on psychoanalysis . . . he was in constant touch with some of the more prominent psychoanalysts . . . and we were able to turn it into a manhunt story wrapped up in pseudo-psychoanalysis." It was one of those plots that with any serious consideration fall apart on several levels, but also the kind that can be glossed over and turned into an entertaining divertissement, which is what Hitchcock and Hecht planned to do.

Selznick was still dubious about the entire set-up, but the idea of a trend-setting murder mystery with a new twist appealed to him. Lacking the time to give the matter more than cursory attention, and still suffering from the severe depression caused by his brother's death, he turned the matter over to the Audience Research Institute, an organization founded in 1935 by Dr. George Gallup, which had pioneered in testing small cross-sections of the public by asking them questions about specific matters, tabulating their answers, and mathematically projecting these for a large percentage of the population. Selznick had first used this service in 1938, when he and Whitney were curious about just what the potential audience for *Gone With The Wind* might be. The ARI predictions had proven accurate, astoundingly so, and Selznick began using them more and more to measure the popularity of stars and test the appeal of various projects.

In June 1944, he asked them to do a survey of the reaction to a picture to be called either *The House of Dr. Edwardes, The Couch*, or *The Man Who Found Himself*, which would be a psychological murder mystery. This was to be augmented with a survey of the popularity of specific combinations of players, among them Gregory Peck, Ingrid Bergman, Joseph Cotten, Joan Fontaine, Olivia de Havilland, Claudette Colbert, and, strangely enough, Greta Garbo. The report delivered to Selznick in July 1944 revealed that "70 percent of moviegoers tested like title *The House of Dr. Edwardes* . . . because of its implications of mystery, murder, and drama. . . . However, acceptance of the story itself [through synopsis] is below average . . . comments indicate people feel it sounds too gruesome, too grisly . . . some said too unnatural. The title *The Couch* had very little appeal, 30 percent share . . . with risqué implications for most of those tested." As to the performers tested, "Since Gregory Peck's first picture has just opened, most moviegoers as yet have no opinion of him. . . . Joseph Cotten has great marquee strength at the moment and is distinctly more popular among women than men, with great appeal among the 'fan' audience, those who go to the movies more than once a week." Ingrid Bergman turned out to have the greatest appeal among the actresses listed, followed closely by Claudette Colbert, with Joan Fontaine twenty-third on the list and Greta Garbo in fortieth place. The reason for Garbo's low rating was that she had not appeared in a movie since 1941.

Somewhat encouraged about the prospects of the film's title and its probable stars, Selznick told his production people to come up with a budget. An estimated cost of $1.25 million was arrived at, which bothered Selznick; through his new production set-up, each of his pictures was financed individually by borrowing from the banks, with David O. Selznick Productions, Inc., acting as guarantor for the loan. Selznick, as president of the company, had to sign for all loans, and he was nervous about extending himself and the company further into debt—there was already a commitment of nearly $3 million on *Since You Went Away*, and the original budget had been estimated as only half that. So *The House of Dr. Edwardes* was causing him some apprehension:

> In view of my guarantee, I am naturally deeply concerned about the cost of this picture. . . . I would much rather face the music now and abandon the Hitchcock picture if it is going to cost too much or if we are so poorly organized that we can't get an accurate estimate that can be depended on . . . we should not even dream of proceeding until it is clear that we can make it for a price that we consider it to be worth. . . . The script is a short one, the sets and the physical action are

"Will he kiss me or kill me?" read the caption on this publicity still for *Spellbound*.

simple. . . . The cast is superb and competent . . . so I certainly don't believe that the picture warrants a 57-day schedule.

With Hitchcock's pledges that the picture would be quickly, efficiently finished, on schedule, Selznick gave his assent.

The House of Dr. Edwardes began filming on Monday, July 7, 1944, and Selznick left Hitchcock almost completely alone to work, unhampered by any interference, script changes, or even his usual on-set conferences. Not being on the set, however, did not mean he wasn't keeping a careful eye on the dailies as they came through, and here his perspective on details caused him to take an active hand in such things as

> creating clothes to suit the role . . . of the girl. In the severity and utter simplicity of line and design we can aid the characterization of a woman of 29 or 30 who has deliberately disinterested herself in frivolity and kids herself that she is aloof from romantic interests, devotes herself entirely to science and yet would have enough pride, fastidiousness and unaffected chic to look distinguished and smartly but severely groomed. . . . It should be borne in mind that the income of this woman . . . would not be over 3,000 a year plus board . . . so let's not have her dressed as though she were a movie star . . . either as to richness of the costumes or as to the way in which they have been tailored.

Ever vigilant that glamour standards be maintained, Selznick was also concerned that "Peck's beard is still showing a little too heavy. . . . I can't understand this as I understand he is now shaving three times a day. . . . I don't want to lose the quality of his face . . . but perhaps a different kind of powder and more of it is indicated. . . . Also the wave in his hair should be changed to make him look more attractive." Most of these criticisms Hitchcock did not argue about, considering that they were minor points well within Selznick's province, and he continued on his unhurried schedule, filming an average of four and a half script pages a day; the crew was functioning smoothly, sometimes managing as many as eleven different camera set-ups a day. The speed and efficiency were such that by the end of the first month, the company was a week ahead of schedule, something that had not happened on a Selznick picture since *Made for Each Other* in late 1938. In recognition of this, Selznick sent a note to his new production manager, Richard Johnston, saying,

> You have had so many squawks out of me in the past that I want you to know that I am capable of speaking up when things are going right. I have seldom seen so smooth-running a crew, or as obviously efficient a company as the "Dr. Edwardes" unit. Please accept my thanks . . . and transmit them to whoever is giving you assistance in accomplishing this fine result.

One of the knottier problems involved in the making of *The House of Dr. Edwardes* was the visualization of the crucial dream sequences whereby the heroine—now a practicing psychiatrist in a private institution for mental cases in Vermont—unravels the mystery of her amnesiac lover's past. Hecht had carefully researched the hero's description of these dreams to make certain they were psychoanalytically accurate in terms of their details, and in his original script they were described by dialogue only. But Hitchcock, ever the visualist, decided after several weeks' shooting that the dreams should be depicted on screen. Of these dream sequences, Hitchcock commented: "Traditionally, up to that time, dream scenes in films were always done with swirling smoke, slightly out of focus. . . . This was the convention and I decided I wanted to go the other way . . . to convey the dreams with great visual sharpness and clarity, sharper than the rest of the film itself. So Ben Hecht and I, in combination, chose Salvador Dali to do these hallucinatory dreams in his style, which had an architectural sharpness to it, with long shadows, the infinity of distance and the converging lines of perspective. . . . I asked Selznick if he could get Dali to work with us, and he agreed, although I think he didn't really understand my reasons for wanting him. . . . He probably thought I wanted his collaboration for publicity purposes."

To Salvador Dali, "Surrealism is an expression of the subconscious . . . no matter what one looks at, other images arise in the mind. . . . The surrealist gives tangible form to these ideas . . . which may sometimes be wish fulfillments." By the early 1940s, Dali's extravagantly eccentric work and personality had given him an international reputation, one that Selznick valued on two levels. "Dali was commissioned to do the job [for us]; he executed it faithfully and extremely well and it added an extra new facet to what I believe was the first film dealing with Freudian psychoanalysis . . . and his work was a minor but still valuable contribution to the eventual success of the picture."

A unique arrangement was made with Dali whereby, after conferences with Hitchcock, he would do a series of sketches for the dream sequence. If his concepts satisfied Hitchcock, and were feasible for picture purposes, he would then render master paintings in oil and supervise the design and décor of these scenes, at the completion of which he would be paid $1,000 for each painting. The original paintings could not be altered in any way; if any adapting of them was done for filming, it would have to be with Dali's permission and under his supervision. Dali delivered five completed master paintings to the Selznick studios in late June 1944. They were then turned over to the art and production departments for budget estimates. According to their figures, using Dali's ideas would cost close to $150,000. To Selznick, this "came as such a ghastly shock . . . and if the figure is correct, the sequence will have to go out of the picture." But Hitchcock showed Selznick how the sequence could be done with minimal sets, relying mostly on miniatures and background projections of Dali's paintings. Once the art department realized the degree of trick work involved, the budget was revised downward to $20,000, much to Selznick's relief. After the sequence had been put together, Selznick looked at it and was not happy. "The more I look at it, the less I like it. . . . It is not Dali's fault, for his work is much finer and much better for the purpose than I ever thought it would be. It is the photography, set-ups, lighting, etc., all of which is completely lacking in imagination and all of which is about what you would expect from Monogram."* There are no comments from Hitchcock about his feelings on the matter; presumably he was satisfied, since the shooting had been done under his supervision and according to his view of the dramatic necessities of the scene. Whatever the case, Selznick put in an emergency call to William Cameron Menzies, who was just finishing directing a picture for Columbia. Menzies looked at the material that had already been filmed, looked at the script and the designs, and spent several weeks working with James Basevi, the art director, trying to make the shots and sequences "more compellingly artistic," as Selznick begged him to do.

Hitchcock had finished all principal photography by Friday, October 13, and had immediately left for England, returning in mid-December to New York, where he had a series of meetings with Dali and several long-distance conferences with Selznick, Menzies, and Basevi. Both Hitchcock and Dali agreed to the changes. Menzies went ahead and revamped the sequence with a week's shooting in early January, boosting the cost by another $4,000. After looking at what Menzies had done, Selznick felt that "as far as I am concerned, the sequence is still a severe

disappointment." The sequence was put back into work, this time by Jack Cosgrove's department, where it was tinkered with, shortened, altered, and otherwise made more presentable; but it never lived up to either Selznick's or Hitchcock's expectations, and rather than spend any more money, they decided to leave it as it was in its truncated form and take the picture to the public.

Before the preview, Selznick decided that the title *The House of Dr. Edwardes* just didn't have the punch this picture needed, and as he often did when he was stumped for a new title, he offered $50 to anyone in the office who could come up with a satisfactory substitute. Ruth Batchelor, Dan O'Shea's secretary, suggested *Spellbound*. Selznick at first was dubious, thinking there was a chance of audiences confusing it with *Gaslight*, but a quick two-week survey by the ARI proved otherwise, and the picture went off to its San Bernardino preview with its new title. The picture played fairly well, the biggest surprise to Selznick being the reaction to Gregory Peck: "We could not keep the audience quiet from the time his name came on the screen until we had shushed them through three or four sequences and stopped all the dames from 'oohing' and 'ahing' and gurgling." The movie was shortened by almost twenty minutes after the preview, and then Selznick decided it must have something unusual and prestigious, or both, in the way of a musical score. At the recommendation of Lionel Barrymore, Selznick asked Miklos Rozsa, the noted Hungarian composer, to look at the unfinished picture. The classically trained, cultured Rozsa had been scoring for films only since 1937, primarily for Alexander Korda; his music for Korda's *The Thief of*

* Monogram Pictures, surpassed only by PRC Pictures as a purveyor of *schlock*.

These frames from *Spellbound* give an indication of the lengths to which director Alfred Hitchcock and writer Ben Hecht went to keep the picture true to Freudian symbolism. In consultation with May Romm, the psychiatric adviser, it was decided that the first kiss of Ingrid Bergman and Gregory Peck should dissolve to a series of doors opening, which is symbolic of trust and giving. The sequence is one of the trickiest and most effective of Hitchcock's many experiments with love scenes throughout his career.

(Top) Salvador Dali in a characteristic pose, standing in front of one of the paintings he did for the dream sequence in *Spellbound*. Dali painted the "more than real world behind the real" to depict "dream, myth, metaphor and the subconscious." He came out to Culver City in early September 1944 to oversee the transferring of his paintings (one of which is seen above) into the film by Hitchcock and art director James Basevi. Hitchcock later recalled, "Some of his ideas were not practical, but we had to carefully film them regardless."

Bagdad and *That Hamilton Woman (Lady Hamilton)* was moody, romantic, and extravagantly imaginative. In 1943 Rozsa had gone to work for Paramount, and it was his scoring of Billy Wilder's *Double Indemnity* that impressed first Barrymore, then Selznick. Rozsa had just achieved something of a first in professional film music circles with the release of his music for Korda's *The Jungle Book* on RCA Victor records; the album had sold 14,000 copies, which made Selznick sit up and take notice. The licensing rights to movie music belonged to the producing company, not the composer, and if Rozsa's music could sell that many copies, then Bergman and Peck on a record cover "could only help the advertising of the picture in addition to bringing us in some extra money."

Selznick asked Rozsa to score a suspenseful sequence with the amnesiac Peck menacingly approaching the sleeping Ingrid Bergman with a straight razor. Hitchcock and Selznick told the composer they wanted "an unusual sound . . . something new" for this scene, and Rozsa, who was an innovator, decided to introduce the sound of the theremin to American audiences. One of the first quasi-electronic musical instruments, its high-pitched sound varied, depending on the distance of the player's hands from the two tuning rods, so that the performer made a series of passes over these, much as a magician made hand passes over a crystal ball, producing an eerie, quivery sound perfect for the scenes of the deranged, paranoiac Peck in the grip of his psychosis. Rozsa's pioneering use of the instrument in *Spellbound* delighted Selznick, who felt that it was an exploitable gimmick and immediately arranged for a small company to record Rozsa's music for release as an album. Rozsa himself later reworked some of the music from the picture into a short concert piece entitled the "Spellbound Concerto," which met with considerable popular success, thereby fulfilling Selznick's other hope, which was to have a hit record of one of the themes from the picture.

After he had finally finished his work on *Spellbound*, Rozsa went back to Paramount to score Billy Wilder's trenchant study of an alcoholic, *The Lost Weekend*, in which he once again made use of the theremin. When Selznick heard about this, he was irritated enough to call Rozsa and ask if it was true. Rozsa is reported to have replied curtly: "Yes, I'm using the theremin and I'm also using the violin, the oboe, and the clarinet as well." Relations between the two men were icily cordial from then on. Even after Rozsa's score for *Spellbound* won the Academy Award the next year, Selznick sent him only a one-word telegram of congratulations. The cause of Selznick's annoyance was the fact that *The Lost Weekend* would probably be released before *Spellbound*, although it had been filmed later. The lengthy delay in the release of *Spellbound* had been compounded by the slow retake schedules on the dream sequence, the difficulty of working out the special effects, and Selznick's continuing depression. In addition, wartime audiences kept pictures playing in the larger first-run theatres for weeks at a time, with a consequent logjam of pictures building up as distributors fought for favorable playing time in the more prestigious metropolitan houses.

Having missed the lucrative summer bookings, United Artists scheduled *Spellbound* for the next best time, which was fall 1945, almost a year since principal photography had been completed. Complicating matters further, *Spellbound* would be the third Bergman picture to be released in New York in October, the other two being Warner Bros.' *Saratoga Trunk*, made in 1944 but held up until then, and *The Bells of St. Mary's*, which Bergman had made after *Spellbound*. Selznick tried desperately to break up this triple threat, but when the other companies proved uncooperative, he decided to turn the situation to his advantage by ordering his publicity department to publicize the event as proof that "1945 is a Bergman year." The combination of the Bergman-Peck star power, the Hitchcock name, and the Selznick "touch" resulted in *Spellbound* (made at a cost of $1,680,377) taking in $4,671,327, outgrossing *Since You Went Away* by several hundred thousand dollars. Selznick found no comfort in this, writing to Neil Agnew, the head of his sales department:

United Artists estimated that *Spellbound* would do close to $5,600,000. . . . It didn't do anywhere near that . . . it did much better than *Since You Went Away*, but this is attributable . . . to the longer running time of the latter, resulting in fewer shows a day . . . so *Spellbound*, which is short and had a greater turnover potential, actually did not do as well as *Since You Went Away*. . . . UA always seems to shrug off the final

The troublesome dream sequence as it finally emerged on the screen, where it helped to solve the mystery of the identity of the character played by Gregory Peck—an amnesiac, masquerading as Dr. Edwardes, the head of Green Manors, an institution for the mentally unstable. It also helped to solve the mystery of who had murdered the real Dr. Edwardes—the crime for which Peck was being hunted by the police. Peck relates his nightmare to Ingrid Bergman, the psychoanalyst who is in love with him, and to her mentor, Dr. Brulov (Michael Chekhov), who helps to unravel the mystery. "I seemed to be in a gambling house," recalls Peck in the film, "but there weren't any walls, just a lot of curtains with eyes painted on them. A man was walking around with a large pair of scissors cutting all the drapes in half. Then a girl came in with hardly anything on and started walking around the gambling room kissing everybody. . . . I was sitting there playing cards with a man who had a beard. . . . He said, 'That makes twenty-one—I win.' But when he turned up his cards they were blank. Just then the proprietor came in and accused him of cheating. The proprietor yelled, 'This is my place and if I catch you

cheating again, I'll fix you.' Then I saw the man with the beard. He was leaning over the sloping roof of a high building. I yelled at him to watch out. Then he went over—slowly—with his feet in the air. And then I saw the proprietor again. He was hiding behind a tall chimney and he had a small wheel in his hand. I saw him drop the wheel on the roof. Then I was running and heard something beating over my head. It was a great pair of wings . . . they were chasing me and almost caught up with me when I came to the bottom of the hill. That's all I remember. Then I woke up." In analyzing the dream, the two psychoanalysts come up with the interpretation that Peck was a patient of Dr. Edwardes, who was to take over as head of Green Manors from the outgoing Dr. Murchison. Edwardes and his patient, "J.B." (Gregory Peck), had stopped off at the 21 Club in New York, where Murchison had an angry confrontation with Dr. Edwardes. Later J.B. sees Dr. Murchison kill Dr. Edwardes and drop the gun off the sloping hill where the deed was done. J.B. is so shocked by the encounter that he loses his memory and assumes the identify of Dr. Edwardes.

349

hundred thousand dollars of business that are still in our pictures . . . I think we should make a study of this situation with a view to seeing what can be done about it.

Selznick's concern with UA's seeming lack of aggressiveness was, of course, a long-standing one, alleviated somewhat by his becoming part owner, which meant that his pictures were distributed at a cost of only 10 percent of the gross, instead of the usual 22 percent that UA charged its other clients. It actually cost UA money to distribute Selznick's pictures, not only his "personal" productions but also the more inexpensive pictures from Vanguard, which were made to fulfill the demands of the UA contract. This type of picturemaking came perilously close to the production of program pictures, which Selznick had so long abhorred. Nevertheless, the UA contract demanded pictures, so Selznick hired forty-year-old Dore Schary to oversee the production of them, under Selznick's careful tutelage.

Schary had begun his film career as a junior writer at MGM in the mid-thirties, winning an Academy Award for co-writing the original story for *Boys' Town* in 1938, after which he had been promoted to producer of some of MGM's more interesting "B" pictures. Considered a liberal and an intellectual, Schary had a penchant for injecting politics and social criticism into his films, which worked to his disadvantage in the very conservative, don't-rock-the-boat atmosphere of MGM. After leaving there in 1943, Schary had been hired by Selznick, who said,

I thought more of him as a picture maker than MGM did. . . . I told him we were miles apart politically—he was a left wing Democrat and I was a Republican—but that I never quarreled with the politics of an associate or an employee and indeed had very few Republicans in my employ. . . . I told him that I didn't try to use my films to sell my politics and I couldn't subscribe to his using his pictures to sell his. Since we were making pictures for audiences that presumably came to be entertained.

Schary was a strong-minded individual, with ideas of his own, and the two men had engaged in some restrained differences of opinion over Schary's handling of the first Vanguard picture, *I'll Be Seeing You,* with

Schary demanding his own way in story and production matters, leading Selznick to remark: "Were I most sensitive, I would deeply resent a man who is working for . . . me, not accepting my opinions, rejecting my criticisms . . . as to new writer, director, etc., and as to story and script changes. For me to put up with this is not alone being tolerant and patient, it is being Christ-like—and I am not Christ-like."

I'll Be Seeing You had made a modest profit, but as Selznick pointed out in late 1944, "Costs are going up tremendously . . . when the war ends and controls are removed, they will go up even further . . . and we won't be able to depend on [our reputation] to overcome costs that are so much in excess of our competitors." Instead of continuing with the making of these cheaper pictures, Selznick reasoned that it would be more to the company's advantage to prepare a package of script, stars, and occasionally a director, and then to sell this for production to another studio, for a set fee and taking 50 percent of whatever profits there might be. "This would relieve us of the effort of making the pictures while still giving us a guaranteed income at little risk. . . ." Accordingly, he made a co-production deal with RKO, giving them the services of Dore Schary as producer, five finished scripts, and the use of several of his stars, including Dorothy McGuire, Guy Madison, Shirley Temple, and Joseph Cotten. Selznick saw nothing questionable in this, but it was obviously in violation of his contract with United Artists, although his rationale was that the UA contract called for pictures "to be produced personally by me." As part owner of the company, he was working against his own interests, although this seems never to have occurred to him, or if it did, he just didn't have the time or inclination to consider it.

As 1945 began, the forty-three-year-old Selznick was immersed in two turbulent situations: he had become emotionally involved with his newest star, Jennifer Jones; and as an indirect result of this, he had embarked on a costly production project, which he thought would not only show off her versatility as an actress but, more importantly, become the kind of spectacular box-office success he felt everyone had been expecting of him since *GWTW.* What emerged from these twin obsessions was a film that marked a turning point in Selznick's personal and professional life, while also presaging the shape of things to come in the Hollywood film industry.

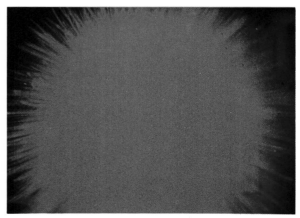

Leo G. Carroll played Dr. Murchison, whom Constance confronts with her interpretation of J.B.'s dream. Hitchcock staged the balance of the scene from Murchison's viewpoint, as he threatens to shoot her. She calls his bluff and leaves, and he commits suicide, firing a shot into the camera. Because it was impossible to keep the hand, the gun, and Bergman all in focus, a larger-than-life-size plaster hand and gun were built, mounted on a special dolly, and turned by two off-camera stagehands. In the original release the gunshot was depicted as a red flash by hand coloring four frames of every print of the film.

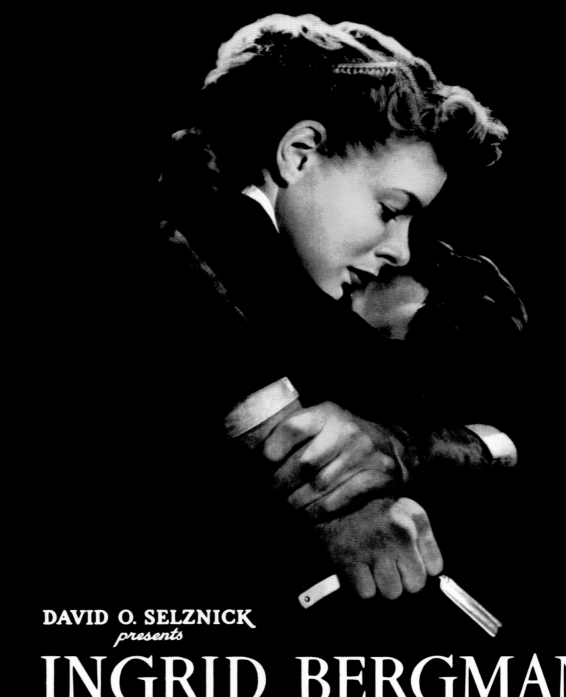

DAVID O. SELZNICK
presents

INGRID BERGMAN
GREGORY PECK
in
ALFRED HITCHCOCK'S

SPELLBOUND

A SELZNICK INTERNATIONAL PICTURE

Screenplay by Ben Hecht • *Released thru United Artists*

JENNIFER JONES as "PEARL CHAVEZ"
Built by the devil...
to drive men crazy

GREGORY PECK as "LEWT McCANLES"
Violent . . . as the
wind-swept prairie

JOSEPH COTTEN as "JESSE McCANLES"
Rebelling against the
tyranny of his father

LIONEL BARRYMORE as "SENATOR McCANLES"
Rich, proud . . . master
of a million acres

HERBERT MARSHALL as "RAOUL CHAVEZ"
Ill-fated son of
creole aristocracy

LILLIAN GISH as "LAURA BELLE McCANLES"
Martyred mother of
a strange brood

WALTER HUSTON as "THE SINKILLER"
Lusty philosopher of
the far-flung prairie

DAVID O. SELZNICK PRESENTS

Duel in the SUN

IN Technicolor

This ad appeared in Sunday tabloids all across the country in the fall of 1945. By the time the picture was ready for release a year later, the name of Herbert Marshall's character had been changed from "Raoul" to "Scott" and all mention of his Creole ancestry had been dropped.

Duel in the Sun

DUEL IN THE SUN had first come to Selznick's attention in mid-1944, when Charles Koerner, the new head of RKO, tried to borrow Jennifer Jones to star in an adaptation of the novel by Niven Busch. Busch had based his story on a legendary lady bandit of Arizona, and had written it with an eye to an eventual movie sale, hoping to star his wife, Teresa Wright, as Pearl Chavez, a half-breed child of nature who disrupts life on the million-acre McCanles ranch in the Staked Plains of Texas in the 1880s. The novel had caused some controversy because of its steamy scenes of sexual activity between Pearl and the elder McCanles son, Lewt, a ne'er-do-well if ever there was one, who rapes Pearl when she is fourteen, the two remaining lovers for several years until Pearl—realizing that Lewt will never marry her because of her Indian heritage, yet will not give her up—kills him in the duel of the title, freeing herself to marry his brother, the bookish, refined Jesse, who loves her in spite of her past and her background. On the strength of its notoriety, RKO had bought the book and hired Busch to adapt his own work and produce the picture. Motherhood prevented Mrs. Busch from playing Pearl, and the same was true of Hedy Lamarr, the next choice. It was at this point that Selznick was asked to lend Jennifer Jones to star opposite John Wayne in a modest black-and-white version of the book.

Selznick's growing obsession with the career of Jennifer Jones had begun to spill over into his private life. He had seen her through the ordeal of her divorce from Robert Walker, helping to soothe its traumatic effects on the nervous, high-strung young woman. Watching her

develop from a shy, sensitive girl to a young woman in whom he saw enormous potential, he began to respond to her on a more emotional level, not an unusual occurrence in a man of his age and temperament. The intense feelings he experienced for her brought on alternate sieges of guilt and depression, as well as fierce emotional and physical urges, and when he read the first draft script that RKO sent him, with its emphasis on seduction, rape, murder, and miscegenation, he wrote to Koerner:

The script is for the most part excellent . . . but I don't think that, as it stands now with the characters as they are and the original ending intact, it is a sufficiently important project to warrant lending Miss Jones. . . . I feel there is a great element of hazard in the casting of John Wayne . . . I know that he is a big favorite right now . . . but he is the exact opposite of what this script requires . . . and if it doesn't come off as a powerful sex story then it is going to misfire as to dramatic importance . . . and I don't think Wayne fills the bill. . . . Niven Busch and I have been friends since boyhood, but this is his first picture as a producer and I don't think that an Academy Award winner should be placed in the hands of a fledgling producer. . . . Miss Jones' career is mine to build and protect exactly as I have that of my other stars and I should be very disappointed if she is not a very great star for the next 10 or 15 years.

Selznick's refusal to lend Jennifer Jones cooled RKO's interest in the project, and after it became known that they had decided to drop production plans, Selznick immediately offered to buy the rights to the novel and the scripts that had been written by both Niven Busch and Selznick's old collaborator Oliver H. P. Garrett. That he would buy this material was surprising, since *Duel in the Sun* was a western, and a pretty pulpy one at that. (Selznick's attitude toward this most despised of all genres was summed up in a response he gave an anonymous interviewer who asked him how far he thought the western had come: "From Wyoming to Arizona—and back.") However, he was evidently excited enough by the prospect of Jennifer Jones playing an innocently sexual temptress to take on the property. Earlier that year Selznick had seen Howard Hughes's notorious saga of Billy the Kid called *The Outlaw,* a picture that promised sex and violence, but delivered only massive close-ups of the generous endowments of its young star, Jane Russell. Yet this, coupled with a blatantly sexual advertising campaign waged by the iconoclastic Hughes, had been sufficient to send crowds of sensation-hungry wartime audiences to the few theatres that played the picture before the Hays office removed its seal of approval. That same year, 1944, had seen the publication of *Forever Amber,* Kathleen Winsor's huge best seller about the career of a courtesan in the Restoration court of Charles II of England. Selznick guessed that audiences were ripe for something sensational, and, as he later related, "Seeing how profitable westerns always were, I decided that if I could create one that had more spectacle than had ever been seen in a western and combine it with a violent love story, then the two elements would give me a great success."

Selznick was reacting very cynically to the current boom in movie attendance; business during the war years had continued to build, and in early 1945 some 88 million people were going to the movies weekly, with no fall-off in sight. It seemed to be just a matter of time until the war in Europe was ended, which would open up the foreign markets again, so the chances were very good for the kind of success Selznick was talking about. Immediately after purchasing the book from RKO, he began working with Oliver Garrett to change, expand, and otherwise "go whole hog ... on the picture." One of the first things he did was to rewrite the ending of the picture so that Pearl, instead of killing Lewt and riding off with brother Jesse into the sunset, shoots Lewt, is in turn shot by him, and then, as Selznick phrased it,

> in a perfectly magnificent finish, that can be played superbly by Miss Jones ... having shot him because it is the only thing she can do, she is still drawn to him and crawls across the face of the mountain to get to him ... and the two play their final love moments together in each other's arms, and as they die we pull back from them until they are lost in the landscape under the blazing, broiling sun.

Selznick felt that this new ending was far more appropriate and

> a lot less unpleasant than the original ... since I don't see how the girl's action in killing [Lewt] can be regarded as anything but murder ... and what kind of bedmates she and Jesse will be after this wanton murder of his brother ... does not present a very pretty picture ... especially since the audience and Jesse both know that she has loved the man she killed unceasingly throughout the entire picture....

The one scene in the novel that Selznick left relatively alone was the rape. It had been the book's most talked-of scene, with its frank depiction of the girl's eventual surrender and ultimate enjoyment of the act. Selznick's main change was to alter the setting from an oppressively hot, dry afternoon to a muggy, ominous, dramatically overcast evening. As Pearl gives in, a tremendous burst of thunder and lightning puts an exclamation point on the scene, endowing the character's sexual awakening with an epic climax. This emphasis on sex was carried through in almost all the scenes between Lewt and Pearl; no punches were pulled about the characters' enjoyment of what they were doing; and eventually their sexual couplings degenerated into a not so thinly disguised sado-masochistic relationship. In one scene, which Selznick dubbed "the degradation," Pearl, in her nightgown, is dragged screaming along the floor, clinging to Lewt's boot, begging him to take her with him to Mexico. He kicks her in the face and goes, leaving her writhing on the floor in a fit of sexual frenzy. This followed a scene showing Pearl trying to arouse Lewt by performing an erotic, seductive dance on the banks of a swimming hole known as "the sump," resulting in a fevered love scene that made even Selznick wonder "if it will get past the censors ... we better have

Joe Breen [from the Hays office] on the set when we film it."

All these changes flew in the face of Selznick's reputation for treating an author's work with respect and fidelity, but as he was quick to point out:

> This does not apply to the adaptation of unsuccessful books, or to books of very moderate success. If the book fails to achieve outstanding distinction in its own medium, there is no reason to believe that a faithful transcription would achieve distinction in another medium; with *Duel in the Sun,* I was enormously attracted by the characters and their relationships ... but felt that the story of the characters got lost in a maze of wild west exploits ... and that the story needed to be expanded in its scope....

His assertion that he was attracted to the characters is interesting, since all the characters and their relationships were completely changed by him in his adaptation except for Pearl and Lewt, and even they underwent a subtle transformation from the psychologically motivated people of the book to mere sexual ciphers whose actions and attitudes are completely controlled by their lust for each other. Selznick's screenplay for *Duel in the Sun* is practically an original, for it uses nothing from the book except the basic plot, deviating even from that in several essentials, with a completely different emphasis in both content and form.

The script is an excellent reflection of Selznick's state of mind at the time and, compared with *The Garden of Allah,* an indication of how much he and his attitudes had changed in ten years. The two pictures are almost opposite sides of the same coin: one concerns itself with the denial of fleshly pleasure, while the other glories in it; one exalts the regenerative power of love, while the other depicts love not as a genuine emotion but as a destructive, neurotic thrill, growing completely out of a sexual attraction. Ten years earlier, Selznick had been young, idealistic, and happily married. Now he was a middle-aged, wealthy businessman, his arrogance no longer tempered by his youthful enthusiasms, his consideration for his co-workers (never one of his strong points) disappearing almost completely under the demands of his ever-increasing ego and his view of himself as a man beset on all sides by ineptitude and stupidity. Self-assured, self-important, losing his humor, he was relentless in pursuit of his goals and could be petty and vindictive with anything or anyone that crossed him. Quick to take offense from those he considered not of his own stature, he became involved in a lengthy and bitter wrangle with Niven Busch over the screenplay credit of *Duel in the Sun,* which was finally settled in Selznick's favor. In ten years he had been transformed from a friendly, appreciative, self-confident, slightly self-indulgent man, who could cheerfully collaborate with others, to an overbearing, querulous autocrat, under the intense pressure of business and the need to maintain his reputation, and holding an almost total conviction and belief in his own infallibility about making movies.

Selznick intended the production of *Duel in the Sun* to be a "test to see whether my theories about the business and public's taste were correct." Where he had once relied on his own instincts and sensibilities in determining the kind of pictures audiences might want, he now began basing his judgment and decisions on what the Audience Research Institute was telling him. Throughout the winter of 1944–45, he was continually testing responses to the title *Duel in the Sun* (which he considered changing when most moviegoers assumed it was the story of an airplane dogfight) and to the theme of the story. In early 1945, the ARI reported that 57 percent of the moviegoing audience would be interested in seeing a picture described as "a sexy story of a wild, passionate girl," and that 58 percent would want to see a picture "where the emphasis was on spectacular adventure, passionate conflict with a western setting." According to these figures, *Duel in the Sun*'s subject matter had only a little above average appeal. But the ARI had the answer to that too; it was called "penetration," and it measured the density of familiarity with a title and "anticipatory knowledge" of a given film. The average penetration index was a 7. On *Duel in the Sun,* in early 1945, it measured out to a 3, and Selznick, deciding to see how far the market and audiences could be manipulated, embarked on an unprecedented advertising campaign concurrent with the picture's production, so that by the time the film was ready for release, every moviegoer in the country would be primed to storm the theatres for a look at it. Nothing like this had ever been tried

(Above) Filming the climactic *Duel in the Sun* scenes 40 miles east of Tucson, March 1945. The temperature hovered at around 25 degrees, and for days at a time the company was forced indoors by snow and icy winds. (Below, left) Director King Vidor (with megaphone), bundled up against the elements, directs a scene while Technicolor cinematographer Hal Rosson (left) looks on. Camera operator Ed Fitzgerald is in front of the camera. (Below, right) King Vidor (left) and Gregory Peck (right) are evidently amused by something Joseph Cotten has said.

before on such a massive, artificially induced scale, but Selznick had always been a firm believer in the power of intensive advertising to lure people into theatres, provided that once in, they were satisfied with what they saw. This publicity campaign was to be waged on several fronts: newspaper and magazine advertising, radio broadcasting tie-ups, cooperative advertising, and good old-fashioned intensive ballyhoo that would start by dropping five thousand tiny nylon parachutes on the seventy-second running of the Kentucky Derby, containing pari-mutuel tickets on the race itself, with a big plug for *Duel in the Sun.* Arrangements were made to have the title plastered on light bulbs, lollipops, ashtrays, T-shirts, sweaters, typewriters, automobile stickers, and several hundred other miscellaneous items that had a high visibility potential.

As plans for this calculated assault on the moviegoer's consciousness were being laid, Selznick was still feverishly injecting into the script everything he could think of to make the picture more salable. He was convinced that only "big" pictures made substantial profits; the success of *GWTW* made him certain that the adage about having to spend money to make money was true. The fact that the story of *Duel in the Sun* was not exactly the highest form of drama did not faze him in the slightest; the quality in this case would come from the production itself. By early 1945, with the publicity well on its way to pounding the title into every semiliterate in the country, Selznick began preparing to make a film that would live up to his campaign for it.

William Dieterle had been Selznick's first choice to direct *Duel in the Sun,* but he didn't like the material, so Selznick went to King Vidor, with whom he hadn't worked since *Bird of Paradise* in 1932, a picture that also dealt with miscegenation and had a high erotic content, as well as a tragic ending in which the heroine sacrifices herself for love. Perhaps remembering these similarities and Vidor's vivid use of landscapes in his *Billy the Kid* (1930), *The Texas Rangers* (1936), and the rugged Technicolor epic *Northwest Passage* (1940), Selznick, according to Vidor, had sent for the director and said, "I want you to produce and direct this thing because I'm going to be doing something else. . . . I'd like you to make a nice intimate little picture out of it." "I read it," continues Vidor, "and I saw it as a very sexy, intense and intimate treatment of the story . . . and if it was done right, I thought I might win an Academy Award with it." After Selznick took it over as a "personal" production, Vidor was not without some qualms about their ability to work together. "David was pretty notorious by then for his antics with directors, and I told him right at the beginning, 'The only thing I won't go for is you coming on the set and yelling and performing in a way that will affect my authority on the set . . . because the crew has to know that there's only one boss on the set.' I told him exactly what I told Sam Goldwyn . . . that if he came out and did that on the set three times . . . then I'd walk off."

By the time filming began, Selznick had completely moved away from the concept of the "nice intimate little picture" Vidor had envisioned. "The first thing I knew," recalls Vidor, "he had me running *Gone With The Wind.* . . . As we were working on the script, he just kept expanding it, adding scenes . . . having the production designer come up with all sorts of wild ideas for the way these scenes should be shot." According to Selznick, "I decided to have some fun with it . . . *Duel in the Sun,* more than any other picture I ever made, was just an exercise in production." The remark was made after the fact; "fun" *Duel in the Sun* wasn't—not for Selznick or for anyone else concerned with its making. In late February 1945, the week before production was to start, Selznick's expansion of the script had escalated the budget close to $3 million, a good chunk of which would be spent on a lengthy location trip to Arizona. A 150-man crew took three vanloads of equipment, 20 tons of props, and a two-story prefabricated ranchhouse set, two barns, and a windmill to a remote hilly area 40 miles outside of Tucson. Once there, the crew spent two months dressing up the location, painting the cacti the proper shade so that it would photograph well in Technicolor, populating the scenery with four hundred head of cattle and a like number of horses. It all added up to a cost of $15,000 a day.

By the time Vidor, Selznick, Jennifer Jones, and her two leading men, Gregory Peck and Joseph Cotten, arrived on March 4, everything that could possibly be taken care of had been, except for the one thing that no one can ever arrange on a location trip: the weather. The second day of shooting, a light snow began to fall; within the first week, high winds

and rain had demolished most of the standing sets; on days that filming could go on, it was so cold that Jennifer Jones's lips, according to the production log, "turned blue." When she wasn't turning blue, she was bleeding from the physical beating she was taking in filming the final scenes of the story, in which she crawls across rocks and up the side of a mountain to reach her dying lover. As Vidor directed these scenes with Jones and Gregory Peck, two second units under action directors B. Reeves Eason and Otto Brower were photographing the spectacular scenes of cattle roundups and the massed riding of hundreds of horsemen over the hills and valleys of the Arizona landscape that would be used to depict what Selznick and Vidor referred to as "the gathering of the clans" to fight off the encroaching railroad, one of the story's subplots. This sequence was patterned after a famous episode in *The Birth of a Nation,* and when Selznick saw the rushes, he commented: "The long shots are enormously impressive . . . I do wish that we had twice as many or three times as many horsemen. . . . I want to shoot the works on numbers of horsemen, wild horses, etc."

While the company was occupied with the location shooting, back in Hollywood a jurisdictional dispute over representation of the set designers and set decorators effectively closed down almost all production activity in the studios, a situation that lasted until mid-April. When *Duel in the Sun's* first unit under Vidor had completed the bulk of its location shooting and returned to Hollywood, it was unable to work on any of the interior sets. It cost Selznick $360,000 just to keep the expensive cast and some of the contract crew on salary until the end of the strike.

Because of poor weather and other difficulties, the company had been two weeks behind schedule by the time they returned to Culver City. The strike delayed them another two weeks. When it finally ended, Vidor began working again, only to find that Selznick had completely revamped the script once more, throwing Vidor's carefully prepared approach completely awry. "I would start to work at nine o'clock in the morning, and I'd be three-quarters through a sequence and here would come David with a new addition to the scene we were working on . . . he'd be very proud of it . . . having stayed up all night to work it out. . . . It would be some silly little thing he had changed . . . and he insisted that I reshoot it." Not content just to rewrite scenes, Selznick began to insist on being on the set when they were shot, as he recounts in a letter he wrote during production: "There were strict orders on the set that not a single scene was to be photographed, not even a single angle of a scene until I was telephoned to come down on the set to check the lighting, the set-up, and the rehearsal . . . I would then not merely check the exact directing of the scene and 99 times out of 100 change it, but I would stay until I personally approved a take." According to Vidor, "This began to happen more and more. . . . And of course it would cost extra money and time to do this. . . . I didn't mind that so much, it was his money and it was his picture . . . and in that sense, David was the only producer I ever worked with who really earned the title of producer because he wanted the best of everything and he worked like hell to get it . . . he made sure you got what he thought was necessary."

With *Duel in the Sun,* Selznick was not above doing things himself if he thought it necessary. On April 12, while Vidor was out sick, Selznick took over the direction of the day's work, and was only prevented from carrying it through by the stunning impact of the news of Franklin Roosevelt's sudden death. Selznick, along with everybody else in the country, was devastated by the event. As a spokesman for the Republican Party, he wrote an eloquent speech, which he delivered over the radio on the night of April 14:

This is our strangest hour. The long awaited victory apparently is ours, but its fruit is bitter. We have regained freedom for the whole world and once again have lost a Great Emancipator . . . but we have the opportunity to prove that we have matured politically . . . to present to the whole world the spectacle of a nation united as never before behind Franklin Roosevelt's dream, a dream which has grown into the determined will of a nation. . . . Here in Hollywood, we of the motion picture business are humbly conscious of the power of the medium which is ours. Along with the radio and the press, that medium will do its share to the end that "my friends" will be not merely a nostalgic phrase, but a national pledge toward all mankind.

SELZNICKS, WED 15 YEARS, PART

By Louella O. Parsons
Motion Picture Editor International News Service

The breaking up of the 15-year-old marriage of David and Irene Selznick came as a shock to their friends, even though rumors have been fast and furious the last few years that all was not well.

Irene, who is the daughter of Mr. and Mrs. Louis B. Mayer, married David Selznick, who was an ambitious and brainy young man, at the home of her parents on April 29, 1930.

Never did a marriage start out more promising.

David, the youngest son of Mr. and Mrs. Lewis J. Selznick, was brought up in the atmosphere of motion pictures. It was a subject he knew and which his bride had known all her life.

WEDDING GUEST—

I was one of the wedding guests, and the two started out with all the good things in the world—money, position and most important—love and happiness.

In the years following their marriage David became one of the most prominent film producers in the world. He has perhaps the greatest lineup of stars of any producer in the business.

Under contract to him are Ingrid Bergman, Jennifer Jones, Shirley Temple, Joan Fontaine, Joseph Cotten, Gregory Peck, Alan Marshall, Dorothy McGuire and many others.

His success has been phenomenal and he has made a fortune. But apparently neither his fame, his money, nor his enviable position in the business world have been enough to make him happy.

He revolutionized motion picture history with "Gone With the Wind," the most publicized motion picture ever made.

The Selznicks have two boys—Lewis Jeffery, aged 13, and Daniel, aged 11. They were with their mother last night in the beautiful Colonial home in Beverly Hills which Irene and David

WAITRESSES WANTED—GOOD SHIFTS. MEALS AND UNIFORMS FURNISHED. APPLY 409 W. FIFTH.—Advertisement.

SEPARATED—Mr. and Mrs. David O. Selznick, who have decided to go their separate ways. Mrs. Selznick, daughter of Louis B. Mayer, confirmed reports of parting yesterday. They wed in 1930.

had planned so proudly only a few years ago.

Irene said when I talked with her last night the decision was hard to make, but seemed the best way.

"We haven't been getting along and under those conditions the only thing to do was separate," she said. "Neither of us plans a divorce."

Irene leaves for New York as soon as she can get transportation. Later, when I talked with David, he said:

"I can't think our separation is final. We have been married so many years and I still con-sider Irene the most brilliant and beautiful woman I know. We haven't discussed divorce, but maybe a separation will clear the air.

"It was all my fault. I'm difficult. Irene has taken a lot of my temperament."

I told both Irene and David I was sorry to have to write this story. I have known them both since they were children. I had thought their difficulty, which seemed much more serious a few years ago, had been ironed out. But, apparently, their difficulties started all over again the last month.

(Above) July 16, 1945–D. W. Griffith with David O. Selznick. Thirty years earlier, the thirteen-year-old Selznick had been awestruck by *The Birth of a Nation.* Now Griffith, almost forgotten, is on the set of Selznick's western epic, which included a sequence Selznick called "the gathering of the clans"—nothing to do with the Ku Klux Klan, but patterned almost shot for shot after the memorable sequence in Griffith's 1915 masterpiece. (Opposite) Jennifer Jones as the half-breed child of nature Pearl Chavez.

On the day of the funeral, April 16, the entire industry closed down in respect. The next day, as the new President, Harry Truman, took over the running of the country and the war, Vidor, recovered from his brief illness, began working on the scenes that Selznick had been trying to direct the previous Thursday: the pivotal and highly charged rape sequence. The scene posed many problems, especially for Jennifer Jones. The part she was playing was completely unsuited to her, as Vidor recalls: "Pearl was a half-degenerate half-breed, dominated completely by her physical emotions, and Jennifer wasn't like that at all ... it was a big struggle for her to play that. ... She has a very expressive face and it signifies her thoughts, and in order to get her in the character of the girl, I had to tell her the story every day up to the point we were at in the script to get her in the mood ... she's like a young girl you're telling a fairy story to ... then she becomes that to the best of her ability.... You'd tell her how to feel in these situations and that's the way she wanted to be directed—she wanted to be told the whole story and the whole character ... she's like putty in your hands."

For Gregory Peck, Vidor had to find a handle, a key, to give to the actor, who was something of a strait-laced, unbending type, more at home in the introspective, sensitive roles that had brought him public acceptance. Lewt, the cold-blooded, sexy seducer and murderer of *Duel in the Sun,* was completely alien to Peck's personality and experience, and in the beginning he was awkward and uncomfortable. Vidor, recognizing this, talked Peck into playing the outward manifestations of the part. "I designed his whole character after the character of Sportin' Life in *Porgy and Bess*—the cigar and the hat slouched over one eye and the easy kind of shuffling walk and drawl. I told Peck about it and he liked the idea and he carried it all the way through the picture." After several days of practice, Peck slipped right into it, delivering an insolent, smoldering sexuality that combined with Jennifer Jones's erotic voluptuousness to give their love scenes and indeed all their scenes together a blatant and unprecedented sexual frankness that would eventually cause major problems for the film.

On April 18, all production in Hollywood was closed down by another of the growing number of disputes between the unions as to who had jurisdiction over the workers. Picket lines were thrown up around the studios and anyone who belonged to any union dared not cross them. Violence greeted those who tried, and as the days stretched on with no settlement in sight, Selznick disbanded the *Duel in the Sun* company for the duration, hoping he could reassemble the technical crew once tempers had cooled. Key cast members, crew, and staff were kept on at reduced pay, while everyone else was laid off. During the hiatus, Selznick had time to take stock of the situation he found himself in: the delays, the strikes, and the escalating costs due to his continual expansion of the script had increased his estimated budget to $4 million, making it, in Selznick's words, "one of the most costly films ever made." In order to maximize cast potential and to keep interest in the picture alive during the anticipated long shutdown, Selznick began signing major character actors for what would normally be walk-ons—"speaking bits" in the picture. These ranged from Walter Huston as a richly comic prairie preacher known as "the Sinkiller," to veterans Harry Carey and Otto Kruger, whose parts were tiny but whose fees were not. Deciding that the only way to insure his ballooning investment was by stepping up the publicity campaign, Selznick allotted $1 million to pound home the fact that *Duel in the Sun* was going to be "the picture of a thousand memorable moments," that it would contain "spectacle, savagery, fury"—a message that was repeated over and over in every newspaper and magazine and on every radio program for which ads could be taken and time bought.

While this campaign was getting under way, Selznick's domestic life was disintegrating. His wife, Irene, told him she couldn't live with him any longer, and during the year the couple separated. The break-up of his marriage marked the loss of one of the few steadying influences in both David's personal and professional life. Over the years Irene Selznick had been more than a wife; she had acted as counselor and adviser, and in many cases had been able to curb his more excessive and questionable enthusiasms through the soundness of her judgment and the logic of her reasoning. Few of his decisions were made without consulting her, and their separation aggravated Selznick's already chaotic state of mind.

(Above) Selznick and Vidor on location in Arizona for *Duel in the Sun.* (Top, right) Selznick caught in a pensive moment by still photographer Madison Lacy just after Vidor has walked off the location at Lasky Mesa in the San Fernando Valley in California following their dispute over the producer's constant interference. Selznick himself directed the balance of the sequence—part of the final bloody confrontation between Pearl and her outlaw lover, Lewt. (Right) Otto Brower (in flowered shirt), second unit director, was, along with B. Reeves Eason, responsible for directing the bulk of the spectacular scenes in *Duel in the Sun.* (Below, left) Josef von Sternberg was in charge of a special unit on the film, advising Selznick and Vidor on lighting effects and the more glamorous aspects of the photography of Jennifer Jones—all under the watchful eye of Selznick (left). Von Sternberg also directed four short scenes in the film. (Below, right) William Dieterle, seen here with Lionel Barrymore and Lillian Gish, took over the direction of the film after Vidor walked off the production. Dieterle (who always wore white gloves when directing) was responsible for thirteen of the picture's sixty-three sequences. Selznick himself directed four scenes in the final film.

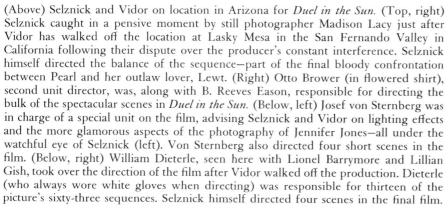

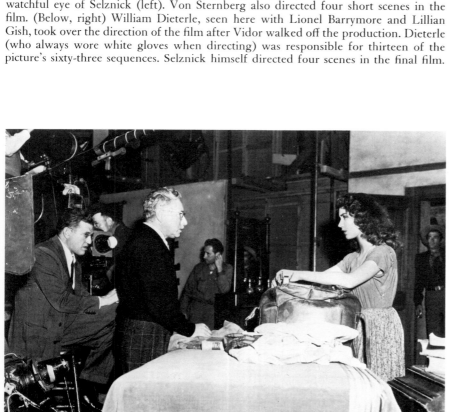

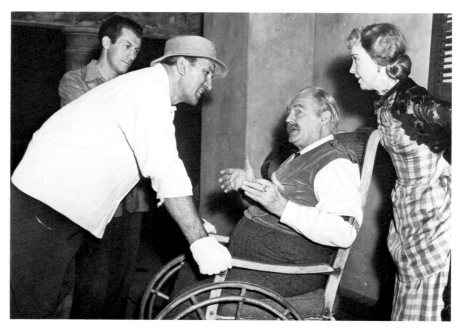

Nowhere was this reflected more than in the financial and artistic morass *Duel in the Sun* had turned into.

Freed now of all restraints, and using the production as an escape from his own problems, Selznick during the strike period began another series of revisions of the story and the characters. When the strike finally ended on June 25, the company was seventy-five days behind schedule and close to $1 million over budget. The actors and the technicians reassembled to be confronted by a script with close to seventy-five more scenes in it and orders to reshoot a considerable portion of the already completed footage. Vidor, instead of jumping right into this, continued to shoot the script he had been working on while arguing with Selznick about the additions. Selznick's constant and maddening script changes were beginning to get to the actors as well. "I was just finishing up with Joe Cotten one day," recalls Vidor. "It was late in the afternoon, and David arrived with what he called a new version of the scene and wanted me to shoot it. I told him we were just finishing with it, that Cotten was taking off his makeup and leaving, but David insisted I get him back and redo it from the new script. All it was was a slightly different speech, but then David, even while we were working on it, began rewriting it again, and we were there until almost midnight.... Joe Cotten had a joke about it. He said, 'Is this the sequence where I have my arm on my lap, or on the edge of the couch?' It was that slight a difference."

Not only Selznick was giving Vidor difficulties: on Monday, July 16, a ghost from the movies' past momentarily haunted the set of *Duel in the Sun.* Vidor recalled that "D. W. Griffith came to visit ... I remember how when I first came to Hollywood we used to sneak under the fence to watch him work on *Intolerance* and now here he was visiting my set. It was pretty hard for the actors. It was a scene between Lillian Gish and Lionel Barrymore—they had both started their careers with him, and his being there made them very nervous. Lionel kept muffing his lines, and after about eight takes I had to go over and ask Griffith to leave because they were going to go up in their lines as long as he was there. He was very nice about it. He said, 'I understand, I've been here long enough as it is.' And he left."

While Vidor worked with the main actors, Otto Brower was busy once again with the large second unit working out on Lasky Mesa in the San Fernando Valley, filming the spectacular scenes of the cavalry coming to the rescue of the railroad people as they try to put tracks across the McCanleses' land. For this he used close to a thousand extras, a genuine 1880 vintage locomotive, a mile of track, and two hundred horses. The tension of the lengthy shooting schedule, the slowness with which work was progressing, and the astronomical outlay of money, plus his own personal situation, were all causing the normally excitable Selznick to become even more irritable and occasionally almost apoplectic. On the afternoon of August 10, Vidor was out on location waiting for one of the Technicolor cameras to arrive so he could begin work. "I'm waiting for the cameras," relates Vidor, "and David arrives and he started yelling, 'My God, you haven't gotten the first shot!' And he starts screaming and kicking the ground. I had warned him not to ever do this, and I had a little megaphone on, so I took it off and just handed it to him and I said, 'You've been wanting to direct a long time, I'm sure—here's your chance,' and I went and got in an automobile and left—he had just gone too far."

Selznick's version of this differs slightly in the details and his reasons:

I went out ... with King to the location. The camera was all set, ready to go. King rehearsed the actors in my presence. Repeatedly I asked him whether the camera was all set and he assured me ... almost impatiently that I need have no worries on this score, [so] I went to a trailer to get caught up on some other work. Hours later, I went back to the set to see how it was progressing and, to my horror, discovered that once again King had completely changed the set-up ... by this one whim, arrived at belatedly, he had thrown another twenty to twenty-five thousand dollars down the drain, since clearly there was no possibility whatsoever of finishing that day.... When I took King to task, he quit. ...

Selznick was shocked—no director had ever walked out on him before—but he recovered quickly and turned the remaining few sequences over to the second-unit directors. Back at the studio, he brought in William Cameron Menzies to lay out and film a colorful party scene involving 320 dancers and extras. They were just finishing a rehearsal of this when Selznick hurried onto the set and announced that the Japanese had surrendered and the war was over. He begged them to stay until they got a good take, and then, as cinematographer Lee Garmes recalls, "We could celebrate the end of the war and the end of the picture." But Garmes reckoned without Selznick's extravagant imagination. Two months later, he hired William Dieterle, who had turned the picture down seventeen months before, to come in and direct an entirely new opening, something to get the story off to a spectacular, bang-up start.

Taking place in a border cantina filled with hundreds of sweating, shouting men, the scene called for Pearl Chavez's mother to do a frenzied dance on top of the bar, to the accompaniment of throbbing tom-toms, punctuated by gunshots and screams, the whole ending with her seductive undulations in front of both her husband and her lover. She leaves with her lover, and the husband kills them both while Pearl watches terrified, thereby setting the plot in motion. The scene was lifted almost intact from a similar one in *The Garden of Allah,* which had ended in a riot instead of a murder, and to make the similarities even more obvious, Selznick hired the same dancer from *The Garden of Allah* to play Pearl's mother in *Duel in the Sun,* the exotic and highly respected Viennese performer Tilly Losch. Miss Losch then tutored Jennifer Jones in the erotic dance that Pearl would perform to arouse Lewt on the banks of "the sump," and as Lydia Schiller recalls: "It was a very revolting piece of dancing.... She was very suggestively weaving around a tree ... it was just so suggestive ... almost a sexual relationship with the tree ... it was just terrible. When we ran the dailies, Mr. Selznick asked me my opinion and I told him I didn't like it.... Then we showed it to Joe Breen, the chief censor, and when the lights came up, he stood up and told Mr. Selznick how unpleasant it was and that we would never, never get an okay to put anything like that on the screen ... and we had to redo it."

After nine months of shooting, Selznick had spent $4,575,000, more than the negative cost of *Gone With The Wind,* and had shot twenty-six hours and thirteen minutes of film. In early February 1946, by dint of backbreaking labor, he and Hal Kern managed to weed this down to a little under four hours for the picture's first preview with temporary stock music at the Grand Lake Theatre in Oakland. The audience reaction veered wildly from appreciation for the spectacle scenes to an unbelieving fascination at the highly charged love scenes and the overt sexuality, with many being repelled by the violence. The heavy melodramatics elicited snickers of derision. The preview cards were the worst Selznick had seen in his entire career, with people calling the story "trash" and the performances "obscene." In an effort to repair what he thought were some of the picture's more obvious faults, Selznick began two months of retakes and added scenes, swelling the budget by another half-million dollars. One thing had especially surprised Selznick at the preview: almost half the audience had never heard of *Duel in the Sun,* and a special study by the ARI confirmed this finding.

The picture was still nowhere near complete; it needed extensive special effects work done on almost every single exterior scene, all of which, to be done by Jack Cosgrove, would be expensive and time-consuming. Selznick reckoned he wouldn't be able to release it before September 1946. That gave him six months to make the United States *Duel in the Sun*-conscious, and he allotted a second million dollars for an expanded advertising and publicity campaign, testing the reaction every month by having the ARI take the moviegoing pulse of the nation, which by late July was beginning to beat faster for the "picture of a thousand memorable moments." By that time, Selznick had reduced the running time to two hours and eighteen minutes, and had hired Dimitri Tiomkin to write an appropriate score. The Russian-born composer had been writing movie music since 1933 for an imposing list of films, ranging from Capra's *Lost Horizon* and *Meet John Doe* to Hitchcock's *Shadow of a Doubt,* but Selznick kept his usual close watch over what he was composing. He was especially concerned about the music for the love scenes between Jones and Peck. Tiomkin relates in his autobiography, *Please Don't Hate Me,* that Selznick would tell him,

"Dimi, [this love theme] is still not right. It hasn't the unbridled, throbbing urge." So I had to write it again, this time giving it plenty of throb, with violent palpitations in the orchestra. (This was my third

The prologue to *Duel in the Sun,* which Selznick referred to as "The Legend." The scene fades in on a mountain in the shape of a face silhouetted against a blood-red sky, while the doom-laden voice of the narrator (Orson Welles) intones: "Deep among the lonely, sun-baked hills of Texas, the great and weather-beaten stone still stands. The Comanches called it 'Squaw's Head Rock.' Time cannot change its impassive face, nor dim the legend of the wild young lovers who found heaven, and hell, in the shadows of the rock. For when the sun is low and the cold wind blows across the desert, there are those of Indian blood who still speak of Pearl Chavez, the half-breed girl from down along the border, and of the laughing outlaw with whom she here kept a final rendezvous, never to be seen again. And this is what the legend says: 'A flower, known nowhere else, grows from out of the desperate crags where Pearl vanished . . . Pearl, who was herself a wild flower, sprung from the hard clay, quick to blossom . . . and early to die.' " As the camera moves in to a close-up of the flower, the scene dissolves to a shot of the thirteen-year-old Pearl dancing for some street urchins in front of a massive Bordertown cantina. Inside, her mother (Tilly Losch) is doing a frenzied, high-class bump and grind on the great square bar, to the throbbing, barbaric rhythms of an Indian orchestra. While her husband—Pearl's father (Herbert Marshall)—looks on, Mrs. Chavez seductively entices her latest paramour (Sidney Blackmer). The two leave to continue their activities elsewhere, followed by Chavez, who kills them both, to Pearl's horror. Condemned to be hanged, Chavez sends his tearful daughter off to Texas to live with his cousin Laura Belle McCanles and recites Omar Khayyám: "One thing is certain, and the rest is lies: /The flower that once has bloomed, forever dies." Then the shadow of the noose appears silhouetted in red on the jailhouse wall. Pearl goes off to live with the McCanles family, thereby setting the story in motion. Squaw's Head Rock was a matte painting by Jack Cosgrove superimposed over previously filmed footage from the Tucson location. The Bordertown cantina sequence was directed by William Dieterle, designed by J. McMillan Johnson, and photographed by Ray Rennahan.

try.) ... When the summons came, I went to his office. ... "What is wrong now?" I restrained myself with difficulty. "Dimi, that is not the way I make love." With that my Russian inflections thickened in a shout of rage: "But it is the way *I* make love!" He burst out laughing. That was the end of it. He agreed I should make musical love in my own way.

Impassioned, pulsating, barbaric, and thunderous, the music matches perfectly the fervid emotionalism of the story.

When Selznick attempted to remove the credit "King Vidor's Production" from the proposed main title, the violation of a contractual obligation met with stiff resistance from Vidor. The dispute grew bitter, especially to Selznick, who fired off a twenty-one-page letter to Vidor's attorney, Henry Herzburn, accusing Vidor of being

> anxious to secure two credits, neither of which he is entitled to. ... I have just received a tally of the present footage of the picture, broken down by directors. ... Mr. Vidor is insisting on sole credit for the direction of the picture of which he directed 6,280 feet, of which he did not direct 7,739 feet.*... It will be up to the Screen Directors Guild to decide a very interesting question; shall a director receive credit for other men's work, both as a director and ... a producer, because of dubious legal precedent, regardless of whether or not he is entitled to this credit?

After seeing the picture, reading the scripts, and listening to testimony from everyone concerned, the Arbitration Board awarded sole directorial credit to King Vidor. Selznick had to accept their verdict, and eventually the two men resumed their friendship, with Selznick remarking in a conciliatory note, "I should hate to think that either of us is so juvenile as to let what happened interfere with a twenty-year friendship."

Almost immediately after this Selznick was faced with another crisis, not of his own making, but having serious repercussions for him. The head of the RKO studio, Charles Koerner, died suddenly, and the company was left without a functioning production authority. Dore Schary, whom Selznick had loaned out to RKO, was approached and asked by the RKO board if he would be interested in taking over Koerner's job. Schary was, and Selznick, after an initial reluctance, let him go with the proviso that RKO buy the stories and casts of several of his planned Vanguard productions: *The Spiral Staircase, The Bachelor and the Bobbysoxer,* and *The Farmer's Daughter.* "We sold the packages to RKO on a partnership basis," related Selznick. "The pictures were produced by Schary and were all great successes. ... We did very well ... RKO did very well ... and so did Schary, who had a percentage." What Selznick neglected to mention was the reaction of his partners in United Artists to this deal. They were outraged to the point of filing a lawsuit, charging him with breach of contract, default in the discharge of his duties and obligations to United Artists, attempting through legal channels to force him out of the company and to return his stock in the company. Particularly serious was their decision, reached at the special stockholders' meeting in late 1946, not to accept *Duel in the Sun* for release. This was almost catastrophic. The picture had already been held up far too long, and Selznick was desperately trying to finish his work on it to open in Los Angeles in time to qualify for the Academy Awards. Without distribution, there would be no way to get back the enormous outlay of money he had tied up in the picture, which was now $5,255,000, most of it in bank loans on which the interest mounted daily and could be the difference between profit and loss.

In a whirlwind of activity, Selznick filed a countersuit, charging UA with improper distribution of his last three pictures, and with repudiating their contract by refusing to distribute *Duel in the Sun.* He filed another suit against Mary Pickford and Charles Chaplin, accusing them of willfully inducing the breach of contract and "maliciously and oppressively conspiring" to deprive him of his distribution agreement for "purposes of injury." Asking a total of $13.5 million in damages, Selznick simultaneously and almost overnight organized his own distribution

*Film editor Hal Kern's breakdown of the individual footage was as follows: Vidor: 6,280; Dieterle: 3,526; Brower: 2,939; Eason: 496; von Sternberg: 473; Kern: 147; Menzies: 104; and C. Franklin: 54.

set-up for the marketing of *Duel* and his other upcoming pictures. Calling it the Selznick Releasing Organization, with the time-honored show business initials SRO for short, Selznick commented:

> I was able to put into effect what I had long preached: that the whole method of distribution was archaic, completely outmoded and very wasteful. Within a few weeks I arranged for the physical distribution of the picture through existing non-theatrical channels on a per shipment basis ... thereby cutting my costs of distribution by sixty percent and got far more efficient distribution.

Arranging for shipping was one thing; getting theatres to play the picture was another. A sales department had to be set up to plan for the exhibition of the picture in the larger first runs, most of which were controlled by the major chains, and the logjam of product still held fast, meaning that initial major bookings could not be negotiated until after the beginning of the new year—a serious loss of the lucrative holiday trade. As Selznick struggled to book a theatre in Los Angeles to show the picture before the end of the year, he was also desperately trying to get a print from Technicolor so that he would have something to show when he finally found an exhibition outlet. The massive publicity campaign had heated up the moviegoing public to a point where the ARI was predicting that 85 percent of all moviegoers were desperate for *Duel.* It was a peak that could not be maintained without additional stoking of the advertising and ballyhoo furnaces. He had already burned up $2 million; any further lengthy delays could result in a backlash, as the public grew weary of the intense hail of publicity propaganda. Compounding everything else was the problem of the normal slow "play-off" of the picture through traditional release procedures. A picture played its first-run engagements, usually at one or two downtown houses, which accounted for the bulk of a picture's intake and impact. This was followed several weeks later by the second, or neighborhood run, at slightly lower prices and in a wider variety of theatres. After this a picture would usually wend its way down the theatrical ladder, ending up eventually in the all-night grind houses and minority theatres. It might take upward of two years before *Duel in the Sun* attained its maximum potential, a situation that would be ruinously expensive for Selznick, all of whose funds were tied up in the picture. He had tentatively tried to interest United Artists in the revolutionary idea of opening the picture in several theatres simultaneously, "preceded by enormously and unprecedentedly heavy newspaper and radio advertising."

The break with UA left Selznick free to experiment with this idea on his own, and he finally made a deal with the Skouras brothers, who owned Fox West Coast Theatres, the largest chain in the state. He could open *Duel in the Sun* at the Egyptian and Vogue theatres on Hollywood Boulevard in time for the Academy Awards, and then follow this engagement up by immediately opening the picture in fifty-six theatres throughout the greater Los Angeles area, thereby accomplishing two things—getting a quick return on his investment, and impressing the other theatre chains with the wisdom of the idea, paving the way for the quick success of the picture throughout the country. All of this, of course, hinged on his ability to get a completed print out of Technicolor. Their strike had been settled, but even with the plant back in operation, Selznick was still only one of Technicolor's dozens of customers, all of whom had several expensive productions waiting to be printed by the company. It was only after Selznick personally beseeched Herbert Kalmus to intervene that a print of *Duel in the Sun* was made up and delivered to the Egyptian Theatre the morning of the premiere. Selznick had already screened a work print of *Duel* for the Hays office, which had to see the picture before it would issue a Code seal. But he had never had the chance to show the film to the other censorship boards, including the National Legion of Decency—not, strictly speaking, a censorship organization, but an organization that rated pictures for attendance by Catholics. In this respect it was extremely powerful, as it could call upon its 22 million members in the United States to stay away from any picture it deemed morally unsuitable. The organization had been in existence since the early thirties, having been formed as a direct result of the Mae West and gangster crazes. It rated pictures on an alphabetical scale: A1—suitable for all; A2—not recommended for children; B—morally objectionable in part for all; and C—Condemned. The last classification had never

(Above) A poignant moment on the set of *Duel in the Sun*. D. W. Griffith, who had given Lionel Barrymore his first film role (*The New York Hat,* with Mary Pickford, in 1912) and had discovered and turned Lillian Gish into a star, visits his two former protégés, as King Vidor rehearses the sequence of the crippled, embittered Senator McCanles's attempt to reconcile with his ailing wife, who dies in his arms. This was one of Griffith's last public appearances; he died of a stroke in his room at the Hollywood Knickerbocker Hotel on July 23, 1948. He was buried not far from his birthplace of La Grange, Kentucky. (Below) Gregory Peck as the ne'er-do-well Lewt McCanles in a sequence with the cook and general cleaning and serving maid of the ranch, Vashti, played by the inimitable Butterfly McQueen. Selznick had a particular fondness for the actress, whose distinctive high-pitched voice and comedic ability had been one of the enduring delights of *Gone With The Wind.* He had later cast her as a WAC platoon leader in the train station sequence of *Since You Went Away,* but her role did not survive the final editing. For *Duel in the Sun* Selznick carefully tailored the role to fit McQueen's ability to shift easily from comedy to poignancy, and the result was one of the most memorable performances in the film.

been given to a major American film, whereas the B had been handed out to practically every picture that dealt with any adult situation, from divorce to excessive drinking. These ratings were decided upon by a small group of priests and lower-middle-class housewives who sat in judgment at specially arranged screenings, and their decisions sometimes meant the difference in hundreds of thousands of dollars, as Catholics were required to take a yearly pledge not to see any films that were rated B.

Because of the threat of economic sanctions, the film industry was eager to stay on the good side of the Legion of Decency; all pictures were screened for it as soon as the Code seal had been granted, but *Duel in the Sun* would be thrown on the screen of the Egyptian Theatre without having been seen by anyone outside the Hays office and the Selznick organization. The night before the opening, Selznick was in a euphoric state: "I have finished my work on it, and I believe we have a really great film ... it should do unprecedented business ... with a good chance of winning several Academy Awards ... our only competition is *The Razor's Edge* and *The Best Years of Our Lives.* ..." His optimism, however, was tempered by a certain grudging awareness: "While I feel that the reviews generally should be very fine [and] I am aware that criticisms are not important to it, I am somewhat nervous about the notices it may receive, particularly on the part of the New York critics [whose] general negative attitude toward me may lead to a patronizing type of review ... [which] would depress everyone connected with the film including myself."

With that, Selznick unveiled his super-western, letting his peers see what two years of his life, $5,255,000 of his money, and a considerable amount of emotional turmoil had finally amounted to. A reporter from *Life* magazine gave the evening's general reaction to

> the story of Pearl Chavez ... whose past is as dark as her cocoa-stained skin ... and who loves everybody, but loves bad Lewt most often.... When a single movie offers murder, rape, attempted fratricide, trainwrecking, fisticuffs, singing, dancing, drunkenness, religion, range wars, prostitution ... sacred and profane love, all in 135 minutes, the fact that it has neither taste nor art is not likely to deter the unsqueamish.

As far as his contemporaries were concerned, Selznick had let himself and the movie business down—for a man of his reputation and stature to have made so contrived and amoral a film came as a great shock to them, and the disappointment that many of them felt soon turned to hostility and sneers. Charles Brackett, for instance, described *Duel* as *"The Outlaw* in bad taste," which surprised and angered Selznick, who replied, *"The Outlaw* is the product of a dilettante in this business.... There were not less than six Academy Award winners associated with the making of *Duel* ... I resent this grouping of my product with such an enterprise." Having flicked off the criticism of the industry, Selznick began badgering Technicolor for more prints so that he could put into effect his multiple theatre exhibition plan. The picture was doing extraordinary business at the two Hollywood Boulevard theatres, with long lines around the blocks all hours of the day; additional showings had to be added to the schedule to take care of the crowds, who were paying road show prices of $1.20 to see it. Selznick confidently predicted that *"Duel* gives every indication of being an even bigger money maker than *Gone."* Then on January 17, 1947, in a completely unexpected action, Archbishop John J. Cantwell of the Archdiocese of Los Angeles, in the Catholic publication *The Tidings,* announced that "pending classification by the Legion of Decency, Catholic people may not, with a free conscience, attend the motion picture *Duel in the Sun* ... it appears to be morally offensive and spiritually depressing." Selznick was flabbergasted: "I am particularly surprised ... at the statement ... in view of the fact that ... we worked very closely with the Production Code Administration ... and followed all their suggestions to the letter ... and we received the ... Code seal of approval without a question." The following week the film critic of *The Tidings,* William Mooring, answered in his column:

> Although *Duel in the Sun* ... has a seal, many critics, myself included, consider it far worse in the moral sense than *The Outlaw....* Mr. Selznick's filming of this immoral story indicates the beginning of a

The visual magnificence of *Duel in the Sun* was maintained consistently in spite of the fact that six different cinematographers and eight directors all had a hand in the proceedings. (Top, left) The stagecoach shot was directed by Otto Brower and photographed by Charles Boyle in Arizona. (Top, right) The approach to the Spanish Bit Ranch was directed by Vidor, retaken by Dieterle, and photographed both times by Hal Rosson; the sky and sign were added by Jack Cosgrove. (Middle, left) Vidor directed this scene of Pearl and Mrs. McCanles, and Hal Rosson photographed it. (Middle, right) Rosson also took this shot of Vashti, which was directed by Josef von Sternberg. (Above, left) This shot of cowboys galloping across the rolling hills was directed by Otto Brower and photographed by Rex Wimpy in Arizona. (Above, right) The confrontation between the McCanles forces and the U.S. Cavalry was photographed by W. Howard Greene and directed by Otto Brower in California.

(Top, left) The barbecue at the Spanish Bit Ranch was directed by both William Cameron Menzies and William Dieterle, and photographed by Lee Garmes and Ray Rennahan. (Top, right) The red-drenched sunset sequence with Lionel Barrymore as "the lonely Senator" was photographed by Lee Garmes and directed by King Vidor. (Middle, left) The bloodied Lewt McCanles was directed by Josef von Sternberg and photographed by Lee Garmes, who also shot the scene (middle, right) of Pearl nursing the wounded Jesse, which was directed by King Vidor. (Above, left) The surreptitious meeting between the outlaw Lewt and his father on the hilltop at sunset was directed by William Dieterle and photographed by Lee Garmes. (Above, right) The long shot was directed by Reeves Eason and photographed by Ray Rennahan.

(Top and above) Pearl's notorious "dance at the sump," where she attempts to arouse Lewt with a variation of the dance that had led to her mother's death at the beginning of the film. Jennifer Jones was coached in this by Tilly Losch, who also played the part of her mother. This sequence, shot three times because of censorship problems, outraged the Catholic Church and led to subsequent cutting of the film. All that remains of it are these publicity stills. (Below) Pearl's efforts resulted in this torrid love scene, which was left in the film. Directed by King Vidor, it was photographed by Ray Rennahan.

new and dangerous trend [and] no amount of argument that the public demands realistic screenplays will ever justify the screen representation of lust as if it were love. . . . Selznick also ignored the Code provision that "Screen treatments of low subjects should be guided always by the dictates of good taste." Jennifer Jones' costumes permitted "undue" if not "indecent exposure."

To Selznick's mind, this last was an unprovoked and unjustified attack on his integrity, and especially on the reputation of Jennifer Jones, something that caused him enormous anguish. In a letter to the editor of *The Tidings,* Selznick lashed out at the

> calloused and diseased mind which has . . . in your columns . . . thoughtlessly attacked [my] reputation, scrupulously built up over a period of twenty years . . . and he has also cast a wicked and wanton slur upon Miss Jennifer Jones . . . a distinguished artist . . . a Catholic who received her education in a convent. . . . She was honored by [the] church for her contribution in the role of Bernadette. . . . After a lifetime of respect and aggressive friendship for the Catholic Church . . . I feel that there should be some sort of retraction and apology for the sake of the record, for the effect upon Miss Jones' children and to eliminate the results upon her own Catholic conscience of this outrage.

Having thus vented his feelings, Selznick now faced up to the problem of what to do about the pending Legion classification. He was prepared for the worst, which would be a C, but this would be a setback of serious proportions to the financial success of the picture. Several days after the archbishop's warning, Selznick had an offer from Marshall "Mickey" Neilan to intercede on his behalf with Martin Quigley, the publisher of the *Motion Picture Herald* and one of the original authors of the Production Code itself. Selznick snapped up the offer gratefully, and in utter secrecy a print of the picture was hurriedly shipped to Quigley in New York for his suggestions on how to cope with the Legion's unstated objections. His reply to Selznick was candid and frightening:

> You should realize that the picture in its present form presents an acute problem . . . for you and for the industry. Because of the power and impact of the film, it is capable, if it goes out in its present form—of creating a wave of political censorship throughout this country and seriously imperiling American prestige throughout the world . . . unless you, earnestly and faithfully, undertake . . . to alter the purport and implication of various scenes and incidents in the picture, the outcome will be disastrous.

Quigley then advised a series of thirty separate cuts in the film, ranging from snippets of dialogue to the complete elimination of Pearl's dance and the rape sequence, and cutting out the "degradation" scene. Meanwhile, Selznick found himself being bombarded from all sides by exhibitors' groups who accused him of "spending seven million dollars [sic] glamorizing murder, rape, lust, passion, carnality, obscenity, smut, bawdry, deceit and stupration."

Selznick now was trying to get some guarantee that if he cut the most offensive scenes from the picture, he could be assured of at least a B rating from the Legion. "I do not believe there is any justification for these cuts . . . but I will make them if it results in an avoidance of a condemnation by the Legion . . . and also because hopefully it will minimize damage to my reputation personally and professionally." He was also furious with the Motion Picture Producers and Distributors Association for standing quietly by while he was attacked. In a letter to Eric Johnston, who had taken over the Association's presidency after Will Hays had retired in 1945, Selznick said:

> the issues arising out of *Duel in the Sun* are due in very large part to the cowardly attitude of the Code Authority and the Producers Association . . . in not backing up its own Code. . . . I have been the victim of a rather shocking betrayal by the industry . . . which has sat silently by while attacks were made upon a motion picture . . . approved in detail by the Code authorities, retaken in part at huge expense under Code supervision. . . . I see I will have to clear my reputation, with or without industry support and without any feeling on my part of further obligation to an industry which has let me down so deliberately and so badly.

The pivotal "rape" sequence of *Duel in the Sun.* In the first version, Pearl tried to escape Lewt's advances, but finally gave in. At the film's premiere at the Egyptian Theatre, this sequence drew gasps from the audience, and several weeks later the ire of the Catholic Church and other religious groups was loosed upon Selznick. Martin Quigley, publisher of the *Motion Picture Herald,* was a leading Catholic layman and one of the original authors of the Production Code; he secretly advised Selznick to eliminate some of the more objectionable sequences. He recommended that the "rape" be dropped completely, but Selznick adamantly refused, arguing that it was necessary for the dramatic development of the story. They compromised by eliminating fifteen shots from the scene, so that instead of Pearl trying to get away from Lewt, she gives in to his advances. The sequence as re-edited opened with a long shot of a lightning bolt splitting the oppressive sky as Lewt returns to the ranch. He hears Pearl mopping her room, goes in, closes the door behind him, takes off his hat, flicks away his cigarette, and stands looking at her. She realizes what he has in mind, throws the rag at him, and tries to get past. In the original version they move back and forth across the room almost as if the sequence were choreographed, until he finally grabs and kisses her. This was deleted, and only her reaction to the kiss was left. A flash of lightning and a roll of thunder underline their emotion as they slowly sink out of the camera's view to the bed below.

(Opposite) *Duel in the Sun* took its title from this sequence, the ultimate confrontation between Pearl and Lewt. She is determined to kill him to be free of his hold on her, he wounds her in return, they both realize they love each other, and Pearl crawls up the side of the mountain to die in his arms as the camera retreats to a spectacular pullback shot and the two figures are swallowed up by the desert landscape under the broiling sun.

Dimitri Tiomkin leads a seventy-five-piece orchestra through his score for *Duel in the Sun,* a scene from which was printed onto the screen at the upper left for this publicity still. The orchestra was augmented by a special percussion section that underlined the shrieking brass and the guttural, wordless chorus of the Hall Johnson Choir that accompanies Pearl's trek to Squaw's Head Rock for the final bloody shootout, providing a fevered, massively dithyrambic finale to a score that is one of the most outstanding aspects of the film.

Johnston's reply was as irritated as Selznick's was aggrieved:

> Your letter is replete with statements to the effect that industry leadership has been yellow, cowardly in attitude and that ... you have been shockingly betrayed. If those remarks are directed at me, I resent them. The injection of personalities can serve only one purpose, and that is to be offensive.... We vigorously defend the Code when challenged by censorship boards. ...

Following more than a month of bickering back and forth, Selznick reluctantly made the recommended cuts, after which the Legion classified the film B, issuing a statement of praise for Selznick: "In effecting this revision the producer has responded with cooperation and understanding to the public criticism of [the picture] and has shown an awareness of responsibility for the moral and social significance of motion pictures." Selznick prominently featured this in a series of ads, which called attention to the fact that "due to this voluntary editing ... the picture is now about three minutes shorter than in its original form ... but not one scene has been lost...." The negative was recut to conform to these eliminations and Technicolor began printing up the 350 copies that would be needed to blanket the country in Selznick's "area saturation" method of presentation.

There was no let-up in the publicity campaign, and as the picture neared its May 7 opening date in New York, the largest movie market in the United States, even Selznick was a bit put off by the undignified nature of the stunts pulled on behalf of the picture. "We are reaching too far and trying too hard," he commented.

> We have broken all our rules as to dignity [on *Duel in the Sun*] and while there was a certain amount of fun in it ... I think now we are in danger of going overboard ... turning people's stomachs and making ourselves and the picture ridiculous. ... I was horrified today to hear ... that there is some sort of contest afoot to select a "Miss Duel in the Sun" ... and there is some plan for dropping a thousand balloons on Times Square with gifts in them. ... I can't believe that a picture of this importance, cost and effort ... requires the type of stunts that are embarrassing us with the public and the press ... and that cause people to think we have a lemon we are trying to palm off. ...

Selznick need not have worried, at least about people being turned off, for audiences in New York—spurred by the censorship controversy and the intensive advertising campaign—flocked by the thousands to the thirty-eight Loew's theatres that simultaneously opened the picture in Manhattan. The response was gratifying to Selznick, who felt vindicated in his belief not only in the potential of the picture but the new method of selling it. "The people at Loew's ... are simply incredulous at the fabulous business being done by *Duel,*" he wired his publicity man Paul MacNamara. "All agree that the multiple run plan is proving ... to be a tremendous milestone in motion picture merchandising and exhibition ... and mark[s] a revolution in the picture business and handling big pictures."

The advertising campaign was a major contributor to the subsequent success of *Duel in the Sun,* but another, often overlooked factor was that the picture was something of a new experience for most moviegoers: all major films up to that time, especially those that approached the costs of *Duel in the Sun,* had served up the tried-and-true virtues of the time, telling stories that left no doubt in the viewer's mind as to just who and what was right and wrong. *Duel in the Sun* marked the first time that audiences were presented with negative emotions, situations, and characters; never before had they been confronted with a film that trafficked so unashamedly and explicitly in carnality and eroticism, and used two major stars to illustrate it in such a massive and attractive package. *Duel in the Sun* is what is now termed a "hot" movie, in every sense of the word. From the moment the pistol shots ring out over the main title, through the blood-red sunset of the prologue with Orson Welles's doom-laden voice intoning the legend, "Deep among the lonely, sunbaked hills of Texas...," to the sun- and blood-drenched romantic ending, the film has a delirious, larger-than-life quality designed to do nothing except titillate and stimulate the viewer. As such, it is a masterpiece of kitsch, a film whose parts are greater than the whole—quintessential Hollywood neurotic romanticism, as much a product of its time as it was a precursor of things to come, a dizzy culmination of both Selznick's and the movie industry's last fling before settling down into responsible middle age and good taste. Audiences paid nearly $10 million to see *Duel in the Sun* in its first year of release, making it the second most successful film of 1947, after *The Best Years of Our Lives,* which presented a nobler and more affirmative view of American character.

The success of *Duel in the Sun* had a price, however, for as Selznick had feared, the critics were merciless, not just in New York but everywhere. In mid-1947, after he had seen the bulk of the reviews from around the country, he commented in a memo to Paul MacNamara: "I am only just commencing to see the reviews and the full extent to which we have been panned, and these have been so violent that I cannot believe they haven't done serious damage." And he followed this up with another memo, urging MacNamara to "spend a great deal of money ... on the regaining of my personal position as it was before *Duel....* I think this campaign ... is needed badly, if only from the standpoint of my own morale and ... there is the matter of my family to think of ... and it is also a fact that if I think the damage has been done, it must affect my state of mind and my work."

Help did come, but not from the direction Selznick had indicated. It arrived in the form of *Gone With The Wind,* which MGM decided to re-release in the fall of 1947, and which did more to bolster Selznick's prestige and ego than any artificially induced publicity campaign could have done.

The Postwar Years

GONE WITH THE WIND had not been seen on American movie screens since November of 1943, when MGM withdrew it after its third reissue had grossed $5.2 million around the country. (It had been playing nonstop in England since April 1940, and in France it had been showing consecutively for four years.) Selznick's office had constantly been receiving requests from individuals and groups who wanted to see the picture again—for instance, the entire student body of Western State High School in Kalamazoo, Michigan, sent him a petition asking for another chance to "enjoy again the superb cast under the direction of David O. Selznick in a supreme film." Margaret Mitchell herself wrote to him, saying, "So many people ask me when the picture will play a return engagement. A number of children who were not old enough to see it when it was last here have requested that I ask you when it will be back. So I am asking for them, and because I'd like to see it myself." Selznick made sure that all this mail was sent to the MGM sales and distribution department. In July 1945, he wrote to J. Robert Rubin, a vice-president of Loew's: "I think the time is about right to revive the film nationally, and I hope you will do this, not merely because of my pride in the film, but also because of what it would mean to [my late brother] Myron's estate, of which I am an executor." (Myron Selznick had a 6 percent interest in the picture, which after his death was divided between his daughter and his mother.)

Reissuing pictures was an old industry practice, dating back to 1921, when *The Birth of a Nation* startled everyone in the business by being spectacularly successful all over again. Since that time, the distributors had occasionally put back into circulation popular films; *King Kong* was the best known of these, but usually reissues were "fillers," which theatres could throw into their mid-week programming. It wasn't until the amazing success of Walt Disney's reissue of *Snow White and the Seven Dwarfs* in 1944 that the distributors began to be aware that certain pictures did indeed have a marketing life far beyond the few thousand dollars the average reissue brought in. In late 1946, MGM cautiously

began experimenting with limited revivals of what they called "masterpiece reprints," offering new prints and ad campaigns for pictures including *The Great Waltz, The Women,* and the 1941 Ingrid Bergman film *Rage in Heaven.* The results were encouraging, and the decision was made early in 1947 to put *Gone With The Wind* back into theatres beginning in July, treating it as a major event with new Technicolor prints, and a huge new ad campaign tailored around a quote from Bosley Crowther in *The New York Times:* "You haven't really seen *GWTW* until you've seen it at least twice"—a remark he had made at the time of the picture's 1942 engagement. Also picked up from that revival was the use of a sketch of Rhett carrying Scarlett in his arms, which became the dominant image for all the subsequent advertising of the film, leading Selznick to remark when he saw the ads that "the art work . . . is likely to get you into trouble with the Johnston office . . . it is perfectly ridiculous [for them] to attempt to create salacious art work . . . when there are so many good stills available."

MGM wanted to cut the film to get in more showings per day, and Selznick halfheartedly assigned Hal Kern the task of trying to eliminate some footage; but after struggling for several weeks, Kern advised Selznick, "It would be impossible to take out [anything] without materially damaging the story," and Selznick told MGM to leave the picture alone, suggesting that they continue to use the phrase "uncut-intact," which had proved so valuable in all the other return engagements. As the re-release date approached, Selznick was insistent that MGM pay scrupulous attention to including the credit billings "David O. Selznick's Production" and "A Selznick International Picture" on all revised ad copy, fearing that they might attempt to call it an MGM picture (which strictly speaking it was, since they now owned most of it). "In view of the tremendous blow to my prestige," Selznick wrote to his lawyers in early 1947, "resulting from the bad press on *Duel,* it is extremely important that my name be used exactly as it was on the first release in connection with the reissue of *Wind* . . . which is to be . . . very widespread . . . and one on

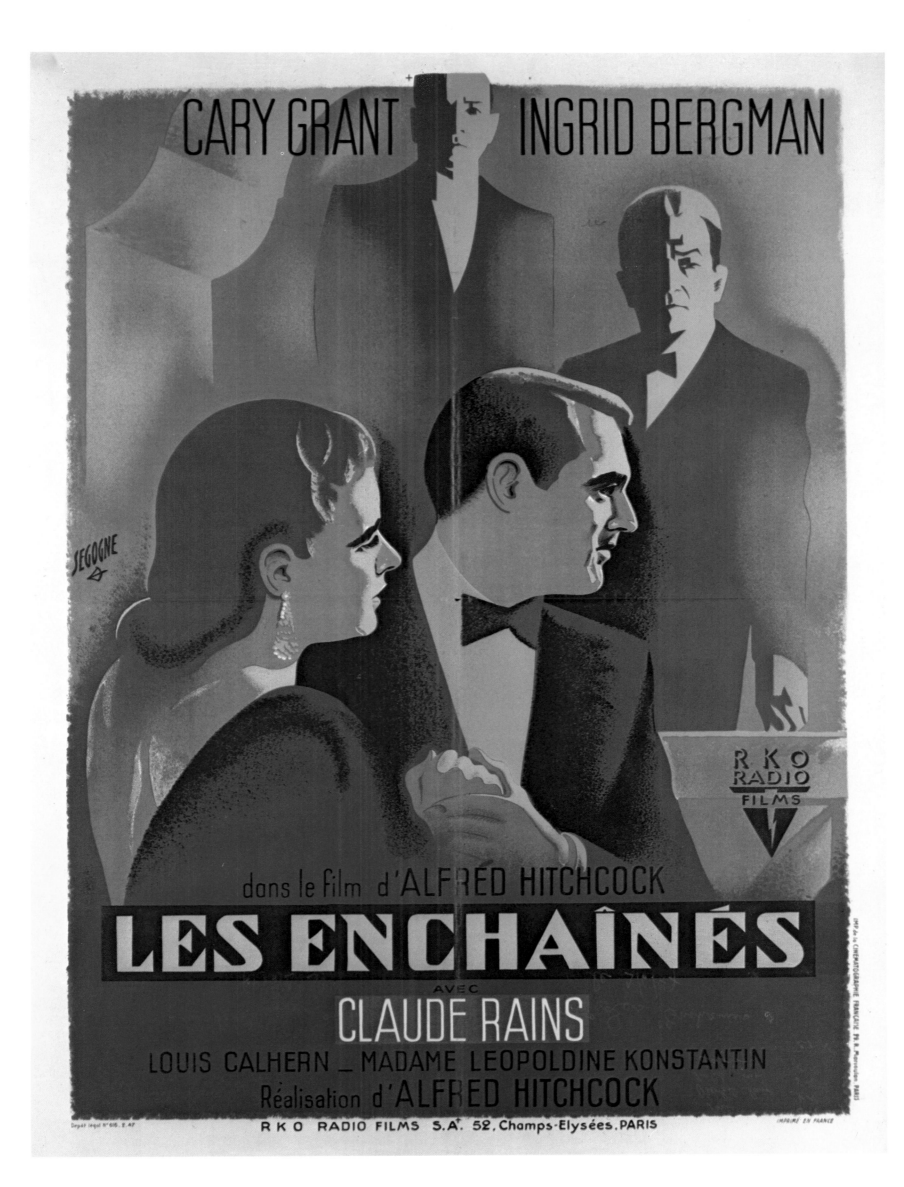

Guy Madison's postwar career with Selznick never quite took off after *Since You Went Away*. Selznick loaned him out to RKO for an adaptation of Niven Busch's novel about returning veterans, *They Dream of Home*, re-christened *Till the End of Time* (1946) to cash in on the Perry Como jukebox hit. He then played opposite Shirley Temple in a trifle called *Honeymoon* (1947). After that Selznick allowed Henry Willson, who had discovered the young man, to loan him out for a series of undistinguished "B" pictures, concentrating on westerns and other outdoor adventure films that capitalized on Madison's physical appeal. Willson turned him into one of the forties' first "beefcake" stars—a phrase coined by columnist Sidney Skolsky to describe actors who looked good with most of their clothes off. Madison left Selznick when he closed his studio; in the early fifties, Madison achieved another kind of fame as television's Wild Bill Hickock.

(Opposite) Rhonda Fleming was the name Henry Willson gave to another of his Selznick discoveries. Born Marilyn Louis, the statuesque redhead caught Willson's attention during her short-lived career as a starlet at 20th Century-Fox—a career that consisted mainly of posing for publicity pictures. After Selznick signed her, she was cast in a small role in *Since You Went Away*, and then was given a larger part as a nymphomaniac in *Spellbound*. Selznick sold her services to RKO as part of the *Spiral Staircase* package (1946), and then to Paramount for their 1949 re-make of *A Connecticut Yankee* with Bing Crosby. It was with this film that she acquired the appellation "Queen of Technicolor," as her complexion and hair photographed spectacularly in color. She had a successful career during the fifties, distinguishing herself as an actress in *Gunfight at the O.K. Corral* (1957) and *Home Before Dark* (1958).

(Top) Selznick and Cary Grant were involved in three projects that Selznick intended to produce: *Notorious* (1946), *The Bachelor and the Bobby-Soxer* (1947), and *Mr. Bland-ings Builds His Dream House* (1948), all of which he sold to RKO, along with Grant's services. (Above) Selznick with director George Stevens, Sr. (left), president of the Screen Directors Guild, and aspiring presidential candidate Harold Stassen in October 1947, when the House Un-American Activities Committee began its investigation into so-called communist infiltration of the Hollywood film industry. Selznick tried to organize a bipartisan group of liberal Democrats and Republicans to combat the Committee's activities, feeling that they were unconstitutional. Stassen headed the group, but disagreements within the ranks soon dissolved the coalition. (Below) One of the projects on which Selznick was executive producer for his Vanguard production subsidiary was *I'll Be Seeing You* (1945). Seen here is the picture's producer, Dore Schary, assistant director Victor Stoloff, and two of its stars, Ginger Rogers and Joseph Cotten.

which they expect a fabulous gross. [MGM] has told me they wouldn't bother to reissue it if they thought they would get less than $5 million ... I mention this because of the ... extent to which it will be publicized and advertised." As it turned out, it was a conservative estimate, for when the picture opened at Loew's Criterion in Manhattan in September, the crowds that turned out to see it were almost as large as those for the original engagements. These audiences were largely made up of people who had vivid memories of the picture, and now they were not disappointed. Nothing about the film was dated; its craftsmanship and production values were still unequaled by any subsequent Hollywood efforts. And to a new generation of moviegoers who were lining up with their parents, the film was every bit as exciting and as satisfying as it had been to their elders. To those who had seen it before, it was more than just a good movie: it represented continuity, a link with their own immediate past—a subliminal repository of memories of themselves in relation to previous screenings.

It was in these original postwar revivals that the picture began to take on the first layers of a patina of nostalgia. The end of the war had brought to moviemaking a new emphasis and appreciation of reality inherited from the documentaries that a number of leading directors had made during the war. As these men returned to commercial filmmaking, the search for a greater realism began to be seen in the widespread use of actual locations for films, and in the choice of stories too; there was a noticeable increase in adult, realistic dramas dealing with themes and topics previously considered taboo. *Crossfire* and *Gentleman's Agreement* were about anti-Semitism, and from anti-Semitism to the problems of racism was a short but courageous step, first taken by independent producer Stanley Kramer in his *Home of the Brave* (1949), followed quickly by *Lost Boundaries, Pinky,* and *Intruder in the Dust.* The novelty of seeing these subjects treated on the screen was fascinating to audiences, but a steady concentration on the unpleasant and the harrowing was more than most moviegoers could absorb, while the escapist films of the time were by now standardized formula, with no surprises and very little satisfaction. Still, moviegoing was a hard habit to break; attendance stayed at its peak level of 90 million all through 1946–47 and into 1948, and *Gone With The Wind* triumphantly rode the crest of this wave. In the last half of 1947 and through most of 1948 it grossed an astounding $9 million, and when Selznick realized what he had sold off five years before he raged: "I could strangle [those tax lawyers] with my bare hands in cold blood." He was particularly angry that MGM, apart from using his credit according to their contract, did not seek him out for any publicity in relation to this new phenomenon, so he took matters into his own hands and issued a lengthy press release, equating the success of *Gone With The Wind* to that of *Duel in the Sun.*

What might have been his share of $9 million, he felt, had slipped through his fingers because he had taken his attorneys' legal advice at face value. He was determined that this would never happen to him again, and in his zeal to make certain it didn't, he became as obsessive in his business dealings as in his production methods. Contracts, pending business transactions, and potential deals were discussed at length, examined from every angle; proposals were met with counterproposals; and all this took so much time that his production activities began to suffer. Scripts that needed work didn't get it, or when they did it was unimaginative, hurried, almost slipshod, a tremendous comedown from the standards he had always prided himself on. As he began devoting more and more of his energies to the business aspects of his empire, his creative people chafed at the inactivity, at the loan outs, or the forced labor on projects they felt were unexciting. He had already lost Ingrid Bergman, who refused to sign another contract with him, wanting the freedom to go out on her own as so many stars and directors were beginning to do, and now the most unhappy of his contract people was Alfred Hitchcock, to whom had been assigned the direction of the next Selznick production, *The Paradine Case.*

Selznick had long been intrigued by this property—as far back as 1935, when at MGM he had tried to interest Greta Garbo in playing the part of the mysterious Mrs. Paradine, whose fascinations prove the downfall of a respected English lawyer hired to defend her from the charge of murdering her husband. Still hoping to intrigue Garbo to

Two publicity stills taken during the making of *The Paradine Case:* (above) standing are Alfred Hitchcock, Louis Jourdan, David O. Selznick, Charles Laughton, Charles Coburn, and Gregory Peck; seated are Joan Tetzel, Ann Todd, and Ethel Barrymore; (below, left) Hitchcock has a sneezing fit while Gregory Peck and Ann Todd indulge in some uncharacteristic torrid lovemaking. (Below, right) Hitchcock makes his traditional cameo appearance in *The Paradine Case,* following Peck out of a train station.

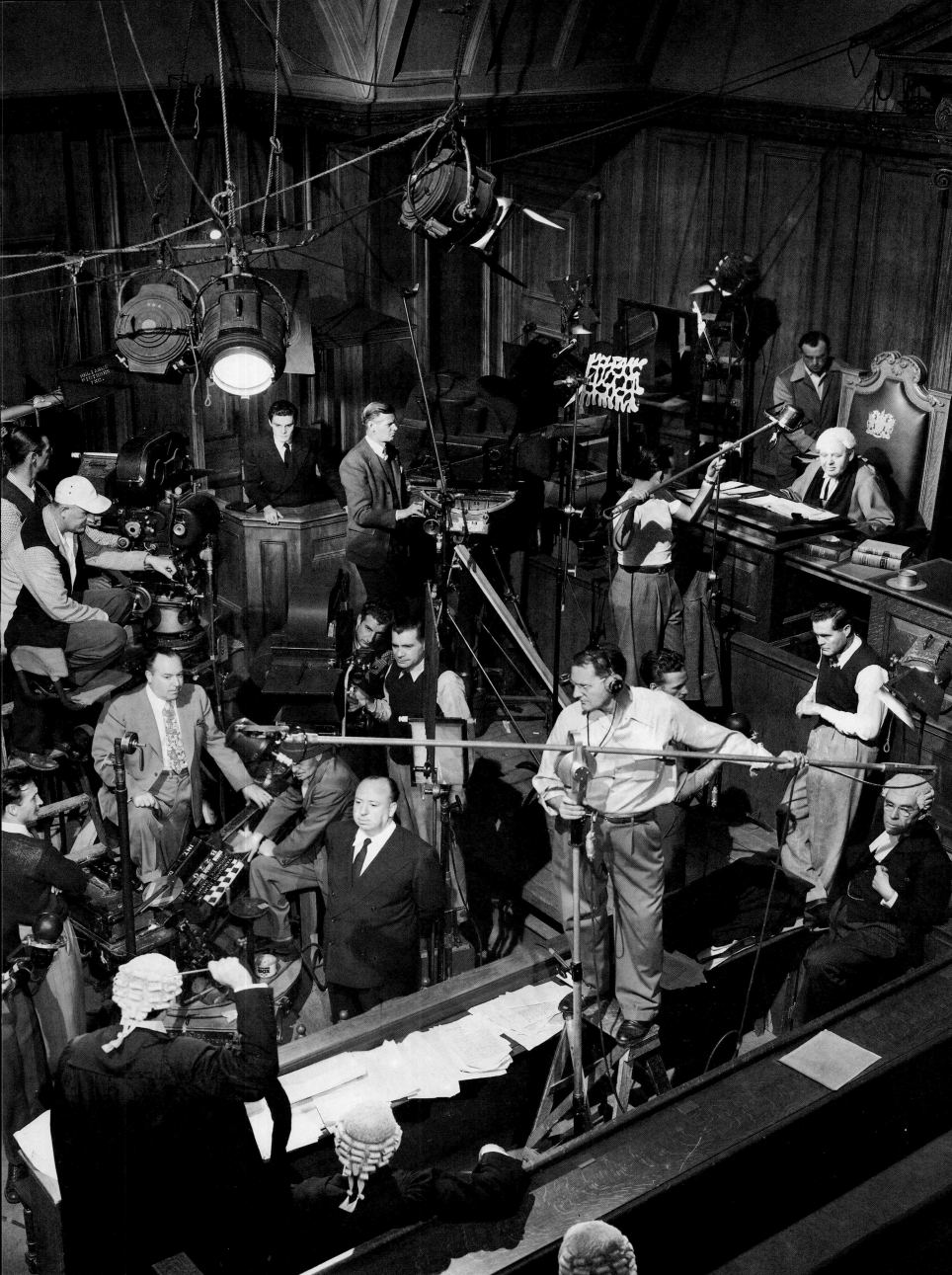

(Opposite) Filming the cross-examination scene on the Old Bailey Courtroom set, designed by J. McMillan Johnson after photographs of the original for *The Paradine Case.* Hitchcock decided to use multiple cameras to film the principals reacting to each other in the emotion-charged scene. Director of photography Lee Garmes (in the light suit and flowered tie) is standing to the left of Hitchcock. Louis Jourdan is on the witness stand, and Charles Laughton is on the judge's bench; Leo G. Carroll is seated at the lower right, and Gregory Peck is standing at the lower left, facing Hitchcock.

(Right) Alida Valli, who played the mysterious Mrs. Paradine, and Louis Jourdan as her lover.

come out of retirement to play the role, Selznick bought the rights to the Robert Hichens novel from MGM and offered it to her. "Unfortunately," related Selznick, "Miss Garbo has always had an aversion to the story, and even today, she won't play in it." Hitchcock didn't much care for the story either, but he was under contract to Selznick for $5,000 a week and felt an obligation to take the assignment. He tried to whip up enthusiasm for it, and finally succeeded in finding some elements of the story that intrigued him. As he related to François Truffaut years later: "What interested me in this picture was to take a person like Mrs. Paradine, to put her in the hands of the police, to have her submit to all their formalities, and to say to her maid, as she was leaving her home between two inspectors, 'I don't think I shall be back for dinner.' And then to show her spending the night in a cell, from which, in fact, she will never emerge." Hitchcock and his wife, Alma Reville, prepared an adaptation of the novel which they felt was acceptable, but Selznick, when he finally found the time to read it, was dissatisfied. He then accepted Hitchcock's suggestion that the reputable Scottish playwright James Bridie be brought from England to work on the script. But Bridie didn't like the United States and quickly returned to England, doing his work there and mailing it to the studio—a situation that proved unacceptable to Selznick, who decided that in spite of his pressing business affairs he would take

over the writing of the screenplay himself. Hoping to make the work go faster, he put in an emergency call to Ben Hecht, but even that didn't have the effect it once would have had. Hecht's schedule didn't allow him to stay on the project very long, and Selznick wasn't able to devote the time he wanted to working with him, with the result that as the scheduled starting date of December 23, 1946, approached, Selznick commented: "I am on the verge of collapse and not thinking clearly, and am having under these conditions to try to patch up and rewrite . . . *The Paradine Case* which I am certain has tremendous flaws [but] it is going to have to go into work, willy-nilly. . . . I simply will have to hope that somehow we will be able to get together the cast for what will inevitably be costly retakes—provided that even when the picture is finished, I have some time to do my job of producing."

For the first time in their long association, Selznick and Hitchcock found themselves having serious differences over the casting of a picture. Selznick had continued in his talent-searching efforts. Hoping to find a replacement for Ingrid Bergman, he imported an Italian actress named Alida Valli; having seen a screen test, and after suitable alterations to make her over into his concept of a Selznick star—including new teeth, a strict diet, and the elimination of her accent and, for publicity purposes, her first name—he cast her as the enigmatic Mrs. Paradine. Selznick also

insisted that Hitchcock use Gregory Peck for the very English lawyer who falls under the spell of his client. "I don't think that Gregory Peck can properly represent an English lawyer," said Hitchcock, who wanted either Laurence Olivier or Ronald Colman. One of the pivotal points in the story revolved around whether Mrs. Paradine had, in fact, killed her husband, as she was accused of doing, for love of a rough-looking stablehand. This offended Selznick: Mrs. Paradine was a woman of sensibility and position; if she were going to take a lover, he would be a person of some refinement, and he cast his newest discovery, a handsome and elegant young Frenchman named Louis Jourdan, thereby negating the central irony of the story.

It was with these drawbacks and compromises that Hitchcock began filming the picture in late December. Selznick was swamped with the problems of opening *Duel in the Sun,* and he had not had time to finish the script. Hitchcock shot everything that had been written, and then, as he related, "[Selznick] would write a scene and send it down to the set every other day—a very poor method of work." This was extremely unsettling to the director, who was having enough trouble maintaining his interest in the project without having to keep worrying about his momentum. Selznick, normally sensitive to the problems of production pacing, somehow felt that in this case the fault lay with Hitchcock, commenting in a memo to Dan O'Shea, now president of Vanguard:

I am deeply concerned about progress on *The Paradine Case.* . . . Hitch has slowed down unaccountably . . . we are more than three days behind in the first six days of shooting. . . . I think he has sensed our

seeming indifference to cost, and the lack of a firm hand, which I . . . once applied to him . . . his indifference to costs and time . . . must be attributable to us, in view of what we . . . know of his extraordinary efficiency when he wants to be efficient. This much I can assure you: you will see an entirely different result when he starts on his own picture; and you can also be sure that he will attribute this efficiency to his own operations, against the gross inefficiency with which he charges us. He told me that he thought it was disgraceful the way we went into this picture with the physical production—photography, sound, etc.—"twenty years behind the time."

In an effort to speed things up, Hitchcock, Selznick, and director of photography Lee Garmes decided to film the climactic courtroom cross-examination scene using multiple cameras and going through the entire dramatic action nonstop, as in a play, getting the entire sequence on film in one day instead of the three or four that it would normally have taken. Yet in spite of this intention, it still took three days for the sequence to be shot, due to cast and camera rehearsals and the setting up of complicated lighting arrangements.

The filming of *The Paradine Case* limped along for several more weeks, finally finishing up principal photography in mid-March 1947. Selznick looked at the first rough assemblage of the footage and was completely discouraged: "It is clear that even though I continue to work eighteen to twenty hours daily . . . *The Paradine Case* [is not] what it should be, and may even be dangerous at its cost, which now will be between $3,200,000 and $3,300,000 with only one star of importance—

December 31, 1947—The world premiere of *The Paradine Case,* held simultaneously at two theatres in the Westwood section of Los Angeles, site of the UCLA campus.

Peck. Clearly I will have neither the time nor the energy nor the clarity of mind to straighten out its problems without worrying about any other pictures." The unfinished picture sat for several months, until Selznick could spare energy from the time-consuming problems of setting up his distribution organization and fighting the censorship battles over *Duel in the Sun.* He managed to cut down the enormous amount of footage on *The Paradine Case* from three hours to a little over two, and after two indifferent previews he ordered several days' worth of retakes, which Hitchcock did quickly, eager to be finished both with the picture and his contract with Selznick so that he could go on to his own independent production plans. The film was completed at last in September, but because Selznick wanted his releasing organization to concentrate all its efforts on *Duel in the Sun,* the release was held up until December. The production costs and interest on the loans to make the picture had pushed the final cost to just a little over the $4 million mark, and the high overhead on Selznick's pictures was beginning to pass the point at which the market could return a profit on investment. The picture had every bit of production value that Selznick could give it—gleaming with a rich upholstered look, beautifully set, costumed, and photographed, with an outstanding musical score by Franz Waxman—but it did not catch dramatic fire; it seemed both talkative and somber, and the patchwork nature of the script showed through in the awkward and flatfooted exposition of much of the central trial sequence. Audiences were not intrigued, either with the story or with Alida Valli, who did not catch on as Selznick hoped she would. Louis Jourdan, however, went on to become a popular leading man over the next decade, specializing in the

type of role that Charles Boyer had been so adept at in the thirties and forties—the smooth, suave, romantic seducer.

The Paradine Case was a major failure for Selznick at a time when he could least afford it, losing most of its investment and shaking his confidence in his ability to make the kind of film the public would want to see at a cost that was economically feasible. He was now confronted with the twin difficulties of having to make pictures to justify the expense of his executive staff and to feed the hungry distribution set-up—a situation he had fought against all through his career, and coming at a time when the economics of the film business clearly indicated it could be suicidal. "We have to have pictures made by other people," he wrote to Dan O'Shea,

> because I haven't the time, nor am I in the state of mind to make more pictures, largely as a result of the increasing amount of deskwork that I have every day—which in turn is traceable to more and more of our people having to report to me directly . . . which is due to our lack of proper organization. . . . We keep adding more and more people in the hope that this will remedy the situation . . . when the remedy is to be found simply in the reorganization of our own work . . . even Metro, with all its wealth, has recognized that the rise in costs throughout the business has necessitated a tremendous shakeup in their organization and entirely different methods of operation. But we go blindly on our way, smug and secure in our own ignorance and in our own inefficiencies.

379

In order to get the help he needed to fill out his picturemaking program, in early 1947 Selznick made a deal with newspaper columnist-turned-producer Mark Hellinger to make three pictures for Vanguard. Hellinger was in partnership with Humphrey Bogart, who had just left Warner Bros. For Universal Hellinger had turned out three of the best of the "new realism" genre: *The Killers,* a hard-bitten adaptation of the Hemingway short story, which made stars of Burt Lancaster and Ava Gardner; *The Naked City,* a gripping, semidocumentary detective thriller filmed on location all over New York City; and *Brute Force,* a trenchant, violent melodrama of prison life. Hellinger would, according to Selznick, "make pictures for my distribution company (and also to absorb my production overhead) with the large number of stars I had under contract." Selznick also hired veteran film executive M. J. Siegal "to produce three smaller pictures yearly to launch and further the careers of a group of younger players I had signed up." Selznick himself planned "to produce only one big picture a year," acting in the role of supervisory producer for the others.

With his immediate overhead and product problems taken care of, and *The Paradine Case* in production, Selznick felt that he could now devote himself to a project that had intrigued him for several years, Robert Nathan's novel *Portrait of Jennie.* The title had immediately caught him as a possible vehicle for Jennifer Jones, and after he read the novel, he fell under its spell. *Portrait of Jennie* told the story of a starving young artist in New York during the thirties, Eban Adams, who meets a strangely dressed little girl on a deserted winter's day in Central Park. She begs him to wait for her to grow up. By a chain of circumstances, he comes to realize that Jennie is the ghost of a young girl who was swept overboard from an ocean liner many years before, but that through eternity she has been searching for someone to love who would have loved her. Eventually the forces that brought them together tear them apart as Adams makes a vain attempt to save her from her original fate; but Jennie, just before she is swept overboard by a huge wave, tells him that love, like time, is endless and undying, and that they will meet again, for they have each other forever. The attraction of the story to a person of Selznick's romantic impulses was enormous, even though he realized the difficulties of adapting the material successfully. Fantasies are the most difficult of all subjects to transfer to film because of the very nature of the medium, which presents everything on a literal plane. If he made *Portrait of Jennie,* it would have to be handled with romantic sensitivity, achieving its mood through photography, music, and the delicacy of the playing, and he did not immediately buy the story, feeling that he would have to give it much more thought and analysis. Meanwhile MGM took an option on it, but the material proved intractable and they let it lapse. Acting quickly, Selznick then snapped up the movie rights, paying $15,000 for the property in late 1944, at which point one of his production people suggested they make it with Shirley Temple, filming it over a period of several years, to take advantage of Temple's emergence from adolescence to young adulthood. Selznick toyed with this idea for a while, liking its novel publicity aspects, but then decided that it would be Jennifer Jones's next picture after *Duel in the Sun.* His emotional situation with her had settled down considerably after the double catharsis of his wife's leaving him and the making of *Duel in the Sun,* and this new state of semiquiet coincided perfectly with the tender, haunting quality of *Portrait of Jennie.*

In mid-1946, during a lull in the frustrations of finishing *Duel in the Sun,* Selznick began auditioning writers and ideas for making the fantasy dramatically believable. After an abortive conference with the author, Robert Nathan, Selznick turned the project over to Mildred Cram, author of *Forever,* a novella with a similar theme, but her suggestions were expensive and complicated the tale even more. Selznick next asked one of his old collaborators, S. N. Behrman, to consider the project. The two men had not worked together since *Anna Karenina* in 1935, but Behrman, after reading the book, commented that he "encountered at once an almost congenital prejudice of [mine]: it was a fantasy, a literary form I have never cared for...." The story was finally given to a young writer named Peter Berneis, who managed to extract a script from the book that Selznick felt was at least a beginning. But just as he was starting to work seriously on rewriting it, the United Artists storm broke almost simultaneously with the censorship problems of *Duel in the Sun,*

and Selznick was forced to give all his attention to these matters plus *The Paradine Case.* Earlier, he had had the ARI take a survey to discover who should be co-starred with Jennifer Jones. Out of the three choices of Gregory Peck, Joseph Cotten, and Laurence Olivier, it was the Peck-Jones combination that scored the highest, with Cotten second, and Olivier last. Peck, however, was committed to a picture at 20th Century-Fox, so Selznick decided that the team of Jones and Cotten would make its fourth picture together. Before *Duel in the Sun* the two had scored a great success in the Hal Wallis production *Love Letters,* one of the better romantic melodramas of the period, and Selznick felt that this casting would work not only commercially but personally too, as the two performers were genuinely fond of each other. The immediate problem was that both of them had heavy commitments in the near future; consequently, the picture would have to go before the cameras fairly quickly. Selznick now decided to do something he had long promised himself to try. He hired an associate producer to work with him on the picture, especially to act as line producer for the location sequences, which Selznick felt had to be made in New York since the city in all its moods and seasons was practically another character in the story. The man he hired for this was David Hempstead, a competent if unimaginative film veteran who had produced a series of successful low-budget pictures for RKO in the mid-forties. Hempstead had one great problem, and it was a drinking one. Selznick knew of this, but hired him in spite of it—alcoholics always received great sympathy and understanding from him, probably in memory of his brother Myron.

Because of the extensive use of New York City backgrounds, Selznick and Hempstead decided to film the bulk of the picture in Manhattan, moving up to Boston Harbor for location work on the climactic storm sequence in which Jennie meets her doom for the second time. An uneasy Selznick stayed in Culver City while Hempstead led a cast and crew of twenty-five players and technicians into the New York winter. William Dieterle had been chosen to direct, largely because of his success in handling the Cotten-Jones team in *Love Letters,* to which he had managed to give a brooding, ominous quality almost supernatural in its effect. The fantasy elements and strong undercurrent of fatalism that ran throughout this new story appealed to Dieterle, and after immersing himself in script preparations and photographic tests with cameraman Joseph August, he accepted the assignment gladly. Dieterle was a man with a strong visual sense; in conjunction with August, who had worked with him before on *The Hunchback of Notre Dame* (1939) and *All That Money Can Buy* (1941), he began a series of tests to find out how far the mood of fantasy could be heightened photographically. Between them, they evolved a mixture of textured overlays, filtered effects, and impressionistic lighting that gave the finished film a poetic pictorialism subtly blending the grim reality of the depression era and the soft romanticism of the love story.

Portrait of Jennie went into production on the Central Park ice rink in February 1947, and continued for two weeks with varying results. Selznick found himself displeased with the way the two stars were being photographed; the harsh winter light was unflattering, and their scenes were not coming across with the proper air of unreality. Compounding the problem was the difficulty of presenting Jennie in her various incarnations, especially in these early scenes in which her age ranged from ten to thirteen. As Selznick, 3,000 miles away, looked at the footage, he realized that the script was not working, that it was "long winded and abstruse." And the script was only one of the problems with *Portrait of Jennie.* Selznick wanted the picture made in New York City "because it will have an atmosphere it won't have here in the studio, thereby improving the quality of the picture immeasurably," but the company hadn't had the opportunity to get organized for proper location work, or even to find suitable backgrounds to film the exterior scenes. As a result, crew and actors were idle for days at a time while Argyle Nelson, the production manager, and Hempstead tried to find satisfactory locations and Dieterle simultaneously began reworking the script under telegraphic and telephonic direction from California. The Selznick memos on *Portrait of Jennie* are among the longest and most anguished in his files; there is one telegram that unfolds to a length of nearly 8 feet, in which he berates Hempstead for, among other things, "the fact that everything I have seen so far will have to be ... redone back here at the

(Top) William Dieterle, Jennifer Jones, and Joseph Cotten during the New York location filming of *Portrait of Jennie*. (Above) Photographing the Central Park ice-skating scenes for the film. The camera is moving ahead of Joseph Cotten. Cinematographer Joseph August is standing fourth from left in the dark coat and hat. (Below) Artist Robert Brackman paints the actual portrait of Jennie used in the film as Joseph Cotten looks on.

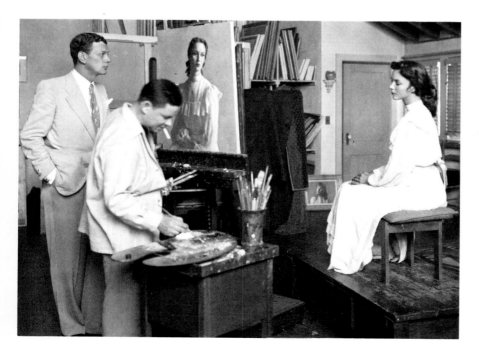

studio . . . since even with retakes it is obvious that you have not been able to lick these comparatively simple problems . . . and when you have handled them . . . it has been with procrastination and weakness."

Hempstead was not used to this kind of complicated and disorganized production, and was completely undone by Selznick's flood of suggestions, demands, and castigations. He began drinking heavily, which left him even less able to cope, and Selznick furiously wired Dan O'Shea, who was with the company in New York: "It should be made very clear to Hempstead that any misbehavior . . . any excess drinking inside or outside the studio is going to result in his instant dismissal. [Hempstead] has great competence and great taste, but if he can't control himself . . . then he is just no use to me . . . this is his last chance." Considerably sobered by this, Hempstead began to assume the role of producer Selznick had hired him for, but in his zeal to oversee all aspects of the production, Hempstead made the mistake of interfering with Dieterle's shooting on the set. Dieterle was an extremely proud and conscientious man; his dedication to his work and his concentration on the end result allowed no interference. He was also a strict disciplinarian, an autocrat who wore white gloves while directing, and his resentment of Hempstead's interference grew until he threatened to walk off the picture unless he was left alone. All of these swirling currents of difficulty, plus the condition of the script, convinced Selznick to close down the production. As he put it:

It is the most dangerous picture we have ever made from the standpoint of its subject matter and its cost, the latest estimate . . . of which was $1,999,000 . . . which figure is ridiculous in light of the fact that we've already spent half a million and only have little more than 10 minutes of usable footage. . . . Our only chance with this picture is if it is an outstanding picture of beauty in every way . . . we are not getting this beauty and we are thereby increasing our gamble to the point where it constitutes the most pessimistic viewpoint about a picture that . . . I have had in twenty-five years of producing . . . if this enterprise of many follies turns out to be a commercial tragedy it will be seriously damaging to our two stars, to me and to the entire organization which we couldn't afford in even the best of times . . . and these are not the best of times.

Selznick put the production into a five-week hiatus and brought in playwright/novelist Paul Osborn, who completely restructured and rewrote the screenplay from a new adaptation by Leonardo Bercovici. Bercovici's new version eliminated much of the confusion in the back-and-forth time flashes of the original, focusing instead on the central love story. There was no doubt in this new version that Jennie was a ghost, and very little explanation of what caused her appearances and involvement with Adams. The emphasis was switched to the inspirational effect she had on the somewhat dour and defeated painter, and with this new, cleaner approach, Selznick reluctantly gave orders to start filming again, saying, "If the picture hadn't run up such a high cost already . . . I would scrap the damned thing . . . as it is we are going to have to be prepared to spend a great deal of extra money to get the quality we want . . . my instincts tell me . . . that this whole *Portrait of Jennie* venture is doomed to be one of the most awful experiences any studio ever had."

His instincts were right. The picture went back into production in late April 1947, still on location in New York and with Hempstead more or less at the helm, although very much under Selznick's thumb. The last shot was finally taken on October 9, 1948. In the year and a half it was before the cameras, the script was rewritten twice, primarily by Selznick; the supporting cast was completely changed; almost every scene was done over three, four, sometimes even five times, and the bulk of the exterior shooting was done on the Culver City stages. The pressure was too much for cinematographer Joseph August, who died of a heart attack on September 25, 1947, while trying to line up a complicated tracking shot (Lee Garmes and Paul Eagler finished the picture). Prior to this, in early July, Selznick had parted company with the last of his old guard, Hal Kern. "It was a quiet Saturday at the studio and I had taken the day off to go to the track to see my horse run," recalls Kern, "and David showed up at the studio with Mary Pickford. He wanted to show her some footage from *Portrait of Jennie* and there wasn't anybody in the editing department, and he got ahold of me and said that I had embarrassed him tremendously, and that he thought he could do without my services from then on. 'Fine with me,' I said, and left." Kern went to work at MGM, and two weeks later Selznick was frantically trying to get him to come back: "One of the worst mistakes I ever made," he wrote,

> was in not keeping Hal on at least long enough to finish this picture.... It has cost us money and on me it is simply murder.... I have to follow up on a hundred little details I never had to do with Hal.... The staff that made the best line-up of pictures in history has been shot to the four winds. Step by step they have been eliminated and a lot of second raters substituted, so that we are left with the most expensive production operation in the history of Hollywood.

Even after principal photography had been finished in December 1947, Selznick had put the picture back before the cameras for two months of retakes and added scenes. Then, after looking at the assembled footage, he felt that the picture did not take fullest advantage of the final scene: a hurricane and tidal wave that tears Jennie from Adams's arms as he tries vainly to keep her fate from overtaking her a second time. Selznick wanted this sequence to be "built up to equal the ... earthquake in San Francisco, the hurricane in the picture of the same name...." This meant additional expense not only in production but in the exhibition plans for the picture, for Selznick wanted the sequence to be shown on an enlarged screen, with multiple sound channels blasting the effects of wind and water throughout the theatre. While these special effects were being added, Selznick began searching for something equally unique and showmanly for the musical accompaniment. As early as 1946, he had considered using Bernard Herrmann, who had supplied the music for Welles's classics *Citizen Kane* and *The Magnificent Ambersons,* but the picture had taken so long that Herrmann was unable to stay on the job. Selznick then tried to interest Arturo Toscanini in selecting classical musical excerpts and conducting them on the track, but when approached, Toscanini, according to information received by Selznick, "was appalled." Margaret McDonnell, the woman who had first suggested filming the story, wrote Selznick another note in late 1947 in which she suggested that he score the film with the music of Claude Debussy. After listening to several of the composer's short romantic mood pieces, Selznick felt that they conveyed perfectly the fragile, delicate nature of the fantasy. A protracted series of negotiations with the Debussy estate ensued before Selznick was able to announce that "permission has been obtained ... to bring to the screen for the first time ... the hauntingly beautiful music of Claude Debussy ... the use of which has been jealously guarded by his estate from being commercialized"—a statement that conveniently overlooked the existence of the popular song "My Reverie," based on a piece by the composer. In late September, composer Dimitri Tiomkin led a seventy-four-piece orchestra and a chorus of twenty-eight voices through the first of what was scheduled to be six scoring sessions but eventually ended up, like everything else about the picture, over budget and over time, taking nearly twenty separate sessions to record the six pieces that served as the backbone of the score. Tiomkin, who had commented in a memo that he wanted to use the music "exactly as written ... because of its dignity, authority and its nostalgic mood," evidently felt that Debussy could stand a little improvement for picture purposes, and he considerably reorchestrated and otherwise altered "The Maid with the Flaxen Hair," "Arabesques 1 and 2," "Clouds," and "Prelude to the Afternoon of a Faun." He was urged on in this by Selznick, who felt that "music, like everything else that pictures make use of to achieve their effects, sometimes has to be adapted. The film medium is not a pure medium, there is nothing in it that isn't derived from something else, and its collaborative nature precludes anything about it not undergoing some sort of alteration, because everything is subservient to the dramatic needs of the story.... Nothing matters except the finished picture." While Tiomkin was writing and recording—then rewriting and rerecording—over a period of six months and at an eventual cost of $160,000, Selznick was taking time out to decide what to do about his production company.

In late 1947, the two men Selznick had contracted to supply pictures for SRO, Mark Hellinger and M. J. Siegal, both died suddenly within weeks of each other, leaving Selznick with an expensive distribution company and no pictures to distribute. He had turned down Howard

(Top) Ethel Barrymore and Cecil Kellaway were two of the numerous character actors in the film, which also included Lillian Gish, Henry Hull, Florence Bates, Felix Bressart, Clem Bevans, and Maude Simmons. (Above) David Wayne and Albert Sharpe were recruited from the Broadway musical *Finian's Rainbow* to play roles in *Portrait of Jennie,* which they did during the day while performing on the stage at night.

(Overleaf) The opening shot of *Portrait of Jennie* was this spectacular view of a sunset over Manhattan, setting the scene perfectly for what the narration called "the haunting legend of a painting ... which hung in the Metropolitan Museum in New York.... There was such a girl, called Jennie, who sat for it. For the rest, science tells us that nothing ever dies, but only changes; that time itself does not pass, but curves around us; that the past and future are forever at our side—together. The truth of our story lies not on our screen but in your heart."

which are perhaps not more than twenty per cent of what they should be.... I have no fears about making pictures and am most eager to make them; but I don't want to make any more until and unless I am properly organized.... Beyond *Portrait of Jennie* I will not go. Whether we liquidate or not, whatever our future course may be, [producing] is a strain ... which I will not longer endure—which I cannot longer endure, even if I were foolish enough to want to.

Portrait of Jennie was finally finished and released at the beginning of 1949, and in spite of excellent reviews and a high-powered publicity and advertising campaign that highlighted everything from the Debussy music to the Cycloramic screen and Cyclophonic sound, the picture never found its audience, which was unfortunate and undeserved, for *Portrait of Jennie* is one of Selznick's most interesting accomplishments. Although the disjointed nature of the narrative and some jarring awkwardnesses in the writing, staging, and acting of some scenes mar its effect, the picture as a whole is the quintessence of Selznick at middle age. *Portrait of Jennie* is suffused with a romantic melancholy that finds its parallel in Joseph August's soft, sparkling images, which move imperceptibly between luminous patches of light, veiled gray and white, and the stark contrast of black and white, imparting a hushed, dreamlike quality to the story. The Debussy themes are a perfect complement to the visuals, echoing the delicate undercurrents of the story and heightening the picture's photographic richness with a score that is tender, evocative, and as haunting as the tale itself. And Jennifer Jones vindicated Selznick's faith in her talent by delivering one of the finest—and most underrated—performances of her entire career. She is completely believable and touching as the ten-year-old child, first seen building a snowman in the park, maturing subtly and believably into the young woman in love, at the same time maintaining the fragile balance between the character's ethereal quality and the romantic demands of the part as written. The final hurricane and tidal wave are an error in production judgment, as the sequence all but overwhelms the fragility of the story. But it is an excitingly staged and crafted error, and a sequence that in its original form on the large screen with multiple sound sources overwhelmed the spectators with some of the loudest sound ever heard in a modern motion picture theatre.

Yet *Portrait of Jennie* was a financial failure of awesome proportions, taking in less than $2 million in film rentals, barely enough to pay for its prints, advertising and distribution expenses, and the additional costs for the special screen and sound effects, the expenses of which were carried by SRO. By the end of 1949, the picture had lost almost all of its $4.04 million investment, and this, coupled with the losses of *The Paradine Case*, was more than Selznick could bear, for as he explained: "My company, as all picture companies, financed itself largely with bank loans, and these loans, with interest, had been extended to a total of about $12,000,000." Ten years after producing *Gone With The Wind*, and five years after he had been quoted in *Time* magazine that he felt he would soon be the master of the industry, David Selznick closed down his Hollywood production activities, reduced SRO to a virtual skeleton staff, and he and Jennifer Jones departed for self-imposed exile in Europe, where, as he commented later, "I wanted to do some of the traveling that I had denied myself during my long concentration on work in Hollywood.... I was tired ... I had been producing pictures for twenty years ... so I stopped ... and decided to combine business with pleasure by exploiting my backlog of films throughout the world."

Hawks's epic *Red River* as being of insufficient stature for his company to handle, an unfortunate decision as the picture went on to become one of the biggest hits of the year for United Artists. Instead, he chose one of the more distinguished British films of the time, *The Fallen Idol,* directed by Carol Reed. Literate, well made, and engrossing, it was exactly the kind of picture he wanted SRO to distribute; the problem was that the return on this kind of film was not lucrative enough to maintain the expenses of the company. The postwar movie market was changing. The boom years of 1947–48 had ended almost precipitously in 1949; weekly theatre attendance was down to 70 million, and even with another admission increase to 50 cents, the total industry gross for the year came to $1.45 billion, a respectable figure, but already starting on the downward slide that would continue for the next fifteen years. The movies were in the same position they had been in in the mid-twenties just before the introduction of sound: audiences were slightly bored with them and began staying home in ever-increasing numbers to watch the hypnotic act that television was fast becoming. By late 1948, the number of video receivers in the Los Angeles area had jumped to 35,000, and ownership was growing by leaps and bounds even as theatre attendance declined. Selznick, alert to the winds of change, sensed that the film industry was in for troubled times, and even as he continued to pour money into finishing *Portrait of Jennie,* he was aware that the picture stood a good chance of not returning its investment. His methods of filmmaking were becoming ruinously expensive, as he pointed out in a confidential memo to his chief executives:

The extent of our wastefulness and excessive costs ... is in the final analysis ... my fault for two reasons: (1) my production methods (2) my tolerance through the years of the wastefulness. But I don't want to be guilty of this any longer, now that it is apparent that many millions of dollars have been eaten up ... and that the most successful series of pictures ever made in the history of the business has produced profits

Hollywood—1954

N UNSUPERSTITIOUS David Selznick left the United States on Friday, May 13, 1949, soon after he had been divorced from his wife, Irene. In July of that year, he and Jennifer Jones were married in Italy. The condition of the European film market had improved considerably immediately after the war, especially for American-made pictures. The film industries of Europe were in disarray, as was the entire economic structure of the war area, but one of the first things people wanted after food and a place to live was movies, and the American companies moved in to take quick advantage of this hunger. By 1948, conditions had improved until there was enough money in circulation to make the marketing of American films extremely profitable. The European governments, however, became alarmed at the amount of money American films were draining out of the various countries—money that was badly needed for reconstruction purposes—and they instituted a crackdown on what could be taken out by foreign companies. Selznick took advantage of this freezing of funds to finance several co-productions in Italy and England.

"During those years," related Selznick, "I learned much about foreign distribution, about foreign production and about the tastes of foreign audiences ... although I had always tried to make pictures for a world market, at last I fully realized the necessity for a world viewpoint in the making of Hollywood films." Although his heart belonged to Hollywood, Selznick quickly became an enthusiastic booster of European filmmakers, and in 1949 he instituted the Golden Laurel Awards, given to non-American-made films "that promote international understanding."

Next, Selznick devised a new method of co-producing European films: "As part of the plans for liquidation of my company and its debts ... we invested certain foreign distribution rights of my pictures in return for acquiring Western Hemisphere rights to these co-productions. ... [We did this] because it was neither easy, nor my desire, to invest money in films in those times." The film industry and the world were as unsettled as Selznick. In June 1950, the United States had become involved in the Korean War, and that same year, movie attendance in the United States dropped to a new low of 60 million people weekly, the worst since the depression year of 1932. The audience had discovered that rather than going to the movies to see mediocrity, it could stay home and see it for free. On Tuesday nights, theatres were empty as millions stayed home to watch "The Texaco Star Theatre," with Milton Berle exhuming a collection of baggy-pants routines and skits that had been buried years before when vaudeville died. The quality was worse than what was available downtown or at the local neighborhood movie theatre, but an evening out at the movies now cost about $4 by the time tickets, babysitters, parking, and refreshments were taken into consideration, while television was free, and not always bad. In the first years of the medium's existence, dozens of outstanding older films found their way into living rooms, reminding many people how good movies used to be, and introducing a whole new generation to the pleasure and excitement of *Stagecoach*, the comedies of Laurel and Hardy, and the low-budget delights of PRC and Monogram Pictures. Sandwiched in between these, ironically enough, were four of the early Selznick International pictures that had been taken over by the Whitney interests and circulated repeatedly throughout the middle and late forties. With the advent of feature films as inexpensive programming for the ninety-seven television stations around the country, viewers were treated to the excellence of *Little Lord Fauntleroy*, *A Star Is Born*, *Nothing Sacred*, and *The Young in Heart*. Even in Europe, Selznick immediately grasped the value of television as a source of income for feature films; in a letter written in July 1950 to Earl R. Beaman, vice-president in charge of distribution for SRO, Selznick commented:

> While it has been my thinking ... to not make our backlog of pictures available to television for two years [after theatrical release], I think we should open our minds to the possibility ... to make at least a number of them available for television immediately.... In my opinion, time will shortly prove that one of the most valuable assets we have is this extraordinary group of films.... I believe that there are television chains that have specialized in [telecasting] pictures, notably ABC ... and many advertisers of tremendous importance and wealth such as Ford, DuPont, General Motors, United States Steel, who have a long range attitude toward television, would be interested in working out a deal even if the pictures were not made available for television immediately.... Television rights for one year or for individual showings have been greater than for preceding years and preceding showings, which is not hard to understand, since the films get more and more word of mouth advertising from their initial showings on television and since more importantly the number of viewers of television is constantly increasing.

Selznick was indeed suggesting a revolutionary concept—that of using television to *increase* the value and appeal of older films—and it was a concept that would eventually prove valid. But in those early days he was a lone voice crying in the television and movie wilderness. The heads of the major studios saw television only as a threat to the theatres and to their own current productions.

Selznick had promised himself that "under no circumstances would I make another film ... until I was free of debt." By dint of careful and shrewd leasing of his films and assets, he began to whittle down the enormous funded debts; in 1951, he sold the screenplay and musical score of *The Prisoner of Zenda* to MGM, where Pandro Berman remade it in Technicolor. Selznick did not see the remake, which starred Stewart Granger, Deborah Kerr, and James Mason, but he related that he'd heard that director Richard Thorpe "did an extraordinary thing ... [he] had a Movieola on the set (with a print of our version) and they copied every single camera set-up." Selznick had figured that it would take him

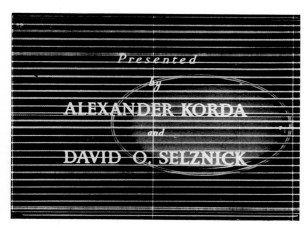

One of Selznick's European co-productions was *The Third Man* (1949), about which he later commented: "The creation of the film was almost entirely [director Carol] Reed's. I did a little work on the script with Reed and Graham Greene, but nothing that contributed greatly to its success. I supplied the stars and I re-edited the film [for the United States]. It was a substantial contribution to making me financially healthy again...."

(Opposite) Jennifer Jones and Montgomery Clift starred in another Selznick co-production, *Stazione Termini*, made in Italy in 1953 with Vittorio De Sica as producer and director. Truman Capote worked on the dialogue. The film was extensively re-edited for the United States, where it was released by Columbia under the title *Indiscretion of an American Wife*.

a little over four years to repay his loans. But he discovered otherwise:

> The costs of operations mounted, and my distributing company had to make millions more out of [my] films to sustain itself ... accordingly it was something over five years before the obligations were paid in full ... when the day finally came that I was able once again to produce personally, I found it difficult to go back: I was enjoying too much freedom from the intensive effort of production as I know it, and I still had no material about which I was enthusiastic.

When Selznick finally returned to Hollywood to set up headquarters officially in late 1953, he found an industry and a town undergoing enormous physical changes. The town of Hollywood, while still a potent name worldwide as a film-manufacturing center, was no longer the only site of industrial activity in southern California. The postwar years had seen the rise of the aircraft, electronics, aerospace, and oil industries to the point where they had quickly eclipsed the entertainment industry as a source of local wealth. Hollywood was now just a section of the huge population mass that made up what the rest of the country referred to as "L.A." But while the movie industry may have suffered a decline in local industrial importance, it still had a hold on the imagination of the public as a center of glamour and excitement. This hold began to be shared equally among radio, television, and the emerging recording industry, which was catering to the hordes of young people who had come of age in the early fifties and were beginning to respond to newer, rawer excitements. These sounds crowded the Frank Sinatras and Doris Days off the best-selling record charts as jukeboxes blared forth the thumping beats of Elvis Presley and Jerry Lee Lewis, a whole new breed of singers, delivering a brand-new vitality to American music—rock 'n' roll. The sound had been introduced to millions of white American teenagers in MGM's 1955 *Blackboard Jungle*, which dealt in a realistic and fairly honest manner with problems and ideas that would have been unthinkable on the screen two years before, and its being made at all was a sign of how much Hollywood had changed since Selznick had left. The eight major studios still ruled the industry, but the studios themselves had different rulers: RKO was now under the thumb of the eccentric millionaire Howard Hughes, who had purchased it in 1948 and had been running it into the ground ever since. And while RKO tottered toward its doom, United Artists, Selznick's one-time ally and erstwhile nemesis,* was beginning a new life under a new management, devising methods of business that would set trends for the Hollywood of the next twenty years. Two theatrical attorneys, Arthur Krim and Robert Benjamin, did this by changing the company from one that was primarily a distribution outfit to one with an emphasis on the *financing* and distribution of independent product. By virtue of this change, and their own shrewd judgments of what and of whom to finance, Krim and Benjamin had been able not only to revive the company but to turn it around financially, giving it a profit of well over $3 million for 1953.

Out in the San Fernando Valley, which was now a thriving section of subcities, the venerable Universal was now Universal-International, having merged with a successful independent outfit in 1948. And it was U-I that startled the industry and started another trend by making a deal with James Stewart by which he would receive a percentage of the profits of any picture he appeared in, thus altering forever the basic power structure of the industry, away from the studios and their producers to the stars and their agents. All of these factors, combined with the final break-up of the production-distribution-exhibition combines, brought about radical changes in the financing and production of films—the loss of guaranteed outlets, the rise of the independent producers—and nowhere was this more obvious than at MGM, which was now ruled by Dore Schary, who had replaced Louis B. Mayer in 1951. Mayer had brought Schary into the company after MGM had fallen prey to the twin terrors of the postwar years, television and poor product. Schary had been hired in the hope that he could rehabilitate the fortunes and prestige of the company as a picturemaker, and his accomplishments eventually led to Mayer's being fired by Nicholas Schenck, the head of

---

* Selznick and UA had settled their respective lawsuits after a short court battle, with UA paying Selznick $164,000 in cash for his stock, returning his initial $300,000, and writing off the $1.5 million it had advanced him in production loans.

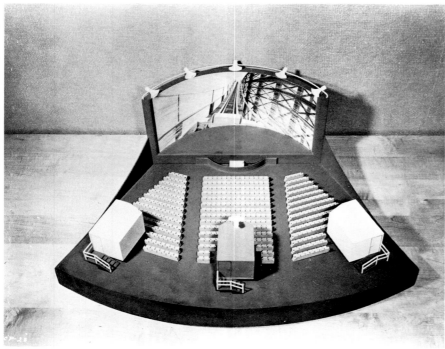

Merian Cooper and Lowell Thomas took an invention of technician Fred Waller and revolutionized the film industry with their production of *This Is Cinerama,* which opened on Broadway in late 1952 and finally came to the Warner Hollywood Theatre in mid-1953. Using three synchronized cameras and projectors, it threw a spectacular wide-angle, 146-degree panoramic picture onto a huge, deeply curved screen six times the size of the average theatre screen, pulling the audience into the picture. This feeling of audience participation was enhanced by the use of multiple sound sources—five speakers behind the screen, five in the back of the auditorium, and five on either side, giving the sound an astonishingly lifelike presence. The costs for production and exhibition of this process were exceedingly high, taking it out of the realm of commercial motion-picture exhibition, but the excitement the technique generated spread quickly across the nation, and the studios tried to jump on the novelty bandwagon that it created by dusting off a twenty-year-old three-dimensional process that required the audience to wear special glasses to see pictures in depth. "A lion in your lap" was the phrase used to advertise the 1952 *Bwana Devil* (opposite, top), the first film shot in this new technique, leading a New York foreign-film exhibitor named Richard Davis to take out ads for the French film *Fanfan la Tulipe* asking audiences, "What do you want—a lion in your lap or a good movie?" Twentieth Century-Fox took another course when it introduced its CinemaScope process, emphasizing the disputable fact that it was a modern "miracle" that audiences could see without special glasses (opposite, bottom). A poor man's Cinerama, it used a special lens on both camera and projector to take and project an image twice as wide as normal, augmenting the visual impact with a variation of Cinerama's stereophonic sound. Three-dimensional movies turned out to be a flash in the pan, and even Cinerama was modified into a single film process, eventually being phased out by the overwhelming success of CinemaScope and its adoption by just about every theatre in the world.

Loew's, with Schary being elevated to head of production. This was a delicate situation for Selznick to contend with as he returned to Hollywood in 1953, for Schary had been a protégé of his and he was gratified to see him rise to the top; but Selznick's affection for and loyalty to Mayer made him personally distressed at what he considered the shameful treatment of the man to whom MGM owed so much. And his ambivalent feelings about Schary were not helped when Schary sponsored the production at MGM in 1952 of a screenplay called *The Bad and the Beautiful,* which dealt with a second-generation Hollywood producer who obsessively interferes both in his own productions and in the private lives of his associates. Selznick felt that "Schary had gone about the business of slandering me, and worse he even tried to involve my late father.... " Selznick was dissuaded by his attorneys from suing Loew's, but the slight to him and his father, real or imagined, rankled quietly for the next two years.

It was not only the power structure of the Hollywood film industry that had changed; close to seven hundred theatres across the country closed in 1951, some being torn down, with others being converted to supermarkets, as people stayed home to watch television.

To combat television's growing popularity, its sense of immediacy, and the novelty of instant reality, the movie producers at first tried creating spectacular entertainments that TV couldn't duplicate, spending great amounts of money on lavish musicals and historical pageants which offered large budgets and little imagination. But audiences continued to defect when they realized that what the movies were offering was available on television, on a smaller scale but at no cost. Clearly, the movie industry would have to find something for audiences that the small screen could not duplicate. Then, on September 30, 1952, in New York City's Broadway Theatre, Merian C. Cooper and Lowell Thomas introduced Cinerama, a process that encompassed the viewer's entire field of vision. The sensation it created caught the industry by surprise. Hoping to cash in on the success of this new technique, Hollywood dusted off a twenty-year-old three-dimensional process which required the audience to wear glasses that added depth to the filmed image, and for a few months the trade papers were rife with the names "3-D," "Natural Vision," "Magnascope," and finally the 20th Century-Fox process, "CinemaScope." It made use of a thirty-year-old device called the anamorphoser, a lens invented by a Frenchman, Henri Chretien, which had the remarkable ability to "squeeze" twice as much image into a normal frame of film; when the same lens was used for projection, the resulting picture spread out to a size two and a half times the normal width. Together, Darryl Zanuck and Spyros Skouras equipped this process with a modification of Cinerama's stereophonic sound system, and announced that all of 20th Century-Fox's productions would be filmed in CinemaScope, the first of which would be Lloyd C. Douglas's best-selling religious novel *The Robe.* This was a gamble of enormous stakes for Fox—they were committing more than $24 million worth of unproduced properties to a process that no theatre in the United States could yet exhibit. But after a series of demonstrations in New York's Roxy Theatre, on a screen 80 feet wide, exhibitors began clamoring for the necessary lenses and sound equipment. By the time of the premiere of *The Robe* in September 1953, more than 1,500 theatres were equipped for the new technique, and CinemaScope had been taken up by MGM, Columbia, Universal-International, and Walt Disney. By mid-1954 *The Robe* had rolled up a box-office gross of $16 million, and audiences began flocking back to the theatres; attendance crept steadily upward to 50 million weekly, giving the industry a twelve-month intake of $1.2 billion, largely from patrons between the ages of eighteen and thirty. But 1953–54 was America's last great moviegoing binge, for after the hype of CinemaScope and big-scale productions had worn off, attendance once more began its incessant decline.

The huge success of *The Robe,* and 20th Century-Fox's claim that it could conceivably topple *Gone With The Wind* from its fifteen-year reign as the industry's top grosser, alternately amused and infuriated Selznick. By 1950, when *GWTW* had played its last domestic engagements, the picture had achieved a phenomenal worldwide gross of $62.7 million. Of this total, $46.7 million had come from the United States and Canada (these figures represent what was paid at the box office; the return to the distributor on this was just over $37 million). Fox was claiming grosses for *The Robe* of $26 million, which was box-office gross, not distributor net, and *The Robe* had been playing at greatly advanced prices. It was conceivable that by the time it had played all the theatres that had yet to be converted to CinemaScope, it might indeed overtake *Gone With The Wind.* To MGM and to Selznick, the possibility of losing this longstanding record was unsettling. For Selznick, it would mean losing the prestige of having produced the industry's most successful motion picture, while MGM prided itself on owning the film and seeing it at the top of *Variety's* list of historic top grossers every year. So in the interest of prestige, pride, and, not so incidentally, the money that would come in from another reissue of the film, MGM let Selznick know in late 1953 that they planned to put the picture back into circulation in the spring of 1954—this despite the fact that it had played its last U.S. theatrical engagement as recently as August 1950. Another reason for issuing it again was that 1954 was the company's thirtieth anniversary, and the picture, even though it had not been made by MGM, was one of its proudest possessions, which could properly be shown off during the birthday celebration. Finally, the sales people felt that exhibiting the picture on the new wide screens that had just come into use would give it a contemporary look and feel, as well as enhancing the spectacle sequences.

The chief difficulty with this latter approach, however, was that most of the maskings of the image necessary to give older pictures a wide-screen proportion were done in the theatre and were largely left up to the projectionists, who took very little care over what they were doing, resulting in heads completely disappearing out of the frame or alternately sitting at the bottom like rows of tenpins. MGM's standards were still the highest in the industry, and many of the people who were working for the company had been entrusted with the care of *GWTW* ever since its original release. They felt an affection for it, and a proprietary interest in its preservation and proper presentation; the thought of its being left to the arbitrary mercies and sloppy projection practices of most theatres was painful in the extreme. So early in 1954, a special assignment was handed to W. D. Kelly of the MGM editorial department: he was to make a survey of the various theatres in the Los Angeles area to determine the proportion in which they projected their image, and how the projectionists framed and centered the picture during a performance. His report to J. Robert Rubin, the vice-president of sales, indicated that "projecting *Gone With The Wind* with present-day standards . . . could lead to certain scenes being damaged from the photographic and dramatic standpoint." He had made a study of the picture projected through the various ratios, and found that if the image was blown up slightly, to a 1.6-to-1 proportion, only five scenes in the film would need careful attention from the projectionist: one in the beginning, when Scarlett runs across the lawn at Tara; the first pullback shot of Scarlett and her father standing under the tree looking out over the plantation; two of the spectacular shots in the Atlanta railroad station; and the final pullback shot at the end of the picture. For these, Kelly recommended that the studio itself "reduce the picture aperture . . . which would obviate the necessity of having . . . theatre projectionists concern themselves with the adjustment." The rest of the picture could be played at the 1.6 ratio with very little loss of the central image.

At the same time that Kelly was making his recommendations, Douglas Shearer of the sound department was concluding arrangements for use of a directional sound process called "Perspecta" in all of MGM's CinemaScope and wide-screen features. Once the decision had been made to exhibit *Gone With The Wind* in wide screen, it was also decided that the picture should be adapted for the Perspecta multi-channel sound process. To achieve this, MGM would need the separate music, dialogue, and sound effects tracks for the picture, and here they faced a tricky situation. When they had bought the rights to the picture from the Whitney interests, they bought only the physical picture and its finished components, which included the three black-and-white color-separation negatives and a composite sound track. Selznick still owned everything else from the film: costumes, unused footage, and the separate music, dialogue, and other sound tracks. On behalf of his brother's estate, which owned a small part of the picture, David had for years constantly bedeviled MGM over what he felt to be improper accounting in the com-

(Above) Loew's Warfield in San Francisco was one of six test theatres that opened the wide-screen reissue of *Gone With The Wind* in May 1954. Heavily publicized and extensively promoted in the showmanly tradition of MGM (which included having models dressed as Rhett and Scarlett tour the city with signs proclaiming "the return to San Francisco of the greatest motion picture ever made"), the picture did astounding business, outgrossing such current MGM spectaculars as *Knights of the Round Table* and *Executive Suite*. It was a success that was repeated all across the country in the fall of 1954 as the picture opened nationwide, grossing $9 million. (Below) To make sure that it would be exhibited properly in wide-screen, MGM carefully masked several scenes in the picture. This shot of the wounded in the Atlanta train station was changed from its original proportion of 1.33-to-1 to a near rectangular 2-to-1 by printing a black strip across the bottom of the image, thereby assuring that audiences would not have the image arbitrarily cut off by careless projectionists. Howard Dietz of the MGM publicity department devised a new slogan for this reissue utilizing the famous initials "GWTW"—only this time it stood for "Greater With The Wide-Screen (and stereophonic—as an added tonic—sound)." Composer Cole Porter liked this latter phrase so much that he appropriated it in 1955 for the song "Stereophonic Sound" in his musical remake of *Ninotchka* called *Silk Stockings*.

pany's remittances to Myron's heirs. Consequently, they were wary of approaching him for the use of the sound track components for the necessary remix. But when they finally did so, in early February 1954, they found him surprisingly tractable; even more amazing was that he would let them have what they wanted for free. As he stated in a letter to J. Robert Rubin, "I don't want one single penny . . . I will gladly donate not only [the tracks] but also my own time and effort to assure the preservation of *GWTW* as the biggest and best picture ever made . . . I will be happy to do this . . . because my pride and my reputation are at stake and I am not going to have my major effort ruined by [my lack of cooperation]."

Selznick's cooperation in this matter, however, was brought to an outraged halt on the evening of February 14, when Ed Sullivan, on his popular Sunday-night television program "The Toast of the Town," devoted the entire evening to celebrating MGM's thirtieth anniversary. The show was made up of a selection of clips from some of the studio's more memorable films, and Selznick, watching it in New York, was "upset at the complete lack of mention of Louis B. Mayer and Irving Thalberg . . . the men who built the company . . . and made most of the pictures that were being excerpted . . . in the course of the program." His upset turned to fury when, at the program's conclusion, a short sequence from *Gone With The Wind* was shown, after which Ed Sullivan introduced a beaming Dore Schary, MGM's production head, and the following dialogue ensued:

> That's quite a treasury of memories, isn't it, Dore? Incidentally, I understand you are re-releasing *Gone With The Wind.*
> Yes, Ed, it opens in May.
> I remember that picture very well, Dore. I was out there when you made it. It was produced by David O. Selznick and released in 1939 . . . and your MGM team is still leading the league.

Selznick's long-simmering resentment of Schary and his treatment of Mayer now boiled over into sputtering rage, not only at the omission of credits for Mayer, Thalberg, Arthur Freed, and the other producers but also at the implication that Schary had in some way been connected with the making of *GWTW*. Almost immediately after the show ended, Selznick was on the phone with his lawyers, and two days later he issued a lengthy statement:

> Dore Schary, representing the current production management of MGM, failed on The Toast of the Town . . . to accord the slightest credit, or acknowledge . . . the past creators whose efforts brought to that studio the eminence it formerly enjoyed. . . . [These omissions] created the impression that the present studio "team" headed by Dore Schary is responsible for the outstanding films produced years ago by MGM. . . . I am also incensed by the startling, and in my opinion, disgraceful and inexcusable attempt on the part of [Schary] to present *Gone With The Wind* . . . as an MGM production. . . . *Gone With The Wind* was produced in its every detail and in its entirety by me and for the Selznick International studio. . . . [On behalf of] the staff and the team that actually made the picture, and for myself, I deeply resent the attempt to mislead the trade and the public and I have instructed my attorneys to take legal steps toward a correction and damages.

Selznick's lawyers studied a kinescope of the controversial sections and demanded that CBS delete all references to *GWTW* before the show was rebroadcast in other parts of the country.

For the next several weeks, the newspapers gleefully printed all the recriminations, accusations, countercharges, and the flow of statements verging on insults from Selznick, Schary, and even Louis B. Mayer, who from the depths of his involuntary retirement fired several long-overdue salvos in Schary's direction, calling him a "ham . . . a man who wrecked an institution that ranked as number one." Asked if he intended to file a suit, Mayer retorted, "What kind of a suit could I file? Can I say I'm the great Louis B. Mayer? This is impossible." Of far more concern to Schary and the rest of the MGM hierarchy was the damage the controversy might do to their plans to reissue *GWTW*. Selznick, who could be a legal terror when he felt he had been unfairly treated, might try to stop the re-release through legal action. Howard Dietz meanwhile was enlisting the aid of Ed Sullivan, who was only too happy to be of help. He invited Selznick to appear on his show in the near future to talk about his career and *Gone With The Wind.* On May 23, Selznick went on "Toast of the Town" with two short sequences from the picture, and in a colloquy with Sullivan, he gave Schary an indirect back of the hand. In answer to Sullivan's question, "What has been your overall philosophy in twenty-nine years as the industry's top producer of films?" Selznick commented, "My feeling is that the first and foremost function of motion pictures is entertainment . . . this is what people pay their money for . . . and I have small patience with those producers who think it their duty to deliver 'messages' with their pictures . . . except incidentally and idealistically. . . . As far as motion pictures are concerned, I think that they must have magic . . . and that they can have no higher purpose than to send people back to their homes feeling a little bit better about life in general."

In the two months preceding this broadcast, MGM's technicians had been feverishly working with the sound tracks Selznick had turned over to them, remixing them for the Perspecta effects, and altering the necessary sections of the picture. They did this by rephotographing portions of the original black-and-white negatives onto a new Eastmancolor single-strip color negative. These altered sections were then inserted into the new Technicolor printing matrices and a completely new set of prints run off, which is why, in certain sections of the 1954 reissue, the color suddenly becomes very grainy and washed-out looking. Selznick commented on this during the several weeks he devoted to overseeing the making of the first batch of new Technicolor prints, remarking that "the color seems much harsher than in my original print." There were several reasons for this, the primary one being that the new prints were made on acetate "safety" film, the more volatile nitrate film base having been outlawed in 1949. All of the prints of *GWTW* made in the United States prior to 1950 had been on nitrate-base stock, and these prints, with their delicate, subdued pastel coloring, were destroyed by government order—except for a few that found their way into the hands of private collectors, and one that was presented to the National Archives in 1941 by Selznick and MGM. The new prints made up by Technicolor for the 1954 reissue differed from the originals in several ways. One, of course, was the transparency of the image—it is much denser in these later printings; another was that the color was much more vivid, what technicians call "saturated"—this was an aesthetic decision, made by MGM and Selznick jointly. (In 1940, it was feared that four hours of Technicolor images would be tiring to the eyes of spectators unaccustomed to color movies, so the coloring was purposely kept subdued.) Adding to the change of hues in 1954 was the fact that the Technicolor staff had changed their dye components, using different ingredients in the chemical mixtures that made up their printing colors. The result of all these seemingly insignificant changes was a version of *Gone With The Wind* drenched in color. Even Selznick mentioned that the color seemed "overly bright and vivid," and at his suggestion, whole reels were printed over again to reduce the chromatic richness of the image. For two months prior to the scheduled "repremiere" in Atlanta in May, Selznick fussed and fretted over the new version, spending days with the MGM and Technicolor technicians in an attempt, as he wrote to Eddie Mannix, one of the vice-presidents of MGM, "to duplicate the original color." He was considerably heartened by the attitudes of the MGM staff, commenting to Mannix:

> It seems obvious that they are trying to do a job worthy of the film . . . but of course none of them has the prior knowledge as to what is necessary to get the full values out of each scene. *GWTW* is a gigantic tapestry, and . . . its overpowering effect is dependent upon the perfection of its thousands of component parts . . . no one of these items would seem important to anyone unfamiliar with how the total effect was achieved. . . . I was very pleased to hear your own staff comment that in all its technical phases [the picture] is still so superior . . . this is a tribute indeed to my staff and our work, considering that we did the job fifteen years ago!

MGM was still bending over backward to do nothing that might further offend Selznick, and even went to the extraordinary effort and expense of printing up special stickers to paste over the already printed posters and other advertising accessories, replacing the words, "A Metro-Goldwyn-

On October 24, 1954, Selznick scored a coup by having his only television production telecast on all three networks simultaneously. A celebration of the seventy-fifth anniversary of Edison's invention of the electric light, the two-hour show was sponsored by three hundred electric companies across the nation. Mixing filmed sections and live sequences, the show starred (clockwise from top right) Joseph Cotten, Helen Hayes, Eddie Fisher (and an unbilled appearance by Debbie Reynolds), Guy Madison, Kim Novak, Thomas Mitchell, Judith Anderson (as the Statue of Liberty), Brandon de Wilde, Erin O'Brien-Moore, and Walter Brennan. Lauren Bacall and David Niven were also in the cast, as was a young comedian named George Gobel, whose explanation of the operation of a computer catapulted him into fame. The show was directed by King Vidor and Chris Nyby, with live sequences directed by Alan Handley. William Wellman flew to Denver to direct a guest appearance by the President of the United States, Dwight D. Eisenhower (seen below with Selznick and Wellman), which was the climax of the program.

Mayer Masterpiece Release" with the simple phrase, "Released by Loew's Incorporated." The company carefully tested the picture in a series of six "pre-release" engagements, kicking these off with the gala reopening in Atlanta. Howard Dietz sent Selznick a special invitation to take part in the festivities, but he declined, stating, "I am delighted to help to maintain the quality of the picture ... but I have no intention of making myself ridiculous by appearing in Atlanta as a member of the 'Schary team' or any other MGM team."

Selznick maintained this standoffish attitude throughout the first months of the picture's revival, softening a bit as letters from moviegoers from all over the country began to arrive at the studio, some from people who had seen it before, but primarily from youngsters, teenagers to whom it was just something their parents had talked about. Some had read the book and were prepared to be critical of the film, but just as with audiences for the past fifteen years, this new generation quickly fell under its spell, many returning to see it several times and leading Selznick to suggest to MGM that they revive the slogan: "How many times have you seen *Gone With The Wind?*" It was the 1954 revival that transmogrified *Gone With The Wind* into more than just an outstanding motion picture, altering its status as the highpoint of the melodramatic, romantic genre. The audiences at the earlier revivals of the picture had been made up largely of people who had seen it before, and their vivid memories were not disappointed in any of the subsequent showings. But in 1954, *Gone With The Wind* was given over to an entirely new generation, who took it for their own as an authentic classic that cut across age and social barriers, its narrative power, the beauty of its images, and its impact potent and undiminished by time, changing attitudes, or technical advances. The 1954 revival turned *Gone With The Wind* into a true folk movie, an heirloom to be handed down from one generation to another.

In August 1954, *Gone With The Wind* finally opened its Hollywood engagement on a glittering, star-studded night at the Egyptian Theatre that was as much a tribute to Selznick as it was to the fifteenth anniversary of the picture. MGM had invited everyone who had worked on the film to attend. Hal Kern, now at MGM as an assistant to Al Lichtman, came to see what had been done to the picture. He hadn't seen it since 1947, and he relates that he was "surprised and disappointed ... the wide screen didn't seem to do what it should, and the new sound just ruined it. I didn't get the thrill from it that I had the last time"—sentiments echoed by Lyle Wheeler, who was now supervising art director for 20th Century-Fox: "I thought all of the things we had worked so hard on, the composition ... all the money and time we had spent on these were gone ... a great deal of it was lost." Absent from the evening's festivities were Victor Fleming, who had died in 1949; Vivien Leigh, who was in England recovering from a nervous breakdown suffered on the set of Paramount's *Elephant Walk;* Olivia de Havilland, who was off making a picture in Europe; and, most conspicuously of all, Clark Gable. Gable and Selznick had patched up most of their differences immediately after the war when, as Selznick related years later to one of Gable's biographers, "I ran into Clark at a party shortly [after he returned] ... he came up, put his arms around me and said, 'I'm so glad to see you ... I have an apology to make to you. I was flying over Berlin on my first mission and I was scared to death, sure I was going to die ... and for some reason you came into my mind ... and I said to myself, What have I got against that man? He has never been anything but kind to me. My best picture was with him ... he did me nothing but good. What have I got against him? And I said if I get out of this thing alive and get back to Hollywood, I'm going to apologize to him. I'm now keeping that promise.'"

Selznick continued, "We met several times, afterwards, very cordially ... and he told me that he learned after the fact how much I had to pay for him for *GWTW* and what a fool he had been because they had given him only a bonus." This latter remark is the key to why Gable was not at the 1954 premiere of *Gone With The Wind*. He had just left MGM, after twenty years as their most popular and durable star, and he was bitter at their treatment of him; the *GWTW* windfall to MGM because of him still rankled; and on his last day at the studio, there was not even a farewell party for him, no gesture of parting, of appreciation. A proud man, he resisted all of MGM's efforts to get him to attend the opening. Even Selznick implored Gable's agent, George Chasin at MCA, to urge Gable to attend, saying in a letter that "Clark's appearance at the opening

means no more (and no less) to me than it does to him. Neither of us will benefit one penny from how *GWTW* is received. But ... it is of great and lasting benefit to us both for *GWTW* to maintain its prestige and its championship. Each of us is likely always to be best remembered for this film ... and it would be folly for either of us ever to turn our back on it." Gable, however, remained unmoved and unwavering. The evening went on without him; but even with his absence, and in spite of the widescreen alterations, the consensus of the celebrity-packed audience that night was that the picture was still "the greatest," a sentiment echoed all across the country. Selznick was considerably buoyed up by the accolades coming his way for the film, and the audience reaction to the picture was exciting, too—he hadn't seen *GWTW* with a theatre audience in almost twelve years, and the reminder of how good it actually was excited him into thinking that the time might be right to make another picture.

The night after the premiere, his life took another upswing when Jennifer Jones presented him with a daughter whom they named Mary Jennifer. In the years since Selznick had given up production, Jennifer had appeared in a number of excellent pictures, some successful, some not, but her appeal at the box office was undeniable. Selznick, of course, oversaw every detail of her career. Pygmalion-like, he advised her on scripts that were submitted, helped her choose the parts she would play, negotiated her loan-out deals, then bombarded the producers and directors for whom she was working with interminable memos about everything from her makeup to camera angles, costumes, and playing styles. Unfortunately, her appearances tended to be either in artistic successes such as William Wyler's *Carrie* (1952) with Laurence Olivier, or in trashy little melodramas such as King Vidor's *Ruby Gentry* (1952), a modern-day follow-up to *Duel in the Sun*. Her last film before temporarily retiring to become a mother had been John Huston's offbeat comedy *Beat the Devil* (1954). But she had not yet had the kind of role or success that Selznick felt her talents demanded and deserved, and in late 1954 he decided it was time for him to do something about it. He would produce another picture, something that would show off her gifts as an actress of sensitivity, depth, and versatility, not to mention great sex appeal. The problem of course was in finding material worthy of her, and incidentally big enough to herald his return to picturemaking.

Selznick found the first answer to that problem in June 1954, when he registered the title *War and Peace* with the Motion Picture Producers and Distributors Association. Title registering was a form of gentleman's agreement within the industry; once it had been registered, no one could use that title or the property without permission from the registrant. Feeling that the part of Natasha Rostova was ideal for Jennifer, Selznick announced to the press: "A large percentage of critics regard it as the greatest novel ever written.... I regard it as one of the greatest stories for motion pictures ... it contains many of the things found in *Gone With The Wind*.... I have thought about making it for almost twenty years." Evidently he was not alone, for immediately after he announced his plans, producer Michael Todd decided that he too would film the story in his new big-screen process called Todd-A-O*; and simultaneously in Italy, Dino de Laurentiis announced plans for a mammoth version to star Audrey Hepburn. Selznick, in the post-*GWTW* honeymoon with MGM, had persuaded Nicholas Schenck to have the company finance and distribute his version, and as he related to historian Rudy Behlmer:

> Paramount made a deal to finance De Laurentiis, and told MGM that if necessary they would release theirs under a different title.... Nick Schenck asked me whether I could [make my version first]. I said I could not and that I would not get into a competition, not as to who made the better picture, but as to who made it first. And so we abandoned it, much to my despair. There are not many pieces of material like *War and Peace*. If Paramount had held the line and been faithful to the registration system, it would not have happened.

And so he began the search for another property. Then, in September 1954, Warner Bros. opened George Cukor's musical remake of *A Star Is Born* with Judy Garland, and the fact of this remake inadvertently led Selznick to the property he was searching for—a new version of Ernest Hemingway's classic novel *A Farewell to Arms*.

---

* A 65 mm process developed by the American Optical Company at Todd's request.

The thirteenth-century village of Venzone, nestled in the Italian Alps in the northwest corner of Italy near the Austrian border, with two thousand Italian troops dressed in World War I uniforms, provides a spectacular backdrop for Selznick's remake of the Hemingway classic *A Farewell to Arms*.

A Farewell to Arms

A FAREWELL TO ARMS, Hemingway's second major novel, had been based in large part on his own experiences and observations on the Italian front during World War I. Its publication in 1929 had taken him out of the ranks of the merely promising and secured his position as one of the foremost American authors of the twentieth century. Hemingway himself is supposed to have referred to it as his *Romeo and Juliet*; the tragic love story between an English nurse and an American serving in the Italian Army depended for its effectiveness not on the tale itself but the manner of the telling, a tough, spare prose style that worked more by indirection and omission than by what was actually said or described. The basic story had been filmed by Frank Borzage for Paramount in 1932 with Gary Cooper and Helen Hayes, but the success of this picture had very little to do with the Hemingway novel, being more a star vehicle with an arbitrary happy ending substituted for the death of the heroine in childbirth. Selznick had left Paramount just as plans were getting under way to film the story, and as an admirer of the author and his novel, he was greatly disappointed by the resulting picture. Later he wrote, "I had wanted to make *A Farewell to Arms* since it was first published; it broke my heart that I was too young a producer to ... make it when it was first filmed ... through many long years I tried to acquire it."

The story had passed from Paramount to Warner Bros. in an involved trading game, and Warner Bros. had refilmed it in a modernized adaptation called *Force of Arms* (1951), setting it during the Korean War; from there, the story had been adapted for a one-hour live television drama starring Guy Madison and Diana Lynn in 1955, and it was this telecast that caught Selznick's eye and renewed his interest in the enormous romantic potential of the story. He tried to buy the story from Warner Bros., but they wouldn't sell; then, according to Selznick:

> There developed a strange situation that at long last made it possible for me to acquire this [property]. Warners had bought the remake rights to *A Star Is Born*, which had passed into other hands at the time of [the dissolution] of Selznick International. I still owned the foreign rights of [the picture] and the negative had a unique value, both for reissue abroad and for initial release in some countries. I refused to sell Warners my rights in these countries [which meant they could not release their picture there], but I suggested I would accept the rights to *A Farewell to Arms* in exchange. After considerable dickering and the addition of a cash payment by me of $25,000, [I] secured *A Farewell to Arms*.

Having obtained the property, he now had to shop it around to the major studios for financing and distribution. He offered it to MGM as a replacement for the aborted *War and Peace*, and the deal with Nicholas

Schenck was almost set, when Schenck, age seventy-two and under pressure because of the poor showing of the Loew's profit and loss statements, unexpectedly resigned in December 1955. Selznick was left on his own. "I had my choice of financing from several sources and accepted a proposal from Spyros Skouras at Twentieth Century-Fox." Not so coincidentally, Jennifer Jones had recently made three of her best pictures for Fox—*Love Is a Many-Splendored Thing, Good Morning, Miss Dove,* and *The Man in the Gray Flannel Suit.* These films had all been successful, and she was now a strong box-office attraction. Fox was also financing and distributing Darryl Zanuck's independent production of an earlier Hemingway novel, *The Sun Also Rises,* for which Jones had been considered, but after she and Selznick read the script, she turned it down.

Now having three important elements of the package, Selznick set about wresting a script from what he described as "a romance . . . a love story . . . almost a fantasy of a love story, born out of some cock-eyed concept of Hemingway's about a girl and a boy that is far from being realistic, or even neo-realistic." The difficulties of trying to adapt the material were not made any easier by what Selznick referred to as "Hemingway's fantastic gift for giving the impression of a scene without actually writing it." To help him catch the elusive qualities of the story, Selznick hired Ben Hecht in the early part of 1956. Hecht had just turned sixty-two; his autobiography, *A Child of the Century,* had created a minor sensation on its publication for his raffish opinions and observations of life in the picture industry. In it, however, he did have high praise for Selznick, calling him "my favorite movie boss." The long, affectionate friendship of the two men, their mutual liking of and respect for each other, and their familiarity with each other's thought processes and feelings about movies would make their working on *A Farewell to Arms* a very smooth and efficient process, for, as Selznick recounted in a letter to Robert Chapman, an instructor at Harvard University:

We actually did five drafts complete, in six weeks! The first of these was *completely* faithful: exactly what Hemingway wrote; it was worthless. Having then put on paper just what Hemingway wrote, we went through [it] to try to put on paper what Hemingway said. . . . This was better. We then proceeded to attack it as a motion picture, visualizing it as we went along, and considering all our other problems besides—tempo, logic, overcoming Hemingway's sloppy introduction of characters and careless handling of time elements, etc., we got closer. I have never seen Ben . . . bring to a job more thorough analysis, more willingness to rewrite than he has. He admired the book greatly as I did, but like me, he has been aware of the failures of others to bring Hemingway off on the screen when they followed him slavishly . . . the only Hemingway stories, without exception, that have been successfully adapted to the screen were those which departed *widely* from Hemingway, notably *The Killers* [1946], a big commercial if not critical hit. . . . Each of our drafts has been getting better and better. . . . If we have done violence in any particular to Hemingway, it has been with great reluctance and only after the most thorough discussion. I don't expect Hemingway to like it; there is ample evidence that if anybody changes a single word or scene or character . . . he is very upset. But I must make a successful motion picture that appeals to audiences, readers of the book, and non-readers alike, not just Hemingway. . . .

To work with Hecht and himself on the various drafts, Selznick brought back into the company Lydia Schiller, who had been living and working in New York since Selznick had ceased active production in 1949. "It was quite extraordinary, the way in which we met again," she recalls. "I had been working for CBS for several years, and one day I was on my way to work and I was passing the Waldorf-Astoria, and a man stepped out of a cab and practically knocked me down. It was Mr. Selznick, and we literally fell into each other's arms—we hadn't seen each other in so long. Well, the first thing he wanted was for me to come to work for him on *A Farewell to Arms,* and I must say I was reluctant . . . I didn't want to go back to Hollywood, New York was such an exciting place to live, but he was persuasive, and told me that the picture would be made in Italy, and I thought, well, I'd give it another try."

While the three of them continued working on the script, Selznick

was mulling over the choice of a director. This was a difficult problem, for, as he remarked candidly to Schiller, "Most directors these days don't want to work with me." Directors were finally breaking free of the restraints of the long-term studio contracts, and the better ones were forming their own companies and signing up for individual projects over which they had absolute approval. It was a situation new to Selznick, but he accepted it as a given and began negotiating with a man who was a close personal friend as well as one of the most individualistic talents of the time—John Huston. The two had worked together tangentially late in the forties when Huston had directed Jennifer Jones in a somber drama of Cuban revolutionaries, *We Were Strangers,* and later when Selznick had been involved in the production of Huston's *Beat the Devil,* also with Jennifer Jones. Huston, a charming roisterer, shared with Hitchcock and DeMille the distinction of being one of the few directors whose name meant something to moviegoers. This personality cult had been built up over the years in Hollywood largely because of his irresponsible attitude toward his chosen field and his cheerful disdain for the formalities of his job, qualities that were captured perfectly by Lillian Ross in her celebrated series of articles in *The New Yorker* on the making of *The Red Badge of Courage* (later published as the book *Picture*), in which she quotes Dore Schary describing Huston: "I love John; when he wants something from you, he sits down next to you and his voice gets all husky, and pretty soon you're a dead pigeon."

Huston's greatest strengths lay in his ability with actors and his sense of the harsh realities of everyday life, softened by an ironic idealism he managed to find in his characters—all of which seemed to make him the ideal choice to direct the Hemingway material. But he was known to be as autocratic and strong-minded as Selznick, something Lydia Schiller pointed out to Selznick when he first broached the idea of having Huston direct. "I asked him if he thought they would get along," she recalls, "and he told me a little sadly that Huston was the only director of any stature who would work with him." Huston was busy finishing up *Heaven Knows, Mr. Allison* (1957) on location in Trinidad when Selznick wired to ask him if he would be interested in doing the film. Huston had earlier written one of the few adaptations of Hemingway's stories that the author had liked, *The Killers,** and the result was a fast friendship between the two men, who were alike in many ways, sharing a love of the rugged outdoor life coupled with an underlying sharp sensitivity and a delight in alcoholic brawls. After finishing *Heaven Knows, Mr. Allison,* Huston stopped off in Paris to talk over the project with Hemingway. According to one of Huston's biographers, William Nolan, "Papa liked his ideas and both men felt that the book would make a powerful film." Huston, however, still had not seen a finished script, so while Selznick and Hecht continued to work on the final adaptation, Selznick dispatched Lydia Schiller to New York with instructions to "sell Huston our version."

"I went up to his suite at the St. Regis," she recalls, "and Huston was there with his agent Paul Kohner. They were all very nice. Huston didn't say much, so I just launched into my recitation of what the script was going to be, the approach we had, and talked about the individual scenes. Huston brightened up a bit after a while, and asked me some questions, and then when I was ready to leave, Paul Kohner took me to the elevator and said, 'You did a good job, I think he likes it.'"

While waiting for Huston to make up his mind, Selznick, who was finishing up the sixth draft of the script with Ben Hecht, was simultaneously arranging the logistics of filming the picture in Italy and trying to decide who should play the male lead of Lieutenant Frederic Henry opposite Jennifer Jones. "We needed a star," related Selznick in a later interview, "and we needed someone young. The picture shows a man in the process of completing his maturity, and if we chose someone for the role who was as old as most of our top leading men then I was afraid that the love story would have a soiled quality. . . . Star personalities are rare and always will be . . . it is a tragedy to see so many youngsters who are passed off as stars these days who photograph well and are talented but who can't hold your attention. A star can't be built . . . you can give the illusion that a person is a star by means of a lot of publicity, but unless he

---

* Huston had surreptitiously worked on the screenplay while in the service, so the credit was given to Anthony Veillar, who did the final adaptation.

Rock Hudson, production manager Arthur Fellows, Jennifer Jones, Selznick, and director John Huston at a pre-production script rehearsal for *A Farewell to Arms*.

is, he won't last." Ironically, Selznick finally chose thirty-one-year-old Rock Hudson for the part; ironic because Hudson, in his immediate post–World War II days as a truck driver, used to stand in front of the Selznick studio in the hopes of being discovered by Selznick's chief talent agent, Henry Willson, who, it was said, had a discerning eye for young male talent. Eventually the 6-foot, 5-inch truck driver, whose name was Roy Fitzgerald, did catch Willson's eye. The agent, impressed by his stature and undoubted sex appeal, took him on as a client, changed his name to Rock Hudson, and arranged a contract for him at Universal-International, where he spent several years as part of the studio's "beefcake brigade"—young men who looked good with most of their clothes off, suitable for westerns, desert romances, and action melodramas. Hudson, however, was a cut above most of the others, being ambitious and eager to learn and with a pleasing honesty to his personality that soon made him a teenager's delight. His appearance in the 1954 remake of *Magnificent Obsession* had turned him into a romantic star, and his excellent work in George Stevens's epic *Giant* had earned him an Academy Award nomination and turned him into one of the top box-office attractions of the time. "Rock Hudson is the first romantic idol since Gary Cooper and Clark Gable," said Selznick. "He's got it—the thing that is indescribable and I was delighted that we could get him. . . . He's got a warm, likable quality that will last for years and years." Meanwhile, Huston told Selznick through his agent that he would take on the project, prompting Selznick to cable his pleasure at the "news of your availability," and then bringing up the difficulties in their working together: "Because of the extent to which I personally produce in every sense of the word, I am . . . worried lest the unquestioned eminence of your present position would cause you to resist and resent functioning as director rather than producer-director (as is your custom). Could you concentrate wholly on *Farewell* until completion of photography after which believe you would feel safe leaving editing and post production in my hands?" Selznick also told him confidentially that the deal he had with 20th Century-Fox was not all that he would have liked it to be: "[We are subject] to extremely severe financial penalties if we go over budget plus contractual ability Twentieth Century [to] take the picture over. . . . We can clearly stay within budget if we make the picture within fourteen weeks which seems extravagant because apart from spectacle scenes three quarters of the film is extremely intimate scenes with small numbers of people."

Selznick and Huston now started work on the final Selznick-Hecht draft of the script, which Huston, as the days went by, began finding serious fault with. The script, in its eighth draft, was being criticized by Huston for all the non-Hemingway material Selznick and Hecht had put into it, with Huston now insisting that they should stay as close as possible to Hemingway's original scenes. This went on all through the beginning of 1957, until finally Selznick called a halt, telling Huston:

> This torturing of the script has, I hope, come to an end—a belated end, for whatever its gains or losses, it has played havoc with proper planning for the film. I went through with Ben every single point that we discussed during his absence. It was not just a case of mollifying Ben, who was very angry, but of listening very carefully to what he had to say about our hasty decisions on [a] script to which he and I had devoted so many months. . . . It is not in the motion picture scenes, original and outside Hemingway, that I think we may have made serious mistakes in recent days. Instead, it is within the dialogue scenes themselves, where we have made cuts of material simply because it was not in the original Hemingway scenes, disregarding the vital fact that it had originally been added to the Hemingway scenes for very solid reasons. And I think we may have gone wrong in adding material simply because it *was* Hemingway . . . approaching the script in these recent days seemingly as though . . . the sole measure of whether the scenes were good or bad was whether they were Hemingway. . . . The responsibility is mine . . . accordingly today I overruled Ben in many of his objections, as I deeply regret I must now overrule you in relation to others.

Huston must have just shrugged this off; he was overheard saying, "I'll just nod, and go ahead and do it my way." Selznick froze the script at number nine, which was made up of what were hoped to be the best aspects of the previous eight, and this "final" script turned out—surprisingly, in view of his past history—to have been just that, for the picture as released follows this version faithfully. Even the dialogue emerged fairly intact, which indicates that Selznick was determined to keep the picture on schedule and on budget—set at $4.2 million, a quite respectable sum indicating the picture would be an important one. MGM was reputedly spending a like amount on its Civil War love story *Raintree County*, closely modeled on *GWTW*, and Columbia Pictures and Sam Spiegel were spending double that on their antiwar adventure drama *The Bridge on the River Kwai*, then filming in Ceylon.

The amount of money involved and the subliminal feeling of being tested must have brought tremendous pressure on Selznick, professionally and psychologically. This was his first picture in nine years, and the challenge of living up to his reputation as the maker of *Gone With The Wind* was upon him, no matter how much he tried to disregard it. Also, he had taken on the responsibility of making the picture an absolutely perfect vehicle for his wife—a dangerous business, no matter how hard he tried to maintain a producer's perspective. He had already made one fundamental error in regard to this, which was that Jennifer Jones neither was the correct age nor had the appropriate temperament for the part. Catherine Barkley, the heroine, is a straightforward romantic twenty-year-old, with a strange maturity in her attitude that doesn't stem from age. Jennifer Jones was thirty-eight when *A Farewell to Arms* went into production, and while her talent and her gifts as an actress were considerable, few performers approaching middle age can convincingly act or project youth on the screen. The innocence isn't there, and it

cannot easily be faked; Jennifer Jones's playing of the part would ring false to most of the moviegoers between the ages of fifteen and thirty, who formed the bulk of the movie audience.

Selznick himself was now fifty-five years old, and he saw everything from the middle-aged vantage point, which puts a peculiar coloration on life, and especially on perceptions of what is emotionally valid. Casting an actual twenty-year-old in the part of Catherine Barkley would have been inconceivable to him at that point in his life, not just because of his feelings for his wife but also because, to him, the love story would not have been believable or interesting. Consequently, it was inconceivable for him to have the part played by anyone other than Jennifer Jones.

Arriving in Rome on March 1, Selznick immediately set about overseeing every minor detail in his characteristic obsessive manner. From his headquarters at the imposingly massive and modern Cinecittà studios, he was determined to move his crew of 250 people all over Italy and into Switzerland, photographing the story as much as possible against the

Charles Vidor (who replaced John Huston), Selznick, and Rock Hudson in the streets of Cortina d'Ampezzo.

actual backgrounds described in the book. The problems of doing this were complicated enormously by the language barrier. In spite of the amount of filming that was being done by American companies in Italy, no one had yet figured out how to overcome this particular obstacle. Interpreters helped, but instructions sometimes became garbled in the translation, resulting in delays and misunderstandings. All of this added to the cost and time of filming, but even with the additional expenses, filming was still cheaper in Italy than in Hollywood. To make *A Farewell to Arms* in Hollywood in 1957 would have cost something like $2 million more than in Italy, without the benefit of the scenery and the actual locations so necessary to the new wide-screen processes, which in their larger compositions revealed so much of the fakery of the back lot. This was especially crucial in the battle scenes of *A Farewell to Arms*, which needed the rugged snow-encrusted Dolomite Mountains to suggest what the war had really been like. Here was one aspect of the production that Huston and Selznick agreed on, but even so there was evidently a wide difference of opinion about just what results to go after and how best to achieve them. Huston liked to keep himself open to any new ideas he might have until just before shooting a scene, which meant that camera set-ups could be—and usually were—changed, lines of dialogue altered, blocking and other staging details revamped, thus giving his scenes an edgy, almost improvised spontaneity. Selznick, on the other hand, wanting as much control over time as possible, and wanting the film to look and sound a certain way, was unalterably opposed to Huston's methods, which he had thought Huston would alter for a picture the size of *A Farewell to Arms*. It was somewhat upsetting to Selznick to find that Huston was not changing his methods, and instead was insisting on

changes in the script, remarking to Selznick in a late-night conference that he felt "like a prostitute" doing a picture from a script that was not his to control and change as he liked.

With filming scheduled to start within a matter of days, and five thousand Alpine troops standing by in the mountain areas around Cortina d'Ampezzo while the weather threatened to produce a major blizzard, preparations came to a halt as Selznick and Huston continued to discuss their different approaches to the entire concept of the story. Selznick argued forcefully in a memo:

> You think you are being faithful to the book but you are only being faithful to your concept of the book.... I most certainly don't want you to be depressed by any feeling that you are not honoring any pledges you may have made to Hemingway.... I have the greatest respect in the world for [him] and my attitude toward his book is best demonstrated by what I have staked on it, but my ego—and also my record—doesn't permit me to think that Hemingway can prepare a better motion picture than I can.... You can only do the job that is essential to this picture by fulfilling your promises to do what I decide, and I emphasize the "I," and do it enthusiastically. It is possible, John, that you have had a change of mind—or a change of stomach since you accepted this assignment. Possibly in the back of your mind is the thought that you would, step by step, bring me round to your way of doing things. I must warn you, John, that I am not easily brought around. I am too old a horse for this. Maybe my way of making pictures is not your way, but it is the only way I know; and at this stage of my life and my career, I cannot change it.... [If I did] it would lead

Jennifer Jones as Catherine Barkley attempting to reach her departing lover, Frederic Henry.

us, not to a better picture, as you and I discussed ... but to a worse one, because it will represent neither what you think the picture should be, nor what I think it should be.

Yet in spite of all the discussions pro and con, and Selznick's insistence on a definite production schedule being set up and adhered to, Huston continued to be maddeningly indecisive regarding his plans for shooting the story. In an effort to calm Selznick, Huston, before leaving for Cortina, began rehearsing on the set at Cinecittà the dramatic scenes involving the first meeting of the two lovers in the British hospital. But the production wasn't functioning yet, and this attempt to accomplish some meaningful work turned into a lengthy fiasco, leading Selznick to fume: "If the shambles of these two days' 'rehearsals' are any criterion ... then I feel that there isn't a chance in hell of our meeting our schedule, or of our coming within cost ... [not with] the kind of 'preparation' we are having. ..."

Huston then left for the Cortina location site in the northern Alps, where he began to work out the logistics of moving and photographing the waiting troops and ancient ambulances, and to organize the special effects necessary for the war scenes. Selznick joined him there four days before shooting was to start. After being briefed by Huston and production manager Arthur Fellows on what the plans were, including Huston's last-minute changes in the sequence as scripted by Selznick, Selznick finally decided that the time had come for drastic action. He went back to his office and began dictating a lengthy memo to Huston, which took him two days to finish and exhausted three secretaries in the process; the editing and typing had to be overseen by Lydia Schiller, working with two other typists. When finished, it ran to sixteen pages of single-spaced admonitions, which started off by saying: "I should be less than candid with you if I didn't tell you that I am most desperately unhappy about the way things are going," and then proceeded to castigate Huston for all the frustrations and fears Selznick was heir to in regard to the picture and Huston's attitude toward it, which he characterized as "unenthusiastic," telling him:

Even your best friends thought I was out of my mind to cast you on a romantic love story of this kind. It was predicted over and over that your interest would be in military matters to the detriment of the love story. You are getting a fabulous amount of money—$250,000—to direct a single motion picture. You are not entitled, therefore, to the privileges of an artist. You are obliged to do a job, just as I am obliged to do a job. The job is to make a picture which will hopefully appeal to critics, but which most importantly will appeal to the tens of millions of people who will have to like it to pay its cost.

Selznick rather tactlessly managed to drag in the relative failure of Huston's version of *Moby Dick,* released the year before, saying: "The trick of fidelity to source was not achieved in *Moby Dick,* not only from the audience standpoint, but even from the standpoint of novel lovers, demonstrated by the lectures given at Harvard University which repeatedly attacked the failure to realize Melville in the film." He even found fault with Huston's choice of locations: "I think it's shocking that the magnificent locations (that I saw in my trip up here) have not been thoroughly studied with a view to better locations than we have now," and then berated him for not having made up his mind about the day-to-day practicalities of the filming. The memo ended up:

Maybe this is the way you have worked, John. It is not the way I have worked. It is not the way I shall ever work. It is not the way I shall work on *A Farewell to Arms.* If you can't decide these things, then we have no alternative but to decide them ourselves. We can't spend hundreds of thousands of dollars because of habits of procrastination or of creating things on the spur of the moment. ... This kind of self-indulgence won't do. ... Let me say in conclusion, John, that fervently as I want you to direct the picture, I would rather face the awful consequence of your not directing it than go through what I am presently going through. I would rather have a worse picture directed perhaps by someone that doesn't have your talent, a director who wouldn't have even the little preparation you have had, than sacrifice my health and my future to this kind of picture-making, which is totally unknown to me, and which in my opinion is no longer remote-

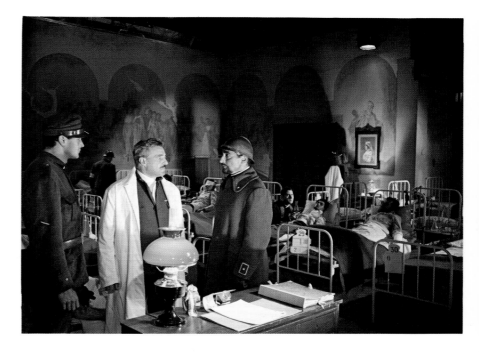

(Top) Rock Hudson, Vittorio De Sica, and Jose Nieto in one of the hospital scenes of *A Farewell to Arms.* The production was designed in color by Alfred Junge, the art direction was by Mario Garbuglia, and the costumes and set decoration were by Veniero Colisanti and John Moore. (Center) Elaine Stritch (left) had one of her first film roles as the tough-talking but sympathetic friend of Catherine Barkley. (Above) Jennifer Jones and Rock Hudson in one of their more romantic moments in the film.

ly tenable in the industry. . . . I therefore ask you to let me know at once your reaction to these comments. Frankly, I have not the slightest idea as to how I will cope with the situation if you resign from the picture. But I would rather face this *right now* than face it later, or face it at an even more difficult time. I am not asking you to resign, I am merely telling you the circumstances, the only circumstances . . . under which I think you can continue. . . . If you decide to resign, you may be sure that I would protect you to the fullest, and that I would be perfectly prepared to emerge, with your New York critical friends and with the entire industry, as the tyrannical producer who didn't understand a gifted artist. I am used to that role. . . . I have learned that nothing matters except the final picture. . . .

After going over the finished copy, Lydia Schiller was appalled at some of the things Selznick had said, and, as she related, "I asked him if he was sure that he wanted to send this, and he said, 'Why?' and I told him, 'When he reads this, he'll walk,' and he looked at me with a sort of smile and didn't say anything, so off it went." Huston's reaction was exactly what Schiller had predicted, and probably what Selznick had wanted. He immediately packed his bags, left the location, and within twenty-four hours was on his way back to the United States. Selznick, true to his word, issued the statement that he and Huston had differed over interpretations and that Huston had chosen to leave. Asked by a reporter if there was any truth to the rumor that he and Huston had disagreed over Jennifer Jones's role, Selznick denied it, saying, "In Mr. Huston, I asked for a first violinist and instead got a conductor."

Meanwhile, the five thousand troops of the Italian Army were still waiting in the snow, and Selznick moved with his customary dispatch in meeting emergency situations. Within a day he had hired Andrew Marton, an experienced action director who had worked with Huston on the second unit for *The Red Badge of Courage* (1951), to come in and film the necessary sequences showing the advance of the Army up the mountains, and the subsequent battle and bombardment scenes. While Marton was doing this quickly, efficiently, and fairly unimaginatively, Selznick was scouring the Hollywood lists for a director of some sensitivity to step in and take over. He decided on the Hungarian-born Charles Vidor (no relation to King), who had just finished his thirty-third film, *The Joker Is Wild* (1957), a hard-boiled autobiography of night club singer/comic Joe E. Lewis, starring Frank Sinatra. Vidor was a cultured, suave director, whose films ranged from the sensuousness of *Gilda* (1946) to the delicacies of *Hans Christian Andersen* (1952). He had come up in the Hollywood ranks under the tutelage (and the thumb) of Harry Cohn at Columbia and Samuel Goldwyn, so he was no stranger to interfering producers. He took over the direction of *A Farewell to Arms* on literally a moment's notice, part of the attraction of the project being that he had served in the Austro-Hungarian Army in the very battles he was now called upon to reconstruct. For the next several weeks, he led his twenty-eight freight cars of troops—cast, crew, and equipment—all over Italy, from Rome to Lake Misurina in the mountains and back down to Brunico on the Austrian frontier, and to eight other major locations around the country. Selznick didn't always accompany the company on these jaunts, but his presence was felt by the number of memos he dogged Vidor with. At one point Vidor was so exasperated that he wired Selznick: "[These memos] indicate that you think you have on your hands a hopelessly inexperienced director. . . . If you don't stop I will think I am stuck with a hopelessly inexperienced producer . . . now for heaven's sake let me function or else come down here and shoot this yourself."

With that, the two men settled down to an uneasy truce, and *A Farewell to Arms* began the long haul toward completion, an estimated four months of shooting marred only by the labor troubles between rival trade unions, which put the picture two weeks behind schedule and close to $300,000 over budget (Selznick supplied the money out of his personal funds rather than breach his contract by asking Fox for it). The final sequence was a complicated one involving night shooting on a lake, and an argument arose between Selznick and production manager Arthur Fellows. Tempers evidently boiled over, for blows were struck. As Lydia Schiller recalls: "A very important floodlight that we needed for the final scene wasn't there and Mr. Selznick was really furious . . . he did tell Arthur off." According to Bob Thomas's book *Selznick*, Selznick thereupon slapped Fellows across the face and Fellows struck back, smashing Selznick's glasses into his eyes. Lydia Schiller disputes this: "I don't remember that he slapped Arthur . . . but Arthur did sock him. . . . I simply cannot believe that Mr. Selznick would lose his temper in that way, he was very gentle, not a physical man at all. . . . It all happened so quickly; fortunately one of the electricians had the presence of mind to pull the plugs so it wouldn't be photographed and get in the press." With this final bit of unpleasantness, *A Farewell to Arms* finished principal photography, and Selznick, Jennifer Jones, and the rest of the company returned to the United States in mid-August 1957, leaving behind a second unit under the supervision of Selznick's older son, Jeffrey, who was a production assistant on the picture.

Back in Hollywood, the final interiors were finished at 20th Century-Fox, and once more Lyle Wheeler found himself overseeing a Selznick set. "He called me," recalls Wheeler, "and said, 'You've got to watch out for me, make sure I get a fair break . . .'—his feeling was that he was going to get charged a lot of extra costs for the work we were doing. . . . We had several sets that duplicated what they had done in Europe, and we redid some of the lake crossing in our tank and the lake up at Malibu." To film these last sequences, Selznick turned to one more old associate, James Wong Howe, who had just finished working on the Warner Bros. adaptation of another Hemingway novel, *The Old Man and the Sea* (1958). Howe completed the last shots on the picture in mid-September. Then Selznick began his customary meticulous editing; but this time, due to his caution about overshooting, the work went relatively fast. By late October he had managed to whittle the picture down to three hours and was continuing to work on getting it down even further when he received the news that Louis B. Mayer was seriously ill with leukemia and was not expected to live more than a few weeks. In the early morning of October 30, 1957, Mayer died; his death marked, more than any other single event, the passing of an era of Hollywood motion picture history. Selznick sat up most of that night—*A Farewell to Arms* temporarily forgotten—to compose a eulogy for the man he saw as a symbol of an era, "a man of great stature . . . a man of contrasts—part sentiment and idealism, part pure practicality . . . for the industry that he loved he fought persistently and unwaveringly. . . . More than any other man, he won for the motion picture industry an esteem that was little more than a dream at the time he first envisioned the future of films. . . . In the future, looking backwards, one will see his head and shoulders rising clearly above the misty memories of Hollywood's past. . . . All the rest is history; the shining epoch of the industry passes with him."

Mayer's death cast a pall over the completion of *A Farewell to Arms,* but much as when his brother had died during the final phases of *Since You Went Away,* Selznick pulled himself together and managed to get the picture ready for its first two previews, one in Burlingame, in northern California, on November 18, to be followed the next night by another at the mammoth Fox Theatre in San Francisco. Both theatres were packed for the screenings, as the previews had been highly publicized. The audiences were extremely enthusiastic at certain moments of the film, but some of the dialogue, including the word "whore," used here for the first time in an American film, was shocking, as were many of the vivid war details. The final ten minutes of the film were given over to an extended and harrowing depiction of Catherine Barkley's death in labor, alienating most of the women in the audience. The realism of the sequence was much too vivid, and it was reduced to just over three minutes in the final editing. For the holidays, 20th Century-Fox had booked the picture into Grauman's Chinese Theatre, the flagship of eight theatres in the Los Angeles area that would simultaneously "world premiere" the picture on the same day, December 19. That was less than a month after the final preview, and the picture still had not been completely edited nor the final sound track mixed, both normally time-consuming technical processes, further complicated in this case by the fact that the score, by Mario Nascimbeni, which had been recorded in Italy, had not yet arrived.

The picture, like so many of Selznick's past efforts, had been previewed with "stock," or already existing, music tracks. Selznick hired Murray Spivack to mix the sound, and as Spivack recalled:

Selznick felt that there might be an Academy Award in it for Jennifer Jones . . . so he said, "You've got to get this ready in ten days, because we've got to get it into the theatres before the last two weeks in December." So I said, "Well, if you guys don't bug me and leave me alone and let me do it, I'll get it out for you, but I don't want anybody screaming about overtime and crews and all of that. . . . It's going to cost you a lot more money." So he agrees, and I go off to start mixing the music and the other tracks, and I start getting these notes from Selznick, one says that in reel three, I want the piano to be soft and build up, and then I get a note ten minutes later saying I want the piano to start with an impact and get softer. So there's no time on these notes, I don't know which one was written first, and I say which one shall I follow? And this was going on all the time. . . . I remember that I was subject to a lot of criticism from some of my colleagues, who said Spivack spent a fortune on this picture when he shouldn't have. I had run up a bill of $35,000 to finish the picture, but these guys didn't understand what Selznick wanted. I saw him a few weeks after the picture opened and I said, "David, I've been getting a lot of criticism from some of my co-workers because of the extra money I cost you to get the picture ready in time." And he said, "Murray, I picked up $175,000 a week by releasing it the two weeks of the Christmas season, so the $35,000 that you cost me was just a drop in the bucket. I'd gladly spend that again because I'm still way ahead of the game." He sent me a $500 bonus soon after that, so I guess he meant it.

Helped along by a large advertising budget and the names of the principals, A Farewell to Arms initially did very well at the box office, clearing just a little over $5 million in its first six months of release, and eking out a small profit margin. But the picture didn't have the staying power that the other blockbusters of the time did. Ironically, it fared little better than MGM's Raintree County, their attempt to duplicate the success of GWTW, even to the use of the ad line, "in the great tradition of Civil War Romance"; but this and A Farewell to Arms were almost throwbacks to another era of moviemaking, and the times were not right for either film. A Farewell to Arms was just out of step with the times. Its melancholy air, the pervasive atmosphere of gloom, doom, and death, coupled with the somberness of the telling, depressed moviegoers, and the word of mouth on the film was not good. The young audiences preferred the sex, youth, and tarnished idealism of Peyton Place or the sex and glamour of Sayonara and turned out in droves to see an antiwar film that had absolutely no romance in it, The Bridge on the River Kwai, which swept that year's Academy Awards. Adding to Selznick's woes was the fact that Jennifer Jones wasn't even nominated for her work, which made the relative failure of the film even more devastating to him, for he had truly expected it to be the capstone of her career. Instead, her critical notices were among the worst she had ever received, with Selznick himself getting the brunt of the drubbing, the picture being called "old-fashioned," "over-produced," and "tedious." Critical reviews seldom meant anything at the box office, but this time the judgment of the public concurred. The elegiac qualities of the picture, its sense of futility and doomed love, were not what excited or affected the bulk of the young people who went to the movies in 1957-58. "I take credit for my pictures when they are good," Selznick said later, "so I must take the blame when they are disappointing. . . . A Farewell to Arms is a job of which I am not especially proud."

Selznick probably realized at this point that he had finally lost touch with his audience. It was the empathy with his audiences that had always given his pictures their vitality; the realization that he had lost this ability to embody their aspirations and fantasies saddened him more than anything else. He had lost his connection with them, they had stopped responding to his stories and the way he told them, and at this point he may have felt that it was best to bow out gracefully and leave the movie industry to those who knew how to speak the language of youth, for as he himself had said so often, "The movies belong to youth."

Epilogue

The crumbling facade of Tara as it looked on the back lot of the Desilu studio in 1959.

SELZNICK spent most of the following year, 1958, attending to the exhibition and marketing of *A Farewell to Arms.* Ultimately, he sold the picture to 20th Century-Fox for $1 million, which, he remarked, "I think it reasonable to assume they wouldn't have paid if they hadn't seen a profit." He continued to market his other pictures through sub-distributors, all the while studying the changing Hollywood situation and wondering whether he wanted to get involved in the new complexities of making pictures.

In early March 1959, Selznick's mother died. Although he had never been as close to her as to his father, the loss slowed him down and depressed him. He wrote to Merian Cooper (whose own mother had died the same day as Selznick's), "It is very strange to be 'little boy lost' at my age, and I am sure you must feel the same way." But Selznick had great emotional recuperative powers, and almost immediately he immersed himself in the second picture due under his contract with 20th Century-Fox—a film of F. Scott Fitzgerald's *Tender Is the Night.* Selznick had known Fitzgerald when they were both young men starting out in Manhattan. According to Selznick:

Fitzgerald was in his early twenties at the time . . . and in the first flush of his success. . . . I persuaded my brother Myron to hire him . . . to write some originals . . . and while they were never made (they were awful!) the relationship with Fitzgerald was a good one. I kept up contact with him, and unsolicited, he made it a practice to send me an autographed copy, with a personal sentiment, of each of his books as it appeared, and I of course value them highly for my library. Not too long before his death, Fitzgerald worked for me, this time in connection with some episodes of *Gone With The Wind* . . . but he was able to

contribute nothing, but here again the relationship was a good one. . . . Throughout a period of some twenty or twenty-five years I saw him only rarely . . . but we never had the slightest misunderstanding about anything, and we always got along very well, both personally and professionally.

To Selznick, *Tender Is the Night* was Fitzgerald's "best . . . and inevitably so since it came out of his maturity, his disillusionments, and his own personal heartbreaks. I think its title is one of the best I have ever heard; its characters the truest and deepest and most fully rounded that he ever created; and its background and period exciting beyond words. . . ." In mid-1951, he had tried to interest the producing team of Jerry Wald and Norman Krasna at RKO in a package of Cary Grant, Jennifer Jones, and *Tender Is the Night.* He intended to make it as a co-production, with George Cukor directing. Unfortunately, the project collapsed because of Grant's reluctance to play the heavily dramatic role of Dick Diver, the psychiatrist who falls in love with his patient. Promptly after *A Farewell to Arms* opened, Selznick began working with Ivan Moffat on an adaptation of the Fitzgerald novel, but Selznick had recently sold a block of his older films to British television, and the British exhibitors' organizations passed a resolution to boycott all further Selznick pictures. They were evidently influential enough to cause Spyros Skouras at 20th Century-Fox to ask Selznick only to prepare the script and then sell it to them, along with the services of Jennifer Jones. He did this reluctantly, on condition that he have approval of casting and that no changes be made in the script without his approval. A young theatre-television producer named Henry T. Weinstein was assigned to the project. He was competent but unimaginative, and Selznick immediately began deluging him with memos on everything from the sets ("They should be as chic and as famous and have the same effect on interior decorating as [the] sets in *Dinner at Eight* ... which revolutionized people's concepts of interior decorating all over the world") to directors ("John Frankenheimer ... my first choice to do the film, who was desperate to do it ... is no longer available.... Henry King ... is wonderful with Jennifer and gets the best results out of her ... and as the senior piece of talent on the Fox lot, they don't push him around the way they do newcomers there") to working conditions ("You can't make a great picture in union hours. If this were my picture, I would be having meetings every night of the week with different department heads, and I would be raising hell to get them to raise their own sights").

In the midst of all this preparation came the shocking news of Clark Gable's death from a heart attack at the age of fifty-nine. He had just finished rugged location work on John Huston's *The Misfits* with Marilyn Monroe, and he and his fifth wife, Kay Spreckels, were expecting a child, his first. All over the world, headlines blazoned word of his death, and in Hollywood, the *Citizen-News* covered its entire front page with a black-bordered photograph of the actor. Selznick once again had the sad duty of memorializing someone he had worked with: "Clark Gable was and will for a long time remain the worldwide symbol of American virility. He was unquestionably the greatest male star of our time...."

Almost simultaneously, MGM announced plans to put *Gone With The Wind* into circulation early in 1961, "to commemorate the Civil War centennial." Selznick's attention was pulled away from the frustrations and compromises resulting from his not being allowed to work on *Tender Is the Night*, and he was once again faced with the accomplishments of his past. His reaction to the ever-growing legendary status of *Gone With The Wind* had taken on an almost schizoid quality: his pride in it was enormous, and yet he had come to hate the looming shadow of the picture, which seemed to blot out everything else in his professional life. Several times over the years he had caustically remarked to intimates about "that damned picture; when I die, the paper will read 'Producer of *Gone With The Wind* died today.'" If he had owned it, his ambivalence would probably not have been as great, but his resentment toward MGM and the millions of dollars it brought to that company every seven years added greatly to his discontent. Yet all this was tempered by his pride, and the esteem that came to him from having produced the industry's top-grossing picture, a position it held until late in 1958, when it was supplanted by Cecil B. DeMille's biblical spectacular *The Ten Commandments*. Consequently, when MGM announced it was putting *GWTW* back into circulation in 1961, Selznick felt bound to cooperate in every way he could to help the picture regain its first-place status. He raised no serious objections when the people at MGM told him in confidence that instead of having Technicolor make new prints for this reissue, the work would be done in MGM's own labs, using the company's "Metro Color" (a trade name for the Eastmancolor process), a quicker, cheaper process that in the fifties had begun to supplant Technicolor as a method for both the photographing and printing of color movies. With careful handling, this process could deliver color that compared favorably with Technicolor's fabled dye transfer system, but it did not offer the control latitude of the Technicolor method, nor did it quite have Technicolor's smoothness and definition in color printing. Finally, it had one distinct disadvantage over the Technicolor dye transfer process: the color, achieved through a chemical process within the layers of the film, was unstable and after several years turned pink as a result of changes in the chemical compositions. The prints made by MGM for the initial 1961 engagements of *Gone With The Wind* lacked the sharpness and definition of the earlier Technicolor prints, and within a year they began to fade, distorting the color values beyond all recognition. When Selznick saw one of these new prints, he was impressed by the lower printing costs but concerned over "the fuzziness and the lack of clarity in some of the exterior scenes and the muddy quality of the interiors, especially in the shadows and the other delicate areas of color that we took such pains to achieve." Many of the Technicolor prints from the 1954 engagements were still in good enough condition to be used in 1961, so that MGM was able to advertise that the picture was in "Color by Technicolor."

In spite of his reservations about the new prints, Selznick was enough of a pragmatist to realize that the changing quality standards of the industry would have to be lived with, and he allowed himself to be persuaded by MGM to attend a three-day celebration in Atlanta for the reopening of the picture in March of 1961. He tried to convince Jock Whitney to attend, wiring him: "Apparently Atlanta is going mad all over again in connection with the reopening of our opus ... climaxing with a new 'premiere.' I tried to persuade MGM that it would be more like a wake, but they insisted that the Georgians wanted this to be the keystone of their centennial, and finally, if reluctantly—I agreed to be present along with the other principal survivors, Vivien and Olivia. I would feel much better about the whole thing if you and I could be there together and have a few drinks over our recollections.... [It] should be fun." Whitney evidently had no stomach for nostalgic recollections, for he declined the invitation, and Selznick instead took his younger son, twenty-five-year-old Daniel, who recalls the event: "Loew's Grand was decorated to resemble the way it had looked in 1939.... Inside the theatre Vivien Leigh sat on one side of my father, with Olivia de Havilland on the other. As the main title appeared on the screen, I saw Vivien clutch my father's hand and whisper, 'Oh, David.' When Clark Gable first appeared on the screen, I heard her gasp, 'Oh look at Clark; he looks so young and gorgeous!' My father turned to her at that moment, put his arm around her, and said, 'So do you, Vivien. And you still do.' The applause at the end of the picture was loud and long; all three rose to share in it. My father seemed to be in very high spirits. But when it was time to leave Atlanta to come back to Hollywood, Dad became very wistful, even melancholy. After such a high, there was no place to go but down."

Selznick's mood was not helped by what was happening to *Tender Is the Night*. Spyros Skouras, the sixty-nine-year-old president of 20th Century-Fox, had assumed an active role in the production activities of the company after the departure of Darryl Zanuck in 1956, and had taken on even more authority after Zanuck's successor, producer Buddy Adler, had died in 1960. But Skouras, a capable executive, suffered from not being a picturemaker; he didn't have the slightest idea about what kind of movies audiences of the time wanted. Within the 1960–61 season, 20th Century-Fox had suffered a series of disastrous flops ranging from *Snow White and the Three Stooges* through *Francis of Assisi* to *Return to Peyton Place*, and the net loss to the once profitable studio had been $25 million. Skouras, deciding that an all-out gamble was called for, had committed the company to what was turning out to be the trouble-plagued, expensive version of *Cleopatra*, whose star, Elizabeth Taylor, had nearly died while the film was in production. Lack of proper organization and conflicting ideas on how and where the picture should be made had boosted the estimated costs upward of $25 million, with the picture not even a third completed.

In an effort to raise the necessary cash to assure that *Cleopatra* could be finished, the 20th Century-Fox board had authorized the sale for $65 million of the extensive back lot acreage in its Beverly Hills studio. In the midst of this welter of mismanagement, near empty treasury, and lack of product for its distribution arm, Skouras and his cohorts had little time for Selznick's obsessiveness or his insistence that they live up to their contracts on the making of *Tender Is the Night*. All during the summer and fall of 1961, Selznick pleaded with the inexperienced Henry Weinstein:

> Please show your producing abilities ... and thoroughness and perfectionism.... If you are going to raise your head above the common or garden variety of so-called producers ... look at the better pictures of the old days that are on television and you will see how much loving care was put into [them]. It is one of the reasons why pictures today are so lousy.... It just makes me sick to my stomach and angers me, to see the sloppiness with which pictures are made today, including, I'm sorry to say, *Tender Is the Night*.... Please don't compromise, Henry ... you have a great opportunity still ... but you are going to muff it if you compromise, compromise, *compromise* and if you rationalize bad things.

Weinstein paid little heed to these entreaties, prompting Selznick to write an anguished letter to Spyros Skouras:

> Studio administrations cannot be calloused and cynical toward the ambitions of, and the promises made to, the creators, without paying

dearly for so hard-shelled an attitude. As things stand, already too many of the top stars and directors and writers and producers in the business have contempt and hatred for their employers.... You cannot simply nominate people to be producers, or to make creative production decisions, regardless of whether they have proven their qualifications or not. It takes endless years of training and experience, as well as talent and insight and knowledge of human behavior and of audience reactions to qualify for the role.... I regret this new evidence of the complete passing of showmanship from the industry, as well as the new attitude of indifference to promises. I can only look back nostalgically on different days that produced different results. I think this is where the bus stops.

Tender Is the Night proved to be the fiasco that Selznick had feared. Though it contained one of Jennifer Jones's best performances, the picture was so badly re-written, so poorly cast, and so botched in its post-production details that it contributed nothing to the Fox treasury, which continued to be drained by *Cleopatra*. (By the time of its release in July 1963, *Cleopatra* had reached the unbelievable cost of $37 million. This led directly to the ouster of Skouras, who was replaced by Darryl Zanuck, whose son Richard was appointed vice-president in charge of production. Thirteen years later, working for a different studio, Richard Zanuck announced plans to film a sequel to *Gone With The Wind*.)

Through the early 1960s, the movie industry seemed not to be affected by the infectious optimism and general prosperity that had begun to be felt across the country. Selznick, who did not make another picture after the disappointment of *Tender Is the Night,* went on with his business dealings in Hollywood, observing the changes in the industry and the content of contemporary films with the rueful knowledge that he could not work within the new system and could not assimilate the values and attitudes of the new audiences. Because he had enough grace to bow out of the moviemaking process, his dignity and his reputation remained largely intact, unlike those of many of his contemporaries who refused to give up their power or change their methods. He divided his time between his home in Beverly Hills and his suite at the Waldorf-Astoria in New York, busied himself continually marketing his films, selling stories, and acting as behind-the-scenes mentor for the career of Jennifer Jones. The specter of *Gone With The Wind* continued to haunt him, even in semiretirement, and he spent a great deal of time, money, and verbal energy in trying to turn it into a stage musical under the title *Scarlett O'Hara.* Various announcements over the years proclaimed that the songs would be written by Richard Rodgers, Harold Arlen, Leroy Anderson, or Dimitri Tiomkin; each of these had a different set of lyricists announced, from Oscar Hammerstein II to Ogden Nash to Kay Swift and Ben Hecht. None of this ever went beyond the stage of speculation, nor did Selznick's efforts to have NBC mount a television version in six parts.

Selznick continued to watch the changes and panic in the industry with amusement and occasional exasperation. Columnist Hedda Hopper, an old friend, obtained a lengthy interview with him in mid-1963 in which Selznick lambasted the current studio hierarchies and what he considered the deceitful and dishonest methods prevalent in the business. After reading a transcript of the session, Selznick asked Hopper not to publish it, saying, "I don't like to be critical and hurt people who've been associated with me, and I don't like to talk when I'm not active; it's easy to sit on the outside and criticize people." Hopper acquiesced and the piece was never used, but excerpts from it give an illuminating view of the film industry circa 1963:

> With the exception of a few men in authority, notably Jack Warner and Walt Disney, the motion picture business is run from New York today ... and that is where the troubles of the business originate. In all but a few cases, basic decisions as to what pictures are made, by whom, and on what budgets, are made by businessmen on the east coast. In the great days of the industry, such decisions were made locally. The basic responsibility for this goes back to the stockholders who elect managements that have no qualifications to make production decisions. Because of their lack of creative and imaginative showmanship, more often than not, they base their decisions on what has succeeded or failed in the past.... Since they know nothing whatsoever about

the creation of a script or the vitally important post-shooting phases of production, they are unable to discern why pictures fail or succeed. Understandably, as businessmen, they are only interested in successes; therefore they do not recognize or even realize that a picture can have brilliant writing or directing or acting and still be a failure, whereas it can be second rate in all these departments and still be a success. The strength of the great studio leaders was their understanding of how to use brilliant talents to achieve the ultimate, and that rare element, showmanship. But the new bosses don't have this, all they have to guide them is their grosses. Most of the so-called independent producers are neither producers nor independent; they're entrepreneurs, agents, opportunists who put together packages, getting a producer's fee and a piece of the picture. They deal with companies whose managements are too inept to do this themselves, with the consequence that some of the most gifted writing and directorial and acting talents in the business are either not being used, or are misused.... The economics of the business are irrational: Motion pictures have become a distributor's racket; unlike any other business in the world, profits are sought from the sales department. It's as though Ford Motors tried to make profits from the sales force rather than on cars. Distribution costs are a carryover from the days before air transportation, when it was necessary to have very many more exchange depots and prints than are required today. Advertising costs are borne almost entirely by the producer.... If a picture fails, the film rental not only suffers in ratio to the box office, as it should, but even the percentage of this lower take is reduced so that the returns are next to nothing. This means that the miserably low film rentals have to equal three times the production cost to pay for distribution fees and costs. It is the very rare picture indeed that can overcome these absurd practices. And the only way the new packagers know to achieve this is by inflating the egos and the values of some stars by paying them million dollar fees and letting them take over the production. So we have things like *Cleopatra* and *Mutiny on the Bounty*, movies of desperation.... At the same time that the new studio heads are bankrolling these undisciplined excesses, they're also maintaining huge overheads to service a series of routine pictures that nobody wants to see. Even the monumental losses of the big companies that have been published reveal only a portion of the sad story. The major companies have taken in tens of millions of dollars from television rental, here and abroad, on pictures made by administrations long since gone. More millions have been taken in from real estate, from reissues and from assets created long, long ago. All of these millions have gone down the drain. There would be drastic changes in the business if the stockholders forced present administrations to segregate profits and losses on current product from windfall profits on assets created in the past. If Hollywood is to get a chance to be resuscitated, it must be on a long range basis, whereas now, with at least some of the companies, everything is dominated by worry about the next annual statement, and whether the stockholders and directors will permit existing managements to stay in their jobs.... People don't tell the truth in this business.... If the truth were revealed, there would be a revolution in picture making and distributing, with great benefit to everyone in the business who belongs in the business.

By early 1963, there were only six producing studios in Hollywood: MGM, Warner Bros., Columbia, 20th Century-Fox, Paramount, and Universal. Even though he wasn't actively involved in production, Selznick still kept his finger in the talent pie, and every now and then would delightedly pull out a plum—a newcomer with talent, or perhaps the promise of talent, who needed help, guidance, or just old-fashioned encouragement. He gave a young actor named Dennis Hopper the assignment of taking movies of his family, because Hopper was desperate to make a film and Selznick knew the feeling. He encouraged a young producer named Alan J. Pakula, who had made *Fear Strikes Out* in 1957, working with Pakula on the script of *To Kill a Mockingbird,* which would earn Gregory Peck an Academy Award as Best Actor of the Year for 1962. At the same time, Selznick was deeply involved in advising a young director named John Frankenheimer on the final editing of his movie *Bird Man of Alcatraz.*

DAVID O. SELZNICK'S FILMATISERING AF MARGARET MITCHELL'S BERØMTE ROMAN

BORTE MED BLÆSTEN

GONE WITH THE WIND

CLARK
GABLE
LESLIE
HOWARD

VIVIEN
LEIGH
OLIVIA
de HAVILLAND

EN FARVEFILM i TECHNICOLOR

ISCENESÆTTELSE:
VICTOR FLEMING

UDLEJNING:

METRO-GOLDWYN-MAYER FILM

This Danish poster for the 1961 reissue of *Gone With The Wind* is similar to the one used in the United States for the picture's Civil War Centennial revival.

Mr. and Mrs. David O. Selznick in a 1963 portrait by photographer John Engstead.

Selznick had by now given up any further hope of putting *Gone With The Wind* on the stage or on television; MGM was still being deluged with offers for the telecasting of the picture, but Selznick controlled the television rights to the story, so they could not license the picture without making a deal with him. Over a period of years, Selznick had paid the Mitchell estate a total of $250,000 for the maintenance of these rights, and in 1963 he finally succumbed to MGM's blandishments, selling them his remaining rights in the story. This allowed MGM to negotiate with the Mitchell family and to get not only the stage and television rights, but the remake rights as well. Three years later, in 1966, the new president of MGM, Robert O'Brian, asked Ray Klune, now a production executive at the studio, to look into the possibilities of reissuing *Gone With The Wind*, this time using a new big-screen 70 mm process. The C. V. Whitney and Myron Selznick interests still held their shares in the film, and their approval had to be obtained before any part of the picture could be tampered with. These permissions were given quickly, and Ray Klune began working with Merle Chamberlin, the head of MGM's technical department, to solve the problem of fitting *Gone With The Wind*'s almost square picture into the long, rectangular shape of the new 70 mm format. Going back to the original black-and-white camera negatives, they were dismayed to find that each negative had shrunk to a different size, meaning that the color would not register without halos. This problem was solved by mounting the negatives on special racks, which could be adjusted individually until they all matched. Having photographed every frame of these black-and-white negatives onto the new Eastman negative stock, Klune, Chamberlin, and the MGM staff then went through every single frame again, laboriously rephotographing each to fit the 70 mm proportion. Unfortunately, this resulted in trimming one-quarter off the top and bottom of the frames, so that the image was cut almost in half, ruining the composition, and in one

For the 1967 reissue of *Gone With The Wind,* MGM converted the image to fit the proportions of the 70 mm process. To do this, it was necessary to recompose every frame for the new ratio. (Right) The original image. (Above, right) The image as cropped and rephotographed on 70 mm Metro Color (Eastmancolor) stock. (Above, left) The original, sweeping main title was replaced by this new version for the 70 mm reissue because the wider proportion cropped too much off the tops and bottoms of the letters. Unfortunately, when MGM struck new 35 mm prints of the film, they kept this uninspiring compromise version instead of returning to the original, which they could easily have done.

inexcusable oversight on everyone's part, changing the original main title—"because of technical consideration," as Merle Chamberlin put it—and so destroying the grandeur of the sweeping title, which was replaced by four tiny words lumped into the center of the screen. All of this, plus making the new six-track enhanced stereophonic sound to boom along with the new version, took almost two years.*

For his part, Selznick badly needed the cash payment he received from the MGM sale. His business activities, legal fees, and methods of operation were eating up money faster than it was coming in, yet he still refused to get back into production. Hedda Hopper interviewed him again in late 1964, and asked him why he didn't get involved in television. "In my one experience in television," Selznick replied, "it took as much time and effort to do a really good TV show as to make a really good film, and I don't want to be connected with anything that is not at least an effort to do the best. Furthermore, my entire life has been spent in motion pictures, and if I am going to go back to screen entertainment, I would prefer it to be in this medium." Hopper closed her interview with a description of the Selznick home and lifestyle:

We talked at his Spanish-type hillside home, set in eight acres of garden and woodland, three minutes from the heart of the city. Atop a piano in the drawing room are pictures of famous close friends of the Selznicks, the William Paleys, the Billy Wilders, the Joe Cottens, Truman Capote, Ben Hecht, Aldous Huxley, Henry Miller . . . on one wall is a magnificent painting of David's wife, Jennifer Jones. Sculpture and canvases cover a wide range from ancient to modern—a carved stone head from the dawn of civilization, originals of a wide range of artists, from Renoir and Vlaminck and Bellows to Augustus John and Grandma Moses. In the den are pictures of his children from babyhood to the present. Across the croquet lawn, and beyond the grotto pool and tennis court and waterfall, is a separate house containing a large office with a huge fireplace, and secretarial offices including even a Telex. There David works and writes. The Selznicks entertain a good deal, but rarely come off "The Hill." Several months

*For a detailed description of how this was done, see *American Cinematographer,* November 1967.

a year, they travel, to New York and Europe and the Far East, to the Caribbean and the Mediterranean. "It's a pleasant life," says Selznick, "too pleasant to give up to make movies with the way things are in the industry now." "Why don't you write your memoirs?" I asked, but he insisted that he wouldn't do that until his old age. He has over 300,000 communications in his files and it would require an enormous amount of time.

What Hopper did not realize was that behind the prosperous veneer, Selznick was fast going broke. Taxes and reduced income were eating up his reserves at an alarming rate. Shortly after the Hopper interview, he closed down his Beverly Hills home, concentrating on his New York affairs and returning to Hollywood only occasionally.

Early in June 1965, while Selznick was in Los Angeles on legal business, Russell Birdwell, whose publicity company had fallen from its former prominence, began running a series of advertisements in *The Hollywood Reporter.* Largely monologues of reminiscences, written in Birdwell's anecdotal style, they related exploits in his career and talked of some of the famous people he had known. Birdwell started discussing Selznick in ad number 4 and was still hard at it in number 10. Selznick was alternately embarrassed, amused, and irritated by the pieces; Birdwell's rough-and-tumble memories were painful to Selznick's dignity, and after the eleventh ad had appeared, he wrote Birdwell:

Dear Russ: I am a little late with this note, but I really didn't think that that "interview" was going to go so long and I am now fearful that it's going to stretch into "Ozzie and Harriet" [a long-running TV favorite]. I do wish Russ that you had checked these things with me before putting them into print . . . also I am frankly embarrassed lest people think I had anything to do with this series and that possibly they are even advertisements of my own! I will be most grateful if you will make clear that it is an advertisement of your own. . . . You have my good wishes and . . . I remember our association with pleasure. . . . As always, cordially David O. Selznick.

This delighted Birdwell, who used the memo as the valedictory to the entire series, printing it in full with a handwritten note appended: "COME HOME, DOS, THE INDUSTRY NEEDS YOU!" The ad ran in the morning edition

"All the News That's Fit to Print"

The New York Times.

LATE CITY EDITION

U. S. Weather Bureau Report (Page 82) forecasts: Fair, hot and humid today, tonight; partly cloudy, warm tomorrow.

Temp. Range: 90—70; yesterday: 91—68. Temp.Hum. Index: about 79; yesterday: 80.

VOL. CXIV..No. 39,232. NEW YORK, WEDNESDAY, JUNE 23, 1965. TEN CENTS

ASSEMBLY PASSES CITY FISCAL BILLS; SESSION NEAR END

Wagner Package, the Last Block to Adjournment, Is Voted With G.O.P. Aid

EXTRA BUDGET ADOPTED

It Includes an Added $1,000 Allowance for Legislators and Payment on L.I.R.R.

By WARREN WEAVER Jr.
Special to The New York Times

ALBANY, Wednesday, June 23—One of the longest, most disorganized, most controversial yet most productive sessions of the Legislature crept toward adjournment this morning.

Through a haze of cigarette smoke and dilatory debate, in chambers carpeted with discarded bills and newspapers, the Senate and Assembly continued after midnight to argue the last of the more than 10,000 bills before them.

The Senate recessed at 1:50 A.M. and the Assembly at 2:40. Both were to meet again at 10 o'clock this morning to wind up the session, which began Jan. 6 and is the longest one since 1911.

Before the recess, the lawmakers took two major steps: they bailed New York City out of its fiscal crisis and they added a record $72 million to the state's current spending program.

Borrowing Authorized

The city fiscal package was approved by the Assembly last night with the key measure—authorizing Mayor Wagner to borrow $255.8 million against future tax receipts—passing by a vote of 79 to 63, just three votes more than needed.

The two other bills authorize the Mayor to borrow $46 million to balance this year's budget and begin action on an amendment to the State Constitution to increase the city's real estate tax revenue by about $250 million a year.

All three measures had been passed by the Senate earlier. Assembly action on them was the last major obstacle to adjournment.

In one sense, the 1965 session ended as it began, with the Republicans giving the Democrats the majorities they could not muster themselves. The key New York City fiscal bill was passed only when five Republican Assemblymen dropped their opposition.

The supplemental budget that

Continued on Page 24, Column 1

United Press International Telephoto

WORKING TOWARD ADJOURNMENT: Assembly Speaker Anthony J. Travia presiding at yesterday's session in Albany. In foreground is John T. McKennan, Assembly clerk.

The Post Halts Publication In a Dispute With Printers

By MURRAY SEEGER

The New York Post suspended publication "temporarily" late yesterday afternoon following an appeal from its publisher that the newspaper be allowed to introduce a new method of setting type. When the members of New York Typographical Union No. 6 rejected the personal request of Dorothy Schiff, the publisher, the management told the entire staff that there was "no work to be performed."

Mimeographed notices posted throughout the plant, at 75

Text of The Post's statement will be found on Page 23.

West Street, told the staff that their pay had ceased with the end of their working shifts. The workers were told that they would be notified when they could return to their jobs.

Computer's Use at Issue

The halting of publication at The Post came exactly a week after a report that The Herald Tribune, The World-Telegram and The Sun and The Journal-American had been holding talks about a possible partial merger or joint, cost-sharing operation of mechanical facilities.

The critical issues in The Post's negotiations with the typographical union involve the potential use of a computer to set type and the sharing of savings made by the paper in the use of punched tape to set stock quotations.

Late in the evening, in an interview on WABC-TV, Mrs. Schiff said The Post could not survive without automation. Asked if the paper might be sold if the dispute could not be settled, she said:

"Yes, that's true, or fold it forever if nobody wants to buy it. I'm not willing to pass the hat to foot deficit financing."

In the composing room yesterday, eight printers were asked to process tape through an International Business Machines Company computer.

The men refused to handle the tape that runs through the

Continued on Page 23, Column 4

GOVERNOR VETOES CONDON REVISION

Says It Would Undermine Deterrent to Strikes by Public Employes

By RONALD SULLIVAN
Special to The New York Times

ALBANY, June 22—Governor Rockefeller quoted Franklin D. Roosevelt today and then vetoed a Democratic measure that would have softened restrictions against strikes by public employes.

"It is fundamental to government that public employes have no right to strike," Mr. Rockefeller said. He then quoted a statement that he said was made by President Roosevelt in 1937:

"A strike of public employes manifests nothing less than an attempt to prevent or obstruct the operations of government until their demands are satisfied. Such action, looking toward the paralysis of government by those who have sworn to support it, is unthinkable and intolerable."

Dismissal Mandatory

Restrictions against strikes by public workers are embodied in the Condon-Wadlin Act, which calls for the immediate dismissal of strikers.

The Democrats, in fulfilling a campaign pledge, tried to take the teeth out of the law by throwing out the automatic dismissal provision.

The Democrats also attempted to mandate for the first time collective bargaining between the state, New York City and all other communities and public workers, except the police.

In his light-blue veto message (yellow means approval) the Governor said that the Democrats "would have set up an involved and ineffective procedure which would (1) undermine the deterrent to strikes by public employes; (2) be unworkable and probably unconstitutional in certain of its aspects; and (3) impair vital functions of state and local government."

Prohibition Retained

Actually, the Democratic measure retained the prohibition against strikes. But it dropped the present law's automatic dismissal provisions in favor of milder sanctions in the Civil Service Law. However, a striking worker could still be dismissed at the discretion of the government.

This, said Mr. Rockefeller, would mean that the law "would contain no effective deterrent to a strike against the people." He said that "it is the certainty of a sanction, rather than its severity, that brings about compliance with a law

Continued on Page 28, Column 2

NEW RACING PLAN LEADS TO THREATS

Legislator Tells of Calls—Quarter-Horse Bill Loses

By SYDNEY H. SCHANBERG
Special to The New York Times

ALBANY, June 22 — The sponsor of a quarter-horse racing bill brought a stunned hush to the Assembly chamber today when he disclosed that he and his family had been threatened by anonymous telephone calls and that the last call had been traced to the Assembly switchboard.

Assemblyman Clarence D. Lane, his voice quavering slightly, told his colleagues: "My family has been through hell this past week."

Many of the legislators were touched by the Greene County Republican's story and several rushed to his side to offer sympathy. The quarter-horse bill was later defeated by the Assembly for the second time.

The margin of defeat this time, however, was only two votes. The first time the bill came up, two weeks ago, it lost by eight votes. The second defeat killed the measure for this year. It would have authorized pari-mutuel betting on quarter-horse racing at up to eight tracks in the state.

The quarter horse is a cross between the American mustang and the thoroughbred and is named and noted for its ability to run a quarter mile at high speed. Mr. Lane had estimated that the state would receive more than $4 million from the additional tracks.

Assemblyman Lane told of the threatening phone calls at the close of his speech in defense of his bill. The state police,

Continued on Page 25, Column 1

EISENHOWER BACKS BIRTH CURB STUDY

Urges Legislation in Letter as Senate Group Begins Hearings on Problem

Text of Eisenhower's letter is printed on Page 21.

By JOHN W. FINNEY
Special to The New York Times

WASHINGTON, June 22 — With a letter of support from former President Dwight D. Eisenhower, a Senate subcommittee began today the first Congressional hearings on the once politically taboo subject of birth control.

The former President and a number of Representatives and Senators made an urgent recommendation that the Federal Government assume a more active, open role in attempting to control the population explosion, both at home and abroad.

What they said, however, was in many ways less significant than the fact that they were saying it publicly before a Congressional committee. The hearing was a landmark in Congressional history, for it marked the first time that a committee has dared discuss the issue of birth control.

The Congressional hearing, in turn, is designed to provoke more open discussion and positive steps within the executive branch.

The impetus for the hearings was provided by Senator Ernest Gruening, Democrat of Alaska, who has been an advocate

Continued on Page 21, Column 5

Suffolk Aide Sees Gangster Influence

Special to The New York Times

PATCHOGUE, L. I., June 22—Charles T. Matthews, 39-year-old Republican assistant district attorney in Suffolk County, bolted his party tonight to accept the Democratic designation for county prosecutor.

Mr. Matthews, accepting the Democrats' support at a convention here, charged that "sinister underworld influences have moved into Suffolk."

The Suffolk Democratic Committee made its surprise selection of a candidate two hours before 800 delegates opened a convention here. The delegates approved Mr. Matthews unanimously.

Mr. Matthews, a lawyer of Cold Spring Harbor and chief of the appeals bureau of the District Attorney's office, has been a Republican committeeman from Huntington for the last decade. He was refused the

Continued on Page 22, Column 4

CITY'S DIRTY AIR CALLED A FACTOR IN RISING DEATHS

Cars, Factories and Heating Listed as Contributors in Special Council Study

By CHARLES GRUTZNER

A special committee of the City Council that has been studying air pollution since early this year reported yesterday that New York's foul air was a contributing factor in an increasing death rate from respiratory diseases and lung cancer.

A research team reported at a Toronto meeting that air pollution was found to be heavily implicated in deaths that occurred during New York's influenza epidemic early in 1963.

The special committee of the City Council here, in its first public report, also asserted the following:

¶Just breathing the city's air causes as much inhalation of benzpyrene, a cancer-inducing hydrocarbon, as would result from smoking two packs of cigarettes a day.

¶There is more sulphur dioxide in the air here than in any other major city—50 per cent more than in Chicago and twice as much as in Philadelphia.

¶New York "is not gaining in the struggle to reduce the amounts of various pollutants in the air." While the level of some irritants has changed little since 1952 or has decreased slightly, other types of pollutants, including carbon monoxide, nitrogen dioxide and sulphur dioxide, are more plentiful than before.

2 Days of Hearings Due

These and other somber findings are contained in the special committee's interim report, which will provide background for two days of public hearings beginning tomorrow at 10:30 A.M. The hearings, with Mayor Wagner as the first witness, will be in the Council chamber at City Hall.

The report pointed out that air pollution had hastened deterioration of the City Hall's marble facade, necessitating its replacement a few years ago at a cost of $4 million.

The committee chairman, Councilman Robert A. Low, Democrat-Liberal of Manhattan, said that these and later hearings would be followed by "very specific legislative recommendations and other proposals to improve the situation."

Other witnesses tomorrow will be James M. Quigley, Assistant Secretary of Health, Education and Welfare; Dr. George James, the city's Commissioner of Health, and Arthur J. Benline, Commissioner of Air Pollution Control.

Ten experts in public health and urban decay and the effects of air pollution on people, plant life, and statuary and other works of art will be heard Friday.

Councilman Low said that al-

Continued on Page 30, Column 1

David O. Selznick, 63, Producer Of 'Gone With the Wind,' Dies

Special to The New York Times

HOLLYWOOD, June 22—David O. Selznick, one of the leading producers in the motion picture industry, died of a coronary occlusion this afternoon at Mount Sinai Hospital.

Mr. Selznick, who was 63 years old, was stricken in the office of his lawyer, Barry Brannen, in Beverly Hills, and was rushed to the hospital. His wife, Jennifer Jones, the actress, was with him at the time of the attack.

Mr. Selznick, who produced "Gone With the Wind," the movies' biggest money-maker, and his wife had returned to their Beverly Hills home last week after spending three months in New York City.

Mercurial, shrewd, self-confident and enormously gifted, David O. Selznick climbed to the pinnacle of power and success in Hollywood with films that are now classics and actors who are considered screen immortals.

His films included "Intermezzo," "Rebecca," "David Copperfield," "Little Women," "The Prisoner of Zenda," "Dinner at Eight," "A Star Is Born," "Duel in the Sun," and, the epic, "Gone With the Wind."

He was instrumental in spurring the careers of such actors as Clark Gable, Vivien Leigh, Ingrid Bergman, Joseph Cotten, Gregory Peck, Katharine Hep-

Associated Press

David O. Selznick

burn, Joan Fontaine, Fred Astaire, Leslie Howard, Myrna Loy and his wife, Miss Jones.

Mr. Selznick, a 6-foot 1-inch 200-pounder, moved quickly, spoke rapidly and worked tirelessly. He produced quality films with three trademarks: top stars, the finest writers and no expense spared.

Even in the twilight of his career, he remained wide-eyed and even brash, although a trace of pessimism and melan-

Continued on Page 38, Column 1

Diplomat Indicates Soviet May Admit Vietnam Panel

In Conversation With Reporter, Russian Hints at Cooperation With Efforts for Peace by Commonwealth

By ANTHONY LEWIS
Special to The New York Times

LONDON, June 22—A Soviet diplomat here has indicated that his Government will let the Commonwealth peace mission on Vietnam visit Moscow.

A statement to that effect was made by the diplomat in a conversation yesterday with an American correspondent. It was one of several talks with Western journalists arranged on short notice by Soviet Embassy personnel.

The Russians had long talks, at their request, with three American correspondents. A report from Paris said a similar approach had been made to a correspondent for Le Monde.

The conversations in London differed considerably from one another. In only one did the embassy official make an affirmative statement that in the end he thought the Soviet Union would have to admit the Commonwealth mission.

But all of the talks had an inquiring character, with the Russians seeking to explore the origins of the Commonwealth peace mission and its possible results. In all, there was the impression of Soviet uneasiness about the expansion of the Vietnam war.

One of the Soviet diplomats even raised the possibility that American troops would seal off South Vietnam and then negotiate with the Vietcong.

With varying degrees of frankness, the Russians distinguished their attitude from the Chinese Communists'. They said they did not think the United States was a paper tiger that could readily be humiliated in Vietnam.

One of the Russians, in another recent talk that he sought with an American correspond-

Continued on Page 2, Column 2

Johnson Ends Suspension On Food Aid for U.A.R.

By FELIX BELAIR Jr.
Special to The New York Times

WASHINGTON, June 22—President Johnson has decided that it is in the national interest to send the United Arab Republic the $37 million in surplus farm products still undelivered under a three-year contract that expires June 30.

In announcing the President's decision, a State Department spokesman said, "there has been a definite improvement in our relations with the U.A.R. since aid was suspended six months ago." He cited Cairo's promise to compensate the United States for the burning of the John F. Kennedy Library in November and to provide interim quarters rent-free.

In an expression of indignation at the burning of the library, operated by the United States Information Agency, the House of Representatives in January approved a measure banning any further aid to the Government of President Gamal Abdel Nasser, including the $37 million in undelivered shipments.

$22.4 in Wheat Included

Secretary of State Dean Rusk and Under Secretary George W. Ball persuaded the Senate Appropriations Committee to modify the House language. President Johnson, at a news conference, made a public appeal for a "free hand" to enable him to work for improved relations with Cairo.

The $37 million remaining to be delivered under the $432 million contract consists of $22.4 million in wheat, $8.9 million in tobacco, $5.6 million in vegetable oil and $100,000 in nonfat dry milk.

The State Department announcement, by Robert J. McCloskey, information officer, said the Egyptian Government "has undertaken in connection with the agreement to enter into discussions with us on any outstanding differences and to resolve these to our mutual satisfaction."

Officials said this statement referred to the question whether the Egyptians had violated their

Continued on Page 3, Column 6

Cigarette Warning Is Voted by House

By United Press International

WASHINGTON, June 22—The House passed legislation today to require that cigarette packages carry a warning that smoking may be hazardous to health.

The measure, approved by voice vote, was similar to one passed by the Senate last week. Both bills call for a label reading: "Caution: Cigarette smoking May be Hazardous to Your Health."

The House measure would permanently ban the Federal Trade Commission from extending the warning to cigarette advertising, as it has proposed to do effective July 1.

The commission felt that advertising was the chief means of encouraging young persons to begin smoking and should be regulated.

The Senate measure would prohibit action against adver-

Continued on Page 68, Column 4

ALGERIAN REGIME GAINING SUPPORT

Most Ben Bella Aides Said to Rally to It—Nasser and Chou Back Parley Now

By PETER BRAESTRUP
Special to The New York Times

ALGIERS, June 22—Amid conflicting reports on the prospects for convening the Asian-African leaders' conference here next Tuesday, Col. Houari Boumedienne's four-day-old regime sought today to show continuity at home and to gain recognition abroad.

[In Cairo President Gamal Abdel Nasser of the United Arab Republic and Premier Chou En-lai of Communist China said that the Algiers conference should proceed on schedule. Page 5.]

To combat a "campaign of false rumors," the Algerian Information Ministry said in a statement tonight that only former President Ahmed Ben Bella, who was deposed last Saturday, and five other top politicians had been arrested.

Three Others Listed

The statement said the others included Hadj Ben Alla, President of the National Assembly, Health Minister Mohammed Nekkache and Minister Without Portfolio Abderrahmane Cherif.

Secrecy shrouded both the membership and the deliberations of Colonel Boumedienne's army-backed Revolutionary Council. It appeared, however, to have rallied most of the old Ben Bella Cabinet as well as several former Boumedienne foes, notably Mohand ou el Hadj, a Berber leader, to its support.

This capital appeared calm under army surveillance through the day after yesterday's sporadic left-wing demonstrations staged in favor of Mr. Ben Bella by 50 to 200 students and some women.

But shortly before 9 o'clock tonight, a new demonstration, apparently organized by Communists and other left-wingers, was begun in downtown Algiers.

About a thousand demonstrators, mostly teen-agers, moved across the square in front of the central post office yelling, "Down with Boumedienne!" A

Continued on Page 4, Column 1

NEWS INDEX

U.S. JETS ATTACK NORTH OF HANOI, NEAR RED CHINA

Planes Strike Ammunition Dump and Barracks Area Beyond the Capital

SHIFT IN TACTICS SEEN

A Readiness to Raid Major Military Facilities in New Zone Is Now Indicated

By JACK LANGGUTH
Special to The New York Times

SAIGON, South Vietnam, June 22 — United States Air Force jets flew north of Hanoi today to bomb a North Vietnamese ammunition dump and a barracks area, the latter 80 miles from the Chinese Communist border.

The selection of the targets indicated that the United States was now prepared to raid the large and important military targets in the northern third of the country.

Since the bombing of North Vietnam began last Feb. 7 almost all the raids have been below the 20th Parallel, which is 70 miles south of Hanoi.

Eight F-105 Thunderchiefs struck the Bannuocchieu ammunition depot 70 miles west-northwest of Hanoi today.

Pilots reported only moderate damage from the 17 tons of 750-pound bombs and rockets they dropped.

Raiders Are Escorted

Another group of eight Thunderchiefs struck the Sonla army barracks, which are 110 miles west-northwest of Hanoi. The pilots said they had destroyed nine buildings and damaged 20 others at the site, with 17 more tons of the same type of bombs and rockets as those used at Bannuocchieu. Escorts of 25 Air Force planes supported the raiders on both missions.

[Sonla was first raided June 18 but was not designated as north of Hanoi at that time, The Associated Press reported. A communiqué had located Sonla as west-southwest of Hanoi. The Pentagon said this was a clerical error.]

The pilots who bombed Bannuocchieu said they had encountered some antiaircraft fire but did not see any enemy aircraft. All of the planes returned safely to their bases.

The United States mission here does not disclose the Southeast Asian land bases used in strikes against North Viet-

Continued on Page 2, Column 6

JAPAN AND KOREA RESUME FULL TIES

Treaty's Foes Clash With Police in 2 Capitals

By ROBERT TRUMBULL
Special to The New York Times

TOKYO, June 22—Japan and South Korea today signed a treaty and 20 related documents restoring full diplomatic relations after a lapse of 55 years. The action was a result of 14 years of intermittent negotiations.

The participants in the historic ceremony wore plain business suits, exchanged handshakes in Occidental fashion instead of making Oriental bows and drank a toast in champagne brought in after the ceremony by white-coated waiters.

The police estimated that 10,000 left-wing unionists and students, under Communist leadership, marched through downtown Tokyo today in a protest against the agreement.

About 30 policemen and demonstrators were injured in scuffles, the police said.

[In Seoul 200 Opposition leaders and 8,000 students were involved in clashes with the police and 573 students were arrested. Page 3.]

The demonstrators in Tokyo, who were relatively orderly, asserted that the rapprochement with South Korea was likely to involve Japan in the Vietnam war through the participation of Korean troops in the conflict on South Vietnam's side.

The leftists were also dissatisfied with a clause in the agreement under which Japan recognizes the administration in Seoul as the "only legal government" in Korea. Tokyo has no official relations with the Com-

Continued on Page 3, Column 2

of *The Hollywood Reporter,* on June 22, 1965, across the page from an MGM studio ad announcing proudly that its entire facility was now busy with television work.

The night before the ad appeared, Selznick watched a new film by the French director Jacques Demy, *The Umbrellas of Cherbourg,* and remarked to his son Daniel that the delicately flavored contemporary musical was one of the best made and most entertaining movies he had seen in years. He was due in New York on Thursday for a lunch with Henry Luce to discuss some business ventures, and he wanted to clear up several pending matters, so his schedule for Wednesday included a long session with his attorney Barry Brannen, starting at noon. Their meeting had been going on for an hour when Selznick, according to published accounts, "complained of feeling faint, put his hand on his chest and sat down. An ambulance was called and he was taken to Cedars of Sinai Hospital, where he died at 2:33 P.M. He was 65 years old."

News of his death stunned everyone in the film business. He had been a legend in his own time, one of the authentic giants who was always there as a reminder of what the movies were capable of accomplishing; inactive as he was, Hollywood still felt his presence. To those who had known him or had worked closely with him, the impact of his death was tremendous. Hal Kern remembers the intensity of his disbelief at the news: "I just couldn't believe it. In fact, I think I didn't believe it for two days. You see, I never associated David with death. He had so much life, so much vitality about him, that it just seemed impossible for him to be dead. I think I only finally believed it at the funeral."

A quiet, dignified affair, Selznick's funeral was held on a gray, overcast morning at Forest Lawn Memorial Park in nearby Glendale. At his own request, the services were brief, the eulogies restrained. Newspaper and other media coverage of his death was worldwide and extensive, and the headlines were much as he had predicted: "Producer of 'Gone With The Wind' Dies." Many of the newspapers concluded their obituaries by quoting a remark he had made in 1959. The set of Tara, still standing on the back lot of what was now Desilu Studios, was about to be dismantled and shipped to Atlanta, where a local promoter intended to reconstruct it on the supposed actual site of the plantation as described by Miss Mitchell. Selznick had presided at a small ceremony as the set was taken down and crated. In one of his more melancholy moods he made a short, untypical speech, saying: "Tara was just a facade; it had no rooms in it. It is symbolic of Hollywood, that once photographed, life here is ended."

But *Gone With The Wind* was not ended. In October 1967, it began its seventh tour of U.S. theatres. Exhibited in the new 70 mm stereophonic version that MGM had spent hundreds of thousands of dollars to prepare, and offered as a reserved-seat attraction for the first time in twenty-seven years, the picture once again demonstrated its unique hold on the imagination of audiences by becoming one of the top-grossing films of the year. The new, younger viewers seeing the film for the first time didn't seem to mind the physical alterations in the look and shape of the film, and were immediately caught up in its narrative drive, its excitement, and the unabashed romanticism. In New York, it stayed at the Rivoli Theatre for almost a year, competing for attention with—and ultimately outgrossing—Stanley Kubrick's masterpiece, *2001: A Space Odyssey.* In Hollywood, *Gone With The Wind* opened at the same Carthay Circle Theatre that had been the scene of its original Hollywood premiere and played there for just over a year; at the conclusion of its run, the theatre was demolished to make way for an office building. Nearly a decade later, MGM, which had always displayed considerable shrewdness in its handling of the picture, finally licensed the rights to NBC for a Bicentennial television presentation. The film was telecast in two parts on the evenings of November 7 and 8, 1976. Reduced to less than lifesize, sandwiched in between endless commercials, with its impact sliced up and delivered like salami and its magnificent color squeezed down to tiny garish blobs, it still had the power, by virtue of its mystique and its craftsmanship, to engage and enthrall 77 million Americans—a record audience that stood until the telecast of *Roots,* a romantic epic of another kind and another sensibility.

T HE HOLLYWOOD that David O. Selznick worked in and loved for forty years is gone. Some of the studios still stand, of course, as do many of the landmarks of the town: the Ambassador and Roosevelt hotels, the Hollywood Bowl, the Brown Derby, Grauman's Chinese and Egyptian theatres. What is gone, and what gave the Hollywood of Selznick's time its vitality and influence, are the people who lived and worked there, the people who made the name Hollywood synonymous with a kind of magic—that mysterious, seemingly inexplicable, and extraordinary power to evoke in the beholder a sense of the inexhaustible resources of the mind and spirit. Remnants of this power can still be found at random moments in the work of some of the newer generation, but by and large the commitment to excellence and the standards of quality to which Selznick and his contemporaries devoted their professional lives are sadly lacking today. The past can never be recaptured, that much is certain. But what can be recaptured, and what makes the films in this book live and reverberate with a life beyond their creators, are the same elements that gave those films their appeal to three generations of moviegoers: taste, imagination, idealism, and a concern for the integrity and intelligence of the audience. In an address that Selznick gave at the University of Rochester in May 1940, he spoke of these intangibles and about his love of the moviemaking process, the pride of craftsmanship, and the satisfaction of carefully, painstakingly laboring over the details of a film because of the deeply held conviction that the motion picture was a powerful force for good in the world. At the end of his speech, he expressed just what the movies had meant to him, to me, and to everyone who ever stared in hopeful anticipation at a blank movie screen:

> To you who feel the burning urge to influence the modes and manners, the social and political ideologies of the future through the medium of the motion picture, I say, Here is a challenge, here is a frontier that is and always will be crying for the courage and the energy and the initiative and the genius of American youth. Here is the Southwest Passage to fame and fortune and influence! Here is the El Dorado of the heart, the soul and the mind.

THE END

A SELZNICK INTERNATIONAL PICTURE

Hollywood—1980

David O. Selznick's Hollywood:
Written & Produced by Ronald Haver
Designed by Thomas Ingalls
Executive Producer: Robert Gottlieb
Associate Producer: Martha Kaplan
In Charge of Production: Ellen McNeilly
Design Associate: Heather McRae
Chief Research Associate: Joan Cohen
  Assisted by:
  Sharon McCormick
  Janet Brunie
  Barbara Lauter
  Rod Dwyer
  David Chierichetti
  Neal Aberman
  Tim Hunter
  Rick Sandford
  Claudia Kunze

Grateful acknowledgment is made to the following institutions and individuals, without whose efforts this book would be less than it is.

In Hollywood

At the American Film Institute—Center for Advanced Film Studies
Anne Schlosser
James Powers
Adam Bedoun

At ABC Entertainment
Arthur Schimmel

At the Academy of Motion Picture Arts and Sciences
Mildred Simpson
Bonnie Rothbart
Robert Cushman
Sam Gill
Carol Epstein
Stacy Endres
Rodney Recor

At Bekins Archival Services
Jimmy Boston
Rico Mancini

At Book City Collectibles
Marci Siegal

At Cherokee Books
Oliver Durnberger

At Collectors Book Store
Malcolm Willits
Mark Willoughby

Everybody's Book Shop

At Eddie Brandt's Saturday Matinee
Eddie Brandt
Mike Hawks

At The Hollywood Reporter
Tichi Wilkerson Miles
Carl Schaeffer

At Graphic Process—Third Street (black-and-white frame blow-ups and photocopying)
Frank Salgado
Steve Higashi

Hank Edow
Jerry Wong

At Larry Edmunds Book Shop
Milt Luboviski
Git Luboviski
Din Luboviski
Phil Luboviski
Claude Plum

At the Los Angeles Herald-Examiner
Judy Jacobson

The Los Angeles Public Library

At the Los Angeles Times
John Snyder
Nancy Tew

At MGM
Frank Davis
Herbert Nusbaum
Dore Freeman
Ben Presser
Florence Warner

At Marie Cowdrey Graphicolor (Technicolor frame enlargements and color photocopying)
Bruce Kohigashi
Buncha Chusub
Jim Inouye
Billie Ackerman

At ReproColor (Technicolor frame enlargements and color retouching and correcting)
Max Jaikin
Bill Hosie
Ray Price
Dorothy McKellar

In Sung Han
Joanne Costa
Elsie Kozuh

At RKO Radio Pictures
Vernon Harbin
John Hall
Karen Murphy
Lloyd Cohn
Jack Curtis

At the Society of Motion Picture and Television Art Directors
Phyllis Harper

At Technicolor Incorporated
Tom Tarr

At 20th Century-Fox
Frank Rodriguez

At the UCLA Film Archive
Bob Epstein
Robert Gitt

The UCLA Map Library

At the UCLA Theatre Arts Library
Bernard Galm

The Doheny Library at USC

Projectionists:
Steve Stuart
Ted Dodd
Jim Farquharson
William Stoddard
Mike Maday
Ron Barth

In New York City

Culver Pictures

At Movie Star News
Paula Klaw
Ira Kramer

At the Memory Shop
Marc Ricci

At the Museum of Modern Art
Mary Corliss
Carlos Clarens
Adrienne Mancia
Larry Kardish
Steve Soba
Mary Lea Bandy

At the New York Times
John J. Stanton, Jr.
Barbara Langenberger

At RKO Radio Pictures
Al Korn

At Time magazine
Marian Powers

The New York Public Library

The Library for the Performing Arts at Lincoln Center

At Alfred A. Knopf, Inc.
Robert Gottlieb
Martha Kaplan
Ellen McNeilly
Karen Latuchie
Neal Jones
Eva Resnikova
Dana Cole
Jane Friedman
William Loverd
Richard Tanner

In Atlanta

At the Atlanta Journal-Constitution
William H. Fields

In San Francisco

McDonald's Book Shop

Loew's Warfield Theatre

The San Francisco Public Library

The Center Theatre

Valuable Assistance Provided By

Robert Bennett
David Bradley
Jeff Capp
Ross Carron
Rich Correll
Doug Edwards
Henry Franklin
Bob Greenberg
Nancy Grubb
Greg Holding
Peter Johnson
David Shepard
Steve Stuart
Jonathan Taylor
Marc Wanamaker
Kent Warner
Bill Whitehead
and John Henry Wilborn, Jr.

Photo Credits

All visual material in this book is from the author's collection and the archives of Selznick Properties, Limited, except as noted below:

Academy of Motion Picture Arts and Sciences—Margaret Herrick Library
4, 8, 11, 17(top), 28–29, 30, 31, 32, 56, 72–73, 94, 99(bottom, left & right)

American Film Institute—Charles K. Feldman Library
98–99(top), 119

Rudy Behlmer
56(top), 88(top)

James Bigwood
348(bottom)

Bison Archives (Los Angeles)
20, 21, 25, 26, 27, 35, 36, 37, 38–51, 66, 67, 68, 114(bottom), 121, 124, 179(bottom, left & right)

Anton Bruehl
184–185

David Chierichetti
371, 381

Coca-Cola
131

Collectors Book Store (Los Angeles)
200

Merian C. Cooper
84, 101

Culver Pictures (New York)
2–3, 5

Linwood Dunn
69 (middle, right)

Eddie Brandt's Saturday Matinee (Los Angeles)
71, 232, 333, 390(top)

Gary Essert
392, 403

Larry Holland
19

The Hollywood Reporter
386

House & Garden
259, 272(top, left & right), 273(top, left & right), 287 (Copyright 1939, 1967 by Conde Nast Publications, Inc.)

Los Angeles Herald-Examiner
34, 120, 356(top)

Metro-Goldwyn-Mayer
All stills and frame enlargements from the following films:

Spoilers of the West © Metro-Goldwyn-Mayer Distributing Corporation 1927; renewed Loew's Incorporated 1955.
Dinner at Eight © Metro-Goldwyn-Mayer Corporation 1933; renewed Metro-Goldwyn-Mayer Inc. 1960.
Night Flight © Metro-Goldwyn-Mayer Corporation 1933; renewed Metro-Goldwyn-Mayer Inc. 1960.
Dancing Lady © Metro-Goldwyn-Mayer Corporation 1933; renewed Metro-Goldwyn-Mayer Inc. 1960.
Viva Villa! © Metro-Goldwyn-Mayer Corporation 1934; renewed Metro-Goldwyn-Mayer Inc. 1961.
Meet the Baron © Metro-Goldwyn-Mayer Corporation 1933; renewed Metro-Goldwyn-Mayer Inc. 1960.
Vanessa: Her Love Story © Metro-Goldwyn-Mayer Corporation 1935; renewed Metro-Goldwyn-Mayer Inc. 1962.
Anna Karenina © Metro-Goldwyn-Mayer Corporation 1935; renewed Metro-Goldwyn-Mayer Inc. 1962.
Reckless © Metro-Goldwyn-Mayer Corporation 1935; renewed Metro-Goldwyn-Mayer Inc. 1962.
Manhattan Melodrama © Metro-Goldwyn-Mayer Corporation 1934; renewed Metro-Goldwyn-Mayer Inc. 1961.
A Tale of Two Cities © Metro-Goldwyn-Mayer Corporation 1935; renewed Metro-Goldwyn-Mayer Inc. 1962.
David Copperfield © Metro-Goldwyn-Mayer Corporation 1935; renewed Metro-Goldwyn-Mayer Inc. 1962.
The Prisoner of Zenda © Selznick International Pictures Inc. 1937; renewed Metro-Goldwyn-Mayer Inc. 1964.
Gone With The Wind © Selznick International Pictures Inc. 1939; renewed Metro-Goldwyn-Mayer Inc. 1967.

Movie Star News (New York)
40, 41, 42, 49, 52, 53, 59, 60, 62, 390(bottom)

Museum of Modern Art Stills Archive
24, 33, 39, 44, 58, 79(top), 98(bottom, left), 132, 145, 288, 289, 316, 370, 408

New York Times
305, 410

Darlene O'Brien
82, 83, 85(top, right), 105(top & right), 110(top), 114(top; left, center, & right), 115(bottom, right)

Fred Parrish
254–255, 275(top), 278

Walter Plunkett
245(bottom)

Alan Rivkin
136

RKO (New York)
76, 77, 88(bottom), 89, 90, 91, 93, 104, 106–107, 109, 110(middle & bottom), 112, 113, 115, 117 (All material copyrighted by RKO Radio Pictures; renewed by RKO General. Reproduced by permission.)

Murray Spivack
74(top), 111

Technicolor Incorporated
96, 178, 249(bottom), 266(top, left), 272(bottom, right), 281(first row, right)

Time-Life Incorporated
307

UCLA Map Library
22

Raul Vega
412

Marc Wanamaker
gatefold

Dan Woodruff
178(top, left)

David O. Selznick Filmography

* Academy Award winner
** Academy Award nominee
Nonfiction short films not included.

Roulette

Aetna Pictures (distributed by Selznick Distributing Co.)
50 minutes (5 reels); silent

Director S.E.V. Taylor *Scenario* Gerald C. Duffy, from a story by William Briggs MacHarg *Adaptation* Gerald C. Duffy and Lewis Allen Browne *Cast* Lois Carrington: Edith Roberts; John Tralee: Norman Trevor; Ben Corcoran: Maurice Costello; Mrs. Harris: Mary Carr; Peter Marineaux: Walter Booth; Mrs. Marineaux: Effie Shannon; Dan Carrington: Montagu Love

New York: January 19, 1924, Loew's

Spoilers of the West

Metro-Goldwyn-Mayer
60 minutes; silent

Director W.S. Van Dyke *Screenplay* Madeleine Ruthven and Ross B. Wills, from a story by John Thomas Neville *Photography* Clyde De Vinna *Costumes* Lucia Coulter *Editor* Dan Sharits *Cast* Lt. Lang: Tim McCoy; The Girl: Marjorie Daw; The Girl's Brother: William Fairbanks; Red Cloud: Chief Big Tree

New York: March 12, 1928, Loew's American; London: January 1929, general release

Wyoming

Metro-Goldwyn-Mayer
50 minutes (5 reels)†

Director W.S. Van Dyke *Scenario* Madeleine Ruthven and Ross B. Wills *Writer* W.S. Van Dyke *Photography* Clyde De Vinna *Wardrobe* Lucia Coulter *Editor* William Le Vanway *Titles* Ruth Cummings *Cast* Lt. Jack Colter: Tim McCoy; Samantha Jerusha Farrell: Dorothy Sebastian; Chief Big Cloud: Charles Bell; Buffalo Bill: William Fairbanks; An Indian: Chief Big Tree

March 24, 1928, general release

† *American Film Institute catalogue notes that "indication in copyright records that the film has sound has not been verified."*

Forgotten Faces

Paramount-Famous-Lasky
80 minutes (8 reels); silent

Director Victor Schertzinger *Scenario* Howard Estabrook, from a story by Richard W. Child *Adaptation* Oliver H.P. Garrett *Photography* J. Roy Hunt *Editor* George Nichols, Jr. *Titles* Julian Johnson *Cast* Heliotrope Harry Harlow: Clive Brook; Alice Deane: Mary Brian; Lilly Harlow: [Olga] Baclanova; Froggy: William Powell

New York: August 5, 1928, Paramount; Los Angeles: August 17, 1928, Metropolitan; London: April 8, 1929, Shepherd's Bush Pavilion

Chinatown Nights

Paramount-Famous-Lasky
82 minutes; part talking

Director William Wellman *Screenplay* Ben Grauman Kohn and Oliver H.P. Garrett, from the novel *Tong War* by Samuel Ornitz *Photography* Henry Gerrard *Art Direction* Wiard Ihnen (uncredited) *Editor* Allyson Shaffer *Cast* Chuck Riley: Wallace Beery; Joan Fry: Florence Vidor; Boston Charley: Warner Oland; The Shadow: Jack McHugh; The Reporter: Jack Oakie

Los Angeles: March 14, 1929, Paramount; New York: March 31, 1929, Paramount; London: December 9, 1929, Stoll, Kingsway, Kensington

The Man I Love

Paramount-Famous-Lasky
74 minutes

Director William Wellman *Screenplay* Herman J. Mankiewicz *Photography* Henry Gerrard *Costumes* Travis Banton *Song* Leo Robin and Richard Whiting *Editor* Allyson Shaffer *Cast* Dum-Dum Brooks: Richard Arlen; Celia Fields: Mary Brian; Sonia Barondoff: [Olga] Baclanova; Curly Bloom: Harry Green; Lew Layton: Jack Oakie

New York: May 27, 1929, Paramount; Los Angeles: June 21, 1929, Paramount; London: February 10, 1930, Kensington

The Four Feathers

Paramount-Famous-Lasky
81 minutes; musical score and sound effects

Directors Merian C. Cooper, Ernest B. Schoedsack, and Lothar Mendes *Screenplay* Howard Estabrook and Hope Loring, from the novel by A.E.W. Mason *Photography* Robert Kurrle, Merian C. Cooper, and Ernest B. Schoedsack *Costumes* Travis Banton *Music* William Frederick Peters *Editor* Ernest B. Schoedsack *Cast* Harry Faversham: Richard Arlen; Ethne Eustace: Fay Wray; Lt. Durrance: Clive Brook; Captain Trench: William Powell; Slave Trader: Noah Beery

New York: June 12, 1929, Criterion; Los Angeles: July 24, 1929, United Artists; London: September 12, 1929, Carlton, Haymarket

The Dance of Life

Paramount-Famous-Lasky
130 minutes; part Technicolor

Directors John Cromwell and Edward Sutherland *Screenplay* Benjamin Glazer, from the play *Burlesque* by George Manker Watters *Photography* J. Roy Hunt *Art Direction* Wiard Ihnen *Costumes* Travis Banton *Songs* Richard Whiting, Leo Robin, and Sam Coslow *Technicolor Supervisor* Natalie Kalmus *Editor* George Nichols, Jr. *Cast* Bonny Lee King: Nancy Carroll; Ralph "Skid" Johnson: Hal Skelly; Harvey Howell: Ralph Theodore; Lefty: Charles Brown; Sylvia Marco: Dorothy Revier; Bozo: Al St. John; Gussie: May Boley; Jerry: Oscar Levant

New York: August 15, 1929, Rivoli; Los Angeles: October 1, 1929, United Artists; London: November 14, 1929, Plaza

Street of Chance

Paramount-Famous-Lasky
75 minutes

Director John Cromwell *Screenplay* Howard Estabrook,** from a story by Oliver H.P. Garrett *Photography* Charles Lang *Art Direction* Wiard Ihnen *Costumes* Travis Banton *Editor* Otto Levering *Cast* John B. Marsden ("Natural" Davis): William Powell; Judith Marsden: Jean Arthur; Alma Marsden: Kay Francis; "Babe" Marsden: Regis Toomey; Dorgan: Stanley Fields; Al Mastick: Brooks Benedict

New York: February 2, 1930, Rialto; Los Angeles: February 20, 1930, Paramount; London: May 1, 1930, Plaza

Sarah and Son

Paramount-Famous-Lasky
80 minutes

Director Dorothy Arzner *Screenplay* Zoë Akins, from the novel by Timothy Shea *Photography* Charles Lang *Art Direction* Van Nest Polglase *Costumes* Edward Gross *Music* Nathaniel Finston *Editor* Verna Willis *Cast* Sarah Storm: Ruth Chatterton;** Howard Vanning: Fredric March; Jim Gray: Fuller Mellish, Jr.; John Ashmore: Gilbert Emery; Mrs. Ashmore: Doris Lloyd; Cyril Belloc: William Stack; Bobby: Philippe De Lacy

New York: March 14, 1930, Paramount; Los Angeles: March 20, 1930, Paramount; London: May 23, 1930, Plaza

Honey

Paramount-Famous-Lasky
75 minutes

Director Wesley Ruggles *Screenplay and Adaptation* Herman J. Mankiewicz, from the novel and play *Come Out of the Kitchen* by Alice Duer Miller and A.E. Thomas *Photography* Henry Gerrard *Songs* W. Franke Harling and Sam Coslow *Dances* David Bennett *Sound Recording* Harry M. Lindgren *Titles* Herman J. Mankiewicz *Cast* Olivia Dangerfield: Nancy Carroll; Burton Crane: Stanley Smith; Charles Dangerfield: Skeets Gallagher; Cora Falkner: Lillian Roth; J. William Burnstein: Harry Green; Mayme: Zasu Pitts

Los Angeles: March 27, 1930, Paramount; New York: March 28, 1930, Paramount; London: February 2, 1931, general release

The Texan

Paramount-Publix
79 minutes

Director John Cromwell *Screenplay* Daniel Nathan Rubin, from the story "A Double-Dyed Deceiver" by O. Henry *Adaptation* Oliver H.P. Garrett *Photography* Victor Milner *Songs* L. Wolfe Gilbert and Abel Baer *Sound Recording* Harry M. Lindgren *Editor* Verna Willis *Cast* Enrique (The Llano Kid): Gary Cooper; Consuelo: Fay Wray; Señora Ibarra: Emma Dunn; Thacker: Oscar Apfel

Los Angeles: May 1, 1930, Paramount; New York: May 16, 1930, Paramount; London: July 24, 1930, Plaza

For the Defense

Paramount-Publix
65 minutes

Director John Cromwell *Scenario & Dialogue* Oliver H.P. Garrett, from a story by Charles Furthman *Photography* Charles Lang *Sound Recording* Harold M. McNiff *Editor* George Nichols, Jr. *Cast* William Foster: William Powell; Irene Manners: Kay Francis; Defoe: Scott Kolk; District Attorney Stone: William B. Davidson

New York: July 18, 1930, Paramount; Los Angeles: August 14, 1930; Paramount; London: October 2, 1930, Plaza

Manslaughter

Paramount-Publix
85 minutes

Director George Abbott *Adaptation* George Abbott, from the 1922 film by Cecil B. De Mille *Photography* Archie J. Stout *Sound Recording* Earl Hayman *Editor* Otto Levering *Cast* Lydia Thorne: Claudette Colbert; Dan O'Bannon: Fredric March; Miss Bennett: Emma Dunn; Eleanor: Natalie Moorhead

New York: July 23, 1930, Rivoli; Los Angeles: July 31, 1930, Paramount; London: March 19, 1931, Astoria

Laughter

Paramount-Publix
81 minutes

Director Harry d'Abbadie d'Arrast *Screenplay* Donald Ogden Stewart,** from a story by Harry d'Abbadie d'Arrast** and Douglas Doty** *Photography* George Folsey *Art Direction* William Salter and Van Nest Polglase *Costumes* Caroline Putnam *Music* Frank Tours *Editor* Helene Turner *Cast* Peggy Gibson: Nancy Carroll; Paul Lockridge: Fredric March; G. Mortimer Gibson: Diane Ellis; Benham: Leonard Carey; Pearl: Ollie Burgoyne

New York: November 14, 1930, Paramount, Paramount (Brooklyn)

The Lost Squadron

RKO
72 minutes

Director George Archainbaud *Screenplay* Wallace Smith and Herman J. Mankiewicz *Photography* Leo Tovar and Edward Cronjager *Aerial Photography* Rob Robinson and Elmer Dyer *Art Direction & Costumes* Max Ree *Music* Max Steiner *Cast* Captain Gibson: Richard Dix; Follette Marsh: Mary Astor; Von Furst: Erich von Stroheim; The Pest: Dorothy Jordan; Red: Joel McCrea; Woody: Robert Armstrong; Fritz: Hugh Herbert; Detective: Ralph Ince; The Fliers: Dick Grace, Art Gobel, Leo Nomis, and Frank Clark

New York: March 10, 1932, Mayfair; Los Angeles: April 16, 1932, Orpheum; London: May 26, 1932, Tivoli

Symphony of Six Million

RKO
94 minutes

Associate Producer Pandro S. Berman *Director* Gregory LaCava *Screenplay* Bernard Schubert and J. Walter Ruben, from the novel by Fannie Hurst *Photography* Leo Tovar *Art Direction* Carroll Clark *Music* Max Steiner *Editor* Archie Marshek *Cast* Felix Klauber: Ricardo Cortez; Jessica: Irene Dunne; Hannah: Anna Appel; Meyer Klauber: Gregory Ratoff; Birdie Klauber: Lita Chevret; Magnus Klauber: Noel Madison; Miss Spencer: Helen Freeman

New York: April 14, 1932, Gaeity; Los Angeles: May 13, 1932, Orpheum; London: (under the title *Melody of Life*) June 15, 1933, Tivoli

State's Attorney

RKO
73 minutes

Director George Archainbaud *Screenplay* Gene Fowler and Rowland Brown, from a story by Louis Stevens *Photography* Leo Tovar *Editors* Charles Kimball and William Hamilton *Cast* Tom Cardigan: John Barrymore; June Perry: Helen Twelvetrees; Vanny Powers: William Boyd

New York: May 5, 1932, Mayfair; Los Angeles: June 23, 1932, Pantages

Westward Passage

RKO
73 minutes

Director Robert Milton *Screenplay* Bradley King and Humphrey Pearson, from the novel by Margaret Ayer Barnes *Photography* Lucien Andriot *Music* Max Steiner *Editor* Charles Craft *Cast* Olivia: Ann Harding; Nick Allen: Laurence Olivier; Harry Lanman: Irving Pichel; Henrietta: Juliette Compton: Mrs. Truesdale: Zasu Pitts; Little Olivia: Bonita Granville

New York: June 3, 1932, Mayfair; Los Angeles: June 11, 1932, Orpheum; London: September 15, 1932, New Victoria

What Price Hollywood?

RKO
78 minutes

Associate Producer Pandro S. Berman *Director* George Cukor *Screenplay* Jane Murfin, Ben Markson, Gene Fowler, and Rowland Brown, from a story by Adela Rogers St. John** *Photography* Charles Rosher *Art Direction* Carroll Clark *Costumes* Walter Plunkett *Music* Max Steiner *Editor* Jack Kitchen *Cast* Mary Evans: Constance Bennett; Max Carey: Lowell Sherman; Lenny Borden: Neil Hamilton; Julius Saxe: Gregory Ratoff; Cassie: Louise Beavers; Butler: James Eddie Anderson

Los Angeles: July 9, 1932, Orpheum; New York: July 15, 1932, Mayfair; London: September 8, 1932, New Gallery

Roar of the Dragon
RKO
68 minutes

Director Wesley Ruggles *Screenplay* Merian C. Cooper, from the story "Passage to Hong Kong" by George Kibbe Turner *Photography* Edward Cronjager *Editors* William Hamilton, Jane Bigelow, and Howard Estabrook *Cast* Captain Carson: Richard Dix; Natascha: Gwili Andre; Busby: Edward Everett Horton; Helen: Arline Judge; Gabby Tourist: Zasu Pitts

Los Angeles: July 23, 1932, Orpheum; New York: July 24, 1932, Palace; London: October 27, 1932, Dominion

Age of Consent
RKO
65 minutes

Director Gregory LaCava *Screenplay* Sarah Y. Mason and Francis Cockrell, from the play *Cross Roads* by Martin Flavin *Photography* Roy Hunt *Editor* Jack Kitchen *Cast* Betty Cameron: Dorothy Wilson; Michael Harvey: Richard Cromwell; Duke Galloway: Eric Linden; Dora: Arline Judge

Los Angeles: August 12, 1932, Orpheum; New York: September 2, 1932, Palace; London: January 12, 1933, Regal

Bird of Paradise
RKO
80 minutes

Director King Vidor *Screenplay* Wells Root and Wanda Tuchock, from the play by Richard Walton Tully *Photography* Sid Hickox and Clyde De Vinna *Art Direction* Carroll Clark *Music* Max Steiner *Dances* Busby Berkeley *Editor* Archie Marshek *Cast* Luana: Dolores Del Rio; Johnny Baker: Joel McCrea; Mac: John Halliday; Thornton: Creighton Chaney; Chester: Richard Gallagher; Hector: Bert Roach; The King: Pukui; Medicine Man: Agostino Borgato; Old Native Woman: Sophie Ortego

Los Angeles: September 2, 1932, Orpheum; New York: September 9, 1932, Mayfair; London: January 10, 1933, New Gallery

A Bill of Divorcement
RKO
75 minutes

Director George Cukor *Screenplay* Howard Estabrook and Harry Wagstaff Gribble, from the play by Clemence Dane *Photography* Sid Hickox *Art Direction* Carroll Clark *Costumes* Josette De Lima *Editor* Arthur Roberts *Cast* Hilary Fairfield: John Barrymore; Margaret Fairfield: Billie Burke; Sydney Fairfield: Katharine Hepburn; Kit Pumphrey: David Manners; Gareth: Bramwell Fletcher; Dr. Alliot: Henry Stephenson; Gary Meredith: Paul Cavanagh

New York: October 2, 1932, Mayfair; Los Angeles: October 21, 1932, Hillstreet; London: March 6, 1933, Regal

The Conquerors
RKO
80 minutes

Director William Wellman *Screenplay* Robert Lord, from a story by Howard Estabrook *Photography* Edward Cronjager *Art Direction* Carroll Clark *Music* Max Steiner *Transitional Effects* Slavko Vorkapich *Editor* William Hamilton *Cast* Roger Standish: Richard Dix; Caroline Standish: Ann Harding; Matilda Blake: Edna May Oliver; Dr. Daniel Blake: Guy Kibbee; Frances Standish: Julie Haydon; Warren Lennox: Donald Cook; Stubby: Harry Holman; Benson: Richard Gallagher

New York: November 20, 1932, Mayfair; Los Angeles: November 24, 1932, Hillstreet; London: February 14, 1933, New Gallery

Rockabye
RKO-Pathé
71 minutes

Director George Cukor *Screenplay* Jane Murfin and Kubec Glasmon, from the play by Lucia Bronder *Photography* Charles Rosher *Editor* George Hively *Cast* Judy Carroll: Constance Bennett; Jake Pell: Joel McCrea; De Sola: Paul Lukas; Commissioner Howard: Walter Pidgeon; Man in Night Club: Sterling Holloway

New York: December 4, 1932, Mayfair; London: February 5, 1933, Alhambra

The Animal Kingdom
RKO
90 minutes

Director Edward H. Griffith *Screenplay* Horace Jackson, from the play by Philip Barry *Photography* Lucien Andriot *Editor* Daniel Mandel *Cast* Tom Collier: Leslie Howard; Daisy Sage: Ann Harding; Cecelia Henry: Myrna Loy; Owen: Neil Hamilton; Regan: William Gargan

New York: December 29, 1932, Roxy; Los Angeles: January 1, 1933, Hillstreet; London: (under the title *A Woman in His House*) August 1, 1933, Plaza

The Half-Naked Truth
RKO
67 minutes

Director Gregory LaCava *Screenplay* Ben Markson, H.N. Swanson, Bartlett Cormack, and Corey Ford, from the autobiographical stories of Harry Reichenbach in *Phantom Fame,* as told to David Freedman *Photography* Bert Glennon *Music* Max Steiner *Editor* C.L. Kimball *Cast* Teresita: Lupe Velez; James Bates: Lee Tracy; Achilles: Eugene Pallette; Farrell: Frank Morgan

Los Angeles: December 25, 1932, Hillstreet; New York: December 30, 1932, Mayfair; London: March 23, 1933, Plaza

Topaze
RKO
78 minutes

Director Harry d'Abbadie d'Arrast *Screenplay* Ben Hecht, from Benn W. Levy's adaptation of the play by Marcel Pagnol *Photography* Lucien Andriot *Art Direction* Van Nest Polglase *Music* Max Steiner *Editor* William Hamilton *Cast* Auguste Topaze: John Barrymore; Coco: Myrna Loy; Henri: Albert Conti; Dr. Bomb: Luis Alberni; Baron de Latour-Latour: Reginald Mason; Baroness de Latour-Latour: Jobyna Howland; Charlemagne de Latour-Latour: Jackie Serle; Dr. Stegg: Frank Reicher

New York: February 9, 1933, Radio City Music Hall; Los Angeles: February 24, 1933, Hillstreet; London: April 2, 1933, Empire

The Great Jasper
RKO
76 minutes

Director J. Walter Ruben *Screenplay* H.W. Hanemann and Robert Tasker, from the novel by Fulton Oursler *Photography* Leo Tovar *Editor* Arthur Roberts *Cast* Jasper Horn: Richard Dix; Jenny Horn: Florence Eldridge; Norma McGowd: Wera Engels; Madame Taime: Edna May Oliver; James Bush: Bruce Cabot

New York: February 16, 1933, Radio City Music Hall; Los Angeles: March 10, 1933, Hillstreet; London: October 9, 1933, Davis, Croyden

Our Betters
RKO
78 minutes

Director George Cukor *Screenplay* Jane Murfin and Harry Wagstaff Gribble, from the play by W. Somerset Maugham *Photography* Charles Rosher *Editor* Jack Kitchin *Cast* Lady Pearl Grayston: Constance Bennett; Pepi D'Costa: Gilbert Roland; Fleming Harvey: Charles Starrett; Bessie: Anita Louise; Thornton Clay: Grant Mitchell; Duchess: Violet Kemble-Cooper

New York: February 23, 1933, Radio City Music Hall; Los Angeles: April 21, 1933, Hillstreet; London: May 13, 1933, Plaza

King Kong
RKO
100 minutes

Directors Ernest B. Schoedsack and Merian C. Cooper *Screenplay* James Creelman and Ruth Rose, from a story by Merian C. Cooper and Edgar Wallace *Photography* Edward Lindon, Verne Walker, and J.O. Taylor *Art Direction* Carroll Clark and Al Herman *Costumes* Walter Plunkett *Music* Max Steiner *Sound Effects* Murray Spivack *Chief Technician* Willis O'Brien *Editor* Ted Cheesman *Cast* Ann Darrow: Fay Wray; Carl Denham: Robert Armstrong; Driscoll: Bruce Cabot; Englehorn: Frank Reicher; Weston: Sam Hardy; Native Chief: Noble Johnson; Second Mate: James Flavin; Witch Doctor: Steve Clemento; Charlie: Victor Wong

New York: March 2, 1933, Radio City Music Hall, Roxy; Los Angeles: March 16, 1933, Grauman's Chinese; London: April 17, 1933, Coliseum

Christopher Strong
RKO
72 minutes

Associate Producer Pandro S. Berman *Director* Dorothy Arzner *Screenplay* Zoë Akins, from the novel by Gilbert Frankau *Photography* Bert Glennon *Art Direction* Van Nest Polglase *Music* Max Steiner *Editor* Arthur Roberts *Cast* Lady Cynthia Darrington: Katharine Hepburn; Sir Christopher Strong: Colin Clive; Elaine Strong: Billie Burke; Monica Strong: Helen Chandler; Harry Rawlinson: Ralph Forbes; Carlo: Jack LaRue

New York: March 9, 1933, Radio City Music Hall; Los Angeles: May 12, 1933, Hillstreet; London: July 1, 1933, Plaza

Sweepings
RKO
80 minutes

Director John Cromwell *Screenplay* Lester Cohen, Howard Estabrook, and H.W. Hanemann, from the novel by Lester Cohen *Photography* Edward Cronjager *Editor* George Nichols *Cast* Daniel Pardway: Lionel Barrymore; Thane Pardway: Allan Dinehart; Fred Pardway: Eric Linden; Gene Pardway: William Gargan; Phoebe: Gloria Stuart

New York: March 23, 1933, Radio City Music Hall; Los Angeles: April 14, 1933, Hillstreet; London: August 21, 1933, Plaza

The Monkey's Paw
RKO
52 minutes

Director Wesley Ruggles *Screenplay* Louise M. Parker and Graham John, from the short story by W.W. Jacobs *Photography* Leo Tovar *Editor* Charles L. Kimball *Cast* C. Aubrey Smith; Ivan Simpson; Louise Carter; Bramwell Fletcher

New York: May 30, 1933, Loew's †; Birmingham (England): June 19, 1933, Forum

† *Played for one day only, on a double bill*

Dinner at Eight
Metro-Goldwyn-Mayer
113 minutes

Director George Cukor *Screenplay* Herman J. Mankiewicz and Frances Marion, from the play by George S. Kaufman and Edna Ferber *Photography* William Daniels *Art Direction* Cedric Gibbons and Hobe Erwin *Costumes* Adrian *Music* William Axt *Editor* Ben Lewis *Cast* Carlotta Vance: Marie Dressler; Larry Renault: John Barrymore; Dan Packard: Wallace Beery; Kitty Packard: Jean Harlow; Oliver Jordan: Lionel Barrymore; Max Kane: Lee Tracy; Dr. Wayne Talbot: Edmund Lowe; Mrs. Oliver Jordan: Billie Burke; Paula Jordan: Madge Evans; Jo Stengel: Jean Hersholt; Mrs. Talbot: Karen Morley

New York: August 23, 1933, Astor; Los Angeles: August 29, 1933, Grauman's Chinese; London: September 16, 1933, Plaza

Night Flight
Metro-Goldwyn-Mayer
84 minutes

Director Clarence Brown *Screenplay* Oliver H.P. Garrett, from the novel by Antoine de Saint-Exupéry *Photography* Oliver T. Marsh, Elmer Dyer, and Charles Marshall *Art Direction* Alexander Toluboff *Editor* Hal C. Kern *Cast* Rivière: John Barrymore; Mme Fabien: Helen Hayes; Jules Fabien: Clark Gable; Robineau: Lionel Barrymore; Auguste Pellerin: Robert Montgomery; Brazilian Pilot's Wife: Myrna Loy; Brazilian Pilot: William Gargan; Daudet: C. Henry Gordon

Los Angeles: October 5, 1933, Loew's State; New York: October 6, 1933, Capitol; London: November 4, 1933, Empire

Meet the Baron
Metro-Goldwyn-Mayer
65 minutes

Director Walter Lang *Screenplay* Allen Rivkin and P.J. Wolfson, from a story by Herman J. Mankiewicz and Norman Krasna *Photography* Allen Siegler *Songs* Jimmy McHugh and Dorothy Fields *Editor* James E. Newcom *Cast* Baron: Jack Pearl; Joe McGoo: Jimmy Durante; Zasu: Zasu Pitts; Ted: Ted Healy; Dean Primrose: Edna May Oliver

New York: October 27, 1933, Capitol, Loew's Metropolitan (Brooklyn); Los Angeles: November 16, 1933, Loew's State; London: May 21, 1934, Metropole

Dancing Lady
Metro-Goldwyn-Mayer
94 minutes

Associate Producer John Considine *Director* Robert Z. Leonard *Screenplay* Allen Rivkin and P.J. Wolfson, from the novel by James W. Bellah *Photography* Oliver T. Marsh *Art Direction* Merrill Pye *Costumes* Adrian *Songs* Burton Lane and Harold Adamson, Richard Rodgers and Lorenz Hart, Jimmy McHugh, Dorothy Fields, and Arthur Freed *Dances* Sammy Lee and Eddie Prinz *Editor* Margaret Booth *Cast* Janie Barlow: Joan Crawford; Patch Gallagher: Clark Gable; Tod Newton: Franchot Tone; Mrs. Newton: May Robson; Fred Astaire: himself; Ward King: Robert Benchley; Nelson Eddy: himself; Steve: Ted Healy; His Stooges: Moe Howard, Jerry Howard, and Larry Fine

New York: November 31, 1933, Capitol, Loew's Metropolitan; Los Angeles: December 28, 1933, Loew's State; London: April 16, 1934, Dominion, Metropole

Viva Villa!**
Metro-Goldwyn-Mayer
100 minutes

Director Jack Conway *Screenplay* Ben Hecht,** suggested by the book by Edgcumb Pinchon and O.B. Stade *Photography* James Wong Howe and Charles G. Clarke *Art Direction* Harry Oliver *Costumes* Dolly Tree *Music* Herbert Stothart *Editor* Robert J. Kern *Cast* Pancho Villa: Wallace Beery; Sierra: Leo Carillo; Teresa: Fay Wray; Don Felipe del Castillo: Donald Cook; Johnny Sykes: Stuart Erwin; Emilio Chavito: George E. Stone

New York: April 10, 1934, Criterion; London: May 3, 1934, Empire; Los Angeles: May 17, 1934, Loew's State

Manhattan Melodrama
Metro-Goldwyn-Mayer
93 minutes

Director W.S. Van Dyke *Screenplay* Oliver H.P. Garrett and Joseph L. Mankiewicz, from a story by Arthur Caesar* *Photography* James Wong Howe *Art Direction* Cedric Gibbons *Costumes* Dolly Tree *Song* Richard Rodgers and Lorenz Hart *Editor* Ben Lewis *Cast* Blackie Gallagher: Clark Gable; Jim Wade: William Powell; Eleanor: Myrna Loy; Father Joe: Leo Carrillo; Spud: Nat Pendleton; Poppa Rosen: George Sidney; Annabelle: Isabel Jewell; Tootsie: Muriel Evans; Mr. Snow: Thomas Jackson

New York: May 4, 1934, Capitol, Loew's Metropolitan (Brooklyn); London: May 24, 1934, Empire; Los Angeles: June 20, 1934, Loew's State

David Copperfield**
Metro-Goldwyn-Mayer
132 minutes

Director George Cukor *Screenplay* Howard Estabrook and Hugh Walpole, from the novel by Charles Dickens *Photography* Oliver T. Marsh *Art Direction* Cedric Gibbons *Costumes* Dolly Tree *Music* Herbert Stothart *Special Effects* Slavko Vorkapich *Editor* Robert J. Kern** *Cast* Mr. Micawber: W.C. Fields; Dan Peggotty: Lionel Barrymore; Dora: Maureen O'Sullivan; Agnes: Madge Evans; Aunt Betsey: Edna May Oliver; Mr. Wickfield: Lewis Stone; David, the Man: Frank Lawton; David, the Child: Freddie Bartholomew; Mrs. Copperfield: Elizabeth Allan; Uriah Heep: Roland Young; Mr. Murdstone: Basil Rathbone; Clickett: Elsa Lanchester; Mrs. Micawber: Jean Cadell; Nurse Peggotty: Jessie Ralph; Mr. Dick: Lenox Pawle; Jane Murdstone: Violet Kemble-Cooper

New York: January 18, 1935, Capitol; Los Angeles: February 8, 1935, Grauman's Chinese; London: March 7, 1935, Palace

Vanessa: Her Love Story
Metro-Goldwyn-Mayer
74 minutes

Director William K. Howard *Screenplay* Hugh Walpole and Lenore Coffee, from the novel *Vanessa* by Hugh Walpole *Photography* Ray June *Editor* Frank Hull *Cast* Vanessa: Helen Hayes; Benjie: Robert Montgomery; Ellis: Otto Kruger; Judith: May Robson; Adam: Lewis Stone

London: March 22, 1935, Empire; New York: April 12, 1935, Capitol, Loew's Metropolitan (Brooklyn); Los Angeles: April 25, 1935, Four Star

Reckless
Metro-Goldwyn-Mayer
96 minutes

Director Victor Fleming *Screenplay* P.J. Wolfson, from a story by Oliver Jeffries (David O. Selznick) *Photography* George Folsey *Costumes* Adrian *Songs* Jerome Kern and Dorothy Fields *Editor* Margaret Booth *Cast* Mona: Jean Harlow; Ned Riley: William Powell; Bob Harrison: Franchot Tone; Granny: May Robson; Smiley: Ted Healy; Blossom: Nat Pendleton

Los Angeles: April 18, 1935, Grauman's Chinese, Loew's State; New York: April 19, 1935, Capitol, Loew's Metropolitan (Brooklyn); London: June 2, 1935, Empire

Anna Karenina
Metro-Goldwyn-Mayer
95 minutes

Director Clarence Brown *Screenplay* Clemence Dane and Salka Viertel, from the novel by Leo Tolstoy *Photography* William Daniels *Art Direction* Cedric Gibbons *Costumes* Adrian *Music* Herbert Stothart *Editor* Robert J. Kern *Cast* Anna Karenina: Greta Garbo; Vronsky: Fredric March; Sergei: Freddie Bartholomew; Kitty: Maureen O'Sullivan; Countess Vronsky: May Robson; Karenin: Basil Rathbone; Stiva: Reginald Owen; Yashvin: Reginald Denny; Dolly: Phoebe Foster; Levin: Gyles Isham

New York: August 30, 1935, Capitol; London: October 2, 1935, Empire, Leicester Square; Los Angeles: October 10, 1935, Grauman's Chinese, Loew's State

A Tale of Two Cities**
Metro-Goldwyn-Mayer
121 minutes

Director Jack Conway *Screenplay* W.P. Lipscomb and S.N. Behrman, from the novel by Charles Dickens *Photography* Oliver T. Marsh *Art Direction* Cedric Gibbons *Costumes* Dolly Tree *Music* Herbert Stothart *Editor* Conrad A. Nervig** *Cast* Sydney Carton: Ronald Colman; Lucie Manette: Elizabeth Allan; Miss Pross: Edna May Oliver; Stryver: Reginald Owen; Marquis St. Evrémonde: Basil Rathbone; Madame Defarge: Blanche Yurka; Dr. Manette: Henry B. Walthall; Charles Darnay: Donald Woods

New York: December 25, 1935, Capitol; Los Angeles: January 8, 1936, Grauman's Chinese, Loew's State; London: April 10, 1936, Empire, Leicester Square

Little Lord Fauntleroy
Selznick International (released by United Artists)
98 minutes

Director John Cromwell *Screenplay* Hugh Walpole, from the novel by Frances Hodgson Burnett *Photography* Charles Rosher *Art Direction* Sturges Carne *Costumes* Sophie Wachner *Music* Max Steiner *Editor* Hal C. Kern *Cast* Earl of Dorincourt: C. Aubrey Smith; Ceddie: Freddie Bartholomew; Dearest (Mrs. Errol): Dolores Costello Barrymore; Havisham: Henry Stephenson; Mr. Hobbs: Guy Kibbee; Dick: Mickey Rooney; Ben: Eric Alden; The Claimant: Jackie Searl; Newick: Reginald Barlow; Rev. Mordaunt: Ivan Simpson; Sir Harry Lorridaile: E.E. Clive; Lady Lorridaile: Constance Collier; Mary: Una O'Connor; Mrs. Mellon: May Beatty; Dawson: Joan Standing; Apple Woman: Jessie Ralph; Higgins: Lionel Belmore

New York: April 2, 1936, Radio City Music Hall; Los Angeles: April 10, 1936, Grauman's Chinese, Loew's State; London: April 29, 1936, London Pavilion

The Garden of Allah
Selznick International (released by United Artists)
80 minutes; Technicolor

Director Richard Boleslawski *Screenplay* W.P. Lipscomb and Lynn Riggs, from the novel by Robert Hichins *Photography* W. Howard Greene* and Harold Rosson* *Art Direction* Sturges Carne and Lyle Wheeler *Costumes* Ernest Dryden *Music* Max Steiner** *Technicolor Supervisor* Natalie Kalmus *Editors* Hal C. Kern and Anson Stevenson *Cast* Domini Enfilden: Marlene Dietrich; Boris Androvsky: Charles Boyer; Count Anteoni: Basil Rathbone; Father Roubier: C. Aubrey Smith; Irena: Tilly Losch; Batouch: Joseph Schildkraut; Sand Diviner: John Carradine; De Trevignac: Alan Marshal; Mother Superior: Lucille Watson; Hadj: Henry Brandon

New York: November 19, 1936, Radio City Music Hall; Los Angeles: January 13, 1937, Grauman's Chinese, Loew's State; London: September 20, 1937, Stoll

A Star Is Born**
Selznick International (released by United Artists)
111 minutes; Technicolor

Director William Wellman *Screenplay* Dorothy Parker,** Alan Campbell,** and Robert Carson,** from a story by William Wellman* and Robert Carson* *Photography* W. Howard Greene* *Color Designer* Lansing C. Holden *Art Direction* Lyle Wheeler *Costumes* Omar Kiam *Music* Max Steiner *Technicolor Supervisor* Natalie Kalmus *Editors* Hal C. Kern and James E. Newcom *Cast* Esther Blodgett-Vicki Lester: Janet Gaynor;** Norman Maine: Fredric March;** Oliver Niles: Adolphe Menjou; Lettie: May Robson; Danny McGuire: Andy Devine; Libby: Lionel Stander; Anita Regis: Elizabeth Jenns; Pop Randall: Edgar Kennedy; Casey Burke: Owen Moore

Los Angeles: April 21, 1937, Grauman's Chinese, Loew's State; New York: April 22, 1937, Radio City Music Hall; London: September 18, 1937, Tivoli

The Prisoner of Zenda
Selznick International (released by United Artists)
100 minutes

Director John Cromwell *Screenplay* John L. Balderston, from Wells Root's adaptation of Edward Rose's dramatization of the novel by Anthony Hope *Photography* James Wong Howe *Art Direction* Lyle Wheeler** *Music* Alfred Newman** *Special Effects* Jack Cosgrove *Editors* Hal C. Kern and James E. Newcom *Cast* Rudolf Rassendyll/King Rudolf V: Ronald Colman; Princess Flavia: Madeleine Carroll; Rupert of Hentzau: Douglas Fairbanks, Jr.; Antoinette De Mauban: Mary Astor; Colonel Zapt: C. Aubrey Smith; Black Michael: Raymond Massey; Captain Fritz von Tarlenheim: David Niven; Cook: Eleanor Wesselhoeft; Johann: Byron Foulger; Detchard: Montagu Love

New York: September 2, 1937, Radio City Music Hall; Los Angeles: October 6, 1937, Grauman's Chinese, Loew's State; London: November 1, 1937, Odeon, Leicester Square

Nothing Sacred
Selznick International (released by United Artists)
75 minutes; Technicolor

Director William Wellman *Screenplay* Ben Hecht, from the short story by James Street *Photography* W. Howard Greene *Art Direction* Lyle Wheeler *Costumes* Travis Banton and Walter Plunkett *Music* Oscar Levant *Editor* James E. Newcom *Technicolor Supervisor* Natalie Kalmus *Cast* Hazel Flagg: Carole Lombard; Wally Cook: Fredric March; Dr. Downer: Charles Winninger; Stone: Walter Connolly; Dr. Eggelhoffer: Sig Rumann

New York: November 25, 1937, Radio City Music Hall; Los Angeles: December 1, 1937, Grauman's Chinese, Loew's State; London: February 28, 1938, London Pavilion

The Adventures of Tom Sawyer
Selznick International (released by United Artists)
93 minutes; Technicolor

Director Norman Taurog *Screenplay* John V.A. Weaver, from the novel by Mark Twain *Photography* James Wong Howe and Wilfred M. Cline *Art Direction* Lyle Wheeler,** William Cameron Menzies, and Casey Roberts *Costumes* Walter Plunkett and Ernest Dryden *Music* Lou Forbes *Technicolor Supervisor* Natalie Kalmus *Editors* Hal C. Kern and Margaret Clancey *Cast* Tom Sawyer: Tommy Kelly; Aunt Polly: May Robson; Huck Finn: Jackie Moran; Muff Potter: Walter Brennan; Injun Joe: Victor Jory; Mary Sawyer: Marcia Mae Jones; Sheriff: Victor Kilian; Mrs. Thatcher: Nana Bryant; Becky Thatcher: Ann Gillis; Joe Harper: Mickey Rentschler; Amy Lawrence: Cora Sue Collins; Judge Thatcher: Charles Richman; Widow Douglas: Spring Byington; Mrs. Harper: Margaret Hamilton

New York: February 17, 1938, Radio City Music Hall; Los Angeles: March 23, 1938, Grauman's Chinese, Loew's State; London: May 10, 1938, Odeon, Leicester Square

The Young in Heart
Selznick International (released by United Artists)
91 minutes

Director Richard Wallace *Screenplay* Paul Osborn and Charles Bennett, from the novella *The Gay Banditti* by I.A.R. Wylie *Photography* Leon

Shamroy** *Art Direction* Lyle Wheeler *Costumes* Omar Kiam *Music* Franz Waxman** *Editor* Hal C. Kern *Cast* George-Anne Carleton: Janet Gaynor; Richard Carleton: Douglas Fairbanks, Jr.; Leslie Saunders: Paulette Goddard; Colonel Anthony "Sahib" Carleton: Roland Young; Marmy Carleton: Billie Burke; Duncan MacCrae: Richard Carlson; Miss Ellen Fortune: Minnie Dupree

New York: November 3, 1938, Radio City Music Hall; Los Angeles: November 30, 1938, Grauman's Chinese, Loew's State; London: December 26, 1938, Odeon

Made for Each Other
Selznick International (released by United Artists)
90 minutes

Director John Cromwell *Screenplay* Jo Swerling *Photography* Leon Shamroy *Art Direction* William Cameron Menzies and Lyle Wheeler *Costumes* Travis Banton *Music* Lou Forbes *Editors* Hal C. Kern and James E. Newcom *Cast* Jane Mason: Carole Lombard; John Mason: James Stewart; Judge Doolittle: Charles Coburn; Mrs. Mason: Lucille Watson; Conway: Eddie Quinlan; Sister Madeline: Alma Kruger; Eunice Doolittle: Ruth Weston; Carter: Donald Briggs; Dr. Healy: Harry Davenport; Cook: Esther Dale; Collins: Russell Hopton; Hatton: Ward Bond; Farmer: Olin Howland; Farmer's Wife: Fern Emmett; Cook: Louise Beavers

New York: February 16, 1939, Radio City Music Hall; Los Angeles: February 22, 1939, Grauman's Chinese, Loew's State; London: March 30, 1939, London Pavilion

Intermezzo: A Love Story
Selznick International (released by United Artists)
69 minutes

Director Gregory Ratoff *Screenplay* George O'Neil, from the original Swedish scenario by Gosta Stevens and Gustaf Molander *Photography* Gregg Toland *Art Direction* Lyle Wheeler *Costumes* Travis Banton and Irene *Music* Lou Forbes** *Theme Song* Robert Henning and Heinz Provost *Editors* Hal C. Kern and Francis Lyon *Cast* Holger Brandt: Leslie Howard; Anita Hoffmann: Ingrid Bergman; Margit Brandt: Edna Best; Thomas Stenborg: John Halliday; Charles: Cecil Kellaway; Greta: Enid Bennett; Ann Marie: Ann Todd; Eric: Douglas Scott

New York: October 5, 1939, Radio City Music Hall; Los Angeles: November 8, 1939, Four Star; London: (under the title *Escape to Happiness*) January 19, 1940, Gaumont

Gone With The Wind*
Selznick International (released by Metro-Goldwyn Mayer)
220 minutes; Technicolor

Director Victor Fleming* *Screenplay* Sidney Howard,* from the novel by Margaret Mitchell *Photography* Ernest Haller,* Ray Rennahan,* and Wilfred M. Cline,* *Production Designer* William Cameron Menzies* *Art Direction* Lyle Wheeler* *Costumes* Walter Plunkett *Music* Max Steiner** *Technicolor Supervisor* Natalie Kalmus *Special Effects* Jack Cosgrove,** Fred Albin,** and Arthur Johns** *Editors* Hal C. Kern* and James E. Newcom* *Cast* Scarlett O'Hara: Vivien Leigh;* Rhett Butler: Clark Gable;** Melanie Hamilton: Olivia de Havilland;** Ashley Wilkes: Leslie Howard; Mammy: Hattie McDaniel;* Prissy: Butterfly McQueen; Gerald O'Hara: Thomas Mitchell; Jonas Wilkerson: Victor Jory; Suellen O'Hara: Evelyn Keyes; Carreen O'Hara: Ann Rutherford; Charles Hamilton: Rand Brooks; Aunt Pittypat Hamilton: Laura Hope Crews; Dr. Meade: Harry Davenport; Belle Watling: Ona Munson; A Yankee Captain: Ward Bond; Bonnie Blue Butler: Cammie King

Atlanta: December 15, 1939, Loew's Grand; New York: December 19, 1939, Capitol, Astor; Los Angeles: December 28, 1939, Carthay Circle, United Artists; London: April 18, 1940, Empire, Ritz, Palace

Rebecca*
Selznick International (released by United Artists)
130 minutes

Director Alfred Hitchcock** *Screenplay* Robert E. Sherwood** and Joan Harrison,** from the novel by Daphne Du Maurier *Photography* George Barnes* *Art Direction* Lyle Wheeler** *Costumes* Irene (uncredited) *Music* Franz Waxman** *Special Effects* Jack Cosgrove and Arthur Johns** *Editor* Hal C. Kern** *Cast* Maxim de Winter: Laurence Olivier;** Mrs. de Winter: Joan Fontaine;** Jack Favell: George Sanders; Mrs. Danvers: Judith Anderson;** Major Giles Lacy: Nigel Bruce; Colonel Julyan: C. Aubrey Smith; Frank Crawley: Reginald Denny; Beatrice Lacy: Gladys Cooper; Robert: Philip Winter; Frith: Edward Fielding; Mrs. Van Hopper: Florence Bates; Coroner: Melville Cooper; Dr. Baker: Leo G. Carroll

Los Angeles: March 27, 1940, Four Star; New York: March 28, 1940, Radio City Music Hall; London: August 5, 1940, Gaumont

Since You Went Away**
Selznick International (released by United Artists)
172 minutes

Director John Cromwell *Screenplay* David O. Selznick, from the book by Margaret Buell Wilder *Photography* Lee Garmes** and Stanley Cortez** *Production Designer* William Pereira *Art Direction* Mark-Lee Kirk** *Set Decoration* Victor Gangelin** *Wardrobe* Elmer Ellsworth and Adele Sadler *Music* Max Steiner* *Special Effects* Jack Cosgrove** and Arthur Johns** *Editors* Hal C. Kern** and James E. Newcom** *Cast* Anne Hilton: Claudette Colbert;** Jane Hilton: Jennifer Jones;**

Lt. Tony Willett: Joseph Cotten; Bridget "Brig" Hilton: Shirley Temple; Colonel Smollett: Monty Woolley;** The Clergyman: Lionel Barrymore; William G. Smollett II: Robert Walker; Fidelia: Hattie McDaniel; Emily Hawkins: Agnes Moorehead; Zofia Koslowska: Alla Nazimova; Harold E. Smith: Guy Madison

New York: July 20, 1944, Capitol; Los Angeles: October 10, 1944, Carthay Circle, Ritz, Los Angeles, Egyptian; London: January 14, 1945, Gaumont, Marble Arch Pavilion

I'll Be Seeing You

Selznick International (released by United Artists)
85 minutes

Producer Dore Schary *Director* William Dieterle *Screenplay* Marion Parsonnet, from the novel *Double Furlough* by Charles Martin *Photography* Tony Gaudio *Art Direction* Mark-Lee Kirk *Music* Daniele Amfitheatrof *Song* Irving Kahal and Sammy Fain *Editor* William H. Ziegler *Cast* Mary Marshall: Ginger Rogers; Zachary Morgan: Joseph Cotten; Barbara Marshall: Shirley Temple; Mrs. Marshall: Spring Byington; Mr. Marshall: Tom Tully; Swanson: Chill Wills

Los Angeles: December 25, 1944, United Artists, Fox Wilshire, Four Star; New York: April 5, 1945, Capitol; London: June 26, 1945, Odeon, Leicester Square

Spellbound**

Selznick International (released by United Artists)
110 minutes

Director Alfred Hitchcock** *Screenplay* Ben Hecht, from the novel *The House of Doctor Edwardes* by Francis Beeding *Photography* George Barnes** *Art Direction* James Basevi and John Ewing (dream sequence based on designs by Salvador Dali) *Costumes* Howard Greer *Music* Miklos Rozsa* *Special Effects* Jack Cosgrove** *Editors* Hal C. Kern and William H. Ziegler *Cast* Dr. Constance Peterson: Ingrid Bergman; "J.B.": Gregory Peck; Matron: Jean Acker; Itarry: Donald Curtiss; Miss Carmichael: Rhonda Fleming; Dr. Fleurot: John Emery; Dr. Murchison: Leo G. Carroll; Garmes: Norman Lloyd; Dr. Alex Brulov: Michael Chekhov; Dr. Graff: Steven Geray; Dr. Hanish: Paul Harvey; Dr. Galt: Erskine Sanford; Sheriff: Victor Kilian; Stranger: Wallace Ford; House Detective: Bill Goodwin; Bellboy: Dave Willock; Norma: Janet Scott; Sgt. Gillespie: Regis Toomey; Police Captain: Addison Richards; Lt. Cooley: Art Baker

New York: November 1, 1945, Astor; Los Angeles: November 10, 1945, Grauman's Chinese, Loew's, Uptown; London: May 19, 1946, London Pavilion, Tivoli

Duel in the Sun

Selznick Releasing Organization
126 minutes; Technicolor

Director King Vidor *Screenplay* David O. Selznick, from Oliver H.P. Garrett's adaptation of the novel by Niven Busch *Photography* Lee Garmes, Harold Rosson, and Ray Rennahan *Production Designer* J. McMillan Johnson *Art Direction* James Basevi and John Ewing *Costumes* Walter Plunkett *Music* Dimitri Tiomkin *Technicolor Supervisor* Natalie Kalmus *Special Effects* Clarence Slifer and Jack Cosgrove *Editors* Hal C. Kern, William H. Ziegler, and John Faure *Cast* Pearl Chavez: Jennifer Jones;** Lewt McCanles: Gregory Peck; Jesse McCanles: Joseph Cotten; Senator McCanles: Lionel Barrymore; Laura Belle McCanles: Lillian Gish;** Sam Pierce: Charles Bickford; Vashti: Butterfly McQueen; The Sin Killer: Walter Huston; Scott Chavez: Herbert Marshall; Mrs. Chavez: Tilly Losch

Los Angeles: December 30, 1946, Egyptian; New York: May 7, 1947, Capitol and 38 Loew's theatres in and around New York City; London:

May 23, 1947, Carlton West

The Paradine Case

Selznick Releasing Organization
131 minutes

Director Alfred Hitchcock *Screenplay* David O. Selznick, from Alma Reville and James Bridie's adaptation of the novel by Robert Hichens *Photography* Lee Garmes *Production Designer* J. McMillan Johnson *Costumes* Travis Banton *Music* Franz Waxman *Editor* Hal C. Kern *Cast* Anthony Keane: Gregory Peck; Gay Keane: Ann Todd; Lord Horfield: Charles Laughton; Sir Simon Flaquer: Charles Coburn; Lady Horfield: Ethel Barrymore;** Andre Latour: Louis Jourdan; Maddalena Paradine: [Alida] Valli; Sir Joseph Farrell: Leo G. Carroll; Judy Flaquer: Joan Tetzel; Innkeeper: Isobel Elsom; Man Carrying a Cello: Alfred Hitchcock

Los Angeles: December 31, 1947, Westwood Village, Bruin; New York: January 8, 1948, Radio City Music Hall; London: January 14, 1949, Leicester Square

Portrait of Jennie

Selznick Releasing Organization
86 minutes; part Technicolor

Associate Producer David Hempstead *Director* William Dieterle *Screenplay* Paul Osborn and Peter Berneis, from Leonardo Bercovici's adaptation of the novel by Robert Nathan *Photography* Joseph August** *Art Direction* J. McMillan Johnson *Costumes* Anna Hill Johnstone and Lucinda Ballard *Music* Dimitri Tiomkin (based on themes by Claude Debussy) *Special Effects* Paul Eagler,* J. McMillan Johnson,* Russell Shearman,* Clarence Slifer,* Charles Freeman,* and James G. Stewart* *Editor* Gerald Wilson *Cast* Jennie Appleton: Jennifer Jones; Eben Adams: Joseph Cotten; Miss Spinney: Ethel Barrymore; Mr. Matthews: Cecil Kellaway; Gus O'Toole: David Wayne; Mr. Moore: Albert Sharpe; Mrs. Jekes: Florence Bates; Mother Mary of Mercy: Lillian Gish; Clare Morgan: Maude Simmons

Los Angeles: December 25, 1948, Carthay Circle; New York: March 29, 1949, Rivoli; London: (under the title *Jennie*) May 21, 1951, general release

The Third Man

British Lion/London Films/David O. Selznick
100 minutes

Producers Alexander Korda and David O. Selznick *Director* Carol Reed** *Screenplay* Graham Greene *Photography* Robert Krasker* *Art Direction* Vincent Korda *Music* Anton Karas *Editor* Oswald Hofenrichter** *Cast* Holly Martins: Joseph Cotten; Anna Schmidt: [Alida] Valli; Harry Lime: Orson Welles; Major Calloway: Trevor Howard; Sgt. Paine: Bernard Lee; Kurtz: Ernest Deutsch; Dr. Winkel: Erich Ponto; Popesco: Sigfried Breuer; Professor Crabbin: Wilfred Hyde-White; Harry's Porter: Paul Hoerbiger; Anna's Housekeeper: Hedwig Bleibtreu

London: September 2, 1949, Plaza; New York: February 2, 1950, Victoria; Los Angeles: April 12, 1950, Fine Arts

The Wild Heart

RKO
82 minutes; Technicolor

Producers Michael Powell, Emeric Pressburger, and David O. Selznick *Directors* Michael Powell and Emeric Pressburger, and Rouben Mamoulian (uncredited) *Screenplay* Michael Powell and Emeric Pressburger, from the novel *Gone to Earth* by Mary Webb Davis *Photogra-*

phy Christopher Challis *Art Direction* Hein Heckroth *Costumes* Julia Squire *Music* Brian Easdale *Technicolor Supervisor* Natalie Kalmus *Editor* Reginald Mills *Cast* Hazel Woodus: Jennifer Jones; Jack Reddin: David Farrar; Edward Marston: Cyril Cusack; Abel Woodus: Esmond Knight; Mrs. Marston: Sybil Thorndike; Andrew Vessons: Hugh Griffith

London: (under the title *Gone to Earth*) August 21, 1950, Rialto; Los Angeles: January 17, 1952, Four Star; New York: May 28, 1952, Paramount

Indiscretion of an American Wife

Columbia Pictures
63 minutes

Producers Vittorio De Sica and David O. Selznick *Director* Vittorio De Sica *Screenplay* Cesare Zavattini, Luigi Chiarini, and Giorgio Prosperi, with dialogue by Truman Capote *Photography* G.R. Aldo *Art Direction* Virgilio Marchi *Costumes* Christian Dior** *Music* Alessandro Cicognini *Cast* Mary: Jennifer Jones; Giovanni: Montgomery Clift; Commissioner: Gino Cervi; Paul: Dick Beymer

Los Angeles: May 27, 1954, Pantages, Hillstreet; New York: June 25, 1954, Astor; London: (under the title *Stazione Termini*) August 8, 1954, Dominion, New Victoria

Light's Diamond Jubilee

produced for television
120 minutes

Directors, filmed sequences King Vidor ("A Kiss for the Lieutenant," "Leader of the People"), Norman Taurog (excerpt from *The Adventures of Tom Sawyer*), Roy Rowland (excerpt from *How to Raise a Baby*), and William Wellman (President Eisenhower sequence) *Directors, live sequences* Alan Handley ("Girls in Their Summer Dresses," "Chance for Adventure," Eddie Fisher segment) *Teleplay* Ben Hecht, from stories by Irwin Shaw ("Girls in Their Summer Dresses"), John Steinbeck ("Leader of the People"), Arthur Gordon ("A Kiss for the Lieutenant"), Max Schulman ("Chance for Adventure"), and Burton Benjamin ("Letter from Tomorrow") *Cast* Judith Anderson, David Niven, Lauren Bacall, Walter Brennan, Joseph Cotten, Helen Hayes, Dwight D. Eisenhower, Kim Novak, Guy Madison, George Gobel, Dorothy Dandridge, Robert Benchley, Erin O'Brien Moore, Harry Morgan, and Debbie Reynolds (uncredited)

Telecast simultaneously on NBC, CBS, ABC, and the DuMont television networks, October 24, 1954, 8:00 p.m.

A Farewell to Arms

20th Century-Fox
152 minutes; CinemaScope; Color by DeLuxe

Director Charles Vidor *Screenplay* Ben Hecht, from the novel by Ernest Hemingway and the play by Laurence Stallings *Photography* Piero Portalupi and Oswald Morris *Production Designer* Alfred Junge *Art Direction* Mario Garbuglia *Costumes & Set Decoration* Veniero Colisanti and John Moore *Music* Mario Nascimbene *Re-recording Supervisor* Murray Spivack *Scenario Assistant* Lydia Schiller *Editors* James E. Newcom, Gerald J. Wilson, and John M. Foley *Cast* Lt. Frederic Henry: Rock Hudson; Catherine Barkley: Jennifer Jones; Major Alessandro Rinaldi: Vittorio De Sica; Father Galli: Alberto Sordi; Bonello: Kurt Kasznar; Miss Van Campen: Mercedes McCambridge; Dr. Emerich: Oscar Homolka; Helen Ferguson: Elaine Stritch

Los Angeles: December 19, 1957, Grauman's Chinese and eight theatres in the Los Angeles area; New York: January 24, 1958, Roxy; London: March 26, 1958, Carlton

Selected Bibliography

Agee, James. *Agee on Film.* vol. 1. New York: McDowell Obolensky, 1958.

Allen, Frederick Lewis. *Since Yesterday.* New York: Harper & Row, 1940.

Alpert, Hollis. *The Barrymores.* New York: Dial Press, 1964.

Astaire, Fred. *Steps in Time.* New York: Harper & Row, 1959.

Balio, Tino, ed. *The American Film Industry.* University of Wisconsin Press, 1976.

————. *United Artists.* University of Wisconsin Press, 1976.

Barker, Felix. *The Oliviers.* Philadelphia: Lippincott, 1953.

Barsacq, Leon. *Caligari's Cabinet and Other Grand Illusions: A History of Film Design.* Revised and edited by Elliott Stein. Boston: New York Graphic Society, 1976.

Baxter, John. *Hollywood in the Thirties.* Cranbury, N.J.: Barnes, 1968.

Beeding, Francis. *The House of Dr. Edwardes.* Boston: Little, Brown, 1927.

Behlmer, Rudy, ed. *Memo from David O. Selznick.* New York: Viking Press, 1972.

Bergman, Andrew. *We're in the Money.* New York University Press, 1971.

Blum, Daniel. *A Pictorial History of the Silent Screen.* New York: Putnam, 1953.

————. *A Pictorial History of the Talkies.* New York: Putnam, 1958.

Bowman, Lynn. *Los Angeles: Epic of a City.* Berkeley: Howell-North Books, 1974.

Brooks, John. *The Great Leap.* New York: Harper & Row, 1966.

Brownlow, Kevin. *The Parade's Gone By.* New York: Knopf, 1968.

Busch, Niven. *Duel in the Sun.* New York: Morrow, 1944.

Bush, Donald. *The Streamlined Decade.* New York: Braziller, 1975.

Cannom, Robert C. *Van Dyke and the Mythical City of Hollywood.* Culver City, Calif.: Murray & Gee, 1948.

Cantrel, Hadley, ed. *Public Opinion, 1935–1946.* Princeton University Press, 1951.

Caughey, John, and Caughey, LaRee. *Los Angeles: Biography of a City.* University of California Press, 1976.

Chierichetti, David, *Hollywood Costume Design.* New York: Harmony Books, 1976.

Clarke, Charles G. *Early Film Making in Los Angeles.* Los Angeles: Dawson's Book Shop, 1976.

Cooper, Merian C. *Grass.* New York: Putnam, 1925.

Cottrell, John. *Laurence Olivier.* Englewood Cliffs, N.J.: Prentice-Hall, 1975.

Crawford, Joan, with Ardmore, Jane. *A Portrait of Joan.* New York: Doubleday, 1962.

Croce, Arlene. *The Fred Astaire and Ginger Rogers Book.* New York: Dutton, 1972.

Crowther, Bosley. *Hollywood Rajah: The Life and Times of Louis B. Mayer.* New York: Holt, Rinehart and Winston, 1960.

————. *The Lion's Share: The Story of an Entertainment Empire.* New York: Dutton, 1957.

Dardis, Tom. *Some Time in the Sun.* New York: Scribner, 1976.

Dietz, Howard. *Dancing in the Dark.* New York: Quadrangle, 1974.

Dreher, Carl. *Sarnoff: An American Success.* New York: Quadrangle, 1977.

Du Maurier, Daphne. *Rebecca.* New York: Doubleday, 1938.

Edwards, Anne. *Vivien Leigh: A Biography.* New York: Simon & Schuster, 1977.

Fell, John L. *Film and the Narrative Tradition.* University of Oklahoma Press, 1974.

Fielding, Raymond. *The Technique of Special Effects Cinematography.* New York: Focal Press, 1965.

Film Daily Yearbook of Motion Pictures. New York: Film Daily, 1926–1959.

Geduld, Harry M. *The Birth of the Talkies.* Indiana University Press, 1975.

Goldmark, Peter S., and Edson, Lee. *Maverick Inventor: My Turbulent Years at CBS.* New York: Saturday Press, 1973.

Goldner, Orville, and Turner, George. *The Making of King Kong.* Cranbury, N.J.: Barnes, 1975.

Goulden, Joseph C. *The Best Years: 1945–1950.* New York: Atheneum, 1976.

Green, Abel, and Laurie, Joe, Jr. *Show Biz: From Vaude to Video.* New York: Holt, Rinehart and Winston, 1951.

Griffith, Richard, and Mayer, Arthur. *The Movies.* New York: Simon & Schuster, 1957.

Guiles, Fred L. *Hanging on in Paradise.* New York: McGraw-Hill, 1975.

Hall, Ben M. *The Best Remaining Seats.* New York: Clarkson N. Potter, 1961.

Hampton, Benjamin B. *A History of the Movies.* New York: Covici, Friede, 1931.

Harris, Warren G. *Gable and Lombard.* New York: Simon & Schuster, 1974.

Harwell, Richard B., ed. "The Hollywood Journals of Wilbur G. Kurtz." *Atlanta Historical Journal,* summer 1978.

————. *Margaret Mitchell's "Gone With The Wind" Letters: 1936–1949.* New York: Macmillan, 1976.

Hays, Will. *The Memoirs of Will H. Hays.* Garden City, N.Y.: Doubleday, 1955.

————. *See and Hear.* Los Angeles: Motion Picture Producers and Distributors of America, 1929.

Hecht, Ben. *A Child of the Century.* New York: Simon & Schuster, 1954.

Hemingway, Ernest. *A Farewell to Arms.* New York: Scribner, 1929.

Hichens, Robert. *The Garden of Allah.* Philadelphia: Lippincott, 1904.

Higham, Charles. *Kate.* New York: Norton, 1975.

————. *Hollywood Cameramen.* Indiana University Press, 1970.

Higham, Charles, and Greenberg, Joel. *Hollywood in the Forties.* Cranbury, N.J.: Barnes, 1968.

Hondel, Leo A. *Hollywood Looks at Its Audience.* University of Illinois Press, 1950.

Hope, Anthony. *The Prisoner of Zenda.* New York: Holt, Rinehart and Winston, 1894.

Howard, Leslie Ruth. *A Quite Remarkable Father.* New York: Harcourt Brace Jovanovich, 1959.

Hoyt, Edwin P. *The Tempering Years.* New York: Scribner, 1963.

Huntly, John. *British Technicolor Films.* London: Shelton, Robinson, 1949.

Irwin, Will. *The House That Shadows Built.* Garden City, N.Y.: Doubleday, 1928.

Jacobs, Lewis. *The Rise of the American Film.* New York: Harcourt Brace Jovanovich, 1939.

Jacobs, Norman. *Culture for the Millions.* New York: Van Nostrand, 1961.

Jobes, Gertrude. *Motion Picture Empire.* Hamden, Conn.: Archon Books, 1966.

Jowett, Garth. *Film: The Democratic Art.* Boston: Little, Brown, 1976.

Keats, John. *You Might as Well Live: The Life and Times of Dorothy Parker.* New York: Simon & Schuster, 1970.

Kennedy, Joseph P., ed. *The Story of the Films.* Chicago: A. W. Shaw Co., 1927.

Kiesling, Barrett C. *Talking Pictures: How They Are Made.* New York: Johnston Publishing Co., 1937.

Klein, Adrien. *Colour Cinematography.* Garden City, N.Y.: Amphoto, 1940.

Knef, Hildegard. *The Gift Horse.* New York: McGraw-Hill, 1971.

Knight, Arthur. *The Liveliest Art.* New York: Macmillan, 1957.

Lambert, Gavin. *On Cukor.* New York: Putnam, 1972.

Latham, Aaron. *Crazy Sundays: F. Scott Fitzgerald in Hollywood.* New York: Viking Press, 1971.

Levant, Oscar. *A Smattering of Ignorance.* Garden City, N.Y.: Doubleday, 1939.

Leyda, Jay, ed. *Voices of Film Experience.* New York: Macmillan, 1977.

Lingeman, Richard. *Don't You Know There's a War On?* New York: Putnam, 1970.

Longley, Marjorie; Silverstein, Louis; and Tower, Samuel A. *America's Taste.* New York: Simon & Schuster, 1959.

Loos, Anita. *Kiss Hollywood Goodbye.* New York: Viking Press, 1974.

————. *A Girl Like I.* New York: Random House, 1966.

Loth, David. *The City Within a City: The Story of Rockefeller Center.* New York: Morrow, 1966.

Lyons, Eugene. *David Sarnoff.* New York: Harper & Row, 1966.

MacGowan, Kenneth. *Behind the Screen.* New York: Delacorte Press, 1965.

Madsen, Axel. *John Huston.* Garden City, N.Y.: Doubleday, 1978.

Maltin, Leonard. *The Art of the Cinematographer.* New York: Dover, 1978.

————. *Hollywood: The Movie Factory.* New York: Popular Library, 1976.

Manchester, William. *The Glory and the Dream.* Boston: Little, Brown, 1974.

Manvell, Roger, ed. *The International Encyclopedia of Film.* New York: Crown, 1972.

Marion, Frances. *Off with Their Heads.* New York: Macmillan, 1972.

Marner, Terence St. John, ed. *Film Design.* Cranbury, N.J.: Barnes, 1974.

Marx, Samuel. *Mayer and Thalberg: The Make-Believe Saints.* New York: Random House, 1975.

Mayer, Arthur. *Merely Colossal.* New York: Simon & Schuster, 1953.

Michael, Paul, ed. *The American Movies Reference Book.* Englewood Cliffs, N.J.: Prentice-Hall, 1969.

Mitchell, Margaret. *Gone With The Wind.* New York: Macmillan, 1936.

Montague, Ivor. *With Eisenstein in Hollywood.* Berlin: Seven Seas Books, 1968.

Motion Picture Almanac. New York: Quigley Publishing Co., 1930–1950.

Munden, Kenneth W. *The American Film Institute Catalog of Motion Pictures.* New York: Bowker, 1971.

Nathan, Robert. *Portrait of Jennie.* New York: Knopf, 1949.

Naumberg, Nancy, ed. *We Make the Movies.* New York: Norton, 1937.

Nolan, William F. *John Huston: King Rebel.* Nashville: Sherbourne Press, 1965.

Osborne, Robert. *Academy Awards Illustrated.* Hollywood: Marvin Miller Enterprises, 1965.

Pennington, L.W., and Baxter, W.K. *The History of Culver City.* Culver City, Calif., 1976.

Pike, Bob, and Martin, David. *The Genius of Busby Berkeley.* Reseda, Calif.: Creative Film Society, 1973.

Powdermaker, Hortense. *Hollywood: The Dream Factory.* Boston: Little, Brown, 1950.

Pratt, George. *Spellbound in Darkness.* University of Rochester Press, 1966.

Quigley, Martin. *Decency in Motion Pictures.* New York: Macmillan, 1937.

Quigley, Martin, Jr., ed. *New Screen Techniques.* New York: Quigley Publishing Co., 1953.

Quirk, Lawrence J. *The Films of Ingrid Bergman.* Secaucus, N.J.: Citadel Press, 1970.

Ramsaye, Terry. *A Million and One Nights.* New York: Simon & Schuster, 1926.

Rivkin, Allen, and Kerr, Laura. *Hello Hollywood!* Garden City, N.Y.: Doubleday, 1962.

Rodgers, Richard. *Musical Stages.* New York: Random House, 1975.

Ross, Lillian. *Picture.* Garden City, N.Y.: Doubleday, 1952.

Rosten, Leo. *Hollywood: The Movie Colony, the Movie Makers.* New York: Harcourt Brace Jovanovich, 1941.

Rotha, Paul. *The Film Till Now*. Rev. ed. London: Vision Press, 1951.

Samuels, Charles. *The King: A Biography of Clark Gable*. New York: Coward, McCann & Geoghegan, 1961.

Harris, Andrew, ed. *Interviews with Film Directors*. Indianapolis: Bobbs-Merrill, 1967.

Schickel, Richard. *The Men Who Made the Movies*. New York: Atheneum, 1975.

Shale, Richard, ed. *Academy Awards*. New York: Frederick Ungar, 1978.

Sherwin, Mark, and Markmann, Charles Lam. *One Week in March*. New York: Putnam, 1961.

Sklar, Robert. *Movie-Made America: A Social History of American Movies*. New York: Random House, 1975.

Smith, John, and Cankwell, Tim, eds. *The World Encyclopedia of Film*. New York: Galahad Books, 1972.

Spehr, Paul. *The Movies Begin*. The Newark Museum, 1977.

Steele, Joseph Henry. *Ingrid Bergman: An Intimate Portrait*. New York: McKay, 1959.

Steen, Mike. *Hollywood Speaks*. New York: Putnam, 1974.

Tanner, Louise. *All the Things We Were*. Garden City, N.Y.: Doubleday, 1968.

Taylor, Deems; Peterson, Marcelene; and Hale, Bryant. *A Pictorial History of the Movies*. New York: Simon & Schuster, 1950.

Terkel, Studs. *Hard Times*. New York: Pantheon, 1970.

Thomas, Bob. *Selznick*. Garden City, N.Y.: Doubleday, 1970.

Thomas, D. B. *The First Colour Motion Pictures*. London: Her Majesty's Stationery Office, 1969.

Thomas, Tony. *Gregory Peck*. New York: Harcourt Brace Jovanovich, 1977.

————. *Music for the Movies*. Cranbury, N.J.: Barnes, 1973.

Thompson, David. *A Biographical Dictionary of Film*. New York: Morrow, 1976.

Thorp, Margaret. *America at the Movies*. New Haven: Yale University Press, 1939.

Thrasher, Frederic, ed. *Okay for Sound*. New York: Duell, Sloan & Pierce, 1946.

Tiomkin, Dimitri, and Buranelli, Prosper. *Please Don't Hate Me*. Garden City, N.Y.: Doubleday, 1959.

Trimble, Lynn S. *Color in Motion Pictures and Television*. University of California Press, 1954.

Truffaut, François. *Hitchcock*. New York: Simon & Schuster, 1966.

Tyler, Parker. *The Magic and Myth of the Movies*. New York: Simon & Schuster, 1947.

Vidor, King. *A Tree Is a Tree*. New York: Harcourt Brace Jovanovich, 1952.

Viertel, Salka. *The Kindness of Strangers*. New York: Holt, Rinehart and Winston, 1969.

Von Sternberg, Josef. *Fun in a Chinese Laundry: An Autobiography*. New York: Macmillan, 1965.

Vreeland, Frank, ed. *Foremost Films of 1938*. New York: Pitman, 1939.

Weinberg, Herman G. *Josef von Sternberg*. New York: Dutton, 1967.

Wellman, William. *A Short Time for Insanity*. New York: Hawthorne Books, 1974.

Whalen, Richard J. *The Founding Father*. New York: Signet, 1966.

Wilder, Margaret Buell. *Since You Went Away*. New York: McGraw-Hill, 1943.

Williams, Chester. *Gable*. New York: Fleet Press, 1968.

Zierold, Norman. *Garbo*. Briarcliff Manor, N.Y.: Stein & Day, 1969.

Zukor, Adolph. *The Public Is Never Wrong*. New York: Putnam, 1953.

Index

All of the people
who worked on this book
have tried to make it look
as if it were

A Note on the Type

This book was photocomposed in Granjon, a type named in compliment to Robert Granjon, but neither a copy of a classic face nor an entirely original creation. George W. Jones (1860–1942) based his designs for this type on the type used by Claude Garamond (1510–1561) in his beautiful French books. Granjon resembles Garamond's own type more closely than do any of the various modern types that bear his name. Robert Granjon began his career as a type cutter in 1523. The boldest and most original designer of his time, he was one of the first to practice the trade of type founder apart from that of printer. Between 1557 and 1562 Granjon printed about twenty books in types designed by himself, following, after a fashion, the cursive handwriting of the time. These types, usually known as caractères de civilité, he himself called lettres françaises, as they were especially appropriate to his own country.

"Selznick," the display face used on the jacket, was taken from the original title design for A Star Is Born (1937) and is named in honor of David O. Selznick.

This book was photocomposed in film by New England Typographic Service, Inc., Bloomfield, Connecticut. Black-and-white reproductions were done by New England Typographic Service and scanned halftones by Alithochrome Corporation, Hauppauge, New York, who also scanned the duotones. Mechanical color separations were done by Creative Lithography, New York, New York. Gatefold separations were prepared by Eureka Photo Offset Engravings, Inc., New York, New York. Color separations in text were done by Offset Separations Corporation, New York, New York, and Milan, Italy. The book was printed by Regensteiner Press, Chicago, Illinois. Special inserts were printed by American Printers and Lithographers, Niles, Illinois. Jackets were produced by Alithochrome Corporation. The book was bound by A. Horowitz and Sons, Fairfield, New Jersey.

Production and manufacturing were directed by Ellen McNeilly. Production assistance by Dana Cole. Manuscript and proofs were supervised by Neal Jones and Eva Resnikova. Typography and design by Thomas Ingalls.